I

MA

A HISTORY
OF
CANADA

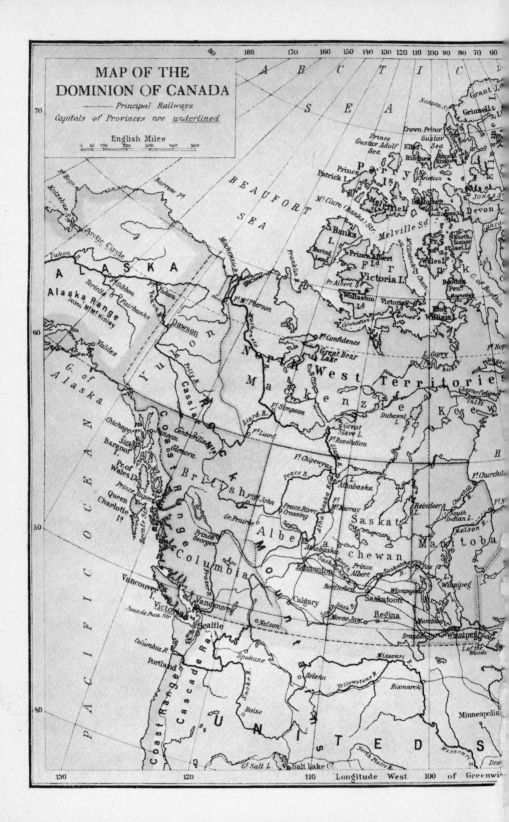

A HISTORY
OF
CANADA

By CARL WITTKE, A.M., Ph.D.

Professor of History, Oberlin College

THIRD
EDITION

NEW YORK

F. S. CROFTS & CO.

1942

COPYRIGHT 1928, 1933, 1941 BY F. S. CROFTS & CO., INC.

First printing, September, 1928

SECOND EDITION
Second printing, October, 1933
Third printing, July, 1939

THIRD EDITION
Fourth printing, June, 1941
Fifth printing, April, 1942

MANUFACTURED IN THE UNITED STATES OF AMERICA

TO

LILLIAN NIPPERT WITTKE

PREFACE

IN RECENT years an increased amount of attention has been given in American colleges and universities to the study of Canadian history. This textbook survey is presented in the hope that it will arouse in teachers and students alike, as well as in Americans generally, a greater interest in this subject. Together with Professor R. G. Trotter's admirable *Canadian History: A Syllabus and Guide to Reading*, it should furnish a summary introduction to the study of a long-neglected field.

An effort has been made to point out the almost constant inter-relation of Canadian and United States history, as well as Canada's rôle in the development of British imperial policies. The period before 1763 has been treated very briefly, not because of any underestimation of its importance, but in order to gain space for a discussion of more recent times. Brief bibliographical notes are appended to each chapter, usually with a suggestion as to where additional material can be found.

It is a difficult, not to say a daring, task to try to produce even a brief summary of the main developments in the history of a country of which comparatively little has been written. My indebtedness to the specialists, especially Canadians, who have written on specific phases of the history of Canada must appear on every page; but it is even greater than mere bibliographical citations can indicate. I am under special obligations to Professor Harry Elmer Barnes; to Professor W. P. M. Kennedy of the University of Toronto, who read the manuscript and made many helpful criticisms and suggestions; and to the reviewers from whose criticisms and suggestions I have profited in preparing this revised edition. My wife, Lillian Nippert, has been of special assistance in seeing the work through the press and in preparing the index.

CARL WITTKE

The Ohio State University
Columbus, Ohio

NOTE TO THIRD EDITION

These lines were written at a time of greatest crisis in Canadian affairs. The future of the British Commonwealth of Nations and of western democracy is at stake in the Second World War. In the struggle against totalitarianism, Canada is playing an important role. Her future in the Empire and as a North American nation is at stake.

Two new chapters have been added, dealing with significant developments since 1932. They describe Canada's experiences during the recent depression, the events that drew the Dominion into another European War, and the record to date of Canada at war. As in earlier editions, the relations between Canada and the United States have received special attention.

CARL WITTKE

May 1, 1941
Oberlin College

TABLE OF CONTENTS

MAPS

A HISTORY
OF
CANADA

CHAPTER I

DISCOVERY AND EXPLORATION

THE present-day Dominion of Canada comprises an area of nearly 3,750,000 square miles. In territorial extent it is larger than the *Size of Canada* United States and almost as large as the entire continent of Europe. Canada's southernmost point is in the latitude of sunny Italy, while its northernmost extreme is hundreds of miles beyond the Magnetic Pole. The province of Quebec alone, if we include the Ungava district, is larger than Belgium, Holland, Germany, Denmark, Sweden, Bulgaria, and the old Austro-Hungarian Empire of the days before the Great War of 1914-1918.

The thousands of miles of frontier that separate Canada from the United States form a political and national boundary which has *Physical* little justification from the standpoint of the physical geography of *features* North America. The narrow Atlantic coastal plain, extending from the Gulf of St. Lawrence to Florida, is flanked on the west by the plateaus and ridges of the Appalachian Mountains, extending diagonally through the eastern section of North America. The eastern maritime provinces of New Brunswick and Nova Scotia are really a part of the great Appalachian system. Westward from the Appalachians to the Rocky Mountains stretches a vast plain, dotted with beautiful lakes and furrowed by majestic rivers. Gradually, in ever-rising plateaus, the prairies and the plains blend into the high, wide ranges of the mountains extending almost to the Pacific Ocean. Topographically, the various sections of the United States and Canada are one, for nature has erected no important barriers between them. The boundaries which divide these two great nations are of artificial creation.

The soil of Canada is the result of century-long glacial action. This entire part of the world was once covered with ice, with the *Soil* result that glaciers have denuded some sections of their soil and enriched others with heavy deposits. In the Laurentian Plateau around Hudson Bay, and extending through most of the modern provinces of Quebec and Ontario, much of the soil is sufficient for a heavy forest growth, but not for extensive agriculture, except in the fertile valleys. In 1924 the province of Quebec produced more than 1,170,000 tons of pulp, valued at over $21,000,000; her total supply of standing pulp-wood was estimated at 345,000,000 cords. In many regions, where the timber has been removed, the land stretches for miles in a barren waste. In the maritime provinces of New Brunswick and Nova Scotia, and in Prince Edward Island, the

3

land is unusually fertile, due to erosion and rock decay, and also to tidal deposits. The lowlands in the St. Lawrence basin, from Quebec to the United States boundary, are among the most fertile areas of the Dominion, due to the decomposition of shale and limestone into a very rich clay soil. The western prairies of Manitoba, Saskatchewan, and Alberta constitute for the most part a drift-covered area of finely powdered rock, the result of ages of glacial action. Here the shale and sandstone have weathered into a clay loam and made this one of the greatest wheat-producing areas in the world. In the cordilleran region, extending from the Rocky Mountains to the Pacific Ocean, agriculture is possible only in the valleys, where rivers arising from glaciers have deposited a rich soil.

Water resources   Canada has the greatest aggregate of water-power of any country in the world. Of her total area of 3,729,665 square miles, 125,755 are water entirely within the country. On the eastern side of the Dominion the St. Lawrence River, Europe's gateway to Canada, drains an area of 530,000 square miles, most of it in Canada. One of its tributaries, the Ottawa, is 700 miles long. For 1000 miles, to Montreal, the St. Lawrence is navigable for large ocean-going steamers, and through a series of lakes and canals large vessels can sail or steam 1400 miles further inland. The area of the Great Lakes, the waters of which the St. Lawrence carries to the sea, is little short of 100,000 square miles. Yet Lake Winnipeg is larger than Lake Ontario, and both Great Slave Lake and Great Bear Lake are larger than Lake Winnipeg. Scores of other lakes in the interior of Canada range from fifty to more than a hundred miles in length, while smaller lakes abound in many parts of the country.

The basin of the Nelson River, which drains the Winnipeg lake system, covers an area of 367,000 square miles, extending from the Rocky Mountains to Hudson Bay. The sources of the great Mississippi, which empties into the warm Gulf of Mexico, and the headwaters of the Saskatchewan, the waters of which eventually find their way over a long course of 1600 miles to the frozen north, are almost within sight of each other on the Canada-United States boundary. For miles the forty-ninth parallel, which constitutes the international boundary between the United States and Canada in the west, almost coincides with the natural watershed dividing the rivers flowing into Hudson Bay from the Missouri and Mississippi river systems. In the northwest, the Mackenzie river system, 2500 miles in length, drains a basin of more than a million square miles, and the Yukon, flowing over a course of 2000 miles, drains an area of 145,000 square miles. The possibilities for hydro-electric power offered by some of these great streams are just now beginning to be developed. In the province of Quebec alone 1,300,000 horsepower were derived in 1925 from the harnessing of some of the almost innumerable rivers.

Nature has endowed Canada with a wide variety of resources.

In the extreme eastern provinces of Nova Scotia and New Brunswick, *Mineral* and in the extreme western province of British Columbia, the most *deposits* important coal deposits have been found. The coal resources of the Appalachian region, including the maritime provinces and the section of Quebec lying southeast of the St. Lawrence River, have been estimated at 6,150,000,000 tons. Coal has also been found in Alberta and Saskatchewan. Newfoundland produces cheap iron ores. Near Thetford, in southeastern Quebec, large open pits yield eighty-three per cent of the world's supply of asbestos. In the lowlands of the St. Lawrence basin no coal or metal has been located, but natural gas, petroleum, salt, and gypsum are among the important products of this section. In the Great Lakes basin valuable deposits of copper, nickel, mica, and silver have been found. In 1903 great silver deposits were discovered in the cobalt field in northern Ontario. In the vicinity of Lake Huron there are salt beds 200 feet deep. In the cordilleran region, extending from the western plains to the Pacific coast, coal, gold, lead, copper, and silver have been found. What mineral deposits may still lie hidden in the frozen basins of Hudson Bay and in the Arctic region have yet to be determined.

The great plains of Canada, extending from the Appalachians to the Rockies, are mainly in the temperate zone, lying between lati- *Climate* tudes 42° and 83°. Here the transition from winter to summer is exceedingly rapid. The province of Ontario has a climate ranging from that of Rome to that of northern Scotland. Vegetables can be grown within the Arctic Circle, especially in the valley of the Mackenzie River, and wheat can be produced in surprisingly high latitudes. Rudyard Kipling's poetic characterization of Canada as "Our Lady of the Snows" is only partially true, and it has helped to give many people a totally false conception of the climate and agricultural potentialities of the Dominion. Settlement in Canada has gradually been expanding northward as well as westward. The Dominion is "no longer a tapeworm, but rather resembles a wasp, with the waist at Winnipeg."

Canada's long and irregular coastline has placed fishing and ship- ping among her fundamental and most prosperous industries. In her *Natural* forests the moose, caribou, deer, bear, wolf, fox, and other fur- *resources* bearing animals have furnished profitable employment to the hunter, the trader, and the trapper from the time of the earliest explorations to the present day. The furs of the beaver, the otter, and the muskrat are still among Canada's most valuable articles of commerce. The vast areas of primeval forests have given rise to the great lumber, pulp, and paper mills now established in that region. Great herds of American bison once roamed the western plains and furnished the meat supply of the aboriginal Indians and early white settlers, until the advance of civilization finally crowded the last of the herds to the northwest. In Wainwright Park, Alberta, and in the Peace River district, the Canadian government is now trying to protect and preserve what is left of these former monarchs of the plains. The area they vacated has proved to be one of the richest wheat-producing regions in the world; but not for a century and a half after the early explorers reached this region did the hand of the plowman turn the prairie soil and reveal its golden riches.

Canadian Indians

Until the beginning of the sixteenth century Canada, with its rich opportunities and marvelous resources, was practically unknown to Europeans. Red-skinned Indians roamed over this vast expanse, though their number probably did not greatly exceed 200,000. Among the most important tribes were the Algonquins, occupying a broad belt from the Atlantic to the Rockies; the Athapascans, scattered over the Mackenzie basin toward the northwest; the Hurons, living on the shores of Lake Huron and Georgian Bay; and the powerful Iroquois, roaming the southern shores of Lake Ontario. Along the barren coasts of Labrador and the Arctic Ocean lived the Eskimos, a short, strong, swarthy people whose racial origin is still to some extent a matter of speculation and controversy.

Norse discoveries

About the year 1000 A.D. a little band of Norse Vikings under Leif Ericson piloted their ships across the treacherous northern waters of the Atlantic and landed somewhere near the coast of Labrador— the first white men to set foot on the soil of North America. Their deeds were recorded and transmitted to posterity through the *sagas*, or legends, of their people. It was not until quite recent times that investigators could identify with any degree of certainty the region where they first landed, and that archæologists, digging for history with pick and shovel, tried to verify the accounts of their settlement. The efforts of these Norse adventurers came to nothing, and the dawn of the sixteenth century found Canada still a vast territory unknown to all save the aborigines who wandered over its plains, quite unconscious of the juggernaut of white civilization which was so soon to grind them under its relentless advance.

Voyages of discovery

In 1497, thirteen months before Christopher Columbus reached the mainland of America, John Cabot, a Genoese navigator sailing under letters patent granted by King Henry VII of England, made a landfall on the shores of Labrador or Newfoundland, and may have reached Cape Breton Island. Two years later a Portuguese navigator, Gaspar Corte Real, explored the east coast of Newfoundland, and in 1500 reached the coast of Greenland. In 1524 a Florentine, Giovanni Da Verrazano, sailing under French auspices, skirted the North American coast from the Carolinas to Newfoundland, and gave to the region around the Gulf of St. Lawrence the name of New France. Fishing vessels followed in the wake of these early exploring expeditions, and from 1504 on, French, English, and Portuguese fishermen, sailing before strong east winds which often took them to the Grand Bank of the Atlantic in less than a month's time, made yearly voyages to fish in the North Atlantic and to trade for furs with the native inhabitants of this region. Before Cartier began his exploration of the lower St. Lawrence valley the American coast had been more or less thoroughly explored from Greenland to Florida, either by fishermen plying their trade or by explorers intent upon finding the mythical northwest passage which would lead them directly to the fabled riches of the East.

It was Jacques Cartier who really laid the foundations for a New France in North America. In a series of three voyages, the first in 1534 and the last in 1541, he thoroughly explored the shores of Newfoundland and the region around the Gulf of St. Lawrence. Entering the St. Lawrence River, he followed it to the Indian settlement of Hochelaga, near the present site of Montreal. There he climbed "Mont Real," and from that elevation he was the first white man to view the beauties of the Lachine Rapids and the winding Ottawa River in the distance. On his last expedition he erected a tiny fort at Quebec, and sowed an acre and a half of the virgin soil with cabbage, turnips, and lettuce in a laudable though futile effort to plant a permanent settlement on the banks of the St. Lawrence. All of this vast region he claimed for the King of France, erecting crosses and markers to warn all intruders against trespassing upon what was thereafter to be considered a part of the domains of the French Crown.

Jacques Cartier

For sixty years French interest in the New World lagged, and France, though one of the leading nations of the world, was the last to appreciate the importance of the newly-discovered continent. Domestic disturbances and problems prevented the development of a French America in these years. But a new era dawned with the coming of Samuel de Champlain. Champlain was thirty-six years of age when he made his first voyage to North America, but his unflagging courage and clear vision made him the superior of all the men with whom he was associated. Champlain came to America with an enviable record behind him as a soldier and sailor, having already, in spite of his youth, visited Mexico, Panama, and the Antilles. In July, 1608, he founded Quebec on a site commanding the way into the heart of North America. Of his band of twenty-eight settlers only eight survived the first winter with its terrible cold and the ravages of scurvy. But for years Quebec remained the only French post in America, an important center for the fur trade, but dependent on the mother-country for practically all of its supplies. In 1609, Champlain accompanied an Algonquin expedition and became involved in a battle against the Iroquois near the southern end of Lake Champlain. Later on the Iroquois, partly from desire for revenge, but more particularly because of the location of their lands around the southern shores of Lake Ontario, and their strategic position as middlemen in the trade with the western Indians, became the natural allies of the Dutch and English and the perpetual enemies of the French. Their alliance with the British was destined to be-

Samuel de Champlain

come an important factor in the final struggles between France and England for supremacy in North America.

For approximately twenty-five years Champlain moved restlessly across the stage of New France. In 1609 he discovered the lake which now bears his name. In 1613 he was vainly following the Ottawa River in quest of a northwest passage through the continent. Two years later he was on the shores of Lake Huron, and by 1634 his agent reached Wisconsin. Jean Nicolet, who at the age of twenty had been sent to live with the Algonquins around Lake Nipissing for the purpose of learning their language, was probably the first European to enter Lake Michigan. This was in the year 1634. From the upper waters of the Wisconsin he might easily have gone on to the Mississippi.

Champlain as colonizer

In spite of opposition and intrigues at the French court, Champlain's courage remained undaunted, and his vision of a great French colony in the New World never failed. In 1627, when the English colony of Virginia had a population of more than four thousand and was beginning to develop a profitable tobacco plantation system, Champlain's Quebec numbered just sixty-five souls, only a fourth of whom were able to work; many were living on roots and herbs and eels, and some had already made off to the neighboring woods. During the last nineteen years of his life Champlain devoted himself entirely to his Quebec project. Once, in 1629, he saw the French flag hauled down in surrender to the English—an ominous portent of the great struggles to come; but in 1632 the post was restored to French hands. In 1635, following a stroke of paralysis, this tireless champion of French power in America passed forever from the scene.

Exploring the interior

By the early 1660's French explorers had reached the region to the north and west of Lake Superior. Radisson and Groseilliers, relishing the profits of the fur trade no less than the adventures of exploration, carried the fleur-de-lys of France far into the interior, and made new Indian alliances with the Sioux, Assiniboines, and other tribes in the far Northwest.

Soldiers of Cross

The missionary was closely associated with the explorer and the trader in the opening of the New World to French contacts. The first permanent Indian mission was established in New France by the Récollet friars in 1615. Ten years later the first Jesuits arrived. With genuine heroism and laudable zeal for the faith these holy fathers made their way into the wilderness amid terrible hardships, intent upon saving the souls of their red-skinned brethren through the Roman Church. One of the most courageous, Jean de Brébeuf, devoted almost a quarter of a century to missionary activities among the Hurons, studying their language, preparing a grammar and a dictionary for those who would follow him, and translating the Catechism into the Huron tongue. He died at the stake, suffering horrible torture at the hands of the Iroquois.

The life of these pious soldiers of the cross was almost always

one of rigorous self-denial. Bravely and without complaint they sub- *Life of*
mitted to the eternal smoke, vermin, and filth of the Indian brethren *missionaries*
whose souls they came to save. They battled, generally in vain,
against the superstitions of the Indians, who only too often remained
entirely unmoved by the solemn litanies, and the sacred pictures,
ornaments, and vestments, with which the Jesuits sought to capture
their imagination. Sometimes the missionaries were regarded as sor-
cerers, and as such responsible for the epidemics and the ill-luck that
befell their Indian flock. But they continued their work, baptizing
the sick and the dying in secret if at last no other means would
serve to lead the Indians into the Catholic fold.

From early in the morning to late at night the Jesuit gave him-
self to his labors. Rising at four, he usually devoted the first few *Day's routine*
hours of the day to private devotion and masses. After breakfast he
began the often thankless task of catechizing and instructing the
Indians—a duty which usually continued, with few interruptions,
until the late afternoon. The evening was left for reading and study,
and for further private devotions. Mission stations sprang up here
and there, usually consisting of a little log chapel, several houses
around it enclosed by a palisade, and some cleared fields around the
station where either converts or hired men carried on the fur trade
and a primitive kind of agriculture. Like many other apostles of an
evangelical religion, these Catholic fathers soon learned that it was
much easier to convert an Indian than it was to hold him rigidly
to his new faith. Moreover, many a Jesuit mission started among
the Hurons and the Algonquins fell a victim to the exterminating
fury of the Iroquois.

Difficult as it may be fully to understand and appreciate the theology
or the methods sometimes employed by zealous priests in making *Record of*
converts, it would be unfair to overlook the record of heroism and *heroism*
devotion which the French missionaries have written across the
pages of American history. In the words of Parkman, "their virtues
shine amidst the rubbish of error, like diamonds and gold in the
gravel of the torrent." Every Jesuit mission station was an outpost
of French influence in North America, and the soldiers of the church
and the soldiers of the king, advancing together, carried the fleur-
de-lys and the cross ever further into the interior of New France.
The Jesuit served his king, as well as his church. He often formed an
important link between the French fur traders and their Indian customers; he made elaborate reports of affairs in the Indian country
to headquarters in Quebec, and he sometimes skilfully combined the
duties of fur trader, interpreter, explorer, and missionary.

The names of many of these missionary explorers have long since
been forgotten. In 1665 Father Allouez ventured into the Lake *Missionary*
Superior country and remained there for twenty-five years. Five *explorers*
years later two Sulpicians were exploring the bounds of Lake Erie,
and Jacques Marquette was learning from the Illinois Indians about

a great river to the west. In May, 1673, Father Marquette, in company with the trader Louis Joliet and five assistants, set out to verify the tale. Starting from the north shore of Lake Michigan, they crossed by the Fox-Wisconsin route to the great Father of Waters, and on June 17 reached the Mississippi at a point near the present site of Prairie-du-Chien. Drifting with the current, and anchoring each night in midstream to avoid trouble with the Indians, the little group passed the mouths of the Illinois, Missouri, and Ohio Rivers, and finally stopped their progress where the Arkansas enters the Mississippi. By September they had returned to their starting-point, having covered approximately 2500 miles. Here Marquette was compelled by an attack of malaria to remain, while Joliet journeyed on to Quebec and reported to Governor Frontenac the results of the expedition. Marquette died two years later, at the age of thirty-eight, in the Illinois country to which he had returned to found a mission.

La Salle

It was left for Robert Cavalier de la Salle, in many respects the greatest of all French explorers, to complete the exploration of the Mississippi. Coming from a wealthy Norman family and trained by Jesuits for a career of learning, his adventurous spirit soon led him to New France, where his brother was serving as a Sulpician priest. In 1667 La Salle was busy laying out his landed estate near Montreal. Two years later he disposed of his seigniory, and with a company of men set out in canoes for Lake Ontario. In the winter and spring of 1669–1670 he probably reached the waters of the Ohio River. With an eye on the profits of the fur trade, he conceived a grandiose scheme to extend this trade to the Mississippi valley. By 1678 he had obtained the consent of the home authorities to build a chain of forts from New France to Mexico, and to exploit the fur trade of the Mississippi valley as a private monopoly. Undismayed by strokes of ill-fortune which would have broken a man of lesser mold, early in 1682 he set out to find the mouth of the Mississippi River. He reached the Gulf of Mexico in the spring of that year, and in 1684 he undertook to plant a French settlement at the mouth of the river. Three years later he was killed by his mutinous followers, who had been driven to desperation by weeks of wandering on the Texas coast. Twelve years after his death France succeeded in planting her first settlement in the lower Mississippi valley, to which the exploration of the unfortunate La Salle had established a French claim.

French posts in the Mississippi valley

New Orleans was founded in 1718. There were earlier settlements of less importance in this region, and French posts were soon erected farther up the valley. It became the ambition of the promoters of New France eventually to consolidate the French settlements along the St. Lawrence with those in the Mississippi valley, and thus crowd out their English and Spanish rivals. Fort St. Louis was begun by La Salle in 1682. Cahokia and Kaskaskia were established

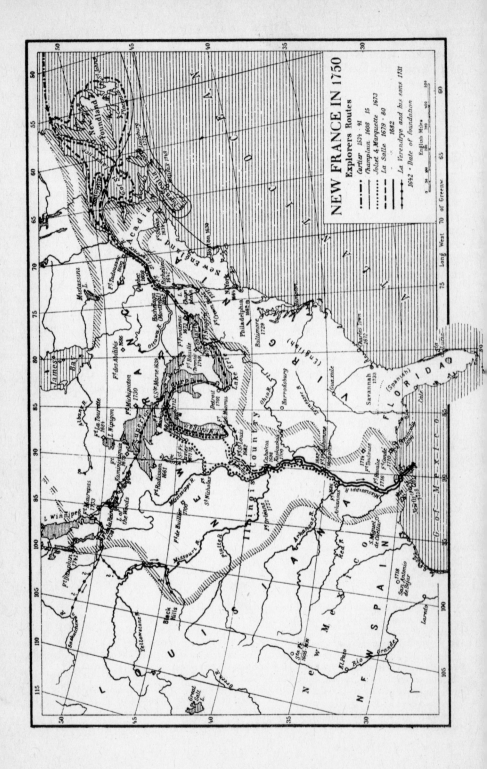

NEW FRANCE IN 1750
Explorers Routes

Cartier   1534 - 41
Champlain   1608 - 15
Joliet & Marquette   1673
La Salle   1679 - 80
                 1682
La Verendrye and his sons 1731
1642 - Date of foundation

English Miles

as mission stations in the Illinois country before the close of 1700, and Detroit was founded in 1701.

The early years of the eighteenth century witnessed the extension of French exploring activities beyond the Mississippi. Again *Westward* the desire for furs and the zeal for making converts were the leading *expansion* motives behind this westward expansion. In 1731 La Verendrye and his three sons planned to carry the fur trade beyond Lake Superior. By the spring of 1733 one son had erected a fort at the mouth of the Winnipeg River, and five years later the party was established on the banks of the Missouri. Still searching for the "Western Sea," some of the group seem to have wandered westward and established contacts with the Crow and Shoshone Indians, but there is still much controversy over the exact route followed by this western expedition. It may have penetrated to the Saskatchewan valley and come within sight of the Rocky Mountains, although recent investigations would indicate that the explorers could not have reached any point west of the Black Hills of South Dakota.

By the close of the French period (1763) the exploration of what may be called Canada proper had extended to Lake Winnipeg and *Extent of* the Lake of the Woods, up the Red River to the Assiniboine, over- *French claims* land into the valley of the Missouri, on the one side, and the Saskatchewan, on the other, and southwesterly into the valley of the Yellowstone. France claimed not only the St. Lawrence valley and the Great Lakes basin, but the region of the Mississippi as well. In the latter region, however, she had encountered the rival claims of England and Spain, and these were adjusted only after a century of warfare.

But France had erected this pretentious superstructure on exceedingly insecure foundations. She had spread her claims over half of North America and had made it part of her glorious colonial empire. It was left for the eighteenth century to reveal how thin this veneer of French influence over most of North America really was.

SELECT BIBLIOGRAPHY FOR CHAPTER I

A good summary treatment of the physical features of Canada and the relation of geographical conditions to national development may be found in CHARLES C. COLBY, *Source Book for the Economic Geography of North America* (Chicago, 1921), pp. 1–141; and R. W. BROCK, "Physical Basis of Canada," in *Canada and Its Provinces* (Toronto, 1914), vol. IX, pp. 9–91.

For a more detailed discussion of the period of French explorations and discoveries in North America, see *Canada and Its Provinces*, edited by Adam Shortt and Arthur G. Doughty (Toronto, 1914), vol. I. This work deals with the founding and development of New France from 1534 to 1760. The twenty-three volumes composing the set are the coöperative work of a number of specialists, and as such they constitute the most exhaustive and authoritative treatment of Canadian history in existence. The work of individual contributors to this series will be cited later.

The work of Francis Parkman is still the standard history of the French period in North America. The twelve volumes comprising his writings appeared at intervals between 1851 and 1892. Of special value for this chapter are PARKMAN'S *Pioneers of France in the New World* (Boston, 1883); *La Salle and the Discovery of the Great West* (Boston,

1879); *The Jesuits in North America* (Boston, 1883). The volumes in the *Chronicles of Canada* which cover this period are: STEPHEN LEACOCK, *The Dawn of Canadian History*, and *The Mariner of St. Malo* (Toronto, 1921); CHARLES W. COLBY, *The Founder of New France* (Toronto, 1921). *The Chronicles of Canada* is a set of thirty-two small volumes, popular in style, but scholarly and authoritative, written by a group of authors under the general editorship of G. M. Wrong and H. H. Langton. *The Precursors of Jacques Cartier, 1497–1534* (Ottawa, 1911), is a collection of documents edited by H. P. Biggar and issued as *Publications of the Canadian Archives*, No. 5. See also *The Voyages of Jacques Cartier, Publications of the Canadian Archives*, No. 11. Other volumes of value are H. P. BIGGAR, *The Early Trading Companies of New France* (University of Toronto Studies in History, 1901); REUBEN GOLDEN THWAITES, *France in America* (New York, 1905); JUSTIN WINSOR, *Cartier to Frontenac* (Boston, 1894) and W. B. MUNRO, *Crusaders of New France* (New Haven, 1921), pp. 1–112, and LOUISE P. KELLOGG's excellent *Early Narratives of the North-west, 1634–1699* (New York, 1917) and *The French Régime in Wisconsin and the Northwest* (Madison, 1925). Winsor's book contains many valuable maps. An excellent recent synthesis is GEORGE M. WRONG, *The Rise and Fall of New France* (New York, 1926)— 2 vols.

An interesting and detailed discussion of Jesuit activities will be found in THOMAS G. MARQUIS, *The Jesuit Missions* (*Chronicles of Canada*, Toronto, 1921). R. G. THWAITES' *Jesuit Relations and Allied Documents* appeared in seventy-three volumes from 1896 to 1901, and is a mine of information. P. F. X. DE CHARLEVOIX, *Histoire et Description Générale de la Nouvelle France*, translated by J. G. Shea, 1866–1872, is written from the Jesuit point of view.

The Journal of La Verendrye (1738–1739) is available in the *Report of the Canadian Archives, 1889* (Ottawa) pp. 1–28, and in L. J. BURPEE, *Journals and Letters of Pierre Gaultier de Varennes de La Verendrye* (Champlain Society, Toronto, 1927). For recent discussions of the careers of the La Verendryes, see *South Dakota Historical Collections*, vol. VII, 1914, pp. 89–402; and A. S. MORTON, "La Verendrye: Commandant, Fur-trader and Explorer" in *The Canadian Historical Review*, Dec. 1928, pp. 294–298.

For a more exhaustive bibliography, see REGINALD G. TROTTER, *Canadian History: A Syllabus and Guide to Reading* (New York, 1926), especially pp. 29–31; 32–35; 37–39; 41–42.

CHAPTER II

THE FRENCH RÉGIME

IN THE seventeenth and eighteenth centuries France, like all other European nations of the time, clung tenaciously to the mercantilist *Mercantile* view of the value of colonies. According to this theory, the aim of *theory* nations was to become self-sufficient unities. Colonies existed for the benefit of the mother-country only, and were to be carefully regulated and exploited for her profit. Home governments had little interest in the development of self-supporting colonies or in the rise of institutions of local government. France's primary object in North America was the promotion of the fisheries and the fur trade—occupations which would yield immediate revenue for the royal treasury and which could best be administered from the seat of government in France.

The fundamental principles underlying French colonial policy were absolute paternalism, close union of church and state, and *Fundamentals* trade monopoly. French Canada was under the direct control of the *of French* French Crown, and the home government insisted on remaining the *colonial policy* sole judge of what regulations were best for developing the resources and the trade of the colony. So close was the supervision exercised by this paternalistic French government that practically nothing was left to private determination and initiative. Moreover, under this theory of government, since it would be impossible for the king to exercise direct control, it became the practice to farm out, either to persons or to companies, a monopoly of the power to plant colonies, establish missions, and exploit the trade of the dependency.

At the opening of the seventeenth century trade was beginning to develop in New France, but colonization and settlement lagged *Trade* far behind. Trade monopolies were granted to individuals and also to a company formed in France for which Champlain served as agent. Companies of this kind usually paid good dividends on the fur trade, but made little progress in promoting settlements along the St. Lawrence River. Indeed, from the very beginning the establishment of permanent settlements seemed incompatible with a maximum profit from the fur trade, for the latter could thrive only in a country that remained a wilderness.

After several earlier experiments, in 1627 monopoly powers over New France were granted to the Company of New France, an enter- *Company of* prise which had the support of no less a personage than the king's *New France* chief minister, Cardinal Richelieu. He conceived the scheme as a part of his general policy to build a world empire for France and dispute with England and Holland the profits to be derived from the New World. The company's headquarters were in Paris, its stockholders were mostly Parisians, and the enterprise was capitalized at 300,000 livres, divided at first into one hundred shares. Like the companies that had preceded it, the Company of New France exercised an absolute control over its territory under the king, and received a perpetual monopoly of the fur trade and a fifteen-year monopoly of all other trade with the colony. The only activities which remained free were the cod and whale fisheries. Colonists might trade with the Indians, but they were required to transfer all furs to the company at a fixed price. All merchandise imported by the company from the mother-country was to be exempt from duty for fifteen years. The company had powers of taxation as well as the right to create courts and appoint all administrative officials. In return for these sweeping concessions, the company undertook to fortify the colony, to send out three hundred faithful Roman Catholic settlers each year, and to provide each settlement with three priests to supervise its religious life and to convert the heathen natives.

Difficulties of company

In spite of the royal patronage, however, the company failed. France's European wars distracted the attention of Richelieu, and the company soon became involved in financial difficulties. A number of its supply-ships were seized by the British, and in 1629 Quebec itself was captured by the English and was not restored until the Treaty of St. Germain-en-Laye in 1632. The hostile Iroquois continued to menace the straggling settlements, and in 1648 and 1649 they virtually exterminated the friendly Hurons. A rival Scottish and English company proved particularly damaging to the French undertaking in the years 1629–1632. Within a few years the company was willing to transfer its trading privileges to an association of merchants in New France (*Compagnie des Habitans*). Interest in the colony was now at low ebb, and for a time French ministers planned to use it as a dumping-ground for criminals and other undesirables.

Government of colony

Notwithstanding these difficulties some progress was made in the development of a governmental system. Soon after the *Compagnie des Habitans* was organized, an agitation arose for the creation of a council to assist the governor of the colony. In 1647 the Council of Quebec, consisting of the governor, the superior of the Jesuits, and the commandant of troops at Montreal, was established. In the following year two citizens were added to the council membership by choice of the other three. There was, however, no suggestion of representative institutions such as were already beginning to develop in the English colonies to the south. The nearest approach to the practice of representation was the formation of the syndics of Montreal and Quebec, a kind of grievance committee, chosen by the citizens to register complaints at the seat of authority. But these bodies had no further voice in governmental affairs, and were without voting power.

After almost thirty years of rule by the Company of New France the population of French Canada was less than 2500. Besides Quebec, *Population* other struggling settlements had arisen, such as Three Rivers (1634), Sillery (1637), Montreal (1642), and Fort Richelieu (1642), but the company had steadily neglected colonization in favor of the fur trade. Nevertheless, the company continued to control the political and commercial destinies of New France until 1663. The French were not a colonizing people, and those who did migrate to the dominions across the sea soon became discouraged by the minute and burdensome governmental regulations to which they were subjected. The population consisted largely of priests, officials, and fur traders, and there was little agriculture or industry. In Quebec, the capital, there were seventy houses and 550 people in 1665. In the lower town were the shops of the merchants, the storehouses, and the residences. In the upper town were the homes of the clergy and religious orders, and the principal buildings. In 1665 Three Rivers had 455 inhabitants, and Montreal 625. The great promoter of New France, Cardinal Richelieu, was too busy with his tasks of crushing feudalism and building up the royal power in France to have much time or energy left for his venture across the Atlantic.

In 1663 the company's charter was cancelled and by a decree of the king New France became a royal province. Its slow progress *Royal province* under the rule of the company, and the bitter quarrels that broke out among the officials who had the government of the colony in hand were the main reasons for this change. Under the personal guidance of the young Louis XIV and his minister Colbert, both of whom were fired with a faith in France's destiny to become a great world empire, conditions in New France began to improve. The Sovereign Council of Quebec, consisting of the governor, bishop, and five councillors, was promptly created, and this body remained, with modifications, an important agency of government to the close of the French régime a century later. This Sovereign Council—later renamed the Superior Council—had a wide variety of powers. It administered the laws of France in the colony, it promulgated all royal decrees, and it made and enforced local ordinances. It also heard the complaints of the syndics, and served as a court of appeal, always subject, of course, to the final power of the French king. The council soon exercised such varied functions as regulating trade, policing the province, fixing prices, and administering all local affairs.

In 1674, and again in 1703, the size of the council was increased by royal decree, until finally it included the governor, the bishop, *Sovereign* the intendant, the attorney-general, the clerk, and twelve other coun- *Council of* cillors. Once a week, on Monday, these men met to dispose of all *Quebec* the minute and vexing details that came to them for settlement, and to hear hundreds of petty disputes that were appealed to them for adjudication. To this routine the Sovereign Council brought an honesty of purpose and a devotion to duty which should not be over-

looked in the face of the many unfavorable criticisms of the French
régime in Canada. Louis XIV took a keen personal interest in the
affairs of the colony, and read with patience and care the hundreds
of dispatches that came from the province.

*Governor and
bishop*

The governor of New France commanded the troops sent out for
the protection of the colony, supervised inter-colonial relations and
Indian affairs, and theoretically, at least, served as the direct representative of the king. As a matter of fact, he found his powers
much curtailed by the presence of two other officials in the council,
namely, the bishop and the royal intendant. Friction between bishop
and governor was very common, and in these struggles the bishop,
as the head of a powerful church organization, exercised no little
power. One of the functions of the intendant was to serve as a buffer
between these two quarreling officials.

Intendant

The first intendant to come to Canada was Jean Talon, who was
appointed in 1665. Professor William B. Munro has appropriately
called this official "the royal man-of-all-work," for the intendant
was the chief instrument of the royal power in the colony. His
office was an old one in France, and his duties were numerous and
diverse. The intendant supervised the administration of justice, and
acted as chief justice in appeals. It was his duty to watch over the
administration of the colonial finances, and the stores and equipment
of the military forces in the colony. In the absence of the governor
he presided over the meetings of the Sovereign Council. His power
reached into every department of government, and deep into the
homes and every-day life of the people. Theoretically, the intendant's powers were supreme in their sphere even over those of the
governor, although the powers of the various government officials
were all too vaguely defined, and there was much overlapping of
jurisdictions and frequent working at cross purposes. The French did
not understand or approve the theory of separation of powers, and
in this muddling of functions lay one of the greatest weaknesses of
the French régime in North America.

Minor officials

In addition to these major officials, the colony had more than its
due share of minor office-holders, judges, church officials, bailiffs,
and deputies of various kinds. Many of these officials were poorly
chosen, and were second- or third-rate men who sought the sinecures
of New France in order to replenish, by judicious grafting, their
depleted family fortunes.

*Progress as
royal province*

In the first ten years of direct royal control the population of
Canada nearly trebled, but as late as 1673 Canada's seven thousand
people remained but a handful as compared with the rapidly increasing number of British colonists along the Atlantic seaboard farther
south. Successful efforts were made to stop the devastating raids of
the Iroquois on the frontier posts of Canada. In 1665 a detachment
of regular French troops, the famous Carignan-Salières regiment,
arrived. In imitation of earlier Roman practice some efforts were

made to furnish these veterans with wives, and to settle them as soldier-farmers along the Richelieu River, where they might serve as frontier guards against the Indians.

Jean Talon, the first and also the greatest of the intendants, showed remarkable enthusiasm and capacity for the performance of his new duties. He sent surveyors to search for copper and iron along the shores of Lake Huron, and at the same time he tried to introduce better agricultural methods and to encourage the importation of better breeds of animals from Europe. By a system of bounties he sought to stimulate the production of necessary commodities such as soap, potash, and tar, and also to promote ship-building. He encouraged fishing, stimulated the manufacture of household wares, and planned to promote trade between Canada and the West Indies. In 1671 Talon wrote joyfully to France, "I am now clothed from foot to head with home-made articles." *Talon, great intendant*

As Talon was the outstanding intendant, so the Count de Frontenac was New France's greatest and most picturesque governor. Possessed of an ungovernable temper and of membership in France's financially embarrassed nobility, Frontenac was nevertheless a man of indomitable courage and surpassing statesmanship. He not only understood the Indian problem but recognized the importance of Indian alliances in the struggle for supremacy in North America. He managed the Indians with flattery and generosity when this seemed the most effective procedure, and with harsh severity when force seemed to be the only alternative. He danced and yelled and smoked with his dusky allies, and punished them too, all with equal zest. Frontenac fully appreciated the importance of the impending intercolonial conflicts between England and France over the interior of North America, and planned a series of fortifications along the Great Lakes and to the Mississippi River, in order to consolidate French power in America. In another direction his political sagacity was revealed by an attempt to convene a Canadian states-general, and to establish municipal institutions in New France; but these efforts, like many others, came to nothing because the governor received little or no support from the home government. A man of his forceful character could not escape numerous conflicts with the intendants and bishops with whom he was obliged to divide his authority, and after ten years of service he was recalled to France (1682). *Frontenac, great governor*

The last years of Frontenac's régime were marked by bitter quarrels with the bishop and intendant, which turned largely on a difference of opinion as to the governor's policy toward the fur traders and his relations with the Indians. All parties concerned sent voluminous reports of these differences to the king, until the latter, driven to distraction by these unseemly controversies, resolved to recall his impetuous governor. But in 1689, when the first great struggle began between England and France over their dominions in America, Frontenac was returned to the scene of his earlier labors and troubles, *End of Frontenac's régime* and against great odds he managed to preserve the territorial integrity of the French possessions in North America, revive their trade, and force the Iroquois to keep the peace.

Population growth

At the close of the French régime the inhabitants of New France numbered approximately 65,000—about one-twentieth of the estimated population of the thirteen British colonies, which by this time were compactly established on the narrow Atlantic seaboard. It had proved impossible to maintain the encouraging rate of immigration which marked the first ten years of direct royal control. Moreover, although this small population was spread over a territory far too extensive to hold, national pride prevented the government from relinquishing territory which its adventurous sons had discovered and explored. Hundreds of French settlers, lured by the larger profits and the more adventurous life of the fur trader, disappeared each year into the wilderness.

Government of New France

The government of New France was a centralized paternalistic autocracy, centered in Versailles. Local government was totally lacking. Supplies, settlers, and even wives for these pioneers were furnished by the same benevolent government which regulated all trade and industry so meticulously as to deprive most of the population of initiative and self-reliance. The Sovereign Council fixed the prices of imports; the accounts of merchants were open to rigid governmental inspection; bad debts could be appealed to the council for settlement; and minute regulations were made for both the import and the export trade of the colony. Inspectors supervised weights and measures, regulated the handicrafts, and fixed the price of bread. Domestics were prohibited from leaving their masters. Revenues often were farmed out to the highest bidder, and many occupations and transactions were subject to an irritating system of licenses. Justification for these measures was found in the argument that without them the struggling colony could not have been kept alive.

The political history of New France virtually ended in 1755. In the few remaining years of the French régime in Canada, military and not political problems were the all-absorbing issues in Canadian life.

Church and State

French Canada was built on the theory of a close union of Church and State. Though this arrangement did not always provide a harmonious combination, the Roman Catholic Church became one of the most powerful agencies in French-Canadian life.

Récollets and Jesuits

The earliest explorers erected crosses alongside the royal insignia, and beginning with the seventeenth century priests and monks struggled against most discouraging odds to convert the heathen Indians to the Catholic faith. On June 24, 1615, the day consecrated to St. John the Baptist, who later became the patron saint of Catholic Canada, Fathers Jamay and Le Caron celebrated the first mass in the province of Quebec. The Récollets arrived in 1615, and the Jesuits made their appearance ten years later. Their importance as agencies for the extension of French influence in North America, and their zeal and devotion to their religious duties, have already been referred to. Their record is all the more creditable because the French government frequently neglected to support the missionaries who were such important aids in the development of the French colonial empire.

By 1620 a Franciscan friary had been projected near Quebec for the brethren of the order and their Indian converts. Montreal began as a settlement consecrated to the Blessed Virgin. Mission after mission arose as the frontier of French Catholic influence moved steadily westward. Many mission stations were destroyed, and their priests and converts cruelly tortured, in the numerous Indian wars which naturally resulted from French expansion. So disastrous were the consequences of these raids that, from a temporal viewpoint, it must be said that missionary activities ended in failure. *Mission stations*

In 1658 François de Laval was appointed the first bishop and vicar apostolic of New France, and in him the Church of Canada found its ablest and most aggressive champion. In 1674 Pope Clement X established the diocese of Quebec, which included within its jurisdiction all French possessions in North America, with Laval as bishop. From the time of his landing in Quebec, in 1659, Laval never wearied of his labors for the Church and for his flock. He fought for the rights of the Church and of the inhabitants; he battled with governor and fur lords alike over the evils of the liquor traffic with the Indians; and in a short time he became the dominating figure of the Sovereign Council. His interest in education led to the founding, at Quebec, of the seminary from which Laval University later evolved. In 1668 Laval virtually forced the summoning of twenty representative colonists to Quebec to consider the whole question of the liquor traffic and its bearing upon the fur trade. In this "Brandy Parliament," the nearest approach to a representative body in the history of New France, and a gathering which might well have established a precedent for the development of representative institutions, all the familiar arguments for and against the liquor traffic were assembled, attested by the Sovereign Council, and communicated to the king. During Laval's régime notable progress was made in consolidating and extending the religious activities of the colony. *Laval, great bishop*

As pointed out earlier, the bishop was not only the head of the ecclesiastical system of the colony, but he also sat on the Sovereign Council as the co-equal of the governor and the intendant. The Church also became the greatest landowner in New France. It controlled about one-fourth of the total area granted for settlement, and occasionally made great efforts to introduce colonists to develop these estates. In many localities the estates of the Church were by far the most valuable and also the best managed. Royal grants helped to fill the treasury of the Church, and after 1667 tithing was fixed by law. *Economic position of Church*

As the colony developed, the number of parishes was gradually extended, and the parish became the unit for the keeping of vital statistics, for the administration of justice, and for the raising of the militia. The parish priest was the unchallenged leader of his flock in practically every field of human activity, and he exerted a tremendous influence upon the minds and lives of his faithful parishioners. It was the church parish which became "the backbone of French-Canadian nationality."

Education was the monopoly of the Catholic clergy and came under their direct and absolute control. Accordingly every effort was made to keep Protestants and Protestant ideas out of the colony. The masses of the people remained illiterate. There were no newspapers in the colony, and very few books, and over the latter the Church tried to exercise a careful censorship. Although Monseigneur de Pontbriand was the sixth and last Bishop of Quebec whose jurisdiction extended over the whole of New France, the Catholic Church did not lose its dominating influence over the lives of the French-Canadian population after the British conquest. French Canada, founded on the principle of a close union of Church and State, never drew a clear line of demarcation between ecclesiastical and political spheres of action, and to this day the Roman Catholic Church continues to be a most powerful factor in every phase of life in French Quebec.

To promote the economic development of New France, large tracts of land were granted to nobles or seigniors, with the understanding that they, in turn, would assemble tenants on their estates for the settlement of the colony. Thus was introduced into the New World a modified form of the feudalism of the Old. The seigniorial system was both a natural and a logical arrangement for the new colony. In the first place, feudalism was still the recognized basis of land tenure and social stratification in the mother-country, and in the second place, such a feudal system seemed to offer the best opportunity for knitting the struggling settlements of France together under a system of control sufficiently coördinated to enable the small number of colonists to defend themselves effectively against both red and white enemies.

Feudalism in Europe originally involved the granting of tracts of land by the landed class to their followers in exchange for a personal allegiance which involved the performance of military service under the lord's banner in time of war. By multiplying this process of land grants many times (the process of sub-infeudation) a great and complicated hierarchy had been created, having its apex in the king, to whom even the most powerful lord was supposed to render service and fealty. In France, however, by the middle of the seventeenth century the older virulent feudal structure had begun to disintegrate before the rise of the royal power, and the employment of mercenaries experienced in the methods of modern warfare was taking the place of the old feudal levy. Military services became less important and were supplanted by other minor obligations, while the feudal nobles, instead of living on their estates and supervising the activities of their vassals, preferred the pleasures of an absentee landlord system which enabled them to bask in the smiles of royal favor at the brilliant Court of Versailles.

When this decayed form of French feudalism was introduced into New France, it acquired new vigor. The old personal bond between lord and vassal was revived, and the obligation of military service gained new significance in a colony planted in a wilderness and surrounded by enemies. *Its revival in New France*

It is probable that the first seigniories in New France were granted prior to 1627. Under Richelieu's Company of New France about sixty seigniories were created, although many of their owners never came to Canada. Later some twenty-five officers of the Carignan-Salières regiment were made seigniors, and as such received grants of land on Canada's most vulnerable frontier along the Richelieu River. *First seigniories*

Seigniors were expected to serve as real-estate agents for the king, and to promote the development of his colony. The seignior swore fealty and homage to his sovereign lord, registered his seigniory at the royal office in Quebec, agreed to reserve a certain kind of lumber from his estate for the royal navy, and undertook to settle his holding with prospective laborers and farmers. The seignior generally made a small payment to the king at the time when the feudal grant was made, although sometimes this payment was entirely remitted. He was expected to render military service in time of need, but this obligation was never specifically prescribed. When seigniories changed hands a small rent was due the king. The size of these feudal holdings ranged from one or two to 1000 square miles, but, large or small, seigniories were always laid out in the shape of oblongs, facing a river. *Seignior*

Seigniories were subdivided among feudal tenants, or *habitants*, whose holdings usually averaged from 100 to 400 square *arpents*.[1] The services and the rents which the *habitant* gave in payment for his land were neither uniform nor burdensome. First of all, the *habitant* paid the *cens*, which amounted to a few *sous* for each farm. At the time when he received his grant the *rentes*, involving annual payments of either money or produce, were determined. These usually consisted of donations of a few fowls or bushels of grain on St. Martin's Day (November 11), one of the numerous festival days of New France. The *lods et ventes*, another feudal obligation of the *habitant*, involved a payment to the seignior, usually fixed at one-twelfth of the estimated value of the holding, but this was made only when the land of the *habitant* changed hands other than by direct descent in the family. Because of the large size of French- *Habitant*

[1] A square *arpent* was a little more than an acre.

Canadian families, which practically always made a direct heir a certainty, such payments were rarely collected.

Feudal dues

Since the seignior had a monopoly of the mills, ovens, wine-presses, and other necessities on the seigniory, the *habitant* was expected to pay for the use of these facilities. These dues, known as the *banalités*, amounted to very little in actual practice, often were ignored, and sometimes proved more burdensome to the owner, who was expected to maintain this service, than to the *habitant* who was expected to use it. By the *corveé*, as applied in Canada, the *habitant* was usually required to work three days a year, and never more than six, for his seignior, but such enforced labor was always commutable into a fixed money payment at the rate of forty *sous* a day. As a matter of fact, the obligation resting upon the seignior to feed his workers made the *corveé* a prerogative of rather doubtful value. There were numerous other seigniorial prerogatives, such as the right to exact contributions of timber, stone, etc., from the tenants, but these were of little importance and often were totally ignored.

Judicial aspects of Canadian feudalism

The judicial powers granted to some of the seigniors likewise were limited, and in every case an appeal lay from the feudal court to the royal judge. These judicial powers were seldom exercised, for they constituted a burden rather than a source of income. Moreover, the amount of jurisdiction granted varied with each seigniory, and there was no relation whatsoever between the range of judicial powers which could be exercised and the size of the seigniorial estate.

Status of habitant

It is evident that Canadian feudalism was never burdensome. The seignior usually had "an abundance of acreage and little cash," and the *habitant* never reached in the social scale the degraded level which marked the lives of many of the peasants of continental Europe at that time. The *habitant's* duties were light, and the royal intendant was always on hand to see that he was not abused by a grasping seignior.

Decline of Canadian feudalism

In spite of many efforts put forth by the royal authorities to compel sub-infeudation on pain of forfeiture of the estate, many seigniories remained devoid of settlers. The *habitant*, moreover, frequently deserted his holding for the more adventurous and more immediately profitable life of the wilderness and the fur trade. By 1712, although several million *arpents* of land had been granted under seigniorial tenure, only about 50,000 were actually under cultivation, and most of these lay along the north shore of the St. Lawrence River from Quebec to Montreal. By the close of the French régime Canadian feudalism had fallen into a state of decay. It had outlived its usefulness, and after the control of Canada passed into British hands the whole feudal system fell into confusion. Nevertheless, it had been useful in welding New France into a homogeneous colony, and undoubtedly it increased the defensive powers of the province at a time when military considerations were of primary importance. On the other hand, because of its paternalistic character, feudalism retarded the political and material development of the colony. Some of the problems and disputed claims arising from this early seigniorial system remained troublesome issues in Canadian politics until after the middle of the nineteenth century.

French Canada stretched for miles along the St. Lawrence River, which served at once as the gateway to Canada and as the one great *Economic* channel of communication for the settlers and traders scattered along *conditions* its banks. Three-fourths of the population of New France lived on farms, and by 1760 there was an average of about five *arpents* of cleared land for every person in the province. Practically all of the cleared land lay along the St. Lawrence River between Quebec and Montreal, and most of it was located on the north shore. Land grants ran back from the river front in thin parallelograms, which grew ever thinner as farms were divided according to the law of equal inheritance for all children. As all of the heirs insisted on getting a frontage along the river, the result was that the back country was neglected and crop rotation became impossible. The homes of the *habitants* came closer and closer together, until the river front resembled a single village street of whitewashed low timber or stone houses.

Agricultural methods were extremely primitive. A few *arpents* were planted in hay, the land lying farther back was plowed and *Agriculture* sown once a year, and behind this strip lay pasture or timber land. Besides wheat (the exports of which actually reached nearly 200,000 bushels in one notably favorable year before the middle of the eighteenth century), hemp, flax, tobacco, garden truck and other grains were produced. The average yield of wheat varied from nine and a half to fourteen bushels an acre. Farm animals were usually of poor stock. No attempt was made to use fertilizers or to introduce any system of crop rotation. Seeds were generally poor, drainage facilities were totally lacking, and most of the farm implements used were primitive and home-made. The long winters and the uncertainties of the Indian wars encouraged idleness and neglect of farm activities; and when the men were called to military service, the care of their farms fell to the women and children.

The industries of New France made little progress, even at those times when some of them received temporary encouragement from *Industry* the government. A little iron was produced, and some lumber was exported. The milling industry suffered from poorly equipped mills, and every craft was minutely regulated and regimented into gilds. Trade was rigidly supervised, and was so hampered by taxes and monopolies that to the end of the French régime exports remained small and consisted almost entirely of raw materials.

From a primitive system of barter, in which moose and beaver skins constituted a standard of exchange, French Canada gradually *Trade and* became familiar with a more complicated currency. French coins *currency* were usually over-valued in Canada by royal decree, in a more or less futile attempt to keep them from passing out of the country.

Copper and silver were very scarce, and at various times wheat served as legal tender for the payment of debts. Successive ordinances were enacted in a vain effort to control or circumvent the intricate workings of economic laws affecting the currency. By 1713 1,600,000 *livres* of "card money" had been issued, but only part of it was ever redeemed, and then at a great discount. The close of the French régime, as the difficulties of the government multiplied, was marked by a veritable orgy of monetary inflation, and by 1759 about 80,000,000 *livres* of paper money were in circulation. After this date no paper money was ever redeemed by the French authorities. Prices rose tremendously, and at times firewood was dearer in Quebec than it was in Paris. Grasping officials, like Bigot, the last of the intendants, sold grain in 1757 at a profit of 400 per cent.

Government regulation

Repeated efforts were made to regulate the trade of the province by price-fixing and by the establishment of public markets to which all goods had to be brought several times a week for sale. House-to-house selling was prohibited; bread prices were fixed by governmental action several times a year; workshops and handicrafts were inspected; and exporters had to make detailed reports on the nature of their shipments and their prices. Imports were supervised as carefully as the export business. Yet, in spite of all these efforts, the illicit trade with the Indians and with the English steadily increased.

Social system

At the head of the social order in New France were the members of the official class, with headquarters at Quebec, the colonial capital. Here the governor, officials, traders, merchants, lawyers, and some of the wealthier landholders assembled to enjoy the gayeties of a miniature Court of Versailles. The winter seasons in this wilderness capital were especially lively, with a round of dances, banquets and occasional dramatic performances—joys of life in which some of the clergy participated, but which others sternly condemned. Only at Montreal and Three Rivers were the other settlements populous enough to permit similar social revelries, and then only on a much less pretentious scale.

Status of seignior

Outside the towns the seignior's house was the center of social activity and influence. The seigniorial system added much to the social life of New France. It was a notable occasion when the seignior appeared, "without sword or spur, his head uncovered and on bended knee," to swear fealty to his royal master. The first day of May was dedicated to the May Pole ceremony, when all the *habitants* appeared at the lord's house to do him honor and to partake freely of his refreshments. There were other feudal and church holidays, meticulously and joyously observed, often to the detriment of the *habitant*, and with a depleting effect upon the fortune of the seignior, who on these occasions was always expected to play the rôle of the gracious and generous host of his people.

Seignior and curé

The seigniory was sometimes co-terminous with the parish, and the *curé* frequently lived and conducted services at the home of the seignior. Where church buildings existed, the seignior was entitled to occupy a special pew at all services, and in religious processions he might march immediately behind the parish priest. At the administering of the sacraments the seignior enjoyed special favors, and when he died his remains were usually buried under the floor of the church. Many seigniories were also held by the Church, or by one of its religious orders, and these were frequently the most prosperous and best-managed estates in the vicinity.

New France never suffered from a rigid caste system, for frontier conditions alone would have made this impossible. Possession of a seigniorial estate did not automatically raise the holder to the rank of the nobility, since that required a special royal grant. Moreover, by the law of equal inheritance a deceased man's rank passed equally to all of his children, and this prevented the development of a small privileged class. It was possible for a *habitant* to become a seignior, or *vice versa*, and many members of the official class in New France were men who had risen from the ranks. The *habitant* never felt himself in a particularly humiliating social position, whereas many seigniors, on the other hand, found it necessary to engage in trade or to perform manual labor in the fields alongside their *habitants*, in order to keep the wolf from the door. *Social classes*

The *habitant* lived in a stone or timber house, some twelve feet high, with a single door and few windows, a projecting roof, and dormer windows above the eaves. His house usually stood close to the road, without lawn or trees to beautify the approach. The houses of French-Canadian peasants had two or three big rooms, and smaller attic chambers used for bedrooms. Each spring the *habitant* applied a coat of whitewash to the outside walls of his dwelling. Behind the house there was generally a small storeroom, and behind this a log stable for the farm animals. Sometimes there was also a specially built house for the preservation and storing of potatoes and other vegetables, although more often vegetables were preserved by the simple process of burying them. Hay and straw were stacked in the fields behind the house. In the rear was the bake-oven, constructed of rocks and clay, where the family baking was usually disposed of for a week or two at a time. *Life of habitant*

The living-room, with its crude furniture and large fireplace, and with kitchen utensils hung about in it, served as sitting-room, kitchen, and dining-room. The adults slept in small bedrooms adjoining this larger room, while the children, of whom there was usually a large number, slept in low rooms upstairs in the attic. The interior of these cottages was as a rule spotlessly clean, with a colored rug spread on the living-room floor, a number of brightly scoured pots and pans hanging over the fireplace, and Catholic ornaments and holy pictures hanging on the walls or resting in the corners of the living-room. *His home*

The *habitant* lived a pious, frugal, carefree life, without luxuries,

Dress

but also without great deprivations, and with little concern about the future. He wore home-made clothes, produced by the women at the family spinning-wheel and loom. Much of his clothing was made of fur, and on his feet he wore deerskin moccasins. In the warmer seasons he went barefoot, and usually wore a straw hat. During most of the year, however, his head was covered by a knitted cap of many gay colors. Only on Sunday, when he went to mass with his gayly dressed wife and daughters, did he exchange his long crude coat and wide trousers for the better suit he reserved for such occasions.

Food

Food was rough, but wholesome. It consisted of coarse wheat and rye bread, corn cakes, salted meat, smoked fish and game for the winter months, and fish for the special days of the Catholic Church calendar. Pea soup was almost a national dish, although beans and potatoes, as well as melons and berries, were in common use. Sour milk and brandy were the national beverages, and home-grown tobacco was smoked almost incessantly by young and old alike.

Joy of living

It was in the long winter season that the *habitant* nourished his pleasure-loving soul. From October to May the social season was in full swing, with much house-to-house visiting, dancing, card-playing, and other amusements, and with the ever-present fiddler contributing much to the gayety of every occasion. The legends that arose from these gatherings have become part of the folk-lore of Canada, and the songs of these early French Canadians now are part of the folk-music of the Dominion. Holidays were many—too many for the good of the colony—and they were celebrated with the utmost punctiliousness and enthusiasm. Sometimes neighbors gathered to husk one another's corn, and these harvest festivals became real social occasions. Each Sunday after mass the members of the parish lingered near the church to exchange the latest gossip about their neighbors and their crops, and to listen to such decrees of the government as might be read to them.

Women of New France

The life of pioneer women at all times and in all places has been notoriously hard, and New France was no exception. Poverty, toil, and care were the lot of most of the wives of the Canadian *habitants*. Frontier conditions compelled them to work in the fields alongside their husbands, and to share the dangers and sufferings of Indian attacks. The men of New France were in a great majority throughout the French régime in North America. Talon had urged the payment of bounties for marriages, and fines were imposed on obstreperous bachelors who refused to assume the responsibilities of matrimony. A paternal king shipped scores of *filles du roi* into the province to meet the shortage of marriageable women in Quebec. Some of the new arrivals were adventurous damsels of loose character, others came from French orphanages, but mostly they were sturdy peasant girls no worse and no better than the average women of their class in France.

Fourteen or fifteen years was considered the marriageable age for

girls in New France, and eighteen or nineteen years for men. Speedy *Family life*
courtships were the rule, and for a time the governor of New France,
in order to encourage family life, endowed each newly-married couple
with a cow, a bull, a hog, a sow, a cock, a hen, two barrels of salted
meat, and a little money. Dowries were expected in New France as
they were in the mother-country, and although they sometimes
amounted to no more than a barrel of bacon they were carefully
specified in the marriage contract. French-Canadian families have
always been large, the number of children ranging from eight to
eighteen. The responsibility of caring for this numerous brood fell
largely upon the mother, who reared her offspring in the stern faith
of the Catholic Church and taught them the needs and duties of
pioneer life. The endless toil and heroic sacrifices of the women of
New France are still largely unchronicled. Not the least important
work of the mothers of New France was the preservation and development of the folk-lore and the folk-songs of the French people in the
New World environment.

The only instances of feminine levity in French Canada which
are comparable in any way with the brilliant feminine types of old *Life in Quebec*
France in the seventeenth and eighteenth centuries are to be found
in Quebec, the colonial capital, and to a lesser extent in Montreal.
In Quebec this gayety reached its height during the closing years of
the French régime. Peter Kalm, a Swedish naturalist who visited
Montreal, Three Rivers, and Quebec in 1749, found the women of
French Canada handsome, well-bred, and virtuous, "with an innocent
and becoming freedom." They were keenly interested in balls and
social gatherings, and especially fond of fancy hair-dressing. The
ladies of society in Quebec curled and powdered their tresses with
great care for hours at a time, and ornamented their heads with gay
aigrettes. Sunday, of course, was the day on which feminine finery
was displayed at its best. For their daily attire the women wore little
jackets, short petticoats "which hardly reach half the leg," and
high-heeled shoes. Flirtations were of common occurrence among the
young ladies of higher rank in Quebec, and scandals were by no means
unknown. Many of the eligible girls of the capital rose at seven,
dressed till nine, and then spent most of the day sitting and sewing
at a window overlooking the street. It was not unusual for an attractive girl of eighteen to have as many as twenty suitors.

In any discussion of the rôle of women in New France the labors
of the nuns must not be overlooked. French Canada was well sup- *Nuns*
plied with women's religious orders, such as the Ursulines, the Nuns
of the Congregation, and the Grey Nuns. The work of these sisters of
mercy was devoted largely to teaching, nursing, and developing
hospitals. The first hospital in Canada was ready for use in 1638, and
in the following year the Archbishop of Rouen sent over three sisters
from the Hospital Nuns at Dieppe to take charge of the enterprise.
The first Ursuline convent in Canada was completed in 1642. The

main occupation of this particular order of nuns was the education of French girls. Others did excellent work among the Indian population, and made great progress in learning the Indian dialects in their efforts to render greater service to the natives.

The *habitants* and their families lived the life of conservative, pious, honest peasants, and thus many of their descendants still live in present-day Quebec. Often poor, the *habitant* was always faithful to the Catholic Church, the leadership of which he accepted in all phases of life. He married early and begat large families. Usually he was content with his lot, and more often than not he was happy with the blessings which Providence had given him.

But not all of the *habitants* of early Canada were content to remain on the land. The profits of the fur trade were so alluring, and the call of the forest was so persistent, that many preferred to exchange the monotonous existence of the peasant farmer for the romantic, adventurous career of the *coureur-de-bois*. All the devices and penalties which an absolute government could invent would not keep these roamers of the forest, these "dare-devils of the wilderness," at home. Year after year hundreds of men deserted their lands, and often their families, to engage in the profits of an illicit fur trade. In 1680 an intendant reported that "there is not a family of any account but has sons, brothers, uncles, and nephews among these *coureurs-de-bois*." Freed from the restraints of organized society, these adventurers and traders often married Indian squaws and became the fathers of dusky half-breeds.

The fur trade remained the heart of the economic system of New France. Each summer a whole fleet of Indian canoes came down to Montreal. An Indian birch-bark canoe, usually twenty feet long and two feet wide, could carry from 800 to 900 pounds, in addition to a crew of four men. White traders built canoes of larger capacity, and later introduced the *bateaux*, which were long and narrow boats, flat-bottomed and high-bowed, built of cedar and propelled by oars and poles. Laden with furs, these craft descended the rivers and lakes each year to dispose of the season's catch. Tents were pitched, and trade began amidst the holding of Indian councils, smoking the peace pipe, and heavy drinking. In Montreal these gala days continued for several weeks, with less elaborate markets and fairs at the smaller posts. After a few weeks of unbridled revelry and conviviality the trappers and traders, laden with new stores of supplies and brandy for the Indian trade, departed again for the solitude of their forest homes.

(margin note: Coureurs-de-bois)

(margin note: Fur trade)

SELECT BIBLIOGRAPHY FOR CHAPTER II

One of the best brief accounts of the institutions of New France is WILLIAM B. MUNRO, *Crusaders of New France* (New Haven, 1921), especially pp. 113–227. The same author's *The Seigniorial System in Canada* (New York, 1907) and *The Seigneurs of Old Canada (Chronicles of Canada)* are more extended treatments of Canadian feudalism. CHARLES W. COLBY, *Canadian Types of the Old Régime, 1608–1698* (New York, 1910) is especially valuable for the social history of the period. WILLIAM B. MUNRO, *Documents Relating to the Seigniorial Tenure in Canada, 1598–1854* (Toronto, 1908), contains a valuable historical introduction. A useful map, showing the seigniories as they were in 1790, can be found in *Canada and Its Provinces,* vol. II, p. 588. The entire volume is a detailed discussion by experts of French-Canadian institutions and life. Vol. XV, pp. 17–117, contains a special article by A. D. DeCelles on "The *Habitant,* his Origin and History." *Documents relating to Canadian Currency, Exchange and Finance during the French Period* edited by Adam Shortt (Ottawa, Public Archives, 1925, 2 vols.) contains a useful introduction, and material that is of value for the whole economic history of the period.

THOMAS CHAPAIS, *The Great Intendant (Chronicles of Canada)* is a good account of the life and times of Jean Talon. Other volumes dealing with phases of the History of New France summarized in the present chapter are FRANCIS PARKMAN, *Count Frontenac and New France under Louis XIV* (Boston, 1877) and *The Old Régime in Canada* (1874); W. KINGSFORD, *History of Canada,* 10 volumes (London, 1887–98) vol. I; C. W. COLBY, *The Fighting Governor, a Chronicle of Frontenac (Chronicles of Canada).*

For all constitutional questions, by far the best book is W. P. M. KENNEDY, *The Constitution of Canada, An Introduction to its Development and Law* (Oxford, 1922). The first twenty-four pages deal with the period before the English conquest. For more detailed references, see TROTTER, *Syllabus,* pp. 41–42; 44–46.

CHAPTER III

ANGLO-FRENCH RIVALRY FOR NORTH AMERICA

Early rivalries

ALMOST from the beginning of their colonizing efforts in North America, England and France watched the development of each other's plans with jealous hostility. Long-standing enmities, arising from the rivalries of European diplomacy, were transferred to the New World, where the interlocking and overlapping of colonial projects furnished new causes for conflict. From the early part of the seventeenth century there were raids by the English and French upon each other's settlements along the Atlantic coast. As early as 1613 English raiders from Virginia tried to destroy the French post of Port Royal in Acadia, and nine years later the King of England undertook to promote an English colony in this region, in spite of its prior occupation by the French.

Anglo-French rivalry in Europe

For nearly a century (1689 to 1763) England and France were diplomatic rivals in the complicated politics of Europe, and for a third of the century they were actually at war. Indeed, the intervals of peace between these Anglo-French wars can be considered hardly more than periods of armed truce. Without going into detail concerning the many causes of these European wars, we may point out that they would have occurred even if there had been no colonies in North America, and that the colonial phase of these struggles was but a reflection of larger contests in Europe. It was logical and inevitable that both parties, once hostilities had commenced, should endeavor to carry the war into every part of the world where there were vulnerable spots in the enemy's colonial dominions.

American aspect

There were, however, several distinctly American or colonial causes for the four inter-colonial wars which were waged to determine the mastery over North America. First of all, there was the overlapping of colonial claims. For hundreds of miles along the St. Lawrence River and the New England frontier the boundaries of New France touched, and frequently overlapped, those of New England, and this proximity provided the cause for friction, rivalry, and bloody struggles in defense of the disputed frontier.

Struggle for interior

Beyond the Alleghenies, stretching from the Great Lakes to the Gulf of Mexico, lay the great Mississippi valley. England claimed it, by virtue of discovery and explorations, and the charters granted to seven of the English colonies along the Atlantic seaboard contained ''sea-to-sea'' provisions; although the mysteries of North American geography were still largely unsolved, it always was contended that the westernmost limit of these colonial claims was at least the Mississippi River. France, because of the explorations of her pioneers such as Marquette, Joliet, La Salle, and others, likewise asserted jurisdiction over much of this territory. She had begun early to erect posts in this region, and, as has been shown, it was her well-established policy to consolidate her claims in the Mississippi valley with her holdings in the St. Lawrence valley, and thus limit the area of British influence to the narrow Atlantic coastal plain. So long as the little English and French settlements were confined to the districts where they were first established, there was small cause for trouble; but before the middle of the eighteenth century the French and English frontiers began to overlap in the interior regions. It was then that both contestants tried to seize and fortify the headwaters of the Ohio River, the strategic point of approach to the Mississippi basin, and thus began the last great struggle to determine whether North America should develop as a predominantly Latin or a predominantly Anglo-Saxon continent.

Rivalry in the fur trade was another source of difficulty. From the earliest days of Canada's history, British fur traders tried by every *Rivalry over* possible means to divert the fur trade of the Great Lakes region from *fur trade* Montreal and Quebec to British posts. In this battle between the English and the French the former used rum to beguile and demoralize their Indian customers, while the latter relied on the appealing force of brandy. But the result was always the same, namely, the wholesale debauchery of the natives. English rum proved to be cheaper than French brandy, and though it was not of as good quality it nevertheless appealed to the Indians, who, for the sake of longer orgies of drunkenness, preferred quantity to quality. The fur trade was the key to the economic history of New France, the motive for much of its exploration, and an important cause of the deadly rivalry with France's English competitors.

Early in the seventeenth century Great Britain gained control of Newfoundland, the fisheries of which passed under the supervision and jurisdiction of "fishing admirals" from Devonshire and London. In 1670 the Hudson's Bay Company, a great British trading corporation patronized by royalty itself, received a charter to trade in the vast undefined region around Hudson Bay, then known as Prince Rupert's Land. A rival British company, cutting in from the north on their fur preserves, naturally proved most exasperating to the French.

Discovered in 1610, by Henry Hudson in his search for a way to the South Sea, the Hudson Bay country had attracted little attention *Hudson's Bay* until 1668. That year marked a revival of interest in the fur trade on *Company* the part of certain Britishers, due largely to rumors of tremendous profits to be made from the fur business in New England, in the Dutch colony of New Netherland, and in New France. In 1668 Groseilliers, the associate of Radisson in exploring expeditions which had carried the French flag as far west as the present state of Minnesota, left the French employ because of alleged bad treatment, and offered his experience and his plans to a group of Englishmen. King Charles II of England, Prince Rupert, the royal cousin, and James, Duke of York, became seriously interested in the organization of a great English fur-trading venture in northern North America. Other notables, including the Earl of Shaftesbury, the Duke of Albemarle, and a number of London merchants supported a fur-trading expedition to the New World in 1668.

Charter of 1670

Only one of the two ships which set sail on this expedition weathered the gales of the Atlantic, but the survivors returned to England with a valuable cargo. The Merchant Adventurers of London now petitioned for a charter, which was granted in May, 1670. By its provisions the Company of Gentleman Adventurers, trading into Hudson Bay, virtually became feudal lords of a dominion as large as Europe. They were to seek a new way to the South Sea, and to become "true and absolute proprietors" of the vast territory the waters of which empty into Hudson Bay, with monopoly rights to the fish, furs, and minerals of the region. The company, which had such men as Prince Rupert and the Duke of Marlborough among its early governors, prospered from the start. It adopted a strictly business policy toward the Indians and in general treated them with scrupulous honesty. Forts and fur-trading stations were erected in the wilderness, and great stores of furs were shipped to England. In a few years shareholders who had begun with an initial investment of £10,500 were collecting large dividends, and by 1720 they were able to increase their capital tenfold by adopting the modern method of "watering" the stock. In 1920 the company, much altered in its organization and business activities, but still very successful, celebrated the two hundred and fiftieth anniversary of its founding.

French and English fur lords

Manifestly French interests along the St. Lawrence River were greatly disturbed by the appearance of these intruders who offered English competition for the fur trade, both to the south and to the north of their settlements. From time to time there was bloody fighting between the rival groups, for bold French Canadians occasionally ventured across the intervening wilderness to attack and plunder isolated fur-trading posts of the Hudson's Bay Company. At times it proved easier to stir up the Indians to do the bloody work. As early as 1673 Count Frontenac and Talon had keenly appreciated the danger of this English competition. From 1685 to 1697 there was sporadic fighting, and the little forts in the wilderness frequently passed back and forth between English and French with the changing fortunes of war. During these skirmishes both parties had the support of their home governments, and several naval battles were fought in the icy waters of Hudson Bay. But the British company managed to survive these darkest years, when it was beset not only by enemies in North America, but also at home by those who attacked its monopoly powers. After 1713 the company began to boom. Its French rival, the "Company of the North," suffering repeatedly from a lack of governmental support and supplies, as also from Indian hostilities, never prospered.

Another important factor in the struggle between the English and the French for supremacy in North America was the Indian. Efforts *Indian relations* were constantly being made to win his support and allegiance for the one or the other of the contestants. Of special importance were the Iroquois, strategically located along the southern shores of Lake Ontario, in a key position between the English and French settlements, guarding the approach to the West. The Iroquois served as the great middlemen in the commercial intercourse between the English at Albany, N. Y., and the Indian tribes of the West. Moreover, this remarkable Indian confederacy had perfected a political and a military organization which made it a powerful ally and a formidable foe. For years British agents and traders used their influence to incite the Iroquois to war against tribes farther inland, in order to break up the latter's fur trade with the French. The French, in turn, tried to lure the Iroquois from their British connections, sometimes by the gentle ministrations of Jesuit missionaries, sometimes by intrigue or war. From 1684 on, the chiefs of the Iroquois confederacy virtually acknowledged the suzerainty of the colony of New York, and accepted its protection. Indian relations like these inevitably involved the British and French governments in many of the troubles of their red-skinned allies. The story of these Indian relations is full of intrigue, violence, and treachery, and in many cases it is difficult to determine whether it was the British or the French who were the worst offenders. The frontier was in an almost continual state of excitement, due to raids and massacres which were the bloody consequences of these rivalries.

As has been suggested, there was enough in the colonial situation as it developed in North America to provoke conflicts between French and English settlers, so that desultory fighting, without any formal declarations of war, was of fairly common occurrence.

In 1689 the first of a series of four inter-colonial wars broke out. The spark came from Europe, where William of Orange, who had *King* just ascended the British throne, launched a great alliance to restore *William's War* the European balance of power and checkmate Louis XIV of France in his ambitious schemes for the extension of French influence and the expansion of French territory. The colonial phase of this war is known in history as King William's War. In this, as in later inter-colonial wars in America, the fighting was of two kinds. There were the usual military expeditions of a more formal nature against the recognized strongholds of the enemy; but owing to the wide distances between rival settlements, most of the fighting was in the nature of guerilla warfare, conducted usually by bands of Indians under white leadership. These murderous raids were the more terrible because they lacked the elements of control which are generally present in formal military expeditions.

King William's War was marked by a series of these frontier raids. The French governor, Count Frontenac, launched a number of attacks on the English frontier settlements of New York, New Hampshire, and Maine. Schenectady, a fortified town in the Mohawk valley, was totally destroyed in 1690. The town itself was burned to the ground and its inhabitants were either murdered or carried off as captives. Similar butcheries occurred at numerous other places along the frontier, and the record of English raiding parties which attacked the Montreal region is quite as bloody as that of their French opponents. In 1690 Sir William Phips, a wealthy Massachusetts shipper, led a naval expedition to Acadia and seized Port Royal in a bloodless encounter. After plundering the place, the expedition proceeded up the St. Lawrence River to take Quebec. But Frontenac dramatically refused to surrender the French capital, and Phips had to abandon the siege. In 1697 King William's War came to an end with the Treaty of Ryswick, which, so far as North America was concerned, left the Anglo-French situation unchanged.

Nature of fighting

The opening of the next century witnessed a resumption of the hostilities. England and France again came to grips over the European balance of power which was threatened this time by a scheme virtually to unite the French and Spanish thrones. What is known in European history as the War of the Spanish Succession, is known in America as Queen Anne's War (1702–1713).

Queen Anne's War

By 1703 the customary frontier butchery was well started, and it culminated in such acts of ruthlessness as the Deerfield (Massachusetts) Massacre of 1704. In 1710 an English fleet, carrying some colonial troops, started for Port Royal, and on October 16 the garrison, in dire straits and outnumbered five to one, surrendered to the British. The captured town was promptly renamed Annapolis.

Port Royal

In the following year a British expedition of some seventy ships sailed from Boston for Quebec. On board were more than 5000 men with seven regiments of British regulars. This powerful armada, however, was commanded by incompetents and became lost in a fog. Eight transports and two supply-ships were dashed against the rocks in the treacherous St. Lawrence channel, resulting in the loss of nearly 1000 lives. The expedition was consequently abandoned, and Quebec rejoiced at what its inhabitants believed to be a miracle of deliverance in answer to their prayers and public fastings.

Quebec

The war was ended by the Peace of Utrecht (1713), the first European treaty seriously to affect the geography of North America. Under its terms France surrendered all claims to Newfoundland, Acadia (Nova Scotia), and the Hudson Bay country. In addition, she formally acknowledged British suzerainty over the Iroquois. The provisions of the treaty of 1713 made the first rift in the great colonial empire of the French in North America. But Cape Breton Island and

Peace of Utrecht

the Ile St. Jean (Prince Edward Island) remained in French hands. Moreover, since no effort was made in the treaty to define the limits of Nova Scotia, its disputed boundary remained a source of friction and strife for several decades longer.

The third inter-colonial war was known as King George's War (1745-1748); in Europe it was called the War of the Austrian Succession. After losing Nova Scotia, in 1713, France built the powerful fortress of Louisbourg on Cape Breton Island. The best French engineering talents were utilized to plan the fortifications and land-batteries of this "Gibraltar of the West," commanding, as it did, the entrance to the St. Lawrence River, and intended as "a pistol held at England's head." In time of war it was expected that Louisbourg would serve as a place of refuge for French ships, and as a base of operations from which expeditions could be launched against the British colonies to the south. In the fort were places for 148 cannon, but unfortunately for the French cause the garrison got little training in the use of these formidable batteries. *King George's War*

In 1745, due largely to the vision of Governor Shirley of Massachusetts, an expedition of New Englanders was organized for the reduction of Louisbourg. Colonel William Pepperell, a rather grandiose New England gentleman without military experience, led a force of four thousand New England militia, many of whom were actuated by the desire for plunder rather than for military glory, in what seemed a foolhardy effort to reduce the greatest military stronghold in America. One historian has described the operations around Louisbourg as "one of the most eccentric sieges ever known." In the attacking party were New England farmers, fishermen, merchants, and clerks; by all the rules of organized, scientific warfare the assault should have failed. Instead, the New Englanders succeeded in effecting a landing west of the town, and pulled their cannon through the marshes to within sight of the fortifications. Some of the bombarding of the French fortress was actually done with captured French cannon. After a forty-seven days' siege Louisbourg, poorly commanded, and with fortifications which were not yet completed, surrendered to the New Englanders. Pepperell became a baronet, and the members of his successful expedition divided much prize money taken from French ships which had been lured into the British trap. A French naval force was sent to the relief of Louisbourg in 1746 and 1747, but it failed in its mission and thus gave further proof of the importance of sea-power as a factor in determining the fate of New France. *Capture of Louisbourg*

The Peace of Aix-la-Chapelle (1748) restored the *status quo ante bellum*, a settlement which involved the restoration of Louisbourg to the French, to the great disgust of the New Englanders. In 1749 New England was indemnified by the British government for the expenses of the siege of 1745. Louisbourg was promptly rebuilt by the French, and by 1758 its walls held 212 guns and seventeen mor- *Peace of Aix-la-Chapelle*

tars, with others in reserve. Roads were built and a serious effort
was made to colonize an agricultural population in the vicinity of
the fort.

Attempts to anglicise Nova Scotia

To offset the menace of Louisbourg, the British built Halifax,
in Nova Scotia in 1749. Three years after its founding, the town
had a population of nearly 4000, a result of the British policy of
anglicising Nova Scotia in order to counteract the influence of the
French Acadian population. The latter remained under the control
of their French priests, and steadfastly refused to take the oath of
allegiance to Great Britain.

Armed truce

The years which intervened between the Treaty of Aix-la-Chapelle
and the outbreak of the French and Indian War six years later were
hardly better than a period of armed truce, with both contestants
preparing for the next and final struggle. By the middle of the eighteenth century both the British and the French were ready to assert
their claims to the region beyond the Alleghenies, and it was over
the struggle for the possession of the forks of the Ohio River, controlling the entry to the Ohio and Mississippi valleys, that the last
of the inter-colonial wars was fought.

De Blainville

Before the middle of the century Virginians began to promote
land companies in order to secure vast grants in the vacant lands
along the Ohio River. In 1750 Christopher Gist, an employee of the
Ohio Land Company, examined the Ohio country with a view to
determining its possibilities for settlement. To offset these plans,
Celoron de Blainville, with a party traveling in twenty-three large
canoes, left Montreal in 1749 to consolidate the French influence
among the Indians of the Ohio valley, and to plant leaden plates
and make inscriptions on the trees. By these methods the French
hoped to reaffirm their ownership of the disputed area. De Blainville
floated down the Ohio River as far as the mouth of the Great Miami
River and returned by way of this stream and various portages to
Lake Erie. During this expedition the French discovered that the
Indians were very friendly toward the British traders, and promptly
decided upon vigorous measures to hold this interior country under
French control.

Race for control of Ohio

A race for the control of the source of the Ohio River followed.
The French determined to erect a fort at the site of the present-day
city of Pittsburgh. Governor Dinwiddie of Virginia, a man of considerable vision and a thorough-going expansionist, promptly dispatched young George Washington, a Virginia surveyor, formally
to warn the French that they were trespassing on British possessions.
The French refused to withdraw, and proceeded with their plans to
construct Fort Duquesne at the fork of the Ohio River. Again Washington was sent with a force of Virginia militia to drive out the
intruders, but on the occasion of his second visit he himself was
compelled to surrender to a superior force, and the French were able
to continue the building of their little fortification.

Thus on the banks of the Ohio River the last of the inter-colonial wars had its beginning. It soon spread to Europe and to other parts of the world where the two main contenders had possessions. In 1755 Great Britain sent General Braddock, with a force of seasoned British veterans, to recapture Fort Duquesne. But Braddock, skilled in the arts of formal warfare, knew little about the frontier methods of fighting, and refused to learn anything from such colonials as George Washington and Benjamin Franklin who were attached to his expedition. Moreover, colonial troops and British regulars had little in common, and not much love was lost between them. After a tedious summer march through Pennsylvania, Braddock's expedition was disastrously defeated by the French and their Indian allies in the forests near Fort Duquesne. Almost immediately the Indians, ever anxious to be on the winning side, went over in large numbers to the French, and soon the torch and bloody tomahawk of the savage were at work among the cabins of the frontiersmen who had ventured too far beyond the settled regions. The frontier of settlement at once receded behind the Appalachians.

French and Indian War

In the year of Braddock's defeat occurred the deportation of the French Acadians from their homes in Nova Scotia. After the transfer of this region to England in 1713, the Acadians were granted one year's time in which to move from their old homes if they desired to do so. The French government wished them to migrate to Cape Breton Island, but the Acadians stubbornly refused to go. Moreover, they were equally persistent in their refusal to take the oath of allegiance to their new British governors. A pledge of neutrality was the greatest concession they were willing to make as a result of the new conditions in which they found themselves. Because Great Britain granted the Acadians the full enjoyment of their religious rights, many French priests, subject to the authorities at Quebec, continued to live and work among them.

Deportation of Acadians

With the renewal of hostilities between England and France, the Acadians, from the point of view of the British of Nova Scotia, were at best dangerous neutrals, menacing Halifax, the British naval base, and likely to be used by the French as "a thorn in Great Britain's side." After rejecting a final opportunity to take the oath of allegiance, in 1755 the Acadians were deported by order of Governor Lawrence and his council, and without the previous knowledge or consent of the British home government.

Military necessity

Herded together in their churches, to some extent by treachery, in October, 1755, the Acadians were loaded on transports and distributed among the ports of the British colonies to the south. About 6000 of them were forcibly expelled, and their farms and houses burned. Approximately one-third were deported to South Carolina, and many eventually made their way to French Louisiana. The American poet, Longfellow, used this incident as the theme of his tragic poem, *Evangeline*, and by his beautiful and sympathetic treatment made it one of the most widely-known events of American history. From the British viewpoint, and according to the stern law of war, the deportation was justified as a military necessity.

French victories   The period from 1754 to 1757 was one of almost unbroken disaster for the British cause in North America. In 1756 the able French commander, the Marquis de Montcalm, embarked at Brest to take command of the defenses of New France. In spite of the constant interference of the vain and incompetent Vaudreuil, the governor at Quebec, and Bigot, the corrupt and grafting intendant, Montcalm made a remarkable record as an efficient military commander. In August, 1756, he surprised and captured Fort Oswego on Lake Ontario. In the following year he seized Fort William Henry, at the southern end of Lake George, and in July, 1758, he defended Ticonderoga, the gateway to Canada along the Lake Champlain route, and compelled the retreat of British and colonial forces, under Abercrombie, which outnumbered his men four to one. Western New York, the strategic route through Lake Champlain, was now under French control.

William Pitt, organizer of victory   By 1758, however, the tide of battle began to turn, for the crisis in British fortunes had brought William Pitt to power in England. As prime minister he not only began to drive corruption, graft, and inefficiency from the British government, as well as from the navy and the army, but with rare statesmanship he began to plan a series of campaigns designed to strike the vulnerable spots of the French Empire in every part of the world. The fighting in Europe he left to his brilliant ally, Frederick the Great of Prussia, whom he kept supplied with a steady stream of British gold. Pitt became the "Organizer of Victory." He perceived at once that England enjoyed a great advantage over her enemy in the matter of naval power, and at the same time realized that sea-power would be the decisive factor of the war.

British victories   Deserving young officers were now promoted to positions of high command in the English armies and sent to America. Jeffrey Amherst was forty years of age, James Wolfe but thirty. Pitt planned the concentration of large supplies and forces at Halifax, and prepared for a new attack on Louisbourg. In 1758 a British fleet mounting nearly 1650 guns left Halifax for the reduction of the French citadel. Land forces, consisting of 12,000 men, were placed under the command of Amherst. The French defenders, under the Chevalier de Drucour, were outnumbered four to one, and the British fleet alone would have been powerful enough to strangle Louisbourg into submission. A landing was effected, and after a siege of forty-eight days Louisbourg fell into British hands. In 1760, after the fall of Quebec, the fortress was completely demolished. In the same year (1758) Fort Frontenac (Kingston) and Fort Duquesne surrendered to the British. The latter was renamed Fort Pitt.

The next great battle was fought for Quebec, the center of French power in North America, and the fall of Louisbourg prepared the *Battle for* ground for this last assault. Montcalm fully appreciated his pre- *Quebec* carious position, and the close of 1758 found him feverishly perfecting the defenses of the city. In this task he was constantly hindered by the governor and the intendant, and the whole corrupt civil service, who repeatedly interfered with the development of his plans. "What a country," Montcalm wrote home in despair, "where rogues grow rich and honest men are ruined."

In February, 1759, a large British fleet sailed for America to begin the siege of Quebec. The British land forces were under the *Nature of* command of General Wolfe. The English colonies along the Atlantic *expedition* seaboard were sufficiently concerned to contribute to the expedition. Even some of the Puritan preachers of New England beat the "drum ecclesiastick" against the hated papal régime in French Canada. Preparatory to the major operations against Quebec, British troops under Amherst forced the French to evacuate Ticonderoga and Crown Point (1759).

The siege of Quebec is one of the decisive events of world history. On June 26, 1759, the British fleet and the British army under Wolfe *Beginning of* arrived at the Isle of Orleans to begin a twelve weeks' siege of the *siege* great citadel. Wolfe was a slight, tall Britisher who had entered the army at the tender age of thirteen, and now, as the great moment of his career approached, was but thirty-two years old. He had participated in the earlier Louisbourg campaign. Though suffering acutely from rheumatism and gravel, and in the very shadow of the grave, he eagerly undertook the almost impossible task of reducing France's most strategically located fortress in North America.

The ancient city of Quebec was situated on a great rock on the north side of the St. Lawrence River, about a mile wide at this point. *Quebec's* Behind it was the St. Charles River. Every conceivable approach by *strategic* which an army could be led up to the high plateau on which the *location* city stood, was covered by French guns and guarded by French pickets. But Montcalm had only about 17,000 troops with which to repel a total British force of 27,000. Only 3500 of Montcalm's army were French regulars, and only these, strictly speaking, were under his immediate command. The militia and the other irregulars were under the control of Vaudreuil, the vain, incompetent, and meddlesome governor.

After weeks of futile manœuvring and bombardment, during which the British made little progress toward penetrating the *Plains of* defenses of Quebec, and French fire-rafts, in turn, failed to demoralize *Abraham* the British blockading fleet, a narrow passageway was discovered by which an army might be led up onto the Plains of Abraham, the plateau upon which the city's defenses stood. Wolfe decided to take the desperate chance. In the dead of night, and behind a screen provided by the British ships, 5000 men crossed five miles of river, and silently, two by two, in the early morning, made their way up the stony cliffs. It was a simple matter to overpower the startled sentry, and when morning dawned, on September 13, 1759, Montcalm found the red-coats drawn up in battle array on the Plains of Abraham, ready for the French attack.

Montcalm and Wolfe

Even now Montcalm's desperate attempts to defend the city were hindered by Vaudreuil. In fifteen minutes the fight was over, and the French were fleeing before the withering fire of their enemies. Quebec soon surrendered to the victors. The city itself was in ruins, and its population reduced to famine conditions. Montcalm, like the rest, had been living on rations of four ounces of horse flesh a day. Neither the victorious nor the vanquished leader lived to see the closing events of the great drama in which they were the last important actors. Both fell, mortally wounded, early in the attack. Montcalm was buried by torchlight in an Ursuline chapel where some days later a British army chaplain read the funeral service for Wolfe.

Second siege

On April 27, 1760, De Levis, the able French commander at Montreal, in an attempt to regain the city, led his troops to the heights of Quebec by almost the same method Wolfe had so successfully employed seven months earlier. De Levis actually won a temporary victory, and General Murray, the British commander at Quebec, was compelled to withdraw into the city proper, where, after several days of anxious waiting, he was saved by the coming of the British fleet. Again British naval supremacy proved the decisive factor in the campaign. At the end of May, 1760, De Levis speedily retired to Montreal, where his little army of 2000 men was besieged by three British forces. On September 8, 1760, Governor Vaudreuil formally signed papers of capitulation. The surrender of the remaining French posts in North America was a foregone conclusion, and by 1763, when the war officially came to a close, two tiny fishing islands off the coast of Newfoundland were all that was left of the French colonial empire in North America.

Treaty of Paris

By the Treaty of Paris (1763) France ceded to Great Britain all of Canada and all of her claims in North America east of the Mississippi River. The British King restored to France the little islands of St. Pierre and Miquelon, to serve as shelter for her fishermen. The region west of the Mississippi, including the Isle of Orleans at its mouth, was transferred to the sovereignty of Spain. Pitt, though no longer in charge when the treaty was made, after long consideration, preferred the annexation of Canada to the annexation of Guadaloupe, a semi-tropical West Indian Island, the acquisition of which had been strongly favored by British merchants. Canada at the time was regarded by many Englishmen as a territorial addition of doubtful value, and, exclusive of the fisheries and the fur trade, of little consequence for the future of the British Empire.

SELECT BIBLIOGRAPHY FOR CHAPTER III

The best and most readable account of the struggle for supremacy in North America is G. M. WRONG, *The Conquest of New France* (New Haven, 1921). Volumes in the *Chronicles of Canada* which are of special importance for this period are WILLIAM WOOD, *The*

Passing of New France, and *The Winning of Canada;* CHARLES W. COLBY, *The Fighting Governor;* and ARTHUR G. DOUGHTY, *The Acadian Exiles.*

The journal of the expedition under Sir William Phips against Port Royal, and other sources dealing with the capture of this position in 1690, will be found in the *Report on the Canadian Archives* (1912), Appendix E, pp. 54–66, 67–83. Special volumes dealing with the fortunes of Louisbourg are WILLIAM WOOD, *The Great Fortress* (*Chronicles of Canada*), and J. S. McLENNAN, *Louisbourg, from its Foundation to its Fall, 1713–1758* (London, 1918). The latter is most exhaustive. See also GEORGE A. WOOD, *The Public Life of William Shirley*, vol. I (New York, 1920), and LAWRENCE SHAW MAYO, *Jeffery Amherst* (New York, 1916) and J. B. BREBNER, *New England's Outpost, Acadia before the Conquest of Canada* (New York, 1927).

Parkman's volumes dealing with the closing scenes in New France are *Montcalm and Wolfe*, 2 vols. (Boston, 1884). See also PARKMAN, *A Half Century of Conflict* (Boston, 1892). G. M. WRONG, *The Fall of Canada* (Oxford, 1914), deals with the last year of the struggle. See also W. T. WAUGH, *James Wolfe, Man and Soldier* (Montreal, 1928).

FRANK H. SEVERANCE, *An Old Frontier of France*, 2 vols. (New York, 1917), deals with the Niagara and the adjoining lake region under French control.

For the history of the Hudson's Bay Company, and its rivalry and struggles with the French, see such histories of the great company as GEORGE BRYCE, *The Remarkable History of the Hudson's Bay Company* (London, 1910), and BECKLES WILSON, *The Great Company* (Toronto, 1899).

For more detailed bibliography, see TROTTER, *Syllabus*, pp. 52–53; 55–58.

CHAPTER IV

BRITISH RULE TO THE AMERICAN REVOLUTION

Reorganizing Empire

THE Treaty of Paris (1763) was of great significance for the future of North America. Not only was French rule expelled, but England now shouldered the burden and responsibility of governing and conciliating a population which was alien in race, in customs, and in religion. This new task was undertaken at a critical juncture in the history of the Empire, when signs of its approaching dissolution were beginning to appear in the thirteen neighboring English colonies. In addition, by her annexations in North America and in other parts of the world England became a world power almost overnight. Consequently, she needed a larger army and navy, and also a reorganization of her system of colonial administration, if she would protect the fruits of the war against her jealous foes. These new burdens, coupled with the desire to have her colonies contribute toward the reduction of a national debt which was the result of long years of warfare, soon led men like the well-intentioned and over-logical Grenville, and his more pig-headed successors, to devise new plans for the raising of imperial revenues and for the reorganization of imperial administrative methods. These new policies soon led to serious friction between the English-American colonies and the mother-country.

Treaty of 1763 and American colonies

The disappearance of the French and Indian menace on the frontiers of New England undoubtedly helped to develop a new spirit of self-reliance among the British colonists, and also a feeling of security which made them less dependent upon the naval and military resources of the home government. As William Burke pointed out when the treaty of 1763 was concluded, "a neighbor that keeps us in some awe is not always the worst of neighbors."

Virility of French stock

When New France was surrendered to the British her total population was somewhere between 65,000 and 70,000 people. Some 15,000 of them lived in towns, the only settlements of appreciable size and importance being Quebec and Montreal. From this little nucleus the present-day French-Canadian population of 3,000,000 has sprung. So great has been the virility of this French stock that, without further immigration from France, and cut off from all spiritual and national ties with the land of their origin, the French Canadians have developed an intense and enduring national spirit which has not only permeated the province of Quebec, but has accompanied the sons and daughters of French Canada in their migrations to the Canadian west and to many parts of the United States.

The articles of capitulation to which the Chevalier de Ramezay agreed when Quebec was surrendered in 1759 permitted the French *Terms of victory* garrison to march to their ships with the honors of war, promised respect for private property, left the inhabitants of Quebec undisturbed in their homes, and permitted the free exercise of the Roman Catholic religion until a final settlement of this question should be made in the treaty of peace. The capitulation signed by Governor Vaudreuil in the following year likewise included a guarantee of the liberties, property, and religion of the Canadian people. The Treaty of Paris (1763) recognized the rights of the people to profess their religion according to the rites of the Roman Catholic Church, "as far as the laws of Great Britain permit." This qualifying clause was deliberately inserted and might have turned out to be a serious limitation of the practice of Roman Catholicism, since many laws were still in force imposing various disabilities on Roman Catholics within the British Empire. Furthermore, the strong-minded and perverse George III had recently ascended the British throne, and his anti-Catholic principles were well known.

Indeed there is some evidence that Great Britain, whatever the guarantees of the treaty, was planning a campaign to encourage the *Great Britain* formation of Protestant schools and to promote the spread of Prot- *and Church of* estantism in the new province of Quebec. The instructions issued to *Canada* Governor Murray in 1763 for the government of the conquered province urged him "not to admit of any Ecclesiastical Jurisdiction of the See of Rome or of any other foreign Ecclesiastical Jurisdiction whatsoever." In actual practice, nevertheless, British rule proved very mild indeed, and the military officials in charge of the conquered province soon learned that it was an excellent policy to respect the rights of the Roman Catholic clergy. The latter, fully aware of the dangers which might arise from the new régime, at once ordered all the faithful to give loyal obedience to their new rulers, and to sing *Te Deums* for their British sovereign.

Immediately after the reduction of Quebec and Montreal the British divided Canada into three military districts—Montreal, *Temporary* Quebec, and Three Rivers—each under a lieutenant-governor, with *military* General Amherst acting as military governor of the entire territory. *government* This temporary military rule was equitable and humane. The religious sentiments of the people were respected, and their property rights were not molested. The old laws and customs, under which French merchants, traders, and landholders had lived for generations, remained undisturbed. The natural result of such tactful conduct was to win the support of the clergy and the seigniors for the new régime, and through these two most influential classes the reactions of the mass of the people could easily be controlled. The treaty of 1763 allowed any who might wish to return to France a period of eighteen months in which to dispose of their holdings, but only a few hundred people left the province. The clergy, almost to a man, decided to remain with their people.

The most discordant element in the population proved to be the recently arrived settlers and traders from New England, who came to take advantage of the new business opportunities which the British conquest of Canada opened to them. Almost at once there was friction between the French-Catholic majority and the steadily growing and aggressive English minority. The latter, familiar with the traditions of New England democracy, clamored for the introduction of British institutions in Canada. As for Governor Murray, who served in Canada as Civil governor from 1763 to 1766, his sympathies were decidedly with the French population. In spite of some restlessness among the *habitants*, Murray was confident that the French Canadians would soon become faithful subjects of the British Crown.

British-American immigration

In October, 1763, the British government, by means of a royal proclamation, tried to institute temporary arrangements for the control of her recent acquisitions in America, and for the handling of the Indian problem, which was always closely bound up with the problem of government. There were abundant reasons to justify the immediate promulgation of these royal orders.

Causes of proclamation of 1763

In the first place, the Indian problem demanded immediate attention and, if possible, prompt solution. Shortly after the conquest of New France most of the British troops were withdrawn, leaving the western Indians under the influence of French fur traders, who were allowed to wander at will through the West. At this critical juncture in Indian affairs the great Ottawa chieftain, Pontiac, a participant in Braddock's defeat in 1755, determined to organize an Indian confederacy to block the British advance into the Mississippi valley. Pontiac, who was a leader of much ability and organizing skill, undoubtedly was aided in his plans by the French. In May, 1763, the Indians rose on all parts of the frontier as part of a well-directed plan of battle. In the eastern half of the Mississippi basin Fort Sandusky was burned, Fort St. Joseph, Fort Miami, Fort Presqu'Isle, and other posts were taken, and within six weeks British influence had disappeared from the entire Great Lakes region, with the exception of Detroit. The latter, which Pontiac had selected as the objective of his own military operations, successfully withstood a fifteen months' siege. Eventually the Indians were beaten back, and in 1768 they were forced to accept the Treaty of Fort Stanwix, which opened to British settlement the region between the Mohawk and Allegheny valleys, and the Ohio valley to the mouth of the Tennessee River. Pontiac was tomahawked by an Illinois Indian, near Fort St. Louis, in 1769.

Pontiac's conspiracy

Pontiac's conspiracy left a deep impression on the minds of British officials, and convinced the government that the Indian problem

Indian line and fur trade

could be solved only by bringing Indian affairs under the complete control of the imperial authorities. It was decided to draw an Indian line through the North American possessions, beyond which whites were not to go except with the special permission of the government. It was also hoped by this means to regulate the fur trade, so that an element in the friction between the whites and Indians which had led to Pontiac's war might henceforth be avoided. Obviously the problem before Great Britain was to draw the Indian line in such a way that the Indians would be assured of an adequate reserve, without unduly restricting the expansion of the seaboard colonies beyond the Alleghenies.

The Royal Proclamation of October 7, 1763, contained many significant provisions. Some dealt with problems in other parts of *Provisions of* North America and therefore may be ignored for our present purpose. *Proclamation* The proclamation created the province of Quebec as the governmental *of 1763* unit for the French-Canadian population in the St. Lawrence valley. A line was drawn along the crest of the Appalachian highlands, extending from northeast to southwest across North America, and beyond this line white settlement was not to go. Thus a great Indian reservation was projected, to be subject to imperial control, and to be administered by the officials of the British Indian Service and the officers of the army. The result of this proposal was that, of all the attractive region beyond the Alleghenies to which the English colonists had been turning covetous glances, only a very small area (what is now the state of West Virginia) was left open to settlement. To enforce this provision, against the natural tendency of the colonies to expand westward, proved to be utterly impossible.

The proclamation of 1763 also laid down detailed regulations for the fur trade in order to promote peace with the Indians and to insure *Governmental* maximum profits. For the province of Quebec it instituted a govern- *regulations* ment consisting of a governor and an appointed council, and promised that an elective assembly should be summoned when conditions in the colony warranted the establishment of this element of self-government. A judicial system was to be established consisting of civil and criminal courts governed by law and equity "as near as may be agreeable to the laws of England," with the right of an appeal, in civil cases, to the British Privy Council. William Pitt declined the governorship, and the formal establishment of civil government in Quebec was brought about by Governor Murray. Murray had the aid and support of a council of twelve appointed by the Crown, but an elective assembly was not considered feasible at this time when there were only about five hundred Protestants in the total population. In view of British practice it seemed impossible to enfranchise the Catholics, and equally impossible to allow a few hundred Protestants, whom Murray called "grab-alls" and "Americanized camp-following traders," to monopolize such representative government as might be established.

Governor Murray's régime was marked by a genuine desire to conciliate the French Canadians. He was an excellent French scholar and had no little appreciation of the psychology of the French people. New courts were established, but most of the ancient customs of the colony were left undisturbed. Indeed, in the legal system inaugurated, Murray deviated strongly from the provisions of the proclamation, which at least implied that English civil and criminal law was to prevail. In spite of his good intentions and humane rule, Murray's term of office was marked by considerable friction. Many poorly qualified officials and judges were sent out from England, and the difficulties with which they had to contend were greatly aggravated by their ignorance of the French language and customs. Friction between the civil and military authorities and between the French agricultural population and the slowly growing British minority of businessmen could not be avoided. The *habitants*, too, were getting restless and felt uncertain as to their exact status under the new dispensation. In 1766 Murray was succeeded by Sir Guy Carleton.

Murray's mild régime

Carleton came of English-Irish stock. He was one of Pitt's "young men" and had served with General Wolfe at Quebec. A man of scrupulous honor and an ardent imperialist, he readily concluded that the way to keep Canada under British control was to allow her to remain French. Carleton exercised great influence on the provisions of the Quebec Act, a new constitutional provision for Canada passed in 1774 and destined to have a basic effect on the history of the province for many generations.

Sir Guy Carleton

For many reasons the arrangements instituted by the proclamation of 1763 were unsatisfactory. Abuses in the administration of justice could be corrected only by settling once for all the system of civil and criminal law which was to prevail. The status and privileges of the Roman Catholic Church needed more careful definition, and the vexing problem of an elective assembly could not be ignored. The problem of governing the great West was as important as ever, and neither the fur trade nor Indian relations had been satisfactorily dealt with. Moreover, in the Illinois country and around the Great Lakes there were a number of unattached French villages for which some kind of civil government had to be instituted. Finally, the constantly increasing friction between the English mother-country and her thirteen colonies made it imperative to conciliate the French population of Quebec and thus minimize the possibility of that province joining them in case they should rebel.

Causes of Quebec Act

The Quebec Act, "the Magna Charta of the French-Canadian race," received the royal assent on May 2, 1774, and became the basic law for the region defined in the act as the Province of Quebec. This included not only the French settlements along the St. Lawrence River and the Great Lakes, as well as Labrador to the eastward, but also that section lying between the Ohio River and the Great Lakes, and extending west of Pennsylvania to the Mississippi River. But the

Quebec Act of 1774

law contained the provision, of dubious significance, that nothing in the statute should in any way affect the boundaries of other colonies, or cancel earlier rights which had been granted. In the confines of the newly-defined province of Quebec the inhabitants were guaranteed the "free exercise of Religion of the Church of Rome, subject to the King's Supremacy," but they were exempted from taking the Oath of Supremacy, and simply swore allegiance to the king, promising to report all treasonable conspiracies to the authorities. The seigniorial system, where it already existed, was left undisturbed. In the administration of justice the old French law was retained for all civil cases, but English law was to prevail in criminal cases. The provisions for the legal system, however, were not rigid, as the act stipulated that they might be changed at any future time by the governor and council. This arrangement was undoubtedly intended to conciliate the British minority. The act provided for the appointment of a council to consist of not more than twenty-three or less than seventeen members, and these royal appointees, together with the governor, were to make the ordinances necessary for the government of the province, subject always to the approval of the Crown. The council did not possess the taxing power, and all of its ordinances dealing with religious questions had to receive the royal approval before they became effective. An elective assembly was considered impossible for the same reasons which had prevented its introduction ten years earlier. Moreover, the French population, inexperienced in the arts of self-government, for the present were content to leave governing problems in other hands.

Much can be said both in justification and in criticism of the Quebec Act, and such comments will depend largely on the length *Criticism of Act* of perspective. The law undoubtedly helped to retain Canada within the Empire at a time when the latter was being disrupted by a rebellion to the south, but it accomplished this by keeping Canada culturally French. The act retained for England, at one of the darkest hours in her imperial history, the loyalty and support of the Roman Catholic clergy and the seigniors, who constituted the two most influential classes in the Canadian population. The law was drawn "with an eye to Boston rather than to Quebec." On the other hand, the Quebec Act stopped such anglicising processes as were suggested or initiated after 1763, and helped to preserve the old French civilization at a time when there were some evidences that it was beginning to disintegrate. As events took their course it perpetuated the rather antiquated and intricate French law, which became a real obstacle to the commercial progress of the province. On the religious side, it prepared the way for that close alliance between Church and State which still complicates the affairs of French Canada. It naturally made the English minority more disgruntled than ever, by practically recognizing a French nationalism which continues even now to affect politics and international relations. The extension of the boundaries of Quebec to include the northern half of the Ohio valley was probably an error, for it deprived the irritated Atlantic colonies of their sea-to-sea claims; and by cutting off their opportunity for westward expansion, it added one more important grievance to the long list of charges which they were preparing against the alleged misrule of George III. In addition, the virtual establishment of the Roman Catholic religion in the province of Quebec proved most irritating to the New England Puritans, who for generations had been thundering against the "Popery" and "bigotry" of their northern neighbors.

Effect on rebellious colonies

It was highly unfortunate that the Quebec Act was passed almost simultaneously with the "coercive" or "intolerable" acts with which a short-sighted British ministry tried to punish the radicals of Boston for their destruction of a cargo of tea in Dorchester Bay. In the minds of the excited English colonists the Quebec Act became one of the worst of the British repressive measures. The relation of the law to the French-Canadian situation was completely lost sight of, and the act was viewed as a purely punitive measure, directed against the American radicals. As a matter of fact, the drafting of the Quebec Act had been begun in England, and its chief principles had been agreed upon before the news of the Boston Tea Party reached London. In the opinion of Professor C. W. Alvord, a careful American student of British policies during this period, the Quebec Act was "one of the few statesmanlike measures of the ministry," being an honest attempt on the part of the mother-country to deal with the Canadian problem, and to protect at least a part of the Mississippi valley from Indian disorders by bringing it under the control of the imperial authorities. As an undeveloped wilderness the Ohio valley seemed to belong, for administrative purposes, more logically to a government in the St. Lawrence valley than to any of the English seaboard colonies which had hitherto laid claim to this hinterland. On the other hand, it must not be forgotten that Carleton had for some years seen the American Revolution on the horizon and had repeatedly urged conciliatory measures for the church and the seigniors of Quebec. Whatever wisdom the boundary provisions of the act may have contained, there is little reasonable doubt that Carleton's presence in England at that time colored it in such a way as to inspire the hope that it would prove an effective weapon for military purposes against the rebellious thirteen colonies.

The Quebec Act remedied many of the legal and religious grievances of the French Canadians, but it left many governmental abuses untouched. The outbreak of the American Revolution made it impossible to put the law into effect on May 1, 1775. But in the trying years which followed the outbreak of the Revolution it gradually came into operation, as the overwhelming importance of military defense left opportunity and time for matters of internal administration.

SELECT BIBLIOGRAPHY FOR CHAPTER IV

For a brief, yet detailed, account of the beginnings of British rule in Canada, see DUNCAN McARTHUR, "The New Régime," in *Canada and Its Provinces*, vol. III, pp. 21–49.

For Pontiac's war, see FRANCIS PARKMAN, *The Conspiracy of Pontiac and the Indian Wars after the Conquest of Canada*, 2 vols. (Boston, 1851).

The most recent discussion of the Quebec Act is R. COUPLAND, *The Quebec Act: a Study in Statesmanship* (Toronto, 1926). The best accounts of British policy as it affected the interior of North America are C. W. ALVORD, *The Illinois Country, 1673–1818* (Springfield, 1920); CLARENCE E. CARTER, *Great Britain and the Illinois Country, 1763–1774* (Washington, 1910). Also see PROFESSOR ALVORD's "Genesis of the Proclamation of 1763" in *Michigan Pioneer and Historical Collections*, vol. XXXVI, pp. 20–52.

For the constitutional history of the period, see W. P. M. KENNEDY, *The Constitution of Canada*, pp. 25–70. Valuable collections of documents are "Correspondence of General James Murray, 1759–1791," in *Report on Canadian Archives*, *1912*, pp. 84–123; "Ordinances for the Province of Quebec from the Establishment of Civil Government to 1767," in *Canadian Archives*, *1913*, pp. 45–86; and Adam Shortt and Arthur G. Doughty, eds., *Documents Relating to the Constitutional History of Canada, 1759–1791*, in *Canadian Archives*, (Ottawa, 1918). See also W. P. M. KENNEDY, *Documents of the Canadian Constitution, 1759–1915* (Toronto, 1918), pp. 1–179.

For other references, see TROTTER, *Syllabus*, pp. 60–62.

CHAPTER V

BRITISH NORTH AMERICA AND THE AMERICAN REVOLUTION

Lexington and Concord

On April 19, 1775, hostilities commenced between American rebels and British troops at Lexington and Concord, near Boston, so that when the Second Continental Congress met in May, 1775, it faced a situation in which rebellion and war were accomplished facts. A final statement to the British King embodied the causes for taking up arms, but this statement was couched in language which left the door open for conciliatory measures in case the British government should desire to present the olive branch rather than the sword. The British reply, however, closed the door to further negotiations and forced a resort to arms—a result which was not at all distasteful to the radical party in the colonies, and for which all preparations had been made.

Causes of Revolution

It is unnecessary for the purpose of this book to discuss at length the causes of the American Revolution—causes which seem to become more complex as historical inquiry penetrates deeper into the sources of this period. Among the most active of them were the application of the mercantile system to the colonies in the form of navigation acts and revenue measures which sought to restrict colonial trade, and a general stiffening-up of imperial control over American commerce, especially since the close of the French and Indian War. Indeed, much of the early agitation against Great Britain had its origin among the colonial merchants whose financial status was affected by the increasingly stringent British regulations. Protests and agitations begun by a conservative merchant class soon passed beyond their control into the hands of more radical leaders who seized the opportunity to demand enlarged self-government, and eventually independence. For a century the colonies had been allowed to shift for themselves, and during these years of "salutary neglect" there had developed a spirit of self-reliance and of national self-sufficiency which was not at all likely to accept lightly any arbitrary interference from the outside. "No taxation without representation" proved an excellent shibboleth to rally the patriot party. The utter tactlessness and lack of political vision on the part of the British ministers gradually consolidated many elements in the colonial population.

Canada— fourteenth colony?

It was natural for the leaders of the American Revolution to speculate upon the possibility of making Canada a fourteenth colony. It was assumed that the French Canadians chafed under British rule, that the English minorities in Quebec and Montreal and in the provinces nearer the sea would welcome an opportunity to join their friends and kinsmen to the south, and that Governor Carleton did not have adequate military forces to defend the long frontier against an invading force of Continental troops. For the moment it was expedient to forget the century of hostility between New England and New France, due to fur-trading rivalries, Indian alliances, frontier raids, and religious differences. It was hoped that "the transcendent nature of freedom" would elevate the minds of all good patriots above "such low-minded infirmities" as religious intolerance and bigotry. So strong was this hope that as early as the fall of 1774 the First Continental Congress at Philadelphia issued addresses to the people of Quebec, and Samuel Adams, the Massachusetts Provincial Congress, and the Boston Committee of Correspondence tried to interest the English minority of Quebec in sending delegates to the Second Continental Congress.

In May, 1775, about 230 Vermont and New Hampshire militiamen, led by three colonels, Ethan Allen, Seth Warner, and Benedict Arnold, won easy victories at Ticonderoga and Crown Point, and thus opened the Lake Champlain route into Canada for the transportation of much-needed supplies for the colonial militia assembled for the siege of Boston. But these incidents also precipitated a real crisis in Canadian relations, for it had been the intention of the leaders of the American Revolution to avoid all friction with their Canadian brethren, in order to convince them that the American rebels regarded them as friends and not as foes, and by subtle propaganda to lure them away from their British allegiance. *Ticonderoga and Crown Point*

The American Continental Congress at once sent several thousand copies of a letter into Canada to reassure the inhabitants of their friendly intentions, and Ethan Allen was dispatched to "preach politics" among the *habitants*. An address "to the oppressed inhabitants of Canada" was prepared by John Jay, Samuel Adams, and Silas Deane, men high in the councils of the revolutionary party, and was translated into French for purposes of propaganda. At the same time steps were taken by the American leaders to prevent the Indians from becoming allies of the British. *"Preaching politics"*

In August, 1775, an American invasion of Canada was definitely agreed upon, on the assumption that a successful assault upon Quebec and Montreal would induce the Canadians to join in the war against England. An army of some 1500 men was assembled at Ticonderoga under General Philip Schuyler of New York. The latter was instructed by Congress to "pursue any measures in Canada that may have a tendency to promote the peace and security of these Colonies," without unduly irritating the Canadians. Consequently Schuyler issued a proclamation announcing his coming, and assuring the Canadian people that the Americans came as deliverers to free them from the yoke of British slavery. Schuyler was soon forced by illness *Friendly invasion* to return to Albany, whereupon his army passed under the command of Richard Montgomery, formerly an officer in the British service.

Military plans
The plan of operation contemplated an advance by Montgomery's army by way of the Lake Champlain route, the seizure of St. John's and Chambly on the Richelieu River, and then the capture of Montreal. This accomplished, Montgomery was to proceed down the St. Lawrence River to Quebec, where his forces were to effect a junction with the army of Colonel Benedict Arnold, who was advancing across the wilderness of Maine. The combined forces could then launch the final assault on Quebec.

Defender of Canada
To Carleton fell the difficult task of defending Canada against both revolutionary propaganda and American troops. His total force of regulars did not exceed a thousand men, and the summoning of the French-Canadian militia to the colors was considered a very precarious move. The majority of the French Canadians were regarded as unreliable in such a crisis, and as a matter of fact many of the *habitants* refused to participate in the efforts to repel the invasion. Carleton's genius and courage made him the savior of Canada.

Fall of Montreal
Montreal and St. John's fell before the American attack, but not until all the stores had been destroyed by the defenders. Carleton managed to leave Montreal while the siege was in progress, and to make a perilous escape past the blockading American troops and ships. On November 19, he suddenly appeared in Quebec to take charge of its defense. Arnold, after a terrible march across Maine, during which his own indomitable courage and his marvelous skill were all that kept his army together in the face of famine, hardship, and disease, had arrived at Quebec five days earlier. Because of the inferior numbers under his command Arnold postponed the attack until the arrival of Montgomery's men, who were coming down the river in hot pursuit of Carleton.

Siege of Quebec
For the second time in sixteen years Quebec was bombarded by an enemy force. Its walls were in poor condition, but so also were the siege guns of the Americans. Carleton had raised about 1800 men for the defense of the city, while the American attacking force numbered nearly 2700, plus a few hundred French Canadians who had decided to support the rebel cause. Carleton had the better cannon and plenty of food, while the American troops were inadequately supplied and suffered terribly from an epidemic of small-pox.

Final assault
Montgomery began the siege early in December. Letters addressed to the city population were attached to arrows and fired over the walls, and in a bombastic note the American commander called on Carleton to surrender the ancient citadel. On December 31, in a snowstorm, the great assault was launched by the Americans. The plans had been well worked out, but at the last moment there was a confusion of signals, and the rockets fired from Montgomery's position as the signal for the general attack were discovered by the

British. After a spirited attack and some bloody street-fighting the Americans were repulsed with a total loss of 700 in killed, wounded, and prisoners. Montgomery was killed, and Arnold was severely wounded.

The siege of Quebec by the Continentals continued through the terrible winter of 1776. The troops suffered from exposure, small-pox, and scanty supplies. The tattered army made a thoroughly bad impression upon the population of the province, and after the failure of the attack on Quebec the American army lost whatever support it had received from the *habitants*. The loose discipline of the troops, the worthless paper money which they tried to force upon the people in payment for supplies, and the steady depletion of their ranks, convinced the people of Quebec that it was time to lose interest in what seemed to be a lost cause. Moreover, American propaganda made little impression on a population for the most part illiterate. *Failure of invasion*

On May 6, 1776, the booming of cannon down the river announced the arrival of a British fleet. The Americans retreated precipitously before these reinforcements, and once more Quebec was saved by the supremacy of the British navy. Arnold skilfully conducted the retreat of his weary troops toward their American base in New York. Montreal also had to be abandoned, and thus the one great offensive campaign planned by the Americans before the Declaration of Independence ended in complete failure. *Retreat of Continentals*

Several hundred Canadians who had joined the American expedition retired with it to the south. By the end of the war these expatriated Canadians constituted a problem for the American government similar to the problem which the British government had to face in dealing with the American Loyalists. Eventually the United States Congress set aside a "Canadian Refugee Tract" in the West as compensation for the Canadians who had served the revolutionary cause, and lands were donated to the claimants in the region now occupied by perhaps the most valuable section of the capital city of Ohio. *Canadian refugees*

Canada continued to be an important factor in the development of the American Revolution in 1776 and 1777, but all prospects of winning the Canadians for the revolutionary cause virtually vanished with the failure to capture Quebec. The simple-minded French-Canadian *habitant* had little understanding of the issues involved and no desire to run after the American goddess of liberty who, his clergy taught him, was after all of rather doubtful divinity. Seigniors and church authorities remained loyal to British rule and to the guarantees of the Quebec Act. Indeed, the Quebec Act served to preserve their loyalty in a population which Carleton denounced in bitter dispatches as "ungrateful" and "blind to honour." As a matter of fact, many of Carleton's hopes concerning the efficacy of the Quebec Act were not realized, but the law did serve well in avoiding a situation in which priests and seigniors might not have been actively *Failure of Revolutionary propaganda* loyal. As for the English minority, it was too small to be of great significance. Moreover, the English merchants of Quebec were profiting greatly from the trade with England which the rebels were boycotting in order to exert pressure on the commercial classes of England.

American plans in 1776

In 1776, before the final collapse of the operations around Quebec, three American commissioners were sent from New York to persuade Canada to join the war, officially to guarantee to her the undisturbed exercise of the Roman Catholic religion, and to promise the clergy complete security in their church estates. A printing-press was brought from Philadelphia and set up in Montreal for the printing of American propaganda. The commission, of which Benjamin Franklin was a member, was an utter failure and only added to the general confusion of the rebel program by seriously interfering with the control of the American army. Late in 1776, after a naval battle with Arnold on Lake Champlain, Carleton retook Crown Point, but Arnold's skilful fighting blocked the British long enough to make a winter campaign against the Americans impossible. Quebec spent a happy winter season in 1776–1777. Carleton was knighted, and 10,000 British troops, quartered in the city, added to the gayety and the security of the inhabitants.

British campaign of 1777

For 1777 the British War Office planned a great three-headed campaign to occupy New York State and to isolate New England, the hot-bed of the rebellion, from the rest of the colonies. General John Burgoyne, who had been appointed commander in May, 1777, because, as is supposed, of Lord George Germain's personal grudge against Carleton, was ordered to proceed into New York by way of Lake Champlain. Colonel St. Leger, with British troops, Loyalists, and Indians, was to enter New York by way of the Mohawk valley, and to join forces with Burgoyne at Albany. In the meantime still a third column was to advance up the valley of the Hudson River from New York City.

Burgoyne's surrender

Howe's decision to launch a campaign against Philadelphia destroyed all chance of reinforcements for Burgoyne, coming up the Hudson from the south. St. Leger's column, after a long siege of Fort Stanwix, the key to the Mohawk valley, was defeated at Oriskany by a band of German settlers under the command of Nikolas Herkheimer, and was forced to return to Canada. Burgoyne slowly made his way from the north toward Albany. His supplies ran low, and foraging parties sent out into the surrounding country fell into the hands of American detachments. As Burgoyne advanced farther into the enemy country, the whole countryside came pouring into American headquarters to help bag the British game. Hopelessly outnumbered and surrounded, Burgoyne at last found it impossible to fight his way out, and on October 17, 1777, he surrendered to the American commander, Horatio Gates, who had arrived in time to profit by the fruits of victories won by others. This victory at

Saratoga was the turning-point of the Revolution. It brought France into open alliance with the United States, and the war spread until its character changed from a mere rebellion to a world struggle in which England stood at bay before a hostile Europe.

After the French alliance of 1778 efforts were renewed to win the adhesion of Canada as a fourteenth state. The French Admiral D'Estaing issued an appeal to the racial pride and memories of his "fellow-countrymen" in Canada, and Congress actually accepted the plan of the youthful Lafayette, who had come to fight for the Continental cause, to invade Canada under French auspices. But Washington, as commander-in-chief of the American forces, foresaw what complications might arise for the new republic if France should regain a foothold in North America, and quietly vetoed the suggestion. Carleton, after three years' retirement, returned to New York in 1782 as commander-in-chief of the British forces in America, and thus it fell to his lot to direct the final evacuation of American territory. *Results of French alliance*

The Treaty of Paris of 1783, which officially closed the American Revolution and recognized the new United States as an independent nation among the family of nations, also had great significance for Canada. To Canada it meant the creation of a world state on her southern border, a state destined to become so powerful that Canada was for many years confronted with the choice of yielding to its powers of absorption, or of remaining faithfully and whole-heartedly attached to the British Empire. *Treaty of 1783*

The treaty of 1783 defined the boundary between these new neighbors. From the mouth of the St. Croix River the international line proceeded to its source, then north to the "highlands" forming the watershed between the Atlantic Ocean and the St. Lawrence River. Thence it proceeded along these "highlands" to the Connecticut River, down that river to the forty-fifth parallel, and thence due west to the St. Lawrence River. Following up this river, the line passed through the middle of the lakes and rivers which form the Great Lakes system, to the northwest corner of the Lake of the Woods. From this point, it was to extend "due west to the Mississippi." *Boundaries*

At a number of points this line was difficult to trace or was absolutely at variance with the facts of geography. Which of several streams was the St. Croix? Where were the "highlands" that separated the streams flowing into the St. Lawrence River from those emptying into the Atlantic Ocean? Finally, a line drawn "due west" from the Lake of the Woods could not possibly touch the Mississippi, which rises considerably farther south. For decades these troublesome problems absorbed much of the time of the diplomats of the United States, Canada, and Great Britain; and closely connected with them were matters of trade, navigation, tariffs, etc., the natural consequences of American independence. *Points in dispute*

But by far the most important result of the American Revolution,

Loyalists

as far as Canada is concerned, was the Loyalist invasion of the British provinces. The American Revolution cannot be properly appraised if one overlooks the fact that it was a great domestic struggle and a civil war, as well as a revolution which grew into a world war. Not all of the people in the thirteen English colonies favored the extreme measures advocated by the more radical leaders of the rebellion. Some joined in the earlier demonstrations against British misrule, only to shrink back when political independence became the goal of the agitation. In some colonies the Loyalist element constituted a large part of the population, possibly a third. New York was often called the Loyalist stronghold, and Pennsylvania "the enemy's country." Some of the hardest fighting in the Revolutionary War was done by such Loyalist regiments as Tarleton's cavalry in the Carolina campaigns, Governor Tryon's forces in New York and Connecticut, and those of Sir John Johnson and Colonel Butler on the western frontier.

Loyalist principles

Many of the Loyalists belonged to the most influential classes in the colonies, and were men of property and education, office-holders and men of social position, who quite naturally were defenders of the established order and opponents of the leveling democracy advocated by radicals such as Samuel Adams and Patrick Henry. While deploring British blunders, these conservatives nevertheless believed there could be no safety, and no law and order, outside the Empire. That the members of this class did not exert an influence commensurate with their number was due largely to the fact that they were unorganized, unarmed, and scattered; and as the war progressed, they became the victims of measures of terrorization and repression launched by their better organized radical adversaries.

Revolution as civil war

In many colonies the battle between "Patriot" and "Tory" was marked by measures to suppress freedom of discussion, and by acts of violence on both sides. Window-breaking, stealing, rioting and tar-and-feather parties were common occurrences in many colonies. After July 4, 1776, the date of the Declaration of Independence, Loyalism became treason, and test oaths were imposed by revolutionary committees upon all persons whose allegiance to the cause of independence seemed open to question. Special offenders frequently were marched through the streets behind a fife and drum corps playing the Rogue's March. Pennsylvania passed bills of attainder against 490 Tories, fines were imposed for evading military service, and in some counties of New York and South Carolina Loyalists had to make good all robberies committed in their localities. It was estimated that New York alone acquired property worth £3,600,000 from Loyalist sources, while the Continental Congress in 1777 recommended the confiscation of Loyalist estates by the various state governments, the proceeds to be invested in bonds for the prosecution of the Revolutionary War. In Pennsylvania some of the expropriated Loyalist property served to swell the endowment fund of the University of Pennsylvania.

Long before the close of the American Revolution many Loyalist families preferred to leave their old homes for more peaceful communities, where they might live under the protection of the British Crown and escape the persecutions and the odium which would follow them as long as they lived in the American Republic. The Loyalists paid the price of supporting a lost cause, and for reasons of necessity and conviction they preferred to migrate rather than yield to a government controlled by those same radicals whose methods they so cordially detested and whose actions they had so vigorously, and often so indiscreetly, opposed.

Beginning of Loyalist migrations

Many American Loyalists went during and after the war to the Bermudas, some returned to England, others sought refuge in Florida. Thousands migrated to the north, and laid the foundations of a British North America. The number who entered Canada will probably never be accurately determined, but it was large enough to affect the whole future of that colony.

Before the British troops evacuated New York City thousands of Loyalists sought refuge within their lines. Carleton refused to leave the city until all had been properly provided for. 5593 sailed for Halifax on the first convoys in April, 1783. 800 migrated from Pennsylvania alone to the western part of Nova Scotia and helped to lay the foundations of the new Province of New Brunswick. Probably 3000 in all moved at this early date to Cape Breton Island. Thousands swarmed across the Canadian frontier from points of rendezvous such as Sackett's Harbor, Oswego, and Niagara, while others followed the familiar Lake Champlain route. Joseph Brant, the Indian chieftain, led his Mohawks into the neighborhood of the present Brantford, Ontario. The total number who finally settled in Nova Scotia, particularly in the valley of the St. John, has been estimated at 28,000. The majority of the Loyalists seem to have preferred this maritime region, for in spite of its rigorous climate it had the advantage of being partially settled, and was under a well-established and orderly government. Some ten thousand braved the perils of the region west of Montreal, at that time a trackless and unbroken wilderness, and with a courage and a persistence which are the pride and the marvel of their descendants, laid the foundations of the great Canadian province today known as Ontario. By 1795 the Loyalist stock of this "Upper Canada" was estimated at thirty thousand. Their coming constituted a second British invasion and conquest of French Canada. This time it was a peaceful penetration rather than a military subjugation, but it changed the whole destiny of Canada.

Loyalist invasion

SELECT BIBLIOGRAPHY FOR CHAPTER V

The most detailed discussion of the efforts of the American revolutionists to make Canada a fourteenth state, is JUSTIN SMITH, *Our Struggle for the Fourteenth Colony*, 2 vols. (New York, 1907). Other briefer accounts are W. C. H. WOOD, "Canada and the American Revolution," in *Canada and Its Provinces*, vol. III, pp. 73-83. The period to 1783 is covered in volumes IV to VII in W. KINGSFORD, *History of Canada*. A detailed account of Arnold's campaign against Quebec is JUSTIN SMITH, *Arnold's March from Cambridge to Quebec* (New York, 1903). See also JOHN CODMAN, 2ND, *Arnold's Expedition to Quebec* (New York, 1903). WILLIAM WOOD, *The Father of British Canada* (*Chronicles of Canada*) and A. G. BRADLEY, *Lord Dorchester* (*Makers of Canada*, 1926), deal in part with Carleton's rôle in the American Revolution.

In the last twenty-five years much has been written concerning the Loyalists. Among the best treatments of this subject may be noted CLAUDE H. VAN TYNE, *The Loyalists in the American Revolution* (New York, 1902); A. C. FLICK, *Loyalism in New York* (New York, 1901); JAMES H. STARK, *The Loyalists of Massachusetts and the other side of the American Revolution* (Boston, 1910); W. H. SIEBERT, *The Loyalists of Pennsylvania* (*Ohio State University Studies*, Columbus, 1920). Other articles by Professor Siebert on phases of the Loyalist question are scattered through the *Transactions of the Royal Society of Canada* for 1913, 1914, 1915, 1916, and in the *Ohio State University Studies*, 1913, 1914, 1916. See also Letters from Governor Parr to Lord Shelburne, describing the arrival and settlement of United Empire Loyalists in Nova Scotia, 1783–1784, in *Report on the Canadian Archives, 1919–1921*, Appendix E. pp, 361–372. The volume in the *Chronicles of Canada* dealing with the Loyalists from the Canadian point of view is W. S. WALLACE, *The United Empire Loyalists.*

Reference to the Vermont affair of 1779–1782, when that frontier community was seeking independence from New York and recognition of statehood from the Continental Congress, and the British authorities in Canada opened negotiations with a view to annexing Vermont as a Canadian province, has been omitted from the text. It is a minor incident in the story of the Revolution, and British negotiations ended in complete failure. Some of the documents dealing with this episode may be found in *Report on the Canadian Archives, 1889*, pp. 53–59. A brief account is W. A. MACINTOSH, "Canada and Vermont: a Study in Historical Geography," in *The Canadian Historical Review*, vol. VII, pp. 9-30. See also J. N. McILWRAITH, *Sir Frederick Haldimand*, in *The Makers of Canada*. This series which originally appeared in Toronto, 1906–1911, has been thoroughly revised and new volumes have been added under the general editorship of W. L. Grant (Clarendon Press, 1926).

For a more detailed account of the Canadian refugees in the American Revolution and the disposition of their claims, see CARL WITTKE, "Canadian Refugees in the American Revolution," in *The Canadian Historical Review*, vol. III, 320–334.

For additional bibliography, see TROTTER, *Syllabus*, pp. 65–69 and 71–72.

CHAPTER VI

LOYALIST PIONEERS AND
THE QUEBEC ACT

THE British government and the British people were keenly aware of the difficulties experienced by the Loyalists in America and fully conscious of a moral duty to aid those who had sacrificed so much in their devotion to the unity of the British Empire. Strenuous efforts were made to have a clause inserted in the treaty of 1783 providing for the protection of the Loyalists and for the restoration of their confiscated estates. But the American negotiators remained adamant and stubbornly refused to consent to an arrangement which in their eyes meant the sanctioning and rewarding of treason. Finally, a clause was incorporated in the treaty of peace by which Congress agreed to recommend to the various state governments composing the weak American Confederation the restoration of the confiscated property of the Loyalists, or compensation for their losses. *Great Britain's interest in Loyalists*

It was one thing for Congress to agree to make a recommendation to the states, but it was quite another thing to get the states to heed such a recommendation. Under the Articles of Confederation, the first experiment in federal government, under which the thirteen American states tried to live from 1781 to 1789, the central government lacked all punitive and executive power and was unable to enforce its decrees on the state governments. The latter ignored the recommendation concerning the Loyalists and made no compensation for their losses; and in some states the work of persecution and confiscation went merrily on. Quite naturally Great Britain concluded that it had been the victim of American duplicity, and her government made bitter complaints about the failure of the United States to live up to treaty obligations. The controversy over this Loyalist provision of the peace treaty complicated the relations between England and her former colonies for many years, and the failure of the United States to observe this feature of the peace settlement was made the justification by the British government for retaining a number of posts along the Canadian border, which were really on American territory. Great Britain did not in the least understand the American "Confederation" and had no idea of its looseness as a national bond. *Loyalist provision of treaty of 1783*

Great Britain undertook the tremendous task of settling in British possessions such Loyalists as wished to leave their old homes. As has been pointed out, Carleton devoted the closing months of *Settling in British North America* his stay in New York to making plans for the transportation of Loyalist emigrés, and he refused to evacuate the city until satisfactory arrangements had been made for these unfortunate victims of the war. Great Britain provided for them transportation and free lands in British North America. Officers of disbanded Loyalist regiments were allowed half-pay when they were mustered out of the service, and a royal commission was created to study the matter of compensation for Loyalist losses. In addition, the English authorities undertook to furnish rations, farm implements, saws, chisels, seed-wheat, clothing, and live-stock, and to erect mills in the newly opened agricultural settlements. It has been estimated that before 1787 no less than 3,200,000 acres of land were granted to Loyalists in Upper Canada alone. In the two Canadas probably $4,000,000 were spent in making surveys and furnishing clothing, food, tools, and stock to the newly arrived settlers. A conservative estimate has placed at $30,000,000 the total amount spent by the British government on behalf of the Loyalists.

Loyalist settlements

Especially in the wilderness west of Quebec, and on the north shore of the St. Lawrence River, between Quebec and Kingston, emigrés were subjected to the greatest hardships and privations while they tried to carve pioneer communities out of the primeval forest. Others established themselves on the Niagara and the Detroit frontiers. Many came in winter, some riding horses or driving teams along the old Indian trails, or in a train of sleighs with runners made from limbs, and laden with food, bedding, clothes, and a few of the most valuable articles which they had been able to preserve from their old homes.

Loyalist pioneers

On their arrival the pioneers frequently camped in tents to await the "drawings," by which the numbers of lots were written on pieces of paper and drawn from a hat. With a short-handled axe the newcomers then set to work at their difficult and often unaccustomed task of making a clearing and erecting a temporary shelter. Usually they lived in one-story log cabins, twenty feet long by fifteen feet wide and some seven or eight feet high, with the logs notched at the corners and the cracks plastered up with clay. Typical cabins had a large stone chimney at one end. In some there was no chimney at all and the smoke escaped through a hole in the roof. Sometimes the cabin had no floor except the ground, and a quilt hung over an opening served as a door. There were seldom more than two little windows in these log structures, and these were covered with oiled paper in the absence of glass which was expensive and very difficult to get. A low attic, reached by a ladder leading into a great hole, served as a second room.

Living conditions

Most of the furniture was home-made—rough benches, tables and a bed, with perhaps an occasional heirloom that had been carried away from the old homestead. A crane usually hung over the fireplace, with an iron kettle, frying pans with three-foot handles, and a griddle for making pancakes. At first there were no mills for the grinding of grain, and so Indian corn and wild rice were crushed between stones or with an axe, or the grain was pounded on a "hominy block," a great stump hollowed at the top. In the house the fire was always kept burning, and smoke often filled the cabin. Bread was generally baked in a large kettle, with the fuel piled above and below it. The fireplace and the tallow dip were the only sources of artificial light. Practically all of the dishes at first were made of wood, until greater affluence and the arrival of a Yankee peddler introduced pewter ware.

Pioneer farming was carried on in a very primitive fashion. At the outset, the clearings were necessarily quite small. Many Indian *Pioneer farming* methods were used, and threshing was done with a flail. Soon chopping frolics and building and husking "bees" for the men, and quilting and paring "bees" for the women, helped to introduce some of the social joys, and to vary the monotony of life in the forest, besides providing the speed and the efficiency which came from the pooling of the labor forces of the region. If there was no fiddler present to enliven these occasions after the work was finished, the boys whistled or the girls sang tunes for the dancing which always followed. Whiskey was fairly cheap, and it added a warmth and a glow to these occasions which did much to compensate for the hardships of the pioneer's existence.

The women managed the spinning-wheels and wove coarse linen from the flax and hemp produced in the little clearings. Boots and *Economic* shoes were also home-made, often from cowhides which had hung *conditions* for weeks in a tanning trough until an itinerant shoemaker happened along and was willing to ply his trade in exchange for a supply of bacon or potatoes. Many of the pioneers wore deerskin clothing. The chief articles of food were pork, preserved in salt water or smoked, corn-meal, coarse flour, maple sugar, and berries growing wild in the forest. For some years the Johnny-cake, so familiar on the American frontier, was too "Yankee" to become established among the Loyalist settlers. Flour in Upper Canada sold at $7.50 a hundred pounds in the 1780's, salt at $4.50 a bushel, tea at $1.50 a pound, wheat and corn at $1.25 a bushel, rum at $3.00 a gallon, and deerskins at sixty-three cents. Wages for a man's day labor were fifty cents. Roads were very poor, and schools and churches extremely rare.

For many of the Loyalists belonging to the more comfortably situated and successful classes of the population of the thirteen *Early hardships* states, this subjection to the most primitive conditions of living on the frontiers of the British provinces entailed the greatest hardship and suffering. In their trials and disappointments not a few grumbled against what seemed to be the neglect of England, and complained that all they had to live on was "His Majesty's rotten pork and unbaked flour." The year 1788 became known as the "Hungry

Year," due to the crop failures of 1787, and American patriots de-
risively referred to the Loyalist settlements in Nova Scotia as "Nova
Scarcity." But these people were made of the stuff which enabled
them gradually to surmount the obstacles which nature set in their
way, and they became the nucleus of a most desirable English element
in the Canadian population.

Political
consequences of
Loyalist
invasion

    The Loyalist migration had most important consequences, so far
as the political development of Canada was concerned. First of all,
it determined that Canada should develop as an English province,
and not along the lines of the old French colonial system which
the Quebec Act of 1774 tended to perpetuate. This very fact, however, induced the French Canadians to consolidate their forces against
this second British invasion, and to defend their religion and language and mode of life against the dangers of British influences. In
other words, as the Quebec Act became unsatisfactory as a method
of government for these newly-arrived people of English stock, the
same act became the great bulwark of French-Canadian liberties
around which the French united their forces in defense of their
peculiar rights and customs. So true is this that in a very large
measure the present-day French-Canadian national spirit is an out-
growth of the Quebec Act and the Loyalist migration at the close
of the American Revolution. Finally, the Loyalist element, with
their strongly anti-republican sentiments, and their bitter experience
with the methods of American democracy still fresh in their memories,
became a permanent barrier to all plans for the annexation of Canada
to the United States.

Loyalists in
the maritime
provinces

    The coming of the Loyalists was the cause of numerous and im-
portant political changes. In Nova Scotia, 10,000 Loyalists had settled by 1783 in that part of the province which lay on the north
side of the Bay of Fundy. The population of the province nearly
trebled within a few years. Towns like Halifax, Shelburne, Annapolis,
and Digby suddenly leaped into prominence as Loyalist settlements.
Up the St. John valley, toward the present Fredericton, the wave
of Loyalist migration advanced steadily, and many of the new arrivals
at once became influential in provincial and local affairs. Lieutenant-
Colonel Abraham Van Buskirk, formerly in command of a regiment
of New Jersey Loyalists, was elected mayor of Shelburne. Christopher
Sauer III, a German Tory printer from Pennsylvania, started a paper
in Parrtown, and soon became a deputy postmaster in his province.
Cases of this kind were rather typical.

Partition of
Nova Scotia

    Much criticism developed among the Loyalists in Nova Scotia
concerning the methods of the royal governor, Parr. He was charged
with failure to look after the new arrivals properly, and with permitting unfair practices in the granting of lands to prospective settlers. There was, moreover, much complaint that Halifax was too
far removed, and communication too difficult, to insure a proper
interest in the problems of the settlers in the part of Nova Scotia

west of the Bay of Fundy. An agitation arose for the dismember-
ment of the province, with the result that pressure was brought to
bear upon London, and in 1784 a new province came into existence
as one of the first fruits of the American Revolution. Nova Scotia
was divided at the isthmus, and the region northwest of the Bay of
Fundy was thereafter to be known as the Province of New Brunswick.

Colonel Thomas Carleton, a younger brother of Sir Guy Carleton, *Loyalist*
became the first governor of the new province, and served the colony *province*
for the next thirty years. Such families as the Winslows, the Coffins,
the Putnams, and the Sewells, representing some of the best blood
of the American states, were among the influential people of early
New Brunswick. A council was created with both executive and
legislative functions, and Loyalists were appointed to these new
positions. On the council were a former attorney-general of the
colony of Massachusetts and three former colonels in Loyalist regiments. The governor's secretary was a minister from New Jersey; a
former judge of the New York Supreme Court became the Chief
Justice of the province. The capital of New Brunswick was soon
moved to Fredericton, and on October 15, 1785, writs were issued
for the election of the first representative assembly. Twenty-six members were chosen to represent eight counties, and the suffrage was
granted to all male adults resident in the province for three months.
The assembly met in January, 1786; it enacted no less than sixty-
one measures, many of which were copied from the statute books of
New York, Massachusetts, and Nova Scotia.

The latter province had been transferred to the British Crown in
1713 by the Treaty of Utrecht. For years the large population of *Early history of*
stolid, pious, and obstinate Acadian peasants, by whom the British *Nova Scotia*
garrisons were virtually surrounded, was governed by a governor or
lieutenant-governor and an appointive council of twelve members
combining executive, legislative, and judicial functions. British control centered at first in the little town of Annapolis Royal. In 1749,
Halifax was founded by an expedition led by Edward Cornwallis,
uncle of the Lord Cornwallis who surrendered at Yorktown, and the
new garrison was rapidly strengthened to serve as a counterpoise to
the menacing French fortress of Louisbourg. Halifax soon superseded
Annapolis Royal as the capital of the province. The British government stimulated a heavy Protestant immigration to Nova Scotia,
and settlers arrived in considerable numbers from Old and New
England, from the upper Rhine valley, and from Ireland and Scotland. Within four years (1750 to 1754) England sent out no less
than 6000 settlers. In 1755 occurred the expulsion of the Acadians
already referred to.

The expulsion of the Acadians, who were Catholics, removed *Establishment*
one of the obstacles in the way of establishing the representative *of*
assembly which had been contemplated and was specifically prom- *representative*
ised in the instructions issued to Cornwallis when he assumed con- *government*

trol over the colony. Cornwallis' instructions contained the significant reference to an assembly to be established "according to the usage of the rest of our Colonies and plantations in America." But these instructions for the time being were ignored. Governor Lawrence was still less friendly to representative institutions than his predecessor, and he deliberately put off the creation of an assembly. The middle of the eighteenth century witnessed the influx of a large number of New Englanders; this element, centering in Halifax, promptly appealed to the home government for the recall of the unpopular governor. Moreover, largely through the efforts of the colony's chief justice, Jonathan Belcher, the question was raised with the Lords of Trade whether laws passed by a governor and council alone could be legally binding upon the people. At this stage in the controversy the British government ordered the summoning of an assembly, and in October, 1758, the first elective assembly in British North America convened at Halifax. For years, however, the real initiative and governing power remained with the governor and his council, and the great struggle for responsible government in Nova Scotia was still to come. After 1760 the colony entered upon a period of real prosperity, which was but slightly affected by the disturbing events of the American Revolution.

Cape Breton Island Loyalists

About 3000 Loyalists went to Cape Breton Island, and in 1784 it too was severed from Nova Scotia and erected into a separate government, with its own lieutenant-governor and a council appointed by the governor of Nova Scotia. No provision was made for an assembly. The establishment of Cape Breton Island as a more or less separate political entity soon proved to be a mistake. Indeed, there seems to have been no particular reason for this change at the time, except a desire to create more political jobs. In 1820 the island was re-annexed to Nova Scotia, with much opposition from the people concerned, who by this time had developed a local spirit which even now has by no means disappeared.

Prince Edward Island Loyalists

Prince Edward Island, which was virtually the possession of a group of absentee proprietors who had secured their estates by lottery in 1767, received an addition of about 600 Loyalists to its sparse population. Most of these had been lured to the island by the landed proprietors, who promptly set about cheating them out of their titles and reducing them to the status of tenants. The governmental evolution of Prince Edward Island proceeded rapidly. In 1763 the island was part of Nova Scotia. In 1769 it was set up as a separate colony under a lieutenant-governor and council, with executive and legislative functions. The calling of a representative assembly was illegally postponed for reasons similar to those which prevailed in Nova Scotia until 1773; in that year an assembly of eighteen members was instituted. Controversies, which continued for many years, arose over the land problem, and between the governor and the assembly over responsible government.

It was to the west of Quebec, in the region which we may hence-
forth call Upper Canada, that the Loyalists exercised their greatest   *Upper Canada*
political influence. Coming in a steady stream since the time of the   *Loyalists*
first arrivals from the Mohawk valley in 1775 and 1776, the number
of Loyalists in what was destined to become the Province of Upper
Canada reached about 10,000 by 1785. Through the aid of Sir Frederick
Haldimand, a British officer of Swiss blood to whom the government
of Canada was entrusted in 1784, the Loyalists were established, for
the most part, in the neighborhood of Kingston and the Niagara
frontier.

Almost immediately there arose among these new arrivals, a
demand for British institutions, the right to writs of *habeas corpus*,   *Demand for*
the English jury system, British commercial law, a more advanced   *British*
educational system, and, above all, an elective assembly, whereby   *institutions*
these Britishers might enjoy that system of representative government and local autonomy with which they had become familiar in
the American colonies, and to which they were no less devoted than
were their radical persecutors in the United States. It soon became
clear that the Quebec Act was unworkable, now that two races, so
widely different in customs, language, religion, and political traditions, lived side by side in Canada. When the British home government was confronted with this problem, the easiest solution seemed
to be to divide Canada into two provinces, in one of which the
French might perpetuate their conception of what constituted a
satisfactory state of society, while the other could be developed
along clearly English lines. This solution was virtually decided upon
by the fall of 1789, and the Government of the younger Pitt sent the
proposed bill for revision and suggestions to Chief Justice Smith (a
New York Loyalist in Canada), and to Governor Carleton. The latter
had returned to Canada in 1786, after having been elevated to the
peerage as Baron Dorchester. It is interesting to note, in view of later
developments, that both men suggested the possibility of federating
the provinces of British North America, and that Dorchester vigorously opposed the division of Quebec into two provinces.

On June 10, 1790, what is known as the Constitutional Act of
1791 was passed by the British Parliament. The new law went into   *Constitutional*
effect on December 26, 1791. At the time of its passage there were   *Act of 1791*
approximately 100,000 French and 10,000 English in Lower Canada,
and perhaps 20,000 English and a very few French traders and trappers
in what became Upper Canada. The "Canada Act" of 1791 left to the
king, acting by order in council, the determination of the exact
boundary between the proposed provinces. The dividing-line was
accordingly fixed at the Ottawa River, and followed this stream
almost to its mouth; but a small region around Montreal was left as
a part of Lower Canada, because the French system of landholding
had been extended into this area.

The bill, as has been said, provided for two provinces, Upper and

Governmental provisions

Lower Canada, each with a separate government. In Lower Canada there was to be a legislative council of not less than fifteen members, appointed for life by the governor, acting on the authority of the king, and an assembly of not less than fifty members, elected on a property-holding franchise. Upper Canada was provided with a legislative council of not less than seven members, appointed by the governor, and an elective assembly of not less than fifteen. As the chief executive officers and the direct representatives of the Crown, a governor and a lieutenant-governor were provided for each province. As a matter of fact, the lieutenant-governor of Lower Canada usually did not function, his duties falling to the lot of the governor, while the lieutenant-governor of Upper Canada, due largely to difficulties of communication, became an executive officer who was often quite independent of the governor-general. The governor and lieutenant-governor could convoke or dissolve their legislatures, refuse assent to bills, or reserve them for the pleasure of the Crown. All acts of the colonial legislatures could be disallowed by the home government within a period of two years. By the terms of the act of 1791 England hoped to create in Canada a miniature of the system of government existing in the mother-country.

Religious provisions

The act contained several other significant provisions. Power to levy customs-duties, and to regulate navigation and commerce, was retained by the English Parliament. The rights of the Roman Catholics were once more recognized and guaranteed, and a provision was included in the law to permit the endowment of a Protestant church in Canada. The act stipulated that the governor, in granting public lands, should reserve for the support and maintenance of a Protestant clergy lands equal to one-seventh of all those granted in the past or to be granted in the future for other purposes. With the advice of his executive council the governor might erect parsonages or rectories and endow them with part of the clergy reserves. The act of 1791 was the first grant of representative institutions by the Imperial Parliament and reveals some modifications in the British colonial policy which were undoubtedly the effects of the disruption of the Empire less than a decade earlier.

Criticisms of act

In the light of later experience it seems that the division of Canada into two separate provinces was a political blunder. It left in Lower Canada, subject to French rule, a dissatisfied and ever-growing British minority. Moreover, it prevented the coalescing of the French and English stocks in Canada, and thus served to perpetuate that French nationalism which had been legally recognized in the Quebec Act seventeen years earlier. If the two peoples had remained a part of one political system, they might eventually have become equally strong, and thus compromise would have been imperative. On the other hand, it is possible that the attempt to force the rapidly growing English element to live under the provisions of the Quebec Act might have led to such an extremely difficult situation that all reasonable compromise would have been out of the question. At any rate, the act of 1791 had the approval of such distinguished English statesmen as the younger Pitt, Edmund Burke, and Charles James Fox. But in the political system it set up in Canada, and in the section dealing with the clergy reserves, the law contained the germs of the most important political controversies of the next half-century.

SELECT BIBLIOGRAPHY FOR CHAPTER VI

In addition to the references for the Loyalists given in the preceding chapter, the following are valuable, especially for a picture of the conditions of life in pioneer Loyalist communities: W. S. HERRINGTON, *Pioneer Life among the Loyalists of Upper Canada* (Toronto, 1915), W. L. SMITH, *The Pioneers of Old Ontario* (Toronto, 1923), and WILLIAM CANNIFF, *History of the Settlement of Upper Canada* (Toronto, 1869). See also the detailed references in TROTTER, *Syllabus*, pp. 84-87.

For the constitutional history of the period, through the Constitutional Act of 1791, see W. P. M. KENNEDY, *The Constitution of Canada*, pp. 71-87, and the following collections of documents, *Documents relating to the constitutional history of Canada*, A. Shortt and A. G. Doughty, eds., in *Report on Canadian Archives* (Ottawa, 1918); Kennedy, *Documents of the Canadian Constitution, 1759-1915* (Oxford, 1918); or *Canadian Constitutional Development*, H. E. Egerton and W. L. Grant, eds. (Toronto, 1907), pp. 99-148. Some of the British correspondence relative to the act of 1791 may be found in *Report on the Canadian Archives, 1890*, pp. 10-41.

For the study of the history of the various maritime provinces, the following may be recommended: BECKLES WILLSON, *Nova Scotia* (London, 1912); A. G. WARBURTON, *A History of Prince Edward Island* (St. John, 1923) and J. W. HARDY, *Prince Edward Island;* J. HANNAY, *The Province of New Brunswick: Its Resources and Advantages* (Fredericton, 1902). See also TROTTER, *Syllabus*, pp. 105-108.

CHAPTER VII

THE FORMATIVE PERIOD (1791–1812)

THE first assembly for Lower Canada met in Quebec, in the old
bishop's palace, on December 17, 1792. It was opened in grand style,
with a military escort, a royal salute, and an address from the throne,
before crowded galleries. Owing to Lord Dorchester's absence in
England, the formalities were carried out under the lieutenant-
governor, Major-General Alured Clarke. At that time the population of the province was something over 161,000. Although the
French Canadians had not asked for representative institutions, and
had no experience in self-government, the membership of the assembly was of high caliber, consisting largely of merchants, lawyers,
and seigniors. In a representative house of fifty members there were
thirty-four Frenchmen and sixteen Britishers, so that from the first
both English and French were the media of debate, and official
records were kept in both languages. The first council was composed
of eight French and nine English members.

Representative government in French Canada

The English population in Lower Canada was in a minority of
one to fifteen, and in some of the rural districts the ratio between the
English and French elements was one to forty. Moreover, the racial
and social differences between the English minority and the French
majority were aggravated by a difference in economic interests. The
English, for the most part, represented the mercantile interests of the
province, while the French element was primarily an agricultural
population. Not unnaturally, therefore, the British merchant class
advocated a land tax as the best means of raising revenue, while the
French landholders preferred a duty on imports. Under the provisions of the Constitutional Act of 1791 the English minority, however small, could generally count on the support of the governor and
the legislative council, who were appointed by the British authorities, and without whose consent no policy could be carried out.
The executive was independent of the assembly and owed responsibility only to the British government. In short, under the structure
of the governmental system it became possible for an official oligarchy,
representing a small minority of the population, to nullify the action
of the assembly, which registered the wishes of the popular majority.
Inherent in this situation was the possibility of long struggles between
the popular party and the official party, and between the legislative
and the executive branches of the government. Although these controversies did not become acute at once, they contained the germs of
the rebellion of 1837. Moreover, political differences of this nature

Problem of British minority

frequently became quite acrimonious because of the sharp racial cleavage in the population.

In the years immediately following the passage of the Constitutional Act of 1791, danger from external foes largely diverted attention from these domestic difficulties. In the last decade of the eighteenth century, relations between Great Britain and the United States became very strained. England charged the United States with failure to execute various provisions of the treaty of 1783, notably the sections dealing with the Loyalists and with the debts owed by Americans to British creditors since the years before the Revolutionary War. In turn, the United States accused Great Britain of duplicity on the score that British forces continued to occupy a number of posts in the American Northwest. As the frontier settlements of the United States pushed steadily westward into the Ohio valley, serious difficulties arose with the Indian population in these regions. The red man realized that he was being slowly crowded out of territory which he still regarded as his own, even though in earlier negotiations he might formally have surrendered his title to it. *Dangers from without*

Of greater importance was the antagonism which developed among American frontiersmen toward British rule in Canada. The Revolution naturally left a heritage of hatred for England, and this antipathy was carefully nursed by the western pioneer, who charged all his troubles with the Indians to the intrigues and machinations of the fur traders and officials of British North America. Great Britain clung to the northwest posts because they gave her fur-trading interests an important leverage in the trade with the Indians of the Middle West and Northwest. Americans accused the British post commanders and traders of deliberately inciting Indian outrages against the pioneers of the Ohio country; these charges occasionally found confirmation in the seizure of Indian captives whose equipment included British guns and supplies. *Friction over fur trade*

In 1791 Indian depredations and butcheries occurred on so extensive a scale that the new United States government determined to send a punitive expedition into the Indian country of the Northwest. Forces were hastily assembled by Arthur St. Clair, first governor of the Northwest Territory, but they were ambushed and cut to pieces in what is now northwestern Ohio. It was not until 1794 that a new army, carefully drilled under the command of General Anthony Wayne, decisively defeated the Indians in the Battle of Fallen Timbers, in the Maumee valley, near the present-day site of Toledo, and forced the natives to accept a treaty opening nearly all of Ohio to settlement by the whites. *Indian relations*

During these campaigns the government of Canada was in a constant state of excitement. General Wayne had threatened to attack a British post in the Ohio country if he should find this necessary for the successful carrying out of his military plans. On the other hand, Lord Dorchester had delivered to an assemblage at Quebec a *Strained Anglo-American relations* somewhat ambiguous speech in which he either deliberately incited the Indians to hostility against the United States, or at least discussed the possibility of using them in case of war with Canada's southern neighbor. In this strained situation, further aggravated by boundary disputes and controversies over commercial rights between the United States and Great Britain during the wars between England and France near the close of the eighteenth century, Edmund Randolph, the United States Secretary of State, made Carleton's Quebec address the occasion for the issuance of a formal protest to the British government. The incident, coupled with some difficulties which Dorchester was having with the lieutenant-governor, eventually led to the former's resignation. Lord Dorchester left Quebec on July 9, 1796, after a long and honorable career of service which has won for him in Canadian annals the honor of being known as "the Father of British Canada."

Anglo-French crisis

While these difficulties were approaching a crisis, England and the new French Republic, established in 1792, had plunged into a war which was destined to continue, with slight interruptions, for the next twenty-five years. Citizen Edmund Genet was dispatched to the United States by the French government, and this enthusiastic young Republican soon won the sympathy of American democrats such as Thomas Jefferson. Differences of opinion concerning the benefits of the French Revolution developed to such a state that the attitude of the United States government toward the French Republic became one of the main causes of bitter party division in the administration of President Washington. But the President wisely refused to be drawn into these European entanglements; when the trouble between England and France was at its height he issued a neutrality proclamation destined to become of vital importance in the development of international law. Genet and one of his successors, Adet, sent agents into Canada to plot against British rule there and to try to enlist the support of the French Canadians under the banner of French Republicanism. Propaganda literature was sent into Lower Canada, there was loose talk of a French invasion of Quebec with the aid of Republicans from the United States, it was reported that the neighboring state of Vermont was buying great stocks of war material in France ostensibly for the equipment of her militia, but probably for use in a raid across the border. With frontier troubles in the Northwest and French intrigues in Lower Canada, these proved anxious years for Lord Dorchester.

Jay's treaty

Fortunately, both of these difficulties were soon removed. President Washington, in a final effort to find a peaceful solution for the many Anglo-American problems that were vexing his administration, dispatched John Jay, "the most English American," to England with instructions to effect a satisfactory settlement. Jay was greatly impressed with the seriousness of the situation, and was keenly aware of the responsibility resting upon him to avoid war. He returned with a treaty which actually settled few of the issues and made its negotiator extremely unpopular among the people of the United States. It did, however, somewhat relieve the Canadian situation, in that it provided for the evacuation of the northwestern posts by the British within a year, and made arrangements for a boundary commission to settle the disputed frontier along the St. Croix River and to the west of the Lake of the Woods.

French intrigues in Lower Canada came to nothing. First of all, Washington's neutrality proclamation of 1793 curbed the ardor and checked the activities of the impetuous Genet as also of the more indiscreet Republicans of the United States who had supported him. *Collapse of French revolutionary propaganda* In Canada, French propaganda was shattered completely against the rock of opposition presented by the Roman Catholic clergy who had become extremely hostile to the French revolutionary movement. They regarded it not only as a political upheaval, but as an atheistic demonstration calculated to enthrone the Goddess of Reason in place of the Catholic religion. The entire effort of the Canadian clergy was directed toward keeping the poison of French rationalism and agnosticism out of Canada. From this time on, there was a sharp cleavage in spiritual and religious matters between the French in Canada and the French in old France. Many French priests exiled by the Revolution found refuge in Quebec. Throughout the Napoleonic Wars the sympathy of the Church of French Canada was with England rather than with France. One French-Canadian bishop welcomed "all events which tend to broaden the gap separating us from France," and when news of Nelson's victory over the French at Trafalgar reached Canada, a *Te Deum* was sung in the cathedral of Quebec.

Lord Dorchester was succeeded as governor-general by General Robert Prescott, a veteran of the French and Indian War and of the American Revolution. Prescott early became involved in a controversy *Prescott and Milnes* over landholding in Lower Canada. There was much confusion in the land system as it then existed, most of it traceable to differences between the French and the English systems of tenure. Moreover, much land had been occupied by "squatters" without titles, or was claimed by speculators who often got control of large tracts of vacant Crown lands by fraudulent methods. Prescott became the implacable enemy of the speculators, but the latter had great influence in the governor's executive council. Friction developed into deadlock, and protests against the governor's methods were sent to England. In 1799 Prescott was succeeded by Robert Shore Milnes. He too had many difficulties with his advisers, and was much disturbed by the growing friction between the British and the French elements in the council. When Milnes retired because of ill health, he was succeeded by Sir James Craig.

Craig had served as a soldier for forty-five years in North America, *Sir James Craig* South Africa, India, and Italy, and he brought to his new duties, in 1807, the psychology of the military commander who is accustomed to giving orders, and is not accustomed to criticism and opposition. Under his governorship the racial antagonisms of Lower Canada became especially marked. Craig was particularly irritated by the criticisms of *Le Canadien*, a newspaper established in 1806 as the exponent of that French-Canadian nationalism which found its best expression in the motto, "*Notre langue, nos institutions et nos lois.*" Craig became sufficiently aroused to arrest the printers and three of the proprietors on charges of treason. He suppressed the journal.

Party politics

During Craig's administration party lines began to take definite form. On the one hand was the Tory or official party, strong among the commercial classes of Quebec and Montreal, fervent in loyalty to the Crown and to British institutions, and extremely intolerant of French customs and religion, which were considered evidences of a less progressive civilization. It was this small Tory group which commonly had the ear of the governor and the legislative council. In opposition to them was the French-Canadian party, growing rapidly in numbers and power, established on the principle of preserving French institutions and the rights of the French race in Canada. Its strength lay in the assembly. As in earlier British colonial history, when the struggle for power developed between these two groups, it came to center more and more around the assembly's demand for control of the purse.

Craig and popular party

Governor Craig was anxious to break down this French-Canadian popular opposition. In 1809 he summarily dissolved the assembly elected during the preceding year, because of the party bickerings that had developed during its sessions. The French party retaliated with the charge that the governor had most outrageously and autocratically interfered with their long-standing rights and privileges. When a new assembly was chosen, it proved to be more obstreperous than its predecessor, promptly inaugurating a fight for the control of appropriations, and for the right to bar judges from membership in the assembly. In 1811 Craig was recalled. He was a not uncommon example of the failure of a successful military man when thrust into a civil office. His successor was Sir George Prevost, a man of a much more conciliatory temperament. By the time the new governor assumed his duties, the war clouds of 1812 were already black on the horizon.

Simcoe— empire-builder

The first lieutenant-governor of the Loyalist Province of Upper Canada was Lieutenant-Colonel John Graves Simcoe, also a veteran of the American Revolution, and an ardent imperialist. He arrived in Kingston on July 1, 1792. Counties were created at once for the election of representatives to the assembly. The first assembly, consisting of sixteen members, was opened at Newark (Niagara) on September 17, 1792. Simcoe valued the impressions made upon the public mind by ceremony, and so he opened his little parliament, in the wilderness capital, with a military procession, the booming of cannon, and an address delivered from a throne built for the occasion.

Laws were passed immediately to provide for the construction of court-houses, and for the introduction of English civil law, legal procedure, and trial by jury. A system of courts was created, and the foundations were laid for local government. Suggestive of frontier conditions, a law was passed legalizing all marriages which had been irregularly contracted because of the absence of a regular clergy in these pioneer settlements. Plans were also made for the establishment of mills, and for the more rapid settlement of the region. *Early laws of Upper Canada*

Simcoe necessarily was greatly interested in the matter of defense. He had an abiding faith that the Loyalists would become the backbone of a British Canada, but he also planned new settlements constructed around detachments of troops as nuclei. He spent much energy in promoting the building of military roads and bridges, and to the great dismay of the Loyalists he even encouraged on occasion, the migration of new settlers from the United States. Among the 30,000 settlers who came into Canada during the five years of the Simcoe régime were many German Mennonites, Quakers from Pennsylvania, disappointed Loyalists from Nova Scotia, and some emigrants from the British Isles. *Problems of defense*

Many of Simcoe's plans were difficult to carry out under the primitive conditions which prevailed during his time. His self-assertion, coupled with the difficulties of communicating with Quebec, led to friction with Lord Dorchester. Moreover, some of his views on government proved too advanced for the home authorities, and in July, 1796, he relinquished his post. *Simcoe's retirement*

After an interregnum, during which the capital was moved to "muddy" York (Toronto), Simcoe was succeeded by General Peter Hunter. The latter's sudden death in 1805 brought another brief interregnum, and during this period the senior member of the council performed many of the duties of the governor. Lieutenant-governor Francis Gore arrived in 1806. It was during his term of office that the first rumblings of opposition to the governing clique, which had come into control of the council in the time of Simcoe, became noticeable. *Interregnum*

In Upper as well as Lower Canada a popular party was arising in protest against the autocratic powers of the governors, and against the clique of Loyalists who were beginning to monopolize the control of the executive and legislative councils, which frequently used their powers to stifle the public will as expressed by the elective assembly. The agitation against a governing oligarchy was greatly augmented by the steady influx of settlers from the United States and Scotland, whose more democratic tendencies and experiences soon set them at odds with the privileged class of Loyalists. This early opposition was led by men such as William Weekes, an Irish lawyer who had been for a time in Aaron Burr's law office in New York, and Robert Thorpe, an Irish judge, but the agitation made comparatively little headway in the period before the War of 1812. Before *Rise of party politics* the opening of hostilities with the United States, Major-General Isaac Brock had succeeded Gore as the lieutenant-governor of Upper Canada.

Progress in maritime provinces

During this same period political developments very similar to these noted for Lower and Upper Canada were taking place in the smaller provinces of Nova Scotia, New Brunswick, and Prince Edward Island. Although the Loyalist population of Nova Scotia remained intensely conservative and devoted to the Crown, this did not prevent some friction between the elective assembly and the appointive council. In New Brunswick, where the first assembly convened in 1786, very slow progress was made in internal development. For twenty-five years little was accomplished in the way of road-building, and the rivers continued to be the most important means of transportation. Nor was there any real self-government in the sense that those charged with the administration of provincial affairs were responsible to the people. The long terms of office of the appointive councillors served to nullify the wishes of the elected assembly as effectively as in the other provinces. An inner ring began to dominate the government, so that the years before the War of 1812 were filled with the familiar tales of conflicts between the various branches of the government. Because of the extremely slow development of the province, many of the original settlers left for Upper Canada or the United States in search of better opportunities. The history of Prince Edward Island during these years presents nothing of particular importance to be noted here.

Trade

The period between the passage of the Constitutional Act of 1791 and the outbreak of the War of 1812, if we consider the British North American provinces as a whole, was a time of slow but steady material progress. The fur trade was still the most important industry of the Canadas, and until 1825, when the building of the Erie Canal across New York State vitally altered the situation, a large part of the American fur trade in the west used the St. Lawrence system as an outlet for its products. Jay's treaty of 1795 opened inland navigation to the inhabitants of both countries, and removed some of the restrictions hampering trade with the United States, but some of the commercial interests of Canada continued to demand even greater freedom of trade. After 1783 the British government applied its mercantile system and its navigation acts to the United States, thus excluding American shipping from the British colonial trade. This arrangement helped to stimulate closer trade relations between British North America and the West Indies, where British-American shippers and traders slowly began to displace their rivals from the United States.

Economic problems

The division of import duties between Upper and Lower Canada became a serious issue between the two provinces. Most of the trade of Upper Canada passed through the ports of Lower Canada, where the duties were collected, and the equitable division of this public revenue was a source of almost constant irritation. The currency was still in an unsatisfactory condition, the lack of a circulating medium was the chief handicap to prosperity, and banks were sadly needed. Much of the inland trade was still carried on by barter. In Upper Canada, especially, many abuses were arising in connection with the public land system, and thousands of acres were passing under the control of speculators who had no intention of using the land for settlement. By 1804 no less than 4,500,000 acres had been alienated in Upper Canada alone.

Transportation and communication were still in a primitive stage. Postal rates continued to be high. A single letter, consisting of one sheet of paper weighing less than an ounce, could be sent from Montreal to Quebec for eight pence. After 1789 post-office stations were opened in Upper Canada, but for a time the courier made but one trip a year, traveling partly on snow shoes in winter and by boat in the open season. It was not until 1810 that a fortnightly courier service was arranged between two points as near each other as Montreal and Kingston. Letters coming across the ocean either arrived in the mail packets (private boats), or else were carried over by the ship's captain, usually at a charge of a penny a letter. As late as 1820 a single letter was carried from London to Quebec by packet for ninety-two cents, and from London to Toronto for $1.12, although the cost was much less if the mail went by American lines. *Difficulties of communication*

Travel and transportation were limited to river traffic or to the crude and often dangerous roads which had been projected through the new country. After 1808 coaches pitched over the rough roads between Montreal and Kingston, but it was not until almost a decade later that stage-coaches were running between Kingston and Toronto. It was not until 1826 that a stage-coach was operated regularly between Niagara and Toronto. Logs laid over muddy parts of the route formed "corduroy roads," over which the coaches rolled and plunged, while the passengers inside strove desperately to maintain their equilibrium. As late as 1838 the trip from New York up the Hudson to York required six days and three nights. As late as 1809 the *bateau* was the only means of river transportation between Montreal and Kingston. In that year American traders from the Mohawk valley introduced the Durham boat, a long, flat boat propelled by poles and larger than the older *bateau*. The Durham boats and the French-Canadian *bateaux* carried most of the commerce of the St. Lawrence between Upper and Lower Canada. Schooners, however, were beginning to replace the *bateaux* on Lake Ontario, and sailing vessels began to carry furs through the Great Lakes. *Modes of travel*

In 1809, two years after Robert Fulton's experiment on the Hudson River, the first Canadian steamboat was launched. Built by John Molson, David Bruce, and John Jackson, it was known as the *Accommodation* and managed to generate six horsepower and a speed of five miles an hour. The fare from Montreal to Quebec was eight *Steamboat* dollars. When the ship's engines proved too weak, teams of oxen pulled her past the troublesome rapids in the river. In 1811 the *Swiftsure*, equipped with engines of twenty-eight horsepower, was procured from England. In 1817 the first steamer on Lake Ontario traveled from Kingston to Toronto, and during the next year the United States steamship *Walk-in-the-Water* made the first trip on Lake Erie from Buffalo to Detroit by steam. The fare for cabin passengers was eighteen dollars and for steerage seven dollars. The boat was able to maintain an average speed of seven and a half miles an hour, and carried a four-pounder on board to announce her approach to the gaping throngs on shore. In spite of these early attempts, steamboat navigation on the lakes did not have its real beginning until after 1830.

Exploring Far West

In the Far West considerable progress was being made during these years in the exploration of new regions. Great Slave Lake had been discovered by Samuel Hearne in 1771, and Peter Pond reached Lake Athabaska in 1778. After the fall of Quebec the fur traders of the Hudson's Bay Company no longer had to confine their activities to the Atlantic coastal plain. The company now sent out men into the Far West, and northward toward the Arctic Ocean. Fur traders of the Northwest Company, one of its competitors, also reached the Pacific.

In 1792–1793 Alexander Mackenzie, one of the greatest of the explorers of the Canadian West, reached the Smoky River, ascended the Peace River and the Parsnip, by portages and overland marches crossed the mountain ranges, and in the summer of 1793 reached the entrance to Vancouver's Cascade Canal. Some years earlier the same explorer had followed the Mackenzie River to the Arctic Ocean. In 1807 an employee of the Northwest Company, thinking he had struck the Columbia, followed the Fraser River almost to within sight of the Pacific Ocean, in a latitude near the present international boundary between the United States and Canada. By 1811 David Thompson, who spent twenty-eight years as an employee of the Hudson's Bay Company and the Northwest Company, finished a careful survey of the Columbia River, and left to posterity a good map of the Pacific Northwest, as well as forty-five volumes of journals. During the same period others were trying in vain to find a way to sail through the Arctic Ocean. Expeditions of this kind meant new contacts with Indian tribes, and a constant expansion of the fur trade.

Life of people

The life of the people changed but little during the period under discussion. In Lower Canada the French Canadian continued to live on his farm as his forefathers had done, although the lumber industry was beginning to develop in some sections of the province. In spite of the fact that the Jesuit society had been suppressed by the British, and many other orders were suffering from a lack of new recruits, the parish priest and the ecclesiastical hierarchy continued to dominate the life of the people in all its phases. Educational facilities were very meager, and for a time they actually decreased because of the disappearance of religious orders which formerly operated the schools. The Catholic clergy dominated those educational institutions which still existed. Most of the population remained illiterate.

The towns continued small, particularly in Upper Canada. Kingston had less than 1000 inhabitants before the War of 1812, and *Towns* York (Toronto), the new capital, had approximately 800. Upper Canada was primarily a pioneer community, where a simple agriculture was carried on by primitive implements, commonly made out of the wood cut in the local forests. Gradually, however, some few comforts began to penetrate even this primitive backwoods province. In 1794 the first brick house was built in Upper Canada. Local "fairs" were arranged in many places, and added to the comforts and social opportunities of the people. Schools were opened in many settlements such as Toronto, Kingston, and Niagara, and gave evidence of the interest of the Loyalist settlers in educational and cultural matters. By 1816 at least a beginning had been made in the development of a common schools system, but the methods of instruction in these pioneer schools and the equipment of their teachers left much to be desired. Textbooks were rare and teachers' salaries extremely low. Moreover, it was expected that the teacher, often a broken-down soldier addicted to drink, would take part of his compensation by "boarding around" among the parents of his pupils.

The settlements of Upper Canada were by 1812 distributed over a strip of territory from six to fifty miles wide, extending for 500 miles along the waterways from the Ottawa to the Detroit River. The total population of the province was about 90,000 and consisted not only of the English Loyalists, but also of Glengarry Highlanders, German Mennonites, some French Canadians along the Detroit River, and numerous recent arrivals from Great Britain and the United States. Indeed, the British and the American settlers constituted two rather sharply defined elements in the population. The life of the people differed little from that of any pioneer section in the neighboring United States.

The first newspaper to be established in Upper Canada was the *Newspapers* *Gazette*, which made its appearance at Newark in 1793. There was no daily paper in the province before 1836, although by 1830 Upper Canada boasted of twenty newspapers. The first paper established in French Canada was the *Quebec Gazette*, founded in 1764 by two Philadelphia printers. The paper had a troubled existence; the present-day *Quebec Chronicle* claims to be its direct descendant. Owing to the difficulties of communication with Europe, especially during the winter months, and the prevailing journalistic ideals of the time, many of the papers filled their columns with "the refined amusements of Literature," and "the pleasing views of well-pointed wit," so that "the youth of both sexes will be improved and persons of all ranks agreeably and usefully entertained."

Formative period

The period from 1791 to 1812 was one of adjustment and slow growth, during which the political machinery of the Constitutional Act of 1791 was set in motion, and the foundations were laid for an English system of government in Canada. There were signs of discontent before 1812, and evidences that the machinery was beginning to creak, but the agitation for reform was temporarily halted by the call to defend the soil of British North America against a foreign foe.

SELECT BIBLIOGRAPHY FOR CHAPTER VII

For brief general accounts of the inauguration of government under the Constitutional Act of 1791, see O. D. SKELTON, *The Canadian Dominion* (New Haven, 1921), pp. 24–47; or H. E. EGERTON, *Canada* (Historical Geography of the British Colonies, vol. V, Pt. II) (Oxford, 1917), pp. 42–78; or *British America*, John Buchan, ed. (Boston, 1923), pp. 73–83.

For the constitutional history of the period from 1791 to 1812, see KENNEDY, *The Constitution of Canada*, Chaps. IX and X. See also E. A. Cruikshank, ed., *The Correspondence of Lieutenant-Governor John Graves Simcoe, with Allied Documents relating to his administration of the government of Upper Canada*, (in progress), (Toronto, 1923, 1924).

The Indian troubles of the Northwest, and the ensuing friction between the United States and Canada, are discussed in DUNCAN C. SCOTT, "Indian Affairs, 1763–1841," in *Canada and Its Provinces*, IV, pp. 693–725. See also C. E. SLOCUM, *The Ohio Country between the Years 1783 and 1815* (New York, 1910). The best and most recent study of Jay's treaty of 1795 is S. F. BEMIS, *Jay's Treaty: a Study in Diplomacy and Commerce* (New York, 1923). Some documents dealing with the designs of the French Republicans upon Canada have been printed in *Report on Canadian Archives, 1891*, pp. 38–84. Others, referring to the relations between the United States and Canada after the peace of 1783, may be found in *Report on Canadian Archives, 1890*, pp. 97–174.

The following are important for various phases of the social and economic history of the period: M. J. PATTON, "Shipping and Canals," in *Canada and Its Provinces*, vol. X, pp. 475–624; WILLIAM SMITH, "The Post Office, 1763–1841," in *Canada and Its Provinces*, vol. IV, pp. 727–757; D. McARTHUR, "History of Public Finance, 1763–1841," in *Canada and Its Provinces*, vol. IV, pp. 491–514; A. SHORTT, "General Economic History, 1763–1841," *Ibid.*, pp. 521–590; A. SHORTT, "Currency and Banking, 1763–1841," *Ibid.*, pp. 599–632. See also W. SMITH, *History of the Post Office in British North America* (Cambridge, 1920).

These biographies in the *Makers of Canada* are useful, A. G. BRADLEY, *Lord Dorchester;* and D. C. SCOTT, *John Graves Simcoe* (Clarendon Press, 1926). The latest biography of Simcoe is W. R. RIDDELL, *The Life of John Graves Simcoe, First Lieutenant Governor of the Province of Upper Canada, 1792–1796* (Toronto, 1926).

For the progress of western exploration, see LAWRENCE J. BURPEE, "Western Exploration, 1763–1841," in *Canada and Its Provinces*, vol. IV, pp. 639–692; his *Pathfinders of the Great Plains*, in the *Chronicles of Canada*, and the same author's *The Search for the Western Sea* (London, 1908). For the rivalry of the North West Company, with the Hudson's Bay Company see G. C. DAVIDSON, *The North West Company* (Berkeley, 1918).

CHAPTER VIII

THE WAR OF 1812

THE War of 1812 is one of the most unsatisfactory episodes in the long story of Anglo-American relations. It was not desired by the *War of 1812* British, and it was not popular with a large and important element of the population of the United States. It contributed little to the military and naval glories of either power, and for the United States it was full of many disgraceful defeats. The one great American military victory was gained by poorly disciplined frontiersmen when the war was officially over. The treaty of peace made no reference to the reasons for which the United States government had entered the war. Only in Canada have the memories of the war been rightly cherished, and Canadian historians point with pride to an heroic and successful defense of their long frontier against a much more powerful invader.

The ostensible and immediate origins of the War of 1812 are to be found in the controversies over the neutral rights of the United States *Causes* during the Napoleonic Wars, and in the prevalent attitude toward Great Britain in the western sections of the United States.

With the renewal of war between France and England, after the rupture of the Peace of Amiens in 1803, the trade of the United States, *Expansion of* the only great neutral nation which had an important merchant *United States* marine, and was not involved in the war, grew by leaps and bounds. *commerce* Much of this commerce was in the form of goods originating in the French, Spanish, and Dutch West Indies, carried to United States ports, and then reëxported as American goods in order to avoid capture by the navies of the belligerents. The United States contended that goods reëxported from her own ports were neutral goods, and that such neutral goods, carried in neutral bottoms by the American merchant marine, were not subject to seizure. The tonnage of United States shipping increased very rapidly during these years, while the unusually prosperous conditions prevailing in American ports attracted ships and sailors into the American service.

English shippers soon became alarmed by this phenomenal expansion of American shipping and commerce, and by 1805 the British *British* courts reversed their earlier attitude and began to authorize the *commercial* seizure of goods shipped between Europe and the West Indies, *via* a *restrictions* United States port, on the ground that the principle of the "broken voyage," when applied to goods that were clearly never intended for the United States, could not protect such shipments from seizure. England now began rigorously to apply the "Rule of 1756" (which

declared that trade not open to a nation in time of peace could not be
legally opened to it in time of war) to cargoes carried by United States
ships between the French and Spanish West Indies and a European
port.

*War of decrees
and orders*

To increase this difficulty, which the United States government
sought in vain to correct by diplomatic negotiations, England and
France soon began a paper war of orders and decrees, by which each
tried to starve the other into quick submission, and during which
neither showed much concern for the technical rights and claims of
neutral nations. Napoleon's Berlin Decree declared the British Isles in
a state of blockade; Great Britain retaliated by a "paper blockade"
closing the coast of Europe from Trieste to Copenhagen, unless neutral
shipping should first stop at a British port and submit to certain
regulations; Napoleon replied at once with the Milan Decree to the
effect that all ships submitting to these British regulations would be
liable to seizure by the French. If these orders and decrees had been
rigidly enforced, the trade of the United States with Europe would
have been virtually ruined. Neither power, however, was able to
enforce its measures, and although these "paper blockades" led to
many irritating captures, American trade continued to develop, and
made large enough profits from increased rates to compensate for the
loss of an occasional ship. The American government repudiated these
orders-in-council and decrees as contrary to international law, insisted that the British Rule of 1756 was illegal, and that "neutral
ships make neutral goods."

*Napoleon's
policy*

It is difficult to determine whether England or France was the
worst offender against the rights of the United States. Napoleon's
object clearly was to involve the United States in war with England,
and to make the American republic the "ally of the Corsican plun-
derer." French decrees against neutral commerce were applied most
treacherously, millions of dollars worth of United States property was
confiscated, and if the number of ships seized by the French in the
five years before 1812 is compared with the number captured by the
British during the same period, little room is left for a choice between
the two offenders.

Impressment

Another controversy, which served as a *casus belli* against England,
was that of impressment. This was not a new quarrel between Great
Britain and her former possessions. England still contended that
British allegiance was inalienable, and frequently resorted to force in
keeping the crews of her ships at full strength. Owing to the hard and
often oppressive conditions of service that prevailed on British men-
of-war, hundreds of British sailors deserted. In the 1780's, and again
after 1793, England began to search United States vessels on the high
seas for deserters from her navy, and after 1803 the question of the
impressment of American seamen again became acute. The better
conditions of employment, and the higher wages offered by the
prosperous United States shippers during this period of trade ex-

pansion, attracted many British subjects into the American merchant marine. A number managed to secure false papers from local magistrates in the United States, certifying that they were American citizens. Indeed, these certificates were sometimes sold or transferred for a small fee. Moreover, because of the use of a common language it sometimes proved very difficult to distinguish between an American and a British seaman.

The United States government tried unsuccessfully to get the British government to admit the principle that the American flag *American* covered the crew, but Great Britain clung tenaciously to the theory of *contention* an inalienable British citizenship, and insisted upon the right of her men-of-war to search foreign vessels on the high seas for deserters from the Royal Navy. Errors were easily made, and required a long time to correct. The practice of impressment led to irritation, hardships, and real suffering for those who were its victims.

In 1807 a crisis in Anglo-American relations resulted when the British ship *Leopard*, with orders to intercept the American battle- *Chesapeake-* ship *Chesapeake* and search for deserters, raked the decks of the Amer- *Leopard affair* ican vessel, killed three and wounded eighteen, and then took off four British deserters who were found among the crew of the unfortunate cruiser. Only the firm determination of President Jefferson to avoid war at all hazards prevented a declaration of hostilities at this point, for the nation was inflamed by what it considered a flagrant insult to its national honor; but Jefferson preferred the channels of diplomacy and a policy of "peaceable coercion." By the latter he meant a self-imposed embargo on United States products, until such a shortage of American products would be created in Europe that both belligerents would be willing to come to terms with the United States, rather than continue to be deprived of products which Jefferson believed were indispensable to England and France alike.

It is unnecessary to follow in detail the long and painful negotiations of Jefferson's government, and that of his successor, James *Policy of* Madison, in the vain endeavor to get a modification of the war *Jefferson and* practices of the belligerents. Nor is it necessary to discuss the treacher- *Madison* ous policies of Napoleon, by which he tried to take advantage of American retaliatory legislation in order to manœuvre the United States into a declaration of war against England. After all, the war cannot be wholly explained by a reference to these interferences with American commercial rights, irritating and serious as they were.

The war was not simply, nor perhaps primarily, a struggle to preserve the neutral rights of the United States. British violations were *Non-commercial* greatest in 1805, 1807, and 1809. By 1812, when war was finally de- *war* clared, the British Parliament was ready to make sweeping concessions to the American demands, and the offensive orders-in-council were actually repealed two days before the United States Congress declared war. It was extremely unfortunate that the United States had no minister either in France or in England in 1811, to keep in constant touch with these new developments. As has been suggested earlier, a war to vindicate the national honor of the United States should certainly have included a declaration of hostilities against France as well as against Great Britain. Moreover, the trouble over impressments had reached a crisis in 1807, and the grievances of the United States were less acute in 1812 than they had been immediately after the *Chesapeake-Leopard* affair. England, suffering from a rapidly mounting war debt, a disruption of her trade, and rising prices, did not care to add to her military burdens in 1812 by aligning the United States among her enemies. On the other hand, a large portion of the Americans, and especially commercial New England, were opposed to war.

Real clue to war   Although the war was technically fought on the issue of impressments, the real clue to the declaration of war against England, at a time when practically all commercial grievances were on the point of settlement, may be found in the situation prevailing in the new American West, beyond the Alleghenies. Here the ever-present Indian menace was charged to British influence in Canada, and this, coupled with a characteristically frontier spirit of expansion which sought the territorial conquest of Canada, seems to furnish the explanation for the beginning and the continuance of the war when England was apparently ready to make sweeping concessions on all the other points at issue, save impressment.

War Hawks   The Congressional elections of 1810 in the United States marked the triumph of an insurgent movement in the Jeffersonian Republican party, which was in part a protest against the weak and vacillating conduct of Jefferson and Madison during the diplomatic controversies with England and France, and in part an evidence of the political influence and patriotic optimism of the "New West." Nearly one-half of the old members of Congress, many of whom had supported the pacific conduct of Presidents Jefferson and Madison, failed to be reelected. Among the new men who now entered the arena of federal politics were Henry Clay of Kentucky, Felix Grundy of Tennessee, Richard M. Johnson of Kentucky, Peter B. Porter of New York, and John C. Calhoun of South Carolina, all of whom soon became famous as national leaders. Most of them came from the West, and favored a more vigorous policy in defense of American rights. Henry Clay was elected to the powerful position of Speaker of the House of Representatives in 1811, and hence was able to exercise a great influence on the course of legislation. The House of Representatives' committee on foreign relations was promptly set to work on a detailed survey of Anglo-American relations; their report clearly was drawn to please this new group of "War Hawks" who held the balance of power in Congress.

Indian menace   The events of 1811 on the western frontier helped to confirm the westerners in their conviction that British power would have to be expelled from North America before the frontier could have peace. The irresistible advance of the white men into the Indian country once more stirred one of the greatest of Indians to attempt the formation of an extensive Indian confederacy to stop further encroachments on their hunting-grounds. This new leader, Tecumseh, was perhaps the greatest statesman the Indian race has produced. He journeyed up and down the Mississippi valley, trying to perfect his confederacy, while his brother, the "Prophet," preached a new religion which called upon the Indians to return to their original simple life and to free themselves from the vices which resulted from alien contacts.

William Henry Harrison, governor of the Indiana Territory, remained adamant to Tecumseh's pleas for the recognition of the *Tecumseh and* Indians' possessions as a basis for an honest and permanent peace. In *Tippecanoe* the fall of 1811, during Tecumseh's absence among the Indians of the south, Harrison began the military occupation of some land ceded by the Indians under treaty two years before. He literally stumbled into a battle with the Indians, under the Prophet, at Tippecanoe. Harrison suffered great losses in beating off the Indian attack, but the alleged victory did good service later, in 1840, when Harrison ran successfully for the presidency of the United States, as the victor of Tippecanoe. British guns and supplies were found on the natives killed or captured in this engagement, and the westerners were more than ever convinced that Tecumseh's plans were traceable to a Canadian source, and that the British must be expelled from Canada. To control the fur trade and the friendship of the Indians, Canadian authorities distributed yearly supplies, and sometimes arms, among the native population, and the Montreal merchants who combined with the Hudson's Bay Company in 1821, carried on trade in the Indiana Territory, but both the government and fur-trading companies always insisted that their policy uniformly aimed at the maintenance of peace on the frontier.

The West determined to seize the opportunity for war with England in order to conquer Canada, to break the strength of the Indians, *New West's* to deprive them of their British allies, and thus to end forever the *demand for war* Indian menace on the frontier. Coupled with this policy relating to what may be called an offensive against Canada for defensive purposes, was a strong desire to realize the "manifest destiny" of the United States to bring all of North America under its jurisdiction. Evidence of this western imperialism, which contemplated the annexation of Florida to the south and Canada to the north, is not difficult to find, particularly in the Congressional debates preceding the declaration of war.

Henry Clay, early in 1810, declared that the conquest of Canada was within the power of the militia of Kentucky alone, and added: "I am *Henry Clay* not for stopping at Quebec or anywhere else; but I would take the *and conquest of* whole continent. . . " In the debate on the report of the House com- *Canada* mittee on foreign relations every phase of the Canadian situation was thoroughly aired. There was discussion of Canada's monopoly of the western fur trade and her consequent wealth, of her influence over the western Indians, of the discontent which was optimistically assumed to exist among the Canadian people, and of the mission of the United States to extend republicanism to the North Pole.

American "manifest destiny"

Peter Porter, chairman of this committee, called for "the destruction of the British fisheries, of British commerce with America and the West Indies, and the conquest of Canada," while Felix Grundy of Tennessee declared his willingness to "receive the Canadians as adopted brethren." The United States Secretary of War announced that "We can take Canada without soldiers," while the venerable and pacifist Jefferson believed that "the acquisition of Canada (was) a mere matter of marching." Richard M. Johnson, a representative from Kentucky, pointed out that "The waters of the St. Lawrence and the Mississippi interlock in a number of places, and the great Disposer of Human Events intended those two rivers should belong to the same people," while many newspaper discussions reflected the sentiments of a correspondent who wrote in the Nashville *Clarion*, in 1812, that "The Canadas, freed from the chains of an European master, shall take the rank of an independent state; or, too weak for sovereignty, shall hover under the wings of the American eagle. . . ."

President Madison's war message

Shortly after the triumph of the "War Hawks" in the elections of 1810, President Madison began to urge preparedness measures for war. On June 18, 1812, at the moment when the British government, for the first time in ten years, was willing to remove the serious obstacles she had placed in the way of American trade, the United States declared war. President Madison's war message, which enumerated the various points at issue between the United States and England, included a reference to the Indian troubles in the West and assumed that British influence was responsible for them. After the repeal of the British orders-in-council, the only two possible grievances left against England were impressment and alleged British intrigues in the West. Clay likened the jubilance of this section, when war was declared, to the enthusiasm and fervor of the crusading ages.

Preparedness of United States

In spite of American optimism the declaration of war found the United States quite unprepared. In the first place, there was cleavage between the commercial interests of New England and those of the rest of the country. In Massachusetts, flags were placed at half-mast when "Mr. Madison's War" was declared, and as the war progressed it became increasingly difficult to get either men or money from the New England states. War loans were most difficult to raise. New England contractors sold beef to the British armies in Canada, and a few bankers of extreme views actually bought British treasury notes in preference to United States bonds. The United States army in 1812 consisted of not quite 7000 men. It was commanded largely by superannuated officers of the days of the Revolution and "politicians in uniform." The secretaries of war and of the navy were incompetent, and the President totally lacked those qualities which make a successful "war president." Moreover, Congress, in spite of its en-

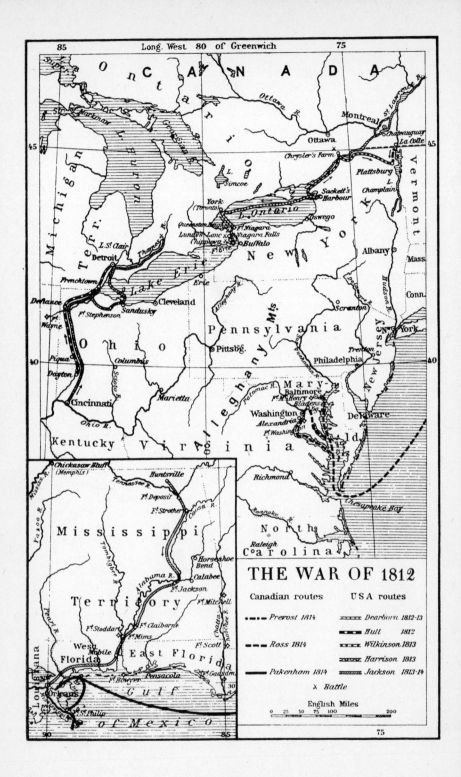

THE WAR OF 1812

Canadian routes   USA routes

-·-·-·- *Prevost 1814*   ┅┅┅ *Dearborn 1812-13*

- - - - *Ross 1814*   ▬▬ *Hull 1812*

───── *Pakenham 1814*   ⋯⋯⋯ *Wilkinson 1813*

    ⋁⋁⋁ *Harrison 1813*

    ▨▨▨ *Jackson 1813-14*

× *Battle*

English Miles

0   25   50   75   100   200

thusiasm for war, steadily refused to pass war taxation and other financial legislation necessary to carry on the war efficiently.

The militia was at best an uncertain quantity, usually little better than an "armed mob." Most frontiersmen were good shots, courageous, and able to endure the hardships of campaigning, but they found it difficult to submit to the discipline of their officers, who were usually elected by vote, according to the prevailing passion for democracy. There was much friction between regiments of militia and regiments of the regular army. The United States navy had been allowed to decline under Jefferson's policy of rigid economy. Some of the ships, particularly Jefferson's coast guards, known as the "Mosquito Fleet," proved absolutely worthless. But the fortunate existence of a large sea-faring population, as also of a great merchant marine from which privateers and crews could be obtained, made the problems in the navy less difficult than those in the army. *Military and naval resources*

Canada faced a very difficult problem of defense in 1812. Her population was hardly more than half a million, and among these were many French Canadians and recent immigrants from the United States, whose attitude toward the war some were disposed to distrust. In every respect Canadian resources were greatly inferior to those of the United States, perhaps in a ratio of fifteen to one. There were 4450 British regulars in Canada in 1812, for the defense of a frontier extending for 1000 miles beyond Montreal, although in General Isaac Brock the British had a commander whose genius was worth regiments of soldiers. Furthermore, the difficulty of moving troops along a wilderness frontier, where roads and bridges were almost unknown, added greatly to the problems of the United States army staff and served as a real help to the Canadian defenders. *Canadian defense*

The total number of Canadian regulars available was 4000. These were men who had been called out for annual muster. Of the militia, in spite of their excellent response, probably not more than 4000 were ever in action, the rest having been used for relief purposes and to protect lines of communication. In the West, Tecumseh led his Indians into the British camp, and they served as useful allies, especially in the Detroit campaign. All in all, there were probably not more than 12,000 men to meet the first shock of the invading armies from the United States. *Military resources*

The plan of the United States was to make a three-headed attack on Canada. Major-General Henry Dearborn was to proceed down the Lake Champlain route and seize Montreal. An army under Stephen Van Rensselaer, a militia commander from New York who represented the politician in uniform, and Alexander Smythe, a regular army officer, was to invade Canada at the Niagara line, while General William Hull, who represented the class of superannuated revolutionary officers, was to seize Detroit and invade the peninsula of Canadian territory lying between Lake Erie and Lake Huron. It was hoped that these great strokes might be executed simultaneously, in *American plan of invasion* which case the way would lie open for a great victorious march through all of Canada. Obviously, the success of these plans depended on perfect coöperation and simultaneous attacks at all points.

Campaign of 1812

The first year (1812) was almost a continuous success for Canada. Dearborn's expedition, after many delays, got as far as the Canadian line. Here his militia refused to cross to foreign soil, and Dearborn was compelled to return to Plattsburg, New York. At the Niagara frontier, Van Rensselaer and Smythe found it impossible to coöperate and their attack was consequently delayed. General Hull's attack at Detroit was doomed to failure, due to the fact that he got no coöperation from the United States troops who were supposed to attack along the Niagara front. Thus General Brock was left free to concentrate his forces at Detroit. Moreover, the United States had no fleet on Lake Erie to protect Hull's line of communication. Hull, who had begun the advance, soon became alarmed by this state of affairs and retreated into Detroit. Brock, upon the arrival of reinforcements, at once began an offensive and demanded the surrender of Detroit. To his great surprise, Hull capitulated in August, 1812, without having fired a shot, and 2000 Americans surrendered to Brock's force of 1300 men, of whom almost one-half were Indians. Together, Brock and Tecumseh, the commander of his Indian allies, entered Detroit in triumph. On the preceding day a small force of Americans evacuated Fort Dearborn (Chicago), and were promptly massacred by the Indians. In July the control of the Straits of Mackinaw, important because of its influence on the Indians in this vicinity, had fallen into the hands of a small British, Canadian, and Indian force, and this post remained under British control to the end of the war.

On Niagara frontier

Within a week after the capitulation of Detroit, Brock was at Niagara, where the United States troops were trying to get in motion. Brock's command consisted of 1000 regulars, 1000 militia, and some Indians. Opposed to him was a force of nearly 7000. On October 13, the Battle of Queenston Heights began. At first victory seemed to perch on the banners of the United States, but in the end, largely due to the utter failure of the regular and militia commanders to coöperate, the battle closed with a defeat for the United States troops. Over 900 Americans were left stranded, to become prisoners on the Canadian side, while the British loss numbered 126, including the brilliant Brock. The spectacular single ship naval engagements won by the Americans in the early months of the war were a slight compensation for this series of military failures.

Campaign of 1813

In 1813 the United States determined to try once more the three-headed attack which had failed at every point during the preceding year. In the West General Harrison in the fall of the year was able to force the British out of Detroit, after Captain Oliver Hazard Perry had defeated the British fleet on Lake Erie, in a brilliant battle, with a squadron of six vessels, built on the lake, and slightly superior to the British ships. Harrison followed the retreating British and

Indians into Upper Canada, up the Thames River, and finally defeated Colonel Proctor's men in a battle in which Tecumseh was killed. Again it was impossible to follow up this initial advantage, because many of Harrison's militiamen promptly set out for home.

Farther to the east, United States troops in April captured York, the capital of Upper Canada, and burned the parliament buildings. *American* In December an American detachment burned Newark, and left the *failures* inhabitants homeless in the dead of winter. For this act of vandalism, which was disavowed by the Washington government, the commander of the troops lost his commission. In the campaign for Montreal the most notable event was the Battle of Chateauguay, where 900 French Canadians and 200 Indians under De Salaberry repulsed a force of at least 3000 invaders under the command of Wade Hampton. Another United States army, under General James Wilkinson, was repulsed in the Battle of Crysler's Farm. It was in 1813 also that the effect of the British blockade of American trade began seriously to be felt in the United States.

The campaign of 1814, from the military standpoint, was more favorable to the United States. By this time many of the incompetents *Campaign of* had been weeded out of the American army. In July, 1814, the in- *1814* vasion of Canada along the Niagara frontier was renewed, under the command of General Jacob Brown. Crossing just below Fort Erie, which easily fell into his hands, Brown encountered the British at Chippewa. The American militia quickly dispersed under the fire of the British, but United States regulars under Winfield Scott valiantly held their ground. The British suffered heavy losses and retired from the field, permitting Brown to reach Queenston. When reinforcements failed to arrive, Brown retired to Chippewa. At Lundy's Lane the forces of Scott and Brown combined against an inferior British army, and one of the best battles of the war, from the standpoint of military tactics, was fought. The Americans seemed to have the advantage in the engagement, but on November 5, after blowing up Fort Erie, they recrossed the river and went into winter quarters on the American side. The fighting along the Niagara River ended in a draw, with both forces exhausted from the strenuous campaigning. Along the upper St. Lawrence River the contending armies remained on their own sides of the line, while from Montreal to the sea the frontier was entirely free of soldiers.

It was in the last year of the war that Great Britain determined to take the offensive in America and "give Jonathan a drubbing." *British* Freed temporarily from the menace of Napoleon in Europe, for the *offensives* first time she was able to concentrate on the struggle taking place on this side of the Atlantic. Her blockading fleet now began to strangle the trade of the United States, and her troops prepared to occupy the enemy's country.

In September, 1814, a British force, supported by a sea attack, invaded Maine, and on September 21 the annexation of "all the eastern side of the Penobscot River and all the country lying between the same river and the boundary of New Brunswick," was proclaimed. In the meantime an army of ten thousand veterans from the European campaigns, under the command of Sir George Prevost, started for Plattsburg, New York, along the familiar Lake Champlain route. By September 6, Prevost was before Plattsburg, but instead of attacking at once he waited for the arrival of Captain George Downie's naval force which had just been completed and was coming up Lake Champlain. The British force, however, was totally annihilated by an American squadron half its size, and Prevost, after a rather half-hearted offensive, retired to Canada.

In August, 1814, a British fleet entered Chesapeake Bay, and landed an army under the command of General Robert Ross, who set out to capture Washington. At Bladensburg, within five miles of the capital of the United States, his troops encountered their first opposition in the form of some 5000 militiamen hastily collected for the defense of the city. Ross's much smaller force completely routed the militia in a battle which soon became known as the "Bladensburg Races." The British entered Washington, President Madison fled from the capital, and in retaliation for the burning of public buildings at York the British applied the torch to the White House and several other government buildings. After an unsuccessful attempt to capture Baltimore, Ross's troops reëmbarked for attacks at other points along the coast.

The third major offensive by the British in 1814 culminated in the Battle of New Orleans. The expedition consisted of nearly 10,000 British veterans commanded by Sir Edward Pakenham, the brother-in-law of Wellington. The United States troops, largely frontiersmen hastily welded into an army under the iron discipline of Andrew Jackson, a typical Tennessee frontiersman who already had displayed his military talents in the Indian wars of the Southwest, seized upon an almost impregnable position and calmly awaited the British attack. Pakenham, probably to show his contempt for the raw American levies, tried on January 8, 1815, to take Jackson's position by assault, but the British, who outnumbered the Americans by at least two to one, were repulsed with tremendous losses. Pakenham was killed, and the loss of the British was twenty-five per cent of their fighting strength, while Jackson's was but one per cent. The victory of New Orleans made Andrew Jackson a popular hero and launched him on the way to the presidency of the United States. It was the one outstanding military success of the United States during three years of fighting. By the irony of circumstances the battle was won fifteen days after the Peace of Ghent had been signed, and thus could exercise no possible influence on the settlement of the war.

The War of 1812 had, comparatively, much less influence on the history of the Atlantic provinces of British North America than on the history of Canada proper. Nova Scotia had developed into an important center of ship-building during the Napoleonic Wars. Its assembly, in a spirit of enthusiastic loyalty, voted money lavishly for carrying on the war against the United States. Privateering flourished, and many a Nova Scotian ship-owner lined his coffers with prize money won during the war. There were practically no hostile operations between Nova Scotia and New England, and considerable trade passed between these two sections in spite of the fact that they were technically at war. New Brunswick, because of New England's opposition to "Mr. Madison's War," had little reason to fear an invasion. In 1814, when British troops occupied a corner of Maine, the New Brunswick legislature petitioned the British government to seize this opportunity to rectify the boundary by annexing the occupied portion. Prince Edward Island was practically unaffected by the war.

As early as September, 1812, when the Czar of Russia offered to mediate between the United States and England, President Madison *Early peace* had appointed peace commissioners. But England preferred to deal *overtures* directly with the Americans, and negotiations were actually begun about the middle of 1814. At that time American and British commissioners met at Ghent, in Belgium. Both parties had considerably modified the war aims with which they had commenced hostilities, while hopes of victory were still running high. England now gave up her demand for an Indian buffer territory in the Northwest, and the United States said no more about the cession of Canada as a *sine qua non* of peace. After long and troublesome discussions, in which not only differences between the two peace commissions had to be overcome, but internal friction had to be eliminated among the American delegates as well, a peace was concluded on Christmas Eve, 1814.

The Treaty of Ghent provided for the mutual restoration of all occupied territory and declared the war at an end. The impressment *Treaty of Ghent* issue was not mentioned in the document. The question of British rights to the navigation of the Mississippi River, and the rights to the Canadian fisheries enjoyed by Americans under the treaty of 1783, were left for future settlement by special commissions. Finally, the treaty included proposals for joint commissions to settle the disputed portions of the Canada-United States boundary.

The results of three years' fighting were most inglorious both for England and for the United States, and it is the judgment of his- *Results of war* torians in both countries that the war was a terrible blunder—that it was absolutely unnecessary and should have been avoided. For Canada, however, the war had important consequences. The heroic defense of their country by the Canadian militiamen against a much more powerful invader became one of the glorious pages in Canadian annals, and a memory which is richly prized. The development of the modern spirit of Canadian nationalism in a sense begins with the experiences of the War of 1812.

For a time, at least, the conflict tended to unite British and French Canadians in defense of their common home, and thus the war became "the blood pledge of the birth of a nation." The Battle of Chateauguay, one of the most brilliant victories of the entire war, was won by French Canadians, under a French-Canadian commander, and the war record of the assembly of Lower Canada was at least as honorable and patriotic as that of Upper Canada. Finally, the war gave the United States one more lesson that British North America was not for sale, and proved that the latter did not care to change her allegiance at the call of a foreigner, even when that invader was the blood brother to the south. The war did much to disabuse the minds of many people in the United States of the belief that it was the destiny of that country some day to annex Canada. The national patriotism which the war developed in the British provinces was conclusive evidence that British North America was determined to go her way alone.

SELECT BIBLIOGRAPHY FOR CHAPTER VIII

For examples of the point of view of modern scholars in the United States concerning the War of 1812, the reader will find it worth while to read H. C. HOCKETT, *A Political and Social History of the United States, 1492–1828* (New York, 1925), pp. 293–333, or D. S. MUZZEY, *The United States of America* (Boston, 1922), I, pp. 224–282.

The most exhaustive discussion of western imperialism as a factor in the declaration of war by the United States is JULIUS W. PRATT, *Expansionists of 1812* (New York, 1925).

Other special volumes by Canadians are W. C. H. WOOD, *The War with the United States (Chronicles of Canada)* (Toronto, 1921); CHARLES P. LUCAS, *The Canadian War of 1812* (Oxford, 1906); WALTER R. NURSEY, *The Story of Isaac Brock* (Toronto, 1923); and W. C. H. WOOD, "Canada in the War of 1812," in *Canada and Its Provinces*, vol. III, pp. 189–252. A. T. MAHAN, *Sea Power in its Relations to the War of 1812*, 2 vols. (Boston, 1905) is valuable, and S. E. MORISON, *Life and Letters of Harrison Gray Otis, Federalist, 1765–1848*, 2 vols. (Boston, 1913) throws much light on the reaction of Federalist New England to the war policy.

The following collections of documents should be noted, W. C. H. WOOD, *Select British Documents of the Canadian War of 1812*, 3 vols. (Toronto, 1923), a Champlain Society publication; Copies of Papers on file in the Dominion Archives at Ottawa, pertaining to the Relations of the British Government with the United States during the Period of the War of 1812, in *Michigan Pioneer and Historical Collections* (Lansing, 1889), vol. XV; and "In Anticipation of the War of 1812," in *Report on the Canadian Archives, 1896*, pp. 24–76.

CHAPTER IX

DRIFTING TOWARD REBELLION

IT WAS unfortunate that the British government did not make use of the enthusiastic patriotism engendered by the War of 1812 to promote more cordial relations with her colony and to foster by wise administration the new war-born friendship between the French and English elements in the Canadian population. Unhappily the period from 1815 to 1837 was marked by a series of controversies which led directly to an appeal to arms in the latter year. Some of the difficulties were due to inherent defects in the Constitutional Act of 1791; some were the result of inter-provincial friction, and were simply the repetition of incidents which had occurred before the War of 1812. Others were caused by the blunders of the British government and its officials, or by the extreme demands of some of the more radical Canadian leaders. A brief discussion of the main events in the political history of the two Canadian provinces, Lower and Upper Canada, will suffice to show how the struggle for popular control of the government and of the purse strings became a struggle for full responsible government. It is notable that this agitation for the democratization of the Canadian government coincides roughly with the era of Jacksonian democracy in the United States, the passage of the Reform Bill of 1832 in England, and the abortive revolutions of 1830 in the countries of continental Europe. *Era of struggle for self-government*

Sir George Prevost, who in 1811 had succeeded Craig as governor of Lower Canada, tried very hard to alleviate the racial antipathies created by his predecessor, and to conciliate the French majority in the population. The patronage of the province was opened to the French on the same basis as to the English, and special favors were shown to the hierarchy of the Roman Catholic Church. Unfortunately for the realization of Prevost's laudable intentions, the Lower Canada assembly refused to act in an equally conciliatory fashion, but plunged headlong into quarrels over taxation, proposals for education, and the independence of the judiciary. These quarrels, owing to the peculiar framework of government under the Constitutional Act of 1791 inevitably led to controversies between the assembly, the legislative council, and the governor, and these, in turn, were aggravated by the fact that the council and the governor represented the British minority and the British government, while the assembly was controlled by the French party. *Friction in Lower Canada*

The popular party was especially insistent that judges of the King's Bench should not sit as members of the appointed legislative *Popular party and judiciary* council. The controversy over this issue eventually culminated in the impeachment of Justices Sewell and Monk, both of whom had been hostile to the French Catholic party. They were charged with violating the legislative powers of the assembly, and with general misconduct in office. Underlying these specific charges was the desire to discredit the judiciary generally. The case was carried to the English Privy Council, where Sewell appeared in person to defend his reputation. The prosecutor selected by the assembly to press the charges was not present because the Upper House (legislative council) refused to pass the appropriation for his expenses. Both judges were exonerated, but this question of the relation between the judicial and the legislative organs continued to prove troublesome. Other attempts at impeachment soon followed, but they were destined to fail because these cases had to be tried before the legislative council. As a last resort the assembly tried to control the salaries of the judges, in the hope that this might prove a more effective remedy.

Sherbrooke's conciliatory policy

After a brief interval under Sir George Drummond, Sir John Coape Sherbrooke was appointed governor of Canada. His views coincided with those of Prevost, to the extent that he favored a policy of compromise and the conciliation of the French population. Through his efforts the Roman Catholic bishop, in 1818, became a member of the governor's executive council. Sherbrooke also favored the enlargement of the legislative council, and the sending of an agent to London, there to represent the interests of the province. In 1818 the British government accepted the proposal of the Canadian assembly to rely entirely on the colonial revenues for the ordinary expenditures of the province. This proved to be a real concession, in that it stopped the illegal practice of earlier years by which the provincial revenue was often used for expenditures concerning which the legislative body had not been consulted.

Papineau

By careful management Sherbrooke was able to live on fairly peaceable terms with the assembly for a time. Louis Joseph Papineau, who had entered the assembly in 1812 at the age of twenty-six, and who served as its speaker with but one brief interruption from 1815 to 1836, was given a special salary for his services as speaker, and Sherbrooke even suggested that the best means of ending the criticisms made by this young firebrand and his followers in the assembly was to offer him a seat on the executive council. It was unfortunate that failing health caused Sherbrooke to resign in 1818. His successor, the Duke of Richmond, found it difficult to deal with the Canadians by the methods he had learned while serving as viceroy of Ireland, and by 1819 the calm of Sherbrooke's administration was rudely interrupted by a storm over the revenues and expenditures of the province.

Revenues

Certain Crown revenues had remained under the control of Great Britain, and were in the nature of a permanent income to the government. These permanent revenues consisted of the proceeds of the

Quebec Act of 1774 (£10,000), the proceeds of the first revenue act passed by the Lower Canadian assembly in 1793, yielding £2,000 annually, and the second revenue act which yielded £5,000 annually to defray the expenses of the administration of justice. In addition, there were the territorial revenues inherited by the British Crown from the King of France, and assigned to the colony in 1794 to meet the expense of civil government. From this source, which included rents from the Jesuit estates and the king's posts, revenue from the forges of St. Maurice and the king's wharf, the timber fund, the *lods et ventes* and the *droit de Quinte*, an annual income of £5,000 was derived. By 1826 these permanent revenues had reached the significant figure of £35,000. In addition, there were old duties levied by British statutes on such articles of commerce as spirits and molasses. All of these constituted the permanent revenues of the Crown in Canada. Theoretically, the only revenue under the control of the assembly were those unappropriated funds which were raised by provincial legislation, such as duties on goods coming into the province, but even in this field the powers of the British and the provincial governments were not carefully delimited.

Attempts to control purse strings

Expenditures usually exceeded the permanent revenues, and appeals had to be made to the legislature for money to meet the deficits. On each such occasion the French popular party seized the opportunity to claim control of all the expenditures of the provincial administration, a demand which was tantamount to control of the entire government policy. As the controversy progressed, the assembly naturally insisted on the right to control the hereditary and permanent revenues of the Crown along with all other sources of income. The legislative council, the creature of the governor, rejected these proposals as violations of the royal prerogatives; it seems certain that yielding on this point would have made the government entirely dependent on the popular will. In that case, what would become of the powers of the king in the province, and what would be the result so far as the imperial connection was concerned? English statesmen were baffled by the problem and as yet knew no constructive way of escape.

Supply bills and redress of grievances

The Duke of Richmond soon after his arrival asked for a large increase in the civil list. The assembly promptly called attention to the desirability of reducing the number of pensioners and useless office-holders, and launched into a long discussion of its right to control all sources of income and to appropriate for each specific expenditure. The governor prorogued the assembly, and stormy times seemed just ahead when the governor fell victim to an attack of hydrophobia and died.

Lord Dalhousie

In June, 1820, Lord Dalhousie took up the duties of governor of Canada, after an earlier and successful régime in Nova Scotia. Dalhousie was an efficient and honest administrator. His efforts were directed toward getting the assembly to appropriate a permanent civil list for the life of the king, so that the government might conduct its affairs without appealing each year to an obstreperous assembly for money with which to pay the salaries of the servants of the Crown. The assembly remained obdurate, and incensed by the receiver-general's defalcations amounting to £96,000 of the public money, which the imperial government refused to make good even though the defaulting official was an imperial officer, it now proceeded carefully to itemize the appropriation bill, and to reduce all salaries by one-fourth. This quarrel over supply bills became the crux of the controversy in Lower Canada. The assembly clung tenaciously to its position, and steadily refused to make permanent provision for government salaries, in order that it might use the government's annual requests for money as a leverage to present other demands.

Union proposal of 1822

In 1822 the British House of Commons proposed the reunion of the provinces of Lower and Upper Canada, primarily because the English minority in Lower Canada, which now numbered forty thousand, continued to object to living under French laws, courts, and institutions. To many leaders in England, and to some in Canada, it seemed high time to undo the results of the Constitutional Act of 1791 which was perpetuating French nationalism in Lower Canada. Moreover, the assembly of Lower Canada was growing yearly more recalcitrant, and it was becoming increasingly difficult to solve the revenue disputes between Upper and Lower Canada. Official opinion in London strongly supported the union of the two provinces. The proposed union bill of 1822 provided for the amalgamation of the two provincial legislatures, the members to be chosen under a high property franchise which would have disfranchised most of the *habitants*. All written procedure was thenceforth to be in English only, and within fifteen years French was to disappear as a language of legislative debate as well. Revenues were to be under the control of the Crown until a permanent civil list had been provided by the assembly. Roman Catholics were confirmed in the enjoyment of their religion, but the Church was to be brought under the Elizabethan Act of Supremacy providing for the approval of the governor for all appointments of the clergy.

Opposition to bill

The bill of 1822 was postponed until Canadian opinion could be sounded. It was clearly designed to stifle the French-Canadian nationality in Lower Canada, and it aroused a veritable storm of protest in that quarter. Papineau at once organized mass meetings throughout the province, and petitions opposing the passage of the bill obtained over sixty thousand signatures. Only the British minority and the official class seemed to favor the measure. In Upper Canada also the majority were opposed to the bill, particularly because of its antidemocratic features.

Canada Trade Act

It is no exaggeration to say that the proposed union bill of 1822 laid the foundation for the rebellion of 1837. While the measure as a whole was dropped as a result of these vehement protests, its financial clauses were passed as the Canada Trade Act. This act made another attempt to bring about an agreement between the legislatures of Upper and Lower Canada with reference to customs' duties, and to apportion by arbitration the income arising from them.

By 1827 the quarrel over supplies reached an impasse in Lower Canada. The assembly had steadily become more aggressive, and many of its demands now invaded the rights of the governor. Dalhousie believed that the time had arrived for strong measures. Consequently he suggested the appointment of new officials in the local districts of the province, as a means of counteracting among the common people the radical propaganda of some of the extremists in the assembly and in the French party. In 1827 he dissolved the legislature. In the abusive campaign which followed, Papineau was one of the most violent opponents of the government. In fiery speeches he denounced the governor, Lord Dalhousie, as a traitor, a renegade, and a thief. Papineau's followers won a sweeping victory and this firebrand was promptly reëlected as speaker of the assembly. *Deadlock of 1827*

Smarting under the unjustified abuse of the campaign, Lord Dalhousie refused to assent to Papineau's election to the speakership, when the latter was presented, according to long-established custom, to the governor for his approval. The assembly denied the right of the governor to withhold his consent, and another deadlock ensued, and again it was necessary to resort to prorogation. In this crisis both sides appealed to England, the petitions of the popular party containing many sound constitutional arguments, as well as much unwarranted personal invective. In 1828 the British Parliament appointed a special committee to investigate Canadian affairs; during the debate many members of the House of Commons pessimistically expressed the belief that Canada would soon cease to be a British possession, and others as seriously contended that the dependency was in any case a losing and entirely useless venture for England. *Quarrel over speakership*

The Parliamentary committee reported that no changes were needed in the constitutional structure of Canada, that a union of the two provinces would be undesirable, and that the chief trouble came from defects in the administration of the government. The committee recommended that the number of public officials appointed to membership in the legislative council be decreased, that all judges, except the chief justice, should be barred entirely, and that the financial troubles of the province be settled by putting all receipts and expenditures under the control of the assembly, in exchange for a permanent civil list which would avoid the necessity of annual grants of salaries. The committee correctly diagnosed some of the grievances of the Canadians, especially those arising from the activities of judges and members of the executive council in the meetings of the legislative council. It was this "chateau clique" of British bureaucrats who virtually nullified all popular measures. Moreover, *Parliamentary investigation* the report confirmed the French Canadians in the enjoyment of their religion and special privileges. The report was accepted as "an imperishable monument of justice and profound wisdom," but unfortunately it had little practical effect upon affairs in Canada. The debates on the report were extremely pessimistic, and in a long array of speakers only William Huskisson revealed a point of view which augured the first dawn of a sound liberal imperialism.

Failure of conciliatory proposals

Before the committee had finished its work, Lord Dalhousie was transferred to India. He was succeeded by Sir James Kempt, who promptly recognized Papineau as speaker of the Assembly and managed to live for several years in comparative peace with the province. In 1829 a law was passed increasing the number of counties in the province, and redistributing representation so that the English minority in the eastern townships received a voice in the assembly. In 1830 Kempt was succeeded by Lord Aylmer, who earnestly desired to continue the conciliatory policies of his predecessor. The assembly, however, again coupled a statement of grievances with the voting of supplies, and now demanded an independent tribunal to try impeachment cases, and also an elective legislative council. To the mind of the British administrator of colonial affairs in these years this was an impossible demand, for an elective council would remove the last safeguard of the rights of the British minority in Lower Canada, and destroy the most important link binding the province to the mother-country. The assembly also called attention to the deplorable conditions resulting from the lack of municipal institutions, and urged some device by which the executive council, which in 1830 contained only two French Canadians, might be made more accountable to the public will.

Transfer of permanent Crown revenues

In 1831 the British government, with a conciliatory purpose, took the fateful step of transferring all of the permanent revenues of the Crown to the control of the provincial assembly. In exchange for these revenues, which amounted to £38,000, the government asked that a civil list of £14,500 be voted by the assembly for the life of the sovereign. The casual revenues retained by the Crown amounted to only £7800. Although the assembly gladly accepted this addition to its powers, it stubbornly refused to make the requested appropriation. Thus the British government weakened its position without securing any compensation for its concessions. As further evidence of an honest desire to live at peace with the turbulent province, municipal government was granted to Quebec and Montreal, judges were removed from the legislature by special act, and an effort was made to remove grievances that arose from a confusion of laws, especially in matters of real property. The English government's surrender of the revenues, without securing in advance the guarantee of salaries, left the governor's party in a very precarious position.

Events now moved rapidly to a crisis. The French nationalists boldly presented proposals to make the judiciary dependent on the *Drifting toward* assembly, and to make the legislative council elective on the basis *rebellion* of a property-holding franchise. Papineau, much influenced by his study of the American and French Revolutions, became more violent, and was carried along by his own passionate eloquence to more extreme positions. A national convention was urged to remake the constitution of the province. Constitutional reformers, such as John Neilson, found it desirable at this stage to withdraw from the agitation because of its increasing violence.

In 1834 the assembly of Lower Canada, under the guidance of Papineau and A. N. Morin, adopted ninety-two resolutions which *Ninety-two* may be called the French-Canadian Declaration of Rights. Like all *resolutions of* documents drafted for purposes of propaganda, some of these resolu- *1834* tions were true statements of fact, others were either partly or wholly false. Beginning with a reference to the loyalty of the French Canadians, the resolutions called attention to the United States as a political model, and bluntly reminded the British Parliament of the American Revolution. Thirty of the resolutions were devoted to an indictment of the legislative council, while others directed attention to various irritating policies of the British government, such as abuses in land tenure, and in the administration of the Crown lands, the British monopoly of patronage, and the failure to provide educational facilities for the people of the province. The resolutions demanded the exclusion of judges from all political affairs, an elective legislative council, complete control of all the revenues by the assembly, and a system of government in which all officers would be subject to the control of the assembly which would have all the rights and privileges of the British House of Commons. Some of the radicals even sought the impeachment of the governor, and a succeeding session of the assembly passed additional resolutions which were even more extreme.

Committees of Correspondence were now organized in Quebec and Montreal to perfect a system of coöperation among the radical *Preparing for* reformers after the model of the committees of the American patriots *emergency* of 1775. The loyal British, fearing that the real aim of the French Canadians was independence, began to form Constitutional Associations, and both parties flooded the home government with petitions setting forth the merits of their respective positions.

At this juncture another Parliamentary committee failed to find a solution for the trouble. Papineau's party, in the meantime, won a *Another* sweeping victory in the election of 1834. A British commission of *parliamentary* three, sent over after the recall of Lord Aylmer, still found it im- *investigation* possible to suggest a remedy for Lower Canada's troubles. Apparently the imperial authorities were quite willing to make additional concessions, but appropriations for a civil list and the demand for an elective council remained the insurmountable obstacles to peace. The excitement over revenue bills increased, and the list of grievances against the British government grew steadily. There was much complaint that petitions from the province were pigeon-holed by British officials in London, that the British failed to develop municipal institutions, and that even in Montreal and Quebec there still were no good streets, no police protection, and no street lights, and that appointive officials wasted money while the country waited in vain for necessary internal improvements.

Deadlock in 1837

Early in 1836 the assembly refused to vote supplies for more than six months, and by September it refused to vote supplies altogether, unless coupled with a redress of grievances. The report of the royal commission suggested no way out of the deadlock because the commissioners were unwilling to recommend responsible government or an elective Upper House. Their only definite recommendation was the repeal of the act of 1831 under which the Crown revenues had been unconditionally transferred to the control of the provincial legislature. In the summer of 1837 the assembly was in session just two days when it was prorogued. Needless to add, the province suffered greatly in its internal development by this constant strife over constitutional issues. In 1838 there was not one good road in all of Lower Canada.

Lord Russell's resolutions

In despair over this endless bickering, Lord John Russell and the British Colonial Office determined to abandon the policy of conciliation and to force a solution by vigorous methods. On March 6, 1837, he introduced in the House of Commons a series of resolutions, in which he summarized the state of affairs in Lower Canada, flatly rejected the demand for responsible government, offered to give the assembly control of all remaining Crown revenues in return for a permanent civil list, and authorized the governor to pay out of the public funds in the treasury, and without vote of the assembly, whatever money was needed to pay the running expenses of government to April 10, 1837. It is one of the ironies of history that Lord John Russell, whose name figures so prominently in the rise of liberalism in nineteenth-century England, should have precipitated the Canadian rebellion, and that Gladstone supported his policy throughout.

Appeal to force

Lord John Russell's resolutions were soon known in Canada, and they convinced Papineau that the British authorities were guilty of the worst duplicity and could no longer be trusted. Mass meetings were organized at which the leaders made addresses calculated to incite the populace to action. The French members of the assembly appeared in homespun in the session of 1837 and absolutely refused to recede from their position on the revenue. The assembly was prorogued on August 26, 1837, by Lord Gosford. To the radical leaders it seemed that the only remaining appeal was to force, and preparations were hurriedly made for this emergency.

Political difficulties in Upper Canada were in many ways similar

to those in Lower Canada, for in both provinces they were in a large *"Family
measure inherent in the Constitutional Act of 1791. The legislative compact" in
assembly of Upper Canada, elected on a rather broad popular basis, Upper Canada*
found its powers constantly curtailed by the legislative council, an
appointive Upper House under the control of the lieutenant-governor
and his executive council. The latter was a mixed body of official
and non-official members practically all of whom also had seats in
the legislative council, and as members of that body held their seats
for life. It is obvious that no measure of which the executive disapproved could pass the Upper House. Similar to the "château
clique" in Lower Canada was a governing clique in Upper Canada,
misnamed the "family compact." As a matter of fact, its members
were neither related nor associated by any formal agreement. Nevertheless, this small group, held together by a community of interests
based on education, social standing, and wealth, and including many
of Loyalist stock, constituted a little oligarchy which controlled
enough of the offices and functions of government to thwart effectively
the popular will as expressed by the assembly. These Tory reaction-
aries came to dominate the governor, controlled the patronage and
sometimes the courts, occasionally packed the assembly with
obsequious office-holders, and in many localities exercised effective
economic control over banking facilities and public works. The
"family compact" also managed to secure the most attractive land
grants at the disposal of the government, and generally manifested
a profound distrust for all newcomers, particularly those who might
have been inoculated with the virus of democracy in the United
States or Ireland.

An opposition party, pledged to carry out certain reforms, had
appeared in Upper Canada before the War of 1812, but their program *Rise of reform
was almost forgotten in the great wave of patriotism and loyalty party*
which followed the declaration of war by the United States. Immediately after 1815 this reform movement began to gather momentum
again, and its leaders were able to organize various discontented
groups into an appreciable opposition party.

The unusual prosperity of the war years was followed by a serious *Effects of
economic depression, the militia was not paid promptly, and the War of 1812*
government was very slow in allotting the military lands promised to
volunteers. Moreover, the existence of vast reserve lands of the
Crown and clergy tended to retard the economic recovery and development of the province, for this land policy left great tracts of unoccupied land in settled areas, a serious obstacle to the development
of farming communities. Furthermore, there was great dissatisfaction
in some quarters because the government had reversed its policy
since the war and no longer sought to attract settlers from the United
States. By 1817 the political agitation in Upper Canada was in full
motion, and as happened in the other province it soon became focused

on the quarrels between the executive and the assembly over supply bills.

*Case of
Robert Gourlay*
In 1817, Robert Gourlay, a Scotch university man with a passion for reform, came to British America. He found employment as a land agent, obtained large holdings, and became greatly interested in stimulating emigration from Great Britain to Canada. In order to advertise the province, Gourlay resolved to prepare a statistical account of Upper Canada and in a circular letter issued to various townships he included a question which solicited the opinion of the residents as to what constituted the greatest obstacle in the way of the development of their districts. Other questions dealt with wages, resources, the number of churches and schools, etc. The "family compact," dominated at this time by John Strachan, a staunch and indomitable Church of England clergyman, and John Beverly Robinson, the solicitor-general, chose to regard this questionnaire and a second address to the resident landowners following close upon the first, as a seditious appeal designed to stir up discontent in the province. The real reason for their disapproval was that they did not wish the light of publicity turned on the administration of the Crown and clergy reserves or on the widespread speculation in public lands. Gourlay retaliated with a bitter personal attack on Strachan, the acting governor, and other high members in the official class, and finally summoned a convention to meet at York in 1818 to adopt a declaration of grievances. A libel suit against Gourlay having failed, his persecutors turned to the assembly which they controlled, and a law was passed declaring meetings such as the York convention unlawful assemblies, and making participants in them guilty of misdemeanor. Gourlay immediately attacked the measure, and his pronouncement was declared a libel against the assembly. In order to bring him under the old Alien Act of 1804 he was ordered to leave the province by proceedings notoriously corrupt. On his refusal to depart, Gourlay was arrested. After a trial which was really a persecution, and during which his mind and his health were seriously affected by long imprisonment, he was found guilty and banished from the country. Gourlay was one of the early organizers of discontent in Upper Canada, and his persecution illustrates the extremes to which the governing clique were prepared to go in order to make criticism of their policies a crime against the government.

*Maitland and
the "family
compact"*
In the year when these troubles with Gourlay began, Sir Peregrine Maitland assumed the duties of lieutenant-governor of Upper Canada and he held this office for the next ten years. Maitland had been in active army service since the age of fifteen. A pronounced Tory, he was soon working hand in hand with the "family compact" group in an effort to suppress all reform movements in the province. Indeed, Maitland was probably the leading man behind Gourlay's persecution. Although immigrants were rapidly filling in the region along the north shores of Lake Ontario and Lake Erie, particularly because

of the colonizing projects of The Canada Company sponsored by the Scotch writer, John Galt, the government continued to turn a deaf ear to all proposals to reapportion representation in the assembly. Obstreperous members whose sympathies were with the reformers were occasionally expelled from their seats by assemblies which, though popularly elected, were sometimes quite subservient to the group which dominated the council.

The Church of England, to which many of the governing oligarchy belonged, enjoyed the privileges of a state church in Upper Canada, *Clergy reserves* much to the dissatisfaction of the Methodists, Baptists, and other dissenters who swarmed into the province as prospective settlers and traders. The Anglicans virtually monopolized education; by means of the clergy reserves they enjoyed a special endowment, and as late as 1824 the legislative council rejected a bill passed by the assembly to allow Methodist pastors to perform legal marriages. This disqualification for dissenting sects was not removed until 1831.

A church establishment in the province had the support of British leaders at this time because it was hoped thereby to check the spread *Source of* of democracy and also to counteract the influence of the Roman *constant friction* Catholic Church in Canada. Even so outspoken an English liberal as Charles James Fox did not object to the principle contained in the clergy reserves section of the act of 1791. By 1825 Upper Canada was suffering from the economic nuisance of having over 2,000,000 acres of land withheld from settlement in the form of clergy reserves. In spite of these and other advantages, such as the monopoly of the solemnization of marriages, the members of the Church of England and Scotland remained in a minority. The Methodist Church, with a type of organization and a kind of theology that appealed strongly to the frontier, soon outstripped all other sects in the number of its adherents. This denomination was the object of particular distrust because of its strong American connections. As late as 1840 Lord Sydenham, in writing to Lord John Russell, declared the clergy reserves "the source of all the troubles in the province; the never-failing watchword of the hustings; the perpetual spring of discord, strife and hatred."

In spite of repressive measures, the reform party grew in strength, and by 1828 it had obtained a clear majority in the assembly. The *William Lyon* most violent of the reformers was William Lyon Mackenzie, who *Mackenzie* came to Canada in 1820 at the age of twenty-five. In Scotland he had been a bookseller and chemist; in Canada he became an editor. In 1824 he founded the *Colonial Advocate*, and born agitator that he was, he soon made it the leading propagandist sheet for reform. Incurring the hatred of the governing ring, he was subjected to many petty annoyances; in June, 1826, his printing establishment at York was destroyed by a mob, following bitter personal attacks on some of the influential citizens which Mackenzie had printed in his paper. Mackenzie brought suit for damages and collected £625, which was paid by subscriptions raised among the friends of the "family compact." This amount proved sufficient to enable the bankrupt editor to continue the publication of his paper.

Reformers and their demands

In 1828 Mackenzie was elected to the assembly of Upper Canada, and he soon acquired notoriety as an agitator. His platform contained many of the demands of the reformers of Lower Canada. He believed that the legislature should have complete control over the provincial revenue, with the exception of the hereditary dues; he demanded an independent judiciary and reform of the legislative council, so that the governor's appointees no longer could block the assembly's proposals; and he argued for religious equality and responsible government. Nevertheless, Mackenzie never assumed leadership in any important issue. He was essentially an agitator, not a constructive thinker, and his chief rôle was to popularize ideas developed by others. The most outstanding leader in the cause of reform undoubtedly was Robert Baldwin, and his name will be associated forever with the evolution of responsible government in Canada. Egerton Ryerson is chiefly remembered in this connection for his fight against the clergy reserves and for the rights of dissenters. The Bidwells, father and son, were important also in the constitutional reform movement; in 1828, when the reformers gained control of the assembly, it was Marshall Spring Bidwell, and not Mackenzie, who received the speakership. Bidwell left Canada in 1837 and his importance has been depreciated on this account. A lesser light who figured prominently during his stormy nine months' stay in Canada was Judge John Walpole Willis. The latter's zeal for reform was undoubtedly whetted by his unsuccessful attempts to secure judicial promotion. Finally, it should be pointed out that most of the rank and file of the reformers belonged to the poorer classes, especially small farmers, and their progressivism was limited rather closely to the field of politics.

Expulsion from assembly

The assembly of 1828, in which the reformers were in a majority and the younger Bidwell served as speaker, set out to hunt trouble with the lieutenant-governor. It is notable that in this radical assembly there were four native Irishmen, six Scotchmen, seven Englishmen, thirteen Canadians, three born in other parts of the Empire, and fifteen born in the United States. Some of the demands of the assembly were extreme and involved little that was constructive. In the session of 1829 and 1830 no less than fifty-eight bills, some of them important and decidedly worth-while, were passed by the assembly, only to be rejected by the legislative council. In 1830 the reform party suffered a severe defeat in the elections, and the new assembly rallied to the support of the governor, Sir John Colborne, by passing a civil list. Mackenzie called it the "Everlasting Salary Bill" and reopened his assaults upon the government party both in the house and in his newspaper. In the session of 1831 he moved repeatedly for inquiries into various abuses. For libelous articles appearing in the *Colonial Advocate* and in other places he was eventually expelled from the assembly. Before this controversy had passed through all of its ramifications, he had been expelled, contrary to the desires of the governor and of Lord Goderich of the Colonial Office, and reëlected, not less than five times; he had been the victim of a personal assault; and he had carried his case to England, where he bombarded the Colonial Office with grievances, secured a hearing and made some impression upon the government. Of course he emerged from this controversy a popular hero, and in 1834, when York became Toronto, Mackenzie was chosen its first mayor.

In the general election of 1834 the reformers again gained control of the assembly, and Mackenzie now became chairman of a special committee on grievances. Though its report was never formally adopted, it became the platform of the Mackenzie group. The Baldwin group never endorsed the demand for an elective legislative council. The report was a bitter arraignment of government by the "family compact." It denounced the abuses of patronage and extravagant salaries and pensions, and it assailed the administration of the public lands, the difficulty in getting correct title deeds, the lack of roads, and the inefficiency of the government surveyors. Much was made of the clergy and Crown reserves, and the militia and Loyalist tracts which were sandwiched in between the farms of actual settlers so that an extraordinarily heavy burden of taxation fell upon the resident settlers who wanted local improvements. It was pointed out that nine-tenths of the people of Upper Canada belonged to some dissenting Protestant sect, and yet all denominations except the Churches of England and Scotland were still excluded from the benefits of the clergy reserves. The Mackenzie reformers asked that the Anglican Church be stripped of its monopoly privileges, and that the clergy reserves be disposed of for the benefit of public education and a system of internal improvements. Among the most important demands contained in this report were those for an elective legislative council and a somewhat vague suggestion of a responsible ministry, to take the place of the executive council, that "nondescript, with which it is folly further to contend." In pursuance of one of these demands the assembly passed bills in 1834 and 1835 to sell the clergy reserves and use the proceeds for public education. Needless to add, these measures were promptly stifled in the Upper House.

Report of Select Committee on Grievances

At this point in the controversy, in January, 1836, Colborne, who had become more and more conservative during his tenure in Canada, was succeeded by Sir Francis Bond Head. We now know that popular control over all revenues, except the post office, was actually in sight in 1835, due to concessions which the Colonial Office had decided to offer. The new lieutenant-governor proved to be an unfortunate selection, for he lacked all experience in handling such a trying political problem. He had served in the Napoleonic

Policy of Sir Francis Bond Head

Wars as an engineer, had had business experiences in South America, and in 1836 was on half-pay. His appointment probably seemed wise to the Colonial Office as a compromise between a military officer and a civilian. Head was tactless even in dealing with some of his own appointees to the council. Although he began with a conciliatory and even a liberal point of view, he quickly developed an intense personal antagonism toward most of the reformers. To Robert Baldwin he offered a place on the executive council. It was accepted only with the understanding that Baldwin need not abandon any of his principles. Two other moderates entered the council at the same time. The three reformers were soon at odds with the governor, who refused to consult them on many important matters of state. Finally, the entire council resigned and was replaced by four men of good repute but without much previous experience in politics.

Crisis   The assembly promptly expressed its want of confidence in the new executive and argued that responsible government was already part of the existing constitution, a position which it would of course have been difficult to support. At this juncture the assembly for the first time in the history of Upper Canada refused to vote supplies and was promptly dissolved. In retaliation, the governor reserved all money bills passed during the session, thus withholding funds amounting to £162,000 and badly needed for public improvements and for educational purposes. By this time it was evident that Head was attempting to throw the responsibility for this dislocation of affairs directly upon the assembly, and in this strategy he was temporarily successful. Staunchly defending the theory that he owed responsibility neither to the assembly nor to the council, but to the King alone, Head took an active part in the campaign. By charging the reformers with disloyalty to the Empire, by raising the bugbear of republicanism among the Loyalists, and by intimidating some of the voters, the governor easily defeated the reform party. The moderate reformers were in despair, and the radicals began to plot revolution. Head's new assembly, dubbed in derision "the Bread and Butter Assembly" to indicate its subservience to the governor, met in November, 1836, and promptly voted the necessary supplies. Head blindly persisted in his course, despite instructions from the government to adopt more conciliatory methods, and to the last remained confident that all difficulties had been surmounted and that upon the loyalty of the Canadians Great Britain could depend "as upon a rock."

Drifting toward   By this time Mackenzie and extremists like him had become *rebellion*   violent agitators. On July 4, 1836, the sixtieth anniversary of the American Declaration of Independence, he launched a new paper, the *Constitution*, in which he preached revolutionary doctrines. The news of Lord John Russell's instructions to the governor of Lower Canada to carry on the government of that province independent of the assembly's appropriations was the signal for great mass meetings in

Upper Canada. Plans were worked out for coöperation with the Lower-Canadian reformers, and the radicals began arming and drilling in preparation for an emergency. As has been suggested, many of the reformers like Bidwell and Baldwin refused to participate in these radical measures. Others, like Egerton Ryerson, probably the most distinguished Methodist in Canada, who had led the fight for the removal of religious disabilities, had been alienated by Mackenzie's tactics some years earlier.

To the extremists it was clear that affairs had reached the stage where an appeal to force was the only remedy. It is significant that the rebellion, which broke out in both provinces, was not due to a deliberately tyrannical policy of England, but rather to the misgovernment, the dishonesty, and the stubborn incompetence of ruling oligarchies in Quebec and Toronto. Nevertheless, the "château clique" of Lower Canada and the "family compact" of Upper Canada were the natural results of defects inherent in the Constitutional Act of 1791, and for these the British government bore the burden of responsibility. Minority rule and class privilege had appeared in the thirteen English seaboard colonies in the preceding century. Prevailing social attitudes and eighteenth century mercantilism were responsible for many of the evils of minority rule.

Fundamental causes of rebellion

SELECT BIBLIOGRAPHY FOR CHAPTER IX

For detailed accounts of the agitation for reform in Lower Canada, culminating in the rebellion of 1837, the following are valuable: DUNCAN MCARTHUR, "Papineau and French Canadian Nationalism," in *Canada and Its Provinces*, vol. III, pp. 275–320. The volumes of W. KINGSFORD's *History of Canada* are written from an anti-French point of view, those of F. X. GARNEAU, *Histoire du Canada* (5th ed., Paris, 1913–20), are from the French viewpoint. R. CHRISTIE, *History of the Late Province of Lower Canada*, 6 vols. (Quebec, 1848–1855) is old, but contains much documentary material. A. D. DE CELLES, *The Patriotes of '37* (1921) *Chronicles of Canada*, and the same author's *Louis Joseph Papineau*, in *Makers of Canada* (1926) are briefer and very readable accounts. For the constitutional history of the period, see KENNEDY, *The Constitution of Canada*, pp. 88–116.

For an account of events in Upper Canada, AILEEN DUNHAM, *Political Unrest in Upper Canada, 1815–1836* (New York, 1927) is the best. The following are also important: DUNCAN MCARTHUR, "The Reform Movement in Upper Canada," in *Canada and Its Provinces*, vol. III, pp. 327–355; W. S. WALLACE, *The Family Compact* (1915), in *Chronicles of Canada;* C. W. ROBINSON, *Life of Sir John Beverly Robinson* (Edinburgh, 1904); J. C. DENT, *The Story of the Upper Canadian Rebellion*, 2 vols. (Toronto, 1885); and D. B. READ, *The Canadian Rebellion of 1837* (Toronto, 1896). CHARLES LINDSEY, *The Life and Times of William Lyon Mackenzie* (Toronto, 1862) is a life of the great reformer by his son-in-law.

The constitutional history of Upper Canada for this period is adequately treated in KENNEDY, *The Constitution of Canada*, pp. 117–155. At the close of each chapter in Kennedy there are excellent bibliographical notes. See also DUNCAN MCARTHUR, "Constitutional History, 1763–1840," in *Canada and Its Provinces*, vol. IV, pp. 431–491. Material for the clergy reserves question may be found in *Report on the Canadian Archives, 1899*, pp. 1–41.

"The Personnel of the Family Compact, 1791–1841" is the title of an article by ALISON EWART and JULIA JARVIS, which appears in *The Canadian Historical Review*, vol. VII, pp. 209–221. The authors give a list of members of the executive council of Upper Canada for this period from 1791 to the Union Act, with brief biographical sketches of each member.

For further references, see TROTTER, *Syllabus*, pp. 90–93.

CHAPTER X

THE REBELLION OF 1837

Radicals of Lower Canada

BY THE summer of 1837 affairs in both provinces had reached a crisis. Indeed, rebellion had been a possibility for some years before 1837, and in 1836 the government in Lower Canada had begun to prepare for hostilities. The members of the radical party also were arming and drilling, under the leadership of Papineau and Dr. Wolfred Nelson. In careful emulation of the patriots who had precipitated the American Revolution, "sons of liberty" wore "liberty caps," met under "liberty trees," and appeared in gaudy home-spun as evidence of their boycott of British products. At public meetings there was much talk of putting an end to British coercion and despotism; some shouted for "*La Nation Canadienne*," and a few for "*Papineau et l'indépendance.*"

Radicals of Upper Canada

In Upper Canada similar revolutionary preparations were being made. At mass meetings the leading agitators advised all good patriots to arm and drill, to adopt declarations of grievances modeled on the United States Declaration of Independence, and to appoint local committees of vigilance. At the same time efforts were made by Mackenzie to secure the coöperation of Papineau's followers in Lower Canada, and plans were made to deliver the great stroke for liberty simultaneously in the two provinces, if such drastic action should become necessary.

Appeal to force

Fighting broke out first in Lower Canada. On November 16, after some preliminary troubles in Montreal between an organization of English and a group of French "sons of liberty," the authorities became excited and ordered the arrest of Papineau, one of his aids, Dr. E. B. O'Callaghan, an Irish radical, and twenty-five others. This order was the signal for the beginning of hostilities. Papineau, on the advice of a priest, had left Montreal for St. Hyacinth, and the government party concluded that he had gone to assume leadership of the rebel forces. When an attempt was made to arrest the ringleaders of the rebellion, the rebel sympathizers naturally rallied to their defense; small groups of rebels congregated in the Richelieu valley, particularly at St. Denis and St. Charles, while government troops were sent to drive them back to their homes.

In Richelieu district

On November 16 the first blood was shed in a conflict between "*patriotes*" and a detachment of British troops on the highway between Chambly and Longueuil. As the troops returned by this same route, with a number of prisoners whom they had been sent to arrest, a mob demanded the surrender of the captives. A scuffle

106

ensued, the troops were routed, and the prisoners freed. Since it was assumed that the ringleaders of the rebellion were in the Richelieu district, the government had decided to begin hostilities there.

On November 23 a government force attacked and eventually dispersed a rebel force at St. Denis. Papineau fled the scene just before the battle, and with O'Callaghan escaped safely to the United States. Whether Papineau deserted his followers out of sheer cowardice, whether he left on Dr. Wolfred Nelson's advice to save himself for greater service later on, whether he had honestly tried to the last to avoid an appeal to force, and then found himself carried to extreme measures by the men whom his own passionate agitation had stirred to action, or whether he tried to avoid heavy casualties by leaving for the United States—these are still debated questions and will probably remain so. *Rebellion suppressed in Lower Canada*

At St. Charles another company of rebels were easily routed; this defeat meant the rapid decline of the rebel cause. The patriot army, always an undisciplined and poorly equipped horde, difficult to control, and often disposed to indulge in plundering and burning expeditions, now disintegrated very rapidly. On December 1 a second attack on St. Denis ended in the burning of the village. There were several other minor engagements, but the only one of any magnitude was the battle at St. Eustache. Here a group of rebels who had assembled in the village church were attacked by a force of two thousand. The church was fired, and the rebels were forced to surrender. In November, 1838, there was a slight recurrence of the revolt along the New York and Vermont frontier, but this was even more easily suppressed by Sir John Colborne than the first outbreak. Hundreds were arrested and faced court martial proceedings, although comparatively few were ever severely punished. *Rebels defeated at St. Charles and St. Denis*

The revolt was a miniature rebellion, confined to an area of some thirty square miles in the immediate vicinity of Montreal. The Quebec and Three Rivers district remained quiet throughout the rebellion. It was the work of an aggressive minority, and it was doomed to failure. There had been little organization and no thorough preparation for the appeal to arms; the little rebel bands fell easy victims to the military forces of the government. The masses of the French-Canadian people remained at home, and at best they remained passively neutral. This was true of the majority of those who had favored the reform program of the leaders of French-Canadian nationalism. *Extent of disaffection*

A determining factor in the situation was the Church. While many French priests sympathized with some of the demands of Papineau's party, they did not want republicanism. They had fared well under the British régime, and did not desire a change which for the Church might prove to be a leap into the dark. Some of the bishops definitely aligned themselves with the government, and in pastoral letters read in the churches issued warnings against the *Causes of failure* deadly sin of rebellion, even threatening the penalties of the Church for those who should participate in this forbidden movement. In this sense it is true, as Professor Kennedy has suggested, "that the Quebec Act saved the situation in 1837–1838," as "it may be said also to have created it."

Later careers of rebel leaders

It is interesting to glance for a moment at the later careers of some of these leaders. Papineau lived for years in the United States and in France. In the latter country he came into contact with the radical forces which were at work there in the decade of 1840–1850. In the late 'forties, after receiving a pardon from the government, he returned to Canada and served for seven years in the Union Parliament. His leadership had never been of the constructive type, and he found it very difficult to readjust himself to the new conditions prevailing in Canada upon his return. Robert Nelson, one of the leaders in Lower Canada who was particularly prominent in the second revolt of 1838, fled to the United States, and practiced medicine in New York until his death. Dr. E. B. O'Callaghan settled at Albany and became the editor of the documentary history of colonial New York, a most scholarly and valuable series. Auguste Morin and Louis Hippolyte Lafontaine served later in the Canadian cabinet, while Georges Etienne Cartier, who as a youth had shouldered a musket at St. Denis, was perhaps the greatest French Canadian among the builders of the present confederation of Canada.

Situation in Upper Canada

In Upper Canada, where there was no French national spirit to complicate and aggravate the issues, the rebellion was more a struggle for constitutional changes, although efforts of the reformers were never concentrated on a single issue. It was perhaps inevitable that a frontier province like Upper Canada should revolt against a government based on such undemocratic principles as a small governing aristocracy, large landed estates, and special privileges for a state Church.

Appeal to Arms

Late in the fall of 1837 Toronto was virtually stripped of troops in order to provide reinforcements to aid the government of Lower Canada in putting down the revolt in that province. Several thousand stands of arms were left in Toronto practically unguarded, in spite of the fact that Sir Francis Bond Head feared trouble, and had been watching Mackenzie for some time. It is doubtful whether Mackenzie really wanted war. He was a born agitator, whose zeal frequently led him to take positions and make statements which his reason would not have endorsed in his calmer moments. He was the type of man known to become temporarily unbalanced in times of great crisis and excitement, and it is generally believed that in later years he suffered from psychopathic troubles. There can, however, be no question of Mackenzie's honesty or of his unselfish devotion to the cause of reform. Fully convinced by the fall of 1837 that no help would come either from England or from the Tory government controlling Canada, he determined to appeal to the sacred right of rebellion for the reform of conditions which a constitutional agitation seemed powerless to modify.

Mackenzie was virtually invited by Head to attack Toronto, probably on the theory that this would be the easiest way to deal *Rebel plans* with the agitator and break his power. Mackenzie planned to take Toronto, seize the governor and the government buildings, and the arms stored in the city, and then demand the immediate creation of a responsible government. If this demand were ignored, he probably planned to create a republican government.

Early in December, 1837, Mackenzie began the attack on Toronto. The rebels, however, had no real plan of action, and instead of the *Attack on* 4000 or 5000 men whom Mackenzie confidently expected to lead *Toronto* against the city, he probably never had more than 800 at his disposal. When the bells of Toronto began to ring, as a signal that the plans of the rebels were known in the city, many of the rebel farmers deserted to their homes. A flag of truce, sent out from the city, further delayed operations and enabled the government party to perfect its plans of defense. A night attack resulted in a precipitous retreat by both sides immediately after the first volley had been fired. Another day was wasted by the rebels in inaction and in conflicts over plans, and finally some eleven hundred Loyalist troops emerged from the city to disperse the rebels. Van Egmond, a brave veteran from the battlefields of Europe, tried to marshal the rebel troops behind the protection of a woods, but as soon as cannon balls began to crash among the trees the rebel forces took to their heels. Van Egmond was captured later and taken to the Toronto jail, where the veteran, his health shattered by exposure and confinement, died before his trial began.

Mackenzie and some of his companions now sought refuge in the United States. Buffalo, New York, was full of boatmen and sailors *Flight of* who at this time of year had little better to do than idle about the *leaders* taverns and hunt for excitement; a number of meetings were held, in which Irish-Americans took a prominent part, to express the sympathy of Americans for the cause of the Canadian rebellion. Mackenzie was enthusiastically received in Buffalo, and given promises of support and gifts of arms, ammunition, food, and other supplies, while some of the officials of New York winked for a time at these violations of the American neutrality laws. On December 13, with a force which probably did not exceed two dozen men, Mackenzie crossed to Navy Island, about two miles above Niagara Falls, on the Canadian side, and there he proclaimed the establishment of a provisional government. Later, land was promised to volunteers, a reward was offered for the capture of Sir Francis Bond Head, and a rebel flag, showing twin stars and a new moon breaking through the clouds, was adopted as the official insignia of the new government. The Canadian rebels held Navy Island for several weeks without interference; their force continued to grow, due largely to the arrival of recruits from the United States. There was considerable cross-firing between the rebels and the Canadian government forces drawn up on shore.

Caroline affair

On the night of December 29, 1837, occurred an incident which for a time threatened to disrupt the peaceful relations between Great Britain and the United States. A small American-owned steamer of forty tons, known as the *Caroline*, had been carrying men and supplies from Buffalo to the rebels on Navy Island. At midnight of December 29 a Canadian force under the leadership of the ardent Loyalist, Allan MacNab, crossed to the American side, loosed the *Caroline* from her moorings at Ft. Schlosser, New York, and sent her, a mass of flames, over the falls. One American was killed in the scuffle. At once the American border was aflame with excitement and resentment over this British violation of United States territory and the consequent murder of an American citizen. For five years the United States and Great Britain carried on diplomatic negotiations before the incident and its results were settled to the satisfaction of both parties.

Border incidents

On January 5, 1838, President Van Buren issued a proclamation urging all United States citizens to refrain from giving aid to the Canadian rebels, and warning them that if they were captured in Canada they might expect no help from the United States government. General Winfield Scott was dispatched at once to the border to prevent further outbreaks. Nevertheless, in 1838 the British steamer *Sir Robert Peel* was burned in United States waters, and the American *Telegraph* was fired on by British soldiers near Brockville.

Mackenzie's arrest

Mackenzie evacuated Navy Island on January 13, 1838. He was arrested by the United States authorities and finally served eleven months in the jail of Rochester, New York, for violating the United States neutrality laws. Some of his followers tried to continue their activities by planning attacks on Canada from Detroit, and by operations on some of the islands in the Detroit River, but serious trouble was avoided by the intervention of the United States government and the vigilance of the Canadian authorities.

"Hunters"

Throughout the year 1838 strained relations continued along the Canada-United States frontier, largely because of the activities of an organization known as the Hunters' Lodges, which sprang into existence all along the border from Vermont to Michigan. The order grew rapidly at a time which marks the triumph of the democratic spirit in the affairs of the American republic. These "Hunters and Chasers in the Eastern Frontier," or "Lodges of Patriotic Masons," as they were known, were a secret organization, with four degrees; their purpose was "to emancipate the British Colonies from British thralldom." Mackenzie was not a member, but many refugees of the Canadian rebellion belonged to the order. A national convention, meeting at Cleveland in the fall of 1838, planned the conquest of Upper Canada, launched a scheme for a "Republican Bank of Canada," and made preparations for a series of frontier raids.

The most serious invasion of Canada by the "Hunters" occurred at Prescott on November 11, 1838. An expedition in which some two hundred men actually crossed to Canadian territory, seized a windmill on a point of land in the St. Lawrence River and held this position for several days. The "Battle of the Windmill," as the engagement was called, resulted in heavy casualties. The defeated filibusterers were under the command of a Polish refugee, von Schultz, who, with eleven others, was eventually convicted and hanged. It is interesting to note that the lawyer who undertook the defense of von Schultz was the young John A. Macdonald, destined within a short time to become one of Canada's greatest statesmen. On December 4, 1838, four hundred "Hunters" marched through the streets of Detroit, shouting "Remember the Caroline!" and intent upon the capture of Windsor, Canada. The expedition was easily repulsed by a Canadian force. The activity of the Hunters' Lodges continued into the 1840's. In 1838 President Van Buren ordered the organization to disband; the president's real desire for peace helped greatly in preventing a rupture in Anglo-American relations as a result of these border disturbances. *Invasion of Canada by "Hunters"*

Mackenzie, after a rather extended residence in the United States, where he was soon disillusioned by the excesses and defects of democracy as exemplified in some of the American states, returned to Canada in 1849. Like Papineau, he was elected to the Parliament of United Canada, but he never regained his earlier influence in Canadian affairs. He died in Toronto in 1861, a poor and disappointed man. *Mackenzie's later career*

The rebellion of 1837 was an abortive, wild, and misguided movement, the work of a small minority led by fiery, and honest zealots. It was hardly more than "a good-sized election row." Many of its causes were inherent in the Constitutional Act of 1791, and in the prevailing policy of nations toward their colonies. In spite of its abortive character, the rebellion probably had greater importance for the future of Canada than a more prolonged conflict with British authority might have had. It directed the attention of Great Britain to certain problems and lessons which might have been learned from the disruption of the Empire in 1776. The rebellion stimulated interest in certain reforms which were absolutely imperative, but which an appeal to reason and peaceful tactics had not been able to arouse. *Nature of rebellion*

The rebellion was evidence that Canada was gradually developing into political maturity, and in the words of Professor McArthur it "marks the beginning of a movement to make colonial independence the basis of imperial unity." There was much truth in what Dr. Nelson, one of the rebels, wrote in the summer of 1838: "We rebelled neither against Her Majesty's person nor her government, but against Colonial misgovernment."

In the maritime provinces the rebellion had little effect save to reveal the fundamental loyalty of the people to the British connection. Pledges of aid in putting down the rebellion came from various groups in New Brunswick and Nova Scotia. *Conditions in maritime provinces*

SELECT BIBLIOGRAPHY FOR CHAPTER X

Most of the references cited in the bibliographical note for the preceding chapter are also useful for the events of the rebellion of 1837. See in addition: DUNCAN McARTHUR, "The Canadian Rebellion of 1837," in *Canada and Its Provinces*, vol. III, pp. 361–383, and C. DURAND, *Reminiscences of the Rebellion of 1837* (Toronto, 1898). E. A. THELLER, *Canada in 1837–38*, 2 vols. (New York, 1841) is a biased account by a participant who escaped to the United States.

CHAPTER XI

LORD DURHAM AND THE AFFAIRS OF BRITISH NORTH AMERICA

THE immediate result of the rebellion of 1837 was the suspension of the constitution of Lower Canada by an imperial act under which *Suspension of* that province automatically lapsed into the stage of government *constitution* which had existed before the Constitutional Act of 1791, namely, government by a governor and council appointed by the Crown. Under this arrangement the initiation of legislation fell to the governor, and for the time being all representative government came to an end.

For the extremely difficult post of governor in this crisis in her *Lord Durham's* imperial relations, Great Britain selected John George Lambton, first *mission* Earl of Durham. Lord Durham was appointed governor-in-chief of all five British-American provinces, with full powers as England's special high commissioner to deal with the critical situation existing in these dependencies. Among his many duties was the task of restoring peace and loyalty among the disaffected people in Upper and Lower Canada, the prevention of a rupture of the peaceful relations between Great Britain and the United States due to continued trouble on the border of Canada, the proper punishment of the leaders of the rebellion, and the suggestion of constructive measures which would make the recurrence of these unhappy events impossible.

Durham belonged to what may be called the radical-liberal group in British politics, and he brought to his difficult task a spirit of *Durham's* devotion to the principles of self-government and a firm faith in the *political views* future of the British Empire. Durham was not afraid to act boldly and to assume full responsibility for his actions, and he believed strongly that an enlightened imperialism, resting on responsible governments in the dependencies, would prove the salvation of the Empire.

Lord Durham was the son-in-law of Earl Grey, famous for the Reform Bill of 1832, the first step toward the democratization of *Qualifications* England's ancient parliamentary institutions. When Durham came *for leadership* to Canada, he was still a comparatively young man, a polished orator, richly endowed with the gifts of a successful student of political affairs, and inclined to emphasize the importance of governmental pomp and ceremony. Perhaps his greatest weakness was a fiery and uncontrollable temper, combined with an extremely sensitive nature, which made it difficult for him to work with other men.

Immediately upon his arrival in Quebec, where he received a

cordial welcome, Lord Durham dismissed the old executive council of Lower Canada, appointed under the suspended constitution, and rudely but wisely turned his back upon the old "château clique" which had dominated the government of the province for many years. This initial step was calculated to conciliate the popular party, and in this Durham was reasonably successful. In his official party was Charles Buller, who served as his secretary, and who had been a pupil of the great Carlyle. Edward Gibbon Wakefield, a careful student of colonial affairs, also accompanied the high commissioner. Commissions were at once appointed to investigate such causes of discontent as the administration of the Crown lands, the status of education, and municipal government in the provinces. Durham personally favored the dismembering of the French province of Lower Canada, and the establishment of a federal union to embrace all of British North America, but he abandoned this suggestion when he discovered that the opposition to confederation was too strong to overcome.

A mission was dispatched to Washington, in order to provide for the more effective guarding of the frontier, and to avoid violence along the border which might provoke a crisis in Anglo-American relations and thus make the rest of Durham's work impossible. Traveling in vice-regal splendor through the two provinces of Canada, Lord Durham paused at Niagara to participate in a banquet at which he toasted the president of the United States. For this incident the governor was severely criticized in some quarters, but Charles Buller, his secretary, ardently defended the act of his chief, insisting that "a million of money would have been a cheap price for the single glass of wine which Lord Durham drank to the health of the American President."

The immediate and pressing problem demanding solution by the high commissioner was the disposal of the political prisoners with whom the jails were crowded at the time of his arrival. Durham did not approve of a vindictive policy toward the rebels of 1837, and he believed that many of the prisoners were simply misguided and discontented folk from the countryside who had been deluded into believing that an appeal to arms would solve their grievances. He was fully conscious, moreover, of the difficulties involved in bringing these rebels to trial. To select a jury fairly from among the French Canadians would probably result in acquittal, whereas to pack the jury with Englishmen, or to tamper with the existing jury laws, was both unwise and contrary to Durham's high sense of honor. In the dilemma in which he found himself he resolved to get a confession of guilt from the accused and to induce them to throw themselves upon his mercy. Lord Durham then issued an ordinance banishing Papineau and fourteen other ringleaders who had escaped to the United States, with the understanding that the death penalty would be imposed if they returned to Canada. Eight others, including

Wolfred Nelson, who pleaded guilty, he banished to Bermuda, and to all the rest he granted complete amnesty.

This merciful course, which has won the full approval of posterity, and now constitutes one of Lord Durham's claims to greatness, also became the cause of his recall. His clemency undoubtedly conciliated many of the British and French Canadians, while the prisoners considered their banishment an act of mercy by which they escaped the gallows. Moreover, a more vindictive policy probably would have stirred the anglophobian fever which was then raging in the United States. *Wisdom of Durham's course*

As a matter of fact, Lord Durham technically exceeded his authority. He did not have the power to banish men to another British colony without a jury trial, even under the special authority exercised by a high commissioner and his council. The English Parliament, instead of legalizing his extraordinary but justifiable procedure by a special act of legislation, began to attack his conduct, largely to make political capital against the party in power. The Government, fearful of losing its slender majority, preferred to allow Lord Durham to become the scapegoat of practical party politics, and disallowed the ordinance. Durham was deeply wounded by this action, which he believed was an evidence of rank duplicity, and his feelings were not improved when he read about the incident for the first time in an American newspaper. Without awaiting the receipt of more formal notification, he at once resigned and left for England on November 1, 1838. On the face of things, it appeared that his mission had ended in failure, for he had not won the support of French Canada, and his conduct of affairs in British North America had been repudiated by the Government to which he was responsible. *His recall*

In February, 1839, after a sojourn of only five months in Canada, Lord Durham submitted to the Queen his epoch-making *Report on the Affairs of British North America*. Little more than a year later, while still under fifty, he died. "Canada has been the death of him," said John Stuart Mill. His last words were, "I would fain hope I have not lived altogether in vain. Whatever the Tories may say, the Canadians will one day do justice to my memory." In that hope he was not to be disappointed, for not only Canadians, but liberals the world over, honor his memory. *Durham's place in Canadian history*

Lord Durham's Report is equally remarkable for its penetrating analysis of British North American affairs, his faith in the future of British North America, and his constructive suggestions for the development of an empire in which colonial autonomy should be the foundation stone. Like all great documents, written during the heat of controversy, the report was neither new nor correct in its entirety. The sections dealing with Upper Canada were probably the weakest, as those dealing with Lower Canada were undoubtedly the most brilliant. The analysis of social and economic factors, though *His famous report* sometimes exaggerated, proved beneficial for the future development of the provinces.

Analysis of causes of discontent

Lord Durham's report was a sweeping condemnation of the whole system of government, as he found it functioning at Quebec and Toronto, and in this respect it was a vindication of the claims of the reformers. Much that the radicals had said about oligarchical government, the meddlesome interference of the British Colonial Office or its failure to act at all, the prevalence of frauds in the management of the public lands, the woeful state of education, and the lack of local government, Lord Durham found true, and he submitted constructive proposals to remedy the situation which he had painted so darkly in his report.

Responsible government

In the first place, he urged the granting of complete responsible self-government, in all matters of colonial concern. Thus far he simply acceded to the demands which had been made by some of the reformers themselves. The problem demanding solution by an enlightened imperialist like Durham was how to reconcile a system of government based on complete recognition of colonial autonomy with the preservation of imperial rights. Durham proposed to divide the functions of government, and to reserve for the imperial government only those powers which he believed absolutely essential to the maintenance of imperial unity. The fields of governmental action included in this category of reserved powers were the control of foreign relations, the regulation of commerce, the determination of the constitution of government for the colony, and the disposal of the public lands. All other powers and functions were to be transferred to the control of the colony. Under this arrangement there would be a division of governmental duties by which responsibility for the exercise of most of them would be lodged in the people of the colony acting through their elected representatives. Responsibility for the four reserved powers remained with the British Crown. Durham believed that any other arrangement would jeopardize the future of the Empire. Yet today, almost all of these functions which Lord Durham thought indispensable to the maintenance of the imperial tie have passed under the complete control of the governments in the Great Dominions, and the British Empire still lives.

Other proposals

Lord Durham recommended that all Crown revenues, other than those derived from the disposal of the public lands, should be left to the colonial government, in exchange for a permanent civil list. On the important question whether revenue bills should originate in the Assembly and be sponsored by the Cabinet, Durham was not altogether clear. He suggested that "good government" would not be attainable "while the present unrestricted powers of voting public money . . . are lodged in the hands of the Assembly." Durham did not advise an elective Upper House, for he believed the legislative council would have to be retained as a wholesome check upon the assembly. By responsible government Lord Durham meant a cabinet responsible to the majority of the elective Lower House. In no other way could collisions between the executive and the legislative branches of the government be avoided. More was probably read into the report on this point in later years than Durham realized. In view of his limitation on the financial powers of the Assembly, and the functions reserved for the Imperial government, no one really knows what Durham meant by responsible government, since he had no opportunity to really work out his theory.

The second important recommendation urged the union of Upper and Lower Canada under one government. By this method Lord *Union* Durham hoped gradually to extinguish the spirit of French nationalism, by absorbing and amalgamating the French group in the ever-growing English population. He believed the English in Upper Canada, plus the English minority in Lower Canada, would be strong enough to control the new union government, and that with the immigration of English settlers Canada would daily become more British. Durham urged the gradual substitution of the English language for French. It is clear that he contemplated a complete union of the two peoples, not simply a coalescing of their two assemblies, and that he had no desire to perpetuate in Lower Canada "two nations warring in the bosom of a single state." Durham advocated representation by population in the Union Parliament, not the equal representation of the two provinces finally written into the law of 1840. It is impossible to say whether an Anglo-French fusion would have been successful under any conditions, but there can be no question that Durham never fully appreciated the tremendous vitality of the French-Canadian people.

Other items in this epoch-making Report were overshadowed by the two major suggestions outlined above. Lord Durham gave valu- *Minor* able advice about economy and efficiency in government, and he *recommendation* urged the immediate development of municipal institutions. These he believed were necessary to serve as a buffer between the people and the legislature, to promote the speedy formation of local communities and to serve as a training school in which citizens could acquire experience for larger political tasks. He also urged a comprehensive program of canal and railroad building to promote the growth of a Canadian national spirit.

Lord Durham's Report, which ushers in a new era in the history of British imperialism, was not accepted at the time with the acclaim *British reaction* which it has since been universally accorded. Many high-minded and broad-minded Englishmen were extremely dubious about many of his proposals, and were especially concerned with the problem of what would become of the governor-general under such a scheme of colonial self-government. Others continued to believe that it was the destiny of the Empire to dissolve soon into its component elements, and that it was therefore unwise to delay the process of peaceful disintegration by such troublesome makeshifts.

Canada's reaction

In British North America the Report was bitterly assailed by the "family compact" in Upper Canada, some of whom honestly questioned its value, while others struggled to hold on to their dominant position under the old régime. In Lower Canada the French-Canadian nationalists vigorously opposed a plan designed to swallow them in a wholly British state. In Upper Canada the governing oligarchy wanted union but not responsible government, whereas in Lower Canada the people wanted responsible government but not union.

Preparing for union

In the summer of 1839 Lord John Russell, whose resolutions had hastened the rebellion of 1837, introduced a union bill, modeled on Durham's Report, for discussion in the British Parliament. Obviously, before much could be accomplished by imperial legislation, it was necessary to prepare the way for the acceptance of a union measure in Canada. For this task, which required tact and ability of an unusual order, the Colonial Office selected Poulett Thomson, better known as Baron Sydenham, the title to which he was raised in 1840. Sydenham had been a candle manufacturer and came from a prominent family of businessmen. He traveled widely and became a master of the social graces. He was a disciple of the economists Mill and Ricardo, and a friend of such distinguished British liberals as Jeremy Bentham and Joseph Hume. At the time of his appointment as governor of Canada he represented Manchester in the British House of Commons, where he had already gained a reputation as a skilful parliamentarian.

Sydenham

Sydenham arrived in Quebec on October 19, 1839. On November 22 he was in Toronto. His delicate task of winning support for the proposed union act had to be performed largely behind the scenes. By many conferences and much persuasion and cajolery, he managed to conciliate some of his opponents. In this campaign of education in Upper Canada he had the support of such moderate reformers as Robert Baldwin and Francis Hincks. Sydenham suggested a solution for the troublesome question of the clergy reserves in Upper Canada by proposing that the remainder of these lands be sold, and the income from this fund be distributed among all the churches. Such a proposal at least had the merit of giving some recognition to the rights of dissenting sects. He urged the establishment of municipal institutions and secured the removal of another grievance by a provision for the accurate registering of deeds and land titles. Kingston was proposed as the new capital of the united provinces.

Upper Canada accepts union

Although the people of the province were divided into many factions, the assembly of Upper Canada finally agreed to union on condition that this province should have equal representation with Lower Canada in the Union Parliament, that a permanent civil list be established large enough to insure an independent judiciary, and that the provincial debt incurred for "public works of common interest" should be assumed as a charge on the combined revenues of the union government. It was this last concession which the governor used most effectively as a lever to overcome the opposition to union of the "family compact" group. Moreover, Sydenham published in the *Upper Canada Gazette* the dispatch from the home government relating to the tenure of public offices. In this it was made clear that no one would be continued in public office unless he made himself of service to the governor and to the province. The governor's strategy worked like magic in silencing further opposition from the "family compact."

In Lower Canada Sydenham established a new judicial organiza- *Problem in* tion. Because the assembly was still under suspension, the governor *Lower Canada* summoned the special council, in existence since the days of virtual dictatorship immediately following the rebellion. This council, composed largely of English, ratified the proposal of union by a vote of twelve to three. Thus in Lower Canada approval of union was given by a body which in no sense represented the people of the province. The council agreed to the assumption of the public debt of Upper Canada by the new union government and promised a permanent civil list. The French Canadians, however, remained extremely skeptical in their attitude toward the new arrangement, and it is doubtful whether even the British minority in the province were entirely satisfied.

With the way thus prepared for union, and with many of its terms virtually agreed upon, a union bill was enacted by the British *Union Act* Parliament. The Union Act became a law on July 23, 1840, to go into operation by proclamation on February 10 of the following year. The law provided for the union of Lower and Upper Canada under a single government to consist of a governor, a legislative council, and an assembly. The governor and the legislative council of not less than twenty members were appointed by the Crown, the members of the council to hold office for life. The Lower House, or House of Assembly, consisting of eighty-four members, was to be chosen by popular suffrage, forty-two members from each of the old provinces. This equal division temporarily gave the advantage to Upper Canada which at that time had a smaller population than the sister province.

The act further provided that all government papers, reports, and records should be kept in the English language, although either *Its provisions* French or English might be used as the vehicle of debate, and the translation of documents and papers into French was allowed. England reserved the right to levy duties for the purpose of regulating imperial commerce, while bills dealing with the Crown lands and with religion were to be reserved by the governor for the action of the home government. All the Canadian revenues were now con-solidated, and the Crown formally surrendered all claims to hereditary and territorial revenues in return for a permanent civil list of £75,000. All bills for the expenditure of money and taxation were to originate with the governor, and were then to be submitted to the House of Assembly for discussion. The debts of the two old provinces were assumed by the union, and the old laws were to continue in force in each province until repealed or amended. The status of such controversial questions as the rights and privileges of the Anglican and the Roman Catholic Churches, religious toleration, and waste lands was carefully defined.

Criticisms of Act

The Union Act left some of the demands of 1837 unfulfilled. The legislative council remained an appointive body until 1856. There was no specific provision in the Act to exclude civil and judicial officers from the legislature, and this reform was not achieved until 1853. The French Canadians objected to the over-representation of Upper Canada in the Union Parliament, and to the saddling of the heavy public debt of Upper Canada upon the consolidated revenue. Nevertheless the act did end the continual friction between Upper and Lower Canada over the division of the proceeds from import duties, this having been one of the insoluble inter-provincial problems before 1837.

Its significance

The union of the two provinces helped to destroy the narrow provincialism and exclusiveness of the French population, at least to the extent that it compelled both the English and the French in Canada to broaden their political horizons and to think of government in larger terms. This duty of participating in the government and the fortunes of a larger area did much to promote the political education of both elements. The most important omission from the Union Act was the fact that the law did not deal with the executive principle at all, and that no reference whatsoever was made to responsible government, the crux of the trouble in 1837. So far as the executive principle was concerned, the law showed no advance over the constitutional legislation of 1791.

Germ of responsible government

The germ from which responsible government developed is to be found in Lord John Russell's dispatches of September 7 and October 16, 1839, to Sydenham. The latter's instructions contained the significant sentence, "The importance of maintaining the utmost possible harmony between the policy of the legislature and of the executive government admits of no question, and it will of course be your anxious endeavor to call to your councils and to employ in the public service those persons, who, by their position and character, have obtained the general confidence and esteem of the inhabitants of the province." Furthermore, Lord John Russell urged the new governor to make it known in the province that good behavior would no longer be a guarantee of life tenure in public office. "Not only will such officers be called to retire from the public service as often as any sufficient motives of public policy may suggest the expediency of that measure, but . . . a change in the person of the governor will be considered as a sufficient reason for any alterations which his successor may deem it expedient to make in the list of public functionaries. . . ."

It is evident from these extracts that Lord John Russell was not yet ready to endorse responsible government as an abstract principle or to accept it as a convention of the constitution, but that he relied on common sense and a policy of moderation to provide the necessary harmony between the legislative and the executive branches of the government. Nevertheless, it is to these phrases that the germs of the concession of responsible government are to be traced, and to nothing whatsoever in the Act of 1840. A long struggle was still necessary before responsible government became fixed as one of the fundamental customs of the Canadian constitution. England had to learn the implications of the responsible principle as applied to colonial affairs, while Canada had to be taught how to use the new machinery of government at her disposal. Most of the 1840's were spent in the struggle to reconcile the imperial interest as represented by the governor, and the local Canadian point of view as manifested in the Canadian Parliament.

SELECT BIBLIOGRAPHY FOR CHAPTER XI

For Lord Durham's mission and report on Canadian affairs, the following are useful brief accounts: DUNCAN McARTHUR, "Lord Durham and the Union of the Canadas," in *Canada and Its Provinces*, vol. IV, pp. 389–406; A. MacMECHAN, *The Winning of Popular Government* (Toronto, 1921), Chap. I, in *Chronicles of Canada;* and KENNEDY, *The Constitution of Canada*, pp. 156–200. The standard edition of Durham's report is SIR CHARLES LUCAS, *Lord Durham's Report*, 3 vols. (Oxford, 1912). This work contains a most valuable introduction and editorial notes. Most of Durham's more important dispatches are available in W. P. M. KENNEDY, *Documents of the Canadian Constitution, 1759–1915* (Oxford, 1918), pp. 223–480; and H. E. EGERTON and W. L. GRANT, *Canadian Constitutional Development* (Toronto, 1907), pp. 111–188. Reference to the *Russell-Sydenham Correspondence*, conveniently found in KENNEDY's *Documents*, pp. 516–528, is vital.

A comprehensive biography of Durham is S. J. REID, *Life and Letters of the First Earl of Durham, 1792–1840*, 2 vols. (London, 1906) and CHESTER W. NEW, *Lord Durham* (Oxford, 1929). The most recent discussion of Buller's share in Durham's mission is E. M. WRONG, *Charles Buller and Responsible Government* (Oxford, 1926).

CHAPTER XII

THE REALIZATION OF RESPONSIBLE GOVERNMENT

THE first Union Parliament met at Kingston, in the refitted General Hospital, on June 14, 1841. The elections had been attended by much excitement and disorder, but through a judicious interference in the campaign, and a ruthless gerrymandering of the Quebec and Montreal districts in the interests of the British element, Sydenham had tried to secure a majority with which he could work in harmony. The membership of the first assembly was, however, so divided that anything like a two-party system was impossible.

In the Lower House were such prominent leaders as John Neilson, the Scotch-Canadian editor of the *Quebec Gazette*, who had opposed union, Robert Christie, a Nova Scotian who represented Lower Canada and is perhaps better known as the author of a history of that province, and Auguste Norbert Morin and Denis Viger, both active in the troubles of 1837, the latter having been a government prisoner during that disturbance. Etienne Pascal Taché and John Sandfield Macdonald also began their parliamentary careers with this session. Allan MacNab was present as the leader of the extreme Loyalist, conservative group, while Francis Hincks, a prominent banker and publisher of Toronto, was already known as one of the outstanding Liberals of Upper Canada. William H. Merritt, one of the promoters of the Welland Canal, and Isaac Buchanan, a leader in the coming struggle to secularize the clergy reserves, were other distinguished members of this interesting and able first assembly. More important than any other member was Robert Baldwin, easily the ablest constructive thinker of the lot, and it was he who immediately opened the battle for responsible government.

Baron Sydenham formally opened the provincial parliament on the second day, with all the ceremonial and precedents which could be borrowed from the procedure of Great Britain. The governor came and went to the accompaniment of salvos of artillery, and made the customary speech from the throne. Sydenham's ideal was undoubtedly to form a non-partisan ministry. Although he selected members from either house to serve in his council, and put each at the head of a department of the government, all his selections were drawn from the English element in Parliament, and the majority of his ministry were Conservatives. Perhaps the most distinguished member of Sydenham's first ministry was William Henry Draper, a Conservative destined to make a long and honorable record on the bench. Robert Baldwin, the ablest friend of responsible government in Canada, at first accepted the office of solicitor-general for Upper Canada, only to resign when he learned that no French Canadians were represented in the Government. While Sydenham generally respected majority opinion in the assembly, it was soon made clear that he fully intended to be his own prime minister and that he held the reins of government firmly in his own hands.

Sydenham was a tireless worker who looked after most of the details of government himself. The decisions of the Government were *Economic* his decisions, and he consulted his council or not, just as he pleased. *progress* Such advice as he sought he usually obtained from individual members, rarely from the council as a body. During his régime in Canada great progress was made in laying the foundations for the sound economic progress of the country. Laws were enacted for public works and for such internal improvements as the completion of the Welland Canal (opened in 1829), to avoid the rapids of the Niagara between Lake Erie and Lake Ontario, the erection of light-houses, and the general improvement of St. Lawrence River navigation, and the construction of highways and bridges. The British government guaranteed a loan of £1,500,000 for this program of public works, and a board of works was created for its more efficient promotion. Municipal government was improved, a better system was devised for the disposal of the public lands, regulations were made for the settlement of immigrants, and reforms were enacted in the criminal law of the province. An act was passed appropriating $200,000 annually for the establishment of a common school system, under a chief superintendent of education for United Canada, with assistants in each of the two provinces. Sydenham also planned to establish a note-issuing national bank, but here he was thwarted by the private banks which opposed such a monopoly.

The governor-general frequently adopted the methods of a "vice-regal pedagogue," in pushing through his program. During his *Sydenham's* governorship, although a remarkable record for constructive legisla- *theory of* tion was made, it was not the work of a responsible government, and *governorship* Sydenham at the time of his death faced a growing opposition in parliament. He steadily opposed all suggestions to diminish the powers of his office, and he honestly believed that the granting of responsible government, in the sense in which the term was used by the reformers, would result in the disintegration of the Empire. The only way Sydenham knew to reconcile his responsibility to both the colony and to the Empire was to guide local affairs as much as he could himself, so that clashes might be avoided. By "responsible government," the reformers of course meant parliamentary government, that is, the English type of executive responsibility through a cabinet responsible to the elected legislature.

In spite of Sydenham's policies, considerable progress was made during his governorship toward the recognition of the principle of

*Sydenham-
Harrison
Resolutions*

responsible government. It was Baldwin who precipitated a discussion of what the governor viewed as "theoretical points of government," by calling for copies of Lord John Russell's dispatches of 1839, and by moving a series of six resolutions the essence of which was the recognition of cabinet responsibility in colonial government. Sydenham at once drew up four amendments to Baldwin's proposals. They were introduced in the assembly by Samuel Bealey Harrison and were adopted. In conjunction with the contents of Russell's dispatch of October 14, 1839, already referred to, the adoption of the Sydenham-Harrison Resolutions made responsible government inevitable. These resolutions represented the greatest concession Sydenham felt he could make. They recognized the right of the people "of having a provincial parliament for the protection of their liberties, for the exercise of a constitutional influence over the executive departments of their government, and for legislation upon all matters of internal government." Although specifically attributing the responsibility of the governor to the imperial authorities alone, the resolutions recognized that "the management of our local affairs can only be conducted by him, by and with the assistance, counsel and information of subordinate officers in the province," and that "in order to preserve between the different branches of the provincial parliament that harmony which is essential to the peace, welfare, and good government of the province, the chief advisors of the representative of the sovereign, constituting a provincial administration under him, ought to be men possessed of the confidence of the representatives of the people, thus affording a guarantee that the well-understood wishes and interests of the people, which our gracious sovereign has declared shall be the rule of the provincial government, will, on all occasions, be faithfully represented and advocated." A few weeks after this event, on September 19, 1841, Sydenham died. His death was due to nervous exhaustion aggravated by an infected leg resulting from a fall from his horse. He was buried under the floor of St. George's Church in Kingston.

*Sir Charles
Bagot*

Sir Charles Bagot was named as Sydenham's successor. Although a life-long Tory, he was never a bitter partisan, and he was willing to administer the constitution of Canada impartially. Bagot had had much experience in the field of diplomacy. Indeed, his appointment was strongly influenced by the idea that he would be acceptable to the United States, where he had gained no little distinction in the Rush-Bagot negotiations for disarmament on the Great Lakes. The new governor assumed his duties after a leisurely journey to Canada *via* Boston and Albany, and after enthusiastic receptions and levees in Toronto, Montreal, and Quebec.

His policy

Bagot soon discovered that in the interests of an efficient and harmonious administration he would have to recognize the French party in the formation of his council. The French group were now under the able leadership of Louis Lafontaine, a former follower of

Papineau, but a constructive and conservative statesman who had accepted the union as an accomplished fact and concluded that further opposition was useless. By a combination of the French followers of Lafontaine and the moderate reformers of Upper Canada led by Robert Baldwin, a coalition was formed in the assembly so powerful that the governor found it necessary to accept a reconstructed ministry under the joint leadership of Lafontaine and Baldwin.

This was a virtual concession of the principle that only a responsible government could get things done in United Canada. The Tory party bitterly resented the presence of "rebels" like Lafontaine in the ministry, and made vigorous assaults upon the governor for accepting such a situation. The newspapers of the old "family compact" accused Bagot of handing "the British over to the vindictive disposition of the French mob," and denounced the governor as a "radical," an "old woman" and an "apostate" for instituting a "radical ministry." But Bagot remained undisturbed by the clamor against his administration, and in due time the British Secretary of State gave his assent to his plan of procedure. *Criticism of Bagot's policy*

Bagot's course did much to reconcile the French Canadians to the new governmental order. Unfortunately, the peaceful evolution toward greater democracy was interrupted by Bagot's serious illness. The governor, suffering severely from dropsy and heart trouble, soon found it necessary to give up the burdens of his office. He met his last cabinet council while confined to his bed, and died in Canada less than two months after he had turned over the government to his successor. The admission of the French Canadians to the ministry during his régime, and the increasing functions exercised by the ministry during his illness, marked great steps forward in the struggle for recognition of the principles of responsible government. *Bagot's retirement*

Sir Charles Theophilus Metcalfe, Bagot's successor, began his turbulent and unhappy career in Canada in 1843. He brought with him years of successful experience in the civil service of India and as governor of Jamaica. Macaulay called him "the ablest civil servant I ever knew in India." The problem of governing Canada proved quite different from that of managing the natives of India and Jamaica, and Metcalfe assumed his new duties without any experience with parliamentary institutions in the dependencies. *Metcalfe*

There is no evidence to show that Metcalfe was appointed deliberately by the British government in order to undo Bagot's work or to give responsible government in Canada a setback. Metcalfe was honestly opposed to party government in the dependencies, because he was fearful that one party would sooner or later favor independence. He could not reconcile the position of the governor-general with the implications of responsible government, nor could he understand how a governor could represent faithfully the interests of the mother-country if he allowed himself to become the spokesman of a colonial faction, even if that faction were dignified by the name of a *Metcalfe's policy* political party. In other words, if the ministry assumed full responsibility for all acts of the Government, what was to become of the governor-general's responsibility to the imperial authorities and to his sovereign? This was the dilemma which Metcalfe found in the Canadian situation as it had developed under his predecessor, and he set to work to undo the evil developments of party government as he saw them. The ministry, of course, was equally determined to consolidate their newly-won powers.

Governor and his ministry

It was not long before Metcalfe stoutly refused to be the ministry's tool. It must be admitted that the ministry frequently treated the governor with scant courtesy, and Metcalfe retaliated by slighting his advisors and frequently seeking the counsel of the opposition leaders. A number of controversies arose over the governor's right to make appointments to public office, without first consulting and securing the approval of the ministry. In November, 1843, matters reached a crisis. Lafontaine and Baldwin virtually demanded that office-holding should become a matter of patronage for the party in power, and be under the sole control of the ministry. This demand the governor considered a violation of the royal prerogative. The conference with the governor on this issue only served to reveal the utter incompatibility of the two points of view, and so the Lafontaine-Baldwin ministry resigned.

Deadlock

The constitutional issues involved in this governmental crisis were aired at great length in the assembly, where the reformers had a majority of nearly three to one. Parliament was prorogued, and for nine months Metcalfe struggled to form a new ministry, while the uproar in the country steadily increased. A shower of pamphlets appeared, in which the reformers were denounced as traitors plotting annexation to the United States, and the governor on the other hand, was called such disrespectful names as "Charles the Simple." Finally, Metcalfe was able to fill six of the cabinet offices. In September, 1844, Parliament was dissolved, and both parties appealed to the electorate to sustain them in their respective positions.

Elections of 1844

The elections of 1844 were marked with rioting, bloodshed, and the use of the militia in some places. Bribery and corruption probably were resorted to by both sides. Largely by raising the loyalty issue, the governor obtained a small majority of six in support of his new ministry. Most of its supporters came from Upper Canada where the charge of republicanism leveled against the reformers did good work among the Loyalist stock. Parliament met in November, and Allan MacNab, a Tory leader who knew no French, was elected speaker of the assembly by the narrow margin of three votes. Among the new members was John A. Macdonald, a young Scotch-Canadian lawyer who had been elected as the Conservative representative for Kingston. Little was accomplished during this session, due to the precariously small majority of the Government, and because friction developed among the majority group. Metcalfe struggled desperately to hold his Government together, and as a matter of fact a personal loyalty to him was practically the only bond which prevented its disintegration.

Metcalfe's devotion to what he considered his duty to the Empire was truly heroic. While the controversy was in progress, his vitality was being sapped unrelentingly by a malignant cancer which robbed him of the sight of an eye, and continued its ravaging course in his throat and face. Parliament was prorogued again in September, after a session barren of results, and near the end of the year 1845 Metcalfe at last resolved to yield to the advice of his friends and resign. He reached Liverpool in December, and nine months later he was dead. It was perhaps a slight compensation for his Spartan fortitude that he was raised to a peerage before his death, as evidence of the high esteem in which his policies were held in the mother-country. Men like Peel, Stanley, and Gladstone, and members of the colonial reform group like Buller and Wakefield, fully approved his course. As for Metcalfe, to quote the words of his biographer, "he felt that he was fighting for his sovereign against a rebellious people." He was utterly impatient with a party system which could boast of no more orderly or disciplined groups than that variety of Canadian organizations which ran the whole gamut of partisan dissensions from the extreme Tories to French rebels and repealers of the union. *Estimate of Metcalfe's policy*

The administration of the Earl of Cathcart, the soldier, who succeeded Metcalfe, was brief, and, on the whole, uneventful, except for friction with the United States over the Oregon country. In January, 1847, Lord Elgin arrived in Canada to assume the rôle of governor-general. A contemporary of Gladstone at Oxford, he came from a Scotch noble family, and had married the daughter of Lord Durham. The four years preceding his arrival in Canada he had spent as governor of Jamaica. Lord Elgin came at a most critical time in the history of Canada and in the history of Canada's relations with the mother-country, as will be pointed out in detail later; but he came with the firm resolve to carry the principles advocated by Lord Durham to their full fruition. *Lord Elgin*

Upon his arrival, Lord Elgin found Metcalfe's last Conservative ministry still holding on to power by the slender majority of two votes. Elgin made no effort to disrupt it, but he also made it clear that he would maintain cordial relations with any other group which might come into control of the legislature. On December 6, 1847, a dissolution took place, and the ensuing election was a triumph for the reformers in both Canada East and Canada West. The new assembly met on February 25, 1848. Among its members was Louis Joseph Papineau, who had returned from his long exile in the United States and France. In less than a week the Conservative ministry suffered an adverse vote and was forced to resign. Lord Elgin had carefully refrained from all interference in the campaign, and on the *His conception of responsible government*

defeat of the Government he promptly summoned Lafontaine and
Baldwin to form a new ministry, thus recognizing again the political
unity of Canada.

Session of 1849

The session of 1849 was one of the great sessions of the Union
Parliament. Among the new members were Georges Etienne Cartier,
who had carried a musket in 1837 against the government, and
Alexander Tilloch Galt, a brilliant spokesman for the British minority in Lower Canada. Both were destined to become leaders in the
building of confederation less than fifteen years later. Lord Elgin
read his speech from the throne in both English and French. Earlier
he had urged the British government to assent to a change in the law
which had made English the sole official language.

*Important
legislation*

Nearly 200 bills became laws during this memorable session.
Among them were bills to refound the University of Toronto on a
non-sectarian basis, to revise the judicial system, to promote railroad
construction, and a municipal corporations act dealing with self-
government for counties, townships, and villages. Efforts were made
to secure a reciprocity trade agreement with the United States,
primarily to offset the evil effects for Canada of the adoption of
free trade by Great Britain. A controversy arose over the arrival of
hordes of Irish immigrants, some of whom became a burden upon
the colony. Lord Elgin was able to steer a course through all of these
complex problems which never once endangered the cordial coöperation of his Government, whatever friction may have developed in
other quarters.

*"Rebellion
Losses Bill"*

The real test of responsible government came with the passage
of the Act of Indemnification, or the "Rebellion Losses Bill," as it
was popularly known. A general amnesty had been passed for all the
rebels of 1837, and of this even leaders like Mackenzie and Papineau
had taken advantage to return to Canada. During the rebellion many
loyal citizens, or innocent bystanders, had suffered losses. Some had
lost guns, cows, or other property, or had had their houses and barns
damaged during the fighting. Sometimes these losses were the result
of violence on the part of the soldiers as well as of the rebels. Compensation for these damages was proposed as early as 1838, and some
funds had actually been voted for this purpose prior to union. Metcalfe had suggested a settlement, compensating all save those who
had actually been sentenced in the courts for rebellion and the issue
had been settled so far as Canada West was concerned. As a matter
of fact, probably not one-tenth of those engaged in the rebellion had
ever been arrested, and to award damages on a liberal basis might
easily have resulted in granting what would virtually have amounted
to a reward for disloyalty.

Bill of 1849

The bill of 1849 was designed for Canada East or Lower Canada.
It provided for a new commission to adjust all "just losses" incurred
during the rebellion, the total not to exceed £100,000 to be raised by
a special sale of bonds. The measure was sponsored by Lafontaine,

the French-Canadian leader of the ministry, and was drawn liberally enough to satisfy the French-Canadian members of the Government, and also to heal old wounds. Specifically excluded from compensation were those who actually had been convicted of treason, or deported to Bermuda, or confined in jail. It is clear that failure to introduce the "rebellion losses" bill would have ended the term of office of the Baldwin-Lafontaine Government.

The bill led to a storm of opposition both inside and outside of Parliament. It was denounced as a disloyal measure, compensating French rebels for their efforts to destroy the unity of an empire which only the efforts of the British element had saved. The Lafontaine-Baldwin coalition was denounced as the "Rebel Ministry," ugly charges were made on the floor of the assembly, and some of the ex-rebels of 1837 were present in person to defend themselves. On several occasions physical violence was narrowly avoided on the floor of Parliament. In spite of this violent opposition, the bill passed the assembly by a vote of forty-seven to eighteen, receiving a majority even among the British members from Upper Canada. *Opposition to bill*

The governor-general's office was promptly flooded with petitions begging him to dissolve Parliament, or at least to reserve his assent to the measure and refer it to the imperial authorities. Protest meetings were organized by the Opposition, and in Toronto both Mackenzie and Baldwin were burned in effigy. The position of Lord Elgin in the face of all this clamor and violence was absolutely correct. He contended that the principle of responsible government demanded that the governor approve all ministerial measures which had the support of both houses of the legislature, unless the governor was certain that the people of the country did not approve of them. He steadfastly and correctly refused to shift responsibility in a matter of purely local concern to the imperial authorities, because he clearly foresaw that such a course might endanger the solidity of the British Empire. Lord Elgin therefore gave his assent to the bill, regarding it as a purely local Canadian measure, with the unqualified support of his ministers and Parliament. *Elgin's attitude*

As the governor-general left Montreal (to which city the capital had been removed) for his place of residence, he was greeted by a storm of hisses and epithets, while missiles rained upon his carriage. An egg struck him in the face, and huge stones damaged his carriage. That night the firebells of Montreal called the people to a protest meeting, and at the meeting a mob formed which set out for the Parliament House, wrecking the office of the *Pilot*, a ministerial organ, on the way. The mob found the assembly in session, but a shower of stones soon drove the members from the chamber. The mob then rushed into the building, broke the chandeliers and the furniture, uprooted benches, tables, and the speaker's chair, and started a fire which destroyed the valuable records in the parliamentary library. The next evening a mob wreaked its vengeance on *Rioting in capital* the houses of members who had supported the "rebellion losses" bill. The rioting continued for three days, and was not checked until the soldiery and a force of 1000 constables were summoned to restore order. Five days later, on April 30, 1849, when the governor came again into the city, his reception was even worse than on the earlier occasion, but Elgin steadfastly refused to meet violence with violence.

Significance of controversy

The extreme Tories sent petitions to England asking Parliament to intervene, and demanding the disallowance of the "rebellion losses" bill. Their point of view was forcefully presented in London by leaders such as MacNab and Cayley. The bill itself was actually discussed in the House of Commons, and in the debate Sir Robert Peel and Lord John Russell supported the policy followed by the governor, while Gladstone sided with the Opposition. In the end Lord Elgin's course was fully sustained, and his offer to resign was refused by the Colonial Secretary. The principle of responsible government thus was established as a practical working principle. The disgraceful mob violence attending its establishment served thoroughly to discredit the extreme Tory party and to sound the death-knell of the "family compact." Parliament's refusal to intervene put an end to the practice of appealing to England by petition, or protesting to Parliament against responsible government in Canada, and thereafter the imperial authorities were much less inclined to intervene in local affairs. Lord Elgin's conduct did much to draw the French Canadians more closely to the government. Following the rioting in Montreal, the capital was at once removed to Toronto.

Toward complete responsible government

By the end of Lord Elgin's administration many of the principles had been recognized for which the reform group contended. No appointments to office were thenceforth to be made by the governor, except after consultation with his cabinet. The civil service had become the patronage, controlled by the leaders of the majority party in the assembly. It was clearly established that the governor must not identify himself with any specific political party, and that he must not interfere in elections. Matters of purely local concern and application were not to be referred to the home government for decision. Finally, it was during Lord Elgin's administration, that the governor ceased to attend regularly at cabinet meetings, a development of great significance for the future status of both the governor-general and the cabinet.

Maritime provinces and responsible government

While these controversies over the meaning of responsible government were raging in United Canada, similar battles were being fought, usually on a smaller scale, in the provinces by the sea.

Problem in New Brunswick

In New Brunswick, established as a separate province in 1784, there was much discontent with a government which was in the hands of a small but firmly-entrenched oligarchy. The latter was closely allied with the Anglican Church, which, though supported by the minority, received special privileges from the government.

The revenue derived from the Crown lands in the province was sufficient to pay the salaries of all government officials, and this made the assembly virtually powerless over the executive. For years the assembly tried to induce the home government to transfer the public lands to its control, in exchange for a permanent civil list.

In 1810 the disability which prevented Roman Catholics from voting in New Brunswick was removed. In 1835 a marriage act *Reform* legalized ceremonies performed by other than Church of England *movement* clergymen. The special privileges of the Anglican Church in educational matters were also gradually extinguished. In the same period the revenues from the customs and from Crown lands were at last transferred to the control of the legislature in return for a civil list. The leader of the reform party in New Brunswick was Lemuel Allan Wilmot, son of a New York Loyalist. Although Lord John Russell, in 1840, agreed that the principle must be followed throughout the British North American provinces that the leaders of the majority in the assembly should be given places in the government, as late as 1842 the opponents of responsible government controlled a majority of the New Brunswick assembly. Naturally they had the support of the lieutenant-governor, who was striving to preserve his power unimpaired by legislative interference.

In 1842 Sir William Colebrook, the lieutenant-governor, tried to follow Metcalfe's policy in making appointments on his own initi- *Success of* ative. But when he appointed his own son-in-law as provincial sec- *reformers* retary, even his Conservative ministry resigned in indignation. The election of 1848 was won by the reformers. In 1847 the British government itself had urged the establishment of responsible government as a means of facilitating efficiency and harmony. It was not until 1855, however, that the evolution of responsible government in New Brunswick can be said to have been entirely completed. In 1851 a law was passed to allow counties to establish a separate form of municipal government.

In Prince Edward Island, a separate province since 1770, the greatest obstacle in the way of political development was the absentee *Prince Edward* landlord system, by which most of the island had passed under the *Island* ownership of English landlords who had promised to promote its settlement, but who, in the main, had not only failed to fulfil their obligations, but had prevented the development of the province by others. The chief struggle of the Prince Edward Island assembly, established in 1773, was not over theories of government, but with these absent landed-proprietors. Not until 1864 were the first steps taken to permit tenants and settlers to buy their farms from the owners. In 1850 the Crown revenues were transferred to the control of the assembly. The specific occasion in the history of Prince Edward Island when the demand was made for responsible government as such, was a quarrel between the lieutenant-governor and the speaker of the assembly, during an attempt to raise the governor's salary.

The principle of the assembly's control of the purse-strings was virtually conceded in 1851. In 1853 the franchise was established practically on a universal manhood suffrage basis. In 1863 the legislative council was made elective, and thus the last stage in the evolution of self-government was completed.

Nova Scotia

The struggle for responsible government in Nova Scotia deserves more extended discussion. "The Tribune of Nova Scotia," the great hero in this battle for responsible government, was Joseph Howe, son of a Massachusetts Tory who became printer and postmaster-general of the maritime region after the American Revolution. Joseph Howe was one of those magnetic and gifted leaders who make the romance of politics. "Poetry was the maiden I loved," he wrote in later years, "but politics was the harridan I married." From 1835 to 1873 Howe's biography is almost a history of the province.

Oligarchy in power

Nova Scotia had had an assembly since 1758, but its government was really in the hands of a little oligarchy centering in Halifax, and closely resembling the "family compact" of Upper Canada. This little group usually controlled the governor, and through its control of the professions, banking, and trade it managed to dominate the economic as well as the political life of the province. The bishop of the Anglican Church sat on the council of Nova Scotia and virtually controlled education in the province. The judiciary also was represented on the council. On one occasion five of the leading bankers of the province were included in its membership, and used their power on the council to prevent the chartering of any competing financial institutions. The Halifax group, however, on the whole, governed the province in a more liberal spirit and with greater ability than the governing cliques at Quebec and Toronto in the days before 1837. Men like Thomas Chandler Haliburton, who as "Sam Slick" probably deserves to be called the founder of American dialect humor, could defend this oligarchical system honestly. "Responsible government," wrote this opponent of democracy, "is responsible nonsense."

Joseph Howe

Joseph Howe began his career in 1828 as editor of the *Nova Scotian.* In 1835 he attracted attention in a libel suit brought against him because of an article in *The Acadian Recorder,* in which he ridiculed some of the Halifax magistrates and accused them of inefficiency and corruption. His address to the court in defense of his statements established his reputation as a brilliant orator, and in 1836 he entered the Nova Scotia assembly as a Liberal member. At once he began the battle to make the legislative council elective, and to force publicity for its deliberations. In a series of letters addressed to Lord John Russell, Howe explained the defects of the old colonial system with a clarity of statement and a penetration that rivals Lord Durham's better known Report. The struggle for responsible government continued until 1847, and for a time a mixed executive council was tried in the hope of allaying party strife. During the governor-ship of Lord Falkland, Howe himself served in the executive council, but resigned when an anti-reformer also was appointed. Howe now launched into most violent controversies with the governor and his Conservative majority. Lord Falkland, driven from office in 1846, was succeeded by Sir John Harvey, an imitator of the principles of Sydenham and Metcalfe.

In 1847 the reformers carried the provincial elections, and in the following year the new lieutenant-governor summoned the Liberals *Success of* to form a cabinet. Thus by 1848 responsible government had been *reformers* achieved in the most important of the maritime provinces. The blood-less victory was in large measure the personal achievement of Howe. To quote a distinguished Canadian historian, who has studied closely the evolution of popular government in Canada, "Howe's achieve-ment must be compared with the failure of Mackenzie and Papineau, if his true greatness is to appear."

SELECT BIBLIOGRAPHY FOR CHAPTER XII

The best detailed account of the achievement of responsible government in the Canadian provinces, is KENNEDY, *The Constitution of Canada*, pp. 182–269. A. MacMECHAN, *The Winning of Popular Government* (Toronto, 1921) in *Chronicles of Canada*, is an interesting and very readable account of the period from the time of Durham's mission to the middle of the 1850's. Briefer accounts are J. L. MORISON, "Parties and Politics, 1840–1867," in *Canada and Its Provinces*, vol. V, pp. 13–77; H. E. EGERTON, *Canada* (Historical Geography of the British Colonies, vol. V, Pt. II), Bk. II, pp. 163–204, and EDWARD PORRITT, *Evolution of the Dominion of Canada: its Government and its Politics* (Yonkers-on-the-Hudson, New York, 1918), pp. 111–146.

J. L. MORISON, *British Supremacy and Canadian Self Government, 1839–1854* (Glasgow, 1919), is a brilliant study of this critical period.

Among the biographies which deal with the leaders in this period, the following are the most important: ADAM SHORTT, *Lord Sydenham* (Toronto, 1908), in *Makers of Canada*—the standard life; J. W. KAYE, *Life and Correspondence of Charles, Lord Metcalfe*, 2 vols. (London, 1854), full of important letters and dispatches; and G. M. WRONG, *The Earl of Elgin* (London, 1905). The latter has now been superseded by W. P. M. KENNEDY, *Lord Elgin* (Clarendon Press, 1926). See also, G. P. DE T. GLAZELBROOK, *Sir Charles Bagot in Canada* (Oxford, 1929).

For the history of the struggle in the maritime provinces, the following are valuable: W. L. GRANT, *The Tribune of Nova Scotia* (Toronto, 1921) in *Chronicles of Canada*, a life of Howe; and J. H. CHISHOLM, *The Speeches and Public Letters of Joseph Howe*, 2 vols. (Halifax, 1909); and J. HANNAY, *Wilmot and Tilley* (Toronto, 1907), a biography of the New Brunswick reformers. W. Ross LIVINGSTON's article, "The First Responsible Party Government in British North America," is a special study for Nova Scotia, and ap-peared in the *Canadian Historical Review*, vol. VII, pp. 115–136. CHESTER MARTIN, *Empire and Commonwealth* (Oxford, 1929) is excellent.

J. C. DENT, *The Last Forty Years, Canada since the Union of 1841*, 2 vols. (Toronto, 1881), is a valuable account, full of intimate and interesting details. Dent's sympathies will be obvious to the reader.

For other references, see TROTTER, *Syllabus*, pp. 98–102.

CHAPTER XIII

ECONOMIC AND SOCIAL PROGRESS
(1815–1860)

Population growth

TEN years after the close of the War of 1812 the population of British North America, not including Newfoundland, was 900,000. By 1830 it had reached approximately 1,400,000, and at the time of the Union Act the population of Upper and Lower Canada alone exceeded 1,000,000. The increase was greater in Upper Canada than in the older province during these years. From 1841 to 1851 the population of Upper Canada virtually doubled, and by 1861 the province boasted 1,396,000 inhabitants. The same census of 1861 indicated a population of 1,111,566 in Lower Canada. Much of this increase in the total population of British North America was due to immigration.

Tide of immigration

The arrivals at Quebec, the chief port of entry, mounted steadily from 12,648 in 1827 to 51,746 in 1832. About two-thirds of these immigrants hailed from Ireland, where political and economic discontent steadily increased until in the late 1840's nearly a fourth of the people left their native isle to settle in new regions. Many came to Canada to stay, while others used it as a half-way station on their way to the United States. Throughout the 1830's about ten per cent of the total immigration to Canada was Scotch, while something over twenty per cent came from England. Most of these immigrants were poor, and generally found it necessary to hire themselves into service for a time, before they could accumulate sufficient money to move out to the frontier and find a cheap pioneer farm.

Competition of United States

It was distressing for Canadian leaders to discover that large groups of the more desirable immigrants, many of them skilled tradesmen who had a little available capital, soon deserted Canada to go to the United States. The latter country was passing through a phenomenal development during this period. This development was much more rapid and varied than that of Canada, and therefore it attracted certain types of immigrants who preferred not to wait for Canada's much slower and more conservative progress. Canada had little free capital, and was largely dependent for her business dealings and for investible money upon the United States and Great Britain. The political upheavals and economic stagnation which marked the decade preceding 1837 stimulated a heavy Canadian migration into the American Northwest, which was just being opened to settlement.

Had Canada been able to maintain the ratio of increase in her population established in the 1820's, her population by 1881 would *Criticism of* have been over 16,000,000. Actually, it did not reach 4,500,000 by *immigration* that year. Near the end of the 1830's the immigration movement *policy* suddenly collapsed for a time, and a heavy drainage of population to the United States set in. No effort was made in these years to sift the more desirable immigrants from the hosts of new arrivals, and Irish lords and British government officials for a time planned to use Canada as a dumping-ground for the undesirables and paupers of the home country. Canada was soon complaining loudly because of "the state-aided export of the lower orders" to her virgin soil.

In the late 1840's, when Irish immigration reached its peak because of the deplorable conditions prevailing in Ireland, the port *Irish* towns of Canada experienced a terrible glutting of the unskilled *immigrants* labor market to which the temporary and artificial stimulation of public works could afford little relief. Frightful overcrowding occurred on immigrant ships, and almshouses and hospitals were filled with diseased and starving immigrants. The industrial development of the country was too slow to absorb this sudden addition to the population, and many Canadians began to question the advantage of a British connection which made their young province a place of refuge for many of the misfits of the mother-country. These distressing features of the immigration problem proved to be only the temporary results of the boiling over of the melting-pot. Gradually the stream of immigration was diverted to the West, and although many continued to cross to the United States, thousands helped to extend the Canadian frontier northward and westward.

At the time of the Union Act five of every six Canadians were engaged either in farming or in lumbering. In Lower Canada the *Economic* unprogressive and often illiterate *habitant* continued to cultivate his *conditions in* ribbon-like farm in the manner of his ancestors a century before. *Canada East* The law permitted even school trustees to affix their marks to their official reports, in lieu of signatures. Agricultural methods were primitive, and the *habitant* seldom rotated his crops. He still lived in the low whitewashed cottages of his fathers, and grumblingly paid the old, inherited feudal dues to the seignioral families.

Montreal had a mixed French and English population of 40,000, and was the commercial center of the province. Quebec in 1845 had *Cities* about 50,000 inhabitants, and was still an almost wholly French city. Quebec, Montreal, and Toronto were the only cities in United Canada with a population exceeding 10,000. Three Rivers was a village of 2500 people. The exports of Lower Canada were limited practically to grain and lumber, and under the prevailing British commercial policy foreign vessels were excluded from the St. Lawrence River, and Canadian ships from foreign ports. At Quebec a beginning had been made in ship-building.

In Upper Canada, or Canada West, as this region was known after the union, development had been more rapid, and agricultural

Agricultural progress in Canada West

methods were somewhat more progressive. While oats, rye, barley, corn, and peas were becoming important products, wheat was still the outstanding crop upon which the farmers concentrated because it yielded the greatest cash returns. By 1841 Upper Canada produced 3,000,000 bushels of wheat. Toronto was the business and social center of the province, and in 1841 had a population of 15,000. Kingston, the first capital of United Canada, still had less than 6000 at the time of the union, while Hamilton had scarcely 3000. Bytown, later the national capital of Ottawa, was little more than a wilderness hamlet in 1841.

Transportation

Most communities were isolated hamlets and towns, virtually self-sufficing, and dependent for transportation on toll-roads and canals. In 1836 the only railroad in Canada had a mileage of sixteen miles. At that time considerable progress had been made in railroad building in the United States. In the next decade almost every important port in the northern part of the United States was bidding for the trade of the West, and was trying to divert it, by railroads and canals, from Montreal to a United States port.

Exports

The exports of Canada in 1841 still consisted largely of timber and grain. A number of flour mills had been built, and as a by-product of the grain business, breweries and distilleries arose near these milling centers. Canada still imported most of her textiles, although Quebec had a growing domestic linen industry, and a few woolen mills were in operation in other parts of the country. There was an iron foundry near Three Rivers. Articles such as soap and candles were manufactured in the homes. Along the coast the fisheries remained the largest source of income.

Labor and prices

In 1836 wheat sold at ninety cents a bushel in Canada, and flour at approximately five dollars a barrel. Milk was sold in the towns at five cents a quart, butter at fifteen cents a pound, and meat at five to eight cents a pound. Labor was cheap. Domestic servants could expect from five to eight dollars a month, plus board and lodging; farm hands were paid from eight to twelve dollars a month; the ordinary artisan earned about one dollar and a half a day. Labor unions of a local and sporadic character were making their appearance in some of the larger cities, beginning, as in the United States, with the organization of the printers, but they made little progress until after 1870.

British preference for Canadian flour and wheat

In the years from 1843 to 1849 the grain and flour business in Canada in some respects enjoyed the advantages of a privileged, vested interest. In pursuance of the old mercantilist principle, by which efforts were made to exclude foreigners from the trade of the Empire, the British Parliament in 1843 passed the Canadian Corn Bill, subjecting Canadian wheat and flour to only about one-fifth the duty paid by foreign producers who imported these products into England. Wheat shipped from the United States to England *via* Canada was not admitted to this privilege, but American wheat, ground into flour in Canada, enjoyed this preferential treatment when reëxported to England. The natural consequence of this preferential trade regulation was to give a great impetus to the milling industry in Canada, and tons of American wheat were converted into flour in Montreal, Toronto, and other Canadian centers. Canadian capitalists, especially in Montreal, at once invested heavily in this new milling industry and in its various subsidiaries, expecting to reap a rich harvest during the continuance of the preferential policy. A real estate boom and a period of speculation followed in the wake of this unexpected prosperity in the milling towns.

Unfortunately for these Canadian interests, in 1846 England decided upon a sharp reversal of her commercial policy, which *England turns* involved the abandoning of her protective tariffs and naviga- *to free trade* tion acts, and a gradual change to a system of free trade which *policy* would open her ports to the traders of all nations on equal terms. Under this new policy the duty on grains imported to England was gradually reduced, and finally extinguished by 1849. At the same time Great Britain began to reduce her duties on foreign timber, especially from the Baltic countries, and at once the lumber interests of provinces such as New Brunswick filed protests against the necessity of facing this new competition. Finally, in 1849, the British Navigation Acts were repealed, depriving Canadian shippers of their special monopoly in the carrying trade with the British West Indies.

These sweeping changes in the British fiscal system brought strenuous protests from the boards of trade of many Canadian towns. *Effects upon* The shipping interests combined with the lumbering and milling *Canada* interests to oppose measures which meant heavy financial losses to Canada, and many influential Canadians objected to a system by which they had to endure a period of depression and bankruptcy as the price of Britain's conversion to free trade principles. Every hope that Canadian millers and grain-dealers would become the great middlemen in the trade with the American West seemed to be destroyed forever. Property values in the booming mill towns fell as much as 50 per cent from 1845 to 1848, and three-fourths of the businessmen in some of these centers became insolvent. Unemployment and stagnation prevailed in parts of Canada, at a time when the United States seemed to be enjoying a period of unusual prosperity and expansion. Instead of trade coming from the United States into Canada, it seemed likely that the current of business would be completely reversed.

In their desperation many Canadian businessmen began to question the desirability of continuing the British connection. Even the loyal- *Canadian* ism of the extreme Tory group was affected by this pinch of the pocket *protests* nerve, and it is not without significance that many of those who suffered most severely from this economic distress should also have been among the bitterest opponents of the "rebellion losses" bill and Lord Elgin's policy, discussed in the preceding chapter. With

England on a free-trade basis, and all pecuniary advantages of the British connection destroyed, why should not Canada assert her fiscal independence, and seek closer trade relations, or even annexation, with the United States? The United States Congress promptly passed a law permitting Canadian goods to go through the United States in bond without paying duty—a measure obviously designed to make New York the distributing point for the Canadian West. Lord Elgin strikingly summarized the situation in a dispatch to the home government: "Peel's Bill of 1846 drives the whole of the produce down the New York channels of communication, destroying the revenue which Canada expected to derive from canal dues, and ruining at once mill-owners, forwarders and merchants. . . . What makes it more serious is that all the prosperity of which Canada is thus robbed is transplanted to the other side of the lines, as if to make Canadians feel more bitterly how much kinder England is to the children who desert her than to those who remain faithful."

Annexation movement of 1849

In their anxiety a minority of Canadian businessmen advised annexation to the United States. There were prophecies that Lord Elgin would be the last governor-general of Canada, although others insisted that the whole annexation agitation was a Tory scheme to compel the governor to turn out his Liberal ministry. A few argued vigorously against closer affiliation with a slave-holding power like the United States.

Annexation Manifesto

In 1849 an Annexation Manifesto was issued at Montreal. This document argued that there were no immediate prospects for relief by a revival of protection in England, or by the adoption of a protective tariff in Canada, or by the federation of the provinces, or by reciprocity with the United States. From such a pessimistic analysis the conclusion was obvious, namely "a friendly and passive separation from British connection and a union upon equitable terms with the great North American Confederacy of Sovereign States." Annexation, it was maintained, would bring United States capital to Canada and inaugurate an era of unusual expansion. Canada would cease to be the bone of contention between the United States and Great Britain, and all political and racial difficulties in Canadian life would immediately disappear.

Its signers

Within ten days more than 1000 people signed the Annexation Manifesto. Among the signers were J. J. C. Abbott, a future prime minister of the Dominion of Canada, John Rose, later minister of finance under Macdonald, a future lieutenant-governor of Ontario, and others of equal prominence. Most of the signers were Conservatives, politically, and only about three per cent were French Canadians, and these were not the important leaders of their group. It is interesting to note, in passing, that at least one American legislature, that of Vermont, passed resolutions urging the peaceable annexation of Canada at this time.

The annexation movement collapsed very speedily. Countermanifestos appeared, and a second manifesto secured few signers. *Collapse of movement* The commercial depression which was the main cause of the movement proved to be of much shorter duration than had been expected, and the end of 1849 brought a bumper harvest. The annexation movement was always limited to a small but influential minority. In Canada East, it had no support outside of Montreal and the eastern townships, where many of the isolated English settlers welcomed a way to escape French domination. A few French radicals favored the movement because of their republican principles. Canada West was almost solidly opposed to annexation, and Mackenzie, back from his exile in the United States, and disillusioned by his first-hand observations of American democracy, strongly advised against it. The Canadian ministry vigorously opposed annexation and considered it virtual treason to the Crown, and the United States government happened to be so absorbed in its own sectional controversy over slavery that it could give no encouragement to the proposal. With the revival of prosperity the agitation was speedily forgotten.

In the minds of Lord Elgin and some members of his Government, the logical solution for Canada's commercial troubles, and the best *Proposal of reciprocity with United States* way to avoid a recurrence of the alarming events of 1849, was to make arrangements for closer trade relations between Canada and her southern neighbor. The discussion of the relative advantages of a freer exchange of products between these two countries finally culminated in the Reciprocity Treaty of 1854. Reciprocity between the United States and Canada had been suggested by some Canadian leaders as early as the 1830's. It had also been discussed in the United States, and several bills, introduced in the late 1840's, either had been defeated in the Senate, or else had become lost in the controversy over slavery then raging in the American states. The discussions of a reciprocity agreement were now extended to include new arrangements for the fisheries and for the use of international waterways, as well as for a free exchange of natural products.

These negotiations reached a tangible form during the administration of President Pierce. Lord Elgin went personally to Washington *Negotiations* to conduct the negotiations with Secretary of State William L. Marcy, and to overcome the opposition of certain Democratic senators to the reciprocity proposals. Dinners, at which champagne flowed freely and Lord Elgin's social graces were charmingly displayed, did much to win the support of Americans who at first seemed hostile. The Elgin Treaty of Reciprocity was concluded on June 5, 1854. In October it went into effect in Canada, and in the following spring, in the United States. It was accepted by all of the British North American provinces except British Columbia.

The treaty contained seven articles of which the most important are summarized below. The first two articles gave United States *Treaty of 1854* fishermen full rights to the inshore fisheries of British North America, except for shell-fish, and guaranteed to the British similar rights in

American waters. Another article gave Americans navigation rights on the St. Lawrence River and on the canals between the Great Lakes and the Atlantic Ocean, on the same terms as British subjects, while Canadians were given similar rights in Lake Michigan, and the United States government agreed to urge the states to grant the use of the state canals on similar terms. Article III enumerated a long list of natural products, such as grain, foodstuffs, meats, cotton and wool, poultry, hides, stone, fruits, vegetables, dairy products, etc., which should be admitted free of duty by both countries. Provision was made for the later adherence of Newfoundland to the treaty, should that province care to accept it, and for a method for the abrogation of the agreement after the ten-year period fixed in the treaty had expired.

Effects upon Canada

The decade following the ratification of the treaty was one of remarkable prosperity in both countries. No doubt Canada also reaped the benefits of her railroad-building program during these years and of the extraordinary market for her goods created by the Crimean War, but there can be no doubt that reciprocity added greatly to this prosperity. The panic of 1857 was but a temporary check on these developments. New towns arose along the new railroad routes, and manufacturing boomed. The prices of Canadian food products increased fully fifty per cent from 1851 to 1857, and the average annual value of goods exchanged between the United States and Canada increased over two and a half times from 1855 to 1866. During the last four years of the treaty Canada's exports to the United States were more than double her imports.

Termination of agreement in 1866

The Reciprocity Treaty was cancelled by the United States in 1866, for a variety of reasons. Perhaps the most important reason was political, rather than economic, for the United States had become distinctly unfriendly to Great Britain because of the latter's attitude and conduct during the American Civil War. Many in the United States opposed what they considered a one-sided bargain. Moreover, reciprocity clearly was contrary to the desires of the protective tariff interests which arose in the United States during and after the Civil War. Some Americans may have believed that the abrogation of the treaty would hasten the time of annexation. The annulment of the treaty was particularly injurious to the maritime region of British North America and to the West, and perhaps on that account it helped to promote sentiment in favor of a federation of all of the Canadian provinces. All attempts to revive reciprocity with the United States have so far been in vain. Only the privilege to use the St. Lawrence River, temporarily granted to the United States in 1854, was restored permanently by the later treaty of 1871, and this was done largely because Canada hoped thereby to attract the products of the American West, and make the St. Lawrence route the outlet to Europe.

This middle period of Canadian history also marked the expansion

of Canadian banking facilities. In 1822 there were but three banks in *Canadian*
Lower Canada regularly chartered by the provincial authorities. *banking*
The number increased slowly in the various provinces. As a rule
Canadian banks had a larger capital stock than the banks operating
during the same period in the United States; branch banks were
established frequently, and in general Canada followed the sound
banking model of Alexander Hamilton's first United States Bank.
In spite of carefully devised banking laws, progress was slow on
account of the scarcity of liquid capital in Canada. The panics of
1837 and 1857 compelled many of the banks to suspend specie payments for a time, and some were seriously involved in the land and
railroad speculation which was rampant in this period. Nevertheless
prior to 1866 no Canadian bank of any importance had failed—a
remarkable record as compared with the history of banking during
these years in the United States. In 1853 Canada adopted the decimal
system of money, and her intimate business relations with the United
States led her to adopt the American dollar, rather than the British
pound sterling, as her unit of currency. Gold became the monetary
standard, and silver was made legal tender for amounts not exceeding
ten dollars. Both the British sovereign and the United States dollar
were acceptable in unlimited amounts as lawful money.

The decade of the 1830's marks the beginning of a great era of internal improvements in Canada. Early travel had been by trails and *Internal*
corduroy roads, and later by plank roads. The latter, consisting of *improvements*
planks laid crosswise, and covered with mud and dirt, was an invention of Upper Canada. Canal-building, to facilitate travel around
the rapids in the many Canadian streams, had begun as early as 1779
along the lower St. Lawrence. In 1824 the Welland Canal, the most
pretentious canal venture of this early period, connecting Lake Erie
and Lake Ontario, was begun under private auspices. The promoter
of this great venture was William Hamilton Merritt; one of the chief
stockholders in his company was J. B. Yates of New York, also one
of the promoters of the Erie Canal. In 1829 the first vessels passed
through the Welland Canal. In 1840 the enterprise was taken over
by the province of Upper Canada, and before the close of the decade
it was possible for vessels drawing nine feet of water to pass from
Chicago to the sea.

The Lachine Canal, along the St. Lawrence route, was built and
opened by the Lower Canadian government in 1825. Many other *Canals*
canals were necessary to complete the St. Lawrence route, such as the
Chambly Canal connecting Lake Champlain with the St. Lawrence,
and the Williamsburg Canal. The Rideau Canal was opened in 1832.
For many years Lower Canada's indifference to her share in improving
the St. Lawrence route was a serious handicap to Upper Canada, and
a cause of friction between the two provinces. This extensive canal
system has been constantly improved in order to keep pace with the
development of lake transportation. In more recent years many of

these canals have been equipped with magnificent electric lock systems, and the St. Lawrence channel itself has been dredged and deepened at various intervals by the government.

Shipping

In the 1840's the first boat lines were established on the Great Lakes and the St. Lawrence River. One of the first of these companies was the *Royal Mail Line*, operating on Lake Ontario and the St. Lawrence. Ship-building developed rapidly in Lower Canada and in the maritime region. By 1852 Quebec alone had eight floating docks and twenty-five ship-building places, and as many as fifty wooden ships were launched in a single year. Magnificent clippers, capable of making fourteen knots an hour, came from the docks of builders like Pierre Brunelle in Quebec. In 1865 Nova Scotia built, mostly at Pictou, a tonnage of 56,000 tons valued at $2,500,000, and in the same year New Brunswick launched 148 vessels. By this time, however, the era of steel ships had come, and since 1865 there has been a steady decline in the building of wooden ships.

Atlantic steamers

The first vessel to cross the Atlantic Ocean under steam power was the *Royal William*, which made the voyage in 1833. This boat was a side-wheeler, built at Quebec, and owned and manned by Canadians. The first line of steamers in the transatlantic service was established by Samuel Cunard, the son of a Philadelphia merchant who had migrated to Halifax during the American Revolution. Cunard secured a subsidy from the British government for carrying the mails. His first steamer crossed the Atlantic in 1840, and by 1855 he began to operate iron ships in this service.

Lake traffic

By the middle of the nineteenth century boat service on the inland lakes and rivers of Canada had to meet the competition of the newly-developed railroad lines, particularly the Grand Trunk, which by 1855 paralleled the water route from Montreal to Toronto. A ruthless rate war followed between the shipping interests and the railroads, and at one time it was possible to travel from Montreal to Quebec, with first class accommodations and meals, for seven dollars, while steerage passengers made the trip for twelve and a half cents. The railroads of course had the advantage in winter when the waterways were frozen over. As late as 1850 prices in Montreal virtually doubled whenever winter closed the river traffic. For a time the steamship companies tried to run a line of stages in winter to keep their business from passing under the control of their competitors during the winter season. It was not until years later that the opening of new areas by the railroads added to lake traffic. When this happened, the railroad companies began to buy or build lake steamers and ocean liners to serve as subsidiaries to the steam roads.

Railroads

The railroad era in Canada begins with the decade of the 1830's. The first Canadian roads were generally "portage roads," built to fill in the gaps between rivers and canals. The primitive cars of such a pioneer road as the Champlain and St. Lawrence Railroad, a little sixteen-mile line from La Prairie on the St. Lawrence River to St.

Johns, operated only in summer, were drawn by horses over wooden "snake-rails" to which iron straps were fastened with spikes. The first steam engine, and the engineer to operate it, were imported from England in 1837. But the European pilot proved unable to handle the engine, and it was necessary to borrow an engineer from the Baltimore and Ohio Railroad in the United States. No great progress was made for another decade. The first steam road in Upper Canada was the Toronto, Simcoe and Huron Union Railroad, developed eventually to make the portage from Lake Ontario to Lake Huron.

In the middle of the century the period of government aid to rail-road building began. Men of vision and statesmanship, like Joseph *Government aid* Howe in Nova Scotia and Francis Hincks in Upper Canada, came to realize how important great railway systems were for the development of a Canadian nationality. In 1847 a survey was made of the route between Halifax and Quebec, and the governments of New Brunswick, Nova Scotia, and Canada cooperated to meet the expenses of this engineering project. In 1854 a railroad was begun from Halifax to Truro, and by 1867 Nova Scotia had 145 miles of railroad radiating from Halifax to the Gulf of St. Lawrence and the Bay of Fundy. New Brunswick found the promotion of railroads more difficult, and her leading road early fell into the hands of receivers. By 1860 the Grand Trunk Railway was completed from Lake Huron to Rivière du Loup. It reached the coast by way of Portland. The road was poorly constructed and badly managed, most of its securities were held in England, and in spite of repeated aids from the Canadian government it never was able to pay dividends on its common stock.

The early railroad policy of United Canada was embodied in the Guarantee Act, drafted by Francis Hincks, and adopted by the *Francis Hincks* Canadian Parliament in 1849. Under the provisions of this law the *and railroad* government of Canada undertook to guarantee 6 per cent interest on *policy* half of the bonded debt of any company which built a railroad in the province at least seventy-five miles long, the guarantee to take effect when one-half of the road had been constructed. The government retained what amounted to a first mortgage on the road's assets after the claims of bondholders had been met. In 1852 the Grand Trunk received a guarantee of £3,000 per mile, in addition to land grants. Subsequent legislation permitted municipalities to take stock in railroad companies and to issue municipal bonds in order to raise the money to finance these enterprises. The result was that the vast majority of towns overspeculated and soon were unable to pay even the interest on these bonds.

A veritable traffic in railroad charters began, and lobbyists appealed for more and more aid to complete their enterprises. One town *Abuses* of less than 9,000 inhabitants borrowed nearly $1,250,000, and was soon $625,000 in arrears on interest alone, as a result of its plunge into railroad promotion. Canada West, perhaps because it was the younger province, was much more deeply involved in these financial troubles than Canada East. Scores of little roads were built which were quite unnecessary and which never paid for themselves. The government soon found it necessary to check this overspeculation, and the heavy public debt incurred in promoting these railroads was one of the causes of the serious financial panic in 1857 and 1858.

Railroad development to 1860

In 1850 Canada had just sixty-six miles of railroad. A decade later, the total mileage for all the British North American provinces was 2,065. The total cost of this construction has been estimated at twenty dollars per capita of the population. The panic of 1857 brought a temporary check to this orgy of railroad building, and many companies were forced to the wall by the prolonged depression following this financial crisis. For a time investors were more cautious about sinking their capital in transportation ventures. The great railway systems of modern Canada were almost all the achievements of a later day.

Postal service

Another improvement in the facilities of communication came about through the reorganization of the post-office department. In 1840 postal rates were still comparatively high; they were not uniform throughout the provinces, and there was much criticism of the way in which the service was managed by the British authorities. In 1847 delegates from the provinces of Canada, New Brunswick, and Nova Scotia met at Montreal and advised a total reorganization of the postal service and a reduction in rates. Two years later the British Parliament passed an act transferring control of the North American postal service to the various provincial governments. The inauguration of the period of local control marks the beginning of an era of expansion and improvement in postal facilities. From 1851 to 1867 the number of post-offices in Nova Scotia increased from 143 to 630; in New Brunswick, from 101 to 438; and in Canada from 601 to 2,333. Although rates were reduced, revenues steadily increased. In 1851 the use of postage stamps was introduced. Before this, the receiver of letters had paid the charges of transportation. A system of money orders and railway post-offices was gradually introduced; by 1853 the first Canadian Ocean Mail Service was established.

Exploration of West and North

The development of internal improvements and the steady increase of population revived an interest in the opening and development of the region west of the settlements of Upper Canada. This section of British North America was still the great fur preserve and the hunting-ground of the Hudson's Bay Company and the native Indians. Explorations during the period from 1840 to the formation of the Confederation in 1867 were largely confined to expeditions into the great north, above latitude 60°, and extending from Hudson Bay to Alaska. The best known of these expeditions into the perilous Arctic was that of Sir John Franklin, who sailed in 1845, equipped with three years' provisions, to seek the northwest passage through the Arctic Ocean. Franklin's ships, after passing Baffin Bay, were never seen again, except by Eskimos. Franklin himself died in 1847, and his party abandoned their ships and started overland on sleds for a Hudson's Bay Company post. None of the missing explorers were ever heard of again and a series of relief expeditions failed to find trace of them. The mystery of their disappearance was not solved until 1857–59, when an expedition financed by Lady Franklin came upon clothing, skeletons and a written record preserved among the stones beyond King William's Land. The ambition actually to sail a ship through the northwest passage of the Arctic was not realized until the beginning of the present century, when the Norwegian explorer, Captain Roald Amundsen, at last negotiated this perilous voyage.

Explorers and traders of the Hudson's Bay Company frequently visited the Yukon region. During the late 1850's numerous surveys were made which added much to the geographical knowledge of the great West between Lake Superior and the Rocky Mountains, and a number of bold and adventurous spirits made important transcontinental journeys. It was during these years that the gaps in the geography of British North America were gradually filled in. *Rounding out geography of British North America*

The year 1830 marked a change in the Indian policy of Canada. The older theory was one of allowing the Indians to manage their own affairs, establishing friendly trade relations with them, and utilizing them occasionally as allies, or at least preventing them from becoming too friendly with a rival power. No effort was made officially to turn the natives from their tribal life and teach them the ways of the white man's civilization, although missionaries of almost every denomination had been at work for decades on a heroic but feeble program of civilizing and Christianizing them. *Indian affairs*

About 1830 a new policy was inaugurated by the British government. This contemplated an attempt to break up the tribal organization and to collect Indians in sufficient numbers to settle them in villages and on lands provided for the purpose. Strenuous efforts were made to stop the rum traffic with the natives, as well as the annual distribution of presents by the government. The latter had long been regarded as one of the Indian's vested rights. The number of presents was reduced gradually, and eventually the right to receive presents was commuted into cash payments. The government made plans to provide religious training and agricultural education for the Indian population congregated in the newly-created villages, and rather generously provided the native farmer with farm implements, seeds, and even rations. *New Indian policy*

Indians remained under the special protection first of the British and later of the Canadian government. It was the plan to permit the natives to vote and hold office as soon as they acquired enough property to meet suffrage requirements. On July 1, 1860, all control of Indian affairs by the imperial authorities ceased. Up to that time the Indian service had been under the direct control of the governor-general. In that year it was transferred to the Canadian provincial authorities. After the Confederation the opening of the new West made the Indian problem one of the most important problems with which the Dominion government had to deal. How well and how honestly this difficult situation was managed, must be left for discussion in a later chapter.

Catholic Church in French Canada

The religious development of the British-American provinces kept pace with their economic progress, and although it is more difficult to appraise because of the intangible nature of religious forces, it was probably of equal significance in the social history of the British North American provinces. The Roman Catholic Church, the oldest of Canada's religious institutions, had made its peace with the English conquerors before the close of the eighteenth century, and was now making steady progress. Undoubtedly the French Revolution did much to strengthen the Canadian Catholic Church. Scores of exiled French priests came to swell the ranks of the Canadian clergy, while the undying hostility of the French Canadians toward the radicalism of the French Revolution served to impress the English government with the loyalty of their new subjects. Bishop Plessis of Quebec loyally supported England in the War of 1812, and gained a seat on the legislative council of Lower Canada. It was under his careful and able leadership that the Catholic Church in Canada was consolidated and firmly established in the eyes of the British authorities as one of the institutions of Canada which must be left undisturbed.

Westward expansion of Catholicism

By 1826 Upper Canada was organized as a separate diocese, and ten years later the Roman Catholic element constituted nearly one-sixth of the population of that province. In the maritime region, the removal of political disabilities of Catholics was a slower and more difficult task. Throughout the nineteenth century the Church continued its educational and charitable work in the provinces, and particularly among the natives and pioneers of the West. Devout Catholic missionaries still lived among their Indian converts, as they had done a century before, enduring great hardships in order to carry the blessings of Roman Catholic Christianity to their red children. One of the most worthy of these pioneers in the cause of religion was Bishop Taché who was ordained a priest in 1845. At that time there were but six regularly ordained Catholic clergymen in the region between Lake Superior and the Rocky Mountains. Bishop Taché became especially active in the Red River valley settlements. At the time of his death, in 1894, he had the satisfaction of seeing five bishoprics and 175 priests at work in the territory where there had been but six when he began his labors.

Church of England

The Church of England, at the beginning of the British régime, and in Upper Canada until the middle of the nineteenth century, enjoyed some privileges of a state Church. Lands were set aside for its support, and the connection between the Church and the government often was very close. The first Anglican bishop, established in Nova Scotia in 1787, had a diocese including virtually all of British North America. The Loyalist migrations after the American Revolution helped greatly to swell the ranks of the Church of England in British North America, and Ontario has remained the great stronghold of this denomination. Anglican missions have been established in great numbers in the northwestern country. A number of denominational colleges, like the King's Colleges of Nova Scotia and New Brunswick, and Wycliffe College at Toronto, give evidence of the interest of this group in higher education.

Most of the so-called dissenting sects came into Canada from the United States. The first ordained Presbyterian minister came to Nova Scotia from New England in 1764. The first Baptist church in Nova Scotia was founded by a minister from Massachusetts, and practically all the early churches in Upper Canada were the result of immigration or of influences originating in the United States. The first preachers of Methodism in Canada were sent by the American Methodist Church, and a formal separation of the Canadian and the American organizations did not occur until 1828, and then largely because the enemies of Methodism frequently charged this group with being "American in their origin and feelings," and with secretly disseminating principles destructive of British institutions in Canada and likely to lead to the establishment of a republican form of government. All of these dissenting sects had a long and hard battle to fight with the Anglican Established Church in most of the provinces, before they could gain sufficient legal status to perform even marriage ceremonies. In this struggle for the recognition of the rights of the dissenters, the name of Adolphus Egerton Ryerson (1803–1882) stands out above all others. *Dissenting sects*

Because of the more equalitarian and emotional type of religion preached by the Baptists and Methodists, these denominations made rapid headway on the frontier. The Methodist circuit rider brought the comforts of salvation to many a lonely pioneer family, and often served as the most important connecting link with the outside world. Indian missions, boarding schools, day schools, and trade schools were established by all of these religious groups, as well as missions and schools for newly-arrived immigrants in the cities. These and other denominations have continued to exercise great influence in the field of social service, in the agitation for temperance reform, and in the promotion of facilities for higher education. *Religion in new West*

Education during this period was emerging from the pioneer stage. Owing to the remarkable gifts of Dr. Adolphus Egerton Ryerson, Upper Canada led all the provinces in educational progress. Here the struggle for free schools was a crucial issue in the long controversy between the champions of aristocracy and democracy culminating in the rebellion of 1837. The "family compact" and its supporters adhered to the belief that education was a privilege of the few, while *Educational progress* the reformers, in the main, demanded educational facilities for all and wished education to be free from sectarian control. In the battle over these conflicting points of view Bishop John Strachan of the Anglican Established Church represented the opponents of universal and non-sectarian education, while Ryerson became the leading champion of the non-conformists. Although of Loyalist stock and in general a believer in Tory principles, Ryerson valiantly championed the cause of education for all of the people, as the "best security of a good Government and constitutional liberty." In 1844 he became super-intendent of education. After a tour of Europe to study its educational systems, he drafted the education bill passed in 1846, which is still the basis of public instruction in Ontario. Grammar schools, which had been providing secondary education, were taken over by the government in 1853 and later became public high schools.

SELECT BIBLIOGRAPHY FOR CHAPTER XIII

The following special articles are extremely valuable for various phases of the economic and social history of the period from the close of the War of 1812 to 1860: ADAM SHORTT, "General Economic History, 1763–1841," in *Canada and Its Provinces*, vol. IV, pp. 521–590; DUNCAN McARTHUR, "History of Public Finance, 1763–1840," *Ibid.*, pp. 491–514; ADAM SHORTT, "Currency and Banking, 1760–1841," *Ibid.*, pp. 599–632; WILLIAM SMITH, "The Post Office, 1763–1841," *Ibid.*, pp. 729–739; ADAM SHORTT, "Economic History, 1840–1867," in *Canada and Its Provinces*, vol. V, pp. 183–257; ADAM SHORTT, "Currency and Banking, 1840–1867," *Ibid.*, pp. 259–291; and DUNCAN McARTHUR, "History of Public Finance, 1840–1867," *Ibid.*, pp. 163–182.

For the story of western explorations and Indian relations the following are important: LAWRENCE J. BURPEE, "Western Exploration, 1840–1867," in *Canada and Its Provinces*, vol. V, pp. 293–328, and DUNCAN C. SCOTT, "Indian Affairs, 1840–1867," *Ibid.*, pp. 329–362.

For the history of transportation and postal facilities, see S. J. McLEAN, "National Highways Overland," in *Canada and Its Provinces*, vol. X, pp. 359–472; M. J. PATTON, "Shipping and Canals," *Ibid.*, pp. 475–624; and WILLIAM SMITH, "The Post Office, 1840–1867," in *Canada and Its Provinces*, vol. V, pp. 363–404; and the early chapters of O. D. SKELTON, *The Railway Builders* (Toronto, 1921) in *Chronicles of Canada*.

O. D. SKELTON's *Life and Times of Sir Alexander Tilloch Galt* (Toronto, 1920) contains much valuable material for the economic and social history of the period, and DENT's *The Last Forty Years* is important. Books like CANIFF HAIGHT, *Country Life in Canada Fifty Years Ago* (Toronto, 1885); W. L. SMITH, *The Pioneers of Old Ontario* (Toronto, 1923), in *Makers of Canada, New Series;* W. L. HIGGINS, *The Life and Times of Joseph Gould* (Toronto, 1887); and W. S. HERRINGTON, *History of the County of Lennox and Addington* (Toronto, 1913) and *Early Days in Upper Canada: Letters of John Langton from the Backwoods of Upper Canada and the Audit Office of the Province of Canada*, edited by W. A. Langton (Toronto, 1926), throw light on the social history of Upper Canada for the early part of the nineteenth century. SIR FRANCIS HINCKS, *Reminiscences of His Public Life* (Montreal, 1884) is also useful. W. J. RATTRAY, *The Scot in British North America*, 4 vols. (Toronto, 1880), and N. F. DAVIN, *The Irishman in Canada* (Toronto, 1877) are efforts to write the history of these two racial groups in Canada.

Special studies of the Elgin Reciprocity Treaty are: F. E. HAYNES, "The Reciprocity Treaty with Canada of 1854," in *Publications of the American Economic Association* (1892), vol. VII, pp. 417–486; and CEPHAS D. ALLIN and GEORGE M. JONES, *Annexation, Preferential Trade and Reciprocity* (Toronto, no date). The former is specially valuable because of many statistical tables on the working of the reciprocity agreement; the latter is a most exhaustive treatment, especially valuable for long quotations from newspapers, proceedings of conventions, and debates. It is almost a source book for the economic history of the years covered.

For the religious history of the period, parts of the following special articles in vol. XI of *Canada and Its Provinces*, should be consulted; CHARLES W. GORDON, "The Presbyterian Church and Its Missions," pp. 249-300; A. G. MORICE, "The Roman Catholic Church West of the Great Lakes," pp. 115-196; J. L. GILMOUR, "The Baptists in Canada," pp. 345-376; L. NORMAN TUCKER, "The Anglican Church and Its Missions," pp. 197-246.

Special articles on educational and cultural developments can be found in *Canada and Its Provinces*, vols. XI, XII, XVI, and XVIII, *passim*. A good article on immigration is FRANCES MOREHOUSE, "Canadian Migration in the Forties," in *The Canadian Historical Review*, Dec. 1928, p. 309-329.

For an excellent and very detailed list of additional references covering such topics as travel, contemporary description, social and cultural progress, etc., for the period under survey, see TROTTER, *Syllabus*, pp. 84-87, and 102. For references on the resources, development and economic and social history of the maritime provinces and Newfoundland during these years, see TROTTER, *Syllabus*, pp. 105-108.

CHAPTER XIV

FOREIGN RELATIONS (1783–1850)

Canadian-American relations

MOST of Canada's international disputes have grown out of questions concerning the thousands of miles of common frontier between the United States and the British North American provinces. At this point it is necessary to review briefly some of these leading controversies and their settlement, in the period from the Treaty of Paris of 1783 to the middle of the nineteenth century.

Controversies raised by Treaty of 1783

A number of these controversies were the result of defects in the Treaty of 1783, by which the United States came into being as an independent nation, and these defects in turn resulted from the imperfect geographical information at the disposal of the negotiators at that time. The famous Mitchell's Map of North America, prepared in 1755, was undoubtedly the one used to define the new international boundary between British North America and the United States, and this map was later found to contain many inaccuracies. The first boundary dispute involved the northeastern limits of the United States.

Maine boundary dispute

By the Treaty of 1783 the boundary between the United States and British North America was described as running up the St. Croix River to its source, thence due north to the highlands in the northwest angle of Nova Scotia, and down these highlands, which served as the watershed between streams running into the St. Lawrence River and those emptying into the Atlantic Ocean, to the north-westernmost head of the Connecticut River. Hence the line proceeded down the middle of that river to the forty-fifth degree of latitude, and then west along this line as far as the Iroquois or Cataraquy River. Many of the terms used in defining this boundary were open to challenge. No less than three rivers might have been the St. Croix, and the watershed and the angle of Nova Scotia mentioned in the treaty were even more difficult to locate accurately.

Locating St. Croix River

From the first, both Massachusetts (which then included the present State of Maine) and Nova Scotia granted land in the area in dispute. When Canadian settlers began to enter the region in controversy, Governor Hancock of Massachusetts requested Governor Parr of Nova Scotia to recall "those subjects of His Majesty who have . . . planted themselves within this commonwealth." Jay's Treaty of 1795 provided for a joint commission to settle the disputed boundary by determining the exact location of the St. Croix River. Three commissioners were appointed, surveys and arguments were prepared with great care, and the commission personally visited and examined the region in controversy. In addition, the commissioners secured depositions from John Jay and John Adams, two of the American peace commissioners of 1783, to ascertain the intentions of the framers of the treaty. Excavations dating from Champlain's time, revealed the remains of a settlement at the mouth of the Schoodic River, and thus it was possible to fix the "Ile Ste. Croix" mentioned by that explorer. In 1799, the commissioners agreed that the Schoodic was the St. Croix. The actual marking of the river was not completed until 1913. The decision on the whole was favorable to Great Britain.

The ownership of several islands in the Bay of Fundy, near the mouth of the St. Croix River continued to be a matter of dispute *Islands in* between the United States and Great Britain. During the War of *Bay of Fundy* 1812 these islands played some part in England's operations, and following the war, Great Britain refused to return one of them, although the basis of the peace was *status quo ante bellum*. The Treaty of Ghent provided for the appointment of a commission to settle this controversy, and in 1817, after much difficulty, a solution was agreed upon by compromise. The United States received Moose Island and two tiny islands dependent on it, while Great Britain got all the rest, including Grand Manan, an important fishing base, and the most valuable of all. The final water boundary in this region was not determined until 1908, when it was settled by arbitration.

The question of the "Highlands line," established by the Treaty of 1783, remained for settlement. The original negotiators probably *"Highlands* had a watershed in mind, but it was soon discovered that highlands *line"* in the sense of mountains did not exist. Several attempts made before 1814 to adjust this dispute ended in failure. In the Treaty of Ghent it was agreed that two commissioners should run the international line from the source of the St. Croix River to the Lake of the Woods, the western extremity of the Great Lakes chain. Thomas Barclay, of Nova Scotia, and Cornelius P. Van Ness, of Vermont, were chosen for this complicated task. For nearly eight years the commissioners wrangled over the method of procedure and the conclusions to be recommended, and in 1822 each filed his own report and agreed that further coöperation was impossible.

Some years later the controversy assumed more than technical significance. In the northeast of the United States a number of Maine *Points at issue* lumbermen began to contest with New Brunswick lumbermen the right to cut timber in this disputed area. In 1827 an American citizen was arrested by New Brunswick officials while at work in this neighborhood, and the United States government made the incident the occasion for a note to Great Britain demanding not only his release, but indemnity for his illegal confinement. In September, 1827, Albert Gallatin, the American representative in London, secured the consent of the British and the American governments to a proposal to submit the issue to a single arbiter for settlement. The King of the

Netherlands was selected, and Gallatin presented the case of the United States very effectively. Without going into too many details, we may remark that the Treaty of 1783 provided that the line should follow "along the said Highlands which divide those rivers that empty themselves into the river St. Lawrence, from those which fall into the Atlantic Ocean." The main question at issue was whether the St. John River, emptying into the Bay of Fundy, flowed into the Atlantic Ocean in the sense in which that term was used in the treaty. About 12,000 square miles of territory were at stake. The main contention of the British was that the "highlands line," insisted upon by the United States, only divided the rivers flowing into the St. Lawrence from those emptying into the Gulf of St. Lawrence, or the Bay of Fundy, and ignored the Atlantic Ocean altogether, and that "highlands," in the sense in which the word was used in the treaty, must be a continuous and well-defined ridge. The British insisted that the boundary must follow the most pronounced line of hills, starting at a point known as Mars Hill, about one hundred miles south of the watershed of the St. Lawrence, and made a distinction between the Bay of Fundy and the Atlantic Ocean.

Failure of arbitration in 1831

In 1831 the King of the Netherlands made his award. He followed neither the British nor the American claims, but proposed a compromise, by which about one-third of the 12,000 square miles in dispute would have been granted to Great Britain, and the rest to the United States. It was very unfortunate that the United States Senate refused to ratify this settlement which was essentially fair. As a result, the controversy dragged on into the 1840's, and as the years passed, the State of Maine became more stubborn, and refused repeatedly to make concessions which might have enabled an adjustment by compromise.

Border troubles

From 1831 to 1839 a number of border disturbances occurred between citizens of Maine and New Brunswick, culminating in the Aroostook War, or the "War of Pork and Beans," as it came to be known in Maine. In 1831 a riot had resulted when Maine tried to hold an election in the disputed area, and clashes between lumberjacks were not infrequent. The British, moreover, were making plans to build a road through the disputed region from Halifax to Quebec.

Aroostook War

In 1838 the Aroostook War began. An officer of the State of Maine, trying to arrest some British lumbermen at work in the Aroostook valley, was himself arrested by the New Brunswick authorities. The Maine legislature promptly appropriated $800,000, raised her militia to fighting strength, and built some defenses, in order to protect the rights which she claimed had been violated. The United States Congress was equally militant, and a credit of $10,000,000 and the calling of 50,000 volunteers were authorized to support the contention of the injured state. New Brunswick retaliated by voting appropriations and by sending 850 militia into the contested district, while her sister province, Nova Scotia, eagerly came to her support.

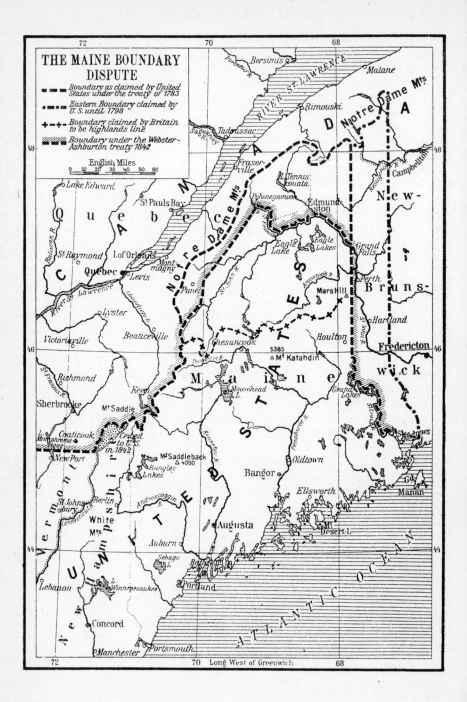

THE MAINE BOUNDARY DISPUTE

- – – – Boundary as claimed by United States under the treaty of 1783
- ·–·–· Eastern Boundary claimed by U. S. until 1798
- +–+–+ Boundary claimed by Britain to be highlands line
- ▨▨▨ Boundary under the Webster-Ashburton treaty 1842

English Miles
0 10 20 30 40 50 60

Governor Fairfield of Maine seemed intent upon war, and the troops at one time were not more than thirty yards apart, with a fordable stream between them. Fortunately President Van Buren was more peacefully inclined. He sent General Winfield Scott, who had already had some experience in dealing with border troubles with Canada, to effect a reconciliation, and for the time being bloodshed was avoided. In 1839 a *modus vivendi* was arranged by the governors of Maine and New Brunswick, by which Maine for the time retained possession of the Aroostook valley, and the British retained possession of the valley of the Upper St. John.

The disputed Maine-New Brunswick boundary was finally settled by the Webster-Ashburton Treaty. At the time of these *Other issues* negotiations the relations between the United States and England were suffering from an accumulation of troubles. About 100,000 acres were in dispute near the head of the Connecticut River. An error in the surveying of the forty-fifth parallel was discovered, and it was found that the fortress built by the United States at Rouses Point, commanding the outlet of Lake Champlain, was really in British territory.

In addition to disturbances along the Maine frontier, the border troubles between the United States and Canada during the rebellion *Caroline affair* of 1837 had reached a critical stage. The destruction by Canadian militia of the *Caroline*, an American vessel carrying supplies to the Canadian rebels on Navy Island, and the consequent loss of at least one American life, had precipitated a diplomatic crisis. The situation was further aggravated when a Canadian militiaman boasted in a New York saloon of his participation in the *Caroline* affair and was arrested and charged before the New York courts with the murder of a United States citizen.

Alexander McLeod, the Canadian in question, claimed that he was not subject to the courts of New York State, since his acts in the *Case of McLeod* *Caroline* affair were the result of orders from his military superiors. England, quite properly, supported his claim, and demanded his immediate release. The United States government was willing to comply, but owing to the American dual system of government the federal authorities had no legal way to interfere with the processes of a state court. It is possible that if McLeod had been executed, Great Britain would have broken off diplomatic relations, and war might have resulted. At any rate the American secretary of state was greatly disturbed by these possibilities.

At this point both nations turned once more to the methods of common sense. Daniel Webster, who became secretary of state of the *Webster-* United States in 1841, was extremely anxious to find a solution for *Ashburton* this accumulation of grievances. In England, Peel's Government *negotiations* proved equally sincere in wanting a compromise, and Alexander Baring (Lord Ashburton), was commissioned to go to Washington to adjust these difficulties. He was a tried friend of the United States, with an American wife, and was personally acquainted with Webster. The British envoy arrived in the United States in April, 1842, and soon had negotiations under way. Both Maine and Massachusetts proved obstreperous about the boundary settlement, and had to be given a voice in the proceedings.

"Battle of Maps"

Webster and Lord Ashburton easily agreed that the northeast boundary of the United States could be settled only by drawing a compromise line, and the negotiators consequently abandoned the hopeless effort to discover the boundary described in the Treaty of 1783. Webster very effectively used a map which Jared Sparks of Harvard College had recently discovered in Paris to convince Maine that she must recede from her extreme demands. On this map, thought to have been used by Franklin at Paris in 1783, a red line marked a boundary which virtually supported the British contention. Webster carefully concealed this map from Lord Ashburton. In the "Battle of the Maps," as this episode has been called, Webster did not know that another early map was in the possession of the British foreign office and was being carefully guarded from American eyes.

Determining boundary

By the Webster-Ashburton Treaty of August 9, 1842, a compromise line was drawn fixing the northeast boundary of the United States as it is today. The boundary followed the Netherlands award up the St. John and St. Francis Rivers to the outlet of Lake Pohenaganook, and then, varying from the award line, it followed a straight southwesterly line to a point on the northwest branch of the St. John more than ten miles distant from the main branch of the river, thence southerly by that branch to its source in the highlands of Metjarmette Portage. From this point the line ran down along the highlands to the head of Hall's Stream, and down this stream to its intersection with the old line of the forty-fifth parallel. Of the disputed territory the United States got 7,015 square miles and England 5,012. Webster estimated that the seven-twelfths awarded to the United States probably equalled four-fifths of the value of the entire strip in controversy. As a matter of fact, the award was 893 square miles less than what the United States might have had if the Senate had accepted the 1831 award of the King of the Netherlands. Maine kept the Aroostook valley, and received the southern part of the valley of the Upper St. John. It was agreed that timber could be floated down the St. John River by Americans on the same terms as applied to British citizens. To compensate Maine and Massachusetts, the United States government divided $300,000 between them. Surveyors were set to work to draw the new international boundary, and it has since been marked with monuments. The American claim to the head of the Connecticut River was allowed to stand, as was also the American ownership of Rouses Point, and thus the international line was completed from Lake Huron to the Lake of the Woods.

The international boundary line ran down the Connecticut River

to the forty-fifth parallel, thence to the St. Lawrence River, and *Line to Rockies*
through the St. Lawrence and Great Lakes system to Lake Superior.
From a point in Lake Superior it followed a complicated line through
little lakes and rivers to the northwest corner of the Lake of the
Woods, whence it was to proceed due west to the source of the
Mississippi River. It was not known at the time the Treaty of 1783
was made that the Mississippi has its rise so far south of this line
that it would be impossible to complete the boundary as stipulated
in the treaty. The Treaty of Ghent provided for the appointment of
two commissioners to run the boundary through the line of rivers
and lakes to the northwest angle of the Lake of the Woods, and to
agree upon a distribution of the islands within these international
waterways. In 1818 the United States and Great Britain agreed to
accept the forty-ninth parallel as the boundary line from the Lake
of the Woods to the Rocky Mountains. The purchase by the United
States of the vast Louisiana territory lying west of the Mississippi,
in 1803, had made this settlement imperative. A number of details of
the British North American boundary to the Rockies remained for
settlement, and these were disposed of by the negotiations of 1842.

At the same time the difficulties arising from the rebellion of
1837 were settled. Great Britain offered her apologies for her violation *Problems*
of United States territory in the case of the sinking of the *Caroline*. *resulting from*
Webster admitted that such a violation was permissible for reasons *rebellion of*
of self-defense, but denied that any necessity had existed in this case. *1837*
Although Lord Ashburton insisted that a necessity did exist, he was
ready to apologize. Fortunately for the United States government,
McLeod was acquitted of the murder charge lodged against him in
the New York courts. The American secretary of state used all his
influence with New York to bring about McLeod's final discharge,
and in order to prevent the recurrence of such incidents he secured an
act of Congress providing that a foreigner on trial in a state court
could be brought before a United States judge by *habeas corpus* proceedings, and dismissed if the court thought proper.

The Treaty of 1842 also contained new provisions for the extra-
dition of offenders against the law, but unfortunately these were not *Other provisions*
inclusive enough to catch the scores of American swindlers and *of treaty*
embezzlers who continued to find safety in British North America
from the wrath of their victims. An effort to reach an understanding
concerning the suppression of the slave trade was not successful.
The Webster-Ashburton Treaty was criticized in the United States,
Great Britain, and British North America. As a matter of fact, it is
the judgment of history that the treaty was an honorable and, on
the whole, satisfactory settlement of issues which might easily have
led to a rupture of friendly relations.

The problem of extending the American boundary from the
Rocky Mountains to the Pacific Ocean still remained to be solved. *Oregon*
It was a problem in which the individual British North American *controversy*

provinces were not directly interested, for the entire West was still
the hunting preserve of the Hudson's Bay Company. The Treaty of
1818, which settled the boundary, except for a few minor details,
as far west as the Rocky Mountains, had specifically postponed the
fixing of the boundary in the region beyond by providing for the
joint occupation of the "Oregon country," for ten years, by the
United States and Great Britain. The region in question once included
everything west of the Rocky Mountains, from 42° to 54° 40′, or
from the Spanish possessions on the Pacific to the Russian colony in
Alaska. Spain, however, had withdrawn her claim to the northwest
coast of North America in the Florida Treaty with the United States
in 1819; Russia by the Treaty of 1824 agreed to withdraw to the
north of 54° 40′. England and the United States, by virtue of discovery,
explorations, and trading expeditions, continued to claim jurisdiction over the Oregon country.

*Early attempts
to determine
Oregon boundary*

All previous efforts to arrive at a settlement involving a satisfactory partition of the Oregon country had failed, because the United
States insisted that the international boundary should follow the
forty-ninth parallel to the Pacific coast, while Great Britain contended
for the Columbia River. This failure to reach an agreement led to
the indefinite extension of the joint occupation arrangement in 1828.
In the race for Oregon, however, the advantage was clearly with the
United States. British interest in the region was largely confined to
the activities of the fur traders of the Hudson's Bay Company, while
in the 1830's and 1840's thousands of Americans migrated over the
Oregon Trail to establish permanent agricultural settlements on the
new frontier. This actual occupation of large sections of the area in
controversy served greatly to strengthen the title of the United
States to the Oregon country.

*Settlement of
1846*

When England continued to reject the 49° line, the United States
began to insist on possession of all of the Pacific coast, as far north
as 54° 40′. "The whole of Oregon," "54° 40′ or fight," and the
"immediate reoccupation of Oregon" were slogans with which
politicians in the United States deluded the voters on election day,
and these were the election cries of the Democratic party in 1844,
when its candidate, James K. Polk, was swept into the presidency.
During Polk's administration notice was given of the abrogation of
the joint occupation agreement, and Congress was asked virtually to
incorporate Oregon as part of the United States. England, anxious
to preserve peace, and probably convinced that President Polk's insistence on the extreme American claims was largely for home consumption, now renewed the suggestion that the forty-ninth parallel
become the international boundary to the Pacific. Polk, after sound-
ing out the United States Senate beforehand, accepted the proposal,
so that in 1846 the boundary line as established east of the Rockies
was extended through the region west of the mountains to the ocean.
When it reached the water's edge, the line was deflected southward,

so as to give Vancouver Island to the British. The Treaty of 1846 guaranteed the free navigation of the Columbia River, and recognized certain property rights of the Hudson's Bay Company and of the Puget Sound Agricultural Company.

Very soon a new dispute arose as to the ownership of the islands in the channel separating the mainland from Vancouver Island, and *San Juan Island* running southward to the Pacific. Any one of three channels seemed possible, according to the treaty provisions of 1846. More specifically, a sharp dispute arose over the ownership of San Juan Island. Proposals to arbitrate proved unacceptable, and the controversy was not settled until 1871, when an award by the German Emperor, to whom the dispute had finally been referred, decided in favor of the United States, by accepting the channel known as Haro Strait as the dividing-line between American and British jurisdiction. In 1908 a treaty between the United States and Great Britain provided for the final demarcation of the Canadian-United States boundary. This task has now been completed.

The question of the rights of the United States in the fisheries of the British North American provinces led to disputes which furnished *Atlantic fisheries* the basis of negotiations extending over 125 years. The American commissioners who made the peace treaty after the close of the Revolution had been specifically instructed by the Continental Congress in no case to give up the rights of Americans to fish in the North Atlantic waters off Newfoundland and in the Gulf of St. Lawrence. This issue was of special importance to the New England states, and John Adams, the representative of this section on the peace commission, worked hard and successfully to get a fisheries provision into the treaty. The Treaty of 1783 guaranteed to United States fishermen equal rights with the British in the North Atlantic, and these fishing rights were not limited to any special distance from the shore line. The only limitation was one which prohibited the drying and curing of fish on the Newfoundland coast. On the other hand, the treaty not only granted fishing rights on the Newfoundland Grand Banks, but also gave Americans the "liberty" to enjoy the inshore fishing privileges, such as getting water, and bait, and drying their catch on shore.

The War of 1812 gave England the opportunity to reopen this question, and in spite of the insistence of John Quincy Adams, who *Fisheries* was a member of the peace commission of 1814 as his father had been *convention of* in 1783, the question of American fishing rights was not settled at *1818* Ghent, but was left for later negotiations. The next four years were years of friction, marked by some collisions between United States fishermen and the authorities of British North America. Finally, in 1818, a convention was agreed upon between England and the United States, which it was hoped, would settle the fisheries dispute. In substance the new convention acknowledged the rights of Americans off the Newfoundland coast, noted in the Treaty of 1783, but the "liberties" of that treaty were declared void, and a new arrangement was entered into giving the United States fishing rights on the southern, western, and northern coasts of Newfoundland, and the right to dry and cure fish on the Newfoundland and Labrador shores so long as these shores remained unsettled. The harbors in settled portions of the coast could be used by American fishermen "for the purpose of shelter and of repairing damages therein, of purchasing wood, and of obtaining water, and for no other purpose whatever." These rights were subject to such restrictions as seemed necessary to "prevent their taking, drying, or curing fish" in these parts, "or in any other manner whatever abusing the privileges hereby reserved to them." In other words, wherever the coast-line contained settlements, it was agreed that the fishing interests must first come to an agreement with the settlers and owners. The United States, in turn, renounced all its rights to fish at other points, or within three miles of any coast, bay, or indentation not included in the limits mentioned above.

Controversial questions

It was difficult to draw the three-mile line accurately along a coast so ragged as the eastern coast of British North America. Here lay the cause for a century of disputes. England insisted that bays whose mouths exceeded six miles were closed waters, while the United States contended for the right to fish in bays much smaller. Moreover, there was nothing in the treaty positively granting the right to buy bait or to use harbor facilities for the reloading of fishing vessels. Some of the port regulations of the British provinces became increasingly burdensome as the rivalry between American and British interests increased.

Three-mile limit

There was no serious trouble, however, until 1836, when the province of Nova Scotia ordered the seizure and search of vessels within three miles of her coast-line. Other provinces passed similar laws, and a violent controversy broke out over the proper extent of the three-mile limit, and whether it should be drawn from headland to headland, or should follow the sinuosities of the coast. The New England fishing interests brought pressure to bear on the United States government to defend their rights against what they considered the unjustified legislation of the British-American provinces. It happened that practically all mackerel suddenly left New England for British North American waters, and this fact undoubtedly added zest to the American contention.

Question still unsettled by 1867

It is unnecessary to follow in detail the long story of diplomatic negotiations between the United States and Great Britain over this difficult problem, or the many incidents of friction and clash between American fishermen and the authorities of British North America. The liberal spirit of the Elgin Reciprocity Treaty of 1854 provided some relief, but its abrogation in 1866 reopened the whole fisheries controversy. After 1867 it became one of the great problems of the Dominion government, and its later phases will be discussed in another chapter. It is sufficient to point out here that the fisheries disputes were not finally disposed of until 1910.

One of the most worthy diplomatic achievements of the period since 1815 was the Rush-Bagot Agreement of 1817. It inaugurated an *Rush-Bagot* era of unbroken peace along 3000 miles of undefended frontier, and *Agreement of* after more than a century it stands out in these troublous days since *1817* the World War of 1914–1918 as a glorious lesson in the practical benefits of real disarmament as a means of preventing war. That it was concluded by the United States and British governments within three years after the close of the War of 1812, when the smell of powder had hardly disappeared, is an indication of the practical common sense of these two English-speaking peoples.

In 1816 John Quincy Adams, as American minister to London, opened the discussion of the limitation of armaments on the Great *Negotiations* Lakes. President Madison was keenly interested in avoiding the expense and the danger of a race for armaments along the Canadian frontier, and Lord Castlereagh proved friendly to the American proposals. Accordingly, in 1817 an agreement was signed by Richard Rush, who was acting as secretary of state in the new Monroe administration pending the return of John Quincy Adams from Europe, and Charles Bagot, the British minister in Washington. Although the agreement was not a treaty, nevertheless President Monroe submitted it to the United States Senate for its formal approval.

The Rush-Bagot Convention of 1817 limited the total number of war vessels on the border lakes to four; all other warships on the *Provisions and* lakes were to be promptly dismantled, and no others were to be con- *importance* structed. Each nation was permitted to maintain one ship on Lake Erie, two on the Upper Lakes, and one on Lake Champlain. No vessel was to exceed one hundred tons burden, and its armament was limited to one eighteen-pound cannon. It is clear that ships of this character could be useful only for combatting smugglers and for the enforcement of the ordinary rules of navigation and fishing on the lakes. Since 1817 Canada and Great Britain have occasionally permitted the United States to have larger ships on the lakes for use as training vessels, but this apparent deviation from the terms of the agreement rests upon permission specifically secured in advance. In July, 1922, the Canadian prime minister, Mackenzie King, journeyed to Washington for a conference with the American secretary of state. One of the purposes of the visit was to convert the Rush-Bagot agreement into a more formal and permanent treaty.

SELECT BIBLIOGRAPHY FOR CHAPTER XIV

A most detailed discussion of boundary disputes and treaties in which Canada has been involved is by JAMES WHITE, "Boundary Disputes and Treaties," in *Canada and Its Provinces*, vol. VIII, pp. 751–958. The complicated negotiations over the fisheries are set forth at length in N. B. WORMWITH, "The Fishery Arbitrations," in *Canada and Its Provinces*, vol. VIII, pp. 681–748.

CHARLES H. LEVERMORE, *The Anglo-American Agreement of 1817*, (World Peace Foundation Pamphlet, Boston, 1924, vol. IV, No. 4) is a detailed account of the Rush-Bagot agreement for disarmament. WILLIAM A. DUNNING, *The British Empire and the United States* (New York, 1914) is a survey of British-American relations during the "hundred years of peace," following the Peace of Ghent, and contains much of value concerning Canadian-American affairs. DAVID R. MOORE, *Canada and the United States, 1815–1830* (Chicago, 1910) also has some value. Some interesting details and local color for the *Caroline* incident and its aftermath are available in CHARLES LINDSEY, *The Life and Times of Wm. Lyon Mackenzie*, 2 vols. (Toronto, 1862).

Canadian-American relations naturally find a large place in histories of American diplomacy. The two best single-volume treatments are C. R. FISH, *American Diplomacy* (New York, 1923) and RANDOLPH G. ADAMS, *A History of the Foreign Policy of the United States* (New York, 1924).

CHAPTER XV

THE FAILURE OF THE ACT OF UNION IN THE CANADAS

THE Lafontaine-Baldwin ministry—the "Great Ministry"—which sponsored the constructive legislation already discussed and secured the acceptance of responsible government as a practical working principle at the time of the "rebellion losses" bill, continued in office until 1851. By the end of its administration it had reformed the system of municipal government, secured important educational and judicial improvements, assumed control of the postal service, abolished the law of primogeniture in Canada West, sponsored the first provincial exhibit of Canadian agricultural and industrial products at Montreal, developed the Canadian canal system, and laid the foundations for the great era of railroad-building. Two major questions only baffled this powerful government coalition, namely, the question of clergy reserves originating in the Constitutional Act of 1791, and the problem of seigniorial tenure, which still survived in Lower Canada. *"Great Ministry"*

Failure to settle these problems was due largely to the rise of internal party friction, and to the slow disintegration of the Reform or Liberal Party. One of the new political factions which was becoming important, was known as the "Clear Grits"—"all sand and no dirt, clear grit all the way through." This group, which cherished radical political ideas, favored popular election of all government officials by secret ballot and universal manhood suffrage, biennial parliaments, free trade, direct taxation, and the abolition of all classes enjoying special privileges of any kind. In matters of foreign relations they felt that only the determination of war and peace, and even "that under certain restrictions," should be left to England. The "Clear Grits" were powerful only in Canada West, where George Brown, of the Toronto *Globe* was their great leader. Brown, who had once denounced the "Grits" as a crowd of radicals, annexationists, and disappointed office-seekers, cast in his lot with the party in the fall of 1850, and at once plunged into the battle for the secularization of the clergy reserves and the elimination of Roman Catholic influence from Canadian politics. His newspaper, the *Globe*, became the most powerful political organ in Canada, and was especially influential among the large Scotch element in Canada West. *"Clear Grits"*

Another group which split from the Reform Party was "La Partie Rouge," composed of ardent young French Canadians under the leadership of Papineau. Their program, more radical in many *"La Partie Rouge"*

respects than that of the "Clear Grits," included the repeal of the
Union Act, the establishment of a republican form of government,
and, for the extremists, annexation to the United States. Many of
these radicals in spite of their membership in the Catholic Church
denounced the system of tithing and clerical intervention in Lower
Canadian political affairs. On the whole, however, this French-
Canadian party could have little in common with the radicals of
Canada West, as long as the latter were led by such a violent anti-
French and anti-Catholic leader as the Scotch editor of the Toronto
Globe.

*Party
realignments*

The Lafontaine-Baldwin ministry was much too moderate in its
point of view on such questions as the clergy reserves and radical
political reforms to satisfy either of these more extreme groups.
On the other hand, it was much too radical to satisfy either the
moderate conservatives or the handful of "die-hard" Tories, led by
Allan MacNab, who had condoned such violent tactics at the time
of the "rebellion losses" bill of 1849 in their opposition to responsible
government. The time was ripe for a realignment of parties, and all
that was needed was a leader astute enough to weld the moderates
of all parties into a new Liberal-Conservative coalition.

*Retirement of
Baldwin and
Lafontaine*

In 1851 Robert Baldwin, finding the party moving along the path
of reform more rapidly than he could follow, refused to coöperate
any longer, and in the next general election he was defeated in his
old constituency and retired to private life. His colleague, Lafontaine,
took a similar course largely because he found himself out of step
with the reformers of Canada West on the question of the clergy
reserves. In 1853 he became chief justice of Lower Canada and in
that high office served with distinction until 1864. It should be added
that both Baldwin and Lafontaine were opposed to the secularization
of the clergy reserves. The former was a devout Anglican and the
latter an equally devout Roman Catholic. With these personal feelings
they undoubtedly felt that they ought not to face the issue to which
they could not bring more independence of attitude.

*"Double
Majority"*

Obviously, under these conditions of political disintegration, it
became difficult on many issues to get the support of both the French-
Canadian Liberals and those of Upper Canada, or Canada West.
Nevertheless, since the fall of the Draper Conservative Government
it had become the accepted principle of Canadian politics that all
important measures must receive the support of a majority of the
representatives of the party in Parliament from both divisions of the
province. This was especially true of bills affecting one division of the
united province more specifically than the other. This principle of the
"double majority" quite obviously was established to avoid friction
between the two divisions, and to make it difficult to enact purely
sectional legislation. With the rapid disintegration of political
parties, and the racial and religious differences between Upper- and
Lower-Canadian Liberals, it became increasingly difficult for the

Government in power to follow this principle. The result was either friction or political stagnation.

This situation can be more specifically illustrated by considering *Clergy reserves* the fortunes of the clergy reserves and the issue of seigniorial tenure *and seigniorial* during the life of the "Great Ministry." Lafontaine himself would *tenure* probably have preferred to let the clergy reserves rest in the lap of the British Government to which they had been transferred in 1840; but his followers in Canada West insisted that he take action to compel England to turn the question over to Canada for settlement. The Protestant dissenters in this section, who did not belong to the Established Church, and were now greatly in the majority, demanded that the Church lands be sold and the proceeds be used for internal improvements and for the development of education. Various make-shift settlements, tried in earlier years, were now denounced as un-satisfactory. The ministry itself was badly divided in the debate over this question. The same confusion existed in the matter of settling the seigniorial rights in Canada East. Lafontaine did not want com-pletely to abolish the dues incident to seigniorial tenure, even though some raised loud protests against the payment of taxes which hindered the free transfer of land, while others advocated the exchange of feudal rights for freehold rights, and the commutation of the old seigniorial dues into a fixed money payment.

In the fall of 1851 the "Great Ministry" was superseded by the Hincks-Morin Government. The new ministry managed to survive *Hincks-Morin* its first general election. Much progress was made in the promotion *Government* of railroads, for which Hincks was chiefly responsible, and some other important measures were passed, but in general the Government steadily lost ground. Hincks was attacked by George Brown for catering too much to the French element in his coalition. Although pledged to secularize the clergy reserves, this ministry found it desirable to leave the question undisturbed as their predecessors had done. Conservatives and Radicals of Canada West therefore combined to oppose the Government for its dilatory tactics. Although in other respects the session of 1852–1853 had been quite fruitful in legislative enactments, such as extension of the franchise, and better trade rela-tions with the United States, the Hincks-Morin Government was defeated in the election of 1854. Both the "Clear Grits" and the Tories fought the Government candidates. The membership of the new assembly, which during the preceding year had been increased from 84 to 130, was divided between "Clear Grits," "Rouges," Conserva-tives under MacNab, and the Moderate-Reform group of the Govern-ment. Lacking a majority, the Hincks-Morin ministry resigned, and was succeeded by a new Liberal-Conservative alliance.

The masterbuilder of this new coalition was the young Scotch-Canadian, John A. Macdonald. In Parliament since 1844, he had *Macdonald and Liberal-* gradually developed those arts of the politician which made him the *Conservative* most successful conciliator, manager of men, and opportunist in *alliance*

Canadian political life. He had long foreseen the possibilities of building a new moderate Liberal-Conservative group from among the remnants of the old Conservatives and the fragments of the Reform Party. Macdonald now undertook to build a new party which was to contain old Conservatives from Canada West, Moderate Reformers from the same province who had been followers of Baldwin and Hincks, and the Liberals from Canada East, led by Morin, who being suspicious of the more radical reformers in the other province, were therefore willing to join the new party. This Liberal-Conservative Party dominated politics for many years. Though the new ministry was under the titular leadership of MacNab and Morin, this fact did not mean that it followed the extreme Tory principles of MacNab. Behind the scenes was the master hand of Macdonald, who resolved to carry out much of the program which the preceding ministry had failed to accomplish. By 1856 MacNab was forced out entirely, and Macdonald became the real head of the Government. In 1854 Lord Elgin was succeeded by Sir Edmund Head, and thus passed the "heroic days of the governor-generalship." From that time on, Canada's own leaders were the responsible men in determining the course of public events, and governors became more or less formal accessories.

"Dishing Whigs" on clergy reserves

Macdonald, convinced that it would be excellent strategy to "dish the Whigs" by stealing their issues and solving them, promptly disposed of the vexing clergy reserves question. England having yielded her control of the matter to Canada, a law was passed providing that all money thenceforth derived from the clergy reserves should constitute a separate fund, to be divided in proportion to population among the counties and cities of the provinces from which the money came, and to be used for secular purposes. What amounted to a pension for the clergy dependent on the reserves at the time of the settlement was made a first charge on the fund.

Extinction of seigniorial rights

Seigniorial tenure was abolished at the same time (1854), and all feudal rights and obligations in United Canada were extinguished. A commission was appointed to study the claims of each parish and seigniory, to prepare a schedule for the commutation of feudal dues into fixed cash rents, and to arbitrate disputes which might arise as a result of these adjustments. A special seigniorial court, composed of fifteen judges, passed on the legality of the claims advanced by the seigniors. The adjustment was definitely completed in 1859; but to this day there are remnants of the feudal ceremonies of old Quebec, and some of the old seigniorial families still enjoy a special social position in their communities.

Gradual breakdown of party government

We need not follow here in detail all the cross-currents of politics in United Canada from 1854 to 1864. The period is significant because it marks the gradual breakdown of party government and, with it, the collapse of the Union policy. From 1854 to 1864 no less than ten ministries were in control of Canadian affairs, some of them, to be sure, differing only slightly in composition from their predecessors. Old leaders like MacNab and Taché gave way to new leaders like Macdonald and Georges E. Cartier. The problem of French nationality remained a great stumbling-block to the practical politician, and "double majorities" became more difficult to manage.

The year 1858 produced the notorious "double shuffle." Taking advantage of a law providing that a minister who resigned and within a month accepted another portfolio did not thereby vacate his seat, a Macdonald Government avoided an appeal to the electorate by shuffling the offices all around, and then reshuffling the same ministers into their old places, all within twenty-four hours. *"Double Shuffle"*

Bad times, following a severe panic in 1857 which was the result of over-expansion and extraordinarily heavy expenditures on railways from 1854 to 1857, added to the distress of the politicians and the people, and left a deficit in the treasury. Instead of the general elections clearing the atmosphere, they served further to complicate the issues and to stir up antagonism between Canada East and Canada West. By 1857 Brown and his "Clear Grits" were fighting to abolish denominational or "separate" schools in Canada, a demand which was especially obnoxious to the French Catholics and which would have proved disastrous for the English minority in French Canada. Brown won Canada West on this issue, but Cartier mobilized the French Canadians against this program of secularization and carried all the seats in Canada East. It became increasingly difficult to build a Government majority out of such conflicting groups. *Sectional antagonisms*

Another demand which created an impassable barrier between the people of the two divisions of United Canada was the demand for representation by population. In 1841 the population of Lower Canada had exceeded that of Upper Canada by several hundred thousand. The equal distribution of representatives in the assembly, provided by the Union Act, had thus proved a decided advantage for Upper Canada, which was greatly over-represented. By 1861 the situation was reversed, and the population of Canada West was now some 300,000 in excess of that of the older province. In the 1850's a great agitation arose to change the basis of representation and to end the domination of the English element by an over-represented French minority. The demand for "Rep. by Pop." was vigorously opposed by the French Canadians, who regarded the proposal as nothing less than an attempt to destroy French institutions and French rights in Canada. Here was another situation which made further coöperation between the leaders of the two divisions of the province increasingly difficult. *"Rep. by Pop."*

Early in 1858 the Macdonald-Cartier Government, having a majority in the assembly, but only a minority of the seats from Canada West, suddenly discarded the "double-majority" practice, and later perpetrated the "double shuffle" described above—a procedure which Cartier justified as meeting the requirements of the law, *Breakdown of "Double Majority" Principle* and at the same time preventing unnecessary elections. Macdonald continued to pass measures affecting Canada West by majorities obtained in the other division of the province. The demand for representation by population steadily increased in English Canada, and it spread from Brown and his "Grits" to some of Macdonald's own followers. As the agitation grew, religious and racial differences became aggravated and there were many suggestions for a separation of the provinces or for some realignment on a federal basis. Canadian politics during these years reached a new level of violence and intrigue.

Governmental instability

The elections of 1861 yielded a majority for the Government in French Canada, and a decided minority in the other division. Within a year the Government was defeated by French-Canadian votes on a militia bill, proposed at the time of strained relations between the United States and Great Britain over the *Trent* affair discussed below. On this particular issue the members from Canada West had voted to sustain the Government. The Cartier-Macdonald Government fell, and was superseded by the John Sandfield Macdonald-Sicotte ministry, which was known to oppose representation by population, and to favor separate schools and a return to the "double-majority" principle. This Government, in turn, was defeated by a vote of want of confidence directed by John A. Macdonald.

Deadlock

Parties were now very evenly balanced, and parliamentary majorities were extremely difficult to maintain. In two years no less than four ministries tried to hold the reins of power. The general elections of 1863 resulted in a virtual deadlock. The "double-majority" principle was more difficult to observe than ever, and responsible parliamentary government was practically impossible. The Union Act had resulted in a governmental deadlock. In this hour of crisis, men of vision and unselfish statesmanship were at hand to work out a constructive solution for the political and constitutional perplexities of United Canada.

Changes in Union Act before 1860

Before discussing the various forces leading to confederation, it will be necessary to summarize briefly the chief modifications of the Union Act which had occurred by 1860. By that year, nearly one-half of the original clauses of the Union Act had been discarded, either legally or as a matter of practice. By 1850 the Canadian government obtained the right to make changes in the civil list which had been guaranteed in 1841. The section providing that English should be the sole official language of the Union Parliament had been repealed, and control of the post-office, and of currency and banking, had been assumed by the Canadian government. As has been shown, the right to settle the clergy reserves question, one of the fundamental stipulations of the Act of 1791, was finally conceded to the Union Parliament. In 1855 Canada undertook to pay for her own militia establishment. Canada's right to regulate immigration was gradually being established, and in 1859 Great Britain recognized the right of the province to raise its own revenues, even when this involved a protective tax on British imports. In that year, when Alexander Galt, the Canadian minister of finance, increased the duties on manufactured articles, the manufacturing interests of Sheffield, England, protested to the Duke of Newcastle, then secretary of state for the colonies, against this tariff legislation. Galt replied in a notable letter which contains really the first clear-cut statement by the government of a growing spirit of autonomy. Although promising the greatest respect and consideration for matters of imperial policy, the Canadian minister of finance insisted that "the government of Canada acting for its legislature and people, cannot, through those feelings of deference which they owe to the imperial authorities, in any manner waive or diminish the right of the people of Canada to decide for themselves both as to the mode and extent to which taxation shall be imposed." Furthermore, Galt pointed out that "in the imposition of taxation it is so plainly necessary that the administration and the people should be in accord, that the former cannot admit responsibility or acquire approval beyond that of the local legislature." Macdonald supported this vigorous assertion of Canadian autonomy, and Newcastle gracefully yielded.

In 1853 the membership of the assembly of United Canada was increased to 130, and a new distribution of seats was arranged. This did *Changes in* not, however, disturb the principle of an equal total representation *legislature* from each division of the province. The law of 1858 fixed a property qualification for the privilege of voting, and in the following year the salary of members of the assembly was raised to six dollars a day, with a mileage allowance for travel. The powers and importance of the Upper House or legislative council steadily declined after the establishment of cabinet government. Attendance dropped off, and many leaders of Canadian opinion, including Lord Elgin, recommended that the Upper House be made elective like the Lower House, but with higher qualifications for membership. In 1856 the size of the legislative council was reduced from sixty to forty-eight members, equally divided between the two divisions. At the same time the Upper House was made an elective body, the members to be chosen by a plan of rotation for eight-year terms. The property qualification for membership was raised to £2000. These changes, however, accomplished very little by way of reviving the importance of the Upper Chamber.

During the 1840's sweeping changes were made in the judicial department, and many of these reforms at last corrected the abuses *Judicial* against which the rebels of 1837 had protested so strongly. The *changes* principle was established that judges should hold office during good behavior, and not during the pleasure of the government, and that they could be removed only on joint address of the two houses of the Union Parliament. At the same time judges were excluded from the Upper House and from the executive council. The beginnings of constitutional right, as against constitutional law, appeared in that the British Parliament refrained from passing laws applicable to the provinces, and the British cabinets exercised less drastic control over provincial legislation with a more restricted use of advice to the Crown to disallow provincial acts. Negotiations between England and Canada were often carried on directly between the two Governments and without the services of the governor-general as intermediary.

Evolution of colonial independence

All these changes gave evidence of the fact that constitutional progress in the direction of greater autonomy was the inevitable result of the introduction of responsible government. In this evolution toward colonial independence the Canadian provinces were leading the Empire. At the same time they continued to function as part of a larger imperial unit. Without these constitutional developments the building of a great, federated Canadian Dominion would have been impossible.

SELECT BIBLIOGRAPHY FOR CHAPTER XV

For detailed treatment of the politics and constitutional developments of the period from 1840 to 1867, the following are valuable: E. KYLIE, "Constitutional Development, 1840–1867," in *Canada and Its Provinces*, vol. V, pp. 103–162; J. L. MORISON, "Parties and Politics, 1840–1867," *Ibid.*, pp. 13–77; and KENNEDY, *The Constitution of Canada*, pp. 249–282. A much briefer account is H. E. EGERTON, *A Historical Geography of the British Dominions*, vol. V, Pt. II, pp. 205–226. O. D. SKELTON, *Life and Times of Sir Alexander Tilloch Galt* (Toronto, 1920) and R. G. TROTTER, *Canadian Federation: Its Origins and Achievement* (Toronto, 1924) also contain valuable chapters on this period. JOHN CHARLES DENT, *The Last Forty Years*, vol. II, gives many interesting details not easily available elsewhere.

CHAPTER XVI

BRITISH NORTH AMERICA AND THE AMERICAN CIVIL WAR

Much of the history of British North America has been determined by fear of the United States or by the example of this larger neighbor to the south. Inevitably the British North American provinces became involved in all controversies between the United States and Great Britain. If such controversies should ever again lead to armed hostilities, Canada would probably become the battle-ground in a war between these great English-speaking peoples. The movement for confederation in British North America was seriously affected by events in the United States during the Civil War period. These incidents were not the sole, nor the most important, cause of confederation, but they were of so serious a nature as to compel both Canadians and Britishers to reflect long and carefully upon the many problems raised by the more or less artificial three-thousand-mile frontier dividing the British dependencies from the American republic. *Neighbor nations*

At the outbreak of the American Civil War the sympathies of the British North Americans were overwhelmingly with the North. The vagaries and technicalities of American constitutional lawyers, both North and South, discoursing at great length concerning the legal rights of the states to secede from the Union, made little impression on the people in British North America. For them, human slavery was the real issue of the conflict. *Uncle Tom's Cabin*, the great propagandist novel of the northern abolitionists, had had a wide circulation in the provinces, several special Canadian editions had been prepared, and the book was translated into French for the people of Quebec. Trade and family connections between British North America and the northern states provided another bond of sympathy. *British North America and slavery*

Lincoln's election in 1860 was viewed with general satisfaction in United Canada, and papers such as George Brown's powerful Toronto *Globe* adopted a strong pro-Northern tone in the early months of 1861. As the war progressed, the United States bought huge supplies of grain and cattle in British North America and the resultant rise in prices created a material prosperity which further strengthened the bond between the provinces and the anti-slavery section of the United States. *Pro-Northern sympathies*

Canada West had first-hand knowledge of the evils and inhumanities of the slave system, for, since early in the nineteenth century she had been the promised land and the haven of refuge which all *Canada and "Underground Railway"* runaway negroes strove to reach. Organizations of abolitionists had developed in the United States, many of their members pious church people, who made it their function to help negro slaves to escape from bondage into the land of freedom to the north. Fugitives were passed from one station to another on what was known as the "Underground Railway," until they were delivered safely on the soil of British North America.

Extinction of slavery in British North American provinces

The first Parliament of Upper Canada prohibited the importation of slaves into the province, and as early as September 28, 1793, provided a system of gradual emancipation for those already in the country. Although slavery was not formally abolished in Lower Canada until the passage of the Imperial Act of 1833, which fixed August 1, 1834, as the date for the emancipation of all slaves in all the British colonies, the slave system had been ended much earlier by a decision of the Court of King's Bench. In the maritime regions climate and soil conditions made the system economically impossible.

Canada's negro population

For years the Canadian provinces had been the destination of the "Underground Railway." In the decade from 1850 to 1860, when the negro population in the United States was especially disturbed by the enactment of a more stringent fugitive slave law, it was estimated that from 15,000 to 20,000 negroes entered United Canada, swelling its total black population to nearly 60,000. Most of these negroes settled along the Detroit River and Lake St. Clair, in the modern counties of Essex and Kent of the province of Ontario. It was along this border that some of the most dramatic incidents were enacted between slave-catchers and negro fugitives in sight of the haven of freedom. Trouble sometimes developed in the Canadian courts when owners tried to have their fugitive slaves returned to them, usually on the plea that they had committed some felony during the escape. At least one of these cases, that of a Missouri negro, Anderson, in 1860 was dragged into Canadian politics, because of an attempt on the part of a British court to exercise jurisdiction in what the Canadians considered a matter of purely local concern. The largest negro refugee colony in Canada West was the Buxton settlement, consisting of some 9000 acres south of Chatham. It is interesting to note that Chatham was selected by John Brown, the fanatical abolitionist who later staged the notorious raid on Harper's Ferry, as the town in which he held a secret convention in May, 1858, to perfect his plans for the forcible freeing of the slaves of the United States.

Employment of negroes

On arriving in Canada the negroes frequently found employment on the railroads which were being developed very rapidly by the middle of the century. In 1851, 2500 negroes found work on the Canada Railway at ten dollars a month pay and board; other companies frequently advertised for negro workmen. Some negroes found employment as farmers and truck-gardeners. A pioneer region like that of western Ontario had little use for barbers, bootblacks, or table-waiters. At the close of the Civil War many Canadian negroes returned to visit their old homes in the South.

The attitude of the Canadian authorities toward the escaped negro was one of welcome and protection. The negro created no special problem in western Canada, either for the provincial or for the local governments. Negroes were urged to take up government lands—they could buy fifty-acre farms at two dollars an acre, paying for them over a ten-year period—and no discrimination was made between black and white purchasers. Fugitive Aid Societies, some Canadian, and some with headquarters in the United States, continued to look after the fugitives during the early stages of their settlement in Canada. Negroes were admitted to citizenship by the provinces on an equal basis with other immigrants, and could vote whenever they could meet the franchise qualifications. Some private schools were opened in the negro sections by religious bodies. Under the Canadian law, negro parents were permitted to send their children to the common schools, or to have separate schools maintained from their share of the school funds. Separate schools were established where prejudice was strong, usually nearest the American border, and it was also in this vicinity that discriminations were sometimes made against negroes in the taverns, on boats, and on juries. The Anti-Slavery Society of Canada, the counterpart of William Lloyd Garrison's American Anti-Slavery Society in the United States, was organized in February, 1851, and counted among its most influential leaders men like Dr. Willis, the Presbyterian principal of Knox College, William McClure, a Methodist minister of some prominence, George Brown of the *Globe*, and Oliver Mowat, later prime minister of the province of Ontario.

Attitude toward negro

Within a few months after the outbreak of war between the United States and the Southern Confederacy, Canada's attitude changed from one of friendliness for the North to one of suspicion, fear, and anger. This was due largely to the strained relations which were developing between the United States and Great Britain out of the latter's attitude and conduct toward the Southern rebels. Into these antagonisms British North America was inevitably drawn.

Change in attitude toward United States

Strained relations began when England issued a proclamation of neutrality—an action which involved the recognition of the South as a government capable of carrying on legal warfare—and accorded to the South the rights of a belligerent power in English ports. President Lincoln had repeatedly insisted that there was no war, but only an "insurrection" of disloyal subjects. The sympathies of the British aristocracy, manufacturers, and governing classes were clearly with the South, although the vulnerability of British North America to attack from the United States undoubtedly served to curb these pro-Southern sentiments somewhat. England was dependent on the cotton supply of the Confederacy for the maintenance of her great textile factories, and it was not long before serious controversies

Anglo-American controversies during Civil War

arose over the naval blockade which Lincoln tried to impose on all Southern ports.

Trent *affair*

In November, 1861, a United States warship stopped a British mail steamer, the *Trent*, on the high seas, and in clear violation of international law took off two Confederate commissioners who were on board, en route from Cuba to England and France. Great Britain at once demanded the release of the prisoners and a disavowal of the act, and dispatched troops to Canada. Canadians were in consternation as they contemplated the results of a possible rupture of Anglo-American relations; steps were taken to call out the Canadian militia. The tension was temporarily relieved when the Confederate prisoners were released and the United States secretary of state penned what amounted to an apology for the action of the American naval commander—a dispatch which was written, as Professor Dunning has put it, "with one eye on the British fleet, the other on the Northern people." The services of President Lincoln, Queen Victoria, and Prince Albert, the royal consort, in overriding the extremists and avoiding a terrible tragedy over the *Trent* affair should never be forgotten. It was a fine bit of irony that Secretary of State Seward actually gave permission to British troops to land in Maine and proceed to their Canadian destination through United States territory because they had arrived too late to pass through the frozen St. Lawrence River.

Jingoism

Another cause of irritation to the people of British North America was the jingoistic attitude of some of the United States newspapers. A number of ardent champions of the anti-slavery cause in the United States shrank in horror from the possibilities of war with their Southern brethren. Some advised a policy of non-resistance toward the Secessionists, while others preferred the familiar device of starting trouble with some foreign power in order to heal the internal sectional wounds by a glorious appeal to a common patriotism. During the presidential campaign of 1860 William H. Seward, later secretary of state under Lincoln, had publicly advocated the annexation of Canada to offset such losses to the Union as might result from the secession of the South, and Lord Lyons, the British Ambassador at Washington, was sufficiently alarmed by these statements to make them the subject of a special communication to Sir Edmund Head, governor-general of Canada. As the first member of his cabinet, Seward had also advised President Lincoln to adopt a vigorous, not to say provocative, foreign policy, against England, France, and other countries, as a means of reuniting the North and South.

American newspapers

Early in 1861 so influential a paper as the New York *Herald* was frankly discussing the possibility of setting up two American confederacies, the Southern to expand to the south, and the Northern to round out its territory by the annexation of Canada. "The Canadians have long been panting for more freedom than they can enjoy under British rule," so ran the argument in one of the most stupid *Herald*

editorials. Other papers in New York City, Utica, Buffalo, and elsewhere repeated these sentiments. Blustering bravado of this kind
only provoked bitter retorts from the Canadian press, even from
that portion which had originally been most friendly to the Washington government.

Another serious difficulty arose between the United States and
Canada from the presence of a large and active group of Confederate *Confederate*
refugees, who found security on Canadian soil, and used that security *refugees in*
to launch intrigues and foolhardy attacks upon Northern border- *Canada*
towns. It was extremely irritating to the United States that, by 1863,
some of these Confederate refugees were actually being welcomed
and dined by a small pro-Southern group in Toronto and Montreal.

Around the person of Jacob Thompson, who had served in Presi-
dent Buchanan's cabinet, a Confederate secret service and propaganda *Border outrages*
organization was built up; Thompson and his colleagues financed
various foolhardy ventures, such as the burning of ships on the Great
Lakes, and on the Mississippi and Ohio Rivers. In September, 1864,
Confederate refugees seized a steamer running on Lake Erie, planning
to release the Confederate prisoners on Johnson's Island, near Sandusky, Ohio, and to raid various lake cities. The expedition was a
complete fiasco. A month later several dozen Confederate ex-soldiers
raided the town of St. Albans, Vermont, plundered three banks,
carried off much loot, and killed a bystander. A Canadian judge refused, on technical grounds, to extradite the prisoners to the United
States for trial, while in Montreal several prisoners were freed on the
ground that they were acting under the orders of their government
and were entitled to the status of belligerents. The closing months of
1864 witnessed much excitement in Detroit and Chicago; it was
rumored that a great plot had been formed to free the prisoners near
Chicago and to stage great demonstrations on the day President Lincoln was up for re-election. At least $75,000 was spent in organizing
peace meetings in Illinois.

It is needless to discuss these absurd ventures in greater detail.
Their psychological effect upon both the American people and the *Effects*
British North Americans is evident. The border was kept in a constant
state of excitement, and friendly relations between the United States
and British North America were difficult to maintain. The enlistment
of some 40,000 Canadians in the Union armies did little to relieve
the situation.

It may be added that the governments in British North America
maintained a policy of scrupulous neutrality throughout the war, and *Neutrality of*
transmitted confidential information of Confederate plots to the *governments*
American government through the British minister at Washington. *of British*
The Canadian authorities repeatedly refused to sell arms and munitions *North America*
to Northern states such as Illinois, Ohio, Massachusetts, and New
York, which tried to buy supplies directly from the government.
Thompson, the head of the Confederate agents in Canada, personally

testified that "the bane and curse of carrying out anything in this country is the surveillance under which we act." On the other hand, some recruiting officers from the Northern states developed a system of "crimping" by which they secured men in Canada for military service through methods that were underhand and illegal. The bounties offered for recruits by some Northern states attracted many Canadians across the border, and at one period of the war the three leading Roman Catholic bishops of Canada East issued letters to their parish clergy, urging them to warn their flocks against enlisting in the United States army.

Anglo-American relations at close of war

The close of the Civil War left Anglo-American affairs in a critical state. Most Northerners were convinced that Great Britain had pursued a pro-Southern policy, and that the war had been unnecessarily prolonged by the hope of the South to secure British recognition and support. The most serious outstanding dispute involved the building of Confederate cruisers in British navy yards during the war. Some of these ships, notably the *Alabama* and the *Florida*, had played havoc with Northern shipping.

Alabama claims

The United States government contended that Great Britain had failed to exercise due diligence in safeguarding her neutrality, and that she could therefore be held liable for compensation to the extent of damage done by these Confederate cruisers to American commerce during the war. Senator Charles Sumner of Massachusetts, chairman of the powerful Senate committee on foreign relations, piled up an enormous bill of damages which he insisted the United States should collect from Great Britain. Sumner hinted that the annexation of British North America might prove an easy means of settlement. Exaggerated statements were made on both sides, and the controversy remained a dangerous issue between the two nations until England finally paid the United States damages of $15,500,000 as a result of an arbitration provided for by the Treaty of Washington in 1871.

Anti-British feeling in United States

Largely because of this anti-British sentiment in the United States, the Elgin Reciprocity Treaty was cancelled in 1866. The disarmament agreement of 1817 on the Great Lakes was also abrogated by the United States, but sober reflection brought about its renewal in 1865. The United States Secretary of the Navy called for additional ships to patrol the international waterways between Canada and the United States, and the Secretary of State began to demand passports from all Canadian immigrants. Senator Sumner's speech on the Alabama claims, in which he made a bitter arraignment of British policy during the war, had the approval of President Grant and most of the United States Congress. The same senator favored the purchase of Alaska by the United States in 1867, because it would "set a watchful Yankee on each side of John Bull in his far-western Canadian possessions," and because it would "drive one more monarch from this continent." The suggestion that it would next be the turn of the English monarch to evacuate North America, hardly requires further elucidation.

One more dangerous incident resulted from the war and served to complicate Canadian-American relations. In some respects, this was the most immediately troublesome of all of the post-war issues. *Fenian Brotherhood* Thousands of Irish-Americans in the United States, organized under the name of the Fenian Brotherhood, decided to take advantage of the hostile attitude of most Americans toward Great Britain as a result of the Civil War for the purpose of launching a movement which should bring freedom and independence to their native Ireland. A revolt in Ireland having been ruthlessly suppressed by Great Britain, the Fenians conceived the foolhardy idea of doing something for Ireland by twisting the tail of the British lion in Canada. Many Fenians were veterans of the Civil War, anxious to put their military experience to good use in Canada. A convention of the organization was held at Cincinnati, Ohio, in 1865; here an Irish republic was created, on paper, with a set of officials composed largely of Irish-American officers of the war. Bonds were sold and elaborate plans were made for the advance on Canada. It was optimistically assumed in many quarters that the Canadians would rise against their British governors as soon as the Fenians had occupied a corner of Canadian territory, and that the United States government would thereupon formally recognize the new republican government of Canada. If war with England followed, so much the better.

On June 1, 1866, the hosts of Fenianism—which had been assembling on the Niagara frontier for several weeks—advanced upon Canada fifteen hundred strong. They seized the Canadian village of *Invasion of Canada* Fort Erie, threw up entrenchments, and issued a proclamation to the Canadian people. The American secretary of state waited five days before he issued a proclamation to guard the neutrality of the United States—a delay which may have been caused by his fear of antagonizing the Irish-American vote in the United States, or by a desire to impress upon England the necessity of settling the claims arising from the Civil War.

Several engagements took place on Canadian territory. The Canadians rallied heartily to the defense of their native soil against these *Battling with invaders* foreign agitators, and soon forced the Fenians to retreat to the United States. Hundreds were arrested by the United States authorities, but eventually were paroled and returned to their homes at the expense of the United States government. A similar raid across the Vermont border by New England Irishmen also ended in failure. The president of the "Irish Republic," Colonel W. R. Roberts, was arrested on a charge of organizing a conspiracy and of violating the United States neutrality laws. In 1870 another attack, for which careful preparations had been made in secret, was launched on the Vermont border, but both United States and Canadian authorities had been warned in advance and were on the alert for the invaders.

The leader, General O'Neil, was finally sentenced to six months' imprisonment in the United States. During this period of strained relations it was extremely fortunate that the Canadian authorities were wise enough not to inflict the death penalty on such Fenians as happened to fall into their hands. The last flurry of Fenian excitement occurred in 1871, when it was charged that some Irish-Americans were plotting to give aid to the rebellious Indian and half-breed population in the Canadian Red River country.

Canada's claims for indemnity

The Canadian government in 1871, during the negotiation of the Treaty of Washington, which was designed to provide the means of settlement for all outstanding Anglo-American disputes, tried to include a section which should provide compensation and damages to Canada for losses incurred during the Fenian movement. England, however, anxious to bring about a settlement of other points which were considered more significant, refused to support the Canadian position, and the Canadian envoys had to drop the matter.

Fear of United States

The effect of these incidents during the Civil War and the period of disagreement which followed was tremendous on the public opinion of both Canada and Great Britain. The United States emerged from the Civil War a great military power, with a large army of veterans, and with a national spirit that seemed to outsiders more militaristic than ever. In the picturesque language of the Irish-Canadian, Thomas D'Arcy McGee, "That shot fired at Fort Sumter (the opening engagement of the Civil War) was the signal gun of a new epoch for North America, which told the people of Canada, more plainly than human speech can express it, to sleep no more except on their arms." In the strained relations which characterized post-war Anglo-American diplomacy, and in such border troubles as the Fenian disturbances, the people of British North America discovered the need for a consolidation of their strength, for in the event of war between England and the United States, Canada and New Brunswick would become the battle-ground. The common dangers faced during these years did much to develop a spirit of greater unity among the British North Americans; spokesmen of the French party, such as Cartier and Langevin, spoke quite as excitedly about the dangers of annexation by the United States as did their contemporaries in the essentially English provinces.

Problem of defense

England, likewise, suddenly awoke to the British North American problem of defense, particularly as it involved the vast and undeveloped West beyond modern Ontario. This region was still the great hunting-ground of the fur trader and the Indian; it was not under the jurisdiction or control of the Canadian provincial government. It was a debatable question whether the region extending westward to the Pacific coast should remain part of British North America, or whether the lusty giant nation to the south might not ignore the artificial international line fixed by diplomats to pour its immigrants out on the British-American prairies as they were at that time overrunning the great American Northwest. British Columbia, separated from the rest of British North America by hundreds of miles of virgin forest and rolling prairie, already was being drawn within the economic orbit of San Francisco. The psychological effect of this state of affairs was to make both Canadians and Britishers seriously ponder the development of a great British North American federation, which should consolidate the latent powers of the existing provinces and make it possible to face the problems of the future with a united strength and a common program.

Finally, it was not only fear of the United States, but also the example of the United States, which affected the development of the federation movement in British North America. During three-quarters of a century this region had been the immediate neighbor of the world's greatest experiment in federalism. The success of that experiment was, to be sure, temporarily clouded by the Civil War, and a policy of "blood and iron" was necessary to determine whether this federal state could survive the shock of Secessionist theories; but the American experiment weathered the crisis of war and embarked on a new period of even greater national unity. To the Canadian observer it seemed that the Secessionist controversy was in a large measure due to a defect in the United States Constitution, by which the central government was given limited and specifically delegated powers, and all the residue of governmental powers was left vaguely to the individual states, and to the people. Therefore, when British North America prepared her plan of federation she reversed the situation. The Canadian provincial governments received specifically defined powers, but all the residue of legislative power, whether or not stated in the instrument of government, was reserved for the Dominion government. Thus the experiences of the United States during the Secessionist controversy not only affected the confederation movement as such, but helped to determine the form which Canadian federation should take. Unhappily, the Canadian courts soon worked havoc with this distribution of legislative powers.

Example of American federalism

SELECT BIBLIOGRAPHY FOR CHAPTER XVI

The field of Canadian-American relations during the Civil War is still comparatively unworked by the scholars of Canada and the United States alike. The only sizable monograph is HELEN G. MacDONALD, *Canadian Public Opinion on the American Civil War* (New York, 1926), *Columbia University Studies in History, Economics and Public Law*, vol. CXXIV. Pages 224–232 contain a detailed bibliography.

The best detailed study of the operations of the "Underground Railway" is that of W. H. SIEBERT, *The Underground Railway* (New York, 1899). Mr. Fred Landon and Justice William Renwick Riddell have written many articles dealing with the negro in Canada. These have been published in various places, such as *Ontario Historical Society Papers*, and the *Journal of Negro History*. Mr. Landon has published a valuable bibliography of the negro in Canada in the *Ontario Historical Society Papers and Records* (Toronto, 1925), vol. XXII, pp. 18–20.

The following papers, dealing with Canadian experiences during the Civil War, can be found in *The Canadian Historical Review:* FRED LANDON, "Canadian Opinion of Southern Secession, 1860," vol. I, September, 1920; FRED LANDON, "The Trent Affair of 1861," vol. III, March, 1922; WILFRED BOVEY, "Confederate Agents in Canada during the American Civil War," vol. II, March, 1921. W. F. RANEY, "Recruiting and Crimping in Canada for the Northern Forces, 1861–1865," in *The Mississippi Valley Historical Review*, vol. X, pp. 21–33, is a study of the activities of Northern recruiting officers along the Canadian border. See also, T. C. BLEGEN, "A Plan for the Union of British North America and the United States, 1866," in *The Mississippi Historical Review*, March, 1918; J. M. CALLAHAN, "The Northern Lake Frontier during the Civil War," in *American Historical Association Report*, 1896; and R. G. TROTTER, "Some American Influences upon the Canadian Federation Movement," in *The Canadian Historical Review*, vol. V, September, 1924.

For the Fenian raids, see JOHN A. MACDONALD, *Troublous Times in Canada* (Toronto, 1910), and CLYDE L. KING, "The Fenian Movement," in *University of Colorado Studies*, vol. VI, No. 3, p. 187.

CHAPTER XVII

CONFEDERATION

By 1864 political conditions in Canada had reached the stage of deadlock, and the legislative Union of Canada East and Canada West thus ended in failure. Government, theoretically based on "double-majorities" and double-headed cabinets from the two divisions, became so unstable that it functioned only with the greatest difficulty. It proved impossible to dispel the prejudices of race and religion which divided the French and the English elements. The average life of ministries was now six months, and even these Governments clung to their lease of power by slender majorities of from one to three votes. Each section, under the system of equal representation, was able to veto the demands of the other; public works were halted because of this unseemly competition, and the general stagnation which ensued gave new stimulation to the heavy Canadian exodus to the United States. *Political deadlock*

The "Clear Grits" under Brown were clamoring for "Rep. by Pop.," a change in the Union Act which French Canada was prepared to oppose to the last. The inequities of the taxation system afforded another argument for these Upper-Canadian reformers, for most of the funds for the Union government were raised through a system of indirect taxation, by which Canada West paid virtually three-fourths of the cost of government for the united provinces. The controversy over internal improvements, separate schools, and alleged Roman Catholic dominance in Canadian affairs reached a stage in which discussion gave place to extremely bitter and abusive personal attacks. The fear and the example of the United States were factors in promoting confederation, while the problem of the West, the *Canada Irredenta* of this period, was calling for solution. Settlers were beginning to enter the western prairie lands; a vigorous governmental policy was necessary to deal with the many problems which this advance of the frontier raised, particularly with the Indian and half-breed population, and with the Hudson's Bay Company. French Canada, however, persistently blocked all proposals to effect a settlement with the Hudson's Bay Company in order to extinguish the claims of that corporation to the West, for westward expansion would have meant territorial aggrandizement for the English section of Canada. *Problems to be solved*

Intimately related to political federation was the need for railroads to unite the isolated provinces of British North America. The maritime provinces were virtually isolated from the rest of Canada, *Need of railroads*

179

and hostile customs duties, coupled with the lack of common standards of currency, banking, and weights and measures, served as barriers to the development of better commercial intercourse. An inter-colonial railway was imperatively necessary, simply to provide a physical bond between the provinces, and also because so many of the railroads of the United States were approaching the Canadian border.

Railway promoters and confederation

The most prominent intermediary between the railroad promoters and the politicians of British North America and the home government was Edward W. Watkin, an associate of the banking houses of Glyns and Barings, and an official of the Grand Trunk Railway. By organizing semi-official excursions to various parts of the provinces, and carrying politicians free on these trips, Watkin subtly convinced them of the need of more railroads, and promoted a better understanding among the leaders of the isolated provinces. Such a project as a great transcontinental railroad could of course be carried out only by combining the resources of all of British North America.

Federation— a minority proposal

Federation, when it came, was not the result of the demand of the majority of the Canadian people. It was the work of a small minority of leaders, "inspired by wide political vision, actuated by economic interest, stimulated by dangers of foreign aggression." It could not have been accomplished had not responsible government already been a reality in British North America and had not England renounced her old commercial policy by which the trade of the colonies had been fettered in the interest of the Empire. As has been shown, responsible government had been achieved in all of British North America except British Columbia shortly after 1849. Confederation was peculiar in the further respect that it is the only case on record to that time in which a group of colonies practically remade their own constitution in an absolutely peaceful way.

Pioneers of confederation

Many pioneers in the field of practical politics for years had urged federation as a solution for British North American problems, perhaps as early as 1783. Among earlier advocates of the movement the names of Guy Carleton, Chief Justice William Smith, and Lord Durham should not be overlooked. Federation was first proposed in the Canadian Parliament by W. H. Merritt in 1851; and in 1856 by A. A. Dorion, of Canada East, as a result of a conference with Alexander T. Galt, the most influential representative of the English minority in the province. But after all, as Professor Skelton has pointed out, the idea of confederation "might occur to any politician of imagination with a map before him and the example of the United States in his mind."

The Brown— Macdonald coalition

In the spring of 1864 affairs in the Union Parliament of Canada reached another impasse. This time, instead of calling new elections, Lord Monck, the new governor-general, suggested a coalition Government, in which Macdonald and his political enemy, Brown, should divide the leadership. Brown had previously moved the appointment of a committee to study the recommendations made by Galt, Cartier, and others in 1858, by which what really amounted to a plan of confederation had been communicated to the British colonial secretary. At that time, however, the mother-country had been cold and indifferent to the suggestion. Brown now intimated his willingness to coöperate with the Government in an effort to settle forever the constitutional difficulties which seemed to make further progress impossible. Galt and Macdonald formally called upon the leader of the "Grits," old party animosities were patched up as well as possible, a memorandum was drawn up pledging the Government to work out, if possible, a plan for the confederation of all the British North American provinces, and certainly for the two Canadas. Delegations were to be sent to England and to the other provinces to get their coöperation. Brown then entered a coalition ministry with Macdonald, his life-long enemy. As a necessary concession, three places in the cabinet were given to the Brown faction.

The new coalition was a tribute to the patriotism of George Brown. For him it meant the virtual wrecking of a party of which he had served as leader for many years, and the acceptance of an inferior position under Macdonald, a personal enemy whose principles he distrusted. Brown's conduct, moreover, meant an entirely new alignment in Canadian political life. Later, when the main purpose of the coalition had been accomplished, Brown resigned his irksome place in the Government, and the two leaders resumed their old positions and "ceased to speak." *Brown's patriotism*

The first definite steps toward confederation were initiated, however, in the maritime provinces. For many years the advantages of a maritime union had been under serious consideration. Union here, after all, involved only the undoing of the disruption of 1784, when old Acadia had been divided into three parts. The movement in the provinces by the sea sprang, not from a breakdown or deadlock in the government, but from a keen realization of the handicaps of isolation, the need for an inter-colonial railway, the removal of tariff barriers, and other advantages which might come from a pooling of resources. Perhaps also the two giants of Nova Scotian politics, Joseph Howe and his younger rival, Dr. Charles Tupper, were seeking a larger arena for the display of their political talents. *Movement for union in maritime provinces*

In 1863 Howe and the Liberals were driven from power in Nova Scotia. The new prime minister, Dr. Tupper, after having received the assurance of the British Colonial Office that there would be no interference from the mother-country, arranged for the calling of a convention of delegates from the maritime provinces to meet in Charlottetown, in September, 1864, in order to consider plans for a legislative union. Practically identical resolutions were adopted in New Brunswick, under the leadership of prime minister, Samuel Leonard Tilley, and in Prince Edward Island, where the people wanted less taxation and a chance to unload the railroad debts of *Call for Charlottetown convention* the province on a larger governmental unit, under the leadership of William Henry Pope.

Work of convention

The Charlottetown convention soon discovered that plans involving only such a small area as the three Atlantic provinces were exceedingly difficult to carry out to the satisfaction of all concerned. The deliberations were interrupted at an early stage by the arrival of a delegation of eight members from United Canada who had previously received permission from the maritime delegates to attend their conference. The Canadian delegation pledged support to the Charlottetown plans and urged the possibility of including all British North America in a plan of federation.

Delegation from Canada

The Canadian delegation consisted of Brown, Macdonald, Galt, McGee, Cartier, Hector Louis Langevin, William McDougall, and Alexander Campbell. They were cordially received and royally banqueted at Halifax and St. John, while the Grand Trunk Railway arranged a free junketing trip for the party and attending newspapermen through the maritime region. The exchange of felicitations on these occasions did much to pave the way for a successful scheme of confederation. Macdonald, Cartier, Galt, and Brown made the most important addresses at these festivities. Galt discussed the financial aspect of union, Brown dealt with the organization, powers, and work of the federal legislature, and Macdonald, a firm advocate of a strong central government, discussed the general framework of government. The work of these men stands out above the rest in constructive greatness. Thomas D'Arcy McGee, a brilliant Irish-Canadian poet, journalist, and orator, became the "Mazzini of Canadian nationalism" and in Parliament and on the lecture platform used his picturesque oratory to proclaim the new gospel of "one great nationality bound, like the shield of Achilles, by the blue rim of ocean."

Call for Quebec Conference

The Charlottetown convention, in secret sessions, agreed on a popularly elected Lower House and a system of equal representation in an Upper House. It adjourned to Halifax and St. John, and finally postponed further deliberations until a conference of all the British North American provinces could be arranged to meet at Quebec in the following month.

Quebec Conference

The Quebec convention assembled on October 10 and adjourned on October 28. Its actual working time did not exceed fourteen days and its sessions were held behind closed doors. Thirty-three members constituted this constitutional convention, the first in the history of the British Empire. United Canada was represented by twelve delegates, five came from Nova Scotia, seven from New Brunswick, and an equal number from Prince Edward Island, and two from Newfoundland. Voting was by provinces, each province having one vote, except Canada, which had two.

Fathers of confederation

Among the most important leaders in the convention was Alexander T. Galt, who occupied a strategic position as the representative of the English minority in French Canada, and who in 1858 had introduced the confederation idea as an issue of practical politics. Galt coupled the proposal for federation with the problem of westward expansion, and it was he who really converted Georges E. Cartier, the French leader of Canada East, to the project. The latter, in turn, undertook the difficult task of converting his fellow racials to an acceptance of the new plan of government, and became the prophet of a new Canadian nationalism. William McDougall, another important member, had long manifested a great interest in the opening of the West, and he particularly stressed this advantage of confederation. McGee did yeoman service in trying to effect a reconciliation between Catholics and Protestants, but his greatest achievement was the passionate and eloquent speeches in which he later argued for ratification of the Quebec resolutions in the Canadian Parliament. It was eminently fitting that his last speech in the Dominion Parliament, before he was struck down by the bullet of an assassin, was in defense of the Union, and an effort to keep Nova Scotia from seceding from the Confederation. Sir Etienne Taché served as chairman of the convention, and Hewitt Bernard acted as executive secretary. The latter performed in a small degree a service to posterity very similar to James Madison's in the United States Constitutional Convention, by keeping careful notes in long-hand of the proceedings of the secret meetings. Years afterwards, these notes were found among the papers of John A. Macdonald and published. Important notes by A. A. Macdonald, a delegate from Prince Edward Island, have also been discovered and made available to students of the convention. It is a significant fact that John A. Macdonald was really the last to be converted to the necessity of confederation, and that even in the Quebec convention he tried to secure a legislative union instead of a federation—a solution that was utterly impractical at the time. Opportunistic to the last, Macdonald nevertheless displayed his unusual quality of managing men in the convention and in the critical controversy over ratification which followed. Macdonald, Galt, Brown, Cartier, McGee, Tupper of Nova Scotia, and Tilley of New Brunswick were "the Big Seven" whose leadership made confederation possible. One of the giants of British North American politics was conspicuously absent, and his absence involved important consequences. Joseph Howe, who had for years been preaching the gospel of closer union and an inter-colonial railway, was invited by Tupper to serve as a delegate from Nova Scotia at Charlottetown. He declined the appointment because his duties as fisheries commissioner under the Reciprocity Treaty of 1854 took him away on his regular cruise of inspection. At the time, however, he promised his coöperation "in carrying out any measures upon which the Conference shall agree."

The results of the Quebec conference were incorporated in seventy-two resolutions which became the basis of the British North America *Quebec* Act of 1867. These the delegates promised to get their respective *resolutions* legislatures to ratify. In many respects the resolutions of the Quebec conference correspond with the detailed proposals which Galt had made in 1858. The Quebec resolutions recommended a federal union of all the British North American provinces under the British Crown. They provided for a federal government, and for provincial governments in each of the provinces, and proceeded to enumerate the powers and duties of the federal and the provincial legislatures, leaving all the undefined residue, or "reserved powers," to the federal government. The federal Parliament was to consist of a Lower House based on population, and an appointive Upper House or Senate. With reference to the Senate, Canada was considered as comprising three divisions—Ontario and Quebec, with the maritime provinces of Nova Scotia and New Brunswick constituting the third. Each division was to be represented by twenty-four senators, those from the maritime section to be divided equally between Nova Scotia and New Brunswick. Only Prince Edward Island supported the American idea of equal representation in the Senate for all members of the Confederation, large or small. The central government was given the right to disallow provincial measures, and the federal ministry could appoint and dismiss the lieutenant-governors of the provinces. Provision was made for the preservation of the British connection by retaining the governor-general, and of course the system of appeal to the Privy Council from the colonial courts, based on old British Acts, was in no way affected by the confederation proposals. The details of the British North America government and of the present government of the Dominion of Canada must be reserved for a later chapter. It is significant that in the Act the word "dominion" was substituted for "kingdom" of Canada because the British minister for foreign affairs, in those gloomy days of Anglo-American misunderstanding, feared that the word kingdom would "wound the sensibilities of the Yankees." In any case, these names were better than Laurentia, Cabotia, Ursalia or Septentrionalia, all of which had been proposed for the new combination of British provinces.

Financial terms

Important financial arrangements also had to be made in order to secure the adherence of some of the delegates to these confederation proposals. For example, the bankers of Prince Edward Island were extremely anxious to unload the burden of their railroad bonds on the new Dominion government; the provincial government wanted to avoid unpopular increases in taxation for these internal improvements. In the past the maritime provinces had depended entirely on taxation levied by the provincial governments, for even the support of clearly municipal enterprises. In exchange for the customs duties, which the provinces now surrendered, it was agreed in the Quebec convention that the dominion treasury should grant annually to each province a sum equal to eighty cents per capita of population, as determined by the census of 1861, and that these federal subsidies should be paid six months in advance. In addition, the debts of the provinces, up to a specified amount, were to be assumed by the new federal government, and each province was to receive a specific contribution for the support of its provincial government. This federal subsidy which was compensation for the surrender of the provincial right to levy customs duties, also served as an additional bond of union by increasing the financial dependence of the provinces upon the central government. From time to time it has been necessary to increase these subsidies and debt allowances in the case of some of the provinces.

The battle over ratification began in earnest when the seventy-two resolutions of the Quebec convention were submitted, *en bloc*, to the respective legislatures. Macdonald dispatched Brown to London to sound out the British government on these proposals, and early in 1865 he introduced a resolution in the Parliament of United Canada praying the Queen to ask the British Parliament for a law incorporating the Quebec Resolutions. Macdonald again revealed his powers of leadership and debate in this controversy over ratification. The opponents of confederation, led by A. A. Dorion, Christopher Dunkin, and John Sandfield Macdonald, criticized the Quebec convention for its hasty action, and pointed out many defects in its work. Some argued that confederation was a step toward independence, others demanded an elective Senate. It was suggested that since the Senate did not follow the American plan of equality for each constituent province it would be inevitable that the executive or cabinet of the federation would be formed on a sectional basis. As a matter of fact, this turned out to be a true forecast of one of the weakest elements in the Canadian federal executive system. The Dominion has never had a cabinet representing the best talents available to the prime minister. During the debate there was much opposition to the financial terms of the settlement, and to the pledge to build an intercolonial railroad. Some criticized the division of powers between the central and the provincial governments; some believed that the federal government would become too powerful, and others expressed the fear of being overwhelmed by the rising tide of French nationalism. There was also a demand for a popular referendum on the whole plan of federation, and this was supported by the claim that the entire scheme had been concocted by politicians in the face of quite widespread apathy among the Canadian people.

Contest over ratification

After a long and exhaustive discussion in which the whole political and economic life of Canada was subjected to close scrutiny, with many a squint at the United States, the Parliament of United Canada ratified the Quebec Resolutions by a vote of ninety-one to thirty-three in the assembly, and forty-five to fifteen in the legislative council.

United Canada ratifies

In the maritime provinces confederation struck unexpected obstacles. In New Brunswick the Opposition raised the bogey of being taxed to support Canada and denounced the federationists

Action of maritime provinces

for selling the New Brunswickers "to the Canadians for eighty cents a head." In the general election, of an assembly of forty-one members, only six supporters of federation were returned. Prince Edward Island rejected the Quebec Resolutions outright, the legislative council unanimously, and the assembly by a vote of twenty-three to five. In Newfoundland the commercial interests were alarmed by the likelihood of higher duties under confederation, and in 1868 the electors of the island declared decisively in favor of a policy of isolation. For all of the maritime provinces confederation seemed to involve a leap into the dark, and the possibility of a higher tariff and larger debts.

Contest in Nova Scotia

In Nova Scotia, Tupper and Howe engaged in a great political duel over confederation—a contest in which Howe had the sympathy of the governor. Howe denounced the "Botheration Scheme," as he called the Quebec conference, with all of the vehement eloquence with which he had once advocated closer union. He appealed to the intense provincial patriotism of the Nova Scotians by warning them that their country would soon swarm with Canadian political tricksters, that confederation would mean higher tariffs and the adoption of a protective tariff policy, and that in every way a legislative union of the maritime provinces would be superior to the impractical plan of federation. Howe also pointed out that federation might arouse the suspicion of the United States and cause trouble on Nova Scotia's exposed frontier. As a matter of fact, confederation was discussed in the United States Congress, and the legislature of Maine called the attention of the federal government at Washington to the establishment of a new form of monarchical government in Canada.

Howe versus Tupper

In all of Howe's arguments, which for the most part were no doubt sincere, one cannot fail to note the spirit of egotism, Howe's greatest failing. It was hard for him to play second fiddle to his younger rival, Tupper, in a matter of such tremendous significance to his province. When New Brunswick rejected confederation, Tupper decided to fall back for the time being upon the proposal of a legislative union of the maritime provinces. Howe carried the first election after confederation, and set out for England to continue the fight there. In the end, however, Tupper defeated his opponent by using Howe's own earlier speeches against him, while Macdonald convinced him that he was fighting for a lost cause. In 1869 Howe entered Macdonald's cabinet as part of a bargain by which he gained better financial terms for his province. His great career ended in 1873. At the time of his death he was serving as lieutenant-governor of his beloved Nova Scotia.

Attitude of Great Britain

It was in the face of these discouragements in the maritime region that a Canadian delegation, of which Macdonald, Cartier, and Galt were the most important members, and a maritime delegation on which were Tupper of Nova Scotia and Tilley of New Brunswick, set out for England, in November, 1866, to frame the details of a bill incorporating the Quebec Resolutions and such changes as the struggle over ratification had made necessary. Resolutions were drawn with the aid of the law officers of the Crown and submitted to the secretary of state. Again it was the genius of Macdonald which harmonized the various prejudices and local interests of the delegates. The British government was, on the whole, quite apathetic. Men like Gladstone and John Bright were considering the proposal of ceding Canada to the United States, in order to avoid further trouble. Many British Liberals believed that the ultimate destiny of Canada was independence, and that no obstacle should be placed in the way of her achieving this destiny as soon as possible. In the words of Professor Kennedy, the Dominion of Canada was "born in a period of mid-Victorian gloom."

Meanwhile, sentiment in the maritime provinces was becoming more favorable to ratification of the plan of federation. Upon direct pressure from the home government, the lieutenant-governor of New Brunswick became reconciled to confederation, and, after a dissolution, Tilley obtained a majority authorizing progress with the plans for federation. Under Tupper's leadership Nova Scotia too swung into line in April, 1866—although a great battle still had to be fought with Howe over the attempt to repeal Nova Scotia's action. *Change of sentiment in maritime provinces*

The British North America Act was passed by the British Parliament in 1867 without a division at any stage of its consideration, with as little interest as if it "were a private bill uniting two or three English parishes." It was substantially unchanged from the proposals presented by the Canadian delegates. A royal proclamation announced July 1, 1867, as the official birthday of the new Dominion of Canada. Simultaneously, a bill was passed guaranteeing £3,000,000 for an inter-colonial railroad. When the British North America Act went into operation, the Dominion consisted of only four provinces— Quebec, Ontario, New Brunswick, and Nova Scotia. *British North America Act of 1867*

At the time of the Confederation all of British North America had a population of 3,500,000, of whom over four-fifths were native born. Most of the population lived east of the Great Lakes. The population of the vast region west of the lakes did not exceed 100,000. There were nine cities in the new Dominion with a population over 10,000. Montreal, with 100,000 people, was the metropolis of Canada, Quebec had grown to 60,000, and Toronto to 50,000. The region beyond Ontario was a wilderness dotted by Hudson's Bay Company posts, and a sea of prairie grass where the American buffalo still roamed in great herds. British Columbia was in its infancy and was an almost unknown Pacific province isolated from the rest of Canada by hundreds of miles of unoccupied land. Ontario was the most progressive of the provinces, with a system of small-scale farming and dairying like that of the middle-western states of the United States. Land sold as low as fifty cents an acre, and the government was greatly interested in a vigorous immigration policy which should extend the Canadian farming frontier toward the Pacific Ocean. *Status of provinces in 1867*

Farming methods had changed little in French Quebec, while the maritime provinces were suffering from a lack of capital and a general depression.

Economic strength

The total lumber exports of the provinces were valued at $14,-000,000 a year, while the fisheries yielded $4,000,000. In Nova Scotia and British Columbia the mining of coal had been begun, but most of Canada's mineral resources were still undeveloped, largely because of a lack of capital. Efforts were being made to develop home manufacturing in order to absorb the country's raw materials, and Montreal was fast becoming the center for the boot and shoe industry, while in Ontario considerable progress had been made in the development of woolen mills. The lack of transportation facilities remained one of Canada's great handicaps.

Confederation raised high hopes for the future. The years of great promise seemed just ahead.

SELECT BIBLIOGRAPHY FOR CHAPTER XVII

The best account of the confederation movement is R. G. Trotter, *Canadian Federation: Its Origins and Achievements: A Study in Nation Building* (Toronto, 1924). Pages 321–332 contain a detailed bibliography. The discussion in Kennedy, *The Constitution of Canada*, pp. 283–321, is excellent. Vol. V of *Canada and its Provinces* contains articles by various authors dealing with the history of the period from 1840 to 1867. A good smaller volume is A. H. U. Colquhoun, *The Fathers of Confederation* (Toronto, 1921) in *Chronicles of Canada;* another important volume is R. E. Gosnell, *The Story of Confederation* (Victoria, 1918).

Many biographies are useful for this period. Among these may be listed: Isabel Skelton, *The Life of Thomas D'Arcy McGee* (Gardenvale, 1925), and Alexander Brady, *Thomas D'Arcy McGee* (Toronto, 1925), a volume in the *Canadian Statesmen* series, edited by W. S. Wallace; E. M. Saunders, *The Life and Letters of Right Honorable Sir Charles Tupper*, 2 vols. (New York, 1916), and Tupper's *Recollections of Sixty Years* (Toronto, 1914); John Boyd, *Sir Georges Etienne Cartier, His Life and Times* (Toronto, 1917); Alexander Mackenzie, *The Life and Speeches of Honorable George Brown* (Toronto, 1882); John Lewis, *George Brown* (Toronto, 1910); O. D. Skelton, *Life and Times of Sir Alexander Tilloch Galt* (Toronto, 1920); W. L. Grant, *The Tribune of Nova Scotia* (Toronto, 1921) in *Chronicles of Canada*, a life of Howe; J. A. Chisholm, *Speeches and Public Letters of Joseph Howe* (Halifax, 1909); Sir Joseph Pope, *The Day of Sir John Macdonald* (Toronto, 1914) in *Chronicles of Canada*, and *Correspondence of Sir John Macdonald* (Toronto, 1921) and *Memoirs of the Rt. Hon. Sir John Alexander Macdonald*, 2 vols. (Ottawa, 1895), by the same author, and G. M. Adam, *The Life and Career of Rt. Hon. Sir John A. Macdonald* (Toronto, 1891). In the *Makers of Canada* series, the following are notable: G. R. Parkin, *Sir John Macdonald;* A. D. DeCelles, *Sir Georges Cartier;* J. Hannay, *Sir Leonard Tilley,* and J. W. Longley, *Sir Charles Tupper.* In 1926 the Oxford University Press, under the editorship of W. L. Grant, issued a new and revised edition of *The Makers of Canada* series, in 12 volumes. This set contains numerous additions and revisions which make it a great improvement over the earlier edition published by G. N. Morang. The new *Dictionary of Canadian Biography* (Toronto, 1926), edited by W. S. Wallace, contains brief and accurate sketches.

For fuller bibliography, see Trotter, *Syllabus*, pp. 120–125.

CHAPTER XVIII

THE GOVERNMENT OF CANADA

THE British North America Act created a federal system of government in which every effort was made to avoid friction between the *Nature of* sphere of functions and powers left to the provincial governments and *Canadian* those vested in the central government. By retaining complete sets of *federalism* provincial governments and superimposing a new machinery of federal government, Canada became, in proportion to her population, the most expensively and elaborately governed country in the Anglo-Saxon world. The British parliamentary system, rather than the system of separation of powers between the executive and legislative branches prevailing in the United States, was retained in Canada, and has become a custom of the constitution in Canada as it is in England. Responsible parliamentary government works in Canada, as in the mother-country, not so much as a matter of law, but as a matter of firmly-rooted tradition.

The distribution of legislative powers can be best understood by referring to sections 91, 92, 93, and 95 of the British North America *Provincial* Act, reprinted in the appendix. The Act of 1867 enumerated a series *powers* of powers which the provinces were to continue to exercise. Among these may be mentioned the power of direct taxation within the province in order to raise money for provincial purposes, the power over municipal institutions, and the right to incorporate corporations for provincial purposes. The solemnizing of marriages, the regulation of shops, saloons, taverns, and other businesses by license in order to raise revenue for local or provincial needs, and the ordinary control over property and civil rights within the province were granted to the provincial legislatures. In all, fifteen enumerated provincial powers were vested in the provincial governments, together with a general exclusive provincial power over matters of purely local and private concern.

The Dominion government has full powers over matters affecting the peace, order, and good government of Canada, insofar as these *Powers of* have not been specifically granted to the provinces. In addition, the *Dominion* entire residuum of governmental powers, after this division of func- *government* tions has been made, is vested in the federal government. But the federal residual power is always limited by the provincial residuary powers over local matters. Twenty-nine powers were specifically enumerated in the British North America Act as granted to the Dominion government alone. Included in these enumerated powers were such matters as the control of the public debt, the postal service, coinage, fisheries, banking, bankruptcy regulations, patents, the army and navy, marriage and divorce, and the wide and important field of criminal law. On two subjects, agriculture and immigration, the central and provincial governments were granted concurrent powers. In case of conflict the federal power will prevail. For the control of education, a subject likely to raise the irritating issue of separate schools in a racially divided country like Canada, a special article (section 93) was included in the Act of 1867, granting provincial legislatures the exclusive right to make educational regulations, but with the proviso that these regulations must never affect any right or privilege enjoyed in law by any separate group or denominational school at the time of federation. Should these guarantees ever be violated, an appeal could be carried to the Dominion cabinet, and the Canadian Parliament was authorized to pass remedial legislation.

Conflicts of jurisdiction

It is significant that this special section on education was sponsored primarily by Alexander Galt, in order to protect the Protestant minority of Quebec, whose spokesman he was. On the other hand, it is doubtful whether the French Canadians would have consented to confederation unless their rights to separate schools had been thus specifically recognized and guaranteed. This section of the British North America Act soon became a source of many disputes, and in later years it proved a stumbling-block for several federal ministries. In spite of careful efforts to avoid conflicts of jurisdiction, the Dominion of Canada has not entirely escaped difficulties over the question of the extent of federal and provincial rights, and scores of court decisions by Canadian courts, as well as by the British Privy Council, have been concerned with the attempt to delimit the powers and jurisdiction of these two spheres of government. Together with the educational clause, the provisions concerning taxation have probably been the most fruitful of legal and political conflicts. After all, federation was the result of compromise between many local, religious, racial, economic, and political prejudices. Necessarily, there was much overlapping in the allocation of legislative powers. The builders of the Dominion deliberately avoided being too logical, and were content to leave much latitude to the courts in settling conflicts of jurisdiction.

Position of the governor-general

Theoretically, the governor-general of Canada is at the head of the Dominion government, as the direct representative of the Crown in Canada. Theoretically, he appoints the lieutenant-governors of the provinces, disallows provincial statutes, makes appointments to the government service, and serves as commander-in-chief of the armed forces of the dependency. Actually, he performs these functions only on the advice of his cabinet, and this advice, according to long-established practice, he is expected to accept and follow on all occasions. The cabinet assumes full responsibility for all acts of the governor-general. By virtue of the dignity of his position as the direct representative of His Majesty the King, and because of his detachment from the conflicts of party politics, the governor-general may exert some influence upon his ministry, and upon the currents of public opinion, but this influence is of a personal rather than a legal nature. He also serves as the visible link of empire, and as the interpreter of Canada to England, and *vice versa*. The term of office of the governor-general now is limited by practice to six years, and a new appointment is usually withheld until Canada has expressed her willingness to receive the king's selection. The governor-general must carefully abstain from talking politics in public, and from all participation in the activities of partisan organizations. In case of his death or absence from Canada, the chief justice of the Canadian Supreme Court usually performs the functions of the governor-general.

The Canadian governor-generalship has long been regarded as a position of great official dignity, rather than one of power and influence. In 1926, when Lord Byng refused to dissolve Parliament on the advice of the legally constituted cabinet, this unexpected assumption of independent power aroused much unfavorable comment in the Dominion and became one of the issues in the elections of that year. Subsequently, in the Imperial Conference held at the close of 1926, the governor-general's position was more clearly defined and his powers still further reduced. It was agreed that the governor-general in any dominion "is a representative of the Crown, holding in all essential respects the same position in relation to the administration of public affairs in a Dominion as is held by his Majesty the King in Great Britain, and he is not a representative or agent of his Majesty's Government in Great Britain, or of any department of that Government." In other words, the governor-general now no longer represents the British home government, but acts simply as a viceroy, whose functions are largely informal, symbolizing the unity of the Empire under a common Crown. Moreover, the recognized method of communication between a dominion and the mother-country is henceforth not to be through the governor-general, but directly from cabinet to cabinet.

Present-day powers

The Parliament of the Dominion of Canada consists of a Senate and a House of Commons. The Senate is an appointive body, selected by the Crown acting through the governor-general, which, of course, really means appointment by the Dominion cabinet. The fathers of confederation entertained high hopes for the future influence and usefulness of this Upper House. Membership was to be limited by an age qualification of thirty years, and the holding of at least $4000 worth of property in the province represented. Membership in the Senate was made appointive in order to avoid the heavy expense of senatorial elections, and to eliminate the possibility of a deadlock which might result if both houses had an equal right to claim to be the people's direct representatives. Another reason was a pledge, made in the Quebec conference, to appoint the first senators

Senate

of the Dominion from among the membership of the provincial councils, since the latter would be abolished with the inauguration of confederation. The Senate originally had seventy-two members, twenty-four from Ontario, twenty-four from Quebec, twelve from Nova Scotia, and twelve from New Brunswick. With the admission of additional provinces to the Dominion, the number has been gradually increased, until in 1921 the membership of the Upper House reached ninety-six. The number of senators may not at any time exceed one hundred and four, unless Newfoundland should decide to enter the Confederation.

Appointment Senators are appointed for life, and in every province except Quebec, they represent the province at large. In Quebec one senator is appointed for each of the twenty-four electoral divisions formerly represented in the legislative council of Lower Canada. Other than through removals by death, a senatorial seat may be vacated by the loss of the property or residence qualifications, by conviction of crime, or by remaining away from the meetings of Parliament for two consecutive sessions.

Procedure The procedure of the Canadian Senate is modeled carefully upon that of the British House of Lords. The Senate chamber is done in red, and contains a throne from which the king's representative addresses the members of Parliament. The officer representing the power and dignity of the Senate is known by the English title of Gentleman Usher of the Black Rod. The Government party and the Opposition always have a leader in the Upper Chamber, but it has long since been a convention of the constitution that the Senate need not be represented in the Dominion cabinet.

Present-day In spite of the expectations of the founders of federation, the
importance Senate has lost most of its importance and functions only sporadically with effectiveness. Finance bills cannot be originated or amended by the Senate, though they may be rejected. A custom has developed by which divorce bills originate in the Upper House. In seven provinces there is a divorce jurisdiction carried over into federation from powers possessed before 1867, but Ontario and Quebec never possessed a divorce jurisdiction, necessitating the use of Parliament as a divorce court. In 1930, a divorce court was set up in Ontario. The Senate's powers over legislation are limited in practice to revising measures which come from the popular house, and only rarely has the Upper House dared to reject really important legislation. Sometimes this power of revision has served as an effective check upon hasty law-making, and in some cases, it has undoubtedly resulted in improvement in the character of bills. In any case of serious deadlock between the two branches of Parliament, the Senate would undoubtedly have to yield to the popular body, although the number of additional Senators who could be appointed to break the deadlock by the party in power is limited by statute to eight. The revision of the

composition of the Senate, and even its total abolition, is a much-discussed issue in present-day Canadian politics.

The salary or "indemnity" of a senator was originally fixed at $2500 for every session of over thirty days, with deductions for *Perquisites and* absences. With a liberal allowance for traveling expenses and clerical *influence* assistance, a senator's total income probably reached $6000 a year. More recently, the salary of members of Parliament was raised to $4000. All senators are addressed as "Honorable" while in office, and are entitled to elaborate offices and club perquisites in the government buildings. Under ordinary conditions very few cabinet ministers have seats in the Upper House, and often the Senate has little to do. Canadian newspapers seldom assign reporters to cover its proceedings, and often decline to print accounts of the debates when they are furnished free by a special reporter hired by the Senate. The average Canadian today knows but few of the members of the Upper House. The Senate has become a "reservoir of party patronage," and appointment to the honors and emoluments of a senatorship is used by party leaders in power to reward men who have served the party well, such as newspaper editors and others who seem to deserve a pension for political services rendered. The result of this practice has been that the average age of the members of the Senate is probably higher than that of any legislative body in the world, and senators eighty and even ninety years of age are not uncommon. There is usually a long waiting-list of men who desire these appointments to a place of honor and leisure and pleasant retirement from the stormy arena of active politics. The Senate has repeatedly been described as a body which "does nothing in particular, and does it very well."

The House of Commons is the important branch of the Dominion Parliament. It is chosen by the qualified voters of the Canadian *House of* provinces by a suffrage fixed by provincial action. At present this *Commons* means virtually universal male and female suffrage. Representation in the Lower House is apportioned according to population. Quebec, by the terms of federation, was guaranteed an unchanging number of sixty-five seats in the Commons. The number of representatives for the other provinces is determined by dividing the population of the province of Quebec by sixty-five, in order to get the federal ratio of representation, and then dividing the resultant figure into the population of each province. Reapportionments are based on the decennial census. At present the membership of the House of Commons is 245.

General elections must be held at least once every five years, but Parliament, under the system of responsible government, may be *Elections* dissolved at any time and new elections ordered by the governor-general on the advice of his ministry. The only specific requirement concerning the time for meetings of Parliament is that twelve months must not intervene between two sessions. Sessions usually begin in November, and may last for shorter or longer periods, depending on the volume of business and the plans of the Government. Canadian constituencies have names, usually geographical, instead of numbers, as in the United States. Any one may be nominated for Parliament who is a British citizen, twenty-one years of age, if he can get twenty-five voters to sign his nomination papers, and if he is willing to make a deposit of $200. If the candidate then fails to poll at least one-half as many votes as the successful aspirant, his deposit is forfeited to the government. The development of rigid party lines has reduced independent candidacies to a minimum. Ballots contain neither party emblems nor party names, but only the name, residence, and occupation of the candidates—an arrangement which puts more of a premium on intelligent voting than is the case in most American states where ballots contain the party column and the party emblem.

Procedure
    At the opening of Parliament the ancient procedure of the British "Mother of Parliaments" is carefully followed. The Commons are summoned to the bar of the Upper House in disorder, and then are advised to retire to their own chamber in order to elect a speaker. When this has been done, and the speaker has taken his chair, the sergeant's mace, which is the symbol of the authority of the Commons, is placed upon the table. The speaker is not a party leader, and is usually selected alternately from the French and English elements. (This custom was broken in 1926.) He occupies a position somewhere between that of the speaker of the English House of Commons, who is an absolutely impartial arbiter of proceedings, and the speaker of the United States House of Representatives, who frankly is expected to be a partisan leader. The Canadian speaker votes only in case of a tie.

Throne speech
    On the day following the election of a speaker the Commons again proceed to the Senate chamber, to hear the throne speech of the governor-general. This is read in both English and French, and usually written, or at least closely supervised, by the prime minister. The speaker is presented officially on this occasion, and makes the ancient petition that the Commons may enjoy the usual privileges of Parliament. This is, of course, a mere formality, and no approval is required or sought from the governor-general for what the Commons regard as their firmly-established legal rights. After the retirement to the House of Commons, a "dummy bill" is introduced before the members proceed to a consideration of the throne speech and the drafting of a reply. This procedure again follows a British precedent, and indicates the power of the House of Commons to act entirely on its own authority and without waiting for the address from the throne.

Party government
    The procedure of the Canadian House is modeled as closely as possible upon that of its British prototype. Much of the work is done in standing committees, the bills of private members have little chance of passing, and all money bills must be sponsored by the Government. Party "caucuses" and party "whips" keep wavering party members in line as supporters of the program of the Government. Both English

and French are the languages of debate. The leader of the Opposition party receives a special salary from the government for the performance of his duties as chief critic of the administration. When bills have passed both houses, they are assented to and signed by the governor-general. The latter has no veto, although theoretically he may reserve bills for the pleasure of the Crown, in which case, again theoretically, they may be disallowed at any time within two years. The last bill to be disallowed was the Oaths Bill of 1873. Since that time the veto power has been dormant.

The dominion cabinet is by far the most powerful organ of the Canadian government, although technically it has no legal existence except as a committee of "the King's Privy Council for Canada." The Privy Council is appointed by the governor-general, on the advice of the ministry. In contrast with British practice, the appointment of Privy Councillors rarely occurs except when necessary to make an individual legally eligible for cabinet office. The Privy Council never meets apart from the cabinet. *Cabinet*

As in all countries where the British parliamentary system prevails, the cabinet consists of a committee of Parliament, representing the majority group in the House of Commons; the cabinet, or "Government," which combines vast executive and administrative duties with responsibility for legislation, can remain in office only so long as it retains the confidence and support of a majority of the Commons. No formal records of cabinet meetings are ever kept, all of its sessions are in secret and are never referred to in Parliament, and there is no fixed membership of the cabinet, although usually, the number ranges from fifteen to twenty. The principle of joint responsibility for all decisions of the cabinet is firmly established. The governor-general has long since ceased to attend these deliberations except for purely ceremonial functions. *Procedure*

The cabinet, under the leadership of the prime minister, furnishes the real governmental leadership in Canada. It brings in and sponsors all Government bills, and as the complexities of government are steadily increasing, these are practically the only measures which have a chance of passage. The cabinet is responsible for all taxation and expenditures, and also constitutes the executive power of the Dominion. While there are always a few ministers without portfolio, most members of the cabinet serve as heads of government departments. On accepting appointment to a cabinet position, members of the House automatically vacate their seats and must appeal to the electorate for reëlection. Recently, there has been some discussion of a proposal to abolish these ministerial elections, which in many cases are mere formalities. The prime minister is technically unrecognized by the Canadian constitutional system. The only law which takes cognizance of his existence is the one giving him a special salary in addition to his regular stipend as a member of Parliament. *Cabinet powers*

Only the most important ministerial positions can be noted here.

Next to the prime minister in importance, is the minister of finance, who together with a subcommittee of the cabinet, directs the financial program of the Government. The auditor-general, who is a civil servant and does not technically hold a ministerial position, serves as virtually a permanent appointee. He examines the public accounts and reports the results of his audits to the House of Commons. The minister of justice is the legal advisor of the government, including the governor-general, and acts as the attorney for the government in all litigation. He also supervises the penitentiaries and the Dominion police, and recommends the appointment of judges. His chief assistant, the solicitor-general, sits in Parliament, but until recent times was not a member of the cabinet. The secretary of state's office takes care of all government correspondence and official papers, and has the responsibility for external affairs, such as passports, and dispatches from other governments. Trade Commissioners operate under the department of trade and commerce. The minister of public works, besides taking care of all internal improvements and the public buildings, for a long time, supervised the post-office. The functions of the minister of railways and canals have become steadily more important with the rapid expansion of facilities of communication and transportation. The minister of the interior is in charge of public lands, Indian affairs, the forests, national parks, the geological survey, and many other matters. In recent years the minister of immigration has assumed new importance with the growing desire to attract settlers to Canada's virgin prairies. The minister of agriculture combines with his more obvious duties the supervision of patents and the census. The functions of the minister of marines and fisheries and the minister of customs are fairly clear from the titles of their positions. In addition, there are the minister of trade and commerce, the minister of labor, the minister of inland revenue, and the minister of militia and defense. There is nothing final about the distribution of functions among these various department heads, nor does the number of cabinet officials remain the same in every decade. Changes and additions are made in accordance with the increasing needs and responsibilities of government. Another important official of the Canadian government who should not be overlooked, is the Canadian High Commissioner, sent to London as a quasi-diplomatic representative of Canada in the mother-country. A permanent Canadian agent is also maintained in Paris. The office of high commissioner was established in 1879, and has been filled by such distinguished Canadians as Galt, Tupper, and Lord Strathcona and Mount Royal.

As in the case of most governments, much of the important expert work in Canada is done by commissions, and by a great host of under-secretaries and government clerks whose names are seldom known to the public. Nevertheless, it is these men who constitute the great permanent staff of experts without whose services the government could not long carry on. At first, appointments to the Canadian civil

service were frankly political. A civil service law in 1868 proved
ineffective, and both parties were guilty of reducing it to a dead letter.
In these early days of civil service reform, not only were examinations
held usually after the appointment was made, but failure to pass led
to a second chance; the examinations themselves were extremely
simple. The Canadian "spoils system," however, differed from that
which flourished in the United States so disastrously after the days of
President Andrew Jackson, in that appointments, once made, were
likely to prove permanent. There was no "rotation in office," a
practice accepted by all parties in the United States, and promotions
generally depended on merit rather than on politics.

The first real effort to substitute civil service reform for the spoils
system was made in 1882, when a law was passed creating a Board of   *Civil service*
Examiners for applicants for government positions. The law was due   *reform*
largely to the indefatigable pioneering work of George Elliot Casey,
who had entered Parliament in 1872 at the age of twenty-two and
devoted himself zealously to the cause of civil service reform. Year
after year he introduced bills modeled on the British civil service acts.
The law of 1882 was a compromise measure, the examinations were
too easy and non-competitive, and politics still played a major rôle in
getting names on the eligible lists.

In 1908 a more effective law was passed providing for the appointment of two commissioners to conduct the competitive examinations   *Law of 1908*
for all positions in government departments below those of deputy-
head. The commissioners were removable only upon a joint address of
the houses of Parliament. All appointments to the civil service were
made provisional for a period of six months. Promotions depended not
only upon the recommendations of department heads, but also upon
certificates of qualification which had to be obtained from the commission.

The ordinary courts of Canada are maintained at provincial expense, but the judges are appointed by the Dominion government. In   *Courts*
each province there is a supreme court of appeal to which cases come
from the lower courts. At the apex of the Canadian judicial system is
the Supreme Court of Canada, created in 1875, and this tribunal, under
certain specified conditions, exercises appellate jurisdiction in both
civil and criminal cases. Most cases now end in the Canadian Supreme
Court, but an appeal still lies, by petition, to the Judicial Committee
of the British Privy Council, which serves as a supreme court for
appeals from all the dependencies. This appellate jurisdiction of the
Privy Council is another of the much-discussed questions of present-
day Canadian political life, and there are many who resent this last
vestige of British control, which seems to them an unwarranted and
unnecessary limitation upon Canada's recently-acquired nationhood.

The provincial governments closely resemble the Dominion government. Quebec alone has a bicameral legislature; the other provinces   *Provincial*
now have the unicameral system. Each has a lieutenant-governor,   *governments*

appointed by the Dominion government, and virtually holding office at its discretion. There are provincial prime ministers and cabinet ministers who function as heads of their respective departments and governments, in accordance with the recognized procedure and custom of responsible parliamentary government. The Dominion power to disallow provincial acts, which is lodged in the governor-general-in-council, that is, the cabinet, is now very infrequently used, and as a rule only when provincial legislation might prove harmful to the Dominion as a whole, or is in clear violation of treaties or imperial rights.

Canadian nationhood

The chief limitations on the self-governing powers of Canada, as fixed by the British North America Act of 1867, were the imperial power to disallow Dominion measures, the control of foreign affairs, the appellate jurisdiction of the Privy Council, and the fact that the Canadian constitution is the result of legislation by the British Parliament, and therefore cannot be amended except by action of the British Parliament. Other minor rights were reserved at the time by Great Britain, such as control of immigration, copyright, the governor's pardoning power, and command of the Canadian defenses by a British officer, but these have now passed under the control of the Dominion government. Many significant modifications have been made in the last generation in the powers of the imperial government over Canada, and the evolution of Canadian nationhood is probably not yet completed. This question of the development of Canadian nationality, and the changing status of Canada in the British Empire, must be left for later consideration.

SELECT BIBLIOGRAPHY FOR CHAPTER XVIII

An interesting discussion of the constitutional basis and the framework of government for the Dominion of Canada is: E. Porritt, *Evolution of the Dominion of Canada* (Yonkers-on-the-Hudson, N. Y., 1918), pp. 211–429, but the book contains many errors and only the last part can be used with safety. In *Canada and Its Provinces*, vol. VI, the following special articles are valuable: Joseph Pope, "The Federal Government," pp. 271–376; and A. H. F. Lefroy, "The Federal Constitution," pp. 209–267.

Another special treatise is: A. H. F. Lefroy, *Canada's Federal System* (Toronto, 1913). A. H. Smith compares Canadian and United States federalism in his *Federalism in North America* (Boston, 1923). Sir J. Bourinot's "Canada and the United States—a Study in Comparative Politics" also has some value, and may be found in *Annals of the American Academy of Political and Social Sciences*, vol. I, pp. 1–26. Bourinot, *Parliamentary Procedure* (Toronto, 1916) is an excellent and accurate work.

Sir R. L. Borden, *Canadian Constitutional Studies* (Toronto, 1922) and W. R. Riddell, *The Constitution of Canada in Its History and Practical Working* (New Haven, 1917), are collections of university lectures which give important interpretations, especially for the more recent period. Another recent publication of much value on a present-day issue is Robert A. Mackay, *The Unreformed Senate of Canada* (Toronto, 1926). A thorough analysis of the nature of Canadian federalism and institutions is available in W. P. M. Kennedy, *The Constitution of Canada*, pp. 378–459.

CHAPTER XIX

INAUGURATING THE NEW RÉGIME

LORD MONK, the governor-general of the Canadian provinces at the time of confederation, summoned John A. Macdonald to build the first ministry to put the Dominion government into operation. The selection was eminently fitting, the only one politically practical. Elections for the Dominion Parliament were held in August and September, 1867, and in three of the provinces the coalition Governments which had sponsored confederation, were sustained by the voters. In Nova Scotia the confederation proposal received what seemed a crushing blow, due to the influence of Howe, when all of its supporters except Tupper went down to defeat. A number of the successful candidates in each of the provinces secured seats in both the provincial and the federal parliaments, and this practice of playing a double rôle in provincial and Dominion politics continued down to 1872. Among the conspicuous builders of confederation who suffered defeat was George Brown; the old "Grit" leader did not make his reappearance in public life until 1874, when he accepted a seat in the Senate.

First Dominion Parliament

It required all of Macdonald's consummate skill as a political strategist to construct a cabinet which would represent the various factions in the Dominion, for this first ministry, if the coalition were to endure, had to please both Liberals and Conservatives. Brown objected to the continuance of this coöperation and tried hard to reunite the Liberals under his leadership. The Catholic and Protestant elements, the French, the English and the Irish Catholics, all had to be recognized in the new cabinet. Macdonald constructed a Government in which the Conservatives had seven and the Liberals six portfolios, and the representation of the various elements in Canadian politics was as fair as could be expected. Ontario received five places in the cabinet, Quebec four, and the maritime region four.

First Dominion Government

Macdonald, of course, assumed the position of prime minister, and in addition, undertook the duties of minister of justice. Other leading figures in this first ministry were Cartier, the most important of the French Canadians, who became minister of militia and defense, Galt, who became minister of finance, and William McDougall, a vigorous "Clear Grit" and chief editorial writer for the *Globe*, who assumed the duties of minister of public works. Among the notable fathers of confederation who for practical political reasons had to be omitted from this first ministry, were McGee and Tupper.

Leading figures in cabinet

The first Dominion Parliament assembled at Ottawa on November

Conftructive legislation

6, 1867. It faced the tremendous task of passing the scores of bills necessary to set the new government in operation. Laws were enacted creating the various government departments and defining their duties. The salary of members of Parliament was fixed at $600. Revenue measures were adopted, and in 1871 the first general banking law for the Dominion was enacted. Largely the work of Francis Hincks, it laid the basis for the sound banking principles to which Canada has steadily adhered. The minimum capital of chartered banks was fixed at $500,000, and the note-issue was limited to the actual amount of paid-up capital. Dividends and profits were limited to eight per cent until the bank had accumulated a reserve fund equalling twenty per cent of its capital, and numerous other regulations as to reserves and double liability of stockholders provided ample security for the banking public. Consolidation has been the rule among Canadian banks, and in 1927 eleven large banks with their branches served the needs of the Dominion. The tendency has been to absorb all local banks just as soon as they become important in their communities.

Railway measures

New railway legislation was enacted and plans were made for the completion of the Intercolonial Railway, this being one of the conditions of confederation. Within six months work was begun on this road to connect Quebec with the maritime provinces and to fill in the blank stretches between those portions of the route which had been built at various intervals from 1853 to 1867. The British government guaranteed a loan of £3,000,000 at four per cent interest for the completion of the project, and in the enthusiasm of the moment, these bonds were oversubscribed at a premium. The Dominion government took over the roads built by the maritime provinces, and after much discussion on the proper route to be developed, completed the Intercolonial as a government system of 950 miles under the control of the department of public works.

Organization of West

One of the immediate and pressing problems was the organization of the great West lying between Ontario and British Columbia, and its incorporation into the Dominion of Canada. Westward expansion was discussed with great earnestness at the Quebec convention in 1864, and the British North America Act made possible the eventual admission of this great western region into the federation. At the time of confederation, the West was Indian country, the fur-trading preserve of the Hudson's Bay Company. It had been thoroughly explored and exploited since early times by rival French and English traders, and the fur-trading frontier had been moving constantly westward and northward. Rupert's Land and the Northwest Territories, as the West was known, belonged to the Hudson's Bay Company which, by virtue of its old charter of 1670, exercised governmental and property rights over it. All rival companies had been either crowded out or absorbed in the older corporation. Hudson's Bay Company posts dotted the interior, and the factors of the company were virtually monarchs of the territory which they supervised. It was, moreover, the deliberate policy of the company to discourage colonization and agriculture, and to encourage the intermarriage of whites and Indians—all in the interest of larger dividends from the fur trade. Roads and internal improvements were obviously unnecessary for a region where settlers were unwelcome.

By 1857, the only colony west of Ontario, not wholly dependent on the fur trade for its subsistence, was the settlement in the Red River valley, founded by Lord Selkirk, a Scotch landowner who planned to establish a refuge for discontented Scotch Highlanders in the wilds of what is now Manitoba. In 1811, Lord Selkirk had bought 100,000 acres from the Hudson's Bay Company in the valleys of the Red River and the Assiniboine. In spite of almost incredible hardships and the constant hostility of the rival Northwest Fur-Trading Company, Selkirk's settlement managed to survive. *Lord Selkirk's colony*

In 1867, the population of the district of Assiniboia was about 12,000, one-half to three-fourths of whom were half-breeds, the offspring of the intermarriage of French traders and Indian women. Scores of "squatters" also made their way into the West and added to its population. The people of this country found employment in hunting and trapping, or in trading and hauling freight. Agriculture was extremely primitive. The village of Winnipeg (the Fort Garry of the Hudson's Bay Company), had begun to develop, and one little Roman Catholic church was located on the Red River to minister to the religious needs of the half-breeds and a few Indian converts. Already some of the Catholic clergy were dreaming of founding a new Quebec in the Red River valley as an outlet for the surplus French-Canadian population of the older province. *Red River settlements*

The first step in the Dominion's program of westward expansion was the extinction of the title of the Hudson's Bay Company. McDougall and Cartier were sent to England for this purpose, and received the hearty support of the British government. An act of the British Parliament was passed as a result of negotiations, providing for the transfer of Rupert's Land and the Northwest Territories to Canada. The terms involved a cash payment of £300,000 by Canada to the Hudson's Bay Company, the reservation for the use of the company of two sections in each township, and some 50,000 acres in the immediate vicinity of the fur posts. In exchange, the company surrendered, with the exception of its trading rights, all other exclusive proprietary and governmental rights to the Dominion together with "all other privileges, franchises, powers, and authorities." *Bargain with Hudson's Bay Company*

In 1914 the Hudson's Bay Company was still deriving profits from its stores, from its fur trade, and from the sale of its lands in Canada. In that year alone, it disposed of 26,000 acres of farm land for nearly $573,000 and town lots valued at $131,170. Its dividends have frequently reached forty per cent, and in 1914 there were still over 4,000,000 acres of unsold land in the possession of the company. In *Present status of company*

1920 the company celebrated the two hundred and fiftieth anniversary of its founding by King Charles II; it still continues as a prosperous business venture with investments in many other fields besides the fur trade.

Extent of new acquisitions

By the transfer of title referred to above, Canada acquired about 2,500,000 square miles of territory with a population of some 175,000 whites, half-breeds, Eskimos, and Indians. These negotiations apparently satisfied all parties except the inhabitants of the region concerned, and perhaps some of the employees of the Hudson's Bay Company. It was extremely unfortunate that the government neglected to prepare the way for this transfer of authority and title by preliminary negotiations with the residents, and still more unfortunate that the act of 1869 did not carry any guarantees as to the political and property rights of these newcomers in the Dominion.

Trouble with Red River settlers

December 1, 1869, was the date set for the official transfer of the West to the Canadian government. William McDougall was appointed lieutenant-governor of the Northwest Territory, and promptly issued a proclamation to the inhabitants announcing his authority. Surveyors were sent into the territory before the transfer had been officially completed, and land speculators followed them in a rush to seize the most desirable areas. The surveying system adopted for the Canadian West was the one in use in the United States by which land was laid off in rectangular plots. These frequently cut across the farms of the half-breeds, which extended back from the river fronts in narrow ribbons similar to the farms in Quebec. This arbitrary division, therefore, of the homesteads of the "squatter" population undoubtedly added to the suspicion and misunderstanding which was developing among the native population concerning the acts of the Canadian government. Friction resulted when working parties of surveyors encountered the natives whose protests to Ottawa were pigeonholed by a busy government for consideration at some later time. The old Hudson's Bay Company men assumed at best a very passive attitude and did little to dispel these misunderstandings, for, having worked hitherto on a profit-sharing basis, they were probably fearful that they would be forgotten when the stockholders of the company came to divide the purchase money obtained from the government. The situation required the utmost tact, a quality which seemed to be utterly lacking in all who were immediately concerned with the problem. Serious trouble was therefore inevitable.

Louis Riel

At this point the striking figure of Louis Riel, a French Canadian with some Indian blood, stalked across the stage of Canadian history for the first time. Riel was destined to remain a storm center of politics until his death. He had studied for the priesthood in his younger days, and had been discouraged from pursuing this career farther because of certain peculiar utopian ideas of religion and politics of which he became a fanatical devotee. Riel was able and fairly well educated; when he settled on the Red River he became quite naturally a leader of the half-breed population living in that neighborhood. In the crisis of 1869, he was the spokesman for the discontented. It is difficult to fathom his innermost plans, for his mind trembled constantly on the brink of insanity. It is certain, however, that he stirred up the half-breeds to stop the surveying parties sent out by the government. Fort Garry was seized by his followers without much opposition from the Hudson's Bay Company men, Governor McDougall was forced to retire across the border into the United States, and his proclamations, designed to quell the disturbance, only served to add fuel to the spreading flames.

Riel called upon the inhabitants of the Red River country to elect a council and form a provisional government. On December 1, *Red River* 1869, a bill of rights was adopted containing such perfectly justifiable *rebellion* demands as the right to elect a legislature, a liberal public land policy, a system of internal improvements, and representation in the Dominion Parliament—demands which the Dominion government eventually granted quite willingly and which, perhaps, should have been conceded in advance in order to avoid trouble. Unfortunately, some fighting occurred between the half-breeds and others who supported Riel and a small English group resident in the valley who regarded their opponents as traitors to the Dominion. At this stage of the controversy, Riel virtually assumed the rôle of president of a new state which he may have planned to make independent of the rest of the Dominion. For six months, the new régime continued without interference from any quarter.

Macdonald's Government now became thoroughly alarmed. Bishop Taché who was believed to have great influence over the Red *Belated* River people was hastily summoned from Rome where he was visit- *compromises* ing. A commission of three men was dispatched to the disaffected region to investigate the situation, remove misapprehensions of the Government's policies, and complete the transfer of the district from the authority of the Hudson's Bay Company to the Canadian government. The most important member of the commission was Donald A. Smith who as a lad had come to Canada from Scotland in 1838, had risen rapidly to a high position in the Hudson's Bay Company, and was later to become one of Canada's greatest railway promoters and capitalists and a member of the peerage as Lord Strathcona and Mount Royal. Smith made the hazardous journey to Fort Garry with all possible speed, but he was only partially successful in carrying out his instructions and ending the insurrection. He did, however, gradually undermine Riel's influence by a conciliatory policy which promised full provincial rights to the region when it should be ready for admission to the Dominion.

The lamentable incident which brought matters to a crisis and induced the government to send an armed force to the Red River *Execution of* country was the execution of a young Canadian named Thomas Scott *Scott* who had persistently opposed Riel's provisional government, and had fought on the side of the small English party against Riel's régime. While an active member of this party seeking the overthrow of the rebel government Scott was captured, and after a very unfair trial was found guilty. Somewhat later when he struck the captain of the guard who had him in custody, he was condemned to death. His execution which was unnecessarily brutal and a crime against justice, stirred up a storm of rage, particularly in Ontario, where the murder of an Englishman and an Orangeman by a French Canadian served to revive all the smouldering anti-Catholic prejudices of the militant Protestants of the province.

Olive branch and sword

Bishop Taché arrived at Fort Garry four days after Scott's execution. By a promise of complete amnesty he induced Riel to release his prisoners. The flag of the Hudson's Bay Company now supplanted that of the rebel government over Fort Garry, and order seemed to be restored. The provincial legislature which Riel had summoned agreed to accept the terms offered by the Dominion government and to enter the Confederation. Macdonald's Government, probably because of criticisms of its lenient policy by the Ontario Protestants, now resolved to approach the rebels with an olive branch in one hand, and a sword in the other. The olive branch was the Manitoba Act, which the Government tardily drew up; the sword was a military expedition of twelve hundred men under Colonel Wolseley sent to enforce peace and order in the disaffected region. In most of the disaffected area Riel was still technically in power because the Hudson's Bay Company had not resumed its jurisdiction, and no government had as yet been provided by Ottawa. After a remarkable march of over 500 miles through an almost trackless country, Wolseley's force arrived before Fort Garry in August, 1870. Riel sought safety in flight and the rebellion collapsed immediately. Lieutenant-Governor A. G. Archibald arrived on September 2, and in January, 1871, the first provincial legislature for Manitoba was organized.

Dealing with Riel

So far as the arch-rebel was concerned, the Dominion Government decided to follow a policy of conciliation and mercy, and it was soon whispered about that Macdonald had paid Riel $4000 on condition that he leave the country. At any rate Riel's temporary exile seemed the only way to avoid violent political controversies, since in the eyes of the majority of French Canadians Riel was a martyr, while to the Ontario Protestants he was a brutal murderer. In 1874 Riel caused further complications by being elected to the Dominion Parliament from Manitoba. On appearing at Ottawa to take the oath he was expelled from the House of Commons only to be reëlected five months later. Finally he was granted amnesty on condition that he absent himself from Canada for at least five years. These years of banishment were spent in the United States where Riel was three times confined in insane asylums at his own wish because of the nervous troubles which came upon him with increasing frequency during his later years.

By the Act of 1870 Manitoba became a province of the dominion with a bicameral legislature and representation in the Dominion *Manitoba Act* Parliament. Donald Smith was the first member to go from the new province to the federal House of Commons. Land grants were made to all the inhabitants and their rights were fully guaranteed. Because Manitoba entered the Confederation without a public debt which the central government could assume as had been the case with the older provinces, the Dominion Government and the province agreed on a sum upon which Manitoba was to receive five per cent interest. In addition, the province received a subsidy of $30,000 a year and an allowance of eighty cents per capita until the provincial population should reach 400,000. Manitoba grew rapidly by immigration from the older provinces, from the United States, and from Europe. By 1881 its population was 180,000, and in 1891 it reached 250,000. It was soon discovered that the new province contained the richest wheat land in Canada.

When Manitoba was created a province, the rest of the West was organized as a territory under a lieutenant-governor and a council *Far West* directly responsible to Ottawa. In 1874, the Northwest Mounted Police was organized to keep order in the Far West. In the 1880's the country west of Manitoba was invaded by the cattle-kings who drove their stock across the border from Montana and established ranches in present-day Alberta. Bull-trains and prairie schooners soon connected this region with Fort Benton at the head of navigation on the Missouri River. In 1882, four territories, Assiniboia, Saskatchewan, Alberta, and Athabasca, were created, and six years later, these territories were granted legislative assemblies. It was not until 1905 that the growth of population warranted the consolidation of these units into two provinces, Alberta and Saskatchewan.

By 1873 the Dominion and the provincial governments were spending over half a million dollars annually to encourage immigra- *Westward* tion. A law was passed granting homesteads of 160 acres to actual *movement* settlers after three years' occupation, reserving sections of land for educational purposes, and permitting the purchase of as much as 640 acres at one dollar per acre. Under these conditions Winnipeg grew from 300 people in 1870 to 3000 in 1876. The real settlement of the West, however, awaited the completion of a Pacific railroad.

Closely related to the problem of the acquisition and government of the West was the Indian policy of the Dominion. In the early dec- *Indian policy* ades of the nineteenth century Indian affairs were considered an adjunct of the military department and were under the direction of British officials. Full control of Indian affairs was transferred to the Dominion in 1867, and in 1868 the Canadian Parliament passed its first law dealing with Indian relations. The policy adopted looked toward the gradual extinction of the Indian title to the West. This was accomplished by a series of treaties with the natives setting aside Indian reservations on the basis of one square mile for each family of five and providing a graduated scale of annuities. In return for the Indian's pledge to preserve the peace and accept the jurisdiction of the white man's government, Canada undertook to provide schools and to furnish agricultural implements, annual supplies of ammunition, fishing nets, and twine. The Canadian government has not only observed these treaties to the letter but has always interpreted them in a spirit of liberality and fairness. As the buffalo herds disappeared, the government after 1879 assumed the additional obligation of furnishing temporary rations for the natives. The agents of the Indian service exercise a paternal control over their charges.

Estimate of its success

In more recent times as Indian reserves have become too large for the needs of the tribes, the excess lands have been sold and the proceeds transferred to an Indian Trust Fund managed by the government. From this the Indians either collect the interest, or make loans to build houses or to improve their farms. By 1910 the government was spending nearly $550,000 annually for Indian schools, much of it in the nature of per capita grants to religious schools. When an Indian returns to his people from one of these schools, it is the duty of the Indian agent to help him get a farm and generally to guard his rights. In Ontario some of the Indian tribes have now been completely absorbed by the whites. Many Indians find work in the lumbering and canning industries, on farms, and in the mines. Canada's history in striking contrast with the bloody Indian annals of the United States has been singularly free from Indian wars. Even the Sioux, regarded as one of the most warlike of the tribes inhabiting the western part of the United States, became a peaceful and law-abiding people when they migrated to Canada.

Progress of Indians

Since 1898 Indians not resident on reservations have been subject to the franchise regulations of each province like any other residents, and in most provinces may vote if they meet the requirements. Special concessions have been made for Indians serving with the Canadian forces. By 1926 the total number of Indians in the Dominion was nearly 105,000. These owned real and personal property valued at $74,502,629, and their total income for 1925–1926 was $10,189,696. The Indian Trust Fund in this same year reached a total of $12,418,460, an increase of over $250,000 over the preceding year. As evidence of their state of civilization, it is significant to point out that the Indians' labor wages far exceed their income from hunting and fishing. In 1926 there were 1570 Indian reservations containing an area of almost 5,000,000 acres throughout the Dominion. These are under the control of the Department of Indian Affairs at Ottawa. Educational facilities have been increasing, and for the year 1925–1926 the cost of Indian education was nearly $2,000,000. The great majority of the Indians have at least formally accepted some kind of Christianity, the Catholic Church claiming by far the greatest number of converts. The Indians today follow many varied occupations. In the three prairie provinces 2500 are employed in agriculture; 106,007 acres of land were under cultivation by Indians in 1926; it has been further estimated that the Indians of these provinces own 26,000 head of cattle. Finally it may be noted that during the Great War, 4000 Canadian Indians saw active service overseas.

The admission of the province of Manitoba was but the first step in rounding out the natural boundaries of the Dominion. Since early *Pacific* in the nineteenth century, a British colony had been developing *settlements* slowly but successfully on the Pacific coast. When the Oregon boundary dispute with the United States was settled in 1846, the Pacific coast was still under the control of the Hudson's Bay Company, and was divided into the three divisions of British Columbia, Vancouver Island, and Stikeen Territory. In 1863 gold was discovered on the Pacific coast, and the inrush of prospectors led to the union of British Columbia and Stikeen Territory under a partly elective legislative council. Vancouver Island had already progressed farther toward self-government. Due to commercial troubles between the two sections, they were united in 1866, and in the following year the legislative council of British Columbia sought admission to the Confederation of Canada on terms which included the assumption of a debt of $1,500,000 by the Dominion, an annual subsidy from the federal treasury, and the completion within two years of a wagon road from Lake Superior westward. At the time when these first overtures were made it is interesting to note that a large and influential group in British Columbia preferred annexation to the United States.

In 1870 negotiations came to a head in an agreement which admitted British Columbia to the Dominion with full provincial *British* status, arranged for a debt allowance, an annual grant of $30,000, and *Columbia enters* an eighty cents per capita grant until the population should reach *Dominion* 400,000. In addition, the Macdonald Government promised to begin a railroad to the Pacific Ocean within two years and to complete the project within ten years. These terms were ratified by the people of British Columbia at a general election, and on July 20, 1871, the province officially became a part of the Dominion of Canada.

Prince Edward Island did not enter the Confederation until July 1, 1873. The main reason for its change in attitude was the crushing *Prince Edward* burden of its railroad debts and its difficulty as a small province to *Island ratifies* attract additional capital. The Dominion government agreed to assume the burdens of this province and to incorporate the Island Railway as part of the Dominion government's railroad system. In addition, the federal government promised to establish a telegraph and to maintain steamship service between the mainland and the island all year round, and further to advance a special sum to the provincial government so that the claims of its absentee proprietors might be liquidated. The usual annual subsidies and per capita grants were allowed as in the case of the other provinces.

Another task which fell to the lot of the Macdonald Government

was participation in the diplomatic settlements relative to the friction and controversies engendered by the Civil War between the United States and Great Britain. The chief point at issue was the effort of the United States to collect an indemnity for damages inflicted upon United States commerce during the Civil War by the *Alabama* and other Confederate cruisers built in British ports. In addition, the disputed boundary in the Portland Channel in the extreme northwest of the United States, the fisheries question, and Canada's claim for compensation for damages inflicted by the Fenian raids into Canadian territory required settlement. Because the last three issues were of particular concern to Canada, the Canadian prime minister was attached to the British commission of five charged with the settlement of these controversies.

Fisheries

Upon cancellation of the Elgin Reciprocity Treaty in 1866, the fisheries question had automatically reverted to the settlement of 1818. By this earlier arrangement, it will be remembered, the Americans had been admitted to the inshore fishing rights on certain coasts, but had been excluded from others, and United States fishermen were compelled to secure licenses and pay small fees annually for these privileges. In 1868 the Canadian government raised these fees considerably, and when Americans began to evade the law the entire license system was abolished in 1870, and Canadian cruisers were sent to protect the fisheries from the Americans. As a consequence, United States vessels were seized under rather irritating conditions. President Grant laid the whole matter before the American Congress in a sharp message. It seems that the Canadian government was using its power over the fisheries as a lever to force the renewal of the cancelled reciprocity agreement.

*Boundary
controversy*

The boundary controversy in the Northwest involved principally the possession of the island of San Juan in the Portland Channel. In the matter of the Fenian raids already discussed in an earlier chapter, Canada seized the opportunity to insist on damages for these unwarranted invasions of her territory.

*Treaty of
Washington*

All these disputes were eventually settled in the Treaty of Washington of 1871, a landmark in the history of the settlement of serious controversies by arbitration. The treaty provided various methods for the adjustment of these causes of friction. We need consider here only those provisions of the treaty which concerned Canada directly. As has been said in an earlier chapter the northwest boundary dispute was referred to the German Emperor for settlement; his award was favorable to the United States. The Atlantic fisheries were opened to the United States for at least twelve years, the cash compensation for this privilege to be determined by a commission to meet at Halifax. In 1877 Canada and Newfoundland were awarded $5,500,000 as the excess in value of Canadian fishing rights granted to Americans over those granted Canadians in American waters, and the United

States grumblingly paid this amount. The United States received the right to navigate the St. Lawrence River in perpetuity and without fees while Canada was granted the free navigation of Lake Michigan, the Yukon River, and some of the rivers in the extreme northwest of the United States. In addition, each nation received the right to ship goods in bond through the other's territory. Compensation for the Fenian outrages was dropped altogether, in spite of Macdonald's insistence upon Canada's claims. The Canadian prime minister received no support from the British government on this point, for the latter evidently preferred to sacrifice this issue in the interest of harmony on other matters which were considered of more vital consequence. The most the British government, then under Gladstone's leadership, would promise was the guarantee of a loan for Canadian defenses.

Macdonald returned to Canada bitterly disappointed because of what he considered the unjustifiable sacrifice of Canadian interests to larger British policies. The treaty settled everything, he observed ironically, "no matter at what cost to Canada." Before the Canadian Parliament, however, the prime minister defended the settlement, "for the sake of peace, and for the sake of the great Empire of which we form a part." *Canada's reaction*

The first five years of the Macdonald Government were marked by great achievements of which those noted in this chapter are only the most important. These measures were not carried without opposition and criticism both in Parliament and in the Dominion. Scott's murder during the Riel rebellion and Macdonald's apparent unwillingness to punish the rebel leader made many enemies for the Macdonald Government among the militant Orangemen of the province of Ontario. In all the English provinces, in fact, Macdonald's leniency and his alleged mismanagement of the Red River insurrection gave rise to the charge of pro-French influences in the Government. The Conservatives, as Macdonald's followers were now generally known, were defeated in the Ontario provincial elections, and Edward Blake, the leader of the Liberal opposition, was elected head of a provincial ministry at Toronto which proved a constant thorn in the flesh of the Dominion authorities at Ottawa. Under the leadership of Blake and Alexander Mackenzie, the Liberals had slowly withdrawn from Macdonald's coalition and had been welded into a vigorous Opposition. In the maritime provinces there was still a strong group opposed to confederation. Many Canadians disliked the opportunistic methods of "Old To-morrow" as Macdonald was called because of his belief that time and delay would solve most problems. Because of its sacrifice of Canadian interests the Washington Treaty of 1871 proved unpopular in many sections, while Macdonald's absence at Washington, followed almost immediately by a period of illness, lessened the grip of the master politician on party affairs. *Party politics*

The general elections of 1872 returned Macdonald to power, but with a greatly reduced majority. Mackenzie and Blake, who had relinquished the premiership at Toronto in order to take a seat in the Dominion House of Commons, led a vigorous Opposition at Ottawa. Shortly after the election the storm broke which was to drive the Conservatives from power.

SELECT BIBLIOGRAPHY FOR CHAPTER XIX

A detailed account of the beginnings of Dominion government may be found in special articles by JOHN LEWIS in vol. VI of *Canada and Its Provinces*. Briefer accounts are available in O. D. SKELTON, *The Canadian Dominion* (New Haven, 1921), ch. IV; SIR J. POPE, *The Day of Sir John Macdonald (Chronicles of Canada)*, and H. E. EGERTON, *A Historical Geography of the British Dominions*, vol. V, Pt. II, 249–297. These pages overlap somewhat the material treated in the following chapter.

Many of the biographies noted in the bibliographical note at the end of chapter XVII are useful here. To the list may be added: H. BECKLES WILLSON, *The Life of Lord Strathcona and Mount Royal*, 2 vols. (Boston, 1915). This has now been superseded by John Macnaughton's brilliant biography (Clarendon Press, 1926).

For the development of the Canadian West, the following are of special value: GEORGE BRYCE, *The Remarkable History of the Hudson's Bay Company* (London, 1910); H. BECKLES WILLSON, *The Great Company* (Toronto, 1899); JOSEPH SCHAFER, *A History of the Pacific Northwest* (New York, 1918); G. C. DAVIDSON, *The North West Company*, in *University of California Publications in History* (Berkeley, 1918), vol. VII; ALEXANDER BEGG, *History of the Northwest*, 3 vols. (Toronto, 1894–5). The problems of westward expansion are considered from the point of view of the constitutional historian in: W. P. M. KENNEDY, *The Constitution of Canada*, ch. XX. See also *The Canadian Northwest, Its Early Development and Legislative Records*, 2 vols., edited by E. H. Oliver, in *Publications of Canadian Archives*, No. 9 (Ottawa, 1914–15). These volumes contain among other things the minutes of the councils of the Red River colony and the northern department of Rupert's Land. For the exploration of the Far West, see especially L. J. BURPEE, "Western Exploration, 1840–1867," in *Canada and Its Provinces*, vol. V, pp. 295–331, and AGNES C. LAUT, *Pioneers of the Pacific Coast*, in *Chronicles of Canada*. A detailed study of the Red River colony by C. MARTIN will be found in *Canada and Its Provinces*, vol. XIX, pp. 13–93. JOHN MACOUN, *Manitoba and the Great Northwest* (London, 1883), is an example of the propaganda literature written to attract immigrants to the Canadian West. C. MARTIN, *Lord Selkirk's Work in Canada* (Oxford, 1916), is an admirable work. For a very complete bibliography on the Canadian West before and immediately after federation see TROTTER, *Syllabus*, pp. 111–115, and p. 132.

The best account of Indian affairs in Canada can be found in the articles by DUNCAN C. SCOTT on "Indian Affairs, 1840–1867" and "Indian Affairs, 1867–1912," in *Canada and Its Provinces*, vol. V, pp. 329–362, and vol. VII, pp. 593–626. A very valuable volume is A. MORRIS, *The Treaties of Canada with the Indians of Manitoba and the Northwest* (Toronto, 1880). This book includes an account of treaty negotiations and other pertinent matter.

For the banking and financial history of these early years of federation, consult J. M. COURTNEY and ADAM SHORTT, "Dominion Finance, 1867–1912," in *Canada and Its Provinces*, vol. VII, pp. 471–517; and ADAM SHORTT, "The Banking System of Canada," *Ibid.*, vol. X, pp. 627–660.

For more detailed references on the history of the first generation of the Dominion, see TROTTER, *Syllabus*, pp. 128–132.

CHAPTER XX

THE LIBERAL ADMINISTRATION OF ALEXANDER MACKENZIE

MACDONALD's triumph in the elections of 1872 proved short-lived, for the Government had hardly entered upon its new lease of power when a storm of scandal broke in the House of Commons and in a few months drove the Conservatives from office. This political upheaval was occasioned by the intimate connection between the leaders of the Conservative party and the promoters of the proposed Canadian Pacific railway which was to connect the rest of the Dominion with the Pacific province of British Columbia. *Short-lived triumph*

It has been pointed out that one of the terms upon which British Columbia entered the Confederation was a pledge by the Dominion government to complete a railroad to the Pacific coast within ten years of the date of admission. Such a transcontinental railroad was imperatively necessary for the realization of Canadian nationhood since communications with the West were unbelievably slow. As late as 1841 the speed record from ocean to ocean in Canada was three months. By 1869 the United States had completed its first transcontinental railway, which served as a new stimulus for the project to bind the Dominion by bands of steel and to promote the rapid settlement of the vast unoccupied area between the isolated Pacific communities and the other provinces. *Plans for transcontinental railroad*

The first Macdonald Government had given serious consideration to various proposals for a Pacific railroad for some time before the elections of 1872, and had reached the conclusion that a government railroad would be too costly, and that the best chances for early success lay in a private road subsidized by the government. The first offer to build a road under these conditions came from a group of United States capitalists and promoters including such distinguished men as Jay Cooke, the greatest banker of his time, General Lewis Cass, a former candidate for the American presidency, and W. G. Fargo, long interested in western transportation problems. Closely associated with these American promoters was a group of Canadian capitalists headed by Hugh Allan of Montreal, the founder of the Allan steamship lines. Competing with Allan's group were a number of Toronto capitalists headed by David L. Macpherson, who had organized the Interoceanic company. The Macpherson interests stressed the fact that they represented a purely Canadian enterprise while Allan's Canada Pacific company had to keep its United States connections *Competing for charter*

secret in order to avoid charges of "Yankee dictation" and intervention in Canadian affairs.

*Government's
railroad project*

In 1872 Macdonald submitted the Government's railroad project
to Parliament. It involved the building of the Canadian Pacific from
Lake Nipissing to the Pacific by a private company with substantial
aid from the government. The Conservatives planned to give the
company fifty million acres of land in alternate blocks twenty miles
deep on each side of the roadway, the government to retain the
intervening sections. In addition, the company was to receive a
$30,000,000 cash subsidy to build branch connections to Lake Superior
and to the American border.

*Rival
companies*

Immediately after announcement of these plans, intense rivalry
developed among the companies contending for the charter rights to
construct the railway. The Government announced that it would
grant the charter to the Canada Pacific, the Interoceanic, or to any
other company which could satisfy the Government that it was best
fitted to carry out the contract in the shortest possible time. After the
elections of 1872 the charter was awarded to Allan's company apparently on condition that it immediately sever its connection with
financial interests in the United States. When the company tried to
comply with this request the American interests associated with it
became dissatisfied, and it is from this source that the Liberal Opposition seems to have obtained the information which eventually led
to a parliamentary investigation and to the fall of the Macdonald
Government.

*Canadian
Pacific scandal*

Early in the session of 1873 Lucius Seth Huntington, a Liberal
member from Shefford, Quebec, rose dramatically from his seat in
the Commons and announced that he had damaging evidence against
the Government to the effect that Allan and the United States capitalists associated with him had contributed huge sums to the Conservative party coffers in order to influence the election of 1872 and
secure the railroad charter for their company. A motion for an investigation was defeated by a strict party vote. Macdonald with his back
to the wall fought desperately to avoid any kind of an investigation except one which he himself could control. On July 3,
1873, Parliament was adjourned until August 13. During the interval
new evidence came to light. A Montreal newspaper published letters
which had passed between Allan and George W. McMullen, a
Chicago capitalist, and which had been stolen by the clerk of Allan's
attorney. McMullen then gave his version of the transactions to the
press, and published letters and telegrams from Macdonald, Cartier,
Abbott, and other Conservative leaders clearly establishing the fact
that they had drawn liberally on Allan to finance their campaign for
reëlection. Macdonald's most damaging telegram to Allan read:
"Immediate, private. I must have another ten thousand—will be the
last time of calling. Do not fail me. Answer to-day." Allan, of
course, had used methods which were not at all uncommon in an age

when "big business" was beginning to lean upon governments for valuable privileges. By a careful distribution of stock where it would do the most good, by putting those who required conciliation on the board of directors, and by judicious campaign contributions, Allan had hoped to smooth the way for his company. Donald A. Smith, for example, who was very influential in the affairs of the Hudson's Bay Company, received a place on the board of directors of the railroad because it seemed desirable to enlist the support of his company, and also because as Canada's greatest capitalist, he could help raise money in the London stock market.

Parliament reassembled amid tremendous excitement. To forestall an investigation it was again prorogued and a royal commission was *Campaign* appointed to sift the facts. This commission was virtually a hand- *contributions* picked body which Macdonald hoped to control. Eventually Allan *and fall of* admitted campaign contributions of $350,000. Macdonald, however, *Macdonald* insisted that these contributions had been accepted not to influence the granting of the charter but to insure the reëlection of his party so that its general railroad policy might not be jeopardized. The prime minister also claimed that he had been forced to collect campaign contributions because the Liberal Government of the province of Ontario was using the patronage in an unwarranted and corrupt fashion to influence the election. Parliament reconvened in October, 1873, and Alexander Mackenzie, the leader of the Liberals, moved a vote of censure upon the Government. After two weeks' debate it became apparent that not even so skilled a parliamentary fighter as Macdonald could avoid defeat. Even Smith, who was personally interested in the Canada Pacific Company, was apparently overwhelmed by the evidence and voted with the Opposition against Macdonald. This change of heart was especially irritating to Macdonald, who made the characteristic retort that he "could lick that man Smith quicker than hell could frizzle a feather." On November 5, without waiting for the passage of a formal vote by Parliament, Macdonald and the Conservatives surrendered control of the government.

The formation of a new cabinet was entrusted to Alexander Mackenzie. Mackenzie was in many respects a remarkable man with *Alexander* those qualities of industry, perseverance, and downright honesty *Mackenzie* which make a man great even though he may not be brilliant. Born in Scotland, he had left school at thirteen to work at the trade of stone-cutter and at the age of twenty, in 1842, he had emigrated from Scotland to Canada. By reading and study he soon acquired the education of which social conditions had robbed him in his younger days. Mackenzie was a stern Baptist, a temperance advocate, and a man of rugged honesty with a flair for reform. After working for a time as a contractor and a newspaper editor, he entered politics in 1861 as a member of the provincial legislature of United Canada. Edward Blake, second in command of the Liberal forces, and in rather sharp contrast with their leader, was the son of an Irish immigrant. Blake was a graduate of the University of Toronto and a man of powerful intellect endowed, however, with an unfortunate hyper-sensitiveness which quickly became a serious handicap to him as a practical politician. In 1867 Blake had been elected to a seat in both the federal government and the provincial parliament of Ontario, and four years later he had assumed the duties of prime minister of that province.

Liberal ministry

In the new ministry Prime Minister Mackenzie assumed the duties of head of the department of public works, a position which soon proved so burdensome that it became impossible for him to maintain adequate contacts with his party and with the voters. Richard J. Cartwright served as minister of finance and Antoine Dorion as minister of justice, while Blake, at first, was a member of the cabinet without portfolio. Four years after the inauguration of the Liberal régime Wilfrid Laurier, a brilliant young French Canadian, entered the cabinet as minister of inland revenue. He was then just thirty-six years of age, but he had already attracted attention as the champion of a political liberalism which sought to reconcile Liberalism in politics with adherence to orthodox Roman Catholicism.

Weakness of new Government

Parliament was dissolved soon after the fall of Macdonald, and in January, 1874, the Liberals won an overwhelming victory in the general elections with a majority of about eighty in a house of 206. Despite this apparent success the Government and the Liberal party were handicapped in their new duties in many ways. As the Opposition party they had not evolved a definite program upon which all members could agree. In fact, the only bond holding the diverse elements of the party together was a common distrust of Macdonald. Leadership in the new Government was virtually divided between Mackenzie and Blake and, with the latter's sensitiveness and self-assertion, this state of affairs could easily lead to serious difficulties. Mackenzie himself soon became so engrossed in the attempt to administer the manifold duties of his department efficiently and honestly that he neglected altogether to keep in touch with the currents of public opinion upon which his lease of power depended. Finally, the Liberals had the misfortune to assume office at a time when Canada was suffering from serious economic depression, unemployment, and a general falling off in revenues following the panic of 1873. This panic, like others, came to Canada from Europe and the United States, and resulted in at least six years of business stagnation and falling prices, and was further aggravated by the practice of the United States of "dumping" its surplus products on the Canadian market and selling them at a loss in order to keep prices up at home. Obviously the economic depression of the 1870's could in no sense be attributed to the Liberals, but rather was the result of fundamental conditions which neither party could do much to control.

In spite of this discouraging situation Mackenzie's administration could boast a fine record of real achievement. The General Election *Mackenzie's* Law of 1874 introduced voting by ballot in Canadian elections, *record of real* abolished property tests for membership in the Commons, and *achievements* eliminated many opportunities for corruption by providing for simultaneous elections throughout the Dominion. In 1875 a law was passed creating a Canadian Supreme Court and the Court of Exchequer with civil and criminal jurisdiction. This measure was sponsored by Blake, now serving as minister of justice, and originally contained a clause prohibiting appeals to the judicial committee of the Privy Council in England unless imperial interests were directly involved. This provision was withdrawn however after a warning from the imperial cabinet to the effect that the Canadian government possessed no such prohibitory power. An act determining the territorial government of the Northwest, excluding Manitoba, was passed, as well as legislation dealing with the homestead policy for the disposal of public lands. The Public Accounts Audit Act was in-´ tended to make the auditor of the public accounts independent of the ministry temporarily in power. In 1878, in response to a rising agitation for prohibition, and as the result of a report of a committee sent to the United States to study various state experiments in pro- hibition, the Canada Temperance Act was passed, permitting, on petition of the voters, local option elections by counties, on the liquor question.

In the realm of external affairs, the most important act of the Mackenzie Government was the attempt to make a new reciprocity *New* treaty with the United States. George Brown, now a senator, was *reciprocity* dispatched to Washington to coöperate with the British minister *proposals* in an effort to secure a treaty which coupled fishing rights with a reciprocal trade agreement for natural products and for many manu- factured articles as well. In 1874 President Grant submitted the pro- posed treaty to the United States Senate near the close of its session, but that body refused to ratify the arrangement. Mackenzie, in international relations insisted as a matter of policy upon the right of Canadian representation on all diplomatic missions involving Canadian questions.

Macdonald's Pacific railway project had collapsed as a result of the scandals of the campaign of 1872. Allan's company disintegrated, *Railroad* financial difficulties multiplied, and the company for the time being *policy of* abandoned all hope of pushing through its plans. The first railroad *Liberals* proposal of the Mackenzie Government was to utilize the great water route from Lake Superior westward as links in the projected transcontinental road, thus advancing the date for completion of the project and also materially reducing the cost. In 1874 Parliament authorized the construction of the Pacific railroad as a government enterprise, if this plan should prove feasible. The Government later tried to enlist the interest of a private company by offering a subsidy of $10,000 and 20,000 acres of land for every mile built and by a guaranteed interest rate on the railroad securities for twenty-five years. No group of capitalists could be found who considered these terms sufficiently attractive, and the Government itself finally let a contract for the construction of 227 miles of road as a public undertaking. By 1878 the strip of road from Pembina to Winnipeg was finished.

British Columbia

The Conservatives fretted about the vacillating policy of the Government and charged the latter with failure to appreciate the necessity of completing the transcontinental line with the greatest possible speed. British Columbia became restless and appealed to both the Dominion and the imperial governments for a fulfillment of the terms of the contract under which it had entered the Confederation. In 1876 Lord Dufferin, the governor-general, journeyed to the Pacific province in order to effect a compromise and to check a rapidly rising secessionist movement in British Columbia. He was successful in his mission, and the province waited patiently for the new elections of 1878 which, it was hoped, would return Macdonald and the Conservatives to power. Before the end of his régime Mackenzie had the satisfaction of seeing the Intercolonial Railway completed in the eastern half of the Dominion and formally opened in 1876.

Mackenzie as party leader

As the elections of 1878 approached, Mackenzie confidently expected to secure the approval of the people for the policies of his administration. No one ever administered the difficult and important department of public works with more painstaking care and downright honesty than Mackenzie; his term of office had been absolutely free from suspicion and scandal. Unfortunately for his followers, the prime minister had paid little attention to those duties by which practical politicians keep their supporters enthusiastic and loyal to their party. He depended solely on the appeal which his record of achievement as an administrator might make to the conscientious and public-spirited voter.

"National Policy".

The great issue by which Macdonald and the discredited Conservatives hoped to return to power was the "National Policy," the "N. P.," which was fundamentally and principally the policy of high protective tariffs, although other features were shrewdly coupled with this proposal in order to build a nationalist program which would appeal to all Canadians who believed in the great possibilities of their country. The protective tariff idea in revenue measures had been introduced as early as 1858 in United Canada, and the incidental protection which various articles enjoyed sometimes ran as high as twenty per cent. The first Dominion tariff of 1867 had been in the direction of lower duties, with reductions on many manufactured articles and an extension of the free list. It retained, nevertheless, the protectionist principle, and duties averaged about fifteen per cent.

The stimulus for greater protection, and the inspiration for Macdonald's "National Policy" came largely from the panic of 1873. The

years from 1869 to 1873 were years of prosperity in which manu- *Reasons fo*
facturing grew rapidly, banking capital and railway mileage doubled, *"N. P."*
the government's revenues steadily mounted, and Canada's exports to
Great Britain doubled. The panic of 1873 burst the bubble, and
Canada entered upon six gloomy years of depression. To meet the
falling off in government revenues the Liberals had increased the
tariff from an average of fifteen to seventeen and a half per cent, but
this was done as a revenue measure and not for purposes of protection. In 1874 an attempt to restore prosperity by renewing the reciprocity arrangements with the United States resulted in failure.

As the effects of the panic continued unabated, it became clear to
the Conservatives that a protective tariff argument, if presented in the
name of a new "National Policy," could be made the leading issue *Parties and*
between the parties in the election of 1878. So far as Macdonald is *tariff*
concerned, there is evidence that he had accepted the protectionist
doctrine as early as 1846. There seems, moreover, to have been considerable doubt for a time as to whether the Liberals or the Conservatives would be the first to seize upon the new issue and make it
the battle-cry in the coming campaign. A slight increase of the tariff
by the Liberals might have sidetracked the issue, but Mackenzie
stubbornly refused to deviate from his low-tariff principles. His free-
trade views were undoubtedly strengthened by the feeling that a
change in the direction of greater protection might ruin the Liberal
strength in the maritime provinces, and that protection would prove
injurious to the interests of the masses of consumers. Mackenzie, it
is apparent, failed to sense among the people the growing opinion in
favor of protection.

By skilfully conducted agitation, Macdonald proceeded to make
political capital for the "N. P." All the devices of the practical *Advertising*
politician were used; Macdonald and his supporters for two years *"N. P."*
before the election of 1878 toured the country, preaching the new
gospel of protectionism at mass meetings and political picnics. All the
stock arguments of the advocate of high tariffs were repeated from a
hundred platforms. It was argued that Canada's infant industries
needed protection until they could meet the competition of their more
lusty and longer-established rivals in the United States. Canada
should become a self-sufficing nation. To arguments like these the
organized manufacturers of Ontario gave their keen support. The
farmer was urged to support protection in order to develop a stable
home market for his products. Much emphasis was laid on the rapid
industrial transformation of Canada's southern neighbor since the
Civil War, and this economic revolution was attributed to the protective tariff policy of the United States. It could be maintained,
moreover, with some plausibility, in the face of the recent refusal of
the United States to make a new reciprocity agreement, that the
only way by which Canada could force her neighbor to bargain for
commercial concessions was by erecting a tariff barrier of her own.

Such a procedure would end the American practice of using Canada as a dumping ground in times of overproduction in order to keep prices up in the United States. Finally, the "N. P." provided a splendid opportunity for an appeal to the rising spirit of Canadian nationalism. It appealed as a policy to Canadian patriotism and seemed to provide the means for knitting the provinces more closely together into a firm commercial union.

Other aspects of "National Policy"
    Intimately connected with the advocacy of a new tariff was a promise by the Conservatives to inaugurate a new era of internal improvements which included projects to develop a canal and railroad system wholly within Canadian territory for the transportation of Canadian products to the sea, and also a plan to stimulate immigration and the rapid opening of the West. The "National Policy" seized the Canadian imagination and became the keystone of Canadian policy for a generation. Within a few years the Conservative party became the traditional high-tariff party, while the Liberal party necessarily advocated a policy of freer trade. The principle of protection became ingrained in large elements of the Canadian population so firmly that when the Liberals returned to power many years later they neither cared nor dared to make radical changes in the tariff system.

Liberal defeat
    The Liberals entered the campaign of 1878 much weakened by factional differences; their leaders had neglected to keep in touch with public opinion, and the continued economic depression in the Dominion served as an insurmountable obstacle to success. The Conservatives won a sweeping victory. In Ontario they captured twice as many seats as the Liberals. Quebec voted Conservative, largely because the Conservatives had taken advantage of a great movement among the Catholic leaders to exterminate political liberalism along with other modernist tendencies. Many of the clergy did not hesitate to use spiritual penalties to induce the faithful to vote for the Conservatives. Nova Scotia, Prince Edward Island, British Columbia, and Manitoba went almost solidly for Macdonald.

Macdonald's return to power
    In the new House of Commons the Conservatives had a majority of eighty-six. They remained in power for the next eighteen years. For thirteen of these years the party was under the adroit leadership of its "grand old man," and during this period Canadian political history is to a large measure the biography of John A. Macdonald. Probably no other Canadian leader ever dominated the political arena and captured the hearts of the people as did Macdonald in these years when he was at the height of his power. He never abandoned the rôle of the opportunist and did little to raise the ethics of Canadian politics. He managed, nevertheless, to achieve much that was fundamentally constructive for the sound development of the Dominion. In 1880 Alexander Mackenzie resigned as leader of the defeated and somewhat demoralized Liberals, giving failing health as his reason.

His first lieutenant, Edward Blake, succeeded him as the titular head of the Opposition.

SELECT BIBLIOGRAPHY FOR CHAPTER XX

In addition to volumes noted at the end of chapters XVII and XIX, special articles by JOHN LEWIS in vol. VI of *Canada and Its Provinces* are useful for a general narrative.

For the railroad history of the last half of the nineteenth century, see especially: O. D. SKELTON, *The Railway Builders* (Toronto, 1921) in *Chronicles of Canada;* H. A. INNIS, *A History of the Canadian Pacific Railway* (Toronto, 1923); R. G. MACBETH, *The Romance of the Canadian Pacific Railway* (Toronto, 1925); K. MORRIS, *The Story of the Canadian Pacific Railway* (London, 1923); L. J. BURPEE, *Sandford Fleming, Empire Builder* (London, 1915). For the history of the Intercolonial, S. FLEMING, *The Intercolonial: An Historical Sketch, 1832–76* (Montreal, 1876), is useful.

For a detailed discussion of the inauguration and operation of the "National Policy," consult: E. PORRITT, *Evolution of the Dominion of Canada*, pp. 430–482, and E. PORRITT, *Sixty Years of Protection in Canada, 1846–1907* (London, 1908). Porritt's books, however, must be used with care and discrimination.

SIR JOSEPH POPE, *The Day of Sir John Macdonald* (Toronto, 1914) in *Chronicles of Canada*, and W. S. WALLACE, *Sir John Macdonald* (Toronto, 1924), in *Canadian Statesmen Series*, are brief but excellent biographical sketches. SIR RICHARD CARTWRIGHT's *Reminiscences* (Toronto, 1912) contain some material presented from the point of view of a Liberal leader. The only biography of Mackenzie is W. BUCKINGHAM and HON. G. W. ROSS: *Hon. Alexander Mackenzie, His Life and Times* (Toronto, 1892).

O. D. SKELTON's brilliant article, "General Economic History, 1867–1912," in *Canada and Its Provinces*, vol. IX, pp. 93–274, contains valuable material for this period. J. C. DENT, *The Last Forty Years*, vol. II, gives interesting details to color the political narrative.

CHAPTER XXI

THE AGE OF MACDONALD

New cabinet

In MACDONALD's new cabinet, the prime minister assumed, responsibility for the department of the interior, S. L. Tilley, a former prime minister of New Brunswick, became minister of finance, H. L. Langevin, representing the French-Canadian element, assumed the duties of postmaster-general, and Mackenzie Bowell became minister of customs. Dr. Charles Tupper, who had returned to his medical practice after the Pacific Railroad scandal, reëntered the cabinet as minister of public works.

Tariff legislation

The Conservatives, true to their campaign pledges, at once inaugurated a series of hearings to gather information for the formulation of a new tariff measure. The manufacturers and other interested elements promptly descended upon Ottawa and were invited by the Government to make their needs and wants known. The resulting protective tariff act, which was passed, rested virtually on the theory that the manufacturers should have all they asked for. The Liberal opposition denounced the new tariff as a flagrant example of class legislation. The duty on cotton goods was raised from seventeen and one half to thirty per cent, and on woolens and sugar it was doubled. The rates on boots and shoes and rubber products were increased to twenty-five per cent. A duty of two dollars a ton was provided for pig iron which had hitherto been on the free list, and great increases were made in the protective rates on iron and steel products. To pacify the farmer, wheat, barley, and corn were put on the list of dutiable articles and protection for Canadian live-stock was increased one hundred per cent. By substituting specific for *ad valorem* duties, the rate of protection on many dutiable articles was still further increased.

Prosperity

Interestingly enough, the economic depression, which had held Canada in its clutches since 1873, came to an end shortly after the Conservatives returned to power. To the delight of the country, good times returned and the party which sponsored the "National Policy" reaped the political benefit. The return of prosperity, however, could hardly be attributed to the new tariff legislation. It was part of a world-wide movement of prosperity and was accentuated in Canada by a series of good harvests and by bad ones in England, by a great boom in the West, and by the revival of the lumber trade with the United States. Without discussing details, it may be added that the general tendency in tariff legislation to the early 'nineties was an upward revision of duties. Obviously as long as prosperity continued there was little disposition to tamper with the "N. P."

In 1880 Macdonald negotiated a new agreement for the completion of the Canadian Pacific railroad. A new group of capitalists was organized with important financial connections in London and New York. Among the leaders of the new syndicate were Donald A. Smith, his cousin, George Stephen, president of the Bank of Montreal, and James J. Hill, a native of Ontario destined to become famous as a railroad promoter in the United States. In 1880 Macdonald journeyed to London to induce English capitalists to invest in the project, and the agreement between the Government and the new Canadian Pacific Company, though actually executed and approved by the Dominion Parliament at Ottawa, was really made in London. *New railroad agreement*

The concessions made by the Government to induce this new company to undertake the completion of the transcontinental road were granted with a lavish hand although, in the long run, the rapid completion of the road was probably worth all it cost the Canadian taxpayer. By the terms of the contract the company received a cash bonus of $25,000,000 and 25,000,000 acres of land. In addition, the company received outright more than 700 miles of road which had already been built at a cost of something like $35,000,000. Land grants were made to the company in alternate sections with the right reserved to the railroad to select other blocks if these sections proved unfit for settlement and sale. Land for the roadbed, station houses, docks, and other necessary equipment was also donated by the government, and all materials needed in construction were to be admitted free of duty. All grounds, capital stock, and rolling stock were exempted from taxation, and the Government agreed to keep any competing company from building a road south of the main line of the Canadian Pacific in western Canada for at least twenty years. On the strength of these lavish promises of support, the company agreed to complete the remaining nineteen hundred miles of track necessary to link the Atlantic with the Pacific. *Canadian Pacific contract*

The announcement of these liberal terms precipitated a storm of protest and indignation from the Opposition even more violent than the attack on the tariff policy of the Government had been. Blake thundered against a contract which virtually gave monopoly powers to a private company, and put the Canadian West at its mercy. It was pointed out that under the contract the Government could not regulate rates until the company was able to pay ten per cent dividends on all its capital and that the people were really building the road and presenting it as a gift to a group of private capitalists. Objection was also raised to the reservation of so many acres of railroad land on the ground that this would retard westward expansion. In spite of these and other objections, the agreement was easily ratified by Parliament, and the people, in a burst of optimism and faith in the future, generally approved the bargain. *Criticisms of project*

*Financing
railroad*

The completion of the railroad is one of the romances of Canadian history. It was uphill work for the promoters; undreamed-of obstacles were encountered, but the company, led by a few dauntless spirits such as Stephen and Smith, adhered fearlessly to its task. There were times when funds in the treasury of the company ran so low that it seemed impossible to continue the work for more than a few days, and the promoters were in immediate danger of losing all of their personal fortunes. In spite of the liberal terms of the charter, the Government had to lend the company an additional $27,500,000 to insure the completion of the enterprise, and there were critical moments when it required all the skill of the promoters to keep the enthusiasm of the Government alive. On occasion the company resorted to such tactics as juggling its capital stock, and paying dividends out of current funds in order to keep the work from collapsing. In 1882 James J. Hill sold all his holdings and withdrew from the venture and by 1886 the stock of the company had dropped to $33.75 a share.

Building road

The work of the engineers and builders was no less heroic than that of the financial promoters. Trestles had to be constructed over turbulent mountain streams and dangerous gullies. In the mountain sections snowsheds were necessary to protect the track and the gangs of workers from great avalanches of snow and ice which swept down into the valleys. Yet in the face of difficulties and discouragements the work went steadily forward. In 1882 the builders averaged two and a half miles of track per day, and there was one three-day period when twenty miles of track were laid. On November 7, 1885, Donald A. Smith, at Craigellachie in the Rockies, drove the iron spike which held the last tie in place, and the first through train over the Canadian Pacific left Dalhousie Square Station in Montreal on June 28, 1886, on its 2905 mile journey to Vancouver over what was then the longest railroad in the world. The road was actually completed five years before the time limit fixed in the contract. The chief engineer of this gigantic undertaking was William Van Horne. The route proceeded around Lake Superior to Winnipeg, and thence through the Indian country toward the Rocky Mountains, through the Kicking Horse and Rogers Pass, and down the Fraser River valley to Vancouver.

*Progress of
Canadian
Pacific*

In a certain sense the real troubles of the Canadian Pacific began with the completion of the road. The road had been built far ahead of settlement and could not expect a profitable business for years. Buffalo bones bleaching on the western plains were loaded in cars to be shipped eastward in lieu of other freight. An extensive immigration propaganda was carried on by the government and the company to provide settlers for the West and traffic for the road, and the company tried hard to lure passengers over its route by advertising the glorious scenery along the way. Eventually the Canadian Pacific began to expand eastward and to absorb smaller lines and build feeders in the West. Today it is one of the most remarkably successful transportation companies in the world. It was the only Canadian railroad system which was able to withstand the shock of the Great War and consequently was not absorbed into the Canadian National system.

The Dominion government has continued its interest in the development of a network of railroads to the present time, and has granted subsidies to many short lines and to many local companies, a practice in which political pressure has often played a more conspicuous rôle than economic necessity. *Railway expansion*

In 1882 when the term of the Macdonald Parliament automatically expired, the Conservatives could turn to the country with all the prestige of the "National Policy," the Canadian Pacific agreement, and returning prosperity to make their party popular at the polls. To make success doubly certain the Conservatives took advantage of the census of 1881 to pass a bill for the redistribution of seats in the Commons. Macdonald made the most of the opportunity while the Liberals protested violently, but in vain, against a measure which ignored many of the old county lines in the Liberal strongholds of Ontario, and "hived the Grits," as Macdonald cynically called the process, in such a way as to reduce materially the representation of the Opposition in Parliament. The process was a skilful application of the "gerrymander" which had become fairly common by this time in the political history of the United States. *Elections of 1882*

In the elections of 1882 the Conservatives received a new lease of power. Macdonald continued to dominate the Government, and his able lieutenant, Tupper, withdrew temporarily in 1883, from the domestic scene, to accept the post of Canadian High Commissioner in London. *New lease of power for Conservatives*

In spite of auspicious beginnings the 1880's turned out to be years of disappointment for many of the optimists who had predicted that confederation would inaugurate an era of boundless development and prosperity for the entire Dominion. Despite the "N.P." and the railroads, and Macdonald's record of success, the promise of Canadian life remained unfulfilled, and honest critics had to admit that Canada's progress had fallen far short of expectations. As a result of this reaction, the decade was one in which some looked again to the United States as the source from which permanent improvement would come. Others, less enamored of a closer connection with the United States, preferred a new form of imperial federation. *Years of depression*

The 1880's also brought to a climax a series of quarrels between Dominion and provincial authorities which resulted in numerous appeals to the courts and to the British Privy Council in an effort to define Dominion and provincial rights more accurately. Despite the best efforts of the fathers of confederation, Canada could not entirely avoid controversies between the champions of provincial rights and those who favored a constant widening of the sphere of federal *Provincial rights* activity. It will be remembered that Macdonald himself had always favored a legislative union in preference to a federal system, and during his years in office he generally used his influence in the interests of a greater nationalism. Most of these quarrels over provincial rights belong in the field of constitutional law, and only a few examples can be treated here.

In Quebec

Near the close of Mackenzie's administration, the lieutenant-governor of Quebec, M. Letellier de St. Just, summarily and without adequate reason dismissed his Conservative ministers. Although this action was at variance with the custom of the constitution, the people of the province seemed to approve the change at the next election, and the Mackenzie Government, therefore, refused to intervene in what it considered a purely provincial matter. When Macdonald resumed office, he recommended that Lord Lorne, the governor-general, remove the lieutenant-governor of Quebec. The issue was referred to the Colonial Office for advice, and, although the opinion rendered was somewhat ambiguous, it did uphold the principle that a governor-general must accept the advice of his ministry. Macdonald insisted on the lieutenant-governor's removal, and Letellier de St. Just was summarily dismissed, a course of action which seemed to many to be an unwarranted intervention by Dominion officials in provincial affairs.

Manitoba-Ontario boundary

In 1881 a controversy developed between Manitoba, Ontario and the Ottawa Government because of a law of that year fixing the boundary between these two provinces. Both the northern and eastern boundary of Manitoba had long been in dispute, and a commission had been appointed in 1878 to arbitrate the controversy. Ontario announced her willingness to accept the unanimous award of the commission, extending Ontario northward to the Albany River and westward to the Lake of the Woods, but the Dominion neglected to take action to carry out the recommendations of the commission. Finally in 1881 the Dominion Parliament in somewhat vague terms fixed a boundary for Manitoba, but this the neighboring province of Ontario was unwilling to accept. The two provinces then entered upon a conflict as to whose officials should exercise authority in the disputed strip. 100,000 square miles were involved, and if this area were incorporated in Manitoba, the Ottawa Government, which had retained possession of the public lands in the prairie province, would be able to profit by the disposal of the disputed region. On the other hand, if the area belonged to Ontario, that province would benefit from the lumber and mineral resources of the district in controversy. After some months of hostilities and mutual arrests by Ontario and Manitoba constables in the neighborhood of Kenora, the controversy was appealed to the British Privy Council in 1884. The latter upheld the boundary line fixed by the arbiters, but ruled that it could not be binding until Parliament should legislate it into effect. For a time, the Dominion Government continued to claim jurisdiction and granted licenses for cutting timber in the disputed area. It was not until 1889 that the British Parliament, on petition from Canada, definitely fixed the boundaries of Ontario.

In 1881 the same province passed a Rivers and Streams bill designed to protect public rights on the waterways of the province. The bill was disallowed three times by the Dominion Government, and each time it was repassed by the provincial legislature. Finally in 1884 this conflict of jurisdiction between federal and provincial authority was settled by a decision of the Privy Council which upheld Ontario's rights in the matter. *Ontario Rivers and Streams bill*

The agitation over the liquor question led to another conflict in jurisdiction. According to the British North America Act of 1867, the licensing of saloons for purposes of local revenue was a power left to the provinces. The Dominion Parliament, however, possessed general police power which included the right to legislate for the peace and order and good government of the country. In 1882 the British Privy Council specifically upheld the power of the Dominion Government to enact the Canada Temperance Act of 1878, popularly known as the Scott Act, on the broad basis of the police power, supported by the contention that violations of laws for the public peace and safety would have to be dealt with by the ordinary criminal procedure which rested solely with the Dominion. But Ontario in 1877 had passed a license law dealing with the control of public houses, and this statute had also been sustained by the British Privy Council as entirely within the power of the provincial legislature. In 1883, in order to get uniformity throughout the Dominion and to legislate more effectively for peace and order, Macdonald chose to regard the Ontario act as invalid and secured the passage of a federal license law. An appeal to the Canadian Supreme Court and to the Privy Council sustained the Ontario law as a police regulation which did not interfere with any federal powers. Most of the Dominion license law was therefore declared *ultra vires* and was repealed. *Temperance legislation*

Other cases illustrating this conflict of jurisdictions might be cited. In another connection the complex issues revolving about educational rights in the provinces as another aspect of this same problem will be considered in detail. These controversies prove the extreme difficulty of drawing an instrument of government which will properly relate local rights and sectional interests to the powers which a central government must exercise over national matters. In most of these cases the provincial governments, if they were sufficiently in earnest and persisted long enough, had their way and they usually succeeded in forcing the federal authorities either to repeal their action or to accept a workable compromise. In a Dominion as large as Canada, sectional interests frequently arose to aggravate these contests. *Twilight zone*

The early 1880's, as has been pointed out, marked the beginning of a period of depression. Farmers suffered from a great increase in agricultural production the world over, particularly in the United States, Australia, Russia, and South America. This increase in production was not accompanied by a proportionate increase in gold production and, as a result, prices of farm products fell rapidly. The West was still in the speculative stage of its development, most farmers rejected a system of diversified agriculture and staked all their hopes for success upon wheat, and there were signs that the western boom was about to collapse. The exodus from Canada to the United States increased steadily, and the net gain in the population of the Dominion during the 'seventies and 'eighties was very disappointing.

Accompanying this agricultural depression, despite operation of the "National Policy," there was a general falling off in foreign trade and a decline in manufacturing. In the face of these disappointments the advocates of a commercial union with the United States again made themselves heard. Some went so far as to urge the complete removal of all tariff barriers between Canada and its neighboring republic and the establishment of common excises and customs on foreign trade. A few even advocated a pooling of all income from commerce and its distribution in proportion to the population of the two pooling nations.

This idea was not a new one, and had received support earlier from such leading statesmen of the United States as Stephen A. Douglas, William H. Seward, and Horace Greeley, and in Canada from leaders such as Isaac Buchanan. On several occasions committees of the United States Congress studied the suggestion. In 1887 the leading advocate of this extreme form of commercial union was Erastus Wiman, a Canadian who was president of the Great North West Telegraph Company. Such responsible papers as the Toronto *Globe* argued that a commercial union of this kind would serve as a permanent link of friendship between the United States and Great Britain without really endangering Canada's political union with the mother-country.

In 1887 Congressman Butterworth of Ohio introduced a bill in the United States House of Representatives to grant free admittance to all Canadian goods whenever Canada should adopt a similar measure for products of the United States. Influential protectionist leaders in Congress, such as Nelson Dingley, gave the measure their support, while in Canada the proposal received the approval of numerous farmers' organizations and a number of important newspapers. Canadian merchants and manufacturers, fearing the ruinous competition that would follow the free importation of American products, vigorously opposed the suggestion, while the great mass of the Canadian people objected to the plan because they believed its acceptance would mean the end of Canadian nationality. Liberal leaders such as Richard Cartwright favored a modified form of commercial union with the United States, while other Liberals opposed the plan altogether. The attitude of the major political parties became rather vague on these proposals for reciprocity with the United States and varied with changes in the economic conditions of Canada. In 1891 the Conservatives, despite their traditions of protectionism and imperialism, sent a mission to Washington to renew the Reciprocity Agreement of 1854 in some form, but they found that the Republican high tariff party was in power in the United States and was absolutely opposed to making any concessions.

Those who rejected what seemed to them the unpatriotic proposal of a closer union with the United States tried to find other solutions for Canada's economic and social ills. A small but enthusiastic group, founded as early as 1869 and known as the "Canada First" group, continued to preach the gospel of unwavering faith in Canadian nationhood and exhorted the people to eliminate all sectional and other prejudices and to support the government in a great program of national development. The most enthusiastic of the founders of this group was W. A. Foster, a brilliant young Canadian lawyer. *"Canada First" group*

Another group, under the influence of such men as Goldwin Smith and Colonel G. T. Denison of the British Empire League, advocated a plan of imperial confederation, although they failed to suggest on what basis the Canadian Dominion should be represented in this new imperial organization. The Toronto *Globe* talked prophetically about a British commonwealth of nations. On the other hand, Laurier, leader of the French-Canadian Liberals, in these early years of his public career believed that Canada's ultimate destiny was independence. In 1886 W. S. Fielding, in later years another prominent Liberal member of the Government, actually carried a Nova Scotia election by a large majority on the issue of secession from the confederation, and a resolution to that effect was passed in the legislature of Nova Scotia by a vote of two to one. *Imperial confederation*

Difficulties like these proved that Canada had not yet been welded into a great national state. Local prejudice was an ever-present menace to the realization of a closer union and a stronger national spirit. The West was beginning its attacks upon the tariff and upon the railroad rates enacted and dictated by the influence of the older East, and was protesting bitterly against the domination of the farmers by eastern capital. Ontario and Quebec were frequently at swords' points in controversies that were not simply political, but were aggravated by bitter religious prejudices. It is upon this background of unrest, disappointment, and sectional differences that Macdonald's achievements of the decade of the 1880's must be interpreted and evaluated. *Lack of national spirit*

In 1885 the gloomy figure of Louis Riel reappeared on the Canadian stage to trouble the closing years of Macdonald's administration. The Dominion government was suddenly faced by another rebellion in the Northwest. This new crisis, like the earlier troubles in Manitoba, might have been avoided. It was due largely to the stupid policy of the government toward the half-breed population in the *Half-breeds in Saskatchewan valley*

Saskatchewan valley and to its utter failure to learn the lessons which should have been obvious from the unfortunate events in the Red River valley during Macdonald's first term of office.

Causes of discontent

As suggested earlier, the half-breeds in the Red River valley received land grants from the Government at the time the province of Manitoba was organized in return for the surrender of their claims. No provision was made for the half-breeds living in the territories further west and north. Furthermore, with the steady march of the frontier into the West, the Indians became more restless and viewed with terror the rapid extermination of their buffalo herds. In 1879 due to constant pressure from the Council of the Northwest Territories and from Archbishop Taché and others, a law was passed authorizing the Government to make whatever arrangements seemed advisable in order to conciliate the native population. What the half-breeds in the Saskatchewan valley demanded was individual grants of 240 acres in accordance with the terms offered the natives of Manitoba nine years earlier. In a wilderness of millions of acres, the total of these demands would probably not have exceeded 50,000 acres.

Blunders of Government

The Government, however, remained curiously inactive in the face of the rising disturbance, while surveying parties, sent in to cut up the elongated farms into the United States system of townships of six miles square, aroused the fears of the inhabitants. Land was sold to speculators at the same time that the Government refused to issue patents to the natives for the land already occupied by them. Petitions from the half-breeds, demanding relief and the recognition of their claims, remained unanswered. A series of crop failures added to the discontent in the West, and conditions were soon ripe for a repetition of the insurrection of 1868.

Riel's return

In 1884 a delegation of the discontented from the Saskatchewan valley set out on foot for Montana, where Riel was then living, to invite him to return to Canada and espouse the cause of the wronged natives. Riel consented at once, and in 1885 the Northwest Rebellion was in full progress. The usual "bill of rights" for the Indians and half-breeds was adopted, and a provisional government was created with Riel as president. When the Government at last gave signs of awakening from its lethargy, the rebels attacked a government station and battled with a detachment of mounted police. The Dominion trembled with fear lest these incidents should lead to a general Indian uprising, but fortunately the great majority of the redskins in the Northwest refused to be drawn into the insurrection. The rebellion was crushed by a military force of several thousand volunteers, under General Middleton, who were rushed to the scene on the newly constructed Canadian Pacific railroad. Several engagements were fought and resulted in the loss of some 200 lives. It was estimated that the whole affair cost the government in the neighborhood of $6,000,000, and the Liberal Opposition in Parliament made the most of its opportunity to flay the Conservatives for their stupid, dilatory tactics.

To add to Macdonald's troubles, Riel was captured and brought to trial on a charge of rebellion against the government and inciting *Riel captured* the Indians to armed hostilities. By this time, Riel clearly was suffering from temporary fits of insanity, and an effort was made to save his life on that ground. He refused, however, to plead this defense, and the insanity experts disagreed. Riel was found guilty, and the judgment against him was confirmed by the higher courts. On November 16, 1885, he was hanged for his alleged crimes.

Riel's execution fanned all the smouldering embers of racial and religious prejudice into flames which for a time threatened to consume *His punishment* the Government. To the French Canadians Riel was a fellow Catholic, guilty of no offense save of championing the rights of the downtrodden half-breeds who had the sympathy of the French element for racial and religious reasons if for no other. The French Canadians demanded that Riel be pardoned; the English element, especially the Orangemen of Ontario, demanded his immediate execution. When Macdonald finally decided that Riel must hang, a storm of protest swept over the province of Quebec. Mass meetings condemned the Government, and the Conservative leader was burned in effigy in Quebec. Soon afterward when Macdonald set out for Europe, he was afraid to sail from Montreal or Quebec. He never recovered his political following in the French province. The Liberals naturally made political capital of the situation. Macdonald found comfort for the losses his party had sustained in Quebec in the thought that the Government would make new gains in Ontario. Here the protests of Quebec against the Government led instantly to counter-demonstrations. The net result of the agitation may have favored the Conservatives. At any rate for years after his execution the ghost of Riel con tinued to stalk across the stage of Canadian politics; his activities while alive, and the manner of his death, threatened at any moment to become a political issue.

One important measure remains to be considered before discussing the elections of 1887. In 1885 the Government brought about *Dominion* the enactment of the Dominion Franchise Law. Contrary to earlier *Franchise Act* practice, which left the determination of suffrage rights to each *of 1887* province, this measure provided for a uniform franchise law, on a low property-holding test, for the entire Dominion. A system of federal registration for voters was also established. Macdonald undoubtedly believed that some of the provincial suffrages were too liberal; he favored a property test for voting as a matter of principle. Indeed, he was quite willing to allow unmarried women with property to vote because he believed that they would naturally affiliate with the Conservative party. The Dominion Government was entirely within its legal rights in sponsoring this legislation, but the Liberals fought the measure with all their resources and finally resorted to a filibuster in Parliament during which long passages of *Robinson Crusoe* and other irrelevant works were read to the assembled Commons in the effort to talk the measure to death. The Liberal Opposition maintained that each province was best fitted to determine the suffrage regulations which suited its peculiar conditions, and that to permit federal officers to scrutinize the list of voters would give the party in power a tremendous advantage in the elections. The measure, after some modifications, was finally passed, but it never became popular. When the Liberals returned to power the law was repealed (1898).

Elections of 1887   Macdonald faced the voters in the elections of 1887 with serious misgivings about the outcome. Nevertheless, his prestige and power, though waning, proved sufficient for another victory, and once again the voters returned the "Old Man" to office, but with a considerably reduced majority. Edward Blake, disappointed by the defeat of his party in this election and suffering from bad health, now resigned his leadership of the Liberal party. Four years later he reëntered the field of politics as an Irish Nationalist member of the British House of Commons. The Liberals, passing over older leaders like Sir Richard Cartwright and David Mills, chose Wilfrid Laurier, who had just turned forty-six, as the new leader of the Liberal Opposition. Laurier was a native son of Quebec and a faithful adherent of the Roman Catholic Church, factors which made it particularly difficult for him to carry on his new duties at a time when religious and racial animosities between Ontario and Quebec were so strong, and when local issues like the Riel case and differences over religious and secular schools were constantly being drawn into the arena of federal politics.

SELECT BIBLIOGRAPHY FOR CHAPTER XXI

Most of the volumes listed at the end of the two preceding chapters are also useful here. A brief account of some of the problems discussed in this chapter is available in H. E. EGERTON, *A Historical Geography of the British Dominions*, vol. V, Pt. II, pp. 293–343, *passim*. J. E. COLLINS, *Canada under the Administration of Lord Lorne* (Toronto, 1884), covers part of the period.

G. T. DENISON, *Soldiering in Canada* (Toronto, 1901) deals with the Northwest Rebellion of 1885.

W. P. M. KENNEDY, *The Constitution of Canada*, in ch. XXIV, deals with the distribution of legislative power between the Dominion and provincial governments.

Most of the references cited for the preceding chapter dealing with the railroad history of Canada also cover the years dealt with in this chapter. See in addition: W. VAUGHAN, *The Life and Work of Sir William Van Horne* (New York, 1920), and S. J. McLEAN, "National Highways Overland," in *Canada and Its Provinces*, vol. X, pp. 359–472. H. BECKLES WILLSON's *Life of Lord Strathcona and Mount Royal* should also be consulted for material on the railroad.

Books which illustrate various views held in the 1880's and 1890's concerning Canada's future relations with the Empire, are: GOLDWIN SMITH, *Canada and the Canadian Question* (London, 1891); G. R. PARKIN, *Imperial Federation, the Problem of National Unity* (London, 1892) and *Canada First, A Memorial of the Late William A. Foster* (Toronto, 1890).

For the boundary disputes of this period, see the special volumes on the various provinces in *Canada and Its Provinces*.

CHAPTER XXII

THE DECLINE OF THE CONSERVATIVE GOVERNMENT

THE span of life still left to Macdonald was a time of anxiety and comparatively meagre achievements. By the close of the 1880's, a decade of commercial stagnation, both political parties were angling again for some kind of trade agreement with the United States in the hope of regaining prosperity. The census of 1891 was very discouraging. While the Canadian population numbered nearly 5,000,-000, United States statistics professed to show that fully 1,500,000 Canadians had been lost to the Dominion, apparently forever. In the decade of the 1880's the Canadian population had increased nearly twelve per cent, but that of the United States had grown more than twice that amount. The "N. P." had not proved a panacea for the country's troubles, and by 1890, the Conservatives were willing to risk their political fortunes in a demand for the renewal of the Reciprocity Agreement of 1854 subject to such changes as new conditions might dictate. The Liberals in 1888 came out for unlimited reciprocity, virtually free trade with the United States. *Continued depression*

In 1891 the Conservatives yielded to a growing demand for lower duties by reducing the tariff on raw sugar, retaining, however, the duty on refined sugar, and three years later further reductions were made in the tariffs on agricultural implements, textiles, and lumber. Iron manufacturers and steel kings continued to enjoy heavy protection. In 1891 it was the turn of the Conservatives to make a pilgrimage to Washington in the interests of reciprocity. Like their Liberal predecessors, however, they met with nothing but rebuffs from the United States government. It happened unfortunately whenever a movement for freer trade arose in one of these neighbor nations, that the other was under the control of the protectionists. *Tariff changes*

The fisheries question, which apparently had been settled by the Treaty of Washington (1871), suddenly became an issue again when the United States, in 1885, terminated that part of the treaty which dealt with this question. New circumstances—in the form of a sudden change in the habits of the mackerel—induced the United States to allow this part of the agreement of 1871 to expire, for the mackerel had suddenly deserted Canadian waters for those of the United States. The privileges guaranteed to United States fishing interests, therefore, proved worthless, and in 1882 only one American vessel made use of them. Nevertheless, the arbiters charged by the treaty of 1871 with fixing the special compensation to be paid Great *Revival of fisheries controversy*

Britain for the excess value of the rights enjoyed by Americans in the Canadian fisheries assessed the United States $458,333.33 a year for concessions which were now no longer of value. Other irritating incidents, such as an attack upon American fishermen by a Newfoundland mob in Fortune Bay in 1878, added to American irritation concerning the fisheries arrangement. For this particular act of violence England finally paid $75,000 damages to the United States.

Crisis in controversy

When the United States Congress ordered the termination of the fisheries agreement in 1885, the controversy was thrown back to its beginning in the convention of 1818, and the whole question as to what right Canada and Newfoundland had to regulate the fisheries was revived and argued with great intensity of feeling. The British North American governments naturally claimed that they were charged with full responsiblity for the protection of their valuable fishing resources and for the maintenance of peace and order and the enforcement of law. The Canadian authorities soon began to enforce regulations that seemed unjustifiable, or at least unnecessarily disagreeable, to the American fishing interests. Canadian patrol boats tried to exclude United States fishing vessels from within the three mile limit and to enforce other irritating regulations. Although American deep-sea fishermen could ply their trade beyond the three mile limit, they were obliged to use Canadian harbors to buy ice, bait, and other supplies. Canada was willing to permit the Americans to get water and shelter and to come in for repairs in accordance with the earlier agreement, but refused to grant additional privileges. In 1887, 400 United States vessels were seized for the violation of Canadian regulations, and a United States war ship was sent to protect American fishermen from Canadian patrol boats. During this controversy several sharp notes passed between Washington and London.

Peaceful adjustment

It was evident that the Canadian Government was using the fisheries as a club to force a renewal of a reciprocity agreement which, among other things, would admit fish caught in Canadian waters to the United States free of duty. President Cleveland was ready to begin negotiations on this basis, and in 1888 the Chamberlain-Bayard treaty, drafted by a commission of which Sir Charles Tupper was the Canadian member, was submitted to the United States Senate for ratification. American fishing interests, who opposed complete reciprocity in fish and wanted the United States government to pay a lump sum for a renewal of their privileges, were powerful enough to secure the defeat of the treaty. Fortunately a *modus vivendi* was arranged by which the United States government got most of what it desired. By this temporary agreement any American vessel desiring the freedom of Canadian harbors paid a license fee of one dollar and a half a ton. The new arrangement proved satisfactory. The Canadian government faithfully adhered to this agreement, and from 1888 to 1905 Canadian-American relations over the fisheries were peaceful and mutually satisfactory. As a matter of fact, with the introduction of more steam-driven fishing vessels United States fishermen had less need for the privileges of Canadian harbors.

New domestic issues arose during the same period to stir the antagonisms and prejudices of Quebec and Ontario. In 1888 a bill was passed by the Quebec legislature dealing with the complicated question of compensating the Jesuits for the confiscation of their estates many years earlier. In 1773 the order of the Jesuits had been suppressed by the Pope himself, "for the peace of the church." The Jesuit estates had been confiscated by the British government and after 1831 were held in trust for Canada to be used for educational purposes. In 1867 the control of these estates passed to the province of Quebec. A quarrel soon arose between the Church authorities and the Jesuits, who had returned to Canada in 1842, as to who had the better title to these estates. The question had disrupted provincial politics for some years, until in 1887 Prime Minister Honoré Mercier, himself a former student in a Jesuit college, courageously undertook to settle the controversy. He secured the passage of a bill legally incorporating the Society of Jesus, and in 1888 a law was enacted appropriating the sum of $400,000 as compensation for their estates, this amount to be apportioned among the Church, the Jesuits, and Laval University at a ratio to be fixed by the Pope. In return, the order relinquished all claims to its former possessions. At the same time that this settlement was made for the Catholics, an appropriation was made for the schools of the Protestant minority in Quebec, since some of these schools had been supported by revenues derived from the Jesuit estates.

It is significant that although the Protestant minority in Quebec supported the Jesuits Estates Act, Ontario flew into a rage at once and denounced this new evidence of what Orangemen called "papal aggression" in Canadian affairs. In their eyes the law violated the principle of separation of Church and State, and amounted to an endowment of a secret papal society. That feature of the law which designated the Pope as the arbiter of the claims of the various groups concerned was considered as particularly obnoxious, and a glaring example of Quebec's willingness to let the Pope enforce an act of a Canadian legislature. Ontario clamored for disallowance. The Liberal leader, Laurier, Quebec's "favorite son," supported the Jesuits Estates Act on the ground that this confiscation of property had been unfair. He opposed disallowance by the Dominion government on the general principle that Ottawa should not interfere with those acts of provincial legislatures which were clearly within provincial legal competency. Macdonald permitted the law to take its course, and a proposal to disallow was decisively defeated in the Dominion Parliament. Nevertheless, a bitter sectional and religious controversy continued to rage outside the halls of Parliament, and eventually led to the formation of militant anti-Catholic organizations in Ontario,

Religious and racial prejudices

Jesuits Estates Act

such as the Protestant Protective Association and the Equal Rights Association.

Separate schools and bilingualism

In 1890 a bill was introduced in the Dominion Parliament to prohibit the use of French in the legislature and in the judicial procedure of the Northwest Territories. The proposed legislation clearly violated the specific guarantee provided by the act of 1875 under which this region had been organized. The measure failed, but it was an ominous symptom of the increase of religious and sectional antagonisms and a sign of the approaching controversies over bilingualism and separate schools which soon involved both political parties in an effort to compromise these opposing points of view.

Corruption in the Government

Finally, there was striking evidence of increasing laxity by the Conservatives in the administration of government departments. After an unbroken dozen years of power with almost nothing to fear from a greatly weakened Opposition, the moral fibre of Macdonald's party began to loosen. The Liberals charged Sir Hector Langevin, for some years head of the department of public works, with such mismanagement, corruption, and graft, that in comparison the notorious Tammany machine of New York was said to "smell sweet." To state the case mildly, Langevin was clearly guilty of negligence in office, and negligence in a department charged with responsibility for the public works left the door wide open to corruption. The charges against the minister received sufficient credence to prevent Langevin later from becoming Macdonald's successor as leader of the Conservative party. Other charges convinced many of the voters that a change in party was necessary to improve the morale of the government service.

Sudden appeal to country

In 1890 Macdonald startled the country by asking for a dissolution of Parliament and a new election. Some of his Liberal critics declared that he chose this as the opportune moment because the Canadian Pacific Railroad was trying to float a huge loan in England in order to get a connection with Chicago, and that therefore it could not afford to let the Conservatives lose control of the Dominion government. The implication was plain that generous campaign contributions would be forthcoming from the company. Sensing the rising tide of tariff reform in the West, Macdonald urged a moderate form of reciprocity with the United States at the same time that he restated the merits of the "National Policy" and stressed protection in districts devoted to manufacturing. He misled his followers by an unwarranted suggestion that the United States had made overtures for a new trade agreement, an assertion which the American secretary of state, James G. Blaine, was quick to deny.

Loyalty issue

The Liberals were on record as favoring unrestricted and complete reciprocity, a platform which the Conservatives easily distorted into a proposal for annexation to the United States, and as a "Yankee" proposition smelling of "veiled treason" and rank disloyalty. All loyal Canadians were summoned to the support of "The old man, the old flag, and the old policy," for what would probably be the last time that Canada's "grand old man" would appeal to them for political support. The Liberals tried to combat such sentimentalism with a cold-blooded analysis of the failures of the "National Policy," and by exposing the tactics of their opponents and the corruption and inefficiency in office with which the Conservative party was now definitely tainted.

In 1891, Macdonald once more won in a campaign which was a strange mixture of abuse, cheap politics, and an appeal to patriotism. *Macdonald's* The Conservatives had the great advantage which came from the *last victory.* support of the manufacturers and the business interests, and they diligently collected campaign funds from these sources and from the Canadian Pacific. Nevertheless, Conservative power was on the wane, and the Government lost heavily in both Ontario and Quebec. It was returned to power only because of the loyal support of the West and the maritime provinces.

Macdonald was exhausted by the strenuous winter campaign. In the spring of 1891 he suffered a stroke of paralysis from which he *His death* could not recover and on June 6, 1891, he died. His death was a crushing blow to his party and to the country. He had been prime minister of the Dominion for nearly twenty of its twenty-four years of existence and had so dominated his party that for many years it did not recover from the loss of his leadership. Among his many achievements three stand out above all the rest—the successful launching of the Confederation, although Macdonald had been one of the last to accept the need of confederation; the opening of the Northwest, even though this was accompanied by needless delays and blunders; and the building of the Canadian Pacific Railroad, a project which in its early stages had driven him from power in disgrace. Any one of these achievements would have been sufficient to place the name of Macdonald among the immortals of Canadian history.

Like most great men who have been long in the public eye, Macdonald's career was a strange mixture of virtues and blemishes. *Estimate of* It was Laurier, his life-long political opponent who called him *his career* "Canada's foremost citizen and statesman." He had the "supreme art of governing men," and as Laurier pointed out, "the fact that he could congregate together elements the most heterogeneous and blend them into one compact party, and to the end of his life keep them steadily under his hand, is perhaps altogether unprecedented." On the other hand, the same eulogist could say with equal truth, that "he did more than any other man to lower the level of Canadian political life. . . . Perhaps his chief disservice was to make his countrymen feel that politics was not only a game but a game without rules."

In the five years which elapsed between Macdonald's death and the expulsion of his party from office, four prime ministers passed rapidly over the stage of Canadian politics while the Conservatives sought in vain for a leader who could rally their wavering ranks and save the party from defeat. The first upon whom the mantle of Macdonald fell was Sir John Abbott, an able Montreal lawyer who had survived his connection with the annexationist movement in 1849, and who now served as the leader of his party in the Senate. As he himself told the House of Commons, he was chosen, as were "candidates for the Presidency of the United States," because he was harmless and was "not particularly obnoxious to anybody." The new prime minister retained his place in the Upper House and left the task of managing the Commons to Sir John Thompson. The latter's task was considerably complicated by the fact that he was a Roman Catholic convert from Protestantism.

Abbott's brief term of office was marked by an avalanche of charges against the administration of the government departments during the Macdonald régime. The department of public works, the department of the interior, and the printing bureau were especially singled out by the Liberals for their charges of inefficiency and corruption. There was loud and vehement discussion of Conservative corruption funds contributed by contractors doing business with the department of public works, and in August, 1891, Sir Hector Langevin, the minister in charge, though previously acquitted by a majority of the committee on privileges and elections, felt it necessary to resign. The only answer to these charges which the Conservatives could make was that the Opposition was tarred with the same stick. Thus they welcomed with delight the revelations of corruption in the Liberal Government of Quebec in the hope that this would counteract the charges against themselves. The session of 1891 was known as the "Scandal Session." In 1892 Prime Minister Abbott, because of failing health, relinquished his onerous duties.

He was succeeded by Sir John Thompson whose sheer ability overcame the religious prejudice which his change from Protestantism to Catholicism had aroused in many quarters. The most significant achievement during his premiership was in the field of foreign affairs, and concerned the settlement of the Bering Sea fur sealing controversy with the United States.

Ever since the United States had acquired Alaska in 1867, it had manifested great concern over the seal fisheries of Bering Sea and had been alarmed at the destructive seal hunting which was being carried on in the open sea. American regulations limited the number of seals which could be killed each year to 100,000 and confined the operations of the Alaska Commercial Company, which had the sole right to hunt seals in American waters, to the Pribilof islands, the seals' favorite breeding ground. Unfortunately for the seals, they were accustomed to wander each year far out into the Pacific and to return to Alaska by way of the coast of British Columbia. Many adventurers, especially Canadians, hunted the Alaskan seals which

swam beyond the three mile limit and by dynamiting they threatened
the rapid extinction of the herds. In 1886, under a law of Congress,
a United States revenue cutter seized three Canadian vessels seventy
miles out from the American coast line. Three years later additional
seizures were made. The British government at once protested against
what it considered the unwarranted exercise of United States jurisdiction over a body of water which was part of the open sea. Matters
might have been satisfactorily settled in 1888 had not Canada,
probably because of the breakdown of the negotiations over the
Atlantic fisheries, suddenly asked the British government to suspend
further negotiations.

The imperialistic American Secretary of State James G. Blaine, *Secretary of*
who came into office in 1889, was disposed to insist upon American *State Blaine's*
rights to the extent of arguing that Bering Sea was a *mare clausum* *standpoint*
(a closed sea) entirely under American control, and he carried the
American Congress with him in this extreme position. Great Britain
proposed to arbitrate the trouble, and in 1892 an agreement to this
effect was signed. The arbitration tribunal met at Paris in the
following year. In addition to two members from the United States
and two from the British Empire, of whom Sir John Thompson was
one, the tribunal contained one representative each from France, from
Italy, and from Sweden.

The United States was forced to recede from its extreme contention
with reference to its jurisdiction over Bering Sea. The substance of *Award*
the award was a denial of American property rights to seals beyond
the three mile limit of the coastline of Alaska or the islands of the
United States; further, Bering Sea was definitely included in the
Pacific Ocean as part of the high seas. Great Britain thus won the
legal issues at stake. The arbiters, however, worked out a set of
regulations for the regulation and protection of the seal fisheries,
and on this point the United States was sustained and probably got
all that Secretary Blaine had originally hoped to attain. Within a
zone of Bering Sea and the Pacific Ocean north of $35°$, seal fishing was
prohibited each year during May, June, and July, and pelagic sealing
was forbidden within a sixty mile zone around the Pribilof islands.
The use of steamers, nets, explosives, or guns was prohibited altogether. Finally, Canada collected damages of $425,000 from the
United States as compensation for the latter's unwarranted interference with her vessels.

Time proved that these regulations were ineffective. In 1911 an
International Seal Conference in which Russia, the United States, *Subsequent*
Great Britain, and Japan participated, made a treaty stopping all *sealing*
open sea sealing for fifteen years, pooling the seal skins that Japan, *regulations*
Russia, and the United States got from the rookeries along their
shores, and pro-rating the killings on land among the nations involved in order to compensate Canada and Japan for the surrender of
their pelagic sealing industry during the period agreed upon.

Tariff issue

The domestic problems of the Thompson ministry were not so easily solved. In the face of a rising demand for tariff reform, which was particularly strong among the farmers, the Government appointed a tariff commission to study the needs of industry. The Liberals eagerly seized upon the tariff issue, but prudently abandoned their demand for unrestricted reciprocity as they saw the time for their return to power approaching. Despite protests from the protected interests, some reductions were made in the tariff rates.

Manitoba schools question

It was the Manitoba Schools question which caused the greatest difficulties for the Government and eventually became the issue which brought about its fall from power. When Manitoba entered the Confederation there were no public schools in the province. The act of 1870 contained the usual guarantee on educational matters, to be found in Section 93 of the British North America Act, namely, that no legislation of the province should prejudicially affect the rights or privileges with respect to denominational schools which any class of persons had by law in the province at the time of union. In case of injury an appeal lay to the federal government. This was in accord with Section 93 of the British North America Act. The first legislature of Manitoba passed a school law like that of Quebec, providing for a board of education in which half the members were Catholic and half were Protestant, establishing a Protestant and a Catholic superintendent of education, and dividing the school funds between these two types of schools. In 1875 the arrangement for prorating the educational fund was changed to correspond with the changing proportion of Catholics and Protestants in the province.

Act of 1890 and separate schools

In 1890 a bigoted religious agitation, as well as the crying need for raising educational standards, especially in the parochial schools of some of the immigrant groups which had settled in Manitoba, led to a radical change in the educational system of the province. The act of 1890 swept away the dual board of education and created a single, public, non-sectarian school system to be supported by local taxes and provincial grants, under a department of education. At the option of the local school boards an hour's non-denominational religious instruction might be added to the curriculum, and parents who disapproved of this arrangement, could have their children excused from attending. Any Catholic citizen or any adherent of another denomination retained the right to support his own schools, but he paid the tax for the maintenance of the public school system in addition.

Appeals for relief

An agitation arose immediately among the Catholic population and among other friends of parochial schools to have the law disallowed on the ground that it violated the rights and privileges specifically granted by the act of 1870 under which Manitoba had entered the Confederation. As the controversy developed both parties became embittered, and the latent religious prejudices of the other provinces toward the Catholic Church were quickly aroused. The

Ottawa Government refused to disallow the Manitoba act when it was passed because of the possible effect of such action upon the general elections of 1891. The matter then went before the courts, and the Canadian Supreme Court declared the Manitoba law *ultra vires*. This decision was soon overruled by the Privy Council on the ground that the only right which the Catholics possessed at the time Manitoba entered the Dominion was the right to support their own schools and that this right was still unimpaired. The aggrieved Catholic minority now based its appeal on that section of the British North America Act providing for remedial legislation by the Dominion Parliament when the governor-general-in-council, that is, the cabinet, refuses to act. The Supreme Court of Canada was again overruled on this question of the nature of the remedy, and the Privy Council in 1895 held that the Dominion Government could grant a remedy, although it did not specify what it should be.

At this critical juncture in the affairs of the Conservative party Sir John Thompson suddenly died while visiting at Windsor Castle. *New premier* He was succeeded by Mackenzie Bowell, a second-rate figure in Canadian politics who had been leader for the Government in the Upper House. It did not contribute to the peaceful solution of the Manitoba schools question that Bowell was a past grand master of the Orange lodges.

The separate schools question now became the football of politics. The English element opposed the French, the Protestants fought with *Separate* the Catholics, the champions of provincial self-government contended *schools and* against federal intervention in Manitoba, and the Liberals, of course, *religious* did what they could to develop the situation to a point where it *prejudice* might be used to drive the Conservatives from power. The Protestant Protective Association, a new and violent anti-Catholic secret order which was the counterpart of the "A. P. A." movement in the United States, spread like wildfire during these years, and its members attacked all party leaders who dared to favor the Catholic demands. The "P. P. A." was especially strong in Ontario where the chief strength of the Conservatives also lay. Laurier tried in vain to pacify the agitators against the Catholics by pointing out that the provision of the British North America Act, designed to protect religious minorities had been inserted in 1867 at the specific request of the Protestant minority in Quebec.

On March 21, 1895, following a recent opinion of the British Privy Council to the effect that Ottawa could devise a remedy, *Manitoba* Bowell's Government issued an order-in-council ordering Manitoba *versus* to alter the law of 1890, to restore the rights of the Roman Catholic *Dominion* minority to separate schools which should share in the provincial *Government* grants for education, and to exempt Catholics from taxation for the support of any schools other than those attended by their children. Manitoba refused to abandon its position on the schools question and demanded an impartial investigation of its schools, confident that such a survey would reveal a lower standard of instruction in the parochial schools than in the public school system. The Dominion Government finally concluded to give Manitoba additional time to comply with its request, but announced that if nothing were done to relieve the situation by 1896 the Dominion Parliament would be asked to pass a remedial law.

Remedial bill

In February, 1896, the Government introduced a remedial bill substantially like the order-in-council which it had issued earlier. A month before, half of Bowell's ministry had resigned, because of this controversy and a general dissatisfaction with the prime minister's leadership. Bowell, therefore, was forced to retire at the end of the session. The proposed remedial legislation had the support of the Catholic Church, but Laurier, despite clerical pressure, opposed it, criticising some of its details and arguing for a policy of conciliation rather than compulsory interference with provincial rights.

Liberal filibuster

At this point Dr. Charles Tupper, the venerable Conservative leader and confrère of Macdonald, was hastily summoned from London where he was still serving as Canada's High Commissioner, to try his hand again as a practitioner on the body politic, to save the party. A conference arranged between the Ottawa and Manitoba authorities produced no solution for the trouble, and the people of Manitoba in an election supported their Government on the schools question by a large majority. After the breakdown of these negotiations, Tupper formally introduced the remedial legislation in the Ottawa Parliament. The Liberals opposed it as did some of the Conservatives also, and when Tupper, therefore, tried to force his measure through the Commons, he encountered a well-directed filibuster. After listening to readings from Mark Twain and Canadian histories and sitting wearily through continuous sessions one hundred hours long, Tupper was ready to capitulate. He obtained the passage of the necessary money bills on the promise to dissolve Parliament immediately and to appeal the question to the country. Before the elections were held, Tupper, now prime minister, reconstructed his cabinet.

Appeal to electorate

The leading issues in 1896 were the tariff and the Manitoba schools question. The Liberals favored a revenue tariff, but assured the manufacturers that they need not fear losses to their business from too sweeping changes in the direction of lower duties. The Liberal attitude on both the tariff and the separate schools question was that of cautious politicians who sense the chance to return to power and therefore try to avoid antagonizing any group which may possibly give them support. In Quebec every effort was made by the Conservatives to represent Laurier as an unfaithful son of the church of his fathers, and many of the clergy vigorously opposed his candidacy. The Liberal leader made a strenuous campaign throughout the country and won many voters by that personal magnetism which easily made him Canada's foremost orator. The Conservatives who had lost most of their leaders by death, struggled bravely on under the leadership of the "little doctor" from Nova Scotia, who, despite his years, fought hard to uphold the banner of his party.

As a result of the election, the Liberals were returned to power at Ottawa for the first time in nearly a score of years. Their majority *Liberal victory* in Ontario proved small indeed, but Quebec's "favorite son" managed to capture forty-nine of the sixty-five seats in the French province, and it was these gains which resulted in the Liberal majority. Henceforth, Quebec was the stronghold of the Liberal party, and Dominion affairs now fell to the direction of a French-Canadian Catholic.

Dr. Tupper remained in Parliament as leader of the Opposition until 1899. Before relinquishing the premiership to Laurier, he tried *Tupper's* to pack the Senate, and even the courts, with Conservative appoint- *retirement* ments. When the governor-general, the Earl of Aberdeen, refused to accede to these eleventh-hour selections, his action was denounced as an "unwarranted invasion of responsible government." Tupper died in 1915.

SELECT BIBLIOGRAPHY FOR CHAPTER XXII

In addition to volumes noted before, the political history of the period is covered in special articles of vol. VI of *Canada and Its Provinces*. The following biographical works are useful: E. M. SAUNDERS, *Life and Letters of the Rt. Hon. Sir Charles Tupper*, 2 vols. (New York, 1916); SIR CHARLES TUPPER, *Recollections of Sixty Years in Canada* (London, 1914) and J. CASTELL HOPKINS, *Life and Work of Sir John Thompson* (Toronto, 1895). Vol. I of O. D. SKELTON's *Life and Letters of Sir Wilfrid Laurier* (New York, 1922) deals with some of the events considered in this chapter from the point of view of Laurier's rôle in them.

For the fisheries negotiations, see especially: N. B. WORMWITH, "The Fishery Arbitrations," in *Canada and Its Provinces*, vol. VIII, pp. 681–748. Brief summaries from the American point of view are available in such histories of diplomacy as C. R. FISH, *American Diplomacy* (New York, 1923) and R. G. ADAMS, *A History of the Foreign Policy of the United States* (New York, 1924).

CHAPTER XXIII

THE RETURN OF THE LIBERALS

Wilfrid Laurier WILFRID LAURIER's policies, as embodied in his program as the first French prime minister of the Dominion of Canada, can only be understood by constant reference to his French-Canadian background and to his early experiences as a citizen of Quebec. Laurier was born in a little village near Montreal on November 20, 1841, of French-Canadian parents whose ancestry went back fully two centuries to the dawn of French-Canadian history. He began his education at the parish school of St. Lin and later entered the little college of L' Assomption. After graduating at nineteen, he attended the law courses of McGill University for three years and then entered upon the practice of his profession.

Political views In spite of his faithful adherence to the church of his fathers, Laurier as a young man began to manifest interest in that moderate form of Liberalism which was the key to his later public life, and which sometimes led him into serious misunderstandings with his own people. In 1865 Laurier served as an officer of *L'Institut Canadien*, an organization which eventually fell under the papal interdict for its advanced political and philosophical views and for its persistence in circulating and discussing books of which the Catholic Church disapproved.

Ultramontanes of Quebec In the late 1860's and the early 1870's the claims of the ultra-orthodox church party (the *ultramontanes*) in Quebec reached their climax in an effort to secure domination of the temporal as well as the spiritual affairs of the province. A church council at Quebec compared the modernist, liberal Catholic movement to the serpent that crawled in Eden to plot the fall of man; a French-Canadian battalion of Papal Zouaves was recruited in Quebec to fight for the Papacy's crumbling temporal possessions in Italy, and the troops left Canada with the blessings of the bishop of Montreal. In 1871 a Catholic program was announced which maintained that those entrusted with the legislative power must be "in perfect accord with the teachings of the Church." The triumph of the theory of papal infallibility in the Church at this time was followed by an attempt of the Quebec clergy to control elections in their province in the interests of the hierarchy. Joint pastoral letters were issued warning the people of the sins of political liberalism and suggesting spiritual penalties to intimidate the faithful who might otherwise be tempted to vote against the policies of the Church. Conservative party leaders flirted with the new movement, and eventually several elections

were declared void by the courts because of unwarranted interference
by the clergy on behalf of Conservative candidates.

It was one of the fundamentals of Laurier's Liberalism that a
man might be a good son of the Catholic Church, and yet accept
liberal principles in the domain of politics. On more than one occasion he courageously denounced the Church when it interfered
unduly in political affairs. The principles he announced in the days
of his political apprenticeship (1877) in an address on "Political
Liberalism," delivered before a group of young Quebec Liberals who
were members of *La Club Canadienne*, remained the guiding principles
of all Laurier's later years in matters affecting the relationship of
Church and State. In this address Laurier insisted that his Liberalism
had nothing to do with religion and that it was the tolerant, moderate Liberalism of England rather than the radicalism of the countries
of continental Europe. He disclaimed all intention of leading an
anti-clerical movement and freely admitted the right of the Church
party to participate in elections as any other group of voters might
do. But he denounced all attempts on the part of the Church hierarchy to interfere with freedom in political affairs by threatening a
system of spiritual terrorism. Throughout his life he was fully aware
of the dangers that would result for his people and his country if
political parties were to be founded on religious and racial differences.

In 1871 Laurier entered the provincial assembly of Quebec as a
Liberal; in 1874 he was elected to the Dominion Parliament and
served in Prime Minister Mackenzie's cabinet at the early age of
thirty-six. A decade later he became the titular head of his party
at a time when the Liberals, completely overpowered by the masterful
tactics of Macdonald, were still hopelessly wandering in the political
wilderness. Laurier had all the qualities of a magnetic leader. Endowed with a striking personal appearance he became a master of
oratory, and was equally eloquent in the French and English languages. He was a skilled parliamentarian and a genial leader whose
gentleness at times belied his hidden strength of purpose. Like most
public men he was often an opportunist and sometimes found it
advisable to sanction bits of political jobbery which seemed to belie
his sterling qualities of character. To several principles, however, he
was passionately and consistently devoted. He had organized the
Liberals of Quebec on a platform which permitted of political Liberalism without anti-clerical tendencies, and he devoted his life to
securing and preserving harmony between the English and the French
elements of the Canadian population. He uncompromisingly opposed
every attempt to make religious belief the basis of party organization.
His course in these matters, it is true, was one which his political
sagacity showed him was the only safe one to take. Yet to say that
political shrewdness alone controlled his public acts would be to
misjudge him entirely. With Laurier these matters were deep-rooted

*Laurier's
Liberalism*

*Early political
career*

convictions to which he clung with the tenacity of an honest and courageous soul.

*Liberal
ministry*

Laurier entered upon his new duties with one of the strongest ministries in Canadian history. The prime ministers of three provincial governments were summoned into the federal cabinet to exercise their talents on this larger political stage. W. S. Fielding, for ten years prime minister of Nova Scotia, became minister of finance; Andrew G. Blair, a former prime minister of New Brunswick, became minister of railways and canals; Henri Joly de Lotbinière, a Protestant ex-prime minister of Quebec, assumed the duties of controller of inland revenue; and Louis H. Davies, who had been prime minister of Prince Edward Island, became minister of marine and fisheries. Other notable figures in Laurier's cabinet of seventeen members (two without portfolio) were Richard W. Scott, secretary of state, who had been in public life for forty years, Sir Richard Cartwright of Ontario in charge of trade and commerce, Sir Oliver Mowat as head of the department of justice, a Scotch Presbyterian with a half century of political experience behind him, and Israel Tarte, of Quebec, who became head of the department of public works. Somewhat later, Clifford Sifton, another powerful figure in the Liberal party, entered the cabinet as minister of the interior. Laurier himself, probably with the mistakes of Alexander Mackenzie fresh in his mind, did not allow himself to become so absorbed in the details of one government department that he had no time left for the game of practical politics. He did not assume responsibility for any department and was content to lead his party and the Commons as president of the council. The Liberal Government made a most favorable beginning, for it had the great advantage of assuming office at a time when the tide of economic affairs began to turn favorably for Canada. Indeed the next decade did bring years of boundless optimism and prosperity.

*Settlement of
Manitoba
schools question*

The new prime minister's first task was the settlement of the long-standing quarrel with Manitoba over the separate schools question. True to his promise to avoid coercion, Laurier arranged conferences between the Dominion and the provincial authorities in order to work out a compromise which would satisfy all parties concerned. The terms finally agreed upon involved an amendment of the Manitoba law, but through the voluntary action of the provincial legislature itself. This change permitted religious teaching for a half hour at the end of the school day when authorized by the school trustees and requested by a specified number of parents. Roman Catholic and Protestant teachers were to be employed to give this instruction whenever attendance upon religious teaching reached a number specified in the law. Wherever ten pupils in a school spoke French or some language other than English as their native tongue, they were to be taught by the bilingual system. This provision was designed to meet the wishes and the needs of many European immigrants, such as the German Mennonites, as well as those of the French element. It was further agreed, though not specifically stated in the law, that the matter of textbooks and Roman Catholic representation on administrative boards should be settled to the satisfaction of all parties concerned.

Laurier's Manitoba settlement was an effort to meet the peculiar needs of minority groups without disrupting the public school system of the province. It probably represented the maximum which could be gained at the time without trying to force the province to do that to which it was resolutely opposed. Coercion undoubtedly would have caused trouble and might have ended in failure. The settlement, on the other hand, definitely removed the controversy as a political issue. Its terms were bitterly opposed by many of the Catholic hierarchy, and once more Laurier heard the familiar command to the faithful to choose between obeying the government and obeying the Church, a command that was often represented as a veritable choice between God and the devil. In Quebec the penalties of the Church were invoked to prohibit the reading of certain Liberal newspapers, and in the end Laurier had to appeal to the Papacy to quiet the clergy, only to bring down on his head the wrath of Ontario Protestants who resented this evidence of "papal intervention." A papal nuncio was finally sent to Canada, and the Pope virtually instructed the Quebec churchmen to cease their agitation. *Acceptance by Dominion*

The tariff was the second major issue of the campaign of 1896, and Laurier decided to tackle this complicated problem by means of a tariff commission which should conduct public hearings in many parts of the country in an effort to determine scientifically the tariff needs of each specific industry. It soon became apparent that, whatever may have been the Liberal promises of lower tariff rates during the campaign, the party did not intend to make radical changes in the protective system now that it was charged with the responsibilities of government. The recent enactment of the Dingley tariff by the United States, the highest since the Civil War, undoubtedly had its effect in convincing Canada that the time for free trade had not yet arrived. The new Dominion tariff measure as finally enacted provided a moderate, but on the whole honest, reduction in many of the tariff rates. The duties on iron, steel, and sugar were reduced, although government bounties on iron and steel offset the effect of some of these reductions; some specific duties were changed to *ad valorem* duties, and the number of articles on the free list was materially enlarged by adding articles needed by the farming population in particular. *Tariff policy*

The most important feature of the law was the provision for preferential rates. On the goods of all countries which granted favorable terms to Canadian trade, a flat reduction of twelve and a half per cent was made at once, with the provision that this preferential treatment would be increased to twenty-five and finally to thirty-three *Preferential rates* and a third per cent. This new arrangement was defended on the ground that it would greatly stimulate trade between Canada and Great Britain, and that it would have the important political effect of forging a new link of empire based on closer commercial union between the mother-country and her far-flung dominions. As a matter of fact, with the exception of New South Wales and the Netherlands, the law under existing trade arrangements applied only to Great Britain. For a time Belgium and Germany, who had most-favored-nation treaties with Great Britain, claimed the same preferential treatment, but in 1897 Great Britain renounced these treaties in order to safeguard Canada's fiscal independence. A brief tariff war resulted between Germany, Belgium, and Canada. The policy of imperial preference, inaugurated in Canada, was gradually extended until by the outbreak of the Great War in 1914, Great Britain and nearly forty of her possessions were united in a tariff union.

Prosperity

This preferential policy was initiated over the protests of Canadian manufacturers who predicted dire consequences from this lowering of the tariff walls. Nevertheless, the enactment of the new tariff law was followed by a period of prosperity during which the volume of trade between Canada and the mother-country steadily increased. The Liberal party naturally claimed the credit for this expansion in trade. The tariff, however, was only one small factor in a development which was world-wide and which was, to a large measure, to be attributed to a rise in prices caused by new gold discoveries in the Yukon region and elsewhere, and to the disappearance of the frontier of the United States which caused the current of immigration to be directed into the Canadian West.

Westward expansion

The Dominion Government became enthusiastically interested in all measures which might stimulate the material development of Canada. Late in 1896 Clifford Sifton of Manitoba entered the cabinet as minister of the interior, and under his skilful and enthusiastic direction great changes were made in the immigration statutes and in the land laws of the Dominion. After having donated 32,000,000 acres in all to the railroads, the Dominion government in 1896 abandoned the practice of land grants and began to support the railroads by cash subsidies and guarantees of bonds. Homestead legislation which had been passed by the Conservatives was continued in force, and the process of securing homesteads was simplified still further.

Homesteads

From 1900 to 1906 the number of homestead claims filed increased over 500 per cent, and a vast immigration service was organized to advertise abroad the attractions of Canada in order to attract desirable settlers. The number of immigrants from the United States and Europe increased very rapidly. Various departments of the Dominion government undertook to give aid to the farmer, and experiment stations, farmers' bulletins, farm exhibits, and other devices were used to stimulate the development of the new West. Canada seemed at last to have reached the years when her dreams of nationhood were to be fulfilled, and the prime minister predicted enthusiastically that "the twentieth century belongs to Canada."

In 1897 Laurier went to London to attend the Diamond Jubilee of the accession of Queen Victoria and to participate in what was the *Imperial* third imperial conference between the representatives of the mother-*conference* country and the spokesmen of her widely scattered dominions. For *of 1897* Laurier the conference proved a wonderful and joyous occasion. His charm and his oratory easily made him the most popular figure among all those who came from the Empire to attend the jubilee of their beloved Queen. The Cobden Club gave Laurier a medal for his services to the cause of freer trade within the Empire, the Queen made him a knight, and in France, ancestral home of his beloved French Canadians, he received the ribbon of the Legion of Honor. Small wonder that Laurier's political foes charged that the great democrat was fast becoming an imperialist. Indeed, it was during this visit that Laurier made speeches that were more imperialistic in tone than any he made before or after that occasion. His latest biographer leaves us to guess whether this new imperialistic note was due to the splendor of the occasion or to the effects of too much champagne at state dinners. Withal Laurier insisted on the preservation of Canadian nationality and on equal status for the dominions and Great Britain within the Empire. Even so, this new conception was a far cry from the belief of the young Liberal of earlier days who had prophesied that Canada's destiny was complete independence.

Laurier's European journey did much to advertise Canada to the Empire and fitted in admirably with Canada's plans to attract the *Laurier visits* attention of prospective settlers to the economic opportunities the *Continent* Dominion had to offer. After visits in Ireland and in Rome, where he had an audience with the Pope, Laurier returned to Canada to be received with a round of honors rivaling those he had won abroad.

It was not long before this new interest in imperial unity was subjected to a critical test. In 1899 England went to war with the *Boer War* Boers of South Africa. The hostilities were the result of British investments and aggressive enterprise in conflict with the Dutch farmers of South Africa who resented the exploitation of their gold and diamond fields by foreigners. In a large degree the war was the familiar story of a small country of pastoral and agricultural people, and with large and undeveloped resources, coming into conflict with the relentless juggernaut which we call modern, progressive, capitalistic civilization. British investors and gold-seekers in the South African republic quite naturally demanded political power to protect their financial interests, and denounced the backward Boers who resisted the spread of more advanced British ideas into their domain. With such a ruthless imperialist as Joseph Chamberlain in control of British diplomacy, war could not be avoided. When it came, its causes were skilfully presented in a way that was calculated to enlist the support of public opinion in England and in the British dependencies for a righteous, defensive war.

Question of
Canadian
participation
Canada and Laurier were placed in a difficult position by the Boer War. Should the Dominion which had pointed the way toward a closer union by preferential tariffs take the lead also in building a new imperial union of defense? Would it be proper and expedient to furnish Canadian troops for a British imperial war overseas in a cause in which Canada was after all not vitally concerned? In earlier wars Canadians had volunteered for service under the British flag, and the government had offered to raise troops at the time of the British war scare with Russia in 1877 and during the troubles in the Soudan in 1884, but Canada had never before officially equipped and supported any contingents overseas.

Differences of
opinion
In response to the rising spirit of nationalism and to the new prestige of a British imperial union, many Canadians began to besiege the Government with requests to participate officially in the Boer War. These demands poured in from mass meetings, and through petitions, and were freely discussed in the public press. On the other hand, Quebec remained luke-warm on the matter of sending her sons to fight on foreign soil. The old French province had behind it a great tradition of pacificism and non-participation in outside affairs which had been carefully and consistently nurtured by the Church. French Canadians regarded themselves as the real Canadian nation, rooted in the soil of North America for centuries, with no ties binding them to the intricate details of British diplomacy on the other side of the globe. The Canadian people and the Liberal cabinet were divided on the issue of participation in the war, and Laurier, therefore, had to formulate a policy which might be defended in Quebec as well as in Ontario.

Laurier's policy
Parliament was not in session when this decision had to be made. An order-in-council was therefore issued to the effect that the Government would equip and transport 1000 volunteers to South Africa, but that it would not send an official Canadian contingent. It was further stipulated that this action should not become a precedent. On October 30, 1899, the Canadian volunteers sailed from Quebec. Most of the French Canadians opposed the Government's decision because it involved Canada in imperial affairs. Likewise many Conservatives denounced Laurier for his imperialistic policy. Henri Bourassa, the grandson of Papineau, and a member of Parliament from Quebec, promptly resigned his seat in protest against the Liberal policy, only to be reëlected immediately by his constituents on an anti-participation platform. As Quebec gradually cooled on the issue of participating in the war, Ontario became red hot for greater support of the British Empire, and once again there was serious danger of racial and religious cleavage in the Canadian Dominion.

Before the close of the war, more than 7000 volunteers went to South Africa from Canada. About one-third of these were sent by the Dominion at a cost of nearly $3,000,000. Nearly twenty-five *Canada's* hundred men were officially recruited and partially supported by the *share in war* government. Most of the others were raised by the British government or by Lord Strathcona with no cost to the government of Canada. One battalion released the British garrison at Halifax for duty in South Africa.

In 1900, at a general election, the Liberal party submitted its record to the people for approval. The Government's policy in the *Election of 1900* Boer War was discussed in the campaign with no little heat and prejudice. Laurier defended his course on the ground that to refuse to lend any support to the Empire in its time of need would have destroyed the unity of the Dominion by arraying the French stock against the English. The venerable Tupper, still actively campaigning for the Conservatives, denounced Laurier in the English sections of Canada for having responded too late and too feebly to the cry of the mother-country for help, while in French Canada he tried to represent the Liberals as too imperialistic. No intelligent discussion of the Liberals' domestic program was possible so long as the war issue could be exploited in this fashion in order to arouse racial and religious prejudices.

In the elections of 1900 the Liberals retained control of Dominion affairs. They lost fourteen seats in Ontario, but this loss was more *Results* than offset by carrying fifty-eight of the sixty-five seats in Quebec, and by substantial gains in the West and in the Atlantic provinces. Dr. Tupper himself went down to defeat, and in 1901, when he was more than eighty, he resigned the active leadership of the Conservative party to Robert Laird Borden of Halifax, an able lawyer and a special student of constitutional problems.

Laurier's power and prestige continued to grow. He now dominated his party and his country as thoroughly as Macdonald had in *Laurier's power* earlier years. Among the routine of administrative details and minor legislative enactments during this second Liberal Parliament, diplomatic negotiations with the United States over the Alaskan boundary and other minor controversies, and the promotion of a second transcontinental railway stand out as the most important achievements.

When the United States acquired Alaska from Russia, its boundary, as fixed by an agreement of 1824 at ten marine leagues from the sea, *Alaska* was of little concern to any one. It was not until after the discovery *boundary* of gold both in territory belonging to the United States and to Canada *controversy* that the accurate delimitation of the Alaskan boundary became important, because the profitable exploitation of the resources of the interior depended very largely on easy accessibility to the ocean. It was discovered presently that if the American definition of the boundary should be accepted, Canada would be deprived of every serviceable harbor on the Pacific Ocean north of 54°40'.

In 1898 the United States and Great Britain agreed upon a joint commission to settle a series of Canadian-American issues, the most important of which concerned the Atlantic fisheries and the boundary between Alaska and Canada. Six commissioners were selected by each country, and it is significant to note that while on earlier occasions, as in 1871 and 1887, the Canadian representatives had constituted a minority of the British commissions, this time they were in a position to control the negotiations. After a number of sessions, the commission adjourned without reaching a satisfactory solution of the Alaska boundary controversy. It was successful, however, in working out new regulations for the Bering Sea and Great Lakes fisheries and in settling other matters such as mining rights and bonding privileges.

Major issues

In 1903 negotiations to adjust the Alaskan boundary were renewed. As has been suggested the controversy had assumed new significance with the great gold rush in the late 1890's to the Klondike fields. According to the treaty of 1825 between Russia and England, the boundary between British North America and Russian Alaska started at the southernmost extremity of Prince of Wales Island and extended northward along the Portland Channel to the fifty-sixth parallel. From this point it was to proceed by a line ten marine leagues from the sea, to longitude 141°, and thence to the Arctic Ocean. Wherever the mountain boundary ran more than ten marine leagues from the sea, presumably the line would follow the sinuosities of the coast. The real significance of the controversy lay in the efforts of each country to control the Lynn Canal approach to the Klondike gold fields. The inlet to this canal lay within the strip of coast claimed by the United States. The chief questions which needed to be answered were: what was the Portland Channel? what mountains were meant in the treaty of 1825 as defining the boundary? and whether the ten league line should follow the curvatures and indentations of the coast? If the United States should succeed in establishing the last contention, it would virtually control all the approaches to the Yukon mines. Ignoring the many details of this complicated boundary question, the controversy may be summarized by saying that the Canadians wanted a boundary line which would run along the more prominent landmarks and especially along the mountain heights which ran parallel to the coast. The United States government, on the other hand, contended for a line which would follow the sinuosities of the coast.

*Method of
settlement in
1903*

The treaty signed between the United States and Great Britain in 1903 stipulated that the dispute be submitted to a board of "six impartial jurists of repute," who should "consider judicially the questions to be referred to them." In other words, these jurists were expected to make a judicial and not a political or practical interpretation of the old Anglo-Russian treaty of 1825 and the American-Russian treaty of 1867 by which Alaska had been transferred to the United States. Great Britain and Canada appointed three jurists of repute to the commission, Lord Alverstone, lord chief justice of

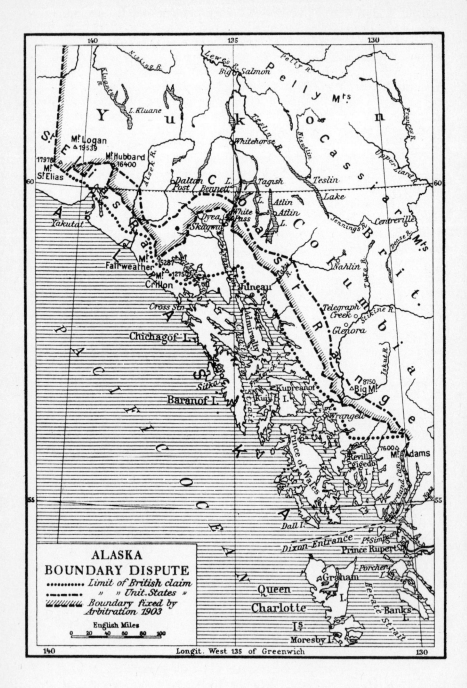

ALASKA
BOUNDARY DISPUTE
.... Limit of British claim
" " Unit. States "
Boundary fixed by
Arbitration 1903

English Miles
0   20   40   60   80 100

Longit. West 135 of Greenwich

England, Judge Armour of the Canadian supreme bench, and Sir Louis Jetté, lieutenant-governor of Quebec, formerly a judge. On the death of Judge Armour, Allen Bristol Aylesworth, a distinguished Toronto lawyer, was appointed to the commission.

Evidence has recently come to light which seems to indicate that President Roosevelt gave assurance in advance to some of the party leaders in the United States as to the personnel of the American delegation. He did this apparently in order to induce the United States Senate to ratify the treaty. At any rate, the American President soon abandoned the suggestions of his secretary of state, John Hay, to appoint members of the United States Supreme Court as the American commissioners—an arrangement which would have carried out the spirit of the agreement with Great Britain and Canada. Instead, the American representatives were Senator Henry Cabot Lodge of Massachusetts, who had already denounced Canada's claims as "baseless and manufactured," Elihu Root, a member of the Roosevelt cabinet, and Senator George Turner from the state of Washington, who had steadily opposed arbitration of the controversy in his speeches in Congress. A recent historian of the diplomatic relations of the United States has called President Roosevelt's appointments "a breach of faith." The Canadians insisted that they were the "victims of a confidence game" and that they had been inveigled to submit their claims to a commission the American members of which had virtually decided in advance to uphold the contentions of the United States at all costs. President Roosevelt, moreover, issued what practically amounted to an ultimatum and threatened to close all discussion of the question if the attempt to arbitrate failed.

"Breach of faith"

The tribunal met in London in the fall of 1903, and its award was signed by the three representatives of the United States and by Lord Alverstone. The Canadian members refused to sign. Great Britain was very anxious at the time to avoid difficulties with the United States and this probably accounts for the action of the British representative. The decision of the commission accepted the American contention that the ten league boundary line must follow the indentations of the coast rather than the crests of the mountains, and thus practically cut off the Canadian Yukon territory from access to the Pacific Ocean through Canadian territory. Lynn Canal and other inlets were awarded to the United States. Up to this point the decision was probably not so unreasonable or unfair as it was thought to be at the time. It is doubtful whether that part of the decision which located the Portland Channel is equally defensible. Here the line was drawn so as to allot to the United States two small islands which the Canadian members of the commission maintained Lord Alverstone had admitted belonged to the Dominion.

Award of tribunal

The Americans were naturally quite satisfied with the results of the arbitration, but in Canada the award led to an outburst of indignation. Once again it was argued that Canada was being sacrificed in the interests of British diplomacy. Lord Alverstone was furiously assailed and accused of holding private meetings with the American commissioners at which he sold out the rights and claims of Canada. Even Laurier made some bitter comments on the results. It is the judgment of later years, however, that the award was perhaps fairer than was originally supposed.

In 1903 the Liberal Government made plans for a second transcontinental railroad to parallel the Canadian Pacific to the north. The rapid development of the West and increasing general prosperity seemed to justify such a vast undertaking. Land values were rising, and the population of western towns like Winnipeg increased four or five times within the short space of a decade. In spite of the rapid extension of the mileage of the Canadian Pacific Railway system, the Government believed that conditions warranted a new road. A contract was entered into with the Grand Trunk Pacific by which the Government undertook to build a transcontinental line from Moncton, New Brunswick, to Winnipeg while the company was to continue the road from Winnipeg to the Pacific coast. The Government agreed to lease its portion of the road to the company for fifty years at a rental based on three per cent of the construction cost, no rent, however, to be paid for the first seven years of the lease. It was stipulated that the western section of the road must be finished within five years, and the Government guaranteed the interest and much of the principal of the company's bonds to an amount equaling seventy-five per cent of the building cost. Provisions permitting the government to regulate rates were included in the agreement.

This Grand Trunk Pacific agreement was forced through Parliament by a strict party vote. Some of the Liberals objected to the terms of the contract and Laurier's minister of railways resigned in protest. It was pointed out by critics of the Government that the country would own the section of the road least likely to pay dividends while it donated the profitable portion to the company. Borden, the Conservative leader, opposed the measure because it tended to postpone the day of government ownership of all the Canadian railway lines.

In 1915 the Grand Trunk Pacific completed the connection between Moncton in New Brunswick and Prince Rupert on the Pacific coast. The road proceeded from Moncton to Quebec and then to Prince Rupert by way of La Tuque, Cochrane, Sioux Lookout, Winnipeg, Melville, Saskatoon, and Edmonton. In its eastern portion the new road opened up much of the back country of Quebec and Ontario. The project was completed at a later date than the contract provided, and the Government found it necessary not only to extend the time limit but also to increase its financial guarantees to the company. The road was excellently built at a total cost of $300,000,000. In 1915 under the stress of war conditions the company refused to lease the government portion of the line, and it was, therefore, retained as another nucleus, like the Intercolonial, for the Canadian National, Canada's experiment in government ownership and operation.

While these plans were going forward, still a third transcontinental route was being developed from Quebec to Vancouver. The promoters of this enterprise, which was known as the Canadian Northern, were William Mackenzie and Donald Mann, two of Canada's greatest financial wizards. Starting with a hundred miles of road in Manitoba, these promoters, by buying lines in all parts of Canada, soon built up a road of ten thousand miles from ocean to ocean. Their route ran from Quebec up the left bank of the St. Lawrence River to Montreal, thence to Hawkesbury, Ottawa, North Bay, southward from Lake Nipigon to Port Arthur, and thence through Rainy River, Winnipeg, Dauphin, Humboldt, and Edmonton, to Vancouver. The phenomenal feature of Mackenzie's and Mann's projects was that these two magnates constructed and secured control of this vast system practically without investing a dollar of their own money. From the Government the company received subsidies and guarantees for its bonds. From these subsidies and bond sales the road was built while the promoters issued all the common stock to themselves in their capacity as managers and constructing agents. From 1903 to 1914 Dominion Governments, both Liberal and Conservative, guaranteed almost $100,000,000 of Canadian Northern bonds while the various provincial guarantees amounted to nearly $135,000,000. In addition the company received subsidies and land grants by skilfully lobbying before the legislatures of the Dominion and the provinces. In 1914 the bubble burst. In spite of feverish expansion into other accessory lines, such as mines, fisheries, lumber camps, and the erection of a chain of hotels and grain elevators, the company found it impossible to continue its process of pyramiding. The government had to come to the rescue, and the road was attached to the government-owned system.

Canadian Northern

To deal more effectively with the increasing complexities of the railroad problem, and particularly to safeguard the public against exorbitant rates and unfair practices by the companies, a law was enacted in 1904 creating a Canadian Railway Commission. This body was given judicial powers to fix rates, regulate matters of railway operation and management, and settle disputes over railway service subject to appeal to the courts on points of law. In many ways the act resembled the legislation of the United States, which had created an Interstate Commerce Commission and had defined its duties.

Government regulation

In the national elections of 1904 the building of the Grand Trunk Pacific was the leading issue before the country. The campaign was comparatively quiet. Laurier was at the height of his power; he appealed successfully to the national spirit of Canada with a plan for a wholly Canadian railroad from the Atlantic to the Pacific. To his

Elections of 1904

opponents, who criticised these expenditures as untimely and unnecessary, the prime minister replied that in view of Canada's unprecedented prosperity and marvellous expansion, delay would be ruinous and unpardonable. The Conservatives had no one to challenge effectively Laurier's popularity with the masses of the people. The elections resulted in a gain of eleven seats for the Government with Liberal majorities in Quebec, Nova Scotia, New Brunswick, and the West.

SELECT BIBLIOGRAPHY FOR CHAPTER XXIII

The best biographies of Sir Wilfrid Laurier are: O. D. Skelton, *Life and Letters of Sir Wilfrid Laurier*, 2 vols. (New York, 1922), and Sir John S. Willison, *Sir Wilfrid Laurier and the Liberal Party*, 2 vols., republished and revised for the *Makers of Canada, New Series* (Toronto, 1926). Other biographies of smaller scope but nevertheless useful are: J. W. Dafoe, *Laurier: A Study in Canadian Politics* (Toronto, 1922); P. McArthur, *Sir Wilfrid Laurier* (London, 1919), and two studies by French Canadians, A. D. DeCelles, *Laurier et son temps* (Montreal, 1920) and L. O. David, *Laurier: sa vie—ses œuvres* (Beauceville, 1919).

The Laurier régime is dealt with more briefly in: O. D. Skelton, *The Day of Sir Wilfrid Laurier*, in *Chronicles of Canada* (Toronto, 1921), and J. Lewis, "The Laurier Régime, 1896–1911," in *Canada and Its Provinces*, vol. VI, pp. 126-209. The latter covers the period to 1912. Most of the references cited here are equally serviceable for later chapters and should be consulted again in that connection. *The Canadian Annual Review of Public Affairs*, published in Toronto, and until the time of his death three years ago under the able editorship of J. Castell Hopkins, made its appearance in 1901 and is indispensable for events since the opening of the present century.

The controversy with the *ultramontane* Church party in Quebec produced a number of pamphlets and books written in the heat of the controversy. They have some value because of the determining influence of the movement in Laurier's evolution as a Liberal leader. Of these books, Charles Lindsey, *Rome in Canada* (Toronto, 1877) is typical of the extreme anti-Catholic point of view. Other volumes which throw some light on the recent clashes of nationalities in Canada are: André Siegfried, *The Race Question in Canada* (London, 1907), and W. H. Moore, *The Clash: A Study in Nationalities* (Toronto, 1918). The latter is decidedly favorable to the French-Canadian element.

For the general economic history of the period, parts of the following special articles are very useful: O. D. Skelton, "General Economic History, 1867–1912," in *Canada and Its Provinces*, vol. IX, 93–174; J. M. Courtney and Adam Shortt, "Dominion Finance, 1867–1912," *Ibid.*, vol. VII, pp. 471–517; W. D. Scott, "Immigration and Population," *Ibid.*, vol. VII, pp. 517–590; and J. A. Ruddick, "National Aid to the Farm," *Ibid.*, pp. 651–677.

A fascinating account of the railroad history of the Dominion with some attention to early beginnings is: O. D. Skelton, *The Railway Builders*, in *Chronicles of Canada* (Toronto, 1921). Some information is also available in S. J. McLean, "National Highways Overland," in *Canada and Its Provinces*, vol. X, pp. 359-472.

George Davidson, *The Alaska Boundary* (San Francisco, 1903) is interesting as a volume written at the time of the controversy for American propaganda purposes for the Alaska Packers' Association. The book contains some good material and several good maps. The most recent discussion of the controversy by an American student of the foreign policy of the United States is in Randolph G. Adams, *A History of the Foreign Policy of the United States* (New York, 1924), pp. 917, *et seq.*

The article by C. F. Hamilton on "Defence, 1812–1912," in *Canada and Its Provinces*, vol. VII, pp. 379–471, throws light on the evolution of Canada's military forces as part of the Empire's defenses.

For more detailed references for these years see Trotter, *Syllabus*, pp. 134–137.

CHAPTER XXIV

THE LAURIER RÉGIME (1904–1911)

LAURIER was destined to guide the Canadian ship of state for seven years longer. Throughout these remaining years of office he dominated the Government so completely that the Liberal party became almost a one-man party, a situation which obviously had its advantages but which at the same time was likely to prove dangerous for the future of the party. During these years Robert Borden toiled steadily and carefully, if without brilliance, to rebuild the decimated ranks of the Conservatives.

Canada continued to prosper. The West was growing rapidly under the generous land policy of the Government and the extensive immigration propaganda carried on by Dominion and provincial governments, as well as by railroad and steamship lines. In 1897 at the beginning of the Liberal régime, only 700 people had crossed from the United States into Western Canada; by 1911 this "American invasion" had reached 100,000. Immigration from Great Britain more than doubled in the short space of a decade, and in the fifteen years that the Liberals were in power the total immigration to Canada passed 2,000,000. Not all of these immigrants stayed in Canada, to be sure, but the greater number remained. The alarming drift of population from Canada to the United States declined, and from 1900 to 1910 the number of native-born Canadians in the United States increased only 11,000. Of the total immigration of 2,250,000 from 1897 to 1912, 961,000 came from the British Isles and 784,000 from the United States. From 1900 to 1910 Canada grew as much as she had grown in the preceding three decades. In 1891 the Dominion population was 4,833,239; in 1901, 5,371,315; and in 1911, 7,206,643. *Years of fulfilment*

In response to Canadian immigration propaganda with its highly-developed circulars, exhibits, special agents, and advertisements, thousands of settlers from the continent of Europe were attracted to the Canadian West. Among them were such widely differentiated groups as Icelanders, Russian and German Mennonites, "spirit wrestlers" like the Doukhobors from Russia, Scotch crofters, Italians, Germans, immigrants from various parts of the Austro-Hungarian Empire, Scandinavians, and numerous others. Fully fifty national and racial groups were represented in this great migration, but Canadians generally were little concerned with the problems of assimilation which might arise in the future. The average Canadian found safety in the great variety of groups represented. *Immigration*

Up to 1885 even Chinese were encouraged to immigrate, because coolie labor was needed for the construction of railroads and other public works. Since that time, largely due to the agitation of organized labor and the province of British Columbia, Chinese immigration has been effectively checked by a head tax which has gradually been raised to $500. By a gentleman's agreement Japan agreed to limit the number of laborers emigrating from her empire for Canadian ports.

Canada's foreign trade expanded more rapidly in the first decade of the twentieth century than that of any other country save Argentina. Foreign capital poured into Canada for investment, and in 1911 these investments reached the astonishing total of two and a half billion dollars. Canadian wheat exports alone were valued at $60,-000,000 in 1912, and this development was accompanied by a steady increase in the exportation of other products, particularly of minerals and lumber. In 1900 the area which now constitutes the western provinces of Manitoba, Alberta, and Saskatchewan, produced 25,-000,000 bushels of wheat; in 1911 its production reached 190,000,000 bushels. To provide for greater transportation facilities 10,000 miles of railways, or an average of two miles per day, were built from 1896 to 1911.

By 1905 Alberta and Saskatchewan had reached provincial status and were ready for admission to the Confederation on an equal basis with the older members of the Dominion. The Northwest Territories passed through various stages of government in their political evolution. Since 1888 these territories had been governed by a lieutenant-governor, a council, and an elective assembly. With the inrush of settlers and the rapid expansion of railroad facilities, the inhabitants of the new West demanded full provincial status. By the Act of 1905 the dominion government retained control of the public lands in Alberta and Saskatchewan; subsidies, however, were granted to the new provinces with a lavish hand. Each province received a $50,000 annual grant, an eighty cents per capita allowance until its population reached 800,000, a special annual grant of nearly $100,000 for a five year term in order to construct public buildings, and an allowance of five per cent on over $8,000,000 because the provinces were free from debt at the time they entered the Confederation. To protect the rights of minorities, the Act contained a provision guaranteeing the right to maintain separate schools (with certain requirements as to standards) and exempting religious minorities from paying taxes for any schools other than their own. All religious instruction was to be limited to the last half hour in the school day, and pupils might be excused from attending these exercises. Although this arrangement was substantially a restatement of the compromise by which the Manitoba schools question had been settled a decade earlier, it led to considerable protest in the cabinet and among certain Protestants who denounced the arrangement as an "endowment of clerical privilege."

A number of important laws were enacted during this period. In

1905 the salary, or "indemnity," of members of Parliament was *New legislation* raised from $1500 to $2500 per year, the prime minister's salary was increased to $12,000, and a salary of $7000 was provided for the leader of the Opposition in Parliament. Proportional increases were provided for judges, and an attempt was made to establish a system of pensions for high government officials. In 1908 in response to a new appreciation of the need for social and humanitarian reforms, an act was passed providing a system of old age annuities by which individuals might begin to contribute to this fund at the age of five while the government met the expense of administration and eventually repaid these savings at four per cent compound interest as a kind of self-earned old age pension. Legislation was enacted to improve further the civil service system and to safeguard the purity of elections by providing publicity for campaign contributions and prohibiting donations from corporations. Severe penalties were also provided for tampering with the voting process. Measures of this kind were increasingly necessary as the influence of big business in politics became more pronounced.

In 1906, due to the influence of the Lord's Day Alliance, a Dominion law was passed prohibiting excursions and performances where *Lord's Day Act* fees were charged, as well as most kinds of labor, on Sunday. The Act, based on a French model, was intended to protect labor against exploitation. A laborer working on Sunday was to have the right to twenty-four continuous hours off duty some other day.

To deal more effectively with transportation problems from the point of view of the public interest, the powers of the Railway *Capital and* Commission were increased and telegraph and telephone companies *labor* were brought under its control. In 1907 because of increasing friction between capital and labor attendant upon Canada's industrial expansion and because of the consequent injury to the public resulting from the industrial anarchy which usually accompanies strikes and lockouts, the Lemieux Act was passed in an attempt to avoid a suspension of operations on public utilities. The law was really drafted by William Lyon Mackenzie King, the young deputy minister in the department of labor which had been created in 1900. The official title of the statute was the Dominion Industrial Disputes Investigation Act. In substance, the act prohibited strikes and lockouts on all public utilities until after a report had been made by an investigating board of three, representing respectively the interests of labor, the employer, and the public. This investigating board was given judicial powers to subpoena witnesses and documents, and the term public utility was defined in a broad way to include mines, gas, electric, and street railway companies, as well as the industries more commonly accepted as utilities. The law did not compel either party to the dispute to accept the findings of the investigating board, but the pressure of public opinion was usually sufficient to force their acceptance. This experiment in preventing industrial disturbances attracted wide attention outside the Dominion. The act, however, was recently declared *ultra vires* by the Privy Council.

New immigration law

The immigration law of 1906, modeled on the legislation of the United States and Australia, provided for an immigration service within and outside Canada for protection of immigrants en route, for the exclusion of undesirables, and for the deportation, at the expense of the transportation company, within three years of their arrival, of those who entered illegally.

Decline of Liberals

In spite of these and other notable achievements, the parliamentary sessions of 1906, 1907, and 1908 were better known for the Government scandals which they brought to light than for their constructive achievements. The Liberal party was beginning to show the effect of long years in office without the checks of a vigorous and powerful opposition. Ugly charges running all the way from inefficiency to positive graft and corruption were made against the department of marine and fisheries and the department of the interior. The interior department seemed particularly to be involved in questionable deals with grazing and lumber interests which came to the department for leases and concessions. The Liberal Government also was charged with favoritism and corruption in the matter of railroad charters and in the administration of the tariff, with tampering with elections and buying votes, and with building up a powerful political machine by manipulating the civil service system so as to satisfy the job-hunters of the party. What in the United States is known as "pork barrel" legislation was also flourishing in Canada, and government funds were being spent on costly post-office buildings, internal improvements, and public works which were more often intended to build up the political fortunes of the local member of Parliament than to meet the crying needs of the community. Laurier tried to disarm his critics by advocating still further extension of the civil service system and by promising a thorough-going investigation of all the charges against his administration.

Effects of industrial revolution

It was apparent that the morale of the Liberal party was deteriorating. There were even charges of personal delinquency and rumors of drunkenness on the floor of Parliament. Canada, moreover, was entering upon that stage of her industrial development when big business tried to control the government, and when industry leaned more and more heavily on the politician. An air of cynicism was beginning to permeate business and politics. In the words of Tarté, a member of the Government, "elections are not won by prayers." Capitalists and active businessmen, dependent on the government for charters, tariff privileges, and other special aids, did not hesitate to justify any methods of political management which promised success for their enterprises. Canadian politics, like those of the United States, began to show the effects of "the tugs and pressures" exerted by the leaders of the new capitalistic order who were none too scrupulous in the methods used to extort special favors or legislative immunity for their investments or in their attempts to create monopolies. In local politics, due largely to the effect of the factory system on the development of congested urban centers, the political "boss" and the party "machine" were slowly rising to a new position of dominance. Canada discovered—though perhaps not so rapidly or so strikingly as the United States—that the industrial revolution brought disadvantages as well as benefits, and that the country was face to face with a rising flood of materialism and cynicism in the field of practical politics. Humanitarian idealism was being rapidly transformed in many quarters into a smug conservatism.

In the election campaign of 1908 the Conservatives devoted much of their energy to the airing of scandals in the government *Issues of 1908* service. On the constructive side they advocated government ownership of public utilities like the railroads, telegraphs and telephones, publicity for campaign expenditures, reforms in the civil service and the Senate, government cold-storage plants and a system of rural mail delivery, more effective government regulation of certain corporations, and a number of internal improvements such as waterways and harbor facilities. Borden and his lieutenants waged an able fight, but the Liberals benefited by the continuing prosperity, by their record of social legislation, and most of all, by the magnetic figure of their great leader who was pleading with the voters for one more endorsement so that he might finish his life's work. The storm center of the campaign was the province of Ontario.

Once more the Liberals received the approval of the Canadian people, this time, however, with a considerably reduced majority. *Another* The Conservatives won a majority in Ontario, Manitoba, and British *Liberal* Columbia, the Liberals in the other six provinces. The total Liberal *victory* majority of sixty-two seats in 1904 was reduced to forty-seven. In the three years left to Laurier as prime minister of the Dominion, relations with foreign countries bulked large and quite overshadowed all other problems of the Government.

In 1909 in response to a growing demand from a large element of the population and the public press, the Liberals were forced to *Naval defense* consider the problem of Canadian naval defense and the possible aid Canada could and should give to the mother-country in case of war. The English-speaking world was greatly excited at the time by the race for naval armaments in which England and Germany were engaged. Great Britain, whose security must necessarily depend on her navy, looked with greatest alarm upon the efforts of Germany to extend her colonial possessions and to provide a navy not only large enough to insure Germany a dominating power on the seas but also to match her military power on the continent of Europe. Stimulated by propagandists and munitions interests desirous of large contracts, Anglo-German relations soon became so tense that many Canadians were convinced that Germany was plotting a European war and that consequently England must arm to the teeth. From many quarters came the demand that Canada as a matter of filial duty and also for her own preservation should bear her share of the ever-mounting burden of armaments which it was generally supposed was the best guarantee for the preservation of the peace of the world.

Laurier's
dilemma

Laurier found himself in a very difficult position. He had participated in all the imperial conferences held during his term of office, and he had helped forge the new commercial bonds which were to unite the Empire in a great economic union. He had pointed with pride to Canada's place in the British commonwealth of nations. On the other hand, Laurier had steadily opposed all attempts of British imperialists, such as Joseph Chamberlain, to reduce this newly achieved unity to the cold, rigid basis of legal enactment or to a new written constitution which should apply to the whole Empire. At the conference of 1902 Laurier had opposed the attempt to create an Imperial Council, and he had not deviated from this position in later meetings of the representatives of the Empire. The conference of 1909 specifically concerned itself with the matter of defense, and the Anglo-German naval competition undoubtedly was the most important issue discussed by British leaders with the dominion prime ministers.

Quebec
nationalists

The situation in the province of Quebec added to the difficulties of the French-Canadian prime minister. Quebec was the stronghold of his party, and the preservation of the solid delegation of Liberal members from the province of Quebec was essential to the prime minister's continuance in office. Yet Quebec was becoming alarmed by the steady development of events which seemed to be drawing Canada more and more deeply into the vortex of Old World diplomacy and rivalries. The French Canadians were true nationalists, in the sense that they believed in a Canadian nationalism absolutely free to determine its own life without entanglements and commitments to British diplomacy. Just as in 1899 many French Canadians could not understand why Canada should participate in a war with the Boers in a part of the world so remote that its affairs could never affect Canada, so in 1909 they feared the results of the rising tide of imperialism. From their point of view it was imperative that Canada preserve her "splendid isolation."

Bourassa

By 1909 this isolationist, and to a large extent pacificist, agitation in Quebec had crystallized into a political movement under the leadership of Henri Bourassa. Bourassa was born in Montreal in 1868 of French-Canadian parents. His father was an author and painter of some note, his mother was the daughter of Papineau, the rebel leader of 1837. Henri Bourassa enjoyed the advantages of an excellent education and gained considerable prominence by his literary ability. In 1896 he entered the Dominion House of Commons as the member for Labelle, Quebec—a seat which he held until 1907 when he resigned to become a member of the legislature of his province. At the time of the Boer war, as has been pointed out, Bourassa had resigned

his seat at Ottawa as a protest against the Government's policy of
outfitting volunteer Canadian contingents for service overseas, and
had been reëlected by his constituents by acclamation.

When Bourassa entered the Ottawa Parliament he was considered
one of the most brilliant of the younger members. He was a masterful   *Bourassa's*
orator in both English and French, he enjoyed the friendship of the   *break with*
prime minister, and there was some talk of including him in the   *Laurier*
Government and raising him to high position in the councils of the
Liberal party. After the break with Laurier in 1899, Bourassa slowly
drifted into opposition and became the organizer and leader of the
Nationalists of Quebec. His friends honored him for his loyalty to
his convictions while his enemies declared that he had left his former
allegiance because his ambition for high office had not been sufficiently
recognized. Bourassa quickly rallied around him all the discontented
groups in French Canada and welded them into a new and powerful
political organization.

Among the Nationalists were to be found many of the Roman
Catholic clergy, who opposed war and all plans to break down   *Background of*
French-Canadian isolation, as well as most of the French Canadians   *Nationalist*
who were by nature anti-imperialistic and had viewed with alarm   *movement*
the work of the various imperial conferences. The controversies with
Ontario Protestants over separate schools, differences in religion, and
the use of the French language, added to their anxiety. On this
background of prejudice, racial antagonisms, and injured pride, it
was comparatively simple to build an organization pledged to defend
French culture and institutions against all attempts to absorb French
Canada in a British dominion or in a British commonwealth of
nations. A program of social and economic reforms was added to
these anti-imperialist principles. Some of the Nationalists may have
contemplated independence as the ultimate goal of their agitation,
but most of them were sincere in maintaining that they represented
the true Canadians who were patriotically interested in preserving
Canadian nationhood.

The Canadian Nationalist League was formed by a group of
Montreal citizens in 1903 under the able leadership of Oliver Asselin. *Program of the*
Its platform asserted the rights of French and Catholic minorities   *Nationalists*
to separate schools, declared French one of the official languages of
the entire country, favored peopling the West with native Canadians
rather than with immigrants, and sponsored the conservation of the
Dominion's resources and the nationalization of the railroads.
For its foreign policy the new organization advocated the greatest
political, commercial, and military autonomy for Canada consistent
with the preservation of the colonial tie. It stood further for the
greatest possible provincial autonomy within the Dominion and the
development of a distinct Canadian nationality. The nationalist
movement grew rapidly after 1903, deriving new support from the
antagonisms aroused by the separate schools question in the bill

organizing Alberta and Saskatchewan in 1905, from the Lord's Day
Act of 1906, and from various happenings in the provincial politics
of Quebec. In 1909 the agitation for a Canadian navy, to help the
Empire cope with the growing German menace led to long and heated
discussions throughout the Dominion, and it was during this controversy that the Nationalist movement reached its highest effectiveness before the outbreak of the Great War in 1914.

*Formation of
Canada's navy*

Liberals and Conservatives alike believed that Canada should
share in the burdens of imperial defense, but they could not agree as
to the best method for making their contribution. In 1910 the Government, after much deliberation and hesitation, decided to sponsor
a naval service bill designed to develop a Canadian navy under the
control of the Dominion government. An initial appropriation of
$10,000,000 was proposed for this purpose, and it was provided that
in case of emergency, and subject to the prior consent of the Canadian
Parliament, the Dominion navy could be turned over to the British
Admiralty for service. It was specifically stated that enrollment for
naval service was to be entirely voluntary. Subsequently the Canadian
government took over the dock yards at Halifax and Esquimalt and
bought two British cruisers, the *Niobe* and the *Rainbow*, to serve as
the nucleus for the Canadian navy and as training vessels for volunteers for the naval service. In 1911 a naval college was opened at
Halifax.

*Laurier's
middle course*

It is clear that with these proposals Laurier was trying to steer
a middle course. England had asked her dominions to create fleet
units consisting of one dreadnought, three armored cruisers, six
destroyers, and three submarines. Some Canadian imperialists favored
a program of contributions by Canada to the British Grand Fleet;
others favored contributing dreadnoughts or their value in an emergency only, and organizing a Canadian navy as a permanent policy.
Bourassa and his Nationalists represented the other extreme and
objected both to a Canadian navy and to contributions to the imperial
navy. Perhaps somewhere between these extreme positions, the great
majority of Canadians took their stand. They probably wished
Canada to develop her naval defenses, but preferred a moderate
Canadian navy to a policy of contributions to Great Britain. It was
this middle group whom Laurier sought to satisfy. F. D. Monk, one of
the leaders of the Quebec Conservatives, opposed all entanglements in
imperial affairs and advocated a popular referendum on the new policy.

*Conservative
opposition*

The naval bill was attacked from many angles in Parliament.
Borden, though favoring some kind of a naval bill, denounced this
particular measure as an extravagant waste of the public funds without
any significant results. The Conservatives as a whole criticized
Laurier's "tin pot navy" and pointed out that the stationing of the
Niobe (11,000 T.) on one coast and the *Rainbow* (3600 T.) on the
other side of the continent was a ridiculous way to defend the Dominion from naval attacks. Borden argued that it would be better policy

to send England the money for the construction of a dreadnought to be added to her battle fleet, but, in any case, he demanded that the people of Canada be consulted beforehand on so important a measure. It is apparent from the foregoing that the Opposition was by no means a unit in the arguments presented.

The debate on the naval service bill furnished the opportunity for a general discussion of Canada's status and obligations in the Empire, and Bourassa and the Nationalists made the most of this opportunity to force the complete issue into the open. The fiery Quebec leader denounced the navy bill in the most violent language and prophesied that the next step would be the drafting of Canadians for gun fodder in Europe's wars. Laurier was described as the tool of the British imperialists and the munitions manufacturers. Bourassa made some able and penetrating analyses of the European system of alliances and secret diplomacy and called attention to the vague features of the bill providing for the use of the Canadian naval force in imperial emergencies. To further his cause, Bourassa, in January, 1910, issued *Le Devoir*, an evening journal which soon became the official organ of the Nationalists. *Canada's status in Empire*

Laurier appealed to French and English Canadians to unite in support of this great national program and argued that it was no longer possible for Canada to stay out of England's wars. "When Britain is at war, Canada is at war," he declared courageously, "there is no distinction." Laurier's "solid Quebec" now became a "house divided against itself." A Nationalist candidate carried Laurier's home constituency of Drummond-Arthabaska, which had voted Liberal since 1887, and Bourassa succeeded in winning for his program the *ultramontane* element of the clergy and many of the younger churchmen and college students of the province as well as some former members of the Conservative party. *Laurier's views on imperial relations*

The Liberals were successful in carrying their naval policy through Parliament, but the issue was projected at once into the next election campaign as an important party question. At the same time government expenditures on the Canadian militia were steadily mounting, and plans were being perfected for the coöperation of Canadian troops with the British General Staff in case of emergency. *Naval policy as election issue*

In 1910 the controversy over the fisheries which had raged intermittently for a century and a quarter was at last definitely settled by reference to the Hague Tribunal. Once again, in 1905, the *modus vivendi* of 1888 had been disturbed by Newfoundland's legislation forbidding the sale of bait and supplies to foreign vessels. This unfriendly legislation was clearly a maneuver to force the United States to open its ports free of duty to Newfoundland's products, but it was promptly circumvented by the device of the American companies of employing Newfoundland fishermen to do their work for them. When this, too, was prohibited by law in 1906, the controversy threatened to become serious. The United States government protested against this *Final settlement of fisheries question* unfriendly legislation; Great Britain disallowed the Newfoundland statute; and a series of notes passed between American Secretary of State Elihu Root, and Sir Edward Grey of the British Foreign Office. The result was a new *modus vivendi*. Finally in 1907 the United States proposed that the entire controversy be submitted to the Hague Tribunal for adjudication and a treaty to this effect was signed in 1909.

Award of Hague Tribunal

The arbitration tribunal was selected from the panel of the permanent court at the Hague. The United States was represented by George Grey, a judge of the Circuit Court of Appeals, and Great Britain's representative was Sir Charles Fitzpatrick, Chief Justice of Canada. Three other members, from Austria, Holland, and Argentina, completed the tribunal. The award was made public on September 7, 1910. On many of the essential points the decision was against the contentions of the United States. The award acknowledged Great Britain's sovereign right to regulate the fisheries, but provided that regulations must be bona fide and in accord with treaty provisions; a mixed commission was created to pass on the reasonableness of these regulations. The three mile line along the Canadian coasts was drawn so that it practically coincided with the claims advanced by Great Britain and Canada during earlier controversies. The award settled other minor issues, and in 1912 other details were disposed of by a treaty. Three years earlier, as further evidence of the new spirit of arbitration and comity between neighbor nations, a treaty had been concluded providing for a permanent International Joint Commission to which Canada and the United States could refer any dispute for settlement, if the United States Senate and the Canadian cabinet agreed to this method of dealing with the controversy.

Closing years of Laurier's régime

Important legislation, such as the law of 1909 which created a commission to conserve Canada's natural resources, was lost sight of in the closing years of the Liberal régime because of the rising tide of tariff agitation. In spite of Liberal professions of interest in a lower tariff, the "National Policy" had remained virtually undisturbed during the period that the Laurier Government was in power. Tendencies to tinker with the tariff and apparent revision of rates downward were often offset by new bounties and subsidies to specially favored industries.

Revival of tariff agitation

The manufacturers of Canada continued to agitate for higher protection, and "infant industries" now grown quite lusty cried for still more milk from the tariff bottle. A new movement for radical tariff reform was coming out of the West, and it was this agitation which compelled the Government to "steer west" in its tariff program. In practically every political campaign promises had been made to the farming, lumbering, and fishing interests to reduce the tariff and to provide closer commercial relations with the United States. These campaign promises, however, were quickly forgotten once the party was safely returned to power. Even if the Canadian government had been seriously interested in tariff reform, it would

not have been possible to get the ear of the United States prior to
1910, for reciprocity proposals. From 1866 to 1898 no less than seven
offers for reciprocal trade agreements were rejected by the United
States government.

In the first decade of the twentieth century prosperity began to
lag in the agricultural regions, and notably in western Ontario and *Agricultural*
the prairie provinces. The disappointed farmer began to complain *unrest*
of the "new feudalism" which made him dependent on eastern capitalists. He argued that the money men of the East controlled the
railroads, the grain elevators, and the banks upon which the farmer
had to rely to get his crops to market. There was a widespread conviction in the agricultural sections that most of the farmer's profits
went into the pockets of these middlemen who controlled the adjuncts
so necessary to the disposal of his crops. As this economic unrest
spread, it was discovered that the protective tariff benefited a group
of vested and specially privileged interests in the manufacturing
towns—Montreal, the center of "Big Business" in Canada, already
had her flock of millionaires—while it did little or nothing for the
farmer or the ultimate consumer save to increase the cost of the
articles they had to buy.

When this was once clearly understood the farmers began to organize for the protection of their interests. From 1900 to 1911 six fed- *Embattled*
erated associations of farmers arose in the West. Some established *farmers*
their own newspapers to voice the political and economic demands
of their section. These Grain Growers' Associations represented a
farmers' insurgent movement against the old parties, and embraced
in their program many of the elements of state socialism. Indeed, the
platforms of these Canadian organizations were very similar to those
of the farmers' non-partisan leagues which arose simultaneously in
the western agricultural states of the American republic. The Grain
Growers' platforms demanded lower duties and reciprocity with the
United States, government ownership and operation of grain elevators
and meat-packing plants, effective railway legislation, and the encouragement of the coöperative movement. In 1910 a delegation of 800
farmers came down to Ottawa in special trains to remind Laurier of
the urgency of their needs and to plead for the farmer's emancipation
from the capitalists of the East. Thus a new division appeared on the
field of Canadian politics, and this independent movement has continued as an important factor in Canadian history to the present day.

At the same time that the Liberals were experiencing this new
pressure for tariff reform from within the Dominion, the United *Tariff*
States government also became interested in closer trade relations *question in*
with Canada. Although the movement for tariff revision in the *United States*
United States had been thwarted by the passage of the Payne-Aldrich
Act of 1909, President Taft felt called upon to defend this protectionist
measure. Thereby he precipitated an insurgent movement in his own
party. The Congressional elections of 1910 resulted in a sweeping

victory for the opponents of the Republican administration, and the
Democrats obtained control of the lower house of Congress. The cost
of living was steadily mounting and there were important groups in
the United States who attacked the tariff as a maker of millionaires
and a vicious form of class legislation. At the same time, American
newspapers wanted Canadian pulp free of duty, and many exporters
were seeking larger markets for their products. President Taft, desiring to do something to reduce the cost of living and to retrieve his
political fortunes, at this critical juncture in the affairs of his administration decided to sponsor an offer of reciprocity to Canada.

*Reciprocity
negotiations*

Formal negotiations for a reciprocity agreement began in November, 1910, between members of the United States and the Canadian
governments meeting at Ottawa. These discussions were later renewed
at Washington. At the suggestion of the Canadian representatives,
it was agreed that a friendly reciprocal arrangement brought about
by mutual legislation would be preferable to a more formal treaty.
The negotiations were conducted in absolute secrecy, and on January
26, 1911, the agreement, together with all official correspondence
pertaining to it, was submitted simultaneously to the national legislatures in the two countries.

*Policy of
Laurier
Government*

To Laurier the offer for a reciprocity agreement came as a distinct
surprise, but the proposal was in complete accord with the lower
tariff demands of large sections of the Canadian Dominion and with
the tendency to negotiate new trade agreements with foreign nations.
In 1907, having by this time gained the right to negotiate such agreements directly and without British intervention, Canada had made a
new commercial treaty with France. In 1910 she had taken steps toward a commercial understanding with Italy. Canadian trade commissioners were established in many parts of the world. Why should
not Canada accept the American offer of reciprocity, especially
since it was offered on such favorable terms and seemed to be new
evidence of the desire of the United States to cultivate closer relations with the rest of the English-speaking world? President Taft
had been very eager to extend to Canada the benefits of the minimum rates provided by the Payne-Aldrich tariff, and there was
no reason to doubt the sincerity of his reciprocity proposals. Indeed,
the offer was far more liberal than had been anticipated.

*Proposals of
1911*

In the agreement as finally worked out, wide reciprocal free trade
concessions, almost as liberal as those of the Elgin Treaty of 1854,
were made. To obtain these concessions Canada had to do little else
than give the United States the reductions already granted to other
countries under the Canadian tariff laws. The reciprocity agreement
provided for mutual free lists on leading primary food products such
as grains, fish, fruits, dairy and poultry products and live-stock; and
for reduced rates on secondary food products such as fresh and canned
meats, cereals, flour, etc. In addition, certain commodities, such as
cotton-seed oil and rough lumber, which had previously been ad-

mitted free by one country were to be made free by the other, while the tariffs on certain commodities, such as plows, agricultural machines, coal, etc., having different rates of duty, were reduced by the country maintaining the larger rate to the lower rate.

In the United States Congress the reciprocity proposal encountered opposition from representatives of the New England fishing interests, *Attitude of* and from some of the grain, lumber, and cattle producers of the West *American* who feared Canadian competition. On the other hand, the proposals *Congress* were supported on the ground that they would open Canadian resources to the United States and provide a wider Canadian market for the surplus farm and manufactured products of the United States. In the final vote on the measure a majority of President Taft's own party voted against the agreement, whereas the Democratic opposition voted practically unanimously in its favor. It was only by the aid of Democratic votes that the measure received Congressional approval.

Laurier probably expected the Dominion Parliament to accept reciprocity without much debate. It was what Canada had been *Reception in* seeking on various occasions since the cancellation of the treaty of *Canada* 1854. The successful negotiation of the reciprocity agreement was hailed at first with enthusiasm by members of the Laurier Government as well as by a large group of Conservatives who still cherished the desire for free trade in the natural products of the two nations, and who regarded the terms of the proposal as a distinct victory for Canadian nationalism. The reading of the astonishingly liberal terms of the agreement by the Hon. W. S. Fielding on January 26, 1911, before the House of Commons was greeted by a storm of applause in which even the Opposition joined.

Slowly, however, a powerful opposition to the agreement developed under the capable leadership of Borden. Some distrusted the *Opposition* liberal nature of the American offer and suspected hidden political *to tariff* motives behind these commercial proposals. Others believed that *agreement* the future of Canada lay in the direction of greater development of the British market. The protected interests and the railroads and banks so intimately connected with them represented reciprocity as the entering wedge for the destruction of the protective tariff policy, and argued against a measure which they believed threatened the Canadian home market and would undermine industries by the "dumping" of cheaper American products upon the Canadian markets. The transportation interests complained that reciprocity would divert Canadian business to the United States.

The Conservative Opposition soon won the support of three of the most prominent Liberal leaders, including the wealthy Clifford *Liberal* Sifton, who had been Laurier's minister of the interior from 1896 to *defections* 1905. The Liberals protested in vain that reciprocity with the United States had been the policy of both Canadian political parties since 1866 and emphasized the splendid market which the American republic, with its population of 90,000,000, would make available to the Canadian farmer.

Loyalty issue again

Unable to attack the agreement very effectively in its economic details, Borden appealed to the country to support the old "National Policy" and to "Let Well Enough Alone" and also raised the loyalty issue with great effect. National unity was at stake, it was alleged, and Conservative orators pointed out that only by rail and the tariff had Canada been welded into a nation. With the tariff wall broken and the railway traffic running north and south, the Dominion would break up into its original parts each to be absorbed by the adjoining section of the American republic. It became impossible for the Liberals to jam their proposal through Parliament, for the Opposition seized upon the issue to force a dissolution and organized a prolonged filibuster. On July 29 Laurier decided to go to the country and the new elections were fixed for September 21.

Campaign of 1911

The campaign of 1911 lasted seven weeks, and in spite of his seventy years the prime minister was the most active figure in it. The campaign was one of the most hotly contested in the history of the Dominion; in four weeks Laurier delivered over fifty speeches. The most effective weapon of the Conservatives was the appeal to Canadian patriotism. Conservative orators represented the reciprocity agreement as a blow at the British connection and the entering wedge for annexation. They denounced "the treason that barters our birthright for the gold of the Kings of the South," and argued that it was the duty of all good Canadians to conserve the natural products of their country and not to export them to an avaricious rival. It was in vain that the Liberals argued, to quote Laurier's latest biographer, that "the Canadian farmer who sold a bushel of good potatoes to the United States no more packed his loyalty with it than did Kipling selling a volume of verse in the same market for the same money." Liberal leaders promised that the "just interests" of the manufacturers would continue to receive adequate protection and warned the eastern capitalists against arousing the new western agrarian movement to still more violent assaults upon the money power and the citadels of privilege.

Indiscretions of American leaders

Unfortunately for the Liberals, the Conservatives in their battle against reciprocity were able to quote the speeches of American leaders to good effect. The speaker of the United States House of Representatives had announced, perhaps jokingly, on the floor of Congress that the United States was preparing to annex Canada, and that he hoped "to see the day when the American flag will float over every square foot of the British North American possessions." A comparatively unknown representative from New York actually introduced a resolution in Congress requesting the President to open negotiations with Great Britain for the annexation of Canada, and, although this stupid proposal was quickly killed in committee, Conservative leaders saw to it that it reached the ears of Canadian voters. Senator Knut Nelson of Minnesota favored annexation, and even President Taft talked rather indiscreetly about Canada being at the "parting of the ways" and held to the British Empire by a "light and imperceptible bond," although his remarks when left in their proper setting were quite harmless. On other occasions the American President described the annexation bogey as "all bosh," and the "dreams of irresponsible imaginations."

In Quebec the Conservatives chose to stress the imperialistic tendencies of the Laurier Government as manifested in the Naval *Sectional issues* Service Bill of 1910, for in this province they could make little headway with the reciprocity issue. Bourassa and the Nationalists insisted that reciprocity was the red herring dragged across the trail to divert attention from the navy question. Laurier vigorously denounced the "unholy alliance" of Nationalists and Conservatives in his home province. In Ontario and farther west, wherever anti-French and anti-Catholic prejudices were strong because of recent controversies over separate schools and bilingualism, Laurier was depicted as the Catholic prime minister who was under the heels of the papal hierarchy while in Quebec he was attacked as the "tool of the imperialists."

The Conservatives used with great effect slogans like the following, "A vote for Borden is a vote for King and Flag and Country," *Campaign* "Empire or Continent, Which?" and "Vote against National *slogans* Suicide." It was in vain that the Liberals tried to start a reaction in Quebec with the slogan, "A vote for Bourassa is a vote for Borden," and in Ontario with the reverse sentiment, "A vote for Borden is a vote for Bourassa." Even Rudyard Kipling figured in the campaign when the Montreal *Star* published his letter warning the Canadians that they were but nine million against ninety million Americans, and therefore would find it impossible to maintain Canada's political autonomy.

In spite of these passionate appeals to prejudice and patriotism, there can be no question that the manufacturers and many of their *Attitude of* employees feared a breach in the protective system and honestly *organized* believed that it was better not to tamper with the *status quo*. As a *capital* result the manufacturers, railroads, and banks in 1911 preferred to contribute to the campaign funds of the Conservatives rather than to the party favoring a change in Canada's protective system. Throughout the campaign the Conservatives were decidedly on the aggressive, for they were "down to fighting weight after fifteen years of hungry opposition." Clifford Sifton, a former Liberal, and one of the most powerful capitalists in Canada, and William Van Horne, the railway magnate, were as important perhaps as Robert Borden in planning and directing the strategy of the Conservative campaign.

In the elections of September 21, the Liberals were driven from power by a Conservative landslide and in the popular vote, the party

Triumph of
Conservatives
of Laurier was in a minority of 47,000. In the Commons the combined strength of the Conservatives and Nationalists was 133 seats while the Liberals obtained only eighty-eight. In Quebec the Liberals carried only thirty-five of the sixty-five constituencies, and these inroads by the Nationalists upon the Liberal stronghold proved decisive. The Conservatives made gains in every province except Alberta. Many of the distinguished figures in the Liberal Government and seven ministers, among whom were Fielding, Fisher, Paterson, and Mackenzie King, lost their seats. In some constituencies young Conservatives with scarcely enough money to qualify for the nomination defeated Liberal veterans who had never lost a political battle, and in several sections of the Dominion the Conservative majorities were so large that some of the Government candidates lost their deposits.

After a premiership of fifteen years Laurier was forced to assume the duties of leader of His Majesty's Opposition. His own judgment concerning the outcome was expressed in a letter written soon after his defeat to an intimate friend. In this he said, "It was not reciprocity that was turned down, but a Catholic premier."

Causes of
Liberal defeat
Students of Canadian political party history, as soon as they had recovered from the shock of this overwhelming political upheaval, began to search for the reasons for the Conservative triumph. No single reason will suffice to explain the results, but among the more important contributing factors may be mentioned, (1) the prosperity which Canada had enjoyed under the old protective policy; (2) the opposition of ultra-Protestants in Ontario to a Catholic prime minister, and of ultra-Catholics in Quebec to a Liberal Catholic prime minister; (3) the superior organization of the Conservatives as contrasted with the decline of Liberal prestige after a long term in office; (4) the opposition of Canadian manufacturers and of transportation and packing interests, and their campaign contributions to the Conservative party; (5) opposition to the Laurier naval bill and to his alleged imperialism; (6) fear that reciprocity would lead to political union with the United States; (7) ill-feeling toward the United States for rejecting Canadian reciprocity proposals in earlier years; (8) the feeling that the Liberals had ruled long enough and that a change in party would benefit the country.

SELECT BIBLIOGRAPHY FOR CHAPTER XXIV

The citations at the end of the preceding chapter should be consulted again for a general narrative of events through the election of 1911.

W. D. SCOTT's "Immigration and Population," in *Canada and Its Provinces*, vol. VII, pp. 517-590, is an excellent summary of Canadian immigration, with some attention to each important immigrant group. ELINA THORNSTENISON, "The Doukhobors in Canada," in *The Mississippi Valley Historical Review*, vol. IV, pp. 1-48, is a special study of what is probably the most curiously interesting of the immigrant colonies.

The fisheries settlement and the entire history of the controversy is well summarized in N. B. WORMWITH, "The Fishery Arbitrations," in *Canada and Its Provinces*, vol. VIII, pp. 681-748. W. A. DUNNING, *The British Empire and the United States* (New York, 1914) also has some value. See also, J. D. ROGERS, *Newfoundland* (Historical Geography of the British Colonies), vol. V, Pt. IV, Appendix F, which gives the award of the Hague Tribunal.

For the rise of the Nationalist movement the following are useful: HENRI BOURASSA, *Independence or Imperial Partnership? A Study of the Problems of the Commonwealth* (Montreal, 1916), and various issues of *The Round Table, a Quarterly Review of the Politics of the British Empire* (London), especially vols. 56 and 78, and the *Canadian Annual Review of Public Affairs.*

The details of the reciprocity negotiations of 1911 are available in the periodical literature of Canada and the United States for the time. The following are the most valuable official documents bearing on the issue: *Reciprocity with Canada: A Study of the Arrangement of 1911,* by the United States Tariff Commission (Washington, 1920), and "Reciprocity with Canada," *U. S. Senate Document No. 80* (62nd Cong. 1st Sess., vols. 13–15) and *U. S. Senate Document No. 56* (62nd Cong. 1st Sess., vols. 5, 6): *House Document No. 1350* (61st Cong. 3d Sess., vol. 124) and *Senate Document No. 787* (61st Cong. 3d Sess., vol. 84). The debates of the Canadian House of Commons are in *Debates House of Commons, Dominion of Canada,* (11th Parl. 3d Sess., 1910–1911). Here again the *Canadian Annual Review of Public Affairs* for 1911 is useful.

CHAPTER XXV

THE CONSERVATIVES RETURN TO POWER

Conservative Government

ROBERT LAIRD BORDEN, the new Conservative prime minister, was fifty-seven years old when he assumed office in October, 1911. A constitutional lawyer of considerable reputation in his profession, and possessor of several university degrees, the new prime minister had made a favorable impression while leader of the Opposition as an able, hard-hitting, and, on the whole, clean politician. The new cabinet contained some well-known figures, but few men of distinction. George E. Foster became minister of trade and commerce, Robert Rogers, minister of the interior, F. D. Monk, the Conservative leader of Quebec, minister of public works, W. Thomas White, minister of finance, Louis P. Pelletier, postmaster-general, and Samuel Hughes, minister of militia and defense. All the French Canadians who held portfolios in the new Government were drawn from the Nationalist group whose stand on the naval issue the Conservatives had utilized so successfully in the recent campaign. Bourassa declined a cabinet position although, in the words of the Liberal Toronto *Globe*, the "Tory Imperialists at Ottawa" had swallowed Bourassa "body, bones and breeches." The new Parliament was opened in state on November 16, 1911, by His Royal Highness, the Duke of Connaught, brother of King Edward VII, who had just assumed the duties of governor-general.

Navy question

On the naval question Prime Minister Borden showed no disposition to press for legislation immediately. He announced that it was "better to be right than to be in a hurry," and the new naval bill of the Conservatives was not introduced until December 5, 1912. In the preceding summer the Canadian prime minister visited England and there consulted with the Liberal Government under Asquith. During his stay as the guest of Winston Churchill, head of the Admiralty, he witnessed a royal review of three hundred and fifteen British fighting ships, and this magnificent procession, fully five miles long, must have made a deep impression upon the visiting prime minister from overseas. In the meantime the Royal Australian Navy was making steady progress, New Zealand had launched a dreadnought of her own and made also a cash contribution to the British treasury, and even the Federated Malay States offered to present the mother-country with a first-class battleship. Germany's new naval bill of 1912 added to the excitement by further endangering Great Britain's naval supremacy.

Borden's bill, introduced soon after his return to Canada, called for the appropriation of $35,000,000 to build three first-class battle- *Introduction* ships as Canada's contribution to the British Grand Fleet. These *of navy bill* ships were to be maintained and controlled by the royal naval authori- *by Borden* ties. There was no pledge of regular or periodic contributions by Canada in the future, and it was understood that if the Dominion ever desired to develop a navy of her own these ships could be recalled to form its nucleus. The Conservatives fully appreciated the signifi- cance of the new policy and freely discussed the desirability of having a Canadian representative on the imperial councils of defense.

In the long debates on the bill the main points stressed by the Conservative leaders were the menacing race for armaments going *Arguments* on in Europe, the collapse of the Anglo-German negotiations for a *in favor* naval holiday which might have called a halt to the frantic building of battleships, the danger spots in the Balkans, and the likelihood of a general European war as the nations of Europe became more solidly united in two opposing alliances. A great array of naval experts, "from Noah to Nelson," were quoted during the debate to decide whether Canada should adhere to the Liberal policy of main- taining her own navy or whether the Dominion should accept the Conservative plan of contributions. The Conservatives justified their proposal as an effective and economical measure by which Canada would help to foot England's bill for policing the world.

The Liberals opposed the naval bill for a variety of reasons. Some demanded the development of a Canadian navy and proposed *Arguments* two naval units, a suggestion which the Conservatives promptly *against* rejected as more costly and less efficient than their own measure. Some asked for a popular referendum on so important a departure in public policy. Laurier denounced the bill as "a cross between jingoism and nationalism," and there was much talk of keeping the navy under the control of the Canadian people and resisting "Downing Street rule" and a status of "colonial inferiority." Some denied the existence of an emergency in imperial affairs and refused to believe that the Empire needed help. Laurier attacked the vicious race for armaments among the powers of Europe as "a circle of fire worse than any described in Dante's Inferno." There were exhaustive speeches on Canada's share in determining the Empire's foreign policy and on the dangers of dragging the peaceful Dominion into the maelstrom of European jingoism and intrigue. Bourassa as the Nationalist spokesman soon came to oppose both the Liberal and the Conservative naval programs, and declared that the whole war scare was the deliberate creation of munitions manufacturers and arma- ment trusts.

After the Liberal Opposition had debated the proposition for a month and had resorted to various obstructionist tactics, the naval *Use of closure* bill, by the use of the closure rule, was finally jammed through the *rule to force* House of Commons in the adjourned session of 1913. The close of the *bill through* debate was marked by much disorder; the Liberals tried desperately *Commons* to force an election, and the House had one continuous session which lasted two weeks.

Its defeat in Senate

In the Upper House the Government encountered a well-directed opposition which it could not control. The Senate by this time had become the stronghold of the Liberal party due to the long period of years in which the Liberals had controlled the Government and had made appointments to the Upper House from their own ranks only. The Conservatives controlled thirty-two votes, the Liberals had a Senate representation of fifty-four. Under the leadership of Sir George Ross, who described the naval bill as "empty as an exploded cartridge and soulless as its plated sides," and as arousing "no sympathy, no sentiment, no emotion of joy or glory," the Senate refused its assent to the bill unless a popular referendum were held. Conservative papers like the Montreal *Star* at once began an agitation for the reform of the Senate, that "band of licensed wreckers" of popular measures, and the agitation gathered considerable momentum at a time when the British House of Commons had just stripped the Lords of some of their ancient powers of obstruction and veto.

Reasons for defeat of bill

Laurier was definitely accused of stirring the Senate to resistance, but many people were undoubtedly glad to see the naval policy dropped in this easy way. Organized labor endorsed a popular referendum on the question; the western farmers favored a program of arbitration and disarmament rather than increased expenditures and imperialism; and others believed the "German scare" had been manufactured for the occasion and now would be heard of no more. It is significant that Prime Minister Borden took no steps to revive the issue or to force the Senate to acquiesce in the Government's program. Apparently he too was not disappointed to see the matter dropped for the time being.

Legislative program, 1911-1914

The Conservative Government soon found itself submerged in the onerous duties and heavy responsibilities which followed the outbreak of the Great War in 1914. Prior to that time the Government had accomplished a great deal in the field of domestic legislation and administration. In July, 1913, a Bank Act was passed through Parliament providing for a number of modifications in the Canadian banking system. The most important new provisions included better inspection of banks and greater security for depositors, and made possible the lending of money to farmers and ranchmen on their products as security. An agricultural education act provided government aid for agricultural instruction, and terminal elevators were built in the West by the Government to facilitate the marketing of the farmer's products. The work for the conservation of Canada's national resources was faithfully continued.

Transportation and communication

Cable rates were reduced and a parcels-post system was established. The mail service between Canada and Europe was changed from a weekly to a tri-weekly basis, and numerous improvements, such as railroad extensions and canal and harbor improvements, were vigorously promoted. By 1914 Canada stood fifth among the nations of the world in total railroad mileage, and first in mileage per population. Much of this railroad building was, to be sure, premature, and involved needless duplication and, as in earlier years, there was much complaint of lobbying, corruption, and high finance on the part of the railroad promoters. The Canadian Northern, one of the newest and one of Canada's most highly speculative railroad ventures, found it necessary to appeal repeatedly to the government for financial aid and in spite of vigorous opposition from many quarters still managed to get new governmental subsidies.

Prime Minister Borden visited the Governor of New York State to discuss the development and use of jointly controlled waterways, *External* particularly from the point of view of developing greater hydro- *affairs* electric facilities, the "white coal" which is to play such a conspicuous rôle in the industrial history of the present century. The Canadian trade commission service abroad was reconstructed. In 1912 delegates from most of the British West Indies and from British Guiana met with Canadian representatives at Ottawa to discuss the possibility of closer trade relations. As a result of the conference, a ten-year trade agreement was made providing for mutual trade preferences by which about fifty Canadian products received a tariff reduction of twenty per cent in the West Indies, thus giving Canada a decided advantage over the United States, her chief competitor. The United States interests in some of the islands tried in vain to prevent ratification of the agreement. In the same year Canada played an important rôle in the eighth Congress of the Chambers of Commerce of the Empire held at the Guildhall in London.

In 1912 the Dominion archives were placed under the jurisdiction of the department of state and in recognition of the importance of *Miscellaneous* archival work, Dr. Arthur G. Doughty, the Dominion's capable *legislation* archivist, was made a deputy minister. An agitation against Canadian knighthoods, "tin-pot titles" in the estimation of many Canadians, reached considerable proportions but the practice of granting titles was not abandoned until some years later. A new Arctic expedition under the command of the noted explorer Vilhjalmur Stefansson was promoted by the Government to discover the secrets of the frozen North. The boundaries of Manitoba, Ontario, and Quebec were extended northward, the additional territory given to the province of Ontario alone being equal to the area of the British Isles.

In the interest of practical party politics the Conservatives sponsored many investigations into the conduct of government depart- *Party politics* ments during the Liberal régime in the hope of uncovering evidence of mismanagement and wrongdoing. The Liberal Opposition countered with sharp attacks on the department of public works and with charges of unnecessary squandering of public funds on unimportant or unnecessary internal improvements ("pork barrel" legislation). A bill creating a tariff commission to make an expert study of the tariff problem passed the Commons but was rejected by the Senate as "a cheap Yankee device." The most significant changes in the cabinet before the war were the resignation of F. D. Monck, of the department of public works, who broke with his colleagues because he favored a referendum on the Dominion's naval policy, and the entrance into the cabinet of Arthur Meighen as solicitor-general in June, 1913. Colonel Sam Hughes, Borden's impetuous and saber-rattling minister of militia and defense, spent his time preaching preparedness, sponsoring boy-scout organizations, and instituting military training in high schools and colleges—a program which stirred up much opposition, especially in the agricultural West, but which the minister vigorously defended as a necessary feature of a better national preparedness program.

Woman's suffrage

The woman's suffrage agitation and the movement for more drastic prohibition legislation made steady progress in the years immediately preceding the outbreak of the Great War. Numerous bills providing for woman's suffrage were introduced in the Ontario legislature, and efforts were made to arouse the interest of the federal government in this reform, but Borden steadily refused to act on the ground that the electoral franchise was a matter to be determined by the provinces.

Activity of organized farmers

There were also signs of renewed activity among the organized farmers of the West. The Grain Growers' Association continued to demand a lower tariff and to denounce the capitalistic interests of the East. The raising of campaign funds, the calling of various provincial conventions, and the launching of newspapers controlled by farmers were ominous signs of a growing political revolt on the western prairies. Coupled with a nation-wide financial depression which struck Canada in 1913, these evidences of discontent caused the Government serious moments of reflection and concern. All these problems were soon submerged in the terrible World War, which broke over Europe in the summer of 1914. In the gigantic struggle for victory all other problems were subordinated to the immediate war needs of the nation and the Empire. Political, social, and economic changes of the most sweeping and fundamental character were the inevitable consequences of a war as extensive and as destructive as the Great War proved to be. The year 1914 therefore in many ways marks the opening of a new era in the history of Canada and the Empire. Before discussing the progress of the war and its effects upon Canadian development, it is necessary to turn back for a brief summary of the Dominion's economic and social progress in the generation before 1914.

SELECT BIBLIOGRAPHY FOR CHAPTER XXV

The most convenient summary of the main events for the years 1911 to 1914 may be found in *The Canadian Annual Review of Public Affairs* for these years. The biographers of Laurier also of necessity devote some attention to these years when Laurier was the leader of the Opposition.

CHAPTER XXVI

ECONOMIC AND SOCIAL PROGRESS SINCE CONFEDERATION

THE three decades following confederation failed to fulfill the promise of Canadian development as it had been pictured by en- *Disappointing* thusiastic advocates in the 1860's. The Dominion did not suddenly *statistics* leap to greatness as a powerful, prosperous nation expanding rapidly from sea to sea. The population at the time of confederation was only 3,500,000, towns of any appreciable size were few, manufacturing and farming were conducted on a small scale, and the region beyond the Great Lakes still awaited the coming of the immigrant to convert its rolling prairies into prosperous homesteads. In spite of the vigorous immigration policy of the government, a liberal homestead plan, and a wide-spread interest in the improvement of transportation facilities by the federal and provincial governments alike, statistical studies of Canada's progress continued to be disappointing until almost the beginning of the twentieth century. For a large part of this period census returns revealed a net loss of Canada's immigrant population to the United Sates.

In spite of these discouraging facts a close study of Canadian economic development reveals that the foundations for the great *Agriculture* progress of the present century were being slowly and often painfully *and fisheries* laid in the disappointing decades immediately following confederation. The census of 1881 revealed an increase of nearly thirty per cent in the number engaged in agricultural pursuits in the four original provinces of the Dominion. Efforts were being made to improve the breed of Canadian live-stock; by 1880 over 30,000 cattle and 100,000 sheep were exported to markets overseas. Cheese factories for which the Dominion was to become famous began to spring up in great numbers, and by 1880, 20,000 tons of cheese were exported to the mother-country. The fisheries under federal encouragement were expanding rapidly and by 1880 the salmon canneries on the Pacific coast were beginning to divert attention from the possibilities of the great Atlantic fisheries to these new resources on the other side of the continent. Manufacturing also developed fairly rapidly until it encountered the panic of 1873 and its damaging results.

The wild years of speculation and expansion preceding the panic of that year were followed by six years of depression and gloom, but *Recovery from* by 1879 industry had recovered from the shock of deflation. It was in *panic of 1873* these years, as has been pointed out elsewhere, that the movement for a protective tariff as a cure-all for their economic troubles caught

the imagination of the Canadian people. The violent economic
fluctuation in Canada during these years is clearly mirrored in the
trade statistics of the Dominion. In 1873 Canada's foreign trade
amounted to $217,801,703; by 1879 it was down to $153,458,682; by
1883, however, it had advanced to $230,339,826. The next dozen
years failed to show any encouraging rate of increase. The number
of cotton spindles, however, quadrupled in the first decade after
confederation; Ontario began to develop her woolen industry; and
the region around Montreal made steady progress as a center for the
manufacture of boots and shoes.

Factory system   Toward the close of the 1880's Canada began to feel the results
of large scale combinations which accompanied the development
of the modern factory system. By the 1880's the first trade agreements
were formed by producers to eliminate competition; in 1887 a "pool,"
a new form of combination, was organized among the oat-millers.
Three years earlier a binder-twine combination had been formed.
Before long "rings," "pools," and trade agreements were organized
by many of the leading manufacturers, paralleling, but on a smaller
scale, the rapid development of large scale production among corporations and trusts in the United States. Indeed many of the new
Canadian combines had close financial connections with firms in the
United States. The ostensible purpose of most of these combinations
was to perfect methods of production and to secure the economic
advantages resulting from large scale enterprise. Some of the consumers, however, feared that these corporations might become
combines in restraint of trade and inflict monopoly prices upon the
helpless public. Consequently they began to urge the necessity of
more stringent government regulation of big business.

Westward   In the decade of the 1880's, due to immigration propaganda and
movement   the liberal land laws of the Canadian governments, a great rush of
settlers set in. The destination of most of the newcomers was the
western prairies. It was estimated that in one year alone (1882)
60,000 settlers entered Manitoba and staked out claims to some
3,000,000 acres of land. Nevertheless, in the ten years from 1881 to
1891 the population of Manitoba and the Northwest Territories
showed a net increase of only 70,000, a figure which clearly indicates
that frosts, dry spells, disappointments, and the counter-attractions
of American territories like Minnesota and the Dakotas induced
many to abandon their homesteads either to enter the United States
or to work their way back slowly to the older centers of population.
The total population of Canada increased less than twelve per cent
during this decade.

Agricultural   The 1880's also witnessed a serious check in the agricultural
depression   expansion of the Dominion. Owing to an increase in the world production of wheat through the opening of new areas to cultivation,
especially in Russia, and because of a scarcity of currency, prices of
agricultural products fell rapidly. Hundreds of farmers who had

entered the prairie provinces as settlers optimistic enough to believe that a few years of honest toil would wipe out the mortgages encumbering their new holdings, now found themselves among the disgruntled debtor class with mortgages coming due and the prices of their products, through which alone these debts could be paid, constantly falling.

The agricultural discontent in the Canadian West differed little in kind from that which prevailed in these years in the western and southern sections of the United States. There the economic depression in the agricultural regions gave rise to such movements as the Farmers' Alliances, the Grange, the Greenback and the Populist parties, all of them attempts to force a panacea for the farmers' ills upon the government by independent political action and generally by an inflation of the currency. So thoroughly, however, was the Canadian grounded in the principles of "sound money" that the demand to expand the currency as a means of restoring prices and good times never became strong in the Dominion, and the "rag baby," as fiat money was called in the United States, never achieved much popularity among the Canadian people. The government, by means of experiment stations and other kinds of aid, tried to furnish some relief, but for the most part, the solution of the economic difficulties of Canada was left to the slower but sounder operation of the laws of time and the general principles of economics. *Similarity to conditions in United States*

It was not until the late 1890's that Canada began to prosper in a way that was comparable with the hopes of the prophets of confederation. After 1896 as a result of new gold discoveries in North America, Africa, and Australia, the volume of the world's currency could be increased on a safe gold basis, and prices began to rise. The disappearance of free lands in the United States stimulated a new influx of settlers into the Canadian West. European capital sought opportunities for investment in the expanding Dominion, and agriculture and manufacturing alike began to boom. Inter-provincial migration increased, while emigration to the United States declined rapidly. A heavy "American invasion" of Canada now set in, and European immigration also increased steadily. *Turn in tide*

In the fifteen years following this revival of prosperity in 1897, over 2,250,000 immigrants arrived in Canada. The immigration from 1900 to 1911 totalled 1,788,369. The population of the Dominion in 1911 was 7,206,643, and the census showed that the greatest percentage of increase was in the new provinces of Alberta and Saskatchewan. The population of Manitoba increased seventy-eight per cent and that of Saskatchewan 439 per cent. Winnipeg became the grain center of North America. Only Prince Edward Island and the Yukon and Northwest Territories showed a net decrease. The net gain in total population for the first decade of the present century was thirty-four and thirteen one-hundredths per cent. Yet in the face of these encouraging returns, the population of Canada still *Population growth since 1896* averaged only one and ninety-three one-hundredths persons to the square mile.

Canada—
melting pot
In the effort to attract settlers to the vacant lands of Canada, the Dominion encouraged the entrance of the greatest variety of racial and national stocks. Some seemed to be more easily assimilable into the Canadian national stock than others, and by the close of the period under consideration Canadians began to raise the question of a more selective immigration policy. Among those most welcome to the Dominion may be mentioned such groups as the ten thousand Icelanders who had arrived in the neighborhood of Lake Winnipeg since 1872, the Scotch-Highland crofters, the Germans, and the Scandinavians who settled for the most part in the four western provinces. These groups were industrious farmers whose mode of life was little different from that of the majority of Canadian citizens, and until the outbreak of the Great War the government made every effort to stimulate greater emigration from these north European peoples.

Immigrant
groups
Like the United States in earlier days the Dominion also became a haven of refuge for many immigrants with unusual religious or social views who desired a new country where they might live out their theories without interference. Thousands of Mennonites migrated in communities into the Canadian West and received guarantees from the government that their religious scruples would be respected and that the new arrivals would be exempted forever from taking legal oaths or rendering military service. From 1887 to 1905 about 10,000 Mormons settled in southern Alberta. Perhaps the most peculiar of these sectarian immigrants to Canada were the Doukhobors, or "spirit wrestlers," from Russia, who turned their footsteps westward to the prairies of Canada after the intervention of Tolstoi had secured for them the necessary permission to leave the land of their persecutors. The Dominion made liberal terms with their leaders and the settlers prospered almost from the first in their new environment. Immigrant groups like these, in spite of their seeming peculiarities, have generally been regarded as valuable additions to the Canadian population save on such occasions as when their religious theories led the Doukhobors into fanatical crusades and pilgrimages, and the Government found itself embarrassed in trying to find methods of dealing with these harmless but somewhat fanatical demonstrations.

"New
immigration"
Of the "newer immigration" from southern and southeastern Europe, Canada attracted nearly 150,000 from Galicia and other parts of the old Austro-Hungarian Empire and more than sixty thousand Italians. The latter were mainly "birds of passage" who planned to return to their native land with their earnings as soon as possible. For the most part these newer immigrants furnished desirable pick and shovel workmen for contractors engaged on public works or other building enterprises. A few Canadian cities developed

Italian quarters where the immigrants clannishly maintained their native languages and institutions.

Chinese immigration was encouraged until 1885, because of the demand for coolie labor to build Canada's railways. It was not long, *Orientals* however, before organized labor began an agitation against the docile celestial who was undermining wages and standards of living. The government instituted a prohibitive head tax which by 1904 reached the sum of $500 per Chinese immigrant. The law has not been uniformly successful in excluding coolie labor, for contractors have at times paid both the head tax and the transportation cost of the Chinese laborer and have compelled him to work off the amount charged against him. Anti-Chinese agitation in Canada, however, has virtually ceased. It has been superseded in recent years by an anti-Japanese demonstration, particularly on the Pacific coast. Alarm over the arrival of fifteen thousand Japanese during the first ten years of the present century led to an agreement with Japan by which the latter promised to limit the number of laborers who could emigrate each year.

It is impossible to discuss specifically the many other immigrant groups attracted to Canada before the Great War put a stop to prac- *Government* tically all immigration. Nor can much be said at this early stage *policy* concerning the social and cultural contributions which these various groups are making to Canadian nationality. The policy of the government has always been to encourage farmers, farm laborers, and domestics to come from the more desirable countries, and to keep out by medical examination and other provisions those who were considered undesirable or likely to become public burdens or who were merely "birds of passage."

The efforts of the government to stimulate immigration have been constantly reinforced and supplemented by the propaganda of railroad *Other* companies with lands to sell. The Canadian Pacific perhaps has done *propaganda* most in this direction; it actually furnishes ready-made farms with *agencies* house, barn, and a portion of the fields under cultivation to prospective settlers, to be purchased on the instalment plan. In spite of some hysterical reactions during the Great War, it is doubtful whether Canada will have to face any serious problems in connection with the assimilation of her immigrant groups for many years to come. The Dominion is still primarily an agricultural country, although the drift from farm to city has begun. In the first decade of the twentieth century Canada's rural population decreased from sixty-three to fifty-five per cent. Canada still needs settlers to develop her great public domain, and her population is so sparsely scattered over her vast area that the problem of assimilating immigrant groups will probably continue to solve itself. It is only in some of the congested manufacturing centers that the immigrant problem is causing any serious concern.

To encourage settlement of the newer sections of the Dominion,

Aid to farmer

the government developed various plans for giving aid to farming communities. By 1912, although nearly 50,000,000 acres of land had been enclosed or acquired for use, this total constituted but one-sixth of the land available for farming and pasturage. It has been only since 1859 that the farm products of British North America have exceeded the value of the products of her forests. Federal aid to the farmer is under the direction of the department of agriculture; a wide variety of activities has been undertaken by this department. Agricultural societies have been promoted, and since 1896 the government has sponsored experimental farms where many discoveries have been made by experts to improve methods of wheat growing and dairying, the use of fertilizers, the breed of farm animals, etc. Many bulletins and reports and sample seeds are available to the farmer without cost.

Dairying

Since 1890 there has been a Dominion dairy commissioner who concentrates his energies upon the growing butter and cheese exports of the country. Many improvements have been introduced in creameries and cold storage plants. The centrifugal cream separator, which has produced a revolution in dairying in many parts of the Dominion, was first used in 1882. Federal, provincial, and local governments have promoted scores of exhibits in all parts of the nation to stimulate interest in more efficient methods of production. Since 1906 a law provides for government inspection of meat and canned goods.

Value of farm products

In 1910 the value of all field crops exceeded half a billion dollars. The annual milk production was valued at $100,000,000, and the value of eggs, wool, and live-stock was estimated at twice that figure. Canada passed the United States as an exporter of cheese in 1890 and the Dominion has never relinquished her position as leader in this field. In 1906 for the first time Canada's wheat exports surpassed the value of cheese exports, and by 1910 Canada ranked second only to Russia as an exporter of wheat and flour.

Railroad development

Of first importance in the development of agricultural resources is the matter of transportation facilities. From 1881 to 1896 the railway mileage of Canada increased from 7260 to 16,387 miles. In the years between 1897 and the outbreak of the Great War, passenger traffic doubled on the Canadian railroads while freight business increased threefold. Most of this increase was attributable to westward expansion.

Great railway systems

The development of new transcontinental lines such as the Canadian Northern and the Grand Trunk Pacific occurred during these years and has already been discussed. The progress of the oldest of the transcontinental lines was phenomenal. From 1901 to 1912 the stock of the Canadian Pacific more than tripled in value, and the gross earnings of the company rose from $30,000,000 to $104,000,000. The company expanded its holdings to include steamboat lines, hotels, irrigation projects, and other developments closely connected with its transportation service. In 1911 a Hudson Bay railroad was proposed to provide a new and shorter outlet to the sea for the agricultural products of the prairie provinces. Another road over 300 miles long was projected into northern Ontario where silver deposits had been discovered and where the government was anxious to colonize settlers.

Railroad expansion and consolidation, as suggested in an earlier connection, were accompanied by a demand for government regula- *Government* tion of this important public utility. Especially from the West, where *control* the depression following the panic of 1873 continued longest, the demand arose for government intervention to prevent exploitation of the producers and consumers by the transportation companies. In the 1880's there was much discussion on the floor of Parliament of the dangers of consolidation. A commission appointed to investigate the question in 1886 favored an increase in the powers of the railway committee of the Dominion Privy Council, but no satisfactory progress was made in the regulation of these public utilities until 1904 when a law was passed creating the Board of Railway Commissioners for Canada. This body meets in all parts of the Dominion. It has power to fix rates and to make regulations in the interest of the public safety, and enjoys other extensive powers over the Dominion's transportation systems. The provincial governments also have provided public utility commissions to safeguard the public interest in provincial issues.

Extensive improvements have been made since confederation in the postal facilities of Canada. Before the completion of the Canadian *Improvements* Pacific, letters posted in British Columbia or Fort Garry for eastern *in postal* parts of the Dominion reached their destination by being carried for *facilities* a large part of the way through the territory of the United States. To transmit a letter from Victoria to Toronto required three weeks, and letters from the maritime provinces to Quebec were sent *via* Maine. The building of transcontinental railways eliminated the roundabout route through the United States and gradually extended the western limit of the railway mail service. A post-office car marked "End of Track, C.P.R." moved forward a little further each day as the construction gangs of the Canadian Pacific proceeded westward. The lowering of postal rates after confederation increased the postal business which in turn increased the revenues of the government. In 1874 the Dominion concluded a postal convention with the United States virtually extinguishing the international boundary so far as the postal service was concerned. A post-office savings bank was organized immediately after confederation, and in 1910 its accounts, serving nearly 150,000 depositors, totalled nearly $44,000,000.

Statistics for manufacturing reveal a steady growth during the last generation. In 1881 the total investment in manufacturing was *Manufacturing* $165,302,623 with a total output valued at $309,676,068. By 1911 the capital invested in Canadian manufacturing equalled a billion and a half, and the total output was valued at one billion dollars annually. Nevertheless, in the face of this great increase the importation of manufactured goods steadily increased; the United States led all other countries in the value of products sold to Canada. By 1912, in spite of an almost unrivalled growth in Canadian exports of grain, fish, lumber, mining, and manufactured products, the excess of imports over exports still amounted to approximately seventy-five per cent. It was not until after the Great War that Canada's visible trade began to show a favorable balance.

"Big Business"

This development in manufacturing was marked by an increase in specialization and by the combination of many small factories into large scale units, a development common to most of the countries of the western world of this period. In this "steel age," Canada's pig iron production increased from 50,000 tons in 1898 to 917,000 tons in 1911, and steel production mounted from 30,000 tons to 876,000 tons. One of the most important centers of the new steel industry was in Nova Scotia where the Nova Scotia Steel and Coal Company developed rapidly into a large and powerful corporation. Mergers were brought about in many industries, resulting in both vertical and horizontal combinations. Trusts and holding companies made their appearance in many fields of production, and the process of amalgamation was often attended by all the evils of watered stock, profiteering, tariff lobbying, and monopoly privileges which generally accompanied this development in older industrial nations. A large part of Canada's industrial expansion was financed by British and American capital. From 1905 to 1912 Canadian loans floated in England amounted to almost a billion dollars. United States corporations also began to invade Canada with branch factories or assembling plants, frequently to avoid high tariffs or to take advantage of the Empire's preferential tariff policy. By 1926 American investments in Canada were estimated at $3,000,000,000 and were said to be increasing at the rate of a quarter billion annually. United States investors controlled many important branches of Canadian industry, such as copper smelting, drugs and chemicals, automobiles, paint and varnish, and patent medicines. On the other hand, there is evidence to show that there has been a slowing up of Canada's borrowing in the United States during the past few years, and it seems likely that Great Britain will be able to absorb a much larger share in the future. Moreover, in recent years, the flow of capital across the international boundary has not all been in the same direction.

Attempts at regulation

Like the United States the Dominion government has experimented with various kinds of legislation designed to prohibit the development of monopoly abuses. In 1898 a loosely drafted statute prohibited combinations in restraint of trade. Eight years later a threat was made to deprive monopoly combines of their tariff protection. In 1910 a new Anti-Combines Act was passed, but corporations have found it comparatively easy, under the law, to avoid interference with their methods. In Canada, as in the United States, but to a lesser degree, the people are facing the problem whether government can control big business or whether, in the end, big business will dominate the government.

Although in Canada industrialism has developed much more slowly than in England or in the United States, nevertheless many *Class consciousness* of the evils of the economic revolution which counterbalance its beneficial results have already made their appearance in Canada. For one thing, the development of class consciousness and stratification in Canadian society is under way, although the movement will be retarded for many years since the Dominion's cheap lands on the frontier may serve as an outlet for the more oppressed populations of the older East. The Dominion had her millionaires before the war, and their ranks during the profiteering orgy of the war years were largely augmented in Canada as in other countries. The muckraking journalist has little trouble in finding cases of special privilege, stock jobbery, and unfair business methods which he may expose to a suspicious public. Although socialism as a party movement has made little progress thus far, some Canadians view with alarm the development of conflicting economic interests and classes in the social structure of the Dominion.

The Canadian labor movement is largely a product of the period since confederation. Before 1870 most labor unions were weak, local, *Labor movement* and often secret organizations exercising but little influence even in their local communities. Indeed, so long as lands were cheap in the West and industry was largely in the domestic stage, there was little stimulus or occasion for labor unions. The industrial revolution did not begin in British North America until after 1860. With the rapid change to a factory system and a capitalist régime in the early 1870's, strikes occurred in many places as ominous signs of the diverging interests of employer and employee. It was not until 1872 that unions and strikes were recognized as legal weapons in this industrial warfare. Before that time labor disturbances had been dealt with under the law as criminal conspiracies against the government. Canada borrowed the technique and mechanism of her labor organizations from the United States although much of the Canadian labor program has been influenced by the progress of the labor movement in Great Britain.

The first great national representative assembly to provide centralized control and direction for the forces of organized labor was *Trades and* held in Canada in 1873 with thirty-one unions represented. This *Labor Congress* organization, known as the Canadian Labor Union, proved very shortlived, although its demands, which involved such issues as the nine-hour day, the restriction of immigration, and the use of arbitration in industrial disputes, were extremely moderate. In 1883 this organization was revived as the Trades and Labor Congress of Canada, and by 1912 it comprised nearly 1000 unions with a membership of over 66,000. The Trades and Labor Congress among its many other duties maintains a parliamentary solicitor to look after the interests of the workers and to secure the enactment of favorable labor legislation. Most of the constituent unions are members of international bodies affiliated with the American Federation of Labor.

Connection with American labor movement

In the years between confederation and the outbreak of the Great War, there has been a steady growth of labor organizations in a wide variety of industries in Canada. The railroad unions, in a strategic position so far as the nation's economic life is concerned, have reached a position of great influence, and practically all Canadian unions have been developing a better spirit of coöperation and a more intelligent leadership. Although a number of national craft unions are not affiliated with the American Federation of Labor, most organizations have been benefited greatly by their American connections through the use of strike funds, sick benefits, and other methods of support. Trade agreements enforced upon employers in the United States in certain industries usually redound to the advantage of the Canadian unions also. On the other hand, this connection with the United States has given employers the opportunity to denounce the meddling of "foreigners" in Canadian industrial problems and to blame the "Yankee walking delegate" for many of their labor troubles.

Labor legislation

Much labor legislation can now be found on the statute books of the various provinces. These laws range all the way from provisions for labor and employment bureaus to statutes for fair wages boards, a minimum wage, factory inspection, child labor, and workmen's compensation acts. By a Dominion Act in 1894, "Labor Day" was definitely fixed as a national holiday. In 1900 a Dominion department of labor was created, and laws have been passed seeking to eliminate the competition of immigrant contract labor. By 1914 Prince Edward Island was the only province which had not yet followed Ontario's lead of 1886 in establishing workmen's compensation systems. Wages generally have been higher in the newer West than in the eastern provinces where by far the greatest number of employees in manufacturing are to be found.

Period of rapid growth

The most rapid growth in the ranks of organized labor prior to the Great War occurred in the first decade of the present century, which was a period of unusual prosperity. In 1911 there were 1752 trade unions in Canada, and in the year following the department of labor estimated the total union membership at 133,132 of which nine-tenths were affiliated with unions in the United States. The greatest number of unions are to be found in the province of Ontario, while the labor organizations of British Columbia are probably the most radical in their demands. Industries having the greatest number of labor organizations, listed in order, are the railroads, building trades, and metal and engineering trades. The Industrial Disputes Investigation Act continued to function to prevent strikes and lockouts on Canada's public utilities, and in 1911, of thirty-one disputes submitted under this law, only four resulted in strikes.

In the field of education the post-confederation period marked *Educational* the triumph of the idea of universal and compulsory public school *progress* education. In 1871 attendance in the free public schools of Ontario was made compulsory, and the educational work of Egerton Ryerson who served as superintendent of education for the province from 1844 to 1876, was consolidated into law. After his resignation the control of education in Ontario passed to a minister with a portfolio in the provincial government. Since 1863 there has been legislation in what is now Ontario recognizing the right of Roman Catholics to maintain separate schools. The Ontario free public school system now extends through the high schools and continuation schools, and since 1919 attendance up to the age of sixteen has been compulsory.

In Quebec education for most of the inhabitants is still largely under the control of the Roman Catholic clergy, although other *In provinces* schools, including technical agricultural schools, have been developing rapidly, and the right of the Protestant minority to have separate schools has been faithfully observed. In Quebec, moreover, there is still a lingering notion that compulsory education somehow interferes with the rights of parents over their children. In the maritime provinces educational development has been retarded by many religious quarrels among sectarian groups; these disputes have necessitated the guaranteeing of special privileges. The development of educational facilities and the struggles over separate schools in the prairie provinces have been discussed elsewhere. Education was not made compulsory in Manitoba until 1916.

Higher education in Canada has not been neglected. To the contrary, sectarian enthusiasm and denominational rigidity have *Higher* \ often led to regrettable duplication of effort and a wasting of re- *education* sources in this field. Universities like Toronto, Dalhousie, and McGill stand at the apex of the Canadian educational pyramid, and have attracted international attention by the merit of their work. The University of Toronto, originally promoted as a sectarian venture, was freed from religious control in 1849, and now receives annual grants from the provincial government of Ontario. Laval University traces its history back to the seminary founded by the great François de Laval, bishop of Quebec in 1674, and has maintained its close connection with the Roman Catholic hierarchy. In 1852 it was chartered in its present form. McGill University was founded in 1821 and has become especially known for its work in medicine and science.

Among other institutions of note may be mentioned Queen's University in Kingston, Western University in London, Ontario, *Canadian* and the younger provincial universities of Manitoba, Saskatchewan, *colleges and* Alberta, and British Columbia. These provincial universities were *universities* created in the present century and are interesting proofs of the genuine concern of the new West for higher and more democratic educational opportunities. In 1912 when the second Congress of Empire Universities assembled in London, nineteen of the fifty-one universities represented were Canadian. In 1925 Canada had twenty-three universities and seventy-nine colleges, many colleges doing work no more advanced than public high schools, and granting no degrees.

Canadian national spirit

Canada is still too young and too undeveloped to resist the overshadowing influences of both Great Britain and the United States and consequently the Dominion has not made much progress in the development of a literature and of fine arts which may be called truly national in spirit. Canadian nationhood is a comparatively recent achievement, and it is still too early to find, with the possible exception of painting, much expression of a distinct Canadian tradition in the art of the Dominion. Nevertheless, Canada's contributions in these fields have become important, and some mention of them must be made in this connection.

Literature of French Canada

French-Canadian literature, the oldest and most fundamentally Canadian, is largely the product of the desire to preserve French nationality in an ever-growing English commonwealth and to give literary expression to the life of the original Canadian stock along the St. Lawrence. Among the first to espouse the cause of French nationalism was the Quebec journalist, Etienne Parent (born 1802). François Xavier Garneau, who died in 1866, became the "national historian" of French Canada. His three volume *Histoire du Canada*, published 1845-48, the result of twenty-five years of toil, while clearly pro-French is a well written and well documented story of French activities in North America from the beginning of colonization to 1840. Michael Bibaud's three volume *Histoire du Canada* is somewhat more friendly to the English element; it stops with 1837. Louis P. Turcotte's *Canada Sous l'Union* deals with the period from the Union to the Confederation. The historical labors of Benjamin Sulté of Three Rivers should not be overlooked in even so brief a list of historical writers, for Sulté's work shows a real appreciation and understanding of those social forces to which modern scholars have given the name of the "new history." Such excellent modern writers as Alfred DeCelles and Thomas Chapais prove that history is still the most fascinating interest of French-Canadian writers.

Poetry

Octave Crémazie, born in Quebec in 1827, is generally regarded as the father of French-Canadian poetry. Louis Fréchette (1839-1908) tells the story of French Canada in his *La Legende d'un Peuple*, and in many of his lyric poems he reveals with rare beauty and charm the simple, pious life of the French peasant folk in old Quebec. Several of Fréchette's poems were crowned by the Institute of France. Louis Hémon's *Marie Chapdelaine* is a more recent and exquisitely beautiful prose version of the same theme. Hémon, in a long list of writers who wrote novels based on French-Canadian life, was the first to achieve real distinction. Needless to say most French-Canadian literature, as well as the legends and folk music of old Quebec, reveal a strong religious flavoring.

Practically all of the noteworthy literary productions of English Canadians date from the time of the Confederation. In the field of history, Robert Christie's six volume *History of Canada* is one of the few exceptions. It covers the period from 1791 to 1841. William Kingsford (1819–1898) trained originally as an engineer, became a follower of the muse of history quite late in life; he began his *History of Canada* at the age of sixty-five. His ten volumes, which are still valuable, carry the story to 1841. Among the historical scholars of present-day Canada it is difficult to make a selection. Arthur G. Doughty has been a notable archivist, and Oscar Douglas Skelton did excellent work until he deserted the profession to become under-secretary in the department of external affairs. George M. Wrong of the University of Toronto during a long career as writer and teacher also has many notable contributions to his credit. Among the newer group of historians especially trained in the new school of scientific research, Chester Martin, Lawrence J. Burpee, W. Jackman, F. W. Howay, W. L. Grant, R. G. Trotter, Adam Shortt, J. L. Morison, W. S. Wallace, Duncan McArthur, and W. P. M. Kennedy have done historical writing which has received recognition not only in Canada but internationally. The valuable *Makers of Canada* series made its first appearance early in the present century, and works like the *Chronicles of Canada* and *Canada and Its Provinces* are coöperative enterprises indispensable to all students of Canadian history. *The Canadian Historical Review* was established in 1920 and quickly took its place among the best historical periodicals.

The field of Canadian fiction is still comparatively barren. Thomas Chandler Haliburton (1796–1865), a native Nova Scotian, stands out as almost the only exceptional genius Canada has produced. His *Sam Slick* ranks with the great figures of humorous literature such as those created later by writers like Artemus Ward and Mark Twain. Among more recent writers are Stephen Leacock, who seems equally at home in half a dozen fields, the Reverend Charles W. Gordon, who as "Ralph Connor" wrote such tales as *The Sky Pilot*, and Norman Duncan, with his Newfoundland stories. Ernest Thompson Seton is internationally known for his animal and nature stories. *Beautiful Joe*, one of the most popular children's books ever written, came from the pen of Margaret Saunders of Halifax. English Canadians have made their greatest reputation in the field of poetry, and most of the best work in this field has been done since 1860. Charles G. D. Roberts, Archibald Lampman, Bliss Carman, William Henry Drummond, D. C. Scott, Marjorie Pickthall, E. J. Pratt, and Wilson Macdonald are among the better known poets of this modern Canadian renaissance.

Canadian journalism has developed rapidly in the last three-quarters of a century, and such papers as the Toronto *Globe*, the Montreal *Gazette*, the Manitoba *Free Press*, and others of the newer

History

Fiction

Journalism

western papers are conducted on a relatively high plane. Canadian periodicals have usually been very shortlived. The flood of magazine literature entering Canada from the United States is primarily responsible for this heavy mortality.

Fine arts
In the fine arts Canadians are just beginning to achieve some distinction. The market for the artist is still very limited in Canada, and consequently many men of talent drift to the art centers of the United States, or send their work to American buyers. Only in painting has Canada developed a school which is distinctively Canadian. Some of the canvases of this newer school have become world-famous and have been hung in the leading galleries of England, Europe and America. The old custom of securing a European training and technique has largely passed for Canadian artists since the Great War. Organizations like the Ontario Society of Artists, founded in 1872, the Royal Canadian Academy established in 1878, and the Group of Seven of recent years have done much to stimulate painting and its recognition by the governments and the people of the Dominion. Schools of art have been established in Toronto, Halifax, Montreal, Winnipeg, Vancouver, and elsewhere. Among the newer group of artists Curtis Williamson and E. Wyly Grier have done excellent work in portraiture, F. S. Challener is noted for mural decorations, and C. W. Jefferys has done some unique historical pictures. Horatio Walker has an international reputation as an interpreter of French-Canadian life and Homer Watson is well known for his paintings of pioneer life. Among earlier artists who won recognition abroad, Paul Peel, Blair Bruce, and James Wilson Morrice should be mentioned. Tom Thomson is one of the greatest landscape painters of recent years.

Recently, moreover, many patrons of art have been recruited among the new aristocracy of industrialism, and most liberal donations have been made from time to time for the advancement of the fine arts in the Dominion. Louis Philippe Hebert is probably the best known Canadian sculptor. In this branch of the fine arts many Canadian artists have found larger fields for the exercise of their talents in the United States. Canadian architecture, with the exception of that of old French Canada, is largely imitative of the United States and England. Many of the art institutes of Canada have benefited greatly at all times by the interest and patronage of various governors-general. Lord Elgin, Lord Dufferin, and the Marquis of Lorne deserve special recognition in this connection. The increasing number of art museums established in many Canadian cities in recent years indicates a very healthy interest in the fine arts. The National Gallery of Canada was established at Ottawa in 1913; it is supported by government appropriations.

Music and
drama
The theatre in Canada, from legitimate drama through musical comedy, burlesque, and moving pictures, is really an appendage of the theatrical activities of the United States and of Great Britain.

At Hart House Theatre, however, has been developed, in a unique way and in a setting of marvellous beauty under the patronage of the Hon. Vincent Massey, a "little theatre" which has attracted the admiration and won the praise of leaders of the theatrical profession throughout the world. The Little Theatre Movement is spreading rapidly to other cities, resulting in much encouragement to native dramatists. Canadian musical life is also closely connected with that of the United States. French Canadians have many lovely folk melodies, and these *chansons populaires* have been faithfully handed down from generation to generation in old Quebec, and constitute, together with a few Indian and Eskimo melodies, the only folk music the Dominion possesses. Most professional performers in Canada are musicians who come from the United States. Edward Johnson, perhaps the greatest living operatic tenor, is a Canadian, but he finds it necessary to go to the Metropolitan Opera of New York to give full range to his extraordinary talents; his countrymen hear him only on occasional concert tours. Municipal orchestras are developing in some of the larger Canadian cities such as Toronto. This city has also become famous for its choral music, primarily through the splendid work of the Mendelssohn Choir, while the Hart House string quartette has made successful tours through many of the larger musical centers of the United States. Montreal maintains a permanent opera company.

In their laudable efforts to develop a truly Canadian culture many Canadians feel the overshadowing influence of the United States very keenly, and there occasionally has been resentment against foreigners (especially Americans) who invade Canada in search of Canadian themes. Although Canada has hitherto lacked the background, the experience, and the leisure to develop a truly national art, the desire for a literature and an art which should give emotional expression to Canada's rise to nationhood has not abated. Some have sought to counteract the relentless permeation of Canadian life by influences from the United States by drawing closer to the mother-country, and Canada is full of various imperial and national organizations, such as the Sons of England, the Imperial Order of the Daughters of the Empire, the Overseas Club, and the Canadian Clubs, which have as part of their program the desire to protect the Canadian national spirit and the imperial connection from too much "Americanization." There has been much protest against becoming a "vassal state" of the United States, and the best corrective for this state of affairs seems to be the preaching of a new and greater appreciation of Canada's own national traditions and mode of life. *Efforts to promote Canadian nationalism*

On the other hand, the peaceful economic and cultural penetration of Canada by forces from the United States was and is unavoidable. The Dominion gets her music, her slang, her tooth-paste, her moving pictures, her periodical literature, almost everything from news dispatches to Kiwanis Clubs, from automobiles to chewing gum, *American penetration* largely from the United States. American baseball rather than English cricket or the Canadian native game of lacrosse is becoming the national game of the Dominion. Much of Canadian economic and industrial evolution closely parallels that of the United States, and many economic and political policies have been directly borrowed from the American republic. The same language, the same customs, the same religious life, and in many cases the same laws prevail on both sides of the international boundary. Canadian and American railroads operate over a standard gauge. Canadian newspapers look more and more like those of the United States and use much the same material. The prices of many Canadian staples are fixed in American markets, as also are the fashions of men's and women's clothes. The Canadian university student has patterned his college yells after those of the United States, and some American national holidays are equally observed in Canada. In a recent debate in the Ontario legislature (1926) an irate member pointed out that 99.5 per cent of all films shown in Canada came from the United States, and the honorable member deplored the showing of films depicting Canadian Royal Northwest Mounted Police operating around a Hudson's Bay Company post over which the Stars and Stripes were prominently displayed.

This spiritual and psychological vassalage to the United States arouses some Canadians to a vigorous defense of their own national ideas and to greater efforts to develop a national culture. Nevertheless, it is doubtful whether this peaceful penetration can be halted or whether it would be possible or desirable to develop a cultural diversity in these neighboring and kindred states. Much of this similarity is undoubtedly due to imitation and to deliberate efforts by American producers to exploit the Canadian market, but much is due also to similar conditions and similar problems in two countries which are separated after all only by a most artificial political boundary.

Nevertheless, the abiding peculiarities of French Canada should not be lost sight of, and in some instances, there is a greater diversity of the traditions of the United States and English Canada than is apparent on the surface. Of late years, American producers with Canadian branches have been exploiting the nationalism of Canada, and General Motors, for example, has not hesitated to use the slogan, "Better because Canadian."

SELECT BIBLIOGRAPHY FOR CHAPTER XXVI

Many of the special articles cited earlier from the volumes of *Canada and Its Provinces* are useful here. Among these may be listed: O. D. SKELTON, "General Economic History, 1867–1912," in *Canada and Its Provinces*, vol. IX, pp. 93–274; J. A. RUDDICK, "National Aid to the Farm," *Ibid.*, vol. VII, pp. 651–677; WILLIAM SMITH, "The Post Office, 1867–1912," *Ibid.*, vol. VII, pp. 629–648; and R. H. COATS, "The Labour Movement in Canada," *Ibid.*, vol. IX, pp. 277–355. For additional information on the development of transportation, consult again: S. J. McLEAN, "National Highways Overland," *Ibid.*, vol. X, pp. 359–472; and O. D. SKELTON, *The Railway Builders* in *Chronicles of Canada*

(Toronto, 1921). For the development of Canada's Indian policy, not touched upon in this chapter, see Duncan C. Scott, "Indian Affairs, 1867–1912," in *Canada and Its Provinces*, vol. VII, pp. 593–626.

Much excellent and specialized material on the history of various religious organizations in Canada is available in the special articles in vols. X and XI of *Canada and Its Provinces*. For the history of Canadian literature and the fine arts, the articles in vol. XII of the same set are indispensable. Frank O. Call, *The Spell of French Canada* (Boston, 1926) is a descriptive volume of the old French-Canadian province of Quebec, and is especially valuable for the information it contains concerning the legends, folk-lore, and folk-music of the French Canadians. Further light on peculiar French-Canadian conditions may be gleaned from such studies as: J. C. Bracq, *The Evolution of French Canada* (New York, 1924); W. H. Moore, *The Clash: A Study in Nationalities* (New York, 1919); Walter A. Riddell, *The Rise of Ecclesiastical Control in Quebec*, in *Columbia University Studies*, LXXIV, No. 1 (New York, 1916).

A. MacMechan, *Headwaters of Canadian Literature* (Toronto, 1924) and J. D. Logan and D. G. French, *Highways of Canadian Literature* (Toronto, 1924) are valuable volumes correlating the literary history of Canada with the development of Canadian life. For the history of the press, consult: *History of Canadian Journalism* edited by a Committee of the Press Association (1908). The volumes of *The Canadian Annual Review of Public Affairs* contain sections which give annual summaries of the progress of Canadian literature, journalism, and the fine arts as well as of the political and economic events of the Dominion. A group of typical French-Canadian folk-songs, with music and English translation, is available in *Canadian Folk Songs, Old and New*, selected and translated by J. Murray Gibbon (Toronto, 1927). See also Wilfrid Bovey, *Canadien, A Study of the French Canadians* (Toronto, 1933).

Two very stimulating articles on Canadian nationality are: W. S. Wallace, "The Growth of Canadian National Feeling," in *Canadian Historical Review*, vol. I, pp. 136–165; and Archibald MacMechan, "Canada as a Vassal State," *Ibid.*, December, 1920. See also, Hugh L. Keenleyside, "American Economic Penetration of Canada," in *The Canadian Historical Review*, vol. VIII, pp. 31–40, and the reply to the same in the succeeding number, pp. 137–141. Keenleyside's *Canada and the United States* (New York, 1928) is devoted to the whole question of Canadian-American relations.

CHAPTER XXVII

CANADIAN PARTICIPATION IN THE GREAT WAR

A BOOK of this kind is not the place for even a brief discussion of the complicated causes of the Great War of 1914–1918. A discussion of war causes is, of course, a perfectly legitimate, and no doubt a highly necessary piece of work, but more space is needed than is available here for a proper balancing of all the pros and cons of the problem of war guilt and for an adequate citation of evidence. It is clear to all well-informed students of the question in every country that the ultimate causes of the war run far back into the history of Europe during the nineteenth century, that they are many and diverse, and that they can be laid at the door of no one European nation. The alignment of the great European powers in two alliances, the mad race for armaments on land and sea in which all participated, the development of sharp rivalries over colonies and commerce, the wave of intense nationalism that engulfed most of Europe before 1914—these and many other factors must be listed among the ultimate causes of the war of 1914. Contrary to the views held during the war in many parts of the world, it is now generally admitted that Germany did not deliberately will the war and that she shares the war guilt with the rest of the great European powers, the only difference among them being one of degree. When war broke out the propaganda bureaus maintained by every nation involved, naturally set out to convince the world that their version of the origins of the conflict was the only acceptable and truthful one. Stories like the Belgian atrocity tales and various slogans like "scraps of paper," "the sanctity of international agreements," the "war to end war," and "the war to make the world safe for democracy" proved most effective in raising the struggle to a seemingly higher plane of idealism.

Whatever were the ultimate causes of the war, the immediate cause took place on June 28, 1914, when the Archduke Ferdinand of Austria and his wife, heirs-apparent to the Austro-Hungarian throne, were assassinated by Serbian plotters in the streets of Serajevo. On July 23, Austria-Hungary, convinced that the murder was traceable to a Pan-Serbian or Pan-Slavic plot to disrupt the ancient empire of the Hapsburgs, despatched a most drastic ultimatum to the Serbian government at Belgrade and demanded a reply within forty-eight hours. Although the Austrian terms seriously impinged upon Serbian sovereignty, the latter nation accepted all but two of the demands, and offered to submit the remainder to arbitration. Austria was not satisfied with the Serbian reply and began mobilization. The wheels of secret diplomacy were set in motion, Europe divided into two opposing alliances, last minute proposals by diplomats to stop the war failed in the atmosphere of intrigue, distrust, and suspicion prevailing in all the European chancelleries, and before the end of the first week in August most of Europe was at war.

So far as Canada was concerned, the Dominion, for all practical and legal purposes, was at war the moment Great Britain entered the conflict. Canada might discuss her technical right of voluntarily coming to the aid of the Empire, but this did not alter her belligerent status as far as the outside world was concerned. Nor was there any disposition to quibble over technicalities. The great majority of Canadians recognized that to give aid to the mother-country was their solemn duty, and were eager to do their share in a war which they considered righteous and unavoidable so far as Great Britain was concerned.

There was no evidence at the outset of racial or political cleavage in Canada over the war issue. Laurier pronounced the war "the most sacred" the Empire had ever participated in, and immediately promised an end of party conflict. He advised volunteering in public utterances that rang with passionate devotion to the Empire and he specifically urged the raising of French-Canadian regiments in addresses at recruiting meetings in Quebec. Even Bourassa, the Quebec Nationalist leader, announced in his newspaper, *Le Devoir*, in September, 1914, that he would not oppose the sending of Canadian contingents to European battlefields. *United nation*

The call for volunteers met with a ready response. The total peace establishment of Canada before the war did not exceed 63,500 men, of whom only 3500 were permanently in service, the rest being enrolled among the active militia. Plans had been made, however, to expand this force to 150,000 in time of war, and Colonel Hughes, the Conservative minister of militia, had been perfecting measures for military training in high schools and universities. By April 10, 1915, over 100,000 men were under arms. *Volunteering*

The first Canadian overseas contingent was landed in Plymouth, England, on October 15, 1914. In the early months of the war more volunteers offered their services than the government could equip, although the minister of militia was frantically rushing about the country, placing war orders, building cantonments in which to train troops, and starting manufacturers to work on munitions. By the end of 1916, 630 munitions plants employing over 300,000 workers were in operation in Canada. The creation of many "Honorary Colonels" helped to mobilize businessmen for war work. By the end of 1915, 212,000 men were under arms, and another 500,000 were called. Recruiting was on the decline by this time, however, and by the end of 1915 the government found it necessary to lower the physical standards for volunteers and to make other changes designed to stimulate recruiting. By the end of 1916, 434,000 men were in *First overseas forces* active service either in Canada or abroad. In all 619,636 men saw service in the Canadian Expeditionary Forces, and of this number 424,589 went overseas.

Recruiting statistics Recruiting statistics show that of the first 250,000 volunteers, over sixty per cent were born in Great Britain, and the general statement may be made that enthusiasm for recruiting varied inversely with length of residence in the Dominion. Official figures issued in February, 1916, indicated that among the Canadian volunteer forces, thirty per cent were native-born and sixty-two per cent came from the United Kingdom. Moreover, the city population seemed to respond in greater numbers than the rural population, and in general the West seemed more enthusiastic for war than the East.

Decline in recruiting By the end of 1916 the use of moving pictures, patriotic speakers, women sent to hunt recruits, and other devices to bring pressure to bear on the timid and the wavering, failed to yield the desired number of soldiers. High wages were attracting many workers into the munitions industries, farmers were loath to leave their farms especially when the government was urging them to increase food production, and many Canadians, in spite of a vigorous propaganda, still lacked understanding of imperial affairs. It was evident by the end of 1916 that recruiting by the volunteer method had virtually reached its limit. In the face of this difficulty, some urged a registration and classification of the man-power of the nation for war work, others favored conscription, and many concluded that Canada had already been bled white by the war and could do no more to help the Empire.

French Canadians and war The situation in French Quebec was watched with keenest interest throughout the Dominion. The first Canadian contingent to go overseas contained twenty-three per cent French Canadians among the total of Canadian-born troops, and some special French-Canadian battalions were raised at the beginning of the war. As late as January, 1916, Prime Minister Borden paid a tribute to Canadians of French stock for their work on the battlefront. In general, however, to the outsider Quebec seemed to be only passively loyal.

Reasons for their attitude There were abundant reasons for this attitude, but unfortunately they were quite misunderstood in the English-speaking provinces of the Dominion. First of all, Quebec was *old* Canada, and its people felt no connection whatsoever with the European world. Reared by church and nationalist leaders in the faith of *La Nation Canadienne*, many of the *habitants* saw no reason why their country should be drawn into the vortex of European intrigues. This inertia was a natural condition which had existed for more than a century. The leaders of the Catholic Church pronounced the war a righteous cause, but probably did not feel it their duty to urge recruiting. It must also be remembered that Quebec was a rural section with few towns, a province of early marriages and large families. Moreover, the Government had done little publicity work among the French

Canadians in the first year of the war, and there were few militia regiments in Quebec which could serve as a nucleus for new volunteer forces. In a sense the passive patriotism of the Quebec *habitant* was in direct proportion to his lack of education in imperial matters. His political responsibilities had hitherto been limited by the boundaries of Canada, and sometimes by the province in which he lived. Moreover, Nationalists like Bourassa and his chief lieutenant, Armand Lavergne, began to criticize the Allies early in the war for their secret diplomacy, and to denounce Ontario's "Prussians" as worse than the Germans.

The new controversy over the bilingual question in the schools of Ontario (there were now 200,000 French in the province) served to add fuel to the flames of racial and religious controversy. The trouble dated back to 1912 when the Ontario Department of Education issued Regulation 17, an order intended to insure the teaching of English in the schools of the provinces. Laurier declared that in actual practice it "created a restricted atmosphere in which French could be taught." The use of French as the language of instruction was permitted where necessary, but pupils were expected to begin the study of English at once and to take up as soon as possible the regular course of study prescribed for public and separate schools. The time for French instruction was, under ordinary conditions, not to exceed one hour a day. *Ontario's bilingual question*

Early in 1916 two teachers in an Ottawa school were dismissed because of the bilingual controversy. Disorders and strikes followed and many bilingual schools were closed for a time. A French-Canadian paper in Ottawa thundered against this "Prussianism and Barbarity" toward the French minority, and the Ontario Orangemen retaliated in kind. A resolution introduced in the Dominion Parliament to effect a compromise failed of adoption largely because Borden did not favor interference in the educational affairs of a province without the latter's prior consent. On the other hand, the Nationalist group of Quebec seemed determined to make this Ontario question a national issue, and claimed that "the constitutional equality of the French and English languages throughout Canada" was at stake. The churches of Quebec made collections for the "wounded of Ontario," and Bourassa attacked both major parties with equal vigor. The Ottawa bilingual controversy however was in itself a language rather than a religious dispute. Indeed, much bitterness developed in the local Separate School Board between French and Irish Catholics, the latter insisting on English education for their children, and fearful lest they lose this arrangement under French influence on the board. *Ontario "Prussianism"*

In the meantime party politics were being revived rapidly. Laurier, as leader of the Opposition, supported the war but did not thereby surrender his right to criticize war methods or the war record of the Government. The Liberals did not, in the main, oppose either the Government's program for raising troops or for financing the war, *Revival of partisan politics* but they did insist on their right, conceived as a patriotic duty, to expose fraud and graft in connection with the development of the war program. The enormous war contracts let in Canada, estimated as early as July, 1915, at nearly $395,000,000, and the hurry incident to the mobilization of the nation's resources, led to opportunities for profiteering and fraud which seem to follow inevitably from the lowering of the national morale accompanying a great war. Before the end of 1915, Parliament and the country were discussing alleged corruption in the awarding of war contracts, and two Conservative members were virtually forced to resign by the prime minister because of graft in purchasing drugs and horses for the government. In response to continued criticism the Government appointed the former chief justice of the Superior Court to make a thorough investigation of all charges of mismanagement. Some disgraceful episodes were uncovered, and several Canadians sought safety from prosecution by flight to the United States.

Colonel Sam Hughes

Much of the controversy centered around the activities of the minister of militia and defense. Colonel Hughes' friends maintained that he was making an unrivaled record for achievement in spite of embarrassing handicaps; his enemies denounced him as a bungling egotist not averse to awarding war contracts so that his friends might profit thereby. The Toronto *Globe* kept up a running fire against what it called "his aping of Napoleon as the world's other military genius." The worst charge against Colonel Hughes concerned the alleged awarding of contracts for shells to United States manufacturers at enormous profits, the deal being arranged through an intimate friend of the minister who was accused of collecting large commissions from American manufacturers. There were other difficulties over the type of rifle to be used by Canadian troops, indiscreet criticisms of British policies at the front, and an undoubted assumption of powers by Colonel Hughes which only the governor-general-in-council could legally exercise. Prime Minister Borden, on Laurier's insistence, instituted an investigation, and gradually stripped the stormy member of his cabinet of his extraordinary powers. Finally, in November, 1916, he requested Hughes' resignation.

Extension of Parliament

In 1916, the Conservative prime minister asked for the extension of the life of Parliament for one year, promising to confine his program to "measures relating to or rising out of the war." The Liberals supported the petition to the British Parliament to amend the British North America Act for this purpose, probably because they wanted to avoid a "khaki election" while the war was at its height. This agreement, however, did not stop Laurier's attacks upon the Government for extravagance, and the Liberal leader insisted more and more on the right of the Opposition to be consulted on all important decisions. By-elections and elections in some of the provinces, moreover, seemed to indicate a slow but steady increase in the strength of the Liberals. The provincial elections of Quebec produced a sweeping

Liberal victory, while in Nova Scotia the Liberals won thirty seats and the Conservatives only thirteen.

In 1916 the prime minister appointed a National Service Board to raise the 130,000 men necessary to fill the required quota of 500,000, and an inventory of the man-power of the Dominion was undertaken in the summer of the same year, because of the continued decline in volunteering. Later in the year many demands were heard for a coalition Government of experts, and this inevitably raised the delicate question of the place Laurier might occupy in such a coalition ministry.

In February, 1917, Borden went to London to attend an imperial conference and to participate in the meetings of the newly devised Imperial Cabinet, the harbinger of a new era in the history of the British Empire. The Canadian prime minister also found time to visit the battlefront. He returned to Canada in May, convinced that the principle had been recognized by England, that the dominions must henceforth be consulted in advance on matters of peace and war, but also convinced that conscription must be adopted in Canada to provide the man-power for the final efforts of the war. From the beginning of the war to the end of 1916, Borden had repeatedly stated that there would be no compulsion used in raising troops in Canada. It is significant that the policy of conscription was announced to the Dominion Parliament on the same day that the draft law was enacted by the United States Congress which by now also had entered the lists against the Central Powers. *Borden visits Europe, 1917*

The Parliamentary session of 1917 was one of the longest and most turbulent in the history of the Dominion. A resolution to extend the life of Parliament to October, 1918, did not receive enough support to warrant Borden to take action. Laurier called attention to thirty unfilled vacancies in the House of Commons and protested against the passage of any important war legislation by a moribund Parliament. Moreover, the Liberal leader refused to enter a coalition Government if this implied acceptance of conscription. To have done so would have given Quebec to the Nationalists. *Parliament in 1917*

At this critical juncture in political affairs, a Military Voters Act was passed, giving the franchise to all Canadian men and women in or out of Canada who were engaged in active war service and denying the vote to conscientious objectors. This was followed by the War Times Election Act, sponsored and drawn by Arthur Meighen, by which the ballot was given to all wives, widows, mothers, sisters, and daughters of Canadians serving overseas, while those of alien enemy birth or those of European birth naturalized since 1902 and using the language of an alien enemy country were disfranchised. *Gerrymandering*

This extraordinary legislation was justified by the Conservatives on the theory that only those who fought for Canada should have the power to determine her political life. Arthur Meighen wanted the coming election to express "the real views of the Canadian *Its justification by the Conservatives* people." Most of the Liberals denounced the "Kaiserism" of the Conservative "Junker aristocracy" as a brazen effort to gerrymander the electorate in the interest of the existing Government. The Liberals pointed out that most of the immigrant groups of the West usually voted their party ticket, that the law was unfair to the aliens whom Canada had lured into the West by her immigration propaganda, and that it disfranchised by federal action many women who had recently received the ballot by action of the western provincial governments. The law was passed, however, by numerous applications of the closure rule.

Conscription

A conscription act was formally introduced on June 11. Its introduction was the signal for the disruption of the Liberal party. Laurier denounced the measure as illegal and contrary to the earlier pledges of the Government, as a political maneuver of a dying Parliament, and as a measure which was unnecessary, inexpedient, opposed by organized labor and the French Canadians, and likely to disrupt the nation. He argued that the measure would not yield the required manpower any more than the volunteering process had done, and he demanded a popular referendum on the question. Laurier's referendum proposal was defeated by a shift of western Liberals to the support of the Government.

Breach in Liberal ranks

Laurier clearly understood the rising tide of opposition in Quebec to such irritating methods of compulsion and saw in the passage of the act the destruction of his life's work to preserve harmony between the French and English elements in Canada, as well as an attempt to break up the Liberal power in Quebec and in the West. Many of the Liberals, however, no longer followed the advice of their veteran leader. Liberals like G. P. Graham, Michael Clark, F. B. Carvell, Clifford Sifton, and others, and Liberal papers like the Toronto *Globe*, the Manitoba *Free Press*, and the Winnipeg *Tribune* supported the draft as a measure necessary for the continuance of the war. The law was passed on August 28, 1917, by a vote in which old party lines were broken. The western agricultural group joined the Conservatives in support of conscription; the Nationalists switched to the Liberal side and demanded a popular referendum.

Provisions of draft law

The draft law provided compulsory registration of all males between the ages of twenty and forty-five and their classification for service in six classes, with exemptions for those engaged in necessary war industries, for the physically unfit, for conscientious objectors, and for those who might suffer a "serious hardship" if called into the army because of "exceptional financial or business obligations or domestic position."

Coalition Government

The demand for a coalition Government now gathered momentum rapidly. Laurier, as has been pointed out, refused to join forces with the Conservatives if this involved the approval of conscription. On July 16, twenty-six dissenting Ontario Liberals caucused without their veteran leader, and endorsed the draft. Liberal conventions were organized in the West and elsewhere on a "win the war" basis, and these gatherings favored a new "national" Government. Borden, largely through the astute Meighen as intermediary, continued to negotiate with prominent Liberals behind the scenes in the hope of perfecting a Union cabinet before the fall elections which were now inevitable. On October 12, 1917, these efforts, partly honest and partly the result of partisan maneuvers, were crowned with success and a Union Government was organized. In the new ministry were such Liberals as N. W. Rowell, F. B. Carvell, T. A. Crerar, and seven others. The Conservatives retained thirteen places in the new cabinet and the Liberals had the other ten. New elections were called for December 17.

Canada's "khaki election" of 1917 was not greatly different from those of other countries where an appeal was made to the electorate while the war hysteria was at its height. The campaign promises of the Conservatives included such pledges as the enforcement of conscription, civil service reform, woman's suffrage, agricultural aids, additional taxes to stop profiteering with its consequent development of war millionaires, and finally the promise to carry the war through to victory at whatever cost. Borden denounced the referendum on conscription as impractical, drew many lurid illustrations from revolutionary Russia, and called on the voters to "keep faith with their fallen comrades." Conservative campaigners shifted the blame for a war-time election to the shoulders of the Liberal leader. *"Khaki election" of 1917*

Laurier, in spite of his seventy-seven years and the rigors of a Canadian winter, undertook a vigorous campaign which carried him as far west as the Pacific coast. He too declared that he would support the war to the bitter end and that he would abide faithfully by the results of the election. He considered conscription untimely and unnecessary, pleaded for the right of the people to express themselves on so vital an issue, and urged one more attempt to raise troops by the volunteering method. Liberals who still followed their aged leader attacked the Government for passing the War Times Election Act, for permitting profiteering, and for other inefficiencies and corruption, and promised, if returned to power, to lower the tariff, care for the returned soldiers and their dependents, and in general, provide more efficient methods for dealing with the problems of war and reconstruction. *Laurier's campaign*

Outside of Quebec Laurier had little newspaper support, but his meetings were attended by large crowds, particularly in the West. In Quebec, his native province, he was often hooted and hissed by former supporters who had been stirred to opposition by Nationalist leaders. Nevertheless, the Nationalists put comparatively few candidates into the field, for after all they were agreed with the Liberal Opposition on the one outstanding issue, opposition to the draft. Bourassa staged large mass meetings in which he denounced conscription as "organized murder" and exposed the secret treaties of *Quebec* the Allies convicting them of imperialistic designs. At some of these anti-draft meetings there were threats of armed opposition, and intervention by the police became necessary. The clergy, while accepting the law as an accomplished fact, were on the whole unfriendly to conscription. Naturally the Conservatives and Unionists made good use of all "unpatriotic" incidents in Quebec in their campaign in the other provinces. "A vote for Laurier is a vote for the Kaiser" and "Don't turn the Liberty Loan over to Quebec to spend" were among the most effective slogans used against the Liberals.

Nature of campaign

The campaign brought to light a curious mixture of honest patriotism and sordid, partisan politics. The Government had most of the English press on its side, and the further advantage of staging simultaneously with the election a great Victory Loan "drive" with its machinery for a nation-wide appeal to patriotism. Most of the Protestant Churches, particularly the Methodists, urged their members to support the Unionists as a matter of Christian and patriotic duty, and, late in 1917, Laurier could write with much truth, "It has been my lot to run the whole gamut of prejudices in Canada. In 1896 I was excommunicated by the Roman priests, and in 1917 by Protestant parsons." Tales of German atrocities were specially exploited, and to good effect, among the newly enfranchised women voters.

Outcome of election

The election results showed that eighty-two Liberals in support of Laurier, thirty-eight Union Liberals, and one hundred and fifteen Conservatives had been elected. The Government thus commanded a majority of seventy-one. The French Canadians had voted almost unanimously against the Union Government, and, in spite of the Nationalists' propaganda, the Liberals carried sixty-two of Quebec's sixty-five seats. In Ontario only eight Liberals were successful, as compared with seventy-four for the Government, although Laurier polled 60,000 more votes in the province than in 1911. In the West only three of the fifty-five candidates elected were Liberals. The popular vote for the Government was 1,057,793; the total Opposition vote was 763,371. Nearly 235,000 soldier votes figured in these election results. Bourassa declared his satisfaction with the results and concluded that "in the conflict between Imperialism and Nationalism the place of the French Canadians is established." Obviously, he was thinking of the days to come when the political alignments of war time would break up again.

Laurier as leader of Opposition

The first session of the Unionist Parliament in 1918 passed many important war measures which will be considered in the next chapter. Laurier studiously followed the policy of avoiding controversies which might widen the breach in the Liberal ranks; he advised his countrymen to obey the conscription law. As far as the operation of the draft was concerned, time proved that Laurier was substantially correct in his objections to the measure. The enforcement of the law in Quebec led to serious draft riots, attributable, in part, to the Government's failure to launch promptly an educational campaign among the French Canadians, and to its failure to select loyal French Catholics to supervise the operation of the law. All this was the more regrettable because the population of Quebec was entitled under the law to many exemptions due to early marriages, large families, and employment in agriculture. Indeed, it seemed needless to antagonize so large a population for so slight a gain in fighting strength.

Anti-draft meetings, mob violence, and police intervention marked the attempt to enforce conscription in many parts of the French province. French Canadians appealed to their provincial prime minister to petition the British Government for relief from the action of the Dominion Parliament. Bourassa counselled resistance to the draft as a national duty "to save the country from ruin, bankruptcy, and suicide," and his paper, *Le Devoir*, found the "germ of conscription" in the "voluntary expedition to South Africa" (in 1899), pointing out how it had been slowly hatched by imperial conferences, by the navy bill of 1910, and by other imperialistic measures. Bourassa argued that Canada had reached "the extreme limit" of her "capacity to pay for destruction." Throughout this bitter controversy, however, the Nationalist leader vigorously opposed all proposals to have Quebec secede from the Dominion. *Draft riots*

In other parts of the Dominion conscription also failed to be a conspicuous success. It did not furnish the men for whom the government was calling, and the number claiming exemption exceeded all expectations. Many defaulted or deserted or appealed to the courts to stop the enforcement of the law. In August, 1918, the acting minister of militia complained bitterly of the "thousands . . . who have failed their country in their country's need." Five months earlier the Government had found it necessary by an order-in-council to cancel all exemptions for those between twenty and twenty-two years of age. The draft law failed to yield as many soldiers per month as volunteering had. *Draft law disappointment*

The controversy over conscription, however, does not detract from Canada's heroic services to the Empire during the war. The total of her expeditionary forces and the total casualties, when compared in percentages of population with the record of other belligerents, reveal a story of sacrifice unequalled anywhere. Canada's total war casualties were approximately 225,000. Of this number over 51,000 were killed in action or died of wounds, and more than 175,000 were wounded or injured. The total number of missing and prisoners of war was a little above 10,000. The Dominion furnished troops for all branches of the military and naval service; Canadian units served in Palestine, Macedonia, and Russia, as well as on the western front. Many Canadians entered the Imperial Royal Flying Corps and became noted for their expert service and their daring exploits. *Canada's fighting forces*

It is impossible to discuss in detail the operations of Canadian troops on the western battlefront of Europe. As has been pointed

On battlefronts out, the first Canadian contingent went overseas in October, 1914, and amid great hardships was trained for service at the front during the winter of 1914-1915. The troops reached France in February, 1915, and took over an important salient on the Ypres front. The "Princess Pat" regiment, as the first Canadian regiment to go over was called, had virtually to be refilled after six months of fighting, largely from the university training corps.

Campaign of 1915   From April 22 to May 13, 1915, the Canadians played a leading rôle in the bloody second battle of Ypres; in spite of gas attacks, they stood their ground valiantly in rolling back a German assault on Calais and the English Channel. The victory was won after French, Turcos and Zouave troops had given way before the withering effects of chlorine gas. The Canadian casualties in these engagements around the villages of Langemarck and St. Julien exceeded five thousand. Before the close of the year, Canadian troops won new laurels in the battles of Festubert and Givenchy.

Campaign of 1916   By the beginning of 1916 there were three Canadian divisions in France, comprising an army corps under Lieutenant-General Sir E. A. H. Alderson, K. C. B. Largely owing to differences with the Canadian minister of militia, he was soon superseded by Lieutenant-General Sir Julian H. G. Byng. During the winter of 1915-1916 the Canadians participated in numerous raids on the German trenches as part of the "nibbling" process in use on the western front at that time. Under the command of General Byng three Canadian divisions and the "Princess Pats" participated in the third battle of Ypres and later, with the addition of a fourth division, fought in the great battle of the Somme. The fall of 1916 found the Canadians engaged in the ceaseless attacks and counter-attacks which constituted the grueling trench warfare in western Europe. The total Canadian casualties at the end of two years' fighting were nearly 68,000. In 1916 alone over 4000 Canadians were decorated for conspicuous gallantry.

Campaign of 1917   Early in 1917 Canadian troops held approximately one-fortieth of the western battlefront. In January they captured important trenches north of Arras. On April 9, four Canadian divisions and one British brigade, under the command of General Byng in the great battle of Arras captured Vimy Ridge from some of the best Bavarian troops on the western front. The assault was preceded by a terrific artillery preparation; after a three days' bombardment the troops advanced over ground torn by shell holes and mine craters, and covered with mud and wire entanglements. At this engagement the "tank," a new weapon of warfare, was introduced on the western front. After the battle of Vimy Ridge the Canadian troops received their first Canadian commander, Major-General Arthur W. Currie. The victory at Vimy Ridge was followed by new operations on the Arras front, particularly by an attack on Lens and, later, on the

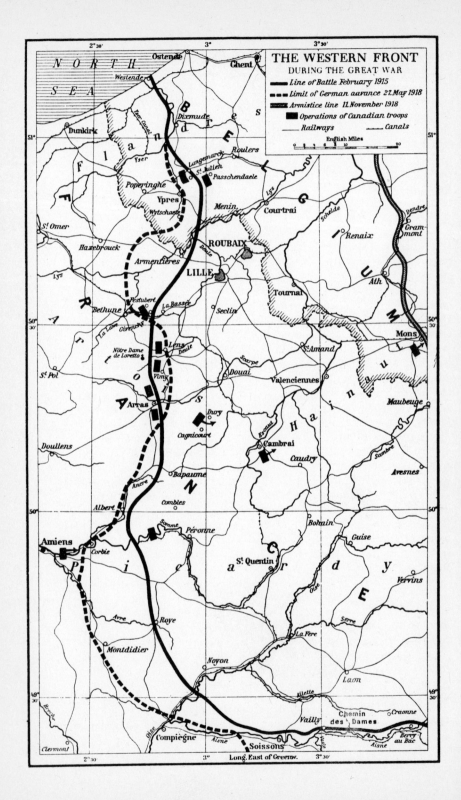

THE WESTERN FRONT
DURING THE GREAT WAR

—— Line of Battle February 1915
━ ━ ━ Limit of German advance 27.May 1918
▨▨▨ Armistice line 11.November 1918
■ Operations of Canadian troops
—— Railways   —— Canals

English Miles
0 1 2 4   6 10   20

Passchendaele Ridge in the fields of Flanders. The fighting in this sector proved indecisive and left the Germans still firmly entrenched in their positions.

In the first stages of the great German offensive in 1918, the last desperate effort of the Central Powers to force the war to a con- *Offensive* clusion on the western front, the Canadians took little part. Their *of 1918* sector was comparatively quiet. In August, when the Allies prepared to launch their great counter-offensive, Canadian troops figured in the advance on Amiens and were active to the southeast of Arras. Early in September, they assaulted and captured Dury and Cagni-court, key positions in the great Hindenburg line of defenses, to which the Germans had been forced to retreat. The end of the month found the Canadians on the outskirts of Cambrai, having captured sixty-nine towns and villages and liberated 175 square miles of territory in a two months' counter-offensive against the retreating enemy. On October 9, after one of the bloodiest battles of the war in which there were 16,000 Canadian casualties, Dominion troops entered Cambrai. In a little over five weeks' fighting they had made 28,000 prisoners and captured 500 guns and over 3000 machine guns. Canadian troops continued to push forward across the Belgian border and on the day of the Armistice, November 11, 1918, the Third Canadian Division entered Mons. On December 13, Canadian soldiers crossed the Rhine and marched into Bonn and Cologne as part of the Allied Army of Occupation.

Of the total number serving in the Canadian Expeditionary Forces, only about eighteen per cent were drafted into service, the *C. E. F.* others being volunteers. Ontario sent 205,808 volunteers, Quebec 52,993. The honors distributed for gallantry among the Canadian contingents reached a total of 17,000; sixty-four Victoria Crosses were won by Dominion troops. The feeling of national pride which greeted the victorious troops at the close of the war was somewhat diminished by a wide-spread controversy, started by charges of Colonel Hughes on the floor of Parliament that General Currie had uselessly sacrificed Canadian lives in the attack on Mons, although, it was claimed, he knew that the Armistice was to go into effect four hours later.[1]

Returning the troops to Canada was a tremendous task carried out not without considerable rioting and unrest and even mutiny *Closing events* among the war-weary veterans who were compelled to wait in British camps for transportation home. From December, 1918, to the summer of 1919, troops were returned at the rate of 3400 per month. About 4000 remained on the Siberian front to battle the Russian revolutionary forces, and one field artillery brigade was kept at Archangel in the futile effort to overthrow the Bolshevik régime in Russia.

[1] On May 1, 1928, Sir Arthur Currie was awarded $500 and costs by an Assize Court jury in an action of libel against certain newspaper publishers, who had printed an article alleging needless loss of life by Canadians at Mons in 1918.

SELECT BIBLIOGRAPHY FOR CHAPTER XXVII

Perhaps the most extreme statement of the "revisionist" point of view concerning the origins of the Great War is HARRY ELMER BARNES, *The Genesis of the World War* (New York, 1926). At the end of each chapter there is a bibliography, and in Appendix I, pp. 709-735, there is a list of books dealing with war guilt together with some critical comments on their value. A briefer, modern account of the causes of the war is available in A. C. FLICK, *Modern World History, 1776-1926* (New York, 1926), pp. 529-564. By far the best treatment is S. B. FAY, *The Origins of the World War*—2 vols. (New York, 1928). For more detailed discussions of Canada's participation in the military events of the Great War, the following recent publications are valuable: C. G. D. ROBERTS, *Canada in Flanders* (Toronto, 1918); H. E. R. STEELE, *The Canadians in France, 1915-1918* (London, 1920); and J. C. HOPKINS, *Canada at War: A Record of Heroism and Achievement* (Toronto, 1919). Other volumes are listed in TROTTER, *Syllabus*, pp. 141-142. The numbers of the *Canadian Annual Review of Public Affairs* for the war years also contain valuable summaries. Some of the books were written during the heat of the war, and often display more heat than light in their treatment of war events.

For the situation in Quebec, besides the lives of Laurier already cited, volumes like W. H. MOORE, *The Clash: A Study in Nationalities* (Toronto, 1920); ARTHUR HAWKES, *The Birthright: A Search for the Canadian and the Larger Loyalty* (Toronto, 1919) are very illuminating. See also: ARTHUR HAWKES, *Canadian Nationalism and the War* (Montreal, 1916) and HENRI BOURASSA, *Que devons-nous à l'Angleterre?* (Montreal, 1916). Additional references on the French-Canadian situation during the war are available in TROTTER, *Syllabus*, pp. 144-145.

CHAPTER XXVIII

WAR WORK ON THE HOME FRONT

MODERN wars are won quite as much by the war work of those
remaining at home as by the more spectacular deeds of those who do *Home front*
the fighting on the battlefront. The mobilization of a nation's
economic resources is as important a function of war-making governments as the mobilization of fighting units. The story of Canada's
domestic reorganization during her greatest national emergency is a
vital and even a dramatic part of Canada's war history.

When news of the declaration of war reached Canada in the
summer of 1914, its first effect upon the financial situation of the *Financial*
Dominion was to cause a run on the leading banks by panicky de- *mobilization*
positors. The Canadian banking laws require that depositors be paid
in gold or Dominion notes; since the latter were also convertible into
gold on demand, there was grave danger that the withdrawal and
hoarding of gold would lead to a serious panic. In this emergency the
Government, after conferences with the leading bankers of the
Dominion, issued an order-in-council authorizing banks to redeem
their liabilities in their own bank notes, and promising them that
the Government would advance Dominion notes to any bank on deposit of proper securities with the minister of finance. By this arrangement the authorized Dominion note issue was increased by $25,000,-
000. These extraordinary provisions were deliberate violations of the
banking laws of the Dominion, and had to be legalized by Parliament
when it reassembled in August 1914. No difficulty was encountered
in securing this approval, because the Canadian people were convinced that only by such drastic provisions for a more elastic currency
could the Dominion be saved from serious financial difficulties.
Nevertheless, the first months of the war brought industrial depression, unemployment, and a general disarrangement of the Canadian
economic structure, and the Government's plan to promote public
works did little to alleviate this situation.

The large amounts of money needed to finance Canada's war
program were raised by loans from her own people in the form of *War loans*
bond sales, by loans from England, and to a small degree, by loans
floated in the United States. By the end of the first year of the war the
Dominion was spending $14,000,000 a month on war activities, and
by the end of 1916 the war was costing Canada $1,000,000 a day.
The Canadian national debt increased from $330,000,000 before the
war to over two and two-thirds billion dollars in 1919. Almost
eighty per cent of this debt was held at home, and bankers and po-

litical leaders derived much comfort from this evidence of the financial stability of the Canadian nation. As late as 1927, however, of the total public expenditures of the Dominion, forty-five and eighteen hundredths per cent was attributable to the war. Most of this amount was needed to pay the interest on the public debt, ten and sixteen hundredths per cent went for war pensions, and two per cent for soldiers' civil reëstablishment.

War orders   During the first few months of the war most of Canada's war purchases were made in England, and from September, 1914, to March, 1915, the British treasury advanced about £12,000,000 to the credit of the Dominion. As the war progressed, the principle followed in this program of war financing was to have Britain lend Canada the money in London to pay for Canadian military expenses overseas, while Canada repaid the mother-country by placing money to her credit in the Dominion. With these credits Great Britain in turn paid for the munitions, food products, and other supplies bought from Canada. To complete the financial circle, it may be added that it was from the sale of these products to the Empire that Canadians derived the money which they subscribed for Dominion war loans.

Foreign and domestic loans   In July, 1915, the Canadian government floated a short time loan for $45,000,000 in the United States through the agency of the great New York banking syndicate of J. P. Morgan and Company. Early in 1916 another loan of $75,000,000 was raised in New York, and in the summer of 1917 an issue of two-year notes for $100,000,000 was placed in New York. The first Canadian domestic loan was attempted in November, 1915, not without considerable fear as to the results of offering to a people who had never subscribed to a loan of even $5,000,000, the chance to contribute $50,000,000. The bonds sold at ninety-seven and a half, and matured in ten years, with interest at five per cent. The loan was a sensational success, and instead of the $50,000,000 asked for the Canadian public subscribed over twice that amount. In 1916 and 1917 two additional loans were floated. The first was a request for $100,000,000 and yielded subscriptions of $200,000,-000; the second was for $150,000,000, and $250,000,000 was subscribed.

Bond "drives"   Elaborate methods of publicity were devised for these bond "drives" to reach as many small investors as possible; bonds were sold in denominations as low as fifty dollars. All possible agencies, such as the schools, the churches, banks, fraternal, and patriotic societies, were mobilized to insure the success of the bond campaigns. These methods reached their maximum efficiency in the three "victory loans" floated in 1917, 1918, and 1919 which yielded in all $1,700,-000,000. By these final loans Canada was enabled to close the war with all her debt funded in the form of obligations, the longest of which ran to 1937.

At the end of the war Great Britain, in spite of heavy Canadian loans in London, owed the Dominion a balance of $400,000,000 for supplies. When peace came the "victory loans" of Canada were quoted at figures above the price of issue, a situation maintained by the work of a Victory Loan Stabilization Committee which bought all offerings of bonds at fixed prices with funds provided by the government in order to protect the value of Canadian securities on the stock market. War savings stamps and thrift stamps were sold by the government, in addition to these bond issues, in order to attract the savings of investors of small means. War savings stamps, issued in 1916, sold at $8.60, and had a maturity value of ten dollars in five years. Most of Canada's war expenditures were met by borrowing, and most of the money borrowed remained within the Dominion to pay for the purchase of war supplies.

Besides borrowing to secure funds, the government resorted to many kinds of war taxation. The budget of 1915, the work of Sir *War taxes* Thomas White, who served as minister of finance from 1911 to 1919, levied special taxes on banking and insurance companies, on checks and other commercial paper, on money-orders, sleeping car and steamboat tickets, wines, patent medicines, and some toilet articles, and increased the postal rates of the Dominion. The tariff duties were uniformly increased seven and a half per cent, and an increase of five per cent was made in British preferential rates. Tampering with the tariff was opposed by the Liberals as a device "based upon protection and politics, not upon revenue and patriotism." But the changes in the tariff were defended by members of the Government on the plea that more revenue was badly needed, and that in the midst of a war was not the proper time to take up the tariff item by item.

The budget of 1916 introduced a new feature in the form of a Business Profits War Tax Act. This excess profits tax was devised *Excess profits* primarily to deal with the swollen fortunes caused by the war, *tax* through unscrupulous profiteering by some producers of war supplies. The excess profits tax, as first enacted, provided for a tax of one-fourth of all profits in excess of seven per cent upon the actual capital of corporations, and in excess of ten per cent upon the capital of individuals or partnerships. The law was made retroactive to the beginning of the war, but, with the exception of manufacturers of munitions, all those whose capital was less than fifty thousand dollars were exempted from the operation of the act. In addition, the law did not apply to those engaged in agriculture or stock-raising. In 1917, the law was made more drastic, and the tax on profits exceeding fifteen per cent was increased to fifty per cent, and that on profits exceeding twenty per cent was raised to seventy-five per cent. In the same year the Dominion Parliament passed an Income War Tax Act.

To the funds officially raised by the government by loans and taxation must be added the millions voluntarily donated by private *Private* individuals and organizations if we would appreciate the full extent *donations* of Canada's financial sacrifices. Voluntary contributions during the war to various kinds of patriotic work may be conservatively estimated at over $100,000,000. Private citizens and many organizations gave money for the purchase of machine guns in the early stages of Canada's preparation for participation in the war. A Canadian Patriotic Fund was raised, primarily to add to the allowances made by the government to widows and dependents of men entering the army, and donations for this purpose were received from individuals, towns and provinces. The city of Toronto insured the life of every soldier who enlisted. Belgian relief organizations were formed and practically all the churches organized units for war work, although some, apparently on moral grounds, refused to contribute for the purchase of tobacco and liquor for the soldiers overseas.

Patriotic societies

Organizations like the Imperial Order of the Daughters of the Empire sent cigarettes, candy, periodicals, knit goods, and hospital supplies to the army camps. Fairs, bazaars, and "tag days" were arranged in order to raise money, canteens were maintained at railroad stations, and thousands of women went to work in munitions plants to take the places of men who entered the service, while others, by a great variety of methods, sought to stir laggard youths to realize their duty to enlist in the sacred cause. Ambulance associations were formed and hospitals established in many places. The Canadian Red Cross alone handled $30,000,000 during the war. As an example of the magnitude of its tasks, it may be pointed out that in 1918 alone, the Dominion Red Cross sent to Europe 1,608,214 socks, 370,000 pajamas, 223,000 shirts, 680,000 towels, and tons of other supplies. The organization continued its activity during the period of demobilization and the repatriation of war prisoners. The individual provinces also spent vast sums in all kinds of war work, from equipping hospitals and soldiers' homes to donating grain and war material to the mother-country.

Munitions industry

The war afforded the stimulus for the creation of a vast munitions industry in Canada; scores of factories were converted from their original purposes and equipped for the production of shells, guns, and other war supplies. By the end of the first year of the fighting, war orders placed in Canada were estimated at nearly $400,000,000; a large percentage of this sum went to the new munitions plants. By the end of 1916, there were 630 munitions factories in the Dominion, employing over 300,000 workers. A government Shell Committee was appointed to supervise the production and distribution of this war material, and this agency was later expanded into the Imperial Munitions Board. By the end of 1916, Canada had loaned Great Britain $175,000,000 to pay for munitions purchased in the Dominion. Altogether, 62,000,000 shells were sent overseas before the close of the war, and $65,000,000 was spent in building ships to carry over these war supplies faster than the German submarines could sink them. In the light of the history of other wars, it was not surprising that this vast program could not be carried out without ugly charges of mismanagement and dishonesty.

The government also sponsored an elaborate program for the conservation of food and for the increase of food production. "Food will win the war," was the slogan which patriotic war workers dinned incessantly into the ears of housewives and farmers alike, in the effort to increase production and reduce consumption, so that food supplies might be liberated for exportation, to counteract the ravages of German submarine warfare which was threatening the life of the allied nations, particularly England. As the war progressed, it became necessary to evolve machinery to prevent hoarding and profiteering in foodstuffs. On June 20, 1917, W. J. Hanna became food controller of the Dominion, under the War Measures Act. After a conference with Herbert Hoover, the food dictator of the United States, he launched a nation-wide program to stimulate production and conserve food supplies without hoarding. *Food conservation*

Most of the work of the food controller was carried on by methods of publicity and by an appeal to the patriotism of the people, and without compulsory regulation of prices. Canada soon accustomed herself to "war menus," "war gardens" were instituted on many vacant lots, even in the cities, and the farmer was urged to increase his production, because "every pound of food raised in the Dominion is another spike in the torpedo tubes of the German submarines." The government fixed the price of wheat for the 1916 crop at $2.40 a bushel, permitted free trading in wheat with the United States, and tried to aid and control the distribution of the entire crop. In 1917 the prices fixed for Canadian wheat were identical with those fixed in the United States. On November 5, 1917, an order-in-council forbade the use of grain in the manufacture of liquor during the rest of the war, and thus furnished the entering wedge for prohibition. Eating houses were regulated and food dealers licensed by the government. An order-in-council of June 8, 1917, created a Dominion fuel controller. Local fuel boards were promptly organized, and early in 1918 the Dominion experienced three "heatless days" in an effort to solve the problem of conservation and distribution of coal for essential war industries. "Daylight saving" was adopted as another method of increasing production in war time. *Food controller*

The number of special commissions and boards created to deal with the emergency needs of the nation during the war was so large that only a few of the more important can be noted here. In 1916, a national service board was appointed to direct the raising of volunteers and to classify the man-power of the nation with a view to determining the needs of commerce and industry, as well as those of the military establishment. Organizations were formed to stimulate industrial research. Early in 1918, a department of public information was created to provide speakers and other means of giving publicity to the reasons for Canada's entry into the war and to explain the war aims of the Allies. This organization was mainly concerned with the maintenance of morale and a united public opinion in support of the *War boards* war on the "home front." A war trade board was organized to coordinate Canadian production, classify the essential industries, grant priority orders for the distribution of their products, and provide coöperation with the industries of the United States in the use of raw materials and the production of war necessities. The Dominion power board was devised to supervise and develop the power and fuel resources of the country, while a commission on conservation dealt with all kinds of problems, from the preservation of natural resources to housing programs and town planning for colonies of war workers.

Other war measures

All purchases of supplies were eventually concentrated in a war purchasing commission. In addition, there were boards of conciliation to deal with impending labor disputes, and an advisory council for scientific and industrial research. Long before the end of the fighting, various governmental agencies were charged with studying the problems of reconstruction, so that the country would not be found unprepared when the readjustment to a peace basis had to be made. A new department, headed by the minister of soldiers' civil reestablishment, was organized early in 1918 to deal with such problems as the employment and housing of returned soldiers and efforts to settle them on public lands, and to provide them with vocational training or government pensions in accordance with the degree of their disabilities. All of these enactments, many of them in the form of orders-in-council, and others in the form of Parliamentary statutes, were the work of the Unionist Government under the direction of Prime Minister, Robert Borden.

Railroads in war time

The railroads constituted a particularly difficult problem, for the extraordinary demands of the war caused a tremendous strain upon the Dominion's railroad facilities. While most of the roads were able to move troops and war supplies with a fair degree of promptness, some found it impossible to maintain their equipment at standards of maximum efficiency. Rolling stock began to deteriorate rapidly, rates could not be raised to keep pace with the advance in wages and the increase in the cost of supplies, and new loans could not be floated easily on a stock market glutted with "victory" bonds and other war securities. In the face of a record volume of business, the number of railroad cars proved inadequate and many costly delays resulted. While the Canadian Pacific managed to weather the crisis, the government soon found it necessary to come to the rescue of other roads which were vital to the Dominion's transportation system and could not be neglected in time of war.

Government support

In 1917, the government had to lend the Grand Trunk Pacific $7,500,000 to enable the road to meet the interest on its securities and to make some extremely necessary improvements. The Canadian Northern was in still greater difficulties, and many other lines were in need of government support. In the fall of 1917, at the Government's suggestion, a Canadian Railway Association was formed, consisting of the presidents of the Canadian Pacific Railroad, the Canadian

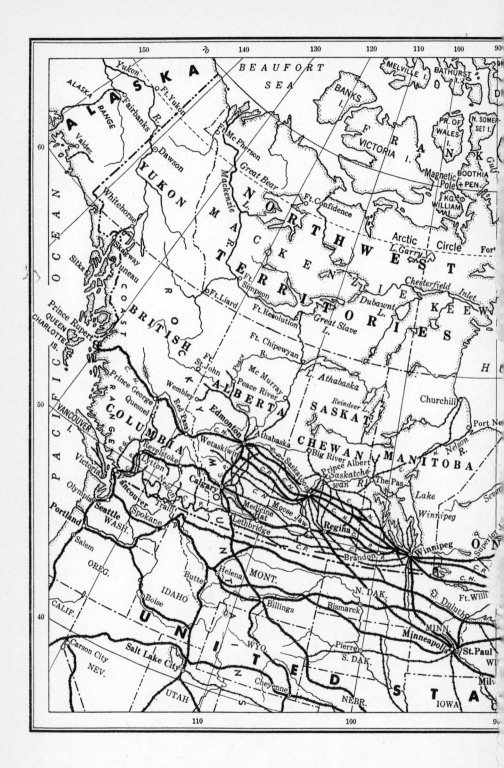

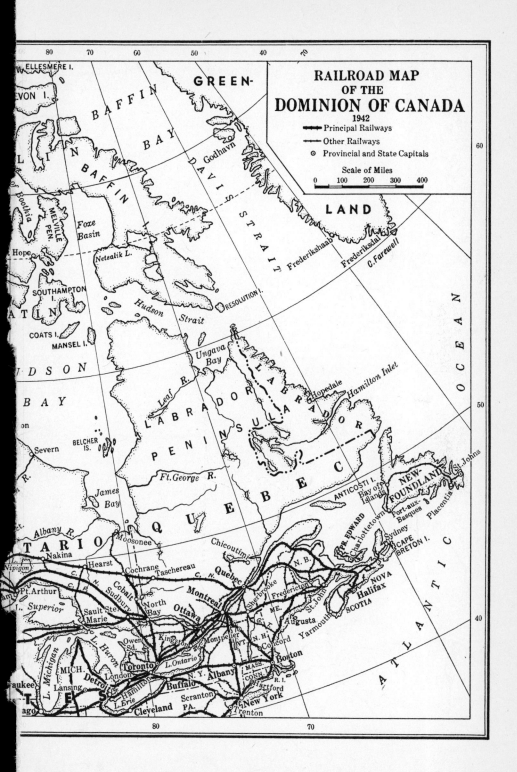

RAILROAD MAP
OF THE
DOMINION OF CANADA
1942

Principal Railways
Other Railways
⊙ Provincial and State Capitals

Scale of Miles
0   100   200   300   400

Northern, the Grand Trunk Pacific, and the New York Central, in an effort to coördinate the railway lines of the country and provide coöperation in the use of each other's facilities. Subsequently, a government board was appointed to study the problem; this body recommended that the Canadian Northern, the Grand Trunk, the Grand Trunk Pacific, the Intercolonial, and the National Transcontinental be consolidated, by act of Parliament, under the control of a board of trustees. This board, a non-political and permanent body, was to control all the railways in the interests of the nation as a whole, the government to guarantee the interest on existing stock issues of the companies concerned. It was pointed out that prior to this emergency the roads involved in this new arrangement had received in one form or another government aid amounting to almost a billion dollars. As another attempt to furnish relief, the Dominion Railway Commission, in the face of a violent protest from the western provinces, permitted an increase of from ten to fifteen per cent in railroad rates.

It is clear from these facts that the Dominion, soon after the outbreak of the war, was face to face with a situation that demanded immediate action and left no time for a theoretical discussion of the relative merits of private and public ownership of the railroads. The Grand Trunk and the Canadian Northern needed help desperately and had reached the limit of their ability to borrow on the stock market. To perhaps a majority of the people, it seemed unreasonable that the government should continue to meet the deficits of private roads without controlling or owning them. The West particularly was strongly in favor of nationalization. *Drift to government ownership*

Before the close of the war, the Canadian Northern was taken over by the government; 400,000 shares of its stock were already in the hands of the government as security for a guarantee of its bond issues, and the other 600,000 shares were acquired at a price of $10,800,000 fixed by a board of arbitrators. Since Canada already owned the Intercolonial and the National Transcontinental from Moncton to Winnipeg, the Dominion now had the roads necessary for the development of a great national railroad system. In 1919, the Grand Trunk Pacific was officially taken over by the government, the price to be fixed by arbitration, although the road was already under the control of government receivers owing to its failure to meet interest payments on its securities. The Grand Trunk was the last great system to be added to the Canadian National Railways. The problems incident to the nationalization of all the great Canadian roads except the Canadian Pacific, and the attempts to operate them profitably, will be treated more in detail in a following chapter. *Nucleus for Canadian National Railways*

The war years also served as a great stimulus to organized labor in Canada. Labor unions have always enjoyed their greatest growth in a time of rising prices and national prosperity, and the experience of organized labor from 1914 to 1918 was no exception to this rule. *Labor and war*

From 1915 to the close of the war, the increase in union membership in Canada was estimated at 100,000. The great majority of organized labor in Canada, as in the United States, supported the Great War as "labor's war" and the "war to end war," and coöperated faithfully with the Government in carrying out its war program. Nevertheless, unrest among the laboring classes steadily increased as the war progressed. War profiteering, the rise of scores of war-time millionaires, and the soaring cost of living, convinced labor leaders that they must insist upon a greater share of the wealth which labor produced. In spite of boards of conciliation and favorable labor legislation in some of the provinces, strikes could not be avoided. In 1917, there were 141 strikes; in 1918, there were 169. A widespread strike of railroad employees was avoided only by applying to Canada the terms of the so-called McAdoo award, by which the United States kept peace in her railroad industry during the war. Strikes of a serious nature occurred in the West in 1918, while the tendency of policemen to organize unions raised a new phase of the labor problem, and thoughtful people questioned whether public servants, charged with the preservation of law and order, had the right to organize unions and resort to strikes.

Strikes

The Government early in 1918 sponsored a general Labor Conference at Ottawa in order to work out the basis for a truce between capital and labor. It also established a national Labor Court of Appeal to review the findings of local boards of conciliation. Finally, an order-in-council, issued in the fall of 1918, sought to prevent strikes and lockouts altogether. A growing minority of radicals began to challenge the leadership of the older union officials, and in various parts of the Dominion plans were made during the war years for the launching of a Canadian Labor Party. The spirit of unrest invaded the ranks of government employees, and the postal workers demanded an increase in wages and asked for the appointment of a board of conciliation to deal with their demands under the Industrial Disputes Investigation Act. When the Government refused this request, a brief strike followed which was finally terminated by a sub-committee of the Government. Labor troubles were among the most serious problems of the reconstruction period and will be referred to again in that connection.

Alien enemies

The problem of alien enemies resident in the Dominion at the outbreak of the war proved a source of worry to a great many Canadians who feared pro-German activities and plots against the government by settlers who had so recently emigrated from the Central Powers. According to the census of 1911, there were 121,340 foreign-born Austro-Hungarians and 39,577 foreign-born Germans in the Dominion. Three-fourths of the immigrants from Austro-Hungary and almost a half of those from Germany had arrived since 1901. If to these be added the number of immigrants born in Bulgaria and Turkey, nations allied with the Central Powers in the war, the total foreign-born from allied countries exceeded those from the enemy countries by only 4,000. There were of course many others of German origin, although not born in Germany, who presumably felt strong sympathy for the cause of their old fatherland or the fatherland of their parents. The general testimony of Ontario and the western provinces, where this "alien enemy" population was concentrated largely, was that the conduct of the vast majority of this class was quite inoffensive during the early months of the war. As a matter of precaution, alien enemies were compelled to register with the government authorities, and were disarmed and then usually paroled, with the understanding that they were to report at stated intervals to the registering officials. By 1916 however, over 6,000 alien enemies had been interned.

As the war dragged on into years, and heavy Canadian casualty lists began to come in, feeling became more tense, and a war hysteria *Increasing* developed in which tales of ordinary indiscretions by those of *friction* German stock often were magnified into horrible conspiracies against the nation. As a result, the treatment of alien enemies and of all those of German blood in particular, became more severe and intolerant, especially after 1916. Some of the German language newspapers in Canada got into difficulties because of their indiscreet or unpatriotic comments on the progress of the war, and a number of leading German-American papers, together with Irish-American and Hearst papers, published in the United States, were barred from the Canadian mails, due to the frankly pro-German attitude which some of these papers maintained in the days before the United States became a party to the war with Germany.

Serious anti-German riots broke out in Victoria, British Columbia, and sedition trials were held in a number of western provinces, but *War hysteria* in spite of this popular excitement, the officers of the Royal Northwest Mounted Police reported in 1916 that they did not need the proposed increase of five hundred men for policing the western provinces. The temporary disfranchisement of all immigrants naturalized since 1902, coming from countries using the language of the enemy, was part of the War Times Election Act of 1917, and has been discussed in that connection. The holding of church services in the enemy tongue was prohibited by organizations of patriots in many parts of the Dominion, and parochial schools also came under the ban. The town of Berlin, Ontario, settled largely by Pennsylvania Germans who had never seen Germany, found it advisable to change its name to Kitchener, and did so as the result of a popular referendum. These anti-German demonstrations reached their climax at the time of the draft and the "drives" for the sale of bonds, when the excitement of the people was at fever heat. Viewed from the perspective of peace days, it is possible to conclude that, on the whole, Canada's alien enemies gave very little trouble, and generally they were content to continue their ordinary routine of life as quietly as their hysterical neighbors would permit.

*Woman's
suffrage*

As in the case of the prohibition movement, which by 1918 had affected eight Canadian provinces, the war did much to quicken the interest of the public in the important political reform of woman's suffrage and helped to bring the agitation to a climax. In the face of the splendid war record of the women of Canada, and in view of the democratic principles avowed as the real goal of the war, it would have been inconsistent and indefensible to bar one-half of the population from voting for the sole reason of sex. In 1916, the cause of equal suffrage triumphed in Alberta, Saskatchewan, and Manitoba. British Columbia authorized a referendum on the question, and woman's suffrage was to go into effect on January 1, 1917, if approved by the voters. In the same year, Ontario gave women the provincial franchise. The War Times Election Act of 1917 provided for partial woman's suffrage throughout the Dominion.

SELECT BIBLIOGRAPHY FOR CHAPTER XXVIII

The details of the mobilization of Canada's resources for war work, and the progress of the various movements referred to in this chapter, can be worked out best by using the volumes of the *Canadian Annual Review of Public Affairs.*

SIR THOMAS WHITE, *The Story of Canada's War Finance* (Montreal, 1921), is a brief and clear account of the financial program of the government during the war by the minister of finance who was responsible for Canada's financial measures from 1911 to 1919. Other special discussions of value are D. CARNEGIE, *The History of Munitions Supply in Canada, 1914-1918* (London, 1925) and A. SHORTT, *Early Economic Effects of the War upon Canada* (Carnegie Peace Foundation, Washington, 1918).

CHAPTER XXIX

THE PROBLEMS OF RECONSTRUCTION

THE immediate and pressing problem after the conclusion of the armistice of November, 1918, was the reëstablishment of the Canadian soldiers in civil life and the readjustment of the nation's industrial activities to the demands of normal peace times.

Demobilization

Canada made every effort to carry out the demobilization of her expeditionary forces and their return to the homeland as speedily as possible, and for the first six months after the close of the war, the men were reëmbarked for Dominion ports at the average rate of 3,400 a month. Nevertheless, this was not rapid enough to suit the wishes of the war-weary veterans, and the demobilization process was therefore accompanied by much unrest and some serious disturbances in the camps where troops waited most impatiently for the order that would release them from the irksome routine of army life. The Canadian Red Cross during these months of demobilization and readjustment proved of great value in caring for the sick and wounded, and gave aid in a dozen ways to the veteran who was trying to reëstablish himself in civil life.

A special department of soldiers' civil reëstablishment was created to deal with the problem of the returned soldier. This work, under the direction of Sir James Lougheed, had many ramifications, but was concerned chiefly with three main tasks: namely, rendering medical service to sick and disabled veterans, retraining the disabled for useful service in some vocation for which they could be fitted, and finding employment for discharged soldiers. During the first few months of readjustment, the government granted subsidies to help meet the most immediate needs of the discharged men and their dependents. A scale of pensions was fixed which compared very favorably with what other nations were doing for their disabled men, and by 1920 the pension for total disability cases amounted to $720 a year, while the allowance for widows or dependent parents of soldiers killed in the war was fixed at $576. In the 1920 session of Parliament, a bill was passed providing for a system of state insurance for returned soldiers. Statistics for March 31, 1925 showed that the total pensions in force at that time for disabled veterans and their dependents amounted to 64,613, with an annual liability to the government of $31,621,205. The number of applications for such relief is still increasing.

Pensions and soldier's civil reëstablishment

A number of special hospitals were opened by the government to care for those whose lives had been wrecked by the war, and the

317

Hospitals and vocational training

skill of some of Canada's best medical and surgical staffs was employed in the effort to rebuild these victims of the war for some kind of service useful to themselves and to the nation. The Canadian Medical Corps had made an excellent record during the war, and many of its members continued to serve the government in this new task of rehabilitating the disabled. Under the supervision of the department of soldiers' civil reëstablishment, vocational training of a wide variety was instituted for those whose education had been prematurely interrupted by the call to arms, and for those who were so disabled that they had to be taught some new means of livelihood.

Government aids

The Canadian government, in addition to its direct expenditures on vocational education, paid allotments to disabled soldiers and their dependents while the former were in training in the government schools. In 1921, additional legislation was passed continuing the financial aids to returned soldiers, giving them preferential treatment in filling offices under the civil service, and providing other means of relief for the disabled who were still unemployed. An effort was made to stimulate business activity by continuing the building of public works, in order to absorb as large a labor supply as possible while the Dominion's war industries were being deflated. The Dominion government also appropriated large sums to help build workers' homes and thus contributed to the solution of the housing problem existing in an acute form in many localities during the early years of reconstruction. In addition to its direct expenditures, the Dominion government granted financial aids to provincial governments which were working out relief programs of their own. In order to provide for a wide range of public health work, the Dominion council of health was established.

Soldiers and land

A well organized effort was made by the government to settle the returned soldiers on the vacant farming lands of the West. Under the direction of a Land Settlement Board, a plan was worked out to enable the prospective settler to acquire a homestead on easy terms. About one-third of the members of the Canadian Expeditionary Forces indicated a willingness to undertake farming or the raising of stock as a means of livelihood, and the government not only prepared to dispose of the public lands still under its control, but also bought some privately-owned lands in the provinces to resell at cost and with easy payments, extending over a period of twenty-five years, to soldier-farmers. To equip the farm the new settler could borrow as much as $2000 from the government for the purchase of live-stock and implements, and an additional $1000 for permanent improvements, the loans to bear interest at five per cent, and to be repaid within four and twenty-five years, respectively.

Land settlement plan

By the end of 1919, the Land Settlement Board had lent over $51,500,000 to 17,000 returned soldiers who had turned farmers. 5,433 soldier entries had been registered covering 869,000 acres of free lands. In addition, two-thirds of the claimants also used their homestead rights as civilians, bringing the total area granted to returned soldiers to nearly 1,500,000 acres. By 1922, 27,000 soldiers were established on the land and government loans for equipment amounted to $88,000,000. In spite of these liberal terms, many war veterans refused to become interested in the possibilities of the new West, and by 1922, 2352 who had tried their luck as farmers decided to abandon their holdings for more attractive, and perhaps more exciting occupations in the densely settled parts of the Dominion.

The latest figures, for 1926, show that 7500 soldiers, for one reason or another, abandoned their undertakings during the nearly nine years in which the plan has been in operation. During this period, over 30,000 ex-soldiers have benefited by the legislation described above. Some 20,000 received financial assistance, and 6500 received free grants of land. For the year 1925–1926, 17,281 settlers were expected to make repayments to the government. Of this number, 8439 met their obligations in full, 6920 made part payments and 4541 were able to make prepayments. Of the total of 30,846 returned soldiers established on the land by the end of 1925, through the work of the soldiers' settlement board, 24,342 received loans from the government totalling nearly $106,000,000. About twenty-seven per cent of the settlers receiving loans either had abandoned their farming ventures, or had suffered foreclosures due to failure to meet payments. In the light of these statistics, it is apparent that in spite of many failures, the scheme has resulted in a greater measure of success than perhaps was anticipated, and the proportion of failures among the soldier-farmers is no greater than that among the general farming public. It may be said in conclusion that Canada made an honest and intelligent effort to deal with this general problem of soldiers' civil reëstablishment. That it was only partially successful was no special fault of the government. The readjustment to civil life and to the ways of peace was not brought about in any of the belligerent nations without severe suffering and discontent in many sections of the population; Canada's record compares very favorably in this respect with that of other nations. In watching over the interests of the returned soldiers, and in giving forceful public expression to their demands, organizations like the Great War Veterans' Association continue to play an important rôle in the Dominion.

Estimate of success of soldier-farmers

By 1920, the national public debt of Canada reached the staggering total of over two and a quarter billion dollars, or $252 per capita, and the total was still rising at that time. In 1919, as has been pointed out, it was necessary to float a third "victory loan" of $300,000,000 to pay off current debts and to meet the costs of demobilizing the military forces. As a result, the close of the war found practically all of Canada's debt funded in the form of bonds of varying dates of maturity. Naturally the public demanded a rapid scaling down of the war taxes as soon as the national emergency had subsided, but for the government this raised a very complicated problem. From some

Public debt

quarters, particularly manufacturing centers, objection was raised to any reductions in the war tariff, other groups insisted upon the retention of the business profits taxes, while the government needed practically all of its revenue to stabilize Canadian exchange and to meet annual deficits incurred by the government-owned railroads.

Tax revisions
In 1919 and 1920, some reductions were made in war tariffs, but most war taxes, including the tax on incomes, were retained. The war tax on excess business profits was soon allowed to expire. The Government retained the excise and stamp taxes, raised the postal rates, and imposed a new one per cent general sales tax, but exempted many necessities from this tax. Slight tariff revisions were also made. By the spring of 1922, the Liberal party was back in power at Ottawa, with Prime Minister William Lyon Mackenzie King pledged to strict economy. The new budget consequently showed a reduction in government expenditures of nearly $140,000,000, saved largely by cuts in the naval and air service, and it provided for moderate tariff reductions on some fifty articles. In the face of such economies, the national debt continued to mount, and now exceeded $272 per capita. It was necessary to retain or increase such taxes as the sales tax, the tax on automobiles, confectionery products, beer, soft drinks, telegrams, gasoline, checks, and insurance.

Budget of 1923
The budget of 1923 also failed to show a net surplus, largely because of continuing deficits on the Canadian National Railways. Nevertheless, in this year further reductions of a moderate nature were made in the tariff, the British preference was increased and the discussion of reciprocity with the United States was seriously revived. Reductions in the tariff, however, were somewhat offset by new bounties for the copper and hemp industry. The sales tax, and taxes on cigarettes, wines, checks and other articles were further reduced, and a beginning was made on the huge task of refunding the war loans at lower rates of interest.

Budget of 1924
The year following brought further changes in the Dominion budget. The sales tax was reduced, and was removed entirely on supplies and machinery needed in agriculture, dairying, fishing, mining, fruit raising and the lumber industry. Exemptions under the income tax law were increased. At the same time, the tariff on agricultural implements was reduced, and raw materials used for the manufacture of these implements were put on the free list when it could be shown that they were imported for this specific use. The theory underlying these tariff changes was the desire to reduce the cost of the "instruments of production" in Canada's basic industries. The new tariff caused some discontent in the Liberal ranks, but it met with the approval of the western Progressives upon whose support King's Liberal Government had to depend if it wished to remain in office. The new budget was clear indication that the Government was "steering west" in the matter of tariff reform, and that the Liberals

were slowly returning to their traditional position as a party standing for freer trade.

The net public debt of the Dominion, on March 31, 1925, was $2,417,437,685. For the fiscal year 1927, the estimated revenue from special war taxes still amounted to $154,000,000, and the principal expenditures for the year attributable to the war reached a total of $162,992,000. Thus, of the Dominion's total public expenditures in 1927, almost a half was traceable to the war, and most of it went to meet the interest on the public debt, which amounted to approximately $140,000,000 annually. There has been some refunding of loans at lower rates of interest, and a beginning was made in applying balances to debt reduction. *National debt in 1925*

The nationalization of most of the Canadian railroad systems greatly affected the progress of financial reconstruction, and in itself, constitutes a problem of the greatest magnitude for the future of the Dominion. By 1921, all the great Canadian roads, the Canadian Northern, the Grand Trunk, and the Grand Trunk Pacific, but not the Canadian Pacific, had been taken over by the government. The virtual collapse of the roads, under extraordinary war conditions, made nationalization inevitable as the only feasible solution of a badly tangled transportation situation. Prime Minister Borden, to be sure, had favored government ownership years before the war, and others had repeatedly suggested that many advantages would result from such centralized control. Nationalization promised improvements in service, the avoidance of duplication and waste, and ample funds for extensions into new and undeveloped sections, and with the exception of some of the capitalists of Quebec and Montreal, it probably had the support of a large part of the Canadian public. The capitalist interests, of course, stressed the dangers of paternalism and the huge costs of government ownership, but Canadian public opinion by the time of the Great War had reached the point where Governments found it increasingly difficult to justify a policy of aiding private railroad companies which were in distress with grants from the pocket of the tax-payer. *C. N. R. and public debt*

The Canadian Railway Board, organized in 1918 to centralize control of the railroads, spent over $70,000,000 in one year for new steel rails, freight cars, and locomotives, and issued numerous regulations to coördinate the service, settle labor troubles, save fuel, and make other improvements in the Canadian roads. In spite of economies and increases in railroad rates, most of the railroads continued to deteriorate, and even the Canadian Pacific, perhaps the finest railway system in the world, experienced a marked falling off in profits. Before the close of 1918, the Canadian Northern, which had been running a steady deficit, was united with the Intercolonial, the National Transcontinental, and some smaller roads to form the nucleus for the Canadian National Railways, representing a total mileage of 13,700 miles. The Grand Trunk and the Grand Trunk Pacific were soon *Organization of C. N. R.*

added to this national system, increasing the government-owned mileage to 22,375 miles, or fifty-two per cent of the total railway mileage of the Dominion. The management of the nationalized roads was centered in a board, non-political and independent of party politics, under the able presidency of David Blyth Hanna.

Economies

Throughout the war and the years of reconstruction the government spent large sums in improvements and in constructing extensions. Ticket offices were consolidated, freight was rerouted over the most direct routes, and attempts were made to economize by more efficient use of the staff of employees, and by a general standardization of methods. Although freight and passenger rates were increased, and many economies introduced, the government railroads showed a most discouraging deficit for many years. In 1919 this deficit reached almost $50,000,000, although much of this apparent loss was due to much-needed and long-delayed increases in wages for railroad workers. In 1920 the operating losses exceeded $70,000,-000, with the old Canadian Northern system showing the largest deficits. Costs of fuel and materials rose steadily, while the general deflation of business accompanying the passing of war orders and war profits, materially reduced the volume of traffic.

Sir Henry Thornton

In 1921, the popular clamor against the high cost of living made necessary a reduction in railroad rates, but this loss in revenue was somewhat offset by a reduction in wages. Statistics for the year showed a reduction in operating expenses, but the net deficit remained virtually unchanged. The year 1922 afforded the first encouragement for the Government and the people, who had now become somewhat disheartened by annual deficits. Largely because of an immense grain harvest, and in spite of further reductions in freight rates on grain and basic materials, the national roads showed substantial net revenues. In this year also, Sir Henry Thornton, a successful British railroad expert, was brought over, at a salary of $65,000 per year, to assume general management of the Canadian National Railroads, and the consolidated lines were placed under a single board of railroads. Sir Henry Thornton was a graduate of the University of Pennsylvania, had served twenty years on the Pennsylvania Railroad in the United States, and brought to the Dominion an enviable record as a successful American railroad manager, as manager of the Great Eastern Railway in England, and as an important figure in the army transportation service during the Great War. Prime Minister King gave the new executive a free hand in his efforts to untangle the Canadian transportation problem, and promised to shield him from political interference, a promise which has, on the whole, been kept faithfully. In return, the new manager cheered the country by promising to show real profits within three years.

Progress under government ownership

Sir Henry Thornton established national headquarters for the Canadian system in Montreal, the city which also contains the main offices of the Canadian Pacific Railroad. Numerous changes were made in the staff and in the regional divisions of the system. The first annual report under the new management showed an increase in net earnings and a decrease in the total deficit. In 1923 and 1924, new economies in management resulted in further reductions in operating costs, but the general business depression of these years, and the resultant decrease in freight traffic, in part attributable to the building of good roads and the competition of the automobile, caused further disappointments and net earnings did not reach the total predicted by the management. Sir Henry answered the critics who challenged his methods by insisting that he was not allowing the railroad properties of the Dominion to depreciate in order to show paper profits, and by welcoming careful scrutiny of the books by experts at any time. For the first time since it was taken over by the government, the net returns of the Canadian National Railways System, during the year 1926, were more than enough to pay all fixed charges due the Canadian public which holds securities totaling nearly a billion dollars, with an annual interest charge thereon of nearly $40,000,000.

While the Canadian National Railways continued to show a deficit, the Canadian Pacific Railroad prospered and paid dividends. *C. P. R.* The *C. P. R.* continues to hold its popularity with the traveling public in Canada; it has assets of over a billion dollars, and continues to expand its investments in many directions. In making comparisons between this private road and the government-owned system, it must be borne in mind that the deficits of the national system are in a large measure attributable to the follies of the pre-war period, for which the present generation of Canadians is paying the bill. Canada has a railway mileage of approximately one mile for every 200 people, as compared with a ratio of one to 400 for the United States, and one for every 2000 in Great Britain. Canadian railway systems have been over-built, far in advance of the needs of the settled sections of the country.

In so far as the nation as a whole has benefited by this over-building through the opening of new areas and the consequent enhancement *Observations* of the national resources, it is economically sound and justifiable to *on Canada's* meet deficits created earlier by taxes on the present generation. *railroad history* Nevertheless, in the period of unregulated private control of railroad building, Canada passed through an orgy of stock-watering, inflation of book values, and other questionable methods of high finance which have added a tremendous load to Canada's present railroad burdens. The most flagrant cases of unethical conduct are associated with the Canadian Northern and the Grand Trunk Railway. The latter repeatedly paid unearned dividends on its preferred shares, it manipulated its bookkeeping to show paper profits, and paid out money in dividends which should have been spent for the maintenance and improvement of its property. The road was allowed to fall into disrepair, and thus the burden which Canadian taxpayers subsequently had to assume was greatly increased.

Case of Grand Trunk

When the Dominion took over the Grand Trunk, an arbitration board, consisting of Chief Justice Taft of the United States Supreme Court representing the road, Sir Thomas White representing the government, and Sir Walter Cassels chosen as an impartial chairman by the other two members, was appointed to appraise the value of the railroad system. This board, by a vote of two to one, decided that the common and preferred stock of the road was absolutely worthless, and their decision was later upheld by the British Privy Council. For years, the government steadfastly refused to give relief to the stockholders of the Grand Trunk on the ground that they had no just claim and that the government had not confiscated their property, but rather had come to the rescue of a bankrupt company.

Proposed settlement

It may be added that the company continued its unethical practices to the end. Some of its dividends actually had been paid from government subsidies, and before the close of business, nearly a half million dollars was voted out of its Fire Insurance Fund for salaries of officials and directors, the latter to be paid for five years in advance. In the fall of 1926, the president of the Canadian National Railways signed a settlement with the holders of the four per cent Grand Trunk Pacific stock, providing for the issue of new securities, to bear interest at two per cent per annum, and to be exchanged dollar for dollar for the old Grand Trunk Pacific stock, of which about $35,000,000 is still outstanding. Under this arrangement, which was submitted to the Dominion Parliament for ratification, most of the stockholders received par value for their holdings, and provision was made for the gradual redemption of their certificates over a period of years. In the light of the past financial history of the company, the settlement seems more than fair.

Government system on trial

Government ownership of the railroads in Canada is still on trial. The experiment in nationalization has been undertaken under the most difficult conditions and with great handicaps. Most of the nationalized roads are not profitable; those which paid dividends have been left in private hands. A large funded debt, and a burdensome annual interest budget have to be carried by the national system. In the face of these staggering obligations, there was much evidence that Canada was succeeding before the panic of 1929 in building a financially sound national system of railways. The annual deficits of 1920 and 1921 were changed into a steadily mounting surplus, and the year 1926 showed net earnings for the Canadian National Railways totaling over $46,000,000. The operating surplus of 1926 showed an increase of 43.81 per cent over the preceding year. Revenues had increased at a greater percentage than operating expenses, mileage had been extended, and coöperative management had been introduced in a number of the railroad shops. With a continuance of prosperity, the government-owned railroads promised to become economically

profitable, as well as extremely serviceable in the development and
settlement of the Dominion.

A number of Canadian municipalities and provinces also are
engaged in great experiments in public ownership of hydro-electric
power facilities and transportation systems. The municipally owned
street railways of Toronto compare most favorably with the privately
owned transportation lines elsewhere, whether in Canada or in the
United States. The great hydro-electric project of Ontario originated
at the beginning of the present century among a group of farseeing
leaders who appreciated the value of Canada's great water-power
facilities and deplored her dependence on coal shipped either from the
United States or from the ends of the Dominion. A Hydro-Electric
Commission was created in the province of Ontario with wide powers
for the production and sale of electric power. Under the devoted and
capable leadership of the late Sir Adam Beck, the commission developed into a great government corporation, owning power plants,
building transformers, transmission lines, turbines and other necessary apparatus to generate electric power which is sold to municipalities. The latter then built the local distributing plants and delivered the current to the ultimate consumers. The commission, at the
present time, furnishes power practically at cost, after allowance
has been made for depreciation charges on the plant and for the
retirement of its bonds, and the municipalities which retail the
current to the user charge a rate approved by the commission.

Other experiments in public ownership

The Ontario hydro-electric project was well under way by the
time the Great War began, and its service has been steadily expanded.
Electric power rates have been greatly reduced, with the result that
home owners and farmers have found it practicable to instal electric
motors and other devices. The cost of electric power on the Canadian
side of Niagara is but a fraction of what it is on the United States
side, although the power is developed from the same source. By 1926,
470 Ontario municipalities served over seventy-eight per cent of the
population with power secured through the Hydro-Electric Power
Commission, and in the years since 1909, when the project was put
before the people by Sir Adam Beck, over eighty municipalities have
paid off their entire indebtedness incurred for the distribution of
electric power. From 1909 to 1926, the savings of the people of
Toronto have been estimated at anywhere from $33,000,000 to
$69,000,000, and those for the province as a whole amounted to
nearly three times the latter figure. In 1926, the "Hydro" had 8600
miles of transmission lines. Ontario has led the world in government
ownership of power. It need hardly be added that Ontario's social
and economic life has been largely made over by the "Hydro."
Additions to the Canadian hydro-electric system are being made every
year, some of them private enterprises and some public, and recent
years have seen many new developments, especially in Quebec and
British Columbia and in the maritime provinces.

Ontario hydro-electric project

The Manitoba Hydro-Electric Commission was established in 1919. In Winnipeg, a city-owned electric light plant was opened in 1911, and its productive capacity now exceeds 100,000 horse-power. In 1922, it furnished current for electric heating at the rate of one cent per kilowatt hour. Recently, plans have been made, both in Canada and in the United States, to develop the great power possibilities of the St. Lawrence River as an international project, and negotiations between the two countries for this purpose have made some progress. In 1924, the water-power resources of the Dominion were estimated at over 18,000,000 horse-power under conditions of ordinary flow, with the possibility of increasing this productivity to over 32,000,000 horse-power. In 1924, the hydro-electric installation for the Dominion, much of it under government ownership and control, averaged 386 horse-power per thousand population, and represented a capital investment of $767,000,000, which exceeded that of any other Canadian industry.

By the end of 1920, the deflation which was the inevitable aftermath of the war had set in in Canada with a vengeance. It was the necessary reaction following the extraordinary boom of the war years, and in Canada, as in other belligerent nations, it produced a severe strain on the whole industrial organization. The movement came gradually, and some attempt was made to control it through the coördinated action of the Canadian Bankers' Association, which inaugurated a uniform and gradual policy of contracting loans and tightening the money supply of the country in order to compel all varieties of industry to return to normal conditions. Nevertheless, prices began to fall, wages likewise, and there was a temporary but serious slump in production.

Deflation proved to be most severe in the agricultural industry, which had been enjoying extraordinarily favorable conditions as an essential war industry. As evidence of these good times, it may be pointed out that between 1914 and 1919 the farm acreage of Canada increased sixty per cent, and the value of field crops 127 per cent. In 1919, a government Wheat Board still marketed the total wheat crop of the Dominion at $2.15 a bushel, distributed the surplus from these sales among the original producers, and prohibited speculating on the exchanges. Agriculture was at that time a specially favored industry and received many aids from the government. By 1920, the Wheat Board no longer functioned, and within two weeks, the price of wheat fell sixty cents per bushel. By 1921, when the deflation process was virtually ended in other industries, the Canadian farmer was still suffering severely.

It was estimated that due to falling prices and a deflated market the Canadian farm crops of 1920 sold at $80,000,000 less than those of the preceding year, and in 1921, the difference in value was $500,000,000. The shrinkage was accompanied by a general decline in most wholesale prices, but this fall in prices was by no means proportional to the losses of the farmer. The Government, in 1919, charged a select committee to investigate the whole question of price levels and secured the passage of a Combines and Fair Prices Act intended to stop profiteering and combinations in restraint of trade. The new law, administered by a Board of Commerce, required detailed reports from all important producers of necessities and provided penalties for unfair practices. The Board also was empowered to fix maximum prices in various localities by limiting profits in such industries as the packing, shoe and clothing businesses. The farmers, and many of the consuming public, denounced the law as a mere sham intended to protect the profiteering manufacturers by throwing sand in the eyes of the public. The farmers insisted that they were receiving but fifty per cent of the values they produced, while textile manufacturers and others continued to make profits ranging from seventy to three hundred per cent. The result of this economic discontent among the agricultural population was the stimulation of coöperative enterprises and the farmers' reëntry into the game of practical politics. These remedies had been tried before and during the war, but now they received a new emphasis.

Shortly after the close of the war, a number of western provinces authorized the establishment of government cold-storage plants, as *Coöperative movement* a means of curbing the power of the meat packers. Coöperative organizations, including various groups of producers and consumers such as live-stock and sheep growers, grain growers, cheese-makers, and distributing and shipping associations, arose in all parts of the Dominion from the maritime provinces to British Columbia, wherever agricultural interests were strong. Saskatchewan authorized the formation of rural credits societies, and permitted these organizations to borrow money from the banks on the corporate security of their members. These funds could then be reloaned at low interest rates to individual members. Provincial and municipal governments often subscribed part of the stock in these new ventures in coöperative banking.

Grain Growers' Associations, formed as early as 1901, assumed new vitality in the years following the close of the war. Under the *Grain growers* capable direction of men like W. R. Motherwell, minister of agriculture for a time in the Saskatchewan Government, the membership of the Grain Growers' Association of that province increased to over 33,000 in 1919, and similar organizations grew with equal speed in other provinces of the West. Grain Growers' newspapers were founded to fight the battle of the farmers against the railroads and the grain elevator combines. As early as 1910, as has been stated, the Grain Growers' Associations virtually had forced Laurier to champion reciprocity with the United States, and in the depression following the war, the farmers prepared for new assaults upon the Government.

The most successful examples of coöperation were the Saskatchewan Coöperative Elevator Company, the Alberta Farmers'

Successful
coöperatives

Coöperative Elevator Company, and the Grain Growers' Grain Company, Ltd., the latter under the able direction of T. A. Crerar. The Grain Growers' Grain Company was especially successful for a time, and in the days of prosperity during the war steadily expanded its coöperative interests, paid substantial profits, and carried on much educational work among the rural population. In 1917, the Grain Growers' Grain Company amalgamated with the Alberta Farmers' Coöperative Elevator Company, under the name of the United Grain Growers' Ltd. Its authorized capital was $5,000,000; by September 1918, its assets were nearly $8,500,000, and it owned 206 grain elevators and leased 137 more, owned 223 flour warehouses and leased eight others, and also owned 181 coal sheds.

U. F. O.

In Ontario, the United Farmers entered politics with striking success, and in the provincial elections of 1919, nominated 68 of their members for the provincial legislature. On a platform pledging the removal of tariff barriers and prohibition, full of denunciations of the railroads and the manufacturers as the enemies of the farmers, they swept most of the older members of the provincial parliament from office, and organized a farmers' Government, under the premiership of E. C. Drury. The new prime minister, to give proof of his sincerity in advocating economy and retrenchment, at once reduced his salary. Much legislation of special interest to the farmer promptly was put upon the statute books of Ontario, including laws for rural credit societies, provincial savings institutions, good roads, a consolidated schools system, and reforestation. Before long, however, the United Farmers showed signs of internal dissension, their membership declined, provincial debts increased, and in the elections of 1923, Prime Minister Drury was driven from power, and the Conservatives resumed control of the Ontario government. A year later, the new administration uncovered frauds in the treasury department of the farmer Government, and a number of former officials were tried and convicted for theft and conspiracy.

National
farmers'
platform

In 1919, the first National Farmers' Platform was drafted to consolidate and coördinate the farmers' movement throughout the Dominion. It denounced imperialism and the protective tariff, favored drastic tariff reductions and reciprocity, attacked corporation methods, favored coöperation, and advocated public ownership of all important public utilities. In addition, the platform sponsored many governmental reforms designed to eliminate the power of the vested interests from Dominion affairs. Grain Growers' conventions were held in a number of the provinces to endorse this declaration of principles. By 1921, the farmers were organized sufficiently to claim a larger share of the seats in the law-making bodies of the Dominion, and early in 1920, they entered federal politics under the name of the National Progressive Party, a party which was officially born at Winnipeg. Crerar, who had resigned from the Unionist Cabinet in 1919, assumed active direction of the new party which was pledged to carry out what it called the "New National Policy." Thus a new sectionalism had arisen in Dominion affairs, and the class consciousness of the western farmer became a vital factor in Canadian politics.

This seething among the discontented farmers was accompanied by a similar wave of discontent and class consciousness in the ranks *Industrial* of the industrial workers of the Dominion. The war had stimulated *discontent* a great development in the iron and steel industry and in the production of chemicals, textiles, flour, paper and other products, and the industrial worker had benefited greatly by the steady rise in wages and by the general war prosperity. In the years of reconstruction, however, he began to complain of the rising cost of living and the steady cutting of wages; stimulated somewhat by the revolutionary ideas liberated everywhere by the war, the producer began to demand a new social order and a larger share of the wealth which his labor created.

By the fall of 1920, many Canadian factories were reducing their labor force, as well as wages and hours of employment. There were *Decline* especially severe depressions in the milling industry, the sugar *in union* refineries and in shipbuilding, and the export trade of the Dominion *membership* slumped badly. Membership in labor unions began to decline, and fell from 378,047 in 1919 to 276,621 in 1922. This slump in the membership of trade organizations was accelerated in the years of depression following 1929, and it has not yet ceased.

Labor disturbances, some of them of a very serious nature, accompanied the passing of the worker's prosperity. The "One Big *"One Big* Union" idea developed rapidly in the West, based on the desire to *Union"* organize all workers by industries, regardless of trades or occupations, in a concerted effort to overthrow the capitalist system. The older craft organizations bitterly opposed this new departure in the labor movement, but often to no avail.

In 1919, a serious strike broke out in Winnipeg, led by R. B. Russell and William Ivens, the latter a Methodist minister. The *Winnipeg* strike, which began with the demand of the Winnipeg metal workers *strike* for the recognition of the right of collective bargaining, and a plea for an increase in wages, spread rapidly until it involved a general sympathetic strike of the building trades, firemen, police and many other employees. The Government's attempts to mediate collapsed over the issue of collective bargaining. By the middle of May, 1919, practically all industrial activities and many municipal functions stopped in Winnipeg, although the committee in charge of the strike ordered policemen, waterworks employees, bakers, and milk wagon drivers to continue their work. For a time, the city virtually was isolated from the outside world by the strike of telegraph and postal employees and all daily newspapers were forced to suspend publication. Needless to add, there was much excitement about alleged support from the Moscow communists; socialist literature was distributed, and rioting occurred in some localities.

On June 17, the Winnipeg strike leaders were arrested, the city's Labor Temple was raided, and the Methodist Conference expelled the radical minister who had turned labor leader. The Department of Justice suppressed the *Western Labor News*, meetings and street parades were prohibited, and because of these drastic measures, the strike soon collapsed. Eight of the leaders were tried for sedition, and were found guilty by a judge and a jury who clearly reflected the hysteria of the time concerning all forms of radical thought. The trial was little short of a travesty on justice. Labor leaders who espoused nothing more radical than pacifism and the single tax were denounced by their enemies as "reds" in the pay of Moscow.

The trouble in Winnipeg was by far the most serious labor disturbance during the reconstruction period. The collapse of the movement proved a death blow to the industrial syndicalists who favored the "One Big Union," and, henceforth, most laborers were content to return to the methods of the older craft organizations. The Canadian Trades and Labor Congress, under the conservative and able leadership of its president, Tom Moore, denounced the general or sympathetic strike as a weapon of industrial warfare, repudiated all revolutionary tactics, and reaffirmed its faith in the traditional principles of the organized labor movement.

The Dominion Government, as a result of these evidences of radicalism in the ranks of the workers, secured the adoption of a measure permitting the deportation of anarchists and alien revolutionists. A national industrial conference was assembled at Ottawa to work out more harmonious relations between labor and capital, and a Royal Commission was constituted to make a general inquiry into industrial matters. In various parts of the Dominion, local labor parties made their appearance during these years, and advocated such measures as old age pensions, labor exchanges, banking and educational reforms, workers' representation in industrial management, and the fixing of rents by the Government. In 1921 the Canadian Labor Party was organized.

By 1923 employment statistics were more encouraging, although membership in the organized labor movement was still declining. There were ninety-one strikes in 1923, six more than in the preceding twelve months, but they were of a less serious nature, and there was every reason to believe that the radical wing of the labor movement had been definitely defeated. The most important strike of the year was that at Sydney, Nova Scotia, among the employees of the Dominion Iron and Steel Company, one of Canada's largest combinations. Although wage demands were involved, the fundamental issue was the recognition of the union. The strike spread with the intervention of the militia, but it was lost by the workers in the fall of 1923. Nevertheless, an investigating commission appointed by the Dominion Government virtually sustained the strikers in their demands. In 1924, a Dominion act provided that the militia could be called out to quell local disturbances only on the request of the provincial attorney-general, and then at the expense of the province. When the British Privy Council declared the Industrial Disputes Investigation Act *ultra vires*, a majority of the provinces passed enabling legislation permitting the federal act to become operative in labor disputes within provincial jurisdiction, thus insuring a continuance of most of the benefits derived from the original federal statute.

Intimately connected with the problems of labor and industry was the question of immigration. During the war, the arrival of immigrants in Canada virtually ceased, but by 1919 there were indications that many Europeans were planning to move to America to escape the burdens which the World War had fastened upon their countries. Some thoughtful Canadians feared the effects of a lenient immigration policy, and Canada's attitude toward immigration after the war may be characterized, in the words of the Toronto *Globe*, as "an open door, with a firm hand on the knob." *Immigration since war*

Unquestionably, the Dominion needed more people to develop her public lands. The census of 1921 fixed the total population at 8,788,-483, but when the natural increase of the native population is taken into account for the preceding ten years, fully 1,750,000 were left unaccounted for. It was clear from these statistics that many Europeans had returned to their native lands after the war, but most of the disappointment was due to another heavy exodus to the United States. Just how heavy this was, it is difficult to determine, for the statistics of the United States seldom agree with those of the Dominion. Because the Dominion's population averaged but 2.43 persons to the square mile, there was a renewed demand for an intelligent and selective immigration propaganda to bring in desirable settlers. Opposition to the plans for encouraging immigration was confined largely to the Great War Veterans' Association, to organized labor, which feared a lowering of wage standards, and to "one hundred per cent Canadians" who distrusted the "hyphenated" citizen. *Present-day policy*

In 1919, a literacy test was tried as a basis of selection, and the government undertook specially to promote the immigration of farm hands. On the other hand, attempts were made to discourage the coming of industrial workers, at least until the distress of unemployment had passed. Government regulations were issued admitting only bona fide farmers and farm hands, domestics reasonably sure of employment, and Britishers and Americans for whose labor there was a real demand. The British Parliament, to cope with the unemployment situation in the mother-country, enacted the Empire Settlements Act which was designed to turn the stream of immigration into the dependencies, but effective coöperation with the Dominion was greatly complicated by the fact that Canada wanted farmers while England wished to export her surplus discontented industrial workers. *Literacy test*

The Canadian immigration office at Paris was reopened, and new offices were established in Warsaw, Danzig, Bucharest and at other *Immigration propaganda*

European points. In 1923, 137,320 immigrants came to Canada, equaling about one-third of the total arrivals of the last year preceding the war. The 1923 budget carried additional appropriations to encourage the immigration of children and domestic servants from Great Britain, to enable British settlers to bring their families, and to aid private colonization associations which were carrying on an immigration propaganda. The Canadian Pacific Railroad sold 180-acre farms and loaned $2000 on easy terms to prospective settlers coming to the Canadian West, while practically all the railroads offered reduced rates to British farm hands employed to harvest the crops, undoubtedly hoping to retain many of the newcomers as permanent settlers. Many provinces likewise gave encouragement to immigrants. Although immigration slowly revived after the war, nothing like the expected after-the-war rush occurred, and the Canadian exodus to the United States continued for a number of years in discouraging proportions. For the calendar year 1926, immigration to Canada reached a total of 135,984, an increase of sixty per cent over the preceding year. What seemed still more encouraging was the fact that in the ten months preceding February 1, 1927, over 50,000 Canadians returned to the Dominion from the United States.

Progress of woman's suffrage

The woman's suffrage movement which made rapid progress during the war through provincial enactment, and received partial recognition in the federal War Times Election Act, achieved its final triumph in the Dominion Franchise Bill of 1920, establishing a uniform suffrage in federal elections for all British citizens male or female who were twenty-one years of age, and had lived in Canada for one year and for two months in the constituency in which they voted. As late as 1927, however, a bill to give women the vote in provincial elections was decisively defeated in the Legislative Assembly of Quebec.

Progress of prohibition

Prohibition in Canada, another by-product of the war years, proved to be a less stable policy. The origins of the prohibition movement go back for several generations in Canadian history; interest in this movement originally spread from the United States into Canada. Since the war the matter of prohibition enforcement has become the great international problem of these neighbor nations. In 1915, Manitoba banished the saloon, but permitted the use of liquor in the home. Saskatchewan and Alberta voted "bone dry" in 1916, and soon British Columbia, Ontario and the maritime provinces adopted laws similar to the legislation in the prairie provinces. Even Quebec, during the last year of the war, largely as a patriotic measure to conserve grain, resolved to adopt prohibition the following year for the remainder of the war. When the war ceased earlier than had been expected, the "wets," in a popular referendum, won a decisive victory in the old French province and that region became the outstanding exception among the provinces in the matter of banishing the liquor trade. Federal orders-in-council and federal legislation authorized individual provinces to prohibit the importation of liquor within their borders. As a war measure, the manufacture of liquor had been prohibited altogether in order to conserve grain.

The prohibition wave apparently reached its crest in Canada by 1921. Although the consumption of liquor was curtailed or prohibited in most of the Canadian provinces, Canadian manufacturers of liquor were permitted to continue the production of their products for consumption in the United States, and these interests found a steady sale for their output in the rapidly expanding market across the border, owing to the passage of the stringent "dry" Volstead Act by the United States Congress. *High tide of prohibition*

The "dry" Canadian provinces soon began to suffer from the advent of the "bootlegger" and the "blind pig" and other agencies for evading the prohibition laws. Canadian brewers and distillers consigned huge shipments of liquor to Cuba and Mexico, and much of the cargoes of the Great Lakes boats engaged in this traffic was diverted clandestinely to the United States. This rum traffic quickly led to wholesale smuggling and corruption in the revenue service of both countries along the international border. *International problem*

By 1924, a great reaction against prohibition had set in in the western provinces and elsewhere, and by that time six of the nine provinces permitted the sale of liquors under a system of government monopoly and on licensed premises. The system prevailing in Quebec is the one most frequently referred to, especially in the United States, and may therefore be discussed a little more in detail. In Quebec, the sale of spirituous liquors is conducted under a "cash and carry" system, in ninety government stores, "a bottle at a time." The last provision may easily be evaded, however, by returning for additional bottles to the same store, or by stopping at another government dispensary. Beer is obtainable by the glass and is supplied direct from the breweries, with no limit on the quantity obtainable. Beers and wines are sold in hotels and restaurants licensed to carry on this business. The whole system in Quebec is controlled by a provincial Liquor Commission, which fixes prices for all liquor, and sees to it that it is analyzed and properly labelled in order to insure the best products at a fair price. The old time saloon has been abolished altogether. Complaints are still heard about bootlegging, but according to the report of the Quebec Liquor Commission, most of the trouble is attributable to the sale of alcoholic drinks in bulk from the United States. *Decline of prohibition*

At the beginning of 1927, most provinces had abandoned the attempt to prohibit the sale and manufacture of liquor altogether. Ontario began with a rigid prohibition law, but in 1925, the alcoholic content of "near beer" was raised from two to four and four-tenths per cent. In December, 1926, the Conservative Government of the province was returned to power on the issue of permitting liquor sales in *Ontario*

Ontario under a system of government control much like that prevailing in Quebec and in some of the western provinces. The Government promised the abolition of the sale of liquor by doctor's prescriptions, and pledged not to restore the saloon. As evidence of his honest intentions, Prime Minister Ferguson of Ontario appointed D. B. Hanna, former general manager of the Canadian National Railways, and a man enjoying the respect of all his fellow citizens, to head the liquor commission which had the difficult task of inaugurating the new program of government control. In June, 1927, the voters of Manitoba endorsed a modification of their "cash and carry" plan, permitting the sale of beer by the glass, but retaining the system of government control and monopoly.

Rum-running

Needless to add, the successes or failures of prohibition legislation are as much the subjects of violent debate in Canada as they are in the United States or anywhere else where this kind of legislation has been attempted. It proved practically impossible to eliminate the fraudulent traffic in liquor along the Canada-United States border, and illicit rum-running and border outrages have become a disgrace to both countries. The "hundred years of peace" on the border came to an end with prohibition.

Educational progress

The years of reconstruction following 1918 have left their mark indelibly on all the institutions of the Dominion, and have affected its social history in directions too numerous to discuss adequately in the space available. The trend in education, particularly in the public schools, has been strongly toward vocational training in these recent years, and a greater emphasis is being placed on what is immediately practical rather than on the older cultural training. Much progress has been made in the field of applied science. Simultaneously, and independently of each other's researches, Dr. F. G. Banting and Dr. J. J. Macleod, both of the University of Toronto, have made perhaps the greatest contribution ever made by Canadians to the world's scientific knowledge, in the discovery of insulin for the treatment of diabetes.

Journalism

Canadian universities have been growing rapidly since the war, and a number of them have received aid from the Rockefeller and Carnegie Foundations of the United States. In the Canadian newspaper world, recent years have witnessed a steady consolidation of newspapers with the decline and gradual disappearance of smaller journals of opinion and the rise of great corporations which sometimes dictate the editorial policy their writers must follow. Since 1917, great efforts have been made to organize and develop a Canadian Press Association, so that Canada might be free from the control of her news service by agencies whose headquarters are in the United States.

Women's clubs

Because of the equal suffrage movement, women have made their entry into politics as office-holders as well as influential voters whose support must be courted. In 1921, women held places in the provincial cabinets of Alberta and British Columbia. Agnes MacPhail, representing an Ontario constituency, was the first woman to win a seat in the Dominion Parliament. Women's economic emancipation is progressing steadily, and the war opened many new opportunities of employment for women. The census of 1921 revealed that there were fully one-fourth as many women employed in Canadian industries as men. Women's clubs of all varieties continue to be active in public affairs and many of them have been federated into the National Council of Women. Besides an interest in social, industrial and civic problems, in public health and in education, many women's clubs are actively carrying on a program of patriotic education, particularly among newly arrived immigrants. Much of this work is strongly colored by efforts toward "Canadianization," which means, in part, the emancipation of Canadian national life from influences coming from the United States.

In the wake of the disruptive forces liberated by the Great War everywhere, Canada, like the United States, experienced a serious *"Crime wave"* "crime wave," although the Canadian system of criminal justice is *and social* generally recognized as greatly superior to that in the states of the *gospel* American republic. In some of the churches, a new interest has been manifested in a gospel of social service, and in efforts to make honest, practical applications of the principles of Christianity to modern industrial and international problems, but religious reforms of this nature, in Canada as in the United States, often encounter opposition from groups who for one reason or another believe that the church has no right to concern itself with business or political affairs. Moreover, much of the energy of the churches has been sapped by the theological battles between "Fundamentalists" and "Modernists." A number of churches have developed great social centers, and for a brief period, the labor churches in Manitoba promised to inaugurate a new era in religious organization.

The census of 1921 showed an increase of approximately half a million church members during the last decade, and a slight pro- *United Church* portional decrease during the last twenty years in the ratio of Catho- *of Canada* lics to Protestants. The movement toward church union has made some progress among the various Protestant denominations, and on June 10, 1925, the United Church of Canada was established by a merger of Congregationalists, Methodists and Presbyterians. However, some of the members of the denominations concerned refused to submerge their denominational identity in this larger body. This great consolidation of 1925 involved a total of 9483 congregations and church property valued at over $100,000,000. The union is the culmination of the efforts of leaders of these three denominations running back for almost half a century. A composite creed has been worked out for the new church. Of the dissenting congregations who refused to participate in the merger, the Presbyterians are by far the most numerous. Nearly 800 Presbyterian congregations with 500,000 members prefer to carry on their separate existence as "continuing"

Presybterians. What the future holds for this experiment in reconciling and extinguishing denominational differences it is too early to say.

Economic stability
In spite of the turbulence and the unrest of these reconstruction years, it may be said with truth that the average Canadian faced the future with optimism and with a real faith in the destiny of his country. Economically, Canada seemed to have returned to sound foundations. Her export trade increased by leaps and bounds, and showed a very favorable trade balance. The average Canadian finds much satisfaction in the fact that Canada with a population of 10,000,000 has developed a volume of export trade which in money value is as large as that of the United States was when the latter had a population of 70,000,000.

New prosperity
Efforts are being made to open up the northern parts of the provinces to settlement, and these efforts have met with much success, particularly in the development of northern Ontario and Quebec, regions especially valuable for mineral deposits and magnificent lumber tracts. Canada today leads the world in newsprint production. Commissions of conservation are at work to preserve and develop the marvelous water-power in these new sections. The good roads movement is spreading, and it has been estimated that the total expenditures on Canadian highways for 1927 reached $35,000,000. Trade statistics for agricultural products showed a remarkable revival in this basic industry also. Canada is now, in a real sense, the granary of the world. In the crop year of 1925-1926, of the total of 488,000,000 bushels of wheat shipments from all the world-exporting countries, Canada alone exported 259,000,000 bushels. The value of this agricultural production has been estimated at one billion and a half dollars. In the face of these staggering totals, it should be added that in 1924, Canada turned out manufactured goods worth nearly twice as much as her agricultural products. The volume of industrial production in 1926 was twenty per cent greater than in 1925 and employment in that year reached its highest level since 1920. The number and the violence of industrial disputes have been decreasing rapidly, and most recent labor troubles have been confined to a few industries such as the mining and clothing business. Banking capital seemed plentiful for purposes of industrial and commercial expansion, and most of Canada's national debt is held by her own people. The one great and immediate need of the Dominion would seem to be a larger population to develop her still comparatively untouched resources and opportunities, although Canadians are not unanimous on the need for a larger population at once.

Labrador boundary dispute
Early in 1927, the map of the Dominion of Canada assumed what will probably be its final delineation when the long-standing boundary dispute between Canada and the self-governing dependency of Newfoundland over the ownership of the Labrador coast was settled by a decision of the British Privy Council. This controversy had been the subject of litigation for many years, and its settlement necessitated

a redrawing of the maps of Canada at the eastern extremity of Quebec. By the award, the ancient British colony of Newfoundland expanded to three times its former area.

Newfoundland, only 1640 miles from the Irish coast, was known to British fishermen long before Virginia was colonized, and Labrador from these earliest times was its dependency. The history of the codfish fisheries is to a large extent the history of Newfoundland, as it is also the clue to most of Newfoundland's international relations from earliest days to the latest controversies with the United States and French fishing interests over the right to catch and dry fish off the Newfoundland Grand Banks. From a colony of British fishermen, Newfoundland and its dependency, Labrador, which was formally annexed in 1763, grew until in 1917 it boasted of a population of over 250,000. During the seventeenth century, the island was under the administration of the "fishing admirals" who arrived each year to ply their trade; they furnished what little government was necessary to keep order among the fisher folk. For a long time, it was the policy of the British authorities to discourage settlement on the island. Newfoundland suffered from the intense Anglo-French rivalries over North America until the peace of Utrecht of 1713. *Newfoundland —early history*

In the nineteenth century, the inhabitants of Newfoundland began to agitate for local self-government, and in 1832, a representative assembly was added to the usual colonial type of government consisting of governor and council for the better administration of affairs in the colony. In 1855, responsible government was granted after a series of controversies which in many respects resembled the struggle for responsible government in the Canadian provinces. At the time of confederation, Newfoundland refused to enter the new Dominion, largely because she believed her economic interests and her basic industry, fishing, would be jeopardized by absorption in the new federation. To this decision, Newfoundland has steadily adhered, and only in the 1890's, when her people were suffering from unusual economic distress, was there a revival of confederation sentiment. Much of the political and constitutional history of Newfoundland in the last two generations has rather closely paralleled the trend of events in the Canadian provinces. *Progress in nineteenth century*

As a result of the boundary settlement of 1927 Newfoundland won practically all its claims in the dispute respecting the Labrador-Canadian boundary. Canada insisted that Newfoundland had title only to a narrow strip of coast, but the decision of the Privy Council, based on documents running as far back as 1763, gave Newfoundland possession of an area of 112,400 square miles. This region includes some 60,000 square miles of spruce forest, valued at a quarter of a billion dollars, and probably the Grand Falls cataract, which is larger than Niagara and has tremendous hydro-electric possibilities, estimated at several million horse-power, or half the total available in the whole province of Quebec. *Boundary settlement of 1927*

SELECT BIBLIOGRAPHY FOR CHAPTER XXIX

Much of the material for the study of the reconstruction period in Canada must be culled from the newspapers and periodicals of the time, and from the annual volumes of *The Canadian Annual Review of Public Affairs*, and reports of various government departments.

For the progress of soldiers' rehabilitation, WALTER E. SEGSWORTH, *Retraining Canada's Disabled Soldiers* (Ottawa, 1920) is valuable. L. A. WOOD, *A History of the Farmers' Movements in Canada* (Toronto, 1924), and W. A. MACKINTOSH, *Agricultural Coöperation in Western Canada* (Kingston, 1924), are useful for a study of the chief economic developments in the agricultural regions.

HARRY W. LAIDLER, *Canada Shows How to Manage Electrical Power* (League of Industrial Democracy Leaflet No. 1, New York, 1924) is a very sympathetic account of the development of Canada's government owned hydro-electric systems. JAMES MAVOR, *Niagara in Politics* (New York, 1926) is a very critical and unfavorable account of the same movement.

Articles in the New York Times *Current History* frequently give brief summaries of recent developments in the Dominion. JAMES MARTIN MILLER, "The Union of Protestant Churches in Canada," in *Current History* (January, 1927) and two articles on Canada's experiment with prohibition in the same periodical for December, 1926, pp. 322–331, may be cited as examples. The *American Review of Reviews* has also paid considerable attention to Canadian affairs in recent years. Consult the *Reader's Guide to Periodical Literature*.

A good analysis, by a trained economist, of conditions in the mother-country, during this period of reconstruction, is available in ANDRÉ SIEGFRIED, *Post-War Britain*, translated by H. H. Hemming (New York, 1924). A valuable contribution to the literature of the labor movement in Canada, is HAROLD A. LOGAN, *The History of Trade Union Organization in Canada* (University of Chicago Press, 1928).

For the history of Newfoundland, to which only incidental reference has been made in this volume, because that colony is not technically a part of the Dominion of Canada, the following are available: J. D. ROGERS, *Newfoundland* (Historical Geography of the British Colonies, vol. V, Pt. IV); D. W. PROWSE, *History of Newfoundland* (London, 1896); LORD BIRKENHEAD, *The Story of Newfoundland* (London, 1920); and W. G. GOSLING, *Labrador: Its Discovery, Exploration and Development* (London, 1910).

CHAPTER XXX

EQUAL STATUS IN THE EMPIRE

A CANADIAN PRESS correspondent, reporting the imperial con- *"Equal* ference of 1926, cabled the following story to Canadian papers: *status"* "While molten metal was being poured at Croydon, England, for one of the great bells of the carillon to be erected in the House of Commons tower at Ottawa, and to be rung for the first time to proclaim the diamond jubilee of Canadian confederation, the prime minister, Mackenzie King, cast in a Canadian cent, coined during the Laurier régime. Apparently as an afterthought, as he watched the Canadian cent disappear in the molten mass, the prime minister took an English halfpenny from his pocket, and tossed it in also, uttering the significant words, 'Equal status.' " Whether or not the incident actually occurred as described, it is symbolic of Canada's new place in the British Commonwealth of Nations, and a truthful comment on the latest developments in British imperial policies. For all practical purposes, the Dominion of Canada today is quite as much the master of its destiny as is the United States or any other independent nation in the family of nations. A full understanding of Canada's new status calls for some reference to the gradual evolution of Canadian autonomy, not only in the field of domestic affairs, but in the conduct of foreign relations as well, for equal status of the dominions in the Empire is the product of a long period of development.

The slow but steady growth of Canadian nationality has been noted in earlier chapters. By the middle of the nineteenth century, *Evolution of* practically all of the British North American provinces had achieved *Canadian* responsible government in the British sense. Responsible government *nationality* implied an increasing emphasis on rights of self-government and inevitable encroachment upon powers which the mother-country had reserved for herself. Since 1867, the development of Canadian nationality has been particularly rapid. Under Laurier the last British garrisons left Canadian territory, and the Canadian navy and militia passed entirely under Dominion control. Since 1879 Canada has virtually enjoyed diplomatic representation in England in the person of its High Commissioner. Twenty years earlier, the Canadian provinces had begun to claim autonomy in the matter of tariff legislation, and the adoption of the "National Policy" under Macdonald involved some prohibitive duties on British goods which could be produced in Canada. After 1877, the Dominion was not bound by British commercial treaties unless she desired to adhere to them; this commercial autonomy was specifically reaffirmed in 1907. In 1899, the

Dominion obtained the right of "separate withdrawal as well as separate adherence" in the negotiations of new commercial treaties. In the light of future developments it is interesting to note that as a general rule during the preliminary negotiations of a treaty, the Canadian plenipotentiaries were associated with the British representative at the foreign court concerned and signed with them, and only once during these years was the principle relaxed in the former connection, but never in connection with the signature. In addition, strict or less strict though the procedure may have been, the rule that the British government's approval was necessary for any treaty was maintained without deviation.

Autonomy in foreign affairs

For more than a generation before the outbreak of the Great War, the principle of appointing Canadians on imperial commissions or to serve as plenipotentiaries for the Empire was followed whenever Canada needed or desired separate trade agreements with foreign powers. In 1883, the signing by Canadians in their own right of the protocol issuing from an international cable conference at Paris augured further developments in autonomous treaty-making powers. The creation of a Canadian department of external affairs in 1909 constituted still another step toward diplomatic autonomy, as well as a further strain on the position of the governor-general, who traditionally, was the only connecting link between the mother-country and the self-governing dependency. Before the war of 1914, it was clearly understood that Canadian participation in, or contribution to, imperial wars depended on the free and unhampered action of the Dominion Parliament, and Canada entered the Great War of her own volition, in the sense that Great Britain made no "demands" of any kind for her aid.

Great War and Empire

The war of 1914 demonstrated in a striking way the marvelous unity of the British Empire, but it also forced a redefinition of imperial relations and precipitated a careful examination into the status of the so-called dependencies, both from the standpoint of constitutional law and of international law. During the war, Great Britain was forced to recognize the fact that the British Empire had really become a Commonwealth of Nations, and that at least in times of emergency it was quite as likely to have imperial destinies decided by the outlying dominions as to have policies formulated and carried out by Downing Street. Statesmen in all the dominions gave much attention to the discussion of their anomalous position in the Empire, and boldly expressed a variety of new theories about the nature of the imperial bond and the future of the British Empire. Lord Milner, in England, spoke of "partner nations," "not yet indeed of equal power but for good and all of equal status," and shortly after the war, General Jan Smuts, the able spokesman of the South African Union, announced that "the British Empire as it existed before the war has in fact ceased to exist as a result of the war," declared that the independence of the dominions was an accomplished fact and that he was opposed to any closer union among the members of the British Empire. As on earlier occasions, Canada played an important rôle in defining this new status of the self-governing nations of the Empire.

In 1917, Prime Minister Borden participated in an imperial conference on war policies in London and at that time he was invited to attend the meetings of the imperial war cabinet, in which the leaders of the self-governing dominions sat on equal terms with the members of the British war cabinet. This arrangement clearly foreshadowed the dawning of a new era in imperial relations, in which the Empire would become a commonwealth of nations. Moreover, when Sir Robert Borden reported the results of his London visit to the Canadian Parliament, he was reasonably sure, in his own mind at least, that henceforth the dominions would be consulted in advance on all questions of war and peace. The war inaugurated the practice of almost constant communication and consultation on important questions between the prime ministers of the dominions and the British prime minister, and in all these exchanges, the equal status of the dominions never was challenged. The older idea of a closer imperial parliamentary federation now gave way to the new conception of a coöperative commonwealth of free and equal nations. As early as 1917, Sir Robert Borden used the phrase "autonomous nations of an Imperial Commonwealth." *Canadian participation in imperial war councils*

The peace negotiations following the armistice of November, 1918, produced a treaty of some eighty thousand words in length. In spite of idealistic professions about a "peace of justice," "a peace without victory," and a peace which "would make the world safe for democracy"—phrases with which President Wilson had captured the support of people everywhere for the war, and which the Allies endorsed, at least in spirit—the Treaty of Versailles was a document imposed by the victors upon the vanquished. The American President, and liberals everywhere, took comfort, however, in the thought that the Covenant for the League of Nations was an integral part of the treaty, and that from this new piece of international machinery might come the gradual modification of the treaty itself. *Peace negotiations*

During the peace negotiations, to quote the words of Professor Dewey, "Dominion nationalism emerged from the shelter of the Imperial Conferences, where it had enjoyed the privacy of a strictly family matter, and asserted itself before an international assembly." At Versailles, Sir Robert Borden had ample opportunity to insist on Canada's rights as an autonomous nation. He maintained that the Dominion was entitled to the same representation at the peace conference accorded to Belgium and to other smaller nations. Secondly, he demanded that some of the British Empire delegates to the conference be selected from a panel of the prime ministers of the various dominions. Both demands were granted, and as eventually constituted, two Canadians served as members of the British delegation, *Canada at Versailles* and Prime Minister Borden, Arthur L. Sifton, Sir George Foster, and Charles J. Doherty alternated in that capacity.

Formulating treaty

The "open diplomacy" so passionately avowed by the opponents of Germany during the war, soon disappeared during the conferences at Versailles, and the treaty was made in an atmosphere of intrigue and secret treaties probably surpassing that of any other European peace conference. The actual work of making the treaty devolved upon a Council of Ten, and finally upon the "Big Four," consisting of the American President, Prime Minister Lloyd George of Great Britain, M. Clemenceau of France, and Prime Minister Orlando of Italy. These four men, behind closed doors and after serious wrangling among themselves, drew the new map of Europe and shaped the destinies of a new generation.

Canada's rôle

Under these conditions, the rôle of the Canadian delegates could hardly be a conspicuous one. Sir Robert Borden made a valiant but unsuccessful effort at Paris to conciliate the hostile factions which claimed to represent Russia; he also served on the committee on Greek boundaries whose chief function was to deal with the extravagant claims for territorial aggrandizement advanced by the pan-Greeks. On several occasions Sir Robert Borden presided over meetings of the British delegation, Canadians were represented on numerous commissions, and the Canadian prime minister was personally much interested in the discussions of the League of Nations Covenant. But the drafting of that document was largely the work of Jan Smuts of South Africa, Lord Robert Cecil of England and President Wilson of the United States.

Canada in the League of Nations

Canada, together with the other dominions, received separate representation in the Assembly of the League. On May 6, 1919, Borden secured the assurance from Clemenceau, Lloyd George, and President Wilson that membership in the Council of the League would also be open to the dominions, and in 1927, Canada's theoretical right to representation on the Council was confirmed by her election to one of the non-permanent seats. Canada likewise secured separate membership in the labor organizations of the League, after an appeal from Borden to the "Big Four," and Canada has participated regularly in all the International Labor Conferences, and has separately ratified all conventions drafted by this body in its effort to work out a new, world-wide agreement on issues affecting labor. The recognition of Canada's nationhood in the League of Nations organization led to much opposition, particularly in the United States, where opponents of the League claimed that the British Empire, by the representation accorded the dominions, virtually had six votes in the Assembly, whereas the United States, if she entered the League, would have but one. This contention appealed to that latent hostility to John Bull in certain classes of the American population which finds expression in the occasional twisting of the tail of the British lion during American election campaigns. The argument assumed, moreover, that the dominions always would support the mother country, a proposition which has not always been true, and it also ignored the fact that the United States, by means of its protectorates and extensive financial interests in the lesser American states, could easily influence additional votes in the Assembly.

All the Canadian delegates signed the Treaty of Versailles, and a Canadian representative also signed the Austrian Treaty of St. Germain. The treaties having been duly signed by the delegates, Canada insisted that they could not become operative, so far as the Dominion was concerned, until ratified by the Canadian Parliament. Indeed, the Dominion Government insisted that separate ratification was necessary before the British King's signature could be affixed to the documents. *Separate ratification*

The debates on separate ratification of the Treaty of Versailles began in the Canadian House of Commons in the fall of 1919, and they revealed points of view strikingly similar to those expressed in the debate in the United States Senate on the question of accepting the treaty and the League Covenant. A minority of the Dominion House of Commons objected to the entire treaty, as unfair, unjust, unworkable, based on revenge, and containing the germs for a score of new European wars, but most of the discussion, in Canada as in the United States, centered around the alleged loss of sovereignty which might result from Canada's acceptance of obligations in the League of Nations. The opposition was focussed on Article X of the League Covenant, which sought to guarantee the political independence and territorial integrity of the European nations against external aggression. President Wilson had called Article X "the heart of the covenant"; Rodolphe Lemieux, a distinguished French-Canadian leader, called it "the teeth." Many Canadians, like their neighbors to the south, believed this much debated article would involve their country in future European wars, by obligating Canada to defend the dangerous territorial settlements imposed by an unsatisfactory treaty. A Liberal member of Parliament denounced Article X as a device which put Canadians at the "beck and call of a Council not responsible to the nation for its actions," and he added, "by one stroke of the pen we are mortgaging our freedom." *The debates on ratification*

Other members of the Liberal party attacked the Government for insisting upon separate representation in the League of Nations, thus sacrificing Canada's independence of action by involving the dominion in dangerous and embarrassing obligations to Europe. A French-Canadian member objected to the transfer of Canadian sovereignty to the League Council, and others actually feared that Canada might at some future time find itself in conflict with the mother-country as a result of its separate membership in the League. An attempt to modify the implications of Article X was defeated in the Canadian House of Commons by a vote of 102 to 70. Criticisms of this nature were met by the argument that all active participation *Objections to the peace terms* in European affairs still would depend on the action of the Canadian Parliament as it did before the League of Nations came into existence. Canada finally ratified without reservations, and on October 10, 1919, the treaty was formally approved by the British King, thus carefully observing the legal fiction that ratification was by "His Majesty on the advice of the Government of Canada."

Attempts to change Article X

In spite of unconditional acceptance of the Versailles settlement, opposition to Article X continued in Canada. Prime Minister Borden had expressed dissatisfaction with Article X during the negotiations at Versailles, and another Canadian delegate suggested that its obligations and guarantees should be assumed by the great powers only. In the first four sessions of the League Assembly, Canada tried in vain to get Article X either modified, or deleted from the Covenant. The attitude of the Canadian delegation on this issue strongly resembled a point of view widely expressed in the United States, and it was evident that the spokesmen for Canada at the League Assembly were eager to serve as interpreters and mediators in Anglo-United States relations. After several attempts to delete Article X failed, Canada proposed two amendments, one of which specifically stated that while the opinions of the League Council would always carry the highest importance, "no member shall be under obligation to engage in any act of war without the consent of its Parliament . . ." Only four of the smaller nations were willing to accept this Canadian amendment; the others urged further postponement of the issue. Finally, a committee of the fourth Assembly undertook to clarify, but not change the substance of Article X by pledging the Council, in case of the necessity for military action, to take into consideration the "special conditions of each state," and specifically recognizing the constitutional right of each state to decide to what degree it was bound to put its military forces at the disposal of the League. When this proposal also failed of adoption, Canada ceased to insist on a change in Article X. Canada's position throughout the controversy revealed her North American "continentalism," and perhaps also a desire to make the Covenant more palatable to the United States. It is perhaps significant that the amendment proposed by Canada in the third Assembly was identical in substance with the reservation of the United States Senate to Article X.

Canada's anomalous position

The Dominion found itself in a somewhat anomalous position at the close of the war period. Some of her leaders advocated an imperial conference to clarify the situation and to work out in detail the meaning of the new imperial relationship, but many Canadians of all parties objected to such an arrangement because it might result in changes in the Canadian constitution, involving too many obligations for Canada. The western farmers, now becoming politically articulate, were strongly opposed to all forms of centralized, imperial control which might bind the Dominion in matters of international policy. An opinion of the Privy Council in 1919, declaring the

Manitoba initiative and referendum law *ultra vires*, revived the agitation to end the appellate jurisdiction of the Judiciary Committee of the Privy Council in Canadian cases. As further evidence of the new spirit of nationality, the Canadian Parliament voted an address to the King asking that no more titles be granted to Canadians except on the specific advice of the Canadian prime minister and for professional distinction only. It was during these years also that Canada raised the question of a special Canadian minister to be accredited to the United States government. Some of the Quebec nationalists continued to talk vaguely of Canadian independence. As late as 1918, a resolution for secession was introduced in the Quebec Legislative Assembly, but it never came to a vote. The visits of Admiral Lord Jellicoe and the popular Prince of Wales in 1919 were probably calculated to counteract some of these tendencies and to stimulate interest in a closer imperial connection.

Canada has taken an active part in League affairs. At the first meeting of the League of Nations Assembly, the Dominion was represented by Sir George Foster, C. J. Doherty, and N. W. Rowell. Her delegates have served on various committees with distinction, and Canada has always insisted that the League must be made a world league and not an organization dominated by European interests. Sir Herbert B. Ames, a member of the Canadian Parliament, was appointed to the commission charged with the supervision of the Saar Basin, a valuable piece of German territory temporarily under the control of a commission of the League in conformity with one of the most complicated stipulations of the peace treaty. The protocol establishing a World Court for the peaceful adjudication of international difficulties was ratified by the Dominion Parliament in 1921. In the session of the sixth Assembly of the League (1925) the Canadian Senator, Raoul Dandurand, was chosen president of the session. One reason for Canada's success in 1927 in her campaign for one of the non-permanent seats on the Council undoubtedly was the personal popularity of Senator Dandurand. Moreover, Canada had always taken a sympathetic view of the problem of European minorities, and this brought the smaller nations to her support. Canada "is far enough away geographically to have the point of view of a deliberate observer," commented *L'Europe Nouvelle*, "and she is near enough spiritually to view European problems sympathetically." The *Manchester Guardian*, on the other hand, explained Canada's election to the Council by the desire of the League Assembly to select "a North American Anglo-Saxon country," "a direct mouthpiece of the Great Republic that holds so obstinately aloof."

In addition to her duties as a member of the League, Canada has participated in most of the international conferences held since the close of the war, and dealing frequently with problems arising from the imperfections of the peace settlement itself. In 1921, the Dominion was represented at the International Emigration Conference at Ge-

Canada in international affairs

International conferences

neva; in 1922, Canada sent two delegates to the Genoa Conference
called by Italy to deal with questions arising from the war settlement, and in 1924, Canadians participated in the Inter-Allied Conference at London which produced the Dawes plan for the payment
of German reparations. Prime Minister Mackenzie King was present
in Paris to sign the Briand-Kellogg pact, and this agreement renounc-
ing war as an instrument of national policy was promptly ratified
by the Ottawa Parliament. At the imperial conference held in London
in 1921, little progress was made toward defining the new constitutional relations of the Dominion with the mother-country, partly
at least because Arthur Meighen, at that time prime minister of
Canada, had gone to London determined to oppose the renewal
of the Anglo-Japanese alliance which was alarming the United States
and arousing opposition in British Columbia. Largely because of
the discussion of British affairs in the Pacific at this conference,
Great Britain agreed to support the United States in calling a great
disarmament conference to meet later in Washington. Although
President Harding did not address separate invitations to the dominions, Great Britain appointed dominion leaders to the empire delegation. Borden was one of the six members representing the Empire.
According to his own statement, "At Washington, the British
Empire Delegation functioned precisely as at the Paris Conference"
(1919), although the dominions generally were somewhat dissatisfied with the inhospitable attitude revealed by the United States
toward them. Each treaty emerging from the Washington Conference was ratified separately by Canada, and the treaties were signed
with the significant formula,—on behalf of "His Majesty the King
of the United Kingdom of Great Britain and Ireland and the Dominions beyond the Seas, Emperor of India—and for the Dominion of
Canada, for the Commonwealth of Australia, for the Dominion of
New Zealand, for India."

"*Canada First*"

That Canada has not always seen eye to eye with the mother-
country and the rest of the Empire in international matters has been
suggested above, in the case of the Anglo-Japanese alliance, but
further examples can be given of an increasing emphasis by the
Dominion upon her right to define her own foreign policy. Canada
has never denied that all treaties are made in the name of a common
sovereign, but she insists that they do not apply throughout the Empire automatically, and that they may be initiated and concluded
by any member acting alone. An Anglo-Russian agreement of March
16, 1921, became binding upon Canada only after prolonged diplomatic discussions between the Dominion and the mother-country.
Moreover, the recognition of the Russian Soviet Republic by Prime
Minister Ramsay Macdonald of Great Britain did not affect the
policy of Canada. Formal recognition of the soviet government by
the Dominion came about only through a communication of the
Canadian prime minister to the Russian trade commissioner at Mon-

treal in March, 1924. It is interesting, however, to add that when Great Britain in 1927 abrogated its trade agreement with Russia, Canada took similar action almost immediately. When a new crisis arose in Near-Eastern affairs, and it seemed possible that the Turkish Nationalists would cross the Dardanelles for an invasion of Europe, England went so far as to ask Canada if she desired to send military forces to help in the settlement of a crisis which seemed to threaten the peace of Europe. Prime Minister Mackenzie King replied with a request for additional information; indicated he could do nothing without the specific sanction of Parliament; and later, at Ottawa staunchly defended Canada's right to decide for herself whether she would participate in an Empire war. In 1925, Arthur Meighen, as leader of the opposition, went so far as to suggest a general election before Canadian troops should be sent to Europe. The incident revived the whole discussion of the value of the imperial connection and the magnitude of Canada's obligations, but fortunately the Near-Eastern crisis passed without serious difficulties.

Apparently because France had objected to separate representation of the dominions at the conference at Lausanne between the allied powers and Turkey, unless Tunisia, Algeria, and French West Africa should be represented also, the dominions were not invited to share in the negotiations with Turkey. Canada thereupon refused to ratify the Treaty of Lausanne. Prime Minister Mackenzie King insisted "that not having been invited, not having been represented directly or indirectly, and not having signed, Canada had no obligations." He agreed later, however, that Canada would be "legally and technically" bound by British acceptance of the treaty, although in a different sense than by the Treaty of Versailles, which imposed "a moral obligation" upon Canada. When the "Security Pact" was signed at Locarno by the leading nations of Europe, to keep the peace in western Europe, Article IX of the pact specifically exempted the dominions from its obligations, unless they separately and specifically indicated their acceptance of its terms. In 1925, the Dominion Parliament ratified a separate reciprocal preferential trade treaty with Australia. As another phase of this autonomy, Canada has insisted successfully on her right to determine her immigration policies, even when this involves discriminations against other races in the Empire. *Lausanne and Locarno*

In 1920, Sir Robert Borden had obtained recognition of the Dominion's rights to establish separate legations in foreign capitals, but it was not until 1927, that the Honorable Vincent Massey assumed his duties as the first Canadian Minister to the United States. Massey's letter of introduction to the President of the United States presented the new envoy as the King's minister, to represent "the interests of our Dominion of Canada," but actually he was designated by the Canadian Prime Minister, and his instructions came from Ottawa. Since 1927, Canada has opened separate legations at Paris *Canadian diplomatic representation* and Tokyo, and this right to separate representation was fully recognized by the Imperial Conference of 1926. In 1925, in recognition of the new importance of the dominions, Great Britain created a Secretaryship of State for Dominion Affairs as an addition to the British ministry. Canada appoints her own trade commissioners to foreign countries, and in 1928, Sir William Clark, who had seen long service in the civil service of England and India, and who had been a former private secretary of Lloyd George and Winston Churchill, was appointed as the first "High Commissioner in Canada for His Majesty's Government in Great Britain," thus providing a form of diplomatic representation for London in Ottawa.

Negotiations with United States

A Postal Conference between the United States and Canada was held in 1922, and in the same year, Prime Minister King, the newly chosen leader of the Liberals who had recently been returned to power, went to Washington to discuss a waterways treaty, the problem of prohibition enforcement, and the development of the St. Lawrence River route as an international waterway and a source of electric energy. In the case of this conference, however, the appointment with the American Secretary of State was arranged through the British Ambassador at Washington.

Halibut fisheries treaty

In 1923 a convention was signed between Great Britain and the United States for the preservation of the halibut fisheries in the northern Pacific Ocean by prohibiting fishing in Alaska during the spawning season. The negotiations, while legally between the United States and Great Britain, again revealed the curious legal fictions necessary to reconcile the Dominion's autonomous powers with her theoretical status in international law. Ernest Lapointe, Canada's minister of marine and fisheries, was designated as His Majesty's plenipotentiary in these negotiations, and the convention was signed by him alone, after he had strenuously opposed the addition of the signature of the British Ambassador to the document. Moreover, during the negotiations Canada insisted on using the words "Dominion of Canada" instead of "Great Britain" in the treaty, and it eventually was found necessary to find other wording to get around this difference of opinion. Finally, the United States Senate refused for a time to accept the convention without inserting an amendment extending its provisions to nationals and vessels of "any other part of Great Britain." To this change Canada stubbornly refused to accede, on the ground that such an amendment would make it necessary to submit the convention to the whole British Empire for acceptance by the various parliaments. At the Imperial Conference of 1923, it was formally agreed that any part of the Empire might negotiate and sign alone treaties affecting only itself, but if other parts of the Empire were affected by such agreements they must be consulted in advance.

The redefinition of constitutional theories is always a difficult task, and the developments in the relationship between Canada and

Great Britain, discussed in the preceding pages, were difficult to reduce, in all details, to the clear-cut statement of cold logic. In 1919, Sir Robert Borden, then the Conservative prime minister of Canada, and a constitutional lawyer of great repute, tried to state the case by characterizing Canada's new status as follows: "Equality of nationhood must be recognized, preserving unimpaired to each dominion the full autonomous powers which it now holds and safe-guarding to each, by necessary consultation and by adequate voice and influence, its highest interests in the issues of war and peace. For each nation complete control in its own affairs; for the whole Empire necessary coöperation according to the will of the people, in all matters of common concern." *Prime Minister Borden on Canada's new status*

Mackenzie King, the Liberal prime minister upon whom has fallen the mantle of Laurier, six years later in a speech at Wiarton, Ontario, tried to clarify his views concerning imperial relationships. His remarks were all the more important because they followed shortly upon the rejection of the Treaty of Lausanne and the halibut fisheries negotiations discussed above. He said, in part, "In regard to foreign affairs there are some things which we in Canada feel to be of our own immediate and direct concern, and of no concern to other parts of the Empire. These things we should manage ourselves. We took that position with regard to the treaty with the United States on the halibut question . . . Just as we have gained self-government in domestic affairs, so in foreign affairs, which are of direct and immediate concern to ourselves, we contend that they should be managed by our own people. In foreign affairs in which we have no immediate or direct interest, we believe these questions should be left to those parts of the Empire concerned. If questions arise which are of a character likely to affect all of us, then we say where our interests come in touch with those of other parts of the Empire, we should take our part in shaping the policy and have our voice heard." *Prime Minister King's views*

In spite of such attempts at clarification, it was apparent that the task of reducing imperial constitutional relations to an intelligible basis was one to which the next imperial conference would have to devote a major part of its attention. Therefore, in the conference which met in London in the fall of 1926, the question of imperial relationships came at once to the front. At the conference were three of the most outspoken champions of dominion "nationhood," Prime Minister Hertzog of South Africa, President Cosgrave of the Irish Free State, and Prime Minister King of Canada. The Canadian delegation consisted of the prime minister and the Hon. Ernest Lapointe, minister of justice, supported by a strong secretariat. *Imperial conference of 1926*

A wide variety of business was discussed at the London conference, such as imperial defense, the establishment of bases for aircraft in the outlying parts of the Empire, imperial trade relations, immigration problems, the interchange of scientific data, and many other matters, and there was the usual review of the British navy by the *Business of conference* visiting prime ministers. All of these matters were overshadowed by the demand for an official statement of the new position of the self-governing states within the Empire, and this demand was squarely and most graciously met by the home government. The result was the issuing of an epoch-making document, the report of the prime ministers on imperial constitutional relations, which has been called "the new Magna Charta of British Imperial Unity."

"New Magna Charta"

According to this report on the reorganization of the Empire full and formal recognition is given to the equality of status as between Great Britain and the dominions, both in domestic and external affairs. The self-governing states are referred to as "autonomous Communities within the British Empire, equal in status, in no way subordinate one to another in any aspect of their domestic or external affairs, though united by a common allegiance to the Crown and freely associated as members of the British Commonwealth of Nations." The document recognizes the tendency toward equality of status as being "both right and inevitable," and proclaims every self-governing member of the British Empire master of its destiny. Equality of status is the "root-principle" governing imperial relations. In the application of this principle, the full treaty-making powers of the dominions are specifically recognized and provision is made for the appointment of foreign consuls to a dominion, on the approval of the dominion government.

Status of Governor-General

The status of the governor-general in the dominions is changed by the statement that this official is "the representative of the Crown, holding in all essential respects the same position in relation to the administration of public affairs in the dominion as is held by His Majesty the King in Great Britain." In other words, the governor-general ceases to be the agent or representative of the British Government, and in the future, the recognized channel of communication between a dominion and the mother-country will be from government to government direct. The title of the dominion governments has been changed and in the case of Canada, the phrase "His Majesty's Government in Canada" is now the only technically correct one to use.

Other changes

Certain general principles were accepted to establish dominion legislatures on a footing of equality with the British Parliament, and the appointment of an imperial committee of experts was recommended to work out a more detailed report on this point. Specific provision also was made in the report for the independent negotiation of treaties by members of the Empire with foreign nations. Such negotiations are to be carried out by the dominions' own representatives, but other parts of the Empire are bound by such treaties only if they desire to be. Finally, in the report of the prime ministers the development of some permanent machinery to insure a more adequate system of communication between the mother-country and the dominions was advised. The report specifically recognized the right of dominion governments to send their own diplomatic representatives to foreign capitals, and to receive accredited ministers. On February 3, 1927, the Washington government designated William Phillips, former minister to Belgium, as the first minister for the United States to Canada.

The Imperial Conference of 1930 concerned itself with a further clarification of dominion status, and sought to remove certain ambiguities that still existed in the relationship of the various parts of the Empire to the mother-country. The proceedings of the Conference were to a considerable degree monopolized by the discussion of possible economic remedies which would provide relief from the existing world depression. Nevertheless, certain resolutions dealing with imperial relations were discussed. Prime Minister Bennett of Canada, however, secured the postponement of the enactment of a statute designed to incorporate these changes until his government could consult with the Canadian provinces. At a conference of representatives of the Dominion and the provincial governments held at Ottawa in April, 1931, it was agreed that nothing in the proposed act should repeal, amend or alter the British North America Acts, or any orders, rules, or regulations made under them, and that the powers to be conferred upon the Dominion Parliament or the provincial legislature should be restricted to laws within the competence of those bodies. *Imperial conference of 1930*

The Statute of Westminster, designed to give effect to the resolutions adopted by the Imperial Conferences of 1926 and 1930, became a law on December 11, 1931. After repealing the Colonial Laws Validity Act of 1865, it provided that Canada may amend or repeal all existing British laws, orders, resolutions or regulations forming part of the law of Canada, with the exception of the British North America Acts, and that any British statute relating to Canada must contain an express declaration that Canada has "requested and consented" to it. No law passed by a dominion was to be void or inoperative on the ground that it was repugnant to a law of England, or to any existing or future act of the Parliament of the United Kingdom. The right of a parliament of a dominion to make laws having extraterritorial operation was specifically conceded. The Statute of Westminster clearly involves the right of a dominion parliament to repeal any act of the Imperial Parliament, with the sole exception of constitutional acts like the British North America Act. Although theoretically the constitution of Canada still derives from an enactment by the British Parliament, it is inconceivable that Canada would be refused any alterations in her fundamental law which her government and her people really desired. *Statute of Westminster*

Opinion has been divided in Canada and elsewhere as to the real value and significance of this new "Magna Charta" of the dominions. In a sense, of course, the reports of 1926 and 1930, and the Statute of Westminster, are merely formal statements of practices *Future co-partnership* and customs which have existed for a number of years in the conduct of imperial relations. The Statute of Westminster meant the abdication of the British Parliament as the supreme authority of the Empire, but it clearly recognized the Crown as "the symbol of the free association of the members of the British Commonwealth of Nations." A few alarmists in Great Britain and Canada have suggested that the new arrangement is the immediate forerunner of the disintegration and collapse of the British Commonwealth of Nations. Most Britishers, whether living in the mother-country or in the dominions, refuse to accept such a pessimistic conclusion. Although the Great War stimulated the spirit of Canadian nationality and brought forth a new insistence by all political parties on complete national autonomy, this did not foreshadow a widespread desire to break the bonds binding the Dominion with the rest of the Empire, even though these bonds consist to a large extent of sentimental considerations. In a discussion of this whole question of what constitutes the basis of unity, it should be remembered, as Professor Martin expressed it, that "The pearl of great price here is mutual confidence, and it is not to be created by the mechanics of government." Or, to repeat the words of Matthew Arnold, "What attaches people to us is the spirit we are of, not the machinery we employ." The habits of trade, reënforced by the ties of sentiment, make for a loyalty which it is difficult to destroy, and the Canadian people, with few exceptions, look forward to continued and mutually beneficial coöperation with Great Britain on a co-partnership basis with other members of the Commonwealth, and with other nationalities represented in the League of Nations. The Empire has been built on common traditions, common policies, and a common political philosophy, and structural technique may prove to be the least important factor in imperial unity. Critical attacks on Great Britain often arouse more resentment in Canada than in the British Isles.

Recent diplomatic events

Canada continues to make full use of her autonomous powers in the field of foreign relations. In 1928, the Dominion ratified the Geneva Opium and Slavery Conventions, and by special act, made three treaties concluded by the Imperial Government with Spain, applicable to Canada. At the Naval Conference of 1930, Canada was represented by her own Minister of National Defence, and she was the first to ratify the ensuing treaty for naval reductions drawn between the United States, Great Britain, and Japan. In 1930, Canada concluded separate treaties on a variety of matters with Germany, Austria, and Bulgaria. Canada separately approved the Hoover Moratorium of 1931 on war debts and reparations by action of her parliament, and in 1932, she concluded treaties with the United States on the development of the St. Lawrence Deep Waterway, and twelve trade agreements with various members of the Empire, as a result of the activities of the Ottawa Conference, discussed elsewhere. Canada participated in all stages of the work leading to the

World Disarmament Conference of 1932, one of her delegates being Miss Winifred Kidd, president of the Canadian National Council of Women. Dr. W. A. Riddell has been kept at Geneva as "Canadian Advisory Officer." Finally, it should be pointed out that in the conferences initiated in 1933 by President Roosevelt to prepare the way for the World Economic Conference held in London in June, Prime Minister Bennett was specially invited to Washington to discuss methods of improving the relations between Canada and the United States, especially in the matter of tariffs and trade. At the London Conference, Bennett played an important rôle, and Canada on several critical issues supported the position taken by the delegates from the United States rather than that of the leading European nations.

Canada's development as a member of the British Commonwealth of Nations has now reached the stage where it may be said that the Dominion, for all practical purposes, is entirely self-governing, in domestic and international affairs. It is true that the Canadian constitution is an act of the British Parliament, and that cases may still be appealed from the Canadian Supreme Court to the British Privy Council. As a matter of fact, these appeals could be stopped at any time Canada resolved to do so, and it would probably prove easier to amend the constitution of Canada than that of the United States. Canada has all the advantages of independence without all its obligations, and on several occasions, the dominions have not been eager to push equal status to its logical conclusion, because such logic would imply added burdens and responsibilities. Writers on constitutional law like to point out that *in law*, Canada is still "an integral part of the British Empire," and that Canada does not have full status in international law because she could not remain neutral in a British war. Britain's enemies might carry the war into all countries over which the British flag flies. Professor Keith, an authority on the dominions, has argued that the dominions neither possess nor claim the right to make war or peace. Professor Kennedy, a Canadian authority, believes that Canada is at war when Great Britain goes to war; that her territory and her citizens are liable to attack, but that "Canada need not fight, need not supply a man or a ship or assist in any way." *Canada's present status*

Membership in the Commonwealth of Nations is only one aspect, and not always the most important aspect, of Canada's foreign relations. Canada's interests are very closely involved with those of the United States, and the Dominion has every reason to desire closer and more friendly intercourse with the great neighbor republic. On many issues, the Canadian viewpoint more nearly approximates that of the United States than that of the mother-country. The American Monroe Doctrine, by its mere existence, has probably been a protection to Canada. Canada has held aloof from the Pan-American Union, though the Latin-American countries are eager to secure the coöperation of the Dominion. A Canadian writer on Canadian- *Canadian-American relations*

American relations frankly pointed out that the World War and subsequent events have created antagonisms and misunderstandings between the Dominion and the United States, and American visitors in Canada have often sensed an attitude of moral superiority on the part of Canadians, probably to counterbalance the Dominion's material inferiority, yet the same writer believes that the United States would coöperate with Canada if any European or Asiatic power should menace her independence. Much has been loosely said and written about Canada's destiny to become an interpreter of the United States to Great Britain. The fact remains that Canada's self-preservation depends, to a considerable degree, on the future of Anglo-American relations. In spite of numerous instances of friction and misunderstanding, Canadian-American relations have been generally peaceful, cordial, and an evidence of the sound common sense of both peoples. On both sides of the international boundary there would be substantial agreement with the thoughts expressed by Charles Evans Hughes, Chief Justice of the United States Supreme Court, in a recent address to the Bar Association of Canada,—

"We rejoice in our long friendship and in permanent peace, and it would be a short-sighted view that either of us has any real interest which is to be promoted without regard to the well-being of the other and the considerate treatment which conditions good will. I am saying this personal word as much to the people of the United States as to the people of Canada; it breathes neither complaint nor criticism, but a keen desire for the coöperation of the closest friends, each secure in independence and in the assurance of amity . . . While we will have much to discuss, we will have nothing to fight about."

SELECT BIBLIOGRAPHY FOR CHAPTER XXX

· A brilliant and brief exposition of the nature of the Imperial tie can be found in W. P. M. Kennedy, *The Constitution of Canada*, pp. 445-458. The periodical literature on recent changes in imperial relations and dominion status is voluminous. Of special value are articles in *The Round Table*, *Fortnightly Review*, *The Canadian Historical Review*, the *Contemporary Review*, and the *North American Review*. Of special interest are F. R. Scott, "The Permanent Bases of Canadian Foreign Policy," in *Foreign Affairs*, X, pp. 617-631; Frederic H. Soward, "The Election of Canada to the League of Nations Council in 1927," in *The American Journal of International Law*, XXIII, pp. 753-765; and "Neighbors: A Canadian View," in *Foreign Affairs*, (April, 1932) pp. 417-430. Consult the various guides to periodical literature. Annual summaries are also available in *The Canadian Annual Review of Public Affairs*.

A vast literature has gathered around the history of Canadian and imperial relations. It can most easily be followed in the *Review of Historical Publications relating to Canada* (*1896-1914*) and in *The Canadian Historical Review* (1920 in progress) where every important book and article is noticed. For a summary interpretation of Canadian development in the field of government and imperial relations, see W. P. M. Kennedy, "The Political Development of Canada, 1867-1927," in *The Edinburgh Review*, April, 927, pp. 209-224. The best and most exhaustive treatment of the question, is A. Gordon Dewey, *The Dominions and Diplomacy, the Canadian Contribution* (2 vols.)—(New York, 1929). Consult also Sir Robert Borden, *Canada in the Commonwealth* (Oxford, 1929); Chester Martin, *Empire and Commonwealth* (Oxford, 1929); Arthur Berriedale Keith, *The*

Sovereignty of the British Dominions (London, 1929), and A. LAWRENCE LOWELL and H. DUNCAN HILL, *The British Commonwealth of Nations* (World Peace Foundation Pamphlets, Boston, 1927).

For Canadian-American relations, the following are important, HUGH L. KEENLEYSIDE, *Canada and the United States* (New York, 1929) and C. J. CHACKO, *The International Joint Commission* (New York, 1932).

A brief bibliography on the Canadian constitution and the external relations of the Dominion is available in TROTTER, *Syllabus*, pp. 135-136; 143-144.

The text of the Report on the reorganization of the British Empire (1926) can be conveniently found in *Current History* (New York), January, 1927, pp. 564-569. The same number also carried several interesting articles by Howard Robinson and Ralston Hayden, commenting on the significance of these changes. Later developments can be followed in *The Canadian Annual Review of Public Affairs* and *The New York Times Current History*.

CHAPTER XXXI

PARTY POLITICS, 1918-1927

Party politics

\ THE coalition Government established by Conservatives and Liberals in 1917 was responsible for most of the legislation, discussed in the preceding chapters, dealing with the war and reconstruction in Canada. This Government guided the Dominion through the last stages of the Great War, it conducted Canada's peace negotiations, and it laid the foundations for the great work of reconstruction. Laurier, the leader of the Opposition composed of those Liberals who had supported him on the conscription issue and who refused to join the Unionist Government, spent the short time still left to him for the game of politics in trying to heal the breach in the ranks of his party. He carefully avoided all controversies which might make the ultimate reconciliation of Liberals and Union Liberals more difficult. He wisely and patriotically urged his fellow Canadians to obey the conscription law, and during the peace negotiations with the vanquished Central Powers, Laurier proved less of a "bitterender" than many of his colleagues. In a spirit of true conciliation, he urged Germany's admission to the League of Nations, and in the domain of domestic affairs, he advocated the enactment of new forms of social legislation.

Death of Laurier

Early in 1919 Laurier's long and honorable career was ended by death, and in that year Parliament met for the first time in forty-five years with the noted French Canadian absent from his seat. At the state funeral with which the Dominion honored her great leader, all parties united to do honor to the memory of a brilliant and patriotic statesman whom many had reviled and whose loyalty some had questioned seriously just a few months before. For nearly forty years, Quebec's favorite son had guided the councils of the Liberal party. Much of his life had been spent in the effort to bring about harmonious relations between the French and the English in Canada, and at the time of his death, it seemed that a large part of his work had been in vain, for the reconciliation of the two races was temporarily defeated by the bitter passions of the war. The great Liberal party which Laurier had piloted for decades was divided into two factions, and the task of rebuilding had to be left to younger hands.

His successor, W. L. M. King

The leader upon whom the mantle of Laurier fell was William Lyon Mackenzie King, grandson of the leader of the Upper Canadian rebellion of 1837, and for years recognized as one of the ablest of the younger Liberals, and a man who had enjoyed the complete confidence of the stricken leader. King was a graduate in political science and law of the University of Toronto, and had advanced degrees from Chicago and Harvard, where he had done special work in sociology and labor problems. At Chicago he had lived for a time in the famous Hull House settlement. After relinquishing a traveling fellowship from Harvard, he declined an instructorship in economics at that institution to enter the government service of the Dominion. In 1900, he began his eight years' service as deputy minister of labor and soon acquired a reputation as a skilful adjuster of industrial controversies. The Lemieux Act of 1907, for the investigation and prevention of strikes and lockouts on public utilities, was really King's work and attracted international attention. In 1909, Laurier promoted his young lieutenant to the position of minister of labor and the confidence which the veteran leader of the Liberals placed in his young colleague at that time steadily grew with the passing of the years. In the Conservative victory of 1911 Mackenzie King lost his seat. At the outbreak of the war three years later, he was engaged in an investigation of industrial problems for the Rockefeller Foundation in the United States, and during the Great War, he remained active in the adjustment of industrial disputes in the United States. King supported Laurier in 1917 in his opposition to conscription. Two years later, over the claims of older men like George P. Graham and W. S. Fielding, Mackenzie King was chosen at a party convention as leader of the Liberal party.

By 1919 signs of the gradual disintegration of the Union Government began to appear. Sir Robert Borden, weighed down by the *Decline of* unusual burdens of guiding the Dominion through the war and the *Union* peace settlement, was in danger of a serious physical breakdown; *Government* his physicians advised at least temporary retirement from public office. T. A. Crerar, a western Liberal and farmer leader who had joined the Union Government, resigned in 1919 to become the spokesman of the agricultural interests in their demands for a lower tariff and reciprocity with the United States. Sir Thomas White, the able minister who so skilfully guided Canada's financial mobilization during the war, also resigned because of ill health and the necessity of resuming his professional affairs. By 1920, only five Liberals were left in the Union Government formed three years earlier, and many of the stalwarts of the Conservative party had retired also. Pardee and Fielding, two of the ablest of the Liberal supporters of the Government, had returned to their Liberal allegiance.

In a party caucus held on July 1, 1920, the old Conservative party, still under the leadership of Sir Robert Borden, was reorganized *Reorganization* as the National Liberal and Conservative Party. Its principles in- *of the party* cluded autonomy within the Empire, revision of the tariff to prevent the formation of oppressive combinations in restraint of trade but without the abandonment of the protective principle, economy in government, expert, non-partisan management of the national railways, government aid to soldiers and farmers, adequate preparedness for war, the encouragement of desirable immigration, a program of internal improvements, and a square deal for labor without class legislation. Obviously, the new platform was calculated to unite all those who favored a middle-of-the-road policy in the troublous days of reconstruction under the banner of the National Liberal and Conservative Party.

Arthur Meighen succeeds Prime Minister Borden

On July 10, Sir Robert Borden resigned the party leadership. Sir Thomas White declined the premiership, and so Arthur Meighen, the minister of the interior, was chosen as Sir Robert Borden's successor. Meighen was then forty-four years of age, the descendant of an Irish immigrant. A distinguished graduate of the University of Toronto, he had been admitted to the Manitoba bar in 1903. In 1908, he entered the House of Commons and soon distinguished himself by his great efficiency, his tremendous industry and powers of endurance, and his ability as a cold, calculating, hard-hitting debater. He was known as an ardent Conservative who believed that the agrarian movement of the West was a dangerous attempt to foist class legislation upon the Dominion, and he had an abiding faith in the saving grace of high protective tariffs. Prime Minister Meighen promptly reconstructed his ministry. Of the sixteen members of the new Government, only four could claim any earlier Liberal affiliations.

Liberal revival

Meantime the Liberals, encouraged by sweeping victories in Quebec and Prince Edward Island, also held a party convention in the summer of 1919. Hundreds of delegates, selected on a broadly representative basis, and eight of the nine provincial prime ministers, attended the three day sessions which developed into a love feast to celebrate the return of the prodigals to the Liberal fold. The platform adopted by the convention contained demands for tariff reduction, and specifically stated what duties should be reduced and what articles should be placed on the free list in order to encourage production and reduce the high cost of living. In addition, under the influence of the party's new leader, resolutions of a very progressive nature, dealing with industrial problems, were inserted. The party endorsed such proposals as labor representation in industry and on government commissions, proportional representation, state insurance, vocational training for disabled workers, federal incorporation of coöperatives, and the restriction of Chinese immigration. The platform opposed any change in Canada's status within the Empire except after an appeal to Parliament and a popular referendum, and contained planks denouncing profiteering, legislation by order-in-council, and the blunders of the Borden Government. To attract the farmers, the party endorsed government grain elevators and rural credits legislation, and the soldier vote was appealed to by the promise to increase the government aid for veterans of the Great War.

Both parties thus reformed their lines for the impending political battle, and in the summer of 1920, the two young leaders undertook *Preparing for* extensive "stumping" tours through the West, for both realized that *election* the greatest and most disquieting single issue in Canadian politics since the war was the revolt of the western farmers against the government, and the rise of a new western sectionalism opposed to a régime accused of truckling to the commercial and capitalist interests of the East. King endeavored to attract the farmer and labor vote by preaching tariff revision, and by denouncing "invisible government" by the big interests, and the "absolutism and autocracy at Ottawa." The latter was a reference to the 35,142 orders-in-council issued by the Ottawa Government between 1914 and 1919. Liberal gains in New Brunswick, Nova Scotia and British Columbia seemed to augur success in the next national campaign.

In the parliamentary session of 1921 the Meighen Government showed further signs of breaking under the load of economic dis- *Session of 1921* content which was the aftermath of the war, and the Opposition, scenting victory in the near future, vigorously assaulted the tottering Government and branded it as a Government without a mandate from the people. In September, the cabinet was reorganized preparatory to an appeal to the country, and four French Canadians were given portfolios, obviously for political reasons. Much of the legislation passed in 1921, dealing with pensions and soldiers' employment in the civil service, and including an act to prevent the dumping of American products on the Canadian market, was hurried through with an eye to the coming elections. Such by-elections as were held went against the Government. At the time of dissolution, Prime Minister Meighen's majority in the Commons had dwindled to twenty-one, with eight vacancies unfilled.

On November 4, 1921, Parliament was dissolved and a general election was called for December 6. The Meighen Government by *Unpopularity* this time had become one of the most unpopular in all of Canadian *of Government* history, and it was destined to go the way of most of the governments which had been in power in the belligerent countries during the war. Greatly weakened by internal friction, the Government was accused of grafting during the war, of encouraging and shielding the war profiteers, of burdening the people with unnecessary war taxes and conscription, of favoring big business, of causing the economic depression following the war, and of autocratically holding on to war powers when the country had returned to a peace basis. Meighen seemed doomed to defeat because the people, now that the war was over, desired a change, although many of the voters did not know just what that change should be.

The National Liberal and Conservative Party manifesto stressed the protective tariff as the leading issue of the campaign. It denied *Issues in* that the tariff protected the "interests," and the party pleaded for *campaign of* support on the basis of its war and reconstruction record. The *1921* Liberals, in an effort to unite all the forces of discontent under their

banner, chronicled the sins of omission and commission of the Borden
and Meighen Governments in great detail. In the list were such
charges as the inflation of the currency, the rising cost of living,
the nationalization of the railroads without a popular referendum,
attacks on the civil service, unemployment, and waste in rehabilitation work. On the tariff issue, the Liberals took middle ground.
They asserted that the "tariff had outlived its usefulness," and they
promised revision, but at the same time, they denied that they were
free traders or that legitimate business had anything to fear from a
Liberal victory.

Farmers'
platform

For the first time the embattled farmers, under the name of the
National Progressive Party, led by Crerar, entered a national campaign, and the old two party system broke down under the attacks
of this new agricultural "bloc." The Progressives demanded a revaluation of the railroads, economy in government, aid to agriculture
and land settlement, proportional representation, the initiative and
referendum, freer trade and reciprocity with the United States. The
party denounced autocracy in government, the war times election
act, and the presence of so many lawyers in political office. These
champions of the "new nationalism" charged that the bankers
controlled the great trusts, and that by a system of interlocking
investments and directorates and by special legislation obtained from
a willing government, a few men were securing a stranglehold on the
industries, railroads, grain elevators, banks, and, in fact, on the
whole economic life of the Dominion. These demands suggest a
marked similarity with those of the Farmers' Nonpartisan League
which was spreading rapidly through the northwestern states of the
United States in this same period.

Nature of
campaign

The political battle of 1921 was waged vigorously in all parts of
the Dominion. A total of 630 candidates were put in nomination for
the 235 seats in the House of Commons. In Quebec, the Nationalists
played an unimportant rôle, and the French-Canadian province, under
the able guidance of Rodolphe Lemieux, Ernest Lapointe, and Sir
Lomer Gouin, returned to its former Liberal allegiance. In Quebec,
both Conservatives and Liberals advocated the "tariff of Laurier."
All parties made a vigorous appeal for the votes of the newly enfranchised women. Prime Minister Meighen, with keen satire and
much truth, described the attempt of the Liberals to get back into
power as a campaign promising "protection for fruit in British
Columbia, free trade in the three prairie provinces, higher tariff on
implements of production in certain sections of Ontario, lower
tariff on implements of production in others, anti-conscription in
Quebec, and humbug in the Maritime provinces." Imperial relations
did not figure much in the campaign. The government ownership
question also attracted comparatively little attention. The Conservatives naturally defended the nationalization of the railroads which
they had brought about as a necessity, the farmers favored public

ownership, and the Liberals confined their comments to an appeal for an honest trial of the new plan.

The elections of 1921 resulted in the defeat of the Meighen Government in every province except British Columbia. On the prairies every *Defeat of* Meighen candidate except one city member went down to defeat. *Government* Quebec, Nova Scotia and Prince Edward Island returned solid Liberal delegations. In the three western provinces, the Progressives won thirty-seven seats, the Liberals five. In Ontario, the organized farmers carried twenty-four seats, and the total representation of the new third party in Parliament was increased from fourteen to sixty-five. The Liberals received a plurality of the popular vote, but controlled only 117 seats in the Commons. This made them the largest single group in Parliament, but obviously they could not command a working majority. Three labor members also won seats in the federal Parliament, and many others were elected to provincial legislatures during these years. Prime Minister Meighen lost his seat to a Progressive, and a new constituency had to be found for him.

The Dominion faced a new political and constitutional problem as a result of the election of 1921. The governor-general summoned *Constitutional* Mackenzie King to construct a new Government, but owing to the *problem* victories of the farmers' third party, the new prime minister could rely on neither a majority in the House of Commons nor in the country. King tried hard to induce several Progressive leaders to enter his cabinet, but the new party preferred to maintain its independent position. Nevertheless, it was clear that the Progressives would be more sympathetic toward the followers of King than they could be toward the followers of Meighen, and so the new prime minister was obliged to steer a course which would propitiate the agrarian "bloc," if he wanted to remain in power. The Progressives were thus in a strategic position to force concessions from the Government, yet they never quite dared to unhorse the Liberal prime minister for fear of bringing the Conservatives back to office.

When Prime Minister King assumed his duties as leader of the Government he was the youngest man ever to have held that high *King's* honor. The new leader promptly reduced the size of his cabinet from *Government* 22 to 19. The prime minister, besides filling the position of president of the privy council, assumed the duties of secretary of state for external affairs. G. P. Graham became minister of militia and defense, James Murdock minister of labor, and W. S. Fielding minister of finance. Sir Lomer Gouin, for years Liberal prime minister of Quebec, entered the federal Government as minister of justice; Ernest Lapointe, another distinguished French Canadian, became minister of marine and fisheries. Rodolphe Lemieux was chosen speaker of the House of Commons, and was soon mentioned as a possible appointee to Washington, should the Government decide to send a special Canadian minister to the United States. W. R. Motherwell, a pioneer in the farmers' movement, became minister of agriculture. The leader of the

Progressives refused to accept the salary set aside for the Opposition spokesman, and so Meighen technically filled that position.

Party situation
The King cabinet contained many able men, and revealed the political skill of the prime minister, who made a very favorable impression in these first years of his leadership. Most of the important legislation enacted between 1921 and 1925 dealing largely with the continuation of reconstruction measures has been noted in a preceding chapter. Because of the unstable party situation, these years, however, were characterized by a notable lack of constructive achievement. By 1922, King had a nominal majority of only two over all parties in the Commons. The Senate remained a Conservative stronghold with a majority of thirty-five, and on occasion displayed real vigor in checkmating the plans of the other house. In 1923, for example, the upper house rejected important railroad bills and liquor legislation.

Rôle of Progressives
The Progressives, still quite undisciplined as a party organization and without many experienced leaders, failed to pursue the rôle of effective critics which many had expected the new radical party to assume, and the year 1922 marked a great falling off in the membership of farmers' organizations, losses to their coöperatives, and differences of opinion among their leaders. In October Crerar resigned his leadership of the National Progressive Party to devote his energies to rebuilding the United Grain Growers' Ltd., which was losing money rapidly. Robert Forke of Manitoba became the new farmer leader, and under his direction, efforts were made to perfect the party machinery and to enlist the support of voters who were not farmers. Three western provinces had farmers' Governments. In Manitoba, the Liberals were turned out of office in the summer of 1922, and Professor John Bracken, President of the Manitoba College of Agriculture, was elevated to the premiership, although he himself was not a member of the United Farmers of Manitoba. By 1923, the crushing defeat of the Drury farmer Government in Ontario gave the first serious blow to the agrarian movement.

Liberal defeats
The Liberals spent much of their time in sparring for position and carefully avoided important legislative measures which might endanger their control of the government. Canada continued to suffer from industrial depression and a heavy loss of population to the United States, and little progress was made in tariff, railroad or other economic legislation. In 1924, the Government lost several by-elections in the maritime provinces, and Sir Lomer Gouin and W. S. Fielding, two of the ablest members of the party, retired from the ministry.

"Steering west" on tariff
The Government now decided to "steer west" on the tariff, and notable changes were made in the budget of 1924, discussed in a preceding chapter. By this emphasis on tariff reform, the Liberals and Progressives were drawn closer together, but the Government's new schedule of railroad freight rates probably antagonized as many westerners as their reform of the tariff could attract. The Government also secured the passage of a redistribution bill increasing the mem-

bership of the House of Commons from 235 to 245, Nova Scotia losing two seats and the western provinces gaining twelve. Thereupon the Government decided to appeal to the country for an increased majority to break the political deadlock which had existed since 1921. The elections were set for October 29, 1925.

It was to be expected that the campaign would lack clear-cut issues, and both Liberals and Conservatives tempered their remarks *Campaign* to please all sections of the country. The Liberals promised tariff *of 1925* reform and tax reduction, but on this point the Progressives fought shy of a Liberal alliance and refused to accept the prime minister's promises at face value. It was notable that the Liberals did not stress tariff reduction in Quebec, because that Liberal stronghold was rapidly turning protectionist. The Progressives attacked the "new feudalism" imposed upon the people by eastern capitalists, and demanded free trade and an elective upper house. They also supported government ownership of the railroads. The Conservatives assailed the Government for alleged attacks on the civil service system, and for squandering money on unnecessary public works. None of the party leaders had much to say about Canada's new international status.

The results of the election reduced the Liberal or Government party's strength in the Commons from 118 to 101. The prime minister *Outcome* and seven of the cabinet failed of reëlection. The Progressive party suffered the most startling defeat in the campaign. Only in Alberta did the Progressives win a majority of the contested seats, and their representation in all the western provinces fell to twenty-three. The Conservatives, although returned with a more than doubled membership, still lacked a working majority in the Commons. Moreover, in spite of a plurality of some 200,000 votes, Meighen lacked an actual majority of the popular votes cast. The result of the election thus gave the Liberals 101, the Conservatives 116, and the Progressives and Independents twenty-eight seats. The balance of power remained with the agricultural "bloc."

A serious constitutional issue was raised by this failure of the people to express their sovereign will more decisively. Neither *"Muddling* Liberals nor Conservatives could claim a mandate to organize the *through"* Government as a majority party, and Prime Minister King was forced to choose among several possible courses. He might have asked the governor-general to call another election, a procedure which would have involved heavy expenditures and probably would have left the party situation as muddled as before. The Conservatives insisted that the only honorable course to follow was to entrust the formation of a new ministry to Arthur Meighen, on the ground that the failure of the Liberals to secure a majority in the election created a moral obligation to call the Opposition to the helm. Mackenzie King preferred to try the third possibility of "muddling through," and announced that he would rebuild his badly riddled cabinet—a new seat had to be found even for the prime minister—by appointing ministers who had been reëlected and Liberal members from the Senate, and that he would leave the fate of his reconstructed Government to Parliament when it reassembled in January, 1926. In the meantime, according to the charge of the Conservatives, the Dominion was virtually governed by order-in-council. King insisted that on the most important issue of the campaign, the tariff, the Progressives would be more likely to give their support to him than to the leader of the Opposition.

Opposition tactics

Prime Minister King's course led to a heated discussion of its constitutional justification, the Conservatives contending that their opponents were defying a well-established custom of the constitution compelling a minority leader to resign immediately when defeated in an appeal to the country. Their argument was unsound. A defeated leader has an absolute right to meet the House and to await its verdict, and King followed excellent precedents. Meighen also denied that the tariff was the leading issue of the campaign, and made serious charges of unethical and unconstitutional conduct on the part of the Liberal prime minister and his followers.

Session of 1926

The Fifteenth Parliament of the Dominion, which met early in 1926 under the nominal leadership of Prime Minister King, found it impossible to enact many important measures and was doomed to an early death. Nevertheless, the King Government managed to push along a budget which was admittedly popular, and an old age pensions and a rural credits bill. The last two measures failed to pass the Senate, after they had received the approval of the Commons. Party tension steadily increased, but for several months, the Liberals received enough votes from the handful of Progressives to remain technically in power. Party "whips" had to exert themselves to the utmost to prevent the unhorsing of the Government on snap votes.

Customs scandal

The Opposition insisted upon a number of investigations into the functioning of government departments, and particularly upon a scrutiny of the customs service and its relation to the growing industry of rum-running across the Canada-United States border. A special parliamentary committee revealed scandals of great magnitude in the customs service. A smuggling industry in alcoholic liquors and narcotics was robbing the Dominion treasury of millions of dollars, and this industry apparently throve through the connivance of some officials in the customs department. Clearance papers for liquor consigned to the United States were signed by the hundreds for vessels technically going to Japan, Mexico or the West Indies. The investigation revealed that a gang of international smugglers had established themselves at Montreal and other points along the border, and not only smuggled liquor into the United States but brought American dutiable products, such as textiles, cigarettes and other articles, into Canada. The latter practice particularly aroused the wrath of Canadian merchants and manufacturers and others who otherwise were inclined to condone the sale of liquor to the United States because it brought money into the Dominion.

The investigation brought to light many facts which seemed to implicate members of the Government. Bootleggers and smugglers had influential friends in the customs service, and political influence had been used on occasion to keep bootleggers out of jail. It was pointed out that a notorious New Brunswick bootlegger had been saved from jail until after the election, because a Liberal member from the province appealed to the minister of customs for a stay of execution of his sentence. *Government involved*

The King Government had to bear the brunt of these disclosures and Meighen pressed for a vote of censure. A conservative estimate placed the loss to the Canadian revenues from smuggling at $35,000,-000 annually. A secret report, supposed to have been suppressed by the investigators, and referring to gay liquor parties on government property by members of the Government, was privately passed around with good effect among the Progressive members. At this critical juncture, it became evident that the latter would no longer support the Government, and the prime minister, faced with defeat, resolved to ask the governor-general, Lord Byng of Vimy, to dissolve Parliament and to call a general election. The governor-general refused to dissolve Parliament on the advice of his chief minister, apparently on the ground that the Opposition leader should first be given an opportunity to construct a Government. Thereupon Prime Minister King resigned (June 28, 1926). *Governor-general raises new constitutional issue*

Meighen was immediately summoned to Government House to form a new ministry, but at this point a new constitutional difficulty arose. The appointment of a new cabinet involved the temporary vacating of the appointees' seats in the Commons, and the necessity of appealing to their constituencies for reëlection. The Conservative majority was so slender that this would immediately make the party pendulum swing back to the Liberals again, and the new Government would suffer defeat before it began to function. Meighen now gave the constitution another wrench, and accepted the post of prime minister, but refused to take the oath of office until he could get guarantees from the Progressives not to oust his Government if he temporarily vacated his seat. The new leader then proceeded to form a temporary ministry of six "acting ministers," all to serve without portfolios. *Government of "acting ministers"*

The Liberals challenged this new departure from the custom of the constitution with great vigor, and on the morning of July 2, the Meighen Government was driven from office by a motion of want of confidence, in which the vote was ninety-six to ninety-five. King, as leader of the Opposition, had threatened to hold up all appropriation bills on the ground that Parliament could not vote the yearly supplies to a Government which had no legal existence. Meighen, after a stormy premiership of hardly three days was thus in turn compelled *Parliament dissolved* to seek a dissolution. Lord Byng this time accepted the advice of his chief minister, and Parliament was dissolved. The fact that the governor-general denied Parliament the courtesy of a formal summons to the prorogation ceremony, and that members were notified by pages that the session was dissolved, added greatly to the excitement over constitutional procedure. A great number of important bills, among them the supply bills, were lost in the constitutional jam at the end of this hectic session.

Campaign of 1926

The campaign of 1926 was the result of years of political floundering following the war, marked by the apparent disintegration of the old two-party system and the rise of a vigorous Canadian sectionalism which seemed to make the task of rebuilding party lines very difficult; 528 candidates contested for 244 seats, one seat in Manitoba going without a contest to a Liberal-Progressive. The candidates were distributed as follows: Conservatives 233, Liberals 199, Progressives twenty, Independents twenty-five, Labor eighteen, United Farmers of Alberta twelve, Liberal-Progressives twenty-one. In forty-eight constituencies the Liberal party, in an effort to avoid three-cornered contests, refrained from making nominations and supported Independent, Labor, or Progressive candidates.

Liberal issues

King insisted at the beginning of the campaign that the unconstitutional procedure of the governor-general in refusing a dissolution to the Liberal prime minister was the "most important issue in the country to-day," and that the election would determine whether Canada would continue as a self-governing nation or be reduced to the level of a Crown colony. He denounced Meighen's appointment of "acting ministers" and accused the Conservatives of awarding contracts and paying out public money without constitutional warrant. Meighen defended the action of the governor-general in what he called "upholding responsible government," accused the Liberals of trying "to cut off the subject's right to go to the foot of the throne," and of planning to weaken the British connection. Mackenzie King was charged with "leaning to the south," an alleged interview was quoted from the *Wall Street Journal* to prove King's American sympathies, and he was forced to explain that he had university degrees from Toronto, Edinburgh and Oxford, as well as from Harvard. By way of retaliation, the Liberals found joy in pointing out that Prime Minister Meighen had christened a son Theodore Roosevelt Meighen.

Conservative issues

According to the Conservatives, King raised "the miserable dust of a constitutional issue to becloud the customs issue on which he was voted out of power." Every effort was made to keep the customs scandal to the front. Meighen accused the Liberals of "helping American thieves make fortunes," and mercilessly exposed the maladministration of the customs department under Bureau and Boivin, two former ministers, the first of whom had since been "sentenced to the Senate at a salary of $4000 a year." The Liberals were forced to admit the truth of many of these charges, but argued that most of the employees were appointees of previous Tory Governments, protected by civil service rules, that both parties were involved, and that the "welter of wickedness" was continuing under the Meighen régime.

The Liberals stressed their record of achievement during the preceding four years. Canada was prosperous, and an unfavorable trade balance of $35,000,000 in 1921 had been converted into a favorable balance of $400,000,000. Manufactured exports exceeded imports by $15,000,000 for the first time in Canadian history, and the Canadian dollar stood above par. King paraded the virtues of the Robb budget, by which cuts had been made in income and sales taxes, postal rates, the tariff on autos and on implements and machinery needed in farming, mining and fishing; he promised further reductions in expenses, taxation and the national debt. "Let Robb Bring in the Next Budget," "Don't Be Robbed of the Robb Budget," and "Put King Back and Keep Prosperity" proved effective Liberal slogans. Meighen replied by attributing Canada's prosperity to a kind Providence and her natural resources, and charged that the Robb budget had made reductions only at the expense of the Treasury, that the budget was "a malodorous sham" and that "tariff tinkering" by the Liberals and their Progressive supporters had closed 3000 factories. *Prosperity and Robb budget*

On the tariff issue neither party was consistent nor clear in its statements of principles. In the West, Mackenzie King appeared on the same platform with Robert Forke, the Progressive leader, and promised real tariff reduction. In protectionist Montreal and Ontario, he advocated a tariff which would build up Canadian industry and not injure any legitimate business, and promised to make cuts with the greatest care. Traditionally the Conservatives are the high tariff party. Meighen championed protection and charged that the Liberals, dominated by western Progressives, were slowly fighting their way to free trade. In Ontario, he advocated a "brick for brick" tariff wall against the United States, but in Saskatchewan Meighen said, "I know the West does not want any high tariff. The Conservative party does not propose to impose any such tariff. Our platform is not what some fellow may say in Toronto or in Montreal." In the East, he consistently denounced free trade as a policy which would set "our best blood flowing into the veins of the United States," and in Brantford, he promised thorough revision to cope with the "big rival to the south." *Trimming on tariff issue*

The Canadian National Railways also figured in the campaign. The Liberals accused the Meighen Government of planning to make them subsidiary to the Canadian Pacific, and although the Conservatives reaffirmed their faith in nationalization, many voters doubted the attitude of Meighen's minister of railways and his Montreal-controlled minister of justice. King promised to reënact the old age pensions law which the Conservative Senate had blocked, and made a special appeal for social justice for the laboring classes. *Other issues*

In various sections local issues assumed importance. In the urban centers of Ontario the chief issue was the tariff, in the western and eastern parts of Canada such issues as railroad rates, the Hudson Bay Railway, alleged preference for American instead of Canadian Atlantic ports, pulpwood exports, Oriental immigration, and even the old Military Service Act of 1917 were important. Finally, both parties appealed to the voters to end the unstable party situation. "Vote Conservative and for Stable Government" was the battle cry of the followers of Meighen, while the Liberals insisted that only their party had a chance to win a majority of the seats in the House of Commons.

Muddled campaign

During the campaign the usual crop of personal attacks, slanders and political "roorbacks" made their appearance. Both King and Meighen conducted strenuous personal campaigns, and in Quebec both repeatedly addressed their hearers in French. Meighen was accused of appealing to the Nationalists of Quebec by promising a parliamentary election before sending Canadian troops abroad to help England, and then refusing to discuss this issue before a Toronto meeting. Henri Bourassa, the fiery Nationalist leader, criticized both parties, but denounced the Conservatives specifically as the "Tory-Orange clique." He promised to support the Liberals who were trying to check the "empire-mongers," rather than vote for "the men who have been the most ardent and the most stubborn in making us drink the cup of the Great War to the dregs."

To an unbiased observer, there was much in the campaign which seemed to prove that "politicians played with principles and policies for the sake of portfolios and power." The Toronto *Globe*, in spite of its Liberal traditions, found it impossible to give unqualified support to either King or Meighen, and claimed that both parties had received secret campaign contributions from the distillers.

Liberal victory

The election turned out to be a crushing defeat for the Conservatives. The result was: Liberals 119, Conservatives ninety-one, Progressives eight, Liberal-Progressives eleven, United Farmers of Alberta eleven, Labor three, Independent two. Prime Minister Meighen and six of his ministers were defeated. British Columbia, Nova Scotia, New Brunswick and Ontario returned Conservative majorities, but in the last named province the great inroads made by the Liberals, even in protected manufacturing districts, were a decisive factor in the defeat of the Meighen Government. The prairie provinces, with the exception of one seat, went solidly against the Conservatives. Although the Liberals did not obtain a clear majority in the House of Commons, a sufficient number of Liberal-Progressives, endorsed by both parties, were elected to give a majority over all others. Moreover, the Independent, Labor, Progressive, and United Farmer of Alberta groups, with twenty-four seats, were expected to support Mackenzie King rather than the Opposition leader on major issues.

The popular vote slightly exceeded 3,100,000, or about seventy per cent of the number of eligible voters in the Dominion. An analysis *Analysis of* of this popular vote shows that there was a relatively slight overturn *popular vote* in public opinion, for the Conservatives polled practically as large a vote as in the preceding election, and the increase in the total Liberal vote was only 100,000. The total minor party vote shrank by 100,000 from that polled in 1925. In Ontario a number of Conservatives and Progressives shifted to the Liberal ticket, and the working agreement between Liberals and Progressives in the West did the rest.

Liberal leaders attributed their gains to tax and tariff reduction and to the prevailing prosperity, with the constitutional issue and *Reasons for* the blunders of the Conservatives having some importance. Prime *Conservative* Minister Meighen's catering to the French Canadians undoubtedly *defeat* antagonized many Conservatives in Ontario. In general, his campaign was destructive rather than constructive, and many of his candidates and associates had records and connections which proved unfortunate in a campaign waged "to clean house." The benefits of the Robb budget, the Liberal promises of further tax reductions, and good times served to outweigh the customs scandal. The victorious leader in a signed pledge, agreed "to continue relentlessly the investigation of the Customs Service and carry out without fear or favor the needed reforms."

Ten days after the election, Prime Minister Meighen and his colleagues tendered their resignations to the governor-general. Mackenzie *New cabinet* King constructed a cabinet notable for its political strength, and for the careful geographical apportionment of the various portfolios so as to conciliate all factions and sections of the party. The new cabinet included seven French-speaking members. Quebec received six places, Ontario five, Saskatchewan three, and the six other provinces one member each. King's greatest success was his conciliation of the Manitoba Progressives. The latter received assurances from the new prime minister that on all important policies affecting the West, such as a moderate tariff, completion of the Hudson Bay Railway, and railway freight rates, the Liberals and Progressives were in complete agreement. To cement the alliance, and in spite of the determined opposition of the United Farmers of Alberta, King induced Robert Forke of Manitoba, the former Progressive floor leader in the Commons, to accept a portfolio. Thus virtually ended the effectiveness of the agricultural "bloc," which for five years had held the balance of power in the House of Commons. This Liberal-Progressive *rapprochement* was a great step toward the return of the two-party system in Canadian politics. The herculean task of cleaning up the department of customs and excises was assigned to William D. Euler, an Independent-Liberal of German stock from Ontario. Other prominent members of the cabinet were J. A. Robb, minister of finance, Ernest Lapointe, minister of justice, C. A. Dunning, minister of railways, and W. R. Motherwell, minister of agriculture.

With the return to power of the Liberals, Lord Byng's term of

*New governor-
general*
office as governor-general expired, and the governor-general, who
raised the constitutional issue which the Liberals insisted involved
the future of Canadian liberty, was succeeded by Lord Willingdon.
When Lord Byng bade farewell to the Dominion, he left with the
plaudits of the people ringing in his ears, and all rumblings of opposition to his recent constitutional course were lost in the farewell
tribute of an affectionate and loyal people to a governor who had
after all been a most popular official.

*New Opposition
leader*
Shortly after the close of the campaign of 1926, Meighen resigned
as the official head of his party. Hugh Guthrie was elected House
leader by a Conservative caucus held at Ottawa in October. The new
leader was a comparatively recent convert to Conservatism. He had
served in the Union Government as solicitor-general and as minister
of militia in the Meighen Governments. A Dominion-wide convention
of Conservatives was planned for 1927, to choose a permanent head
of the party organization. The fact that the convention was to meet
in the West was evidence of the party's desire to woo that section
politically. At this convention, Richard Bedford Bennett of Calgary,
was chosen as leader of the party on the second ballot. The new
leader was born in New Brunswick, studied law, and in 1897 migrated
to the West, where his legal talents and successful investments,
notably in railroads and paper mills, made him a man of millions.
After some service in the provincial legislature, he entered the federal
Parliament in 1911. Closely associated with Sir Robert Borden, he
rose rapidly in party councils. Defeated in 1921, after having served
as minister of justice, Bennett was returned to Parliament in 1925,
and held the post of minister of finance, during the brief Meighen
régime of 1926. In the Liberal sweep of that year, Bennett had the
distinction of being the only Conservative to be returned to the
Commons from the prairies.

*First session
of 1926-1927*
The tactics of the Conservative Opposition in the Parliament of
1927 were those of assisting rather than unnecessarily obstructing
the new Government in the enactment of its program. The first session
of Parliament after the campaign of 1926 proved to be much freer
than its predecessors from petty political maneuvering and partisan
tactics. Stable two-party government seemed to have been reëstab-
lished for the moment. Besides participating in the notable Imperial
Conference of 1926, discussed in the preceding chapter, Mackenzie
King's Government concentrated its efforts on the stimulation of trade
and immigration, a new budget, an attempt to secure the old age
pensions law previously blocked by the Senate, and social legislation,
particularly a system of annuities for the workers of Canada. Negotiations were begun for new trade treaties with Cuba, Germany and
other countries, and new plans for the stimulation of immigration
were worked out by Robert Forke, the Manitoba Progressive who had
become minister of immigration. Talk of Senate reform continued,
and all appointees of the King Government to the Upper House were

pledged in advance to support such reform proposals whenever they may be brought forward.

The investigation and reform of the customs service progressed slowly, but apparently with great effectiveness. A commission was instructed to study the causes of discontent in the maritime provinces. Nova Scotia in particular has frequently expressed its dissatisfaction with the fiscal results of confederation as far as the maritime region is concerned. The province has been isolated, virtually, by high tariffs dictated by the central Canadian provinces. Geographic conditions make it difficult to develop manufacturing in the maritime provinces, and the Dominion policy of protection has resulted in heavy loss in the American market. Relief legislation has now been passed as a result of the report of the investigating committee. The new Robb budget introduced in February, 1927, provided for further tax reductions, in income, stamp, and sales, or so-called "nuisance taxes," but it made no tariff changes. A special tariff board was at work studying the needs and demands of specific industries and the Government apparently preferred to wait for its report before tampering again with the tariff policy of the Dominion. The tax reduction of the Robb budget was estimated to involve a loss of $27,000,000 in government revenues. The finance minister, in the budget speech, reported that nearly $100,000,000 had been paid off on the national debt during the preceding four years and that the estimated debt reduction for 1927 was $31,000,000. For the first time since the war, Parliament was asked to increase expenditures for national defense, the addition of $3,000,000 to be applied primarily to the development of aviation.

Budget

On July 1, 1927, the Dominion of Canada began the celebration of the Diamond Jubilee of the Confederation, by the Governor-General touching a signal on Parliament Hill in Ottawa, which set the new carillon in the Parliament tower ringing, while radio stations broadcast the glad tidings of the nation's sixtieth birthday to the most distant parts of the Dominion and to Europe. Distinguished visitors from the mother-country and many foreign nations, including the popular Prince of Wales, Prince George, Stanley Baldwin and others participated in the happy celebration before the close of the summer. From ocean to ocean Canadians linked hands in pride of their country. His Majesty George V cabled his congratulations in a message which began,

Canada's diamond jubilee

"To-day my people of Canada unite to celebrate the Diamond Jubilee of Confederation, and on such a day they may well look with a just pride at the achievements of the past, and with a confident hope to the promises of the future.

"In sixty years the boundaries of Confederation have extended tenfold, and its Governments are now responsible for the welfare of nearly ten million inhabitants. By labor, peace, and sacrifice of war, Canada has become a mighty nation. Aims as lofty and labors as strenuous await her in the future. Within her own bounds her people have before them the task of developing the heritage which their fathers have left them.

"In a yet wider sphere she has to take an ever-increasing share in guiding counsel and solving problems of the Great Commonwealth of which she is a part, conscious that within it there is perfect freedom, and that the unity of the British Empire is the surest guarantee of the peace of the world to-day. . . ."

SELECT BIBLIOGRAPHY FOR CHAPTER XXXI

Besides *The Canadian Annual Review of Public Affairs*, the periodical literature of the period should be consulted. OWEN E. McGILLICUDDY, *The Making of a Premier* (Toronto, 1922) is a very laudatory account of the rise of Prime Minister King to political prominence.

Special articles on recent elections are H. L. KEENLEYSIDE, "The Canadian Election of 1925," in *Current History*, January, 1926; CARL WITTKE, "The Conservative Defeat in Canada," *Ibid.*, November 1926; and WALTER R. SHARP, "The Canadian Election of 1926," in *The American Political Science Review*, February, 1927, pp. 101–113. For a brief account of the customs scandal, see J. A. STEVENSON, "Scandals in Canada," in *The New Republic*, July 14, 1926, pp. 223–224.

CHAPTER XXXII

A NEW ERA AND ITS PROBLEMS

THE DIAMOND JUBILEE of Confederation filled the patriotic Canadian with that justifiable sense of pride that comes from contemplating a long past full of real achievements. The years just ahead seemed to promise even greater material prosperity. For a little more than two years after the celebration of 1927, all signs continued to point toward an economic development of astounding rapidity and proportions. The railways reported increased tonnage and earnings, and considerable expansion of trackage, and although the Canadian National still could not wipe out its net income deficit, the Canadian taxpayer was confident that the financial burden of the railways was becoming less. By the middle of 1925, the turn in the tide following the depression after the war, was evident. Wheat crops in the next few years were among the largest in the history of Canada, and the curve of general employment showed an encouraging turn upward. Wages advanced, and strikes were comparatively few. Immigration was increasing, and the construction industries showed great activity. Business mergers were reflected in enormous stock market transactions, on a stock market that was unusually active and buoyant. In 1928, 128 Canadian stocks appreciated $1,110,000,000 in value. No-par common stock had become the most fashionable security to hold, and bond sales were almost at a standstill in view of the lure of greater profits on the stock market in more speculative investments. The volume of corporation finance reached a new high level in 1927; the total life insurance in force in Canada increased by a billion dollars in two years, and the revenue from general agriculture was larger than at any time since the "boom years" of the war. In 1927 alone, at least a quarter billion dollars of foreign capital were invested in Canadian enterprises. The Canadian Pacific Railway had greater net earnings in 1928 than at any other time in its history, and its newest hotel, the Royal York of Toronto, was built at a cost of $16,000,000. Both the Canadian National and the Canadian Pacific were spending millions on equipment and extensions. The production of pig iron, steel, and automobiles reached new high records in 1928. In 1929, Canada boasted of the second largest per capita export trade of any nation in the world, and in absolute volume of exports she ranked fifth. The trade balance was favorable, and taxes were coming down. The Canadian West was in the midst of a new era of railway expansion, mining, and hydro-electric development. It would be no exaggeration to say that 1928 marked the

Prosperity

highest point of industrial and trade activity ever reached by Canada, and the Governor-general, in opening Parliament the following year, pointed out that "never in the history of Canada has there been such industrial and commercial expansion as that which has taken place during the past twelve months." The banks were in excellent condition, and no more able to stop the wave of speculation than the Federal Reserve system in the United States; optimism pervaded all business statements, and the few voices raised in warning against the evils of overspeculation were studiously ignored or speedily silenced.

Budget of 1928

Under these conditions of prosperity, the way of the Liberal Government of Mackenzie King was comparatively easy, and there was little disposition to quarrel with the party in power as long as business was good. The Robb budget of 1928 was built on a huge favorable trade balance of $147,000,000 in the preceding year, and provided further reductions in the income and sales taxes, as well as a downward revision of the tariff, especially in the textile groups. The attacks of the opposition upon the policy of the prime minister were comparatively few; every important vote in the session of 1928 resulted in comfortable majorities of twenty-five or thirty for the Government, and Bennett's speeches were mostly devoted to redefining and clarifying the Conservative position on such questions as the tariff, imperial relations, and immigration.

The Customs investigation

The Royal Commission on Customs and Excise, appointed as an aftermath of the customs scandal, issued its final report in January, 1928. It had found evidences of smuggling, and it urged some reorganization of the customs service, but it attributed much of the trouble to the international liquor trade, and urged that clearances to vessels and vehicles carrying liquor to the United States should be prohibited by the Government. It was not until March, 1930, however, that the Canadian House of Commons could be persuaded to pass an act refusing clearance of prohibited beverages consigned to the United States. Almost immediately, the two little French islands, St. Pierre and Miquelon, the last remnants of the French colonial empire in Canada, leaped into unexpected prominence as a base of operations in the lucrative liquor trade with the "dry" American states.

Provincial subsidies

A conference of Dominion and provincial leaders held at Ottawa in November, 1927, to discuss various constitutional and economic questions, led to a renewal of the discussion of increased federal subsidies to the provinces, and stressed the necessity for a new inquiry into the whole field of provincial and dominion taxation. As a result of these discussions, and considerable political maneuvering, new arrangements were finally concluded early in 1930 with the three western provinces of Manitoba, Alberta, and Saskatchewan, and including the belt of railroad lands in British Columbia, by which all public lands were transferred to the provinces, and some readjustments were made in the financial subsidies. These changes were submitted to the British Parliament, for formal approval as an amendment to the British North America Act. In July, 1930, Manitoba celebrated the diamond jubilee of her birth as a province of the Confederation, and on this occasion, which also marked the official return of the natural resources by the Dominion to the province, Prime Minister Mackenzie King handed Prime Minister Bracken of Manitoba a check for $4,584,212.49, due the province to cover the value of her resources for the years when they had been under dominion control. It is interesting to add that the settlement of the natural resources question proposed by the King Government for the three western provinces aroused considerable agitation in Alberta and Saskatchewan. Probably at the insistence of the French-Canadian Liberals, the proposed settlement involved guarantees of school lands and certain rights of Catholic schools. The proposal led to an outburst of religious agitation in Alberta, and in Saskatchewan the Ku Klux Klan attained temporary prosperity by arousing its members against the Catholic clergy, and by insisting that Canada's immigration policy, dictated by Quebec, was flooding the west with Catholics from the backward countries of Central Europe.

Maritimes settlement

The settlement of the natural resources question was an issue of special significance to the Canadian West. In the preceding chapter, it was suggested that the provinces in the maritime region also were dissatisfied and demanded new concessions from the Dominion Government to lighten their economic burdens. As the result of the recommendations of a Royal Commission on Maritime Claims, the King Government agreed to make special annual grants of $875,000 to Nova Scotia, $600,000 to New Brunswick, and $125,000 to Prince Edward Island. In addition, five bills were passed. One reduced railway rates to the Maritimes; another, in order to stimulate the development of a national fuel policy, provided a subsidy to by-product coke plants which would use Canadian coal, thereby reducing the use of anthracite coal from the United States. Provision was also made for the division of the department of marine and fisheries into two departments, and for the creation of harbor boards in St. John and Halifax. This legislation, designed to satisfy the grievances of the maritime region, was not opposed by the Conservative leader, and was criticised only by the western members of the House of Commons.

Immigration

The immigration policy of the Liberal Government was repeatedly challenged on two counts, on the ground that it was ineffective, and that it did not bring in the most desirable settlers. Robert Forke, minister of immigration in the King Government, had been active since 1926 in formulating a policy which should bring "the landless man to the manless land." Preference was given to British immigrants, and to farm laborers and household servants, and reduced rates on ocean lines were offered to selected groups. In the early years of Forke's activity, there was a widespread interest in his program, and the only sizable group which opposed his policies were the leaders of organized labor. In the year ending March 31, 1929, 167,722 immigrants entered Canada, 16,000 more than in the preceding year. Antagonism to the Liberal immigration policy was developing, however, even before the effects of the depression of 1929 became apparent. Forke was accused of using Roman Catholic clergy to recruit immigrants for his department on the continent of Europe, and although he insisted that every preference was given to immigrants of British stock, and that those from Central and Southwestern Europe had to pay the full transportation charges to North America, the antagonism to Central and South Europeans continued to grow. Indeed, many Canadians who were not specially influenced by religious or nativist prejudices, contended that Canada should close its doors until all recent arrivals in her population had been assimilated to the Canadian pattern. Forke finally withdrew to the Senate, and in March, 1930, Charles Stewart, his successor in the department of immigration, announced that "assisted immigration is at an end." The Dominion ceased to give encouragement to prospective immigrants, and the determining influence in immigration policy thereafter passed to the provinces.

Immigration to the United States

An interesting corollary to the immigration problem was Canada's difficulties with the United States when the latter country undertook to keep out Canadians who had commuted across the border for years as workmen in American factories. The controversy led to long diplomatic discussions, and several references of the question to the United States Supreme Court. The latter eventually sustained the stringent regulations enforced by the United States Department of Labor, and in 1929, the United States government decided that only native Canadians were exempt from the quota restrictions imposed by United States law on immigrant groups. If native Canadians were provided with the necessary *visa*, they might continue to enter the United States; all other residents of Canada were subject to the quotas applying to the country of their origin. The whole controversy was of course precipitated by the panic of 1929, and widespread unemployment in both Canada and the United States led both countries to look with disfavor on the arrival of newcomers.

Social legislation

During 1927 and 1928, a number of provincial legislatures had enacted workmen's compensation, mother's allowance, and old age pension laws. In 1929, the Dominion Government secured the passage of an old age pension bill, to establish a pension for indigents with less than $365 a year, the payments to begin at the age of seventy. Under the terms of the act, the Dominion government agreed to assume equal shares with the provincial governments, for amounts not to exceed $240 a year. Ontario accepted the Dominion's proposal, and put the plan into operation, November 1, 1929. Quebec and the Maritimes rejected the proposal, on the ground that the financial obligations were unfairly distributed. As evidence of the increasing importance of women in Canadian politics, Prime Minister Mackenzie King tried to appoint a woman to the Canadian Senate. Thwarted by a unanimous decision of the Canadian Supreme Court, which in April, 1928, decided that "qualified persons" in the British North America Act did not include women for places in the Senate, an appeal was taken to the British Privy Council. The latter declared women eligible to the Senate, and in 1930, the Honorable Cairine Rhea Wilson became the first woman Senator of the Dominion.

In the parliamentary sessions of 1928 and 1929, there was some discussion of the development of the St. Lawrence waterway, as a *The* joint Canadian-United States project, but no action was taken until *St. Lawrence* after the Bennett Government had assumed office. The Canadian *waterway* Supreme Court gave rather inconclusive answers to ten hypothetical questions which had been submitted to it in order to clarify the issue of dominion and provincial jurisdiction over the proposed St. Lawrence waterway and power project, and so the Dominion Government resorted to conferences with the Quebec and Ontario Governments. The Dominion insisted that it would retain exclusive authority over any water power created on the Canadian side under any treaty for the improvement of the St. Lawrence, while the provinces insisted on full control of water power in their areas. Some Canadians were fearful of the loss of their sovereignty rights, and the Conservative prime minister of Ontario talked patriotically about developing an all-Canadian waterway, just as some in the United States advocated an all-American route through New York State. An agreement was concluded in 1928 between the two countries to allow more diversion of water from Niagara Falls for power purposes, without damaging the beauty of the falls.

The parliamentary session of 1929 was comparatively brief. Both the Government and the Opposition leader had spent considerable *Session of* time on speech-making tours the preceding summer. The stars on the *1929* political horizon of 1929 still seemed to favor the Liberal party. Although Ontario was overwhelmingly Conservative, Quebec, under the leadership of Prime Minister Taschereau, remained almost solidly Liberal. An election in Prince Edward Island, in 1927, in which the Conservatives had sponsored a liquor control bill similar to the law of Ontario, had resulted in a Liberal triumph. The western farmers still were prosperous, and farmers' organizations and coöperatives were doing an expanding business. The chief discussions in the parliamentary session of 1929 centered around the tariff and relations with the United States. A cloud, still no bigger than a man's hand, had arisen on the horizon in the form of new tariff legislation by the United States, but it was hoped that the large American investments and business interests in Canada, and the desire for coöperation in developing the St. Lawrence waterway might outweigh the demand of the farmers of the United States for a higher tariff, and thus avert a tariff war with Canada.

President Hoover had been elected in 1928 on the promise to provide relief for American agriculture. Although there was no desire
originally on the part of the American President to have an entirely
new tariff bill enacted, the United States Congress, after a continuous and stormy session of nearly fourteen months, in June, 1930,
passed the notorious Hawley-Smoot tariff act. The bill, as signed
by the President, levied duties on 3,218 articles imported by the
United States. It was passed in the face of opposition from a thousand
American economists and experts on international trade, and over
the protest of many industrialists and bankers, who in the face of a
growing financial depression, had joined the academic economists in
rejecting the protectionist doctrine as synonymous with prosperity,
and who pointed out the dangers inherent in artificial trade barriers,
at a time when the United States had become the largest creditor
nation in the world. The "limited tariff revision" promised by the
Republican party in the campaign of 1928, thus resulted in a general
tariff in which 887 of the rates of the preceding high tariff (the
Fordney-McCumber act) were revised upward. While the bill was
under discussion, the United States received protests from no less
than 42 foreign governments and dependencies, objecting to more than
300 items in the proposed law.

That the bill was especially alarming to Canada is self-evident,
in view of the fact that Canada has been the best customer of the
United States, and that her trade relations with her southern neighbor were more important than with the mother-country. Needless
to add, in the session of 1929, the Opposition leader criticized the
utterances of various public men in the United States as suggesting
a tariff war between the United States and the British Empire. Bennett upbraided the Liberal Government for its supine submission
to the tariff legislation under discussion in Washington, and demanded
a "red-blooded" Canadian policy in retaliation. The Liberal leader
deplored Bennett's jingoistic utterances, the budget of 1929 (the
last to be prepared by Robb) contained no retaliatory proposals,
and Prime Minister King argued that a "cool-headed attitude" was
more essential than a "red-blooded attitude" toward the United
States. He characterized the tariff policy of his Government as one
intended to "encourage production at home and the marketing of
our excess of production abroad," and promised to await the effect
of the United States tariff proposals before taking any action that
might be interpreted as "provocative." The most determined attack
of the Opposition in the session of 1929 was launched against Peter
Veniot, the Postmaster-General, who was criticised for his system
of awarding contracts for rural mail delivery, but particularly because
he had cancelled an appointment of a crippled war veteran to the
postmastership of Simcoe, Ontario, after he had been recommended
by the Civil Service Commission. The Postmaster-General replied
that he had appointed another veteran to the position, solely because

it was necessary to get an able-bodied man, and he successfully answered charges of irregularities in the postal service in New Brunswick. The session ended with Veniot still in office.

After the close of the session of 1929, there were rumors of a Dominion election, and the leaders of both parties made extended tours of the provinces. Both Mackenzie King and Bennett devoted much of their time to a discussion of the tariff question, the Conservative leader insisting that the United States was dumping its products in Canada. Both the prime minister and the opposition leader advocated an imperial conference to stimulate trade, and Mackenzie King promised retaliatory legislation against such United States tariffs as might affect Canada unfavorably, although he opposed a tariff which aimed at a monopoly of the Canadian home market. *Party politics*

Before the fourth and final session of the Sixteenth Parliament opened, the panic of 1929 had fallen like a great blight upon Canada, the United States, and the other leading nations of the world. Business quickly came to a standstill, and the prosperity of recent years tumbled like a house of cards before an economic storm of unprecedented violence. Experts on business cycles are not in complete agreement as to the causes of the depression which has held the world in its grips from 1929 to the present and it is unnecessary to discuss the question in detail here. Part of the trouble could be traced to the destruction caused by the World War, and to the reparations and debt burdens it imposed; partly the panic was due to a mania of unprecedented stock market gambling and overspeculation; to a degree the speeding up of the processes of production by labor-saving inventions may have been responsible, for production had greatly outstripped consumer buying power. But whatever the specific causes, there could be no doubt about the destructive force of the economic storm. The crash on the Canadian stock market on October 29 and November 13, 1929 was the greatest in its history, and the losses of the investors were estimated at five billion dollars, as it became apparent that common stocks which had been preferred during the speculative craze to sound investments were of very doubtful value. The railroads were affected almost immediately, and by 1930, freight traffic in Canada was the lightest in nine years, and passenger traffic had fallen to the level of 1909. The deficits of the Canadian National mounted with alarming rapidity, and even the Canadian Pacific eventually had to pass its dividends. In 1931, 161 stocks on the Canadian exchange declined $1,173,000,000; in the year following, the decline of 50 stocks was nearly five and one-half billion dollars. Tax receipts fell rapidly and Dominion and provincial budgets faced huge annual deficits. The spectre of unemployment raised its ugly head everywhere, and threw new burdens on the government in the form of unemployment and poor relief. The suffering in the agricultural west became so acute that political upheavals *The bubble bursts* of great significance occurred on the prairies; the collapse of the grain market brought suffering to thousands of farmers, and the Dominion Government found it necessary to give financial relief not only to prevent suffering, but to keep some of the provinces from defaulting on their public debts,—a policy which would have endangered the financial structure of the entire Dominion. The external trade of Canada in spite of heroic efforts to find new markets fell off rapidly in 1930 and 1931, especially with the United States. The riots staged by Communists and unemployed in Toronto and elsewhere, and the mobbing of the prime minister and the government buildings in Newfoundland early in 1932, were striking symptoms of a social disease that seemed to reach far down into the vitals of the body politic.

Session of 1930

The King Government, which for several years had been basking in the sunshine of prosperity, now felt the first blows of the financial storm, although its worst effects did not appear until the Liberal party was no longer responsible for the conduct of dominion affairs. The final session of the Sixteenth Parliament opened February 20, 1930, with the tariff the main issue, although unemployment became increasingly important as the debate progressed. For the first time in a number of years, the Liberal budget was brought down by some one other than Robb. The former minister of finance had died quite unexpectedly, and the budget of 1930 was in charge of his successor, C. A. Dunning. The proposed tariff changes called for numerous additions to the free list under British preference, increases in the duty on butter, fruits, and vegetables, upward revisions of the steel and iron schedules, and countervailing duties to be applied in identical amounts to a special list of products whenever another country imposed duties on these articles. This provision was aimed directly at the United States, whose Hawley-Smoot tariff had struck specially hard at Canadian potatoes, livestock, and other agricultural products. Bennett promptly attacked the Government's conciliatory policy toward the United States, declared the proposed protection would prove inadequate, and opposed the extension of the free list for Empire trade, pleading instead for an out-and-out policy of "Canada First." Prime Minister King replied that tariff wars were always unwise. When the prime minister announced his intention to call a general election soon after prorogation, opposition to the budget diminished, and Dunning's proposals were enacted into law.

The unemployment problem

In addition to the budget debate, there was considerable discussion of the unemployment situation. The Liberals, at the outset, opposed direct federal relief, contending that the provinces and municipalities must assume the major responsibility, and proposed unemployment insurance as the long-time solution for the problem. In the heat of the debate, the prime minister was reported to have said that his Government might be willing to contribute to the relief of several western provinces with Progressive Governments, but that not "a single cent"—or "a five-cent piece" would be contributed to a province governed by Tories. Mackenzie King denied the accuracy of the report, and rejected the implications of his words, but the "five cent speech" assumed real importance in the coming election campaign. An Order-in-Council fixing an eight-hour day for all direct employees of the Dominion government was issued before the Liberal Government left office, and several prominent Liberals, among them Rodolphe Lemieux, former speaker of the Commons, and Robert Forke, minister of immigration, retired to the Senate before the election. In preparation for the appeal to the country, fixed for July 28, 1930, a new system of registering voters in urban areas was adopted.

Late in 1929, after twenty-four years of Liberal rule, a Conservative Government had been returned in Saskatchewan. The result *Political* might have been accepted as an omen for the Dominion election of *issues* 1930, for there can be no doubt that the party in power during a depression suffers at the polls. Prime Minister King, in his first campaign speech, stated the issues to be the record of the Government, the Dunning budget, and the question of which party should represent the Dominion at the coming imperial conference. The Liberals denied responsibility for the unemployment situation, blamed Prime Minister Ferguson of Ontario for delaying the St. Lawrence waterway project, denied the implications of the "five-cent speech," and revived the old conscription issue in Quebec. Mackenzie King maintained that Bennett's plan of "blasting his way" into closed world markets with a high tariff would prove unsound and unworkable. Bennett promised new markets, favored a tariff policy based on "Canada First, then the Empire," pledged the carrying out of the St. Lawrence project, and promised a special session of Parliament to deal with unemployment which he blamed on the Liberals, although the leadership of that party had already summoned a conference on unemployment. The Conservatives also urged an old age pension system in which the federal government alone would bear the financial responsibility.

As might have been expected, relations with the United States were vehemently discussed. The Conservatives charged that a million *Canadian-* of Canada's best population had been drained off to the United States *American* in the last ten years because of the ineffectiveness of the Liberal *relations* administrations. As usual, Mackenzie King was represented as pro-American, for had he not permitted $900,000,000 worth of United States goods to be sold in Canada each year, while Canada sold less than half that amount to the United States? Bennett promised an aggressive tariff policy, not only against the United States, but one by which Canadian preference to British products would be counterbalanced by a British preference for the Dominion. The issue, according to the Conservative leader, was whether Canada would be "an annex or a country," and he promised aid to agriculture, the completion of the Hudson Bay railway, and a thorough overhauling of the transportation system of the Dominion. To the Liberal tariff slogan, "Let Uncle Sam go his own way; our way is with John Bull," the Conservatives replied with "Canada First."

Election results

The result of the campaign was a Conservative victory, which gave that party control of 136 of the 245 seats in the House of Commons. The minor parties lost heavily in this political upheaval, only the Labor party retaining its three seats. The Communist vote, in spite of hysterical predictions, proved negligible. The Liberal Government lost heavily because of the depression and a desire for change after ten years of government by that party, and even Quebec, in spite of the Laurier tradition and the scars left from the World War, gave twenty-five of its seats to the Conservatives. The result in Quebec was probably decisive. In Ontario, the Conservatives gained only six seats; on the prairies their representation rose from one to twenty-three, and in Prince Edward Island and New Brunswick the party also made gains. In British Columbia the Liberals increased their mandates from one to five. The strength of the independent group fell from 36 to 20. Five cabinet members, including Dunning and Crerar, were defeated. Robert Gardiner, the U. F. A. leader, and Henri Bourassa were returned without opposition, and Agnes Macphail retained the seat in the House of Commons which she had held since 1921.

The new government

Prime Minister Bennett announced his new Government on August 7, 1930. Besides serving as President of the Privy Council, the Conservative leader also assumed the duties of minister of finance, and secretary of state of external affairs,—a multiplicity of offices which the Liberals were quick to attack as "one-man government." Hugh Guthrie, former leader of the party, became minister of justice, Henry Stevens of British Columbia received the portfolio for trade and commerce, Dr. Robert J. Manion became the minister of railways and canals, and E. N. Rhodes, former prime minister of Nova Scotia, entered the cabinet as minister of fisheries. It was clear from the outset that the prime minister would dominate the Government, and he inaugurated his program in a vigorous and effective fashion.

Special session

True to his campaign promise, the new prime minister summoned Parliament in special session for September 8, 1930. A four-sentence speech from the throne forecast the upward revision of the tariff. During the usual sparring for political advantage Mackenzie King, as the leader of the Opposition, twitted Bennett for his shift in explaining the causes of unemployment, but the measures proposed by the Government were adopted in record time. The prime minister was eager to leave for London to attend the imperial conference and he agreed to give the Liberals full opportunity to discuss the proposed fiscal changes at the next session of Parliament.

On August 25, the Employment Service Council of Canada had outlined a complete program embracing twelve recommendations for executive and legislative action, to alleviate the effects of the growing depression. The prime minister's emergency program to deal with unemployment included an appropriation of $20,000,000 for public works, the repeal of countervailing duties, and tariff revision upward on agricultural products and a long list of key industries, and an increase from 15 to 50 percent in the anti-dumping rate. The tariff legislation authorized the reduction in rates by order-in-council whenever it could be shown that protection was being used to raise prices unfairly. Prior to the meeting of Parliament, the Government had announced the end of immigration from Europe, except in the case of experienced farmers with ample means of support, and wives and children of immigrants already in Canada. In the fall of 1930, a new immigration regulation of the United States excluding residents of Canada who had been without employment in the United States for six months or more, seriously affected commuters who had been employed in Detroit factories. There could be no question about the nature of the Conservative tariff of 1930. It was an emergency measure, and a direct answer to the Hawley-Smoot tariff of the United States. On most commodities, three levels of rates were contemplated, the first giving preference to British goods, an intermediate rate for countries with special trade agreements with the Dominion, and the highest rates for nations which had not lowered their tariff walls against Canadian goods.

Emergency measures

Almost immediately after the close of the special session of 1930, the prime minister hurried to England to attend the imperial conference. In London, Bennett played a prominent part in the proceedings, and raised a storm of debate by his startling proposals. It must be remembered that while protective tariff sentiment was growing in Great Britain, the Labor Government, with its strong free trade views, was still in power. Prime Minister Bennett proposed that all members of the British Commonwealth surround themselves with tariff walls, so that preferences could then be given to promote Empire trade. Specifically, it was suggested that after all members of the Commonwealth had enacted protective tariffs, an additional ten percent should be imposed on imports from all non-British nations. Australia, Ireland, New Zealand, and Newfoundland supported the Canadian plan, but Canada's "offer" elicited a divided response in Great Britain. The British Secretary of State for the Dominions described Bennett's "four square" "Canada First" policy as "humbug." It was obvious that no British Government including such free traders as Philip Snowden and Ramsay Macdonald could accept the Canadian proposal, and it was not until the following year, when the British Labor Government had been superseded by a National Government in which the Conservatives had an overwhelming majority, that the Bennett plan had any chance of success. The imperial conference ended with the understanding that it would meet again in Ottawa in the following summer. Mackenzie King blamed the prime

Imperial conference of 1930

minister for its failure to achieve more tangible results. In December, 1930, Lord Willingdon became viceroy of India, and the following February, the Earl of Bessborough, an Irish peer who had been a Conservative member of the English House of Commons, was appointed as the new governor-general of Canada. Vincent Massey, who had been transferred by the Liberal Government from Washington to London as High Commissioner, resigned and G. Howard Ferguson, the aggressive Conservative leader of the province of Ontario became Canada's enthusiastic representative in London.

Session of 1931

Parliament reassembled on March 12, 1931. In the debate on the address, Mackenzie King characterized Bennett's policy of "blasting a way into the markets of the world" as "coercion"; hinted that the Conservative leader apparently did not wish to deal with the British Labor Government, and had made a secret alliance with the English Tories, and blamed the prime minister for the failure of the conference. The budget for 1931 made numerous tariff revisions upward, largely on foodstuffs, and left the British preference untouched. The corporation income tax and postage rates were raised, and the rates on automobiles, magazines, and periodicals were increased, obviously as a blow at the United States. Mackenzie King denounced the tax on periodicals as "a tax upon international goodwill." Bonuses and subsidies were provided for soft coal from the western and maritime provinces, in order to reduce the reliance of Canadian industry upon coal exports from the United States. The new rates on steel and iron, construction material, and automobiles were designed to induce foreigners to establish factories in Canada, and within one year of the passage of the Hawley-Smoot tariff, the total of American branch factories in Canada reached 524, an increase of 87 in about a year. The usual provisions against dumping were enacted, and the Government was authorized to put excise taxes on any manufacturer who used the tariff to raise prices. United States exports to Canada declined over thirty percent between 1929 and 1930, and Canadian sales to the United States fell off by twenty percent in the same period. Every effort was made to stimulate trade with Europe. On November 25, 1931, the Canadian prime minister, at a dinner given in his honor by the High Commissioner in London, was served the first loaf of bread baked from wheat exported over the Hudson Bay rail and water route.

Relief legislation

On July 31, 1931, Parliament passed another unemployment and farm relief act, which conferred virtually dictatorial powers on the Government for the next nine months, and permitted it to govern in the emergency by order-in-council, "to provide employment, farm relief and preserve peace, order and good government." Before the close of the year, camps of unmarried men were organized to complete a trans-Canadian motor highway. Under the Government's public works plan, the Dominion furnished fifty percent of the costs, and expected the provinces and municipalities to furnish the rest.

In spite of these attempts to deal with the crisis, unemployment increased steadily. The National Railways were running deeper into debt, and the prime minister insisted that they had been operated during the past eight years at a total loss of $346,000,000. In spite of new taxes, the budget deficit of the Dominion was expected to reach $150,000,000. In 1931, an Ontario court outlawed the Communist party and sentenced a number of its leaders to jail sentences, and the more conservative section of the population and portions of the public press expressed fear of a great social revolution, whose signs were believed to be visible even then among the unemployed in the larger cities, and in the agricultural areas of the west. To the United Missionary Congress held in Toronto in the fall of 1931, the prime minister himself confessed his fears that "nothing but the Grace of God will save the world." Harassed by the growing world-wide depression, and the fall in the value of the Canadian dollar when Great Britain abandoned the gold standard, Bennett nevertheless refused to artificially peg agricultural prices. He was criticised frequently for not taking the press and the public into his confidence, and his reticence was compared with that of a "Tammany magistrate before a grand jury."

The growing depression

The sessions of 1931 were enlivened by the so-called Beauharnois inquiry, which promised for a time to disclose a political scandal comparable with the Canadian Pacific scandal which had driven a Conservative Government from office nearly sixty years earlier. This time the accusations were levelled mainly against the recent Liberal Government, but the issue was the same—campaign contributions by a corporation which sought government favors. Between Lake St. Francis and Lake St. Louis, the St. Lawrence, on its way through Quebec, has a fall of eighty-three feet, and as early as 1845, the old Beauharnois canal had been built to avoid the cascades in the river. In June, 1928, the Beauharnois Light, Heat and Power Company secured authorization from the legislature of Quebec to build a new power canal between these lakes with a huge electric power house at the end. A diversion of one-fifth of the normal river-flow was granted for power purposes. Application for a permit had to be made by the company to the Ottawa Government also, because the navigation rights of the river were under dominion control. The negotiations with the federal government dragged on, and numerous protests were filed against the request of the company, on the ground that the project would interfere with the proposed St. Lawrence waterway, and render the navigation rights of the river dependent on a private power group. The president of the Beauharnois Company gave assurances that there would be no interference with navigation, that one half of the power output would be sold to Ontario, and none to the United States. The Montreal power interests and shipping companies vigorously opposed the plan, but in 1929, after modifica-

The Beauharnois project

tions suggested by government engineers had been accepted, and with the understanding that the development would become the property of the Dominion if the canal should be used as part of a greater St. Lawrence shipway, the federal government gave its consent to the project.

In 1930, and again in May, 1931, Robert Gardiner, chairman of the United Farmers of Alberta group, and a member of the House of Commons from Acadia, Alberta, fired several oratorical broadsides against the Beauharnois Company, and the prime minister consented to the appointment of an investigating committee, consisting of five Conservatives, three Liberals and one Progressive. Both the prime minister and the leader of the opposition argued that the investigation was not of urgent public importance, but both voted to create the committee. After a long, exciting and dramatic inquiry, data were brought to light, which greatly embarrassed the Liberals, but which also raised enough suspicion about certain Conservatives to bring the investigation to a rather sudden end. The vice-president and general manager of the Beauharnois Power Corporation had been deputy minister of railways and canals at the time the King Government issued its order-in-council authorizing the project. A Liberal Senator, reputed to be a close friend of the former prime minister, president of the Montreal Harbor Commissioners and a member of the St. Lawrence Waterways Committee, had become chairman of the power company, and had received cash and stocks in the new enterprise. The president of the company, it was revealed, had made campaign contributions estimated variously from $864,000 to $954,000; $300,000 was taken from company funds, and the rest had been raised by him personally. The contributions to the Liberal party totalled between $600,000 and $700,000, had been paid to two Liberal senators, and some funds had gone to the Liberal party in Quebec. With reference to contributions to the Conservative party, the memory of the witness proved hazy, although he admitted small contributions to that party, and there was at least a suspicion that $125,000 had gone into the coffers of the Conservative party in Ontario. The law firm of one of the senators involved had received a substantial retainer from the company, and the promoters of the enterprise were said to have pocketed a cash profit of $2,189,000 and a million shares of Class A common stock, all from money borrowed by the company through its sale of bonds. The facts seemed to indicate that the entire development was based on borrowed money, while an inner ring of promoters were reaping rich rewards. There were securities outstanding totalling well over $300,000,000 to develop a project which would cost about one-sixth that amount. The only immediately tangible asset of the company was a contract with the Ontario Hydroelectric Commission for 250,000 horsepower. The prime minister insisted that his party had refused a $200,000 campaign contribution from the company on his instructions, but the Liberals hoped, by pressing the inquiry farther, to unearth evidence of contributions to the Ontario Conservatives.

Mackenzie King insisted that the whole matter was an affair of the province of Quebec primarily, and that it was his job as Liberal leader to define the policy of his party, but not to assume responsibility for the details of the financing of a political campaign. He demanded the appointment of a Royal Commission of three members, one Judge to be selected by the Liberals, one by the Conservatives, and the third by the Independent group, to investigate the origin of party funds in the last three elections. When the prime minister refused to accept this proposal it was easy to conclude that the Conservatives, having derived enough political capital from the investigation to seriously embarrass the opposition, did not wish to carry the inquiry any further. In the end, the Senate, probably prodded to action by Arthur Meighen, who had entered the upper chamber as Government leader, censured two of the senators involved in the scandal; one of the accused resigned, and another, who was ill, was expected to vacate his seat by the customary method of nonattendance. It was clear that the Conservatives had resolved not to let the Beauharnois project fail, and eventually, it was continued, under new guarantees and restrictions imposed by the government. *The outcome*

The 1932 session of Parliament assembled with little evidence of improvement in the economic status of the Dominion. A loan of approximately $220,000,000 had to be floated to provide for unemployment relief, the continuation of a public works program, and to assist some of the western provinces in meeting their financial obligations. The fact that the bond issue was floated in Canada and oversubscribed, afforded some basis for encouragement. Salary cuts were imposed on the civil service and on large groups of government officials, and wages generally continued to decline, and unemployment to increase. By restricting imports, the Government had created a small "favorable" balance in trade, but nevertheless found it necessary to virtually impose a gold embargo. The value of Canada's international trade decreased from $2,505,000 in 1929 to $1,245,-000,000 in 1931. *Business conditions*

The budget for 1932, prepared by Edgar N. Rhodes, who had recently become minister of finance, provided for an increase in the sales tax to six percent, additions to the excises, "nuisance taxes" and income taxes, and revived some of the old war taxes, but made no major changes in the tariff. Mackenzie King denounced economic nationalism, blamed the Government's tariff policy for the increase in unemployment, and maintained that the favorable trade balance had been achieved only by drastic cutting of imports. The Liberal leader also objected to what he called the "blank check" granted the Government by invoking the closure rule on parliamentary debate. and authorizing the expenditure of an unspecified amount *Budget of 1932* for unemployment relief during the next few months. Although expressing his willingness to vote for a bill for any amount the Government might request, the Liberal leader raised serious constitutional objections to a procedure which gave the Government the authority to spend public funds without specific appropriation by Parliament, and he denounced the practice as dangerous to the whole theory of responsible government.

Radio

In 1932, the Bennett Government also secured the adoption of a bill creating a Canadian Radio Broadcasting Commission, to consist of three members, whose duty it was to gradually build up a national monopoly of broadcasting, by acquiring private stations and collecting a fee of two dollars on every receiving set in the Dominion. Advertising matter should not exceed five percent of the program time. One factor which greatly influenced this decision to establish a government radio monopoly undoubtedly was the offensive nature of many broadcasts that came from the United States.

Railway reorganization

In the fall of 1932, a drastic reorganization of the Canadian railways was undertaken. Most private and government roads were in dire distress because of the continued depression, and immediate relief seemed imperative. Sir Henry Thornton resigned as president of the Canadian National, and a Royal Commission on Canadian Transportation, in a report filed May 20, 1932, recommended that the government roads and the financially embarrassed Canadian Pacific Railway should retain their separate identities, but that immediate steps be taken to compel the elimination of competition and duplication of service between them. In addition to recommending economies, salary cuts, stricter control of expense accounts, and a strict limitation of further capital expenditures, the Commission proposed that the government-owned roads be put under the control of three trustees, appointed for seven-year terms, and that an arbitral tribunal be created to supervise the joint use of terminals, tracks, and the pooling of freight and passenger traffic by the government and privately owned lines. The report of the Commission left no doubt about the critical situation in which all the roads found themselves, and urged a reduction in their bloated capital structure. It was especially emphasized that hereafter the trustees of the Canadian National should spend only what Parliament had appropriated, and that the system must go to Parliament to meet deficits, instead of following the older practice of issuing new bonds. The Commission also pointed out that "political considerations (had) led to unwise and unnecessary capital expenditures." Prime Minister Bennett promised prompt action, and in October, 1932, instead of presenting a Government measure, he laid the bill implementing the report of the Commission on the table of both houses, and invited free discussion and amendment, regardless of party lines.

Overshadowing all other events of the year, was the Ottawa Conference, held in the Dominion capital in July and August of 1932.

In origin, it was the postponed meeting of the economic section of the Imperial Conference of 1930, but in the months that had elapsed, *Empire* the Macdonald Labor Government in London had given way to a *trade* National Government. That Government in February, 1932, had passed the Imports Duties Act imposing a ten percent duty on many articles imported by Great Britain, and granting an exemption to all the dominions from this general tax. The problems confronting the statesmen who assembled at Ottawa were legion. All agreed that preferred markets for their products must be obtained, but none wanted to curtail the volume of their world trade. The many conflicting interests of the dominions and the mother-country quickly came to light, especially since two-thirds of England's exports went to countries outside the Empire. England, as the greatest shipowner and international banker with long-term investments in various parts of the world, could hardly jeopardize these vast interests in return for a more or less uncertain intra-Empire trade, nor could the cost of living of her people be raised simply to satisfy the trade demands of the dominions. The dominions wanted preference for their foodstuffs in the markets of the mother-country; Great Britain wanted an outlet for her manufactured goods, but the dominions insisted on protecting their infant industries.

After the ceremonies at the opening of the conference were concluded, Canada asked for preference in the British market for her *The Ottawa* lumber, wheat, bacon, cheese, and butter, but offered only partial *Conference* preference to British textiles and steel products, and none at all for boots and shoes. Great Britain sought a general lowering of tariffs throughout the Empire. Canada wanted to base preferential treatment on a general raising of the tariff on the products of foreign nations. The Dominion was particularly concerned with stopping the alleged "dumping" of Russian lumber in Great Britain. Sharp discussions arose over conflicting interests, and Prime Minister Bennett was criticised for assuming too domineering and overbearing an attitude, although it must be admitted that he worked with unusual persistence for the attainment of his objectives.

Nine countries participated in the Ottawa Conference, and in the end not one all-inclusive agreement was signed, but twelve separate *The* trade treaties, most of them bilateral. The question of setting up *Ottawa* an Empire bank and an equalized currency was found too difficult *pacts* to handle, and was buried by reference to a committee. It is impossible to give more than a general impression of the nature of the many trade agreements signed at Ottawa, for they involve hundreds of details. Perhaps the most significant result of the negotiations was the agreement of the British Government to continue for five years the provisions of the tariff act of 1932 by which most dominion goods entered Great Britain duty free, thus enjoying on many imports a ten percent preference over foreign nations. The principal products of Canada accorded preferential treatment included wheat, butter, cheese, certain fruits, eggs, poultry and condensed milk, copper, zinc and lead, cattle, meat, and tobacco. The preference for these articles was guaranteed for a definite period only in certain cases, and was subject to the proviso that the dominions could furnish enough of these products at world prices to satisfy the British demand. In return for these concessions, Canada granted free or preferential entry to a list of about two hundred British manufactured products, although in most cases, the preference to Great Britain was given by first raising the Canadian tariff on these imports from foreign countries. Canada also obtained a concession which allowed the Dominion, in fixing its tariff rates, to take into consideration the status of her "infant industries" and the lower labor costs prevailing in England. A Canadian Tariff Commission was to determine such controversial questions, but much to the dissatisfaction of the British, the Commission did not actually begin its hearings until July, 1933. It was the duty of this panel of experts to see that protective duties imposed by Canada did not exceed a level which would give producers in the United Kingdom full opportunity for reasonable competition on the basis of relative costs.

Canadian reaction to Ottawa pacts

The Ottawa trade pacts were vehemently debated in the Dominion Parliament in the fall of 1932. Some independent papers, like the *Toronto Globe*, urged support of the agreements as a way out of the depression. Mackenzie King announced his readiness to accept the treaties as a political campaign issue, and criticised the agreements because they raised Canadian duties, granted only slight concessions to the mother-country, tied the hands of Canada as far as world trade was concerned, and made more difficult a tariff *rapprochement* with the United States. The latter result was especially stressed because unless Canada could exchange its goods freely with its southern neighbor, the Dominion would have to meet its heavy financial obligations to the United States by an increasing drain on its gold supply. Many Dominion manufacturers and the lumber interests were left unsatisfied by the Ottawa agreements, and the attitude of the farmers of the west might be described as lukewarm and skeptical. On the surface, at least, the Ottawa pacts suggested a step toward "Empire free trade." The tendency henceforth may be either to raise or lower the tariff levels of all the members of the Commonwealth.

The St. Lawrence waterway

In the same year that Canada played such a leading rôle in the negotiation of new Empire trade agreements, the long negotiations with the United States over the development of the St. Lawrence waterway finally reached the stage of signing a formal treaty. Negotiations had been begun by the preceding Liberal administration, but little headway was made until the spring of 1932.

There was a sharp division of opinion in both the United States and Canada as to the feasibility and desirability of a waterways development that would eventually make the lake ports on the upper lakes accessible to ocean-going vessels. Quebec opposed the proposal, Ontario favored it. In the United States, the western states were seriously interested in the project, while New York feared the loss of her favored position in handling the export products of the inland region. Proposals for a vast electric power development in connection with the improvement of the waterway further complicated the problem. New York State challenged the proposals of the United States federal government, while in Canada the whole matter of whether the provinces or the dominion government had jurisdiction over electric and water power had been referred to the Canadian Supreme Court for decision, with unsatisfactory results. There was much sentiment in Canada in favor of "keeping the St. Lawrence Canadian," and the business interests of Montreal put up a vigorous fight to keep that city "at the head of navigation." The railways feared the ruinous competition of the new water route. Quebec objected to the cost of the project and insisted that her resources were ample for years to come to satisfy the hydro-electric needs of that section of the Dominion. In spite of discussions of this kind on both sides of the international line, the St. Lawrence Deep Waterway Treaty was signed in Washington, July 18, 1932, by the American Secretary of State and W. D. Herridge, the new Canadian minister to the United States.

The treaty contained ten articles. It contemplated a channel of not less than 27 feet from the Great Lakes to the Atlantic, probably *Terms of* adequate to enable ninety percent of all sea-going vessels to pass *treaty* through the Great Lakes to ports like Chicago, Port Arthur, and Duluth. In the International Rapids section of the St. Lawrence, the work was to be carried out as a joint undertaking of the United States and the Canadian governments, under the supervision of a commission of five from each country, and with the United States providing the funds. Each nation agreed to construct the canal and locks in its own territory, and to use its own engineers, labor, and material on its side of the boundary. Each nation agreed to build its own power house equipment to generate electric power, and it was stipulated that the quantity of water diverted for this purpose was not to exceed one-half the available river flow. Neither country was to exercise proprietary rights or jurisdiction in the territory of the other. Canada agreed to complete the waterway through Quebec, and to widen and deepen the canals around the Lachine and Soulange Rapids; the United States was to deepen the existing channels above Lake Erie, and connecting the upper lakes. The estimated cost, not including power house machinery and equipment, has been stated at nearly $550,000,000. A credit deduction of $128,000,000 was given to Canada for the Welland Canal, and the Dominion was also to receive $67,202,500 from Ontario for 1,100,000 horsepower, thus leaving the net cost to Canada at a figure considerably below the estimated expenditures of the United States. Prime Minister Taschereau promptly denounced the treaty as "a national crime," but Ontario and the west favored it. It was agreed that the treaty should be submitted to the Ottawa Parliament for ratification after it had been approved by the United States government. To date the United States Senate has not ratified the agreement.

Budget of 1933

The budget of 1933 revealed no encouraging figures which might indicate that the Dominion was emerging from the depression. Huge deficits continued to accumulate, and the minister of finance proposed further increases in the corporation, income, and internal taxes. A few tariff reductions were made, but not enough to make any substantial breach in the tariff wall. The index of employment and trade continued to fall early in 1933; the western provinces, the gigantic newsprint business, and the railways were in dire distress, and the Government suddenly became more enthusiastic for coöperation with other nations in bringing about an international recovery. On February 20, 1933, the prime minister unexpectedly intimated that his Government would welcome a reciprocal trade treaty with the United States; and the newly elected Democratic President of the United States, Franklin D. Roosevelt, seemed at least in the early months of his administration, to favor a policy of "reciprocal trade treaties." Although there were some preliminary exchanges of views between Washington and Ottawa, nothing came of the proposal. Canada looked toward the World Economic Conference held in London in June to furnish a check to a growingly destructive and worldwide program of economic nationalism, but this conference also ended in disappointment. Meanwhile, the United States became so engrossed in the improvement of business conditions shortly after the inauguration of the administration's "New Deal," that the United States devoted all its energies to questions of internal policy.

Agrarian unrest

In the meantime, and as a result of the acute suffering in the industrial cities, and more especially, in the agricultural west, a new, radical political group, which caused no little anxiety to the leaders of the major parties, was emerging. For several years before 1933, the farmer's coöperatives had been organizing for a new social order, and insisting that coöperation was impossible under the present capitalistic competitive system. In the parliamentary session of 1932, there was evidence of a growing coöperation between the agrarian and labor groups. The leader of the U. F. A. group demanded nationalization of the banks, currency inflation to raise price levels, and taxes which would prohibit incomes above $25,000 a year. Although the group got little comfort from either Bennett or Mackenzie King, the former accused the latter of flirting with J. S. Woodsworth, the labor leader in parliament, and of pleading with him to remember the Liberals "when thou comest into thy kingdom."

Conditions in west

Conditions in the west grew steadily worse in 1932. Manitoba was suffering acutely from drouth and unemployment, and from a serious derangement of provincial and municipal finances. The

United Farmers of Manitoba, in 1931, declared that social ownership and coöperative, non-profit production was the only basis for
a sound economic order, favored nationalization of all utilities and
natural resources, and urged the establishment of a coöperative
commonwealth. In Saskatchewan, 100,000 people were being fed
by the government, and 150,000 head of live-stock had to be moved
to more fertile areas. At meetings of farm leaders of the province,
a new "Charter of Liberty" was drafted, and a petition was addressed
to Prime Minister Bennett, reviewing the farmer's plight, and threatening to organize "for the political conquest of this Province along
with such other provinces as will join us for the purpose of forming
a coöperative commonwealth within the British Empire, trading
directly with Great Britain on a free trade and barter basis." In 1932,
Prime Minister John Bracken of Manitoba proposed a union of his
province with Alberta and Saskatchewan into a single administrative
unit in order to reduce expenses, and on several occasions, the federal
treasury had to come to the relief of the four western provinces to
meet interest and principal of their maturing obligations. A moratorium on mortgages was declared in many parts of the west.

Suffering and unrest led the farmer and the worker to seek new
panaceas in the field of political and economic experimentation. *The*
The Saskatchewan section of the United Farmers of Canada entered *C. C. F.*
into a pact with the Independent Labor Party of the Dominion to
enter politics on a platform of a "coöperative commonwealth,"
similar to the one already agreed to by some of the farmer's organizations in Alberta and Manitoba, and in Alberta, the "Coöperative
Commonwealth Federation" was launched as a new federal party.
It sought to unite labor and agriculture on a program of state socialism. The C. C. F., with J. S. Woodsworth as its outstanding leader,
made such rapid progress that the major parties soon considered it
worthy of serious attention. Both the Liberal and Conservative
leaders trained their heaviest oratorical guns on the radicals who
threatened once again to destroy the two-party system of the Dominion. Ernest Lapointe, former Liberal minister of justice, hastened to
assure his Quebec followers that there was a vast difference between
liberalism and "socialism and communism," and on July 6, 1933, the
solicitor-general of the Bennett Government announced that the
"next election will be a battle between the forces of law and order
and subversive elements of political, economic, and socialistic disorder." He referred to a "Woodsworth dictatorship," akin to communism, implied that the C. C. F. meant "revolution and the overthrow of our institutions," and called upon the Conservative party
to stand as the last remaining bulwark against the mounting tide
of radicalism.

The first national convention of the C. C. F., held in July, 1933,
in Regina, issued a manifesto containing the following outstanding *National*
demands,—socialization of all financial machinery, industries and *convention*

services essential to a socialized economic order; security of tenure for farmers and progressive removal of their debts; the regulation of imports and exports by a national board; a national labor code, publicly organized health, hospital, and medical services, the promotion of peace and international economic coöperation, and a new program of taxation to remove inequalities and raise funds for the socialization of industry. The C. C. F. convention is the first political gathering, national in scope, which was called for the purpose of fundamentally changing the present economic system of the Dominion. That the new radical party is attracting much attention in Canadian political circles cannot be denied. Its future will probably depend on how soon the Dominion emerges from the depression.

The first faltering signs of returning prosperity in Canada seemed to appear in the summer months of 1933, and coupled with a spectacular and sudden business revival in the United States, gave new hope to the people of the Dominion. Wholesale prices were rising, wheat was selling at a higher level, car loading and canal traffic seemed to reveal a revival of business activity, stock market buying was beginning again, and bank clearings showed substantial gains. The closing weeks of the parliamentary session of 1933 may be described as a period of marking time to see whether the corner of the depression had really been turned.

In the last four years the Dominion has passed through an economic crisis and a financial storm unprecedented in all its history. Although there has been much disagreement among Canadians about the proper methods of dealing with the emergency, few have lost confidence in the destiny of the Dominion and their faith in a great, happy, and prosperous future has remained unshaken.

SELECTED BIBLIOGRAPHY FOR CHAPTER XXXII

In addition to the volumes of *The Canadian Annual Review of Public Affairs*, consult the guides to periodical literature and the files of leading Canadian dailies.

For the Ottawa Conference, the following articles are especially useful,—H. V. Hodson, "Before Ottawa," in *Foreign Affairs*, July, 1932, pp. 589-599, and J. M. Macdonnell, "After the Ottawa Conference," in the same periodical, for January, 1933, pp. 331-346. A series of articles by J. Bartlett Brebner, on "British Imperial Issues at Ottawa," "The Imperial Conference at Ottawa," and "Imperial Conference Results," appeared in *The New York Times Current History*, July, 1932, pp. 423-428; Sept., 1932, pp. 729-730; and Oct., 1932, pp. 57-62. A succinct statement of the results of the conference appeared in *Foreign Policy Bulletin* (New York), vol. XI, No. 43.

CHAPTER XXXIII

BATTLING THE DEPRESSION

AFTER four years of depression, there could no longer be much doubt that the crash of 1929 had precipitated an economic collapse of *Continued* such unusual magnitude as to raise serious questions about the future *depression* of capitalism and the so-called American system of free enterprise. The depression was a profound challenge to nations like Canada and the United States, whose industrialism was protected by high tariffs, but whose agriculture depended upon world markets. In both nations, economic problems raised constitutional issues of great significance. In Canada, controversies and deadlocks over the constitutional powers of the Dominion and the provinces seriously affected many attempts to deal with the economic disaster which had overwhelmed the Dominion.

A careful analysis of Canadian society revealed that in spite of several decades of significant industrial progress, farmers still con- *National* stituted the largest occupational group in the population. Business *Income* still was being carried on predominantly in small units, although large factories, equalling one sixth of the total number of production units, were producing over half of the gross output. By 1940, about 55% of the Canadian population was urban. In Ontario, the percentage was 61%; in New Brunswick it was half that size. The depression started a new flight from the town to the farm. It was discomforting and disturbing to learn that in 1931, one half of all the breadwinners of Canada earned between $500 and $1500 a year; that two thirds of all married men employees got not more than $1200 a year; and that over 40% of this group were actually earning less than ten dollars a week. The number of family men who received over $3000 a year was less than 5% of the total. Nearly half of the farmers of Canada had a revenue less than what is required for a reasonable standard of living, and between 35,000 and 53,500 were on relief during the depression years. That these conditions involved a marked decline in farm ownership and an increase in tenant farming is obvious. At the beginning of the 1930's, the average Canadian skilled steel worker had an annual income of $1037. Workers in the building trades earned $960, and in the clothing business, $878. The average salary for women in professional work was $1100. Only 12,000 people had incomes at or above $10,000, and the number of really wealthy families was extremely small. According to generally accepted figures, the minimum living income for the average Canadian family, judged by urban standards, was $1040 in 1930–31. Thus, the so-called Canadian standard of living was unattainable save by a minority of the Canadian people.

Equally disturbing were certain observations concerning the youth of Canada. Two thirds of each year's crop of young men were without occupation during the depression years, and all non-farm boys had to expect two years of idleness on the average before they could hope for satisfactory employment. Youth training projects were organized in British Columbia and elsewhere, and a National Forestry Program, which had many features in common with the Civilian Conservation Corps in the United States, was inaugurated to deal with projects of reforestation, soil conservation, and the construction of highways and airports, projects especially designed to furnish employment for unmarried men. The government also sponsored a farm resettlement program. Unskilled workers were of course affected most by the depression, and thousands of the elderly became unemployable during the decade of the 1930's. It was estimated that three fourths of those on the relief rolls would probably become chronic indigents. At the beginning of 1933, the Minister of Labor reported 1,357,562 on relief. The problem of the transient, migratory worker, so effectively dramatized for the United States by Steinbeck's *Grapes of Wrath*, was not unknown in the Canadian West, and four of the western provinces organized camps to take care of these homeless, drifting wanderers. Occupants of labor camps received twenty cents a day pocket money besides their board and lodging.

It became apparent that Canadian society was being sharply divided between the "haves" and the "have nots." Federal deficits continued to mount, and refunding operations and the floating of new loans became a regular part of depression financing. By the fall of 1934, the rate of recovery from the depression was actually slowing down again and droughts and duststorms in the West added to the terrific debt burden which weighed down the farmers. By the end of 1934, 1,207,345 Canadians were either on direct or drought relief, or in labor camps. The capital goods industries apparently were not expanding either, except under the artificial stimulus of costly public works programs. Many municipalities were in dire distress, as several conferences of mayors made abundantly clear. The Mayor of Vancouver suggested going into bankruptcy as the best way to lift the staggering debt and relief burden. Prices were still declining; agriculture and the newsprint industry seemed sick past the hope of recovery, and many leading business concerns, including the Canadian Pacific Railway, passed their dividends. Only the Canadian banks, in vivid contrast with the banking crisis in the United States, remained stable and sound. Strikes in the labor camps of British Columbia forecast serious breaches of law and order, and groups of the discontented began a march from Vancouver on Ottawa in the summer of 1935, clashing with the police along the way at Regina. Canadians were alarmed by accounts appearing in the public press about subversive, alien and Communist activities.

During these perilous years, Canada anxiously watched the experience of Great Britain, and more particularly, of the United States, *Financial* under the recovery program advocated by President Roosevelt as *policy* "The New Deal." Indeed, portions of the Canadian lumber and newsprint industry were so closely integrated with United States business that they were informally under the codes of the American National Industrial Recovery Act, and their employees demanded a revision of wages in accordance with the scale agreed upon across the boundary. Canadians remained somewhat confused by the New Deal, which seemed to be riding off in all directions at once, in search of both recovery and reform, and they could not be quite sure whether Canada could afford to initiate such economic experimentation with profit to the Dominion, whose economy was so largely dependent on export markets. As Professor Brebner pointed out, Canada, being on the periphery of both North American and British Imperial affairs, is never quite a free agent, and is likely to experience a time-lag in working out her policy in any given emergency. For four years, following the crash of 1929, the Canadian government had been content to wait and profit by the experiences of the United States and Great Britain. Canadian exchange is always at the mercy of the United States and the mother country, so Canada had followed both off the gold standard, hitching "the Canadian car to the Roosevelt engine" in this respect. Prime Minister Bennett, though forced to favor a policy of "easy money" by means of bank loans and the issuance of bank notes, successfully resisted several proposals made in the House of Commons to inflate the currency, and announced that the Government would maintain the proper legal coverage. Fortunately, Canadian banks and insurance companies remained solvent. Dominion financing could therefore be directed toward helping the provinces and municipalities to carry their relief burdens, and bolstering up the railways. Millions were spent directly by the federal government on a Trans-Canada Highway, and other public works. More millions were contributed by the Dominion treasury to help pay the cost of public works by municipal and provincial governments. To the former, the federal government contributed from 25% of the cost in the eastern provinces to 50% of the cost in the west; and in the case of provincial enterprises, the federal government usually paid half the cost. But no amount of pump-priming seemed to be able to start the usual flow of credit. As public credit was expanded, bank loans contracted. The efforts of the government were supplemented by nationwide appeals for relief funds to be administered by the Red Cross.

When Parliament convened in January, 1934, Mr. Bennett gave no evidence that he had decided upon more drastic and unprecedented measures to end the continuing depression. The speech from the throne by the Earl of Bessborough promised additional public works, with and without provincial and local participation, more direct relief for unemployment, a central bank, an agricultural marketing board, revisions in the Companies Act to provide more effective control over corporations, and the usual promise of cuts in operating expenses. A loan of £10,000,000 was floated in London. The budget, prepared by the Minister of Finance, E. N. Rhodes, contained no novelties of any great significance, as far as internal and customs taxes were concerned, with the exception of a 10% tax to be imposed on the gold production of Canada. To this proposal, the mining companies strenuously objected. The annual budget deficit seemed to be a little smaller and the Government continued to rely on low rate borrowing.

The usual relief bills were passed during the session. Increased credits were provided for the farmers, and legislation was enacted to facilitate compromise agreements between the farmers and their creditors in the matter of their indebtedness. The leader of the Opposition attacked a $40,000,000 appropriation for public works as a brazen attempt to influence the results in the next general election. Although business statistics rose slowly in the summer of 1934, strikes and labor disturbances continued, and agriculture remained in a desperate state in spite of the passage of a Natural Products Marketing Act, which contained some of the features of President Roosevelt's program for recovery among the farmers, and some features borrowed from Great Britain. The act provided for the creation of marketing boards with power to regulate exports, imports and price spreads. It had the support of the C.C.F., but it was opposed by the Liberals, who had recently derived much encouragement from the results of by-elections held in Nova Scotia, Ontario and British Columbia.

Convinced at last of the need for a more radical approach to Canada's economic problems, the House of Commons, in February, 1934, launched an exhaustive investigation of price spreads, mass buying, the operation of chain and department stores, the marketing of live-stock and farm products, wages and labor conditions. Under the stimulus of Henry H. Stevens, Minister of Trade and Commerce, who served as chairman of the investigating commission, a whole year was spent in hearings and publicity. The investigation uncovered some scandalous abuses, including sweatshop conditions in certain Canadian industries, as well as other unethical business practices. Conditions seemed to be especially shocking in the larger cities like Toronto and Montreal. Employees in the needle trades were earning from four dollars to nine dollars a week. In Montreal, girls were receiving as little as two dollars a week; a Montreal biscuit factory was paying wages ranging from five to eleven cents an hour; girls in a shoe factory in rural Quebec received a dollar and a half for a seventy-five hour week. Certain chain and department stores were

among the worst offenders, and the minimum wage laws were frequently ignored or flouted.

Eventually, the Price Spreads Commission reported in favor of a
Federal Trade and Industry Commission, with power to supervise   *The Stevens*
business practices and repress unfair methods, but months before these   *Report*
recommendations were submitted, the findings of the Commission had
become a matter of public knowledge and serious and bitter party
controversy. A speech made by Mr. Stevens at a private meeting of a
study club of some forty Conservative members of Parliament was
published in pamphlet form. In this pamphlet, Mr. Stevens denounced
Canadian business practices in unrestrained terms, and maintained
that "unscrupulous financiers and business men had exploited Canada's consuming public, starved her producers, sweated her workmen,
'gouged' her pulp and paper and other industries and had left the
country faced with a choice of reform, dictatorship or revolution."
Whether the Minister of Trade and Commerce had spilled the apple
cart in all innocence, or whether he had perpetrated a calculated indis-
cretion, is of no great importance now. He had exploded a bombshell
which amounted to an indictment of the whole Canadian capitalist
system, and his findings did not spare some of the Prime Minister's
friends and business associates.

Apparently, the pamphlet was suppressed for a time and Canadian
papers gave the incident no publicity until the *New York Times* reported   *A party*
it on August 4. Three days later, the material was published by   *controversy*
The Winnipeg Free Press. Mr. Stevens had acted without informing his
Cabinet colleagues, and there were immediate demands for his resignation and hints of impending libel suits. Mr. Stevens started on a
speaking tour to British Columbia, taking two thousand copies of the
controversial document with him. Mr. Bennett suppressed all copies
in the Ottawa area, and telephoned his recalcitrant minister in Winnipeg. The latter expressed his regrets for publishing the material, and
denied any desire to bolt the Conservative party. The embarrassment
to the government mounted as the newspapers continued to publish
summaries of Mr. Stevens' charges. Finally, after an exchange of
letters with the Prime Minister, Mr. Stevens resigned from the
Cabinet on October 26, 1934. He continued to serve on the investigating commission, and he carried his speaking crusade into all parts
of the Dominion. The Liberal Opposition sat quietly by and watched
the growing dissension in the Conservative ranks. In June, 1934, the
Liberals had won sixty-six of the ninety provincial seats in Ontario,
and in Saskatchewan they made almost a clean sweep of the election,
save for five seats won by the C.C.F.

It was becoming evident that more drastic measures were needed
to bring Canada back to prosperity, and that the Dominion could no   *Evolving a*
longer wait for a more normal return to good times. The Liberals,   *new policy*
not charged for the moment with direct responsibility, continued

officially to espouse their traditional doctrines of laissez-faire individualism, and waited with great optimism for the next general election. Prime Minister Bennett had always been a conservative individ-
ualist and a staunch defender of the capitalist system of free enterprise.
But he was honest and frank, sincerely devoted to his country's welfare, and bold enough to assume personal responsibility for a new
course of action whenever more conservative and traditional palli-
atives proved inadequate. As early as the fall of 1933, the Prime
Minister had said in Toronto that the alternative to Conservatism was
Socialism or Communism. In May, 1934, in an address before the
Royal Empire Society in Montreal, he had referred to the many experiments going on in the United States, and the "explosive material
nearby." Undoubtedly, he was greatly influenced by his brother-in-
law, Mr. W. D. Herridge, who, as minister to Washington, could
observe the "New Deal" of President Roosevelt at first hand. By the
end of 1934, stronger phraseology began to appear in the Prime
Minister's public addresses. "The day of the robber barons is over,"
he said. "The policy of laissez-faire is no longer sufficient." Two years
later, when Mr. Herridge was openly credited with co-authorship of
Mr. Bennett's "New Deal," he expressed the new attitude as follows:
"This is the end of an economic era. Capitalism will never again work
in the old way. The only system which can work hereafter is the
system controlled and guided by the state."

Announcing
the New Deal

Mr. Bennett decided to expand state control over economic enterprise in the hope that government regulation would end the inequalities and injustices of the present social order. Early in 1935, in a series
of radio addresses, the Prime Minister announced his intentions to the
Canadian electorate, and asserted that "if we cannot abolish the dole,
we should abolish the system." Thereafter, Mr. Bennett became
steadily more radical and Mr. King more conservative. The Prime
Minister boldly proclaimed a war on avaricious and unscrupulous
promoters, denounced the evils of stock-watering and unfair
business practices, accused the Liberals of becoming Tories under
Mackenzie King, and predicted that the continuance of laissez-faire
methods would lead only to fascism. He advocated a national economic council for Canada to be charged with making plans for a more
perfect social justice.

Party
controversy

The Canadian Parliament, by almost unanimous vote, but only
after considerable wrangling, enacted the Prime Minister's program
of reform in the spring of 1935. The Liberals refused to oppose the
"New Deal" openly, but insisted that most of it was unconstitutional.
Mackenzie King demanded an election and exposed the schism in the
Conservative ranks by goading Mr. Stevens into further indiscretions
about the alleged insincerity of his former Cabinet colleagues in
matters of reform. Mr. Bennett's illness early in 1935 slowed down the
tempo of legislation somewhat, and the House leadership had to be

left temporarily in the hands of Sir George Perley. During the Prime Minister's absence in Great Britain, where he attended His Majesty's Silver Jubilee, the Liberal leadership attacked Mr. Bennett for alleged entangling commitments to England, although the Prime Minister had left the conference before the important discussions of imperial defence had begun. Mackenzie King extolled the Canadian constitution and provincial rights, predicted that the courts would throw out most of the Bennett legislation, accused the Conservatives of "calculated unconstitutionality," and insisted that their policy of regimentation would lead to fascism. But the Liberal leadership had no counter proposals to make. Obviously, they could not very well attack the purpose of the Bennett reforms.

The Bennett program may be described in terms of eight legislative acts which were intended to implement the findings of the Price *The Bennett* Spreads Commission, and repair the economic structure of the Do- *program* minion along lines of greater social justice and a better distribution of the national income. The program, expressed in simple terms, provided for a wages and hours law which would strike at child labor and establish the eight hour day and forty-eight hour week, with one day of rest in seven. It sought to establish minimum wages, a scheme of unemployment and social insurance, and a national employment service, with an Employment and Social Insurance Commission to administer the program. Unemployment insurance was fixed at the moderate rate of six dollars a week, after workers had contributed twenty-five cents a week for forty weeks. Employers were to contribute a like amount, and the federal government would add its quota also. The system was carefully protected against having to pay strike benefits; the duration of payments was strictly limited, and government employees, workers with an income over two thousand dollars a year, and the normal victims of seasonal unemployment were ineligible altogether.

The Natural Products Marketing Act and the Farmers' Creditors Arrangement Act, though passed in the preceding year, were amended *Agriculture* in important details. Under the former, producers could apply for *and industry* market controls. Under the latter, direct settlements could be made to alleviate the debt burden on farmers, or the matter could be referred to a board of review for arbitration. The act really was an agricultural bankruptcy act, and in some of its details like the Frazier-Lemke Act which had passed the United States Congress. A Dominion Trade and Industry Commission was provided as a central, governmental agency to regulate and control trusts and monopolies, strike at unfair business practices, and help adjust existing merchandizing procedures to the new standards of trade and production. The Criminal Code was amended to strike at false advertising, to deal with employers who paid less than the minimum wage, and to provide for the prosecution of business men guilty of unfair practices and "chiseling" against established good business standards. The Companies Act Amendment of 1935 was devised to eliminate speculative, "high finance" features in business and industry. It dealt with the structure of corporations, the rights of directors and officials, and was designed to compel public statements which would show the company's solvency. The Canadian Wheat Board Act created a board empowered to take over the grain elevators, control export marketing, and fix the buying and selling price. The carry-over of wheat from earlier years amounted at that time to the staggering total of 225,000,000 bushels. It was destined to go much higher. In addition to these measures, relief legislation, public works, a bill to assist in the development of a housing program, and a bill providing long-term credit for distressed fishermen, were enacted in 1935. Legislation also was passed to rehabilitate the areas of the prairie provinces which had suffered from drought and soil erosion. Preliminary soundings were made in Washington for a new reciprocity agreement. The budget of 1935 contained slight changes in the tariff, and in income and excise taxes, raised the corporation income tax one per cent, and also increased the surtaxes on the higher individual incomes. Finally, a National Economic Council was created. It was to consist of an unpaid advisory group of fifteen members, with the Prime Minister acting as chairman, to deal with social and economic problems by means of research, advice, and reports. The Senate made many amendments to some of these proposals, and for the most part the House of Commons concurred in the changes proposed by the upper chamber.

The constitutional issue

This in substance constitutes the remarkable achievement of the Bennett Government in the ten months preceding the general election of 1935. Many of the measures suggest a close affinity with the New Deal legislation passed in the United States during the 1930's. The Prime Minister himself had doubts about the constitutionality of part of his program. In Canada, as in the United States, the question of judicial review of hitherto unprecedented social and economic legislation, passed to cope with a grave national emergency, became a matter of violent partisan controversy. Mr. Bennett had tried to circumvent some of his constitutional problems by using the Dominion's treaty-making power to ratify the conventions of 1928, of the International Labor Office of the League of Nations, concerning wages, hours and a labor code, thus providing for their acceptance in Canada. The Canadian Parliament in fact expressed its adherence to these labor reforms by formal resolutions which ratified six of the draft conventions of the International Labor Office, rather than by specific legislative enactments. The question of a possible re-allocation of powers between the federal and provincial governments, in view of present-day economic and financial needs, had been the subject of discussion in several provincial conferences. No tangible results had been achieved, and the problem continued to plague succeeding governments. In the United States, President Roosevelt, whose New Deal legislation had suffered mutilation at the hands of the Supreme Court on grounds of constitutionality, had not hesitated to denounce a constitutional system which applied the concepts of the "horse and buggy age" to modern industrial problems. In Canada, Prime Minister Bennett maintained that the judges must learn how to apply sound principles of constitutional growth to the conditions of modern society. In February, 1935, a special parliamentary committee considered the whole question of how the Canadian constitution of 1867 was working in the present emergency, and the Royal Commission on Business Practices recommended constitutional revision to permit Parliament to promote wages and hours legislation, and collective bargaining. Mr. Bennett espoused a new doctrine of federal emergency powers, based on an elastic interpretation of the "peace, order and good government" clause of the British North America Act.

Soon after the election of 1935, in which the whole Bennett program was of course the leading issue, the Liberal Government submitted the eight leading reform measures of their predecessors to the Canadian Supreme Court for a ruling on their constitutionality, and the next year carried appeals to the Privy Council. The Canadian Supreme Court divided equally on the labor code, sustained the social security legislation, the Criminal Code Amendment, the Marketing Act and the Trade and Industrial Commission Act. The British Privy Council, on January 28, 1937, sustained only the Farmers' Creditors Act, the Criminal Code Amendment, and the Dominion Trade and Industrial Commission Act. It declared invalid all the legislation dealing with unemployment and social insurance, the minimum wage, the forty-eight hour week, and the Natural Products Marketing Act. Thus it may be said that the Privy Council was in substantial agreement with the Canadian Supreme Court, provided we remember that the latter had given a tie vote on the labor code. Because unemployment insurance affected the civil rights of employers and employees in each province, the Privy Council declared it *ultra vires*. The labor code generally was considered to be a violation of provincial rights, and the learned judges of the Privy Council added, by way of explaining their constitutional views more fully: "While the Ship of State now sails on larger ventures and into foreign waters she still retains the water-tight compartments which are an essential part of her original structure."

In spite of adverse legal decisions, the need and demand for a system of unemployment insurance could not long be evaded. Mr. Bennett's plan having been knocked out by the courts, the Liberal Government which came into power after the election of 1935 got the previous consent of all the provinces for an amendment to Section 97 of the British North America Act in order to bring unemployment insurance under the jurisdiction of the federal government. The British

Ultra vires

Unemployment insurance

Parliament complied with the request for an amendment. In July, 1940, the Minister of Labor introduced a bill in the Dominion House of Commons, providing for a graduated levy on workers and employees to raise an insurance fund, to which the federal government added an annual quota of $11,200,000 as well as meeting the costs of administration. The total cost of the plan was estimated at about $75,000,000 a year. The insurance was to be administered by a commission of three, one a representative of labor, another an employer, and a third to represent the general public. The benefit to be paid per week to a worker with a wife and four children amounted to only $9.60. All parties endorsed the measure.

Bank of Canada

One other piece of fiscal legislation needs to be considered before turning to a discussion of the general election of 1935. This deals with the establishment of a Central Bank of Canada. Despite the remarkable stability of the Canadian banking structure throughout the depression years, there were frequent demands for a better integration of Canadian banking facilities, and for a more elastic currency. In 1933, a Royal Commission on banking and monetary matters had been created. It toured the Dominion from Halifax to Vancouver, and made a thorough study of the complicated problems assigned to it. Its report, presented in the fall of 1933, and with the two banker members dissenting, recommended the immediate creation of a central bank, with an initial capital stock of $5,000,000. The bank was to be strictly non-political. It was to have the sole right of note issue. It was to serve as the banker for the government, handle its national debt and credit policy, and control the currency and foreign exchange. The recommendations of the Commission were immediately attacked by many of the banking fraternity, and in some of the Conservative newspapers. The Liberals were generally in favor of a central bank, but fought for complete government ownership and control. Some French Canadian leaders purported to find in the proposal a thinly disguised scheme to make the Dominion the slave of England. An attempt on the part of the French to make the bank notes bilingual was defeated. The bank bill was introduced in Parliament in February, 1934. Essentially, it provided for what may be described as a privately owned bank under public control. Ownership of stock was limited to British shareholders, and no one was to own more than fifty shares. The bank was to regulate internal credit and foreign exchange, to give expert advice to the government in fiscal matters, and to provide an elastic control of currency and bank credit in order to mitigate fluctuations in business and the price structure. All private banks had to surrender their gold holdings to the Bank of Canada, which was to act as a bank of rediscount for them and maintain a 25% gold reserve. Over a period of time, the note-issuing privileges of all existing banks were to be curtailed until the central bank eventually had a monopoly of issuing paper money. By these various provisions, it was expected to produce a currency that would always be both sound and elastic. Like the Federal Reserve System in the United States, the bank could lower or raise its rediscount rate to the banks. The headquarters of the Bank of Canada was to be at Ottawa, and its chief executive officers were to be appointed by the Government. Directors were to be elected by the shareholders among the diversified occupations, and not from the boards of directors of the chartered banks. Dividends were limited to $4\frac{1}{2}\%$, and as eventually passed, the bill provided that no shareholder was to own more than fifteen shares at fifty dollars par value. In March, 1935, the bank began business with Graham Ford Towers as its first governor. It assumed responsibility at once for $220,000,000 of Dominion notes, and it stood ready to make loans based on Dominion and provincial obligations as collateral, at an initial interest rate of $2\frac{1}{2}\%$. In 1938, when the Liberals were in power, the government bought the 100,000 shares previously issued to individuals, and the Bank of Canada became a government bank.

The general election campaign of 1935 really began with Prime Minister Bennett's broadcasts in January, forecasting his Canadian *Election* "New Deal." His Government, throughout its existence, and in spite *of 1935* of its bold and courageous attacks on the nation's economic and social ills, had suffered from the unpopularity that any government inevitably experiences if it holds office in bad times. Many Conservatives were shocked by the radical proposals which Mr. Bennett had enacted into law in 1935. *The Montreal Gazette* accused the Prime Minister of having done "violence to every Conservative principle." Others, with frequent references to the influence of his brother-in-law in Washington, accused the Prime Minister of drawing "a red Herridge across the political trail" for purely political purposes. The C.C.F. questioned the sincerity of the Prime Minister's sudden conversion to the cause of reform by drastic government intervention, and shouted regimentation and fascism. As late as 1933, Mr. Bennett had declared that Canada was "not a country in which we can make experiments." The Prime Minister had upset the whole strategy of the Liberal Opposition by his bold program, and shocked the Liberal leaders out of their smug complacency. The Liberal party now became an asylum for frightened conservatives.

Under the Redistribution Act of 1933, based on the census of 1931, and passed after an acrimonious debate and some evidence of "gerry- *The campaign* mandering," Nova Scotia had lost two seats, and New Brunswick one, in the federal parliament, and British Columbia and Alberta had gained two and one seats, respectively. Parliament was prorogued in July, 1935, in an atmosphere that made a Liberal victory seem virtually certain. The election was announced for October 14, and the Canadian Thanksgiving was moved from October 14 to October 24. 896 candidates presented themselves for the fall elections, a larger

number than in any preceding campaign. Fifteen were women, most
of whom were more radical in their views than the major parties.
By-elections had been going steadily against the Government ever
since 1933.

*Conservative
campaign
tactics*

Mr. Bennett carried on a vigorous campaign in spite of a serious
illness earlier in the year. He presented his program as an honest
attempt to reform and preserve, not destroy, the capitalist system.
Throughout the Dominion, and over the air waves, he stoutly defended his record, and promised new reforms, such as an old age pension for all over sixty, a reduction of the debt, an end to tax-exempt
bonds, a more equitable distribution of the tax burden, and further
relief to property owners. The Prime Minister maintained that the
Ottawa trade agreements had saved Canada during the depression,
and accused the Liberals of wanting to scrap empire trade for the sake
of a tariff agreement with the United States. He denounced seditious
and subversive activities, and apparently believed that Nature would
solve the problem of surplus wheat.

*The Liberal
strategy*

Mr. Mackenzie King had little to do except wait for the political
tide which promised victory to roll in. He was canny enough to
avoid many specific references to the issues, and he was especially
careful in his utterances about the tariff. He talked in general terms of
freer trade and freer competition. More specifically, he insisted that
he had no intention of scrapping the Ottawa agreements, and he
argued that he desired to reduce the rates to the 1930 level and bring
about a trade treaty with the United States. He advocated the repeal
of the Natural Products Marketing Act and favored selling Canada's
surplus wheat in the world market for whatever it might bring. He
urged converting the Bank of Canada into a state institution. He
attacked the Prime Minister for having announced his program to the
people by radio instead of in Parliament, and seemed to suggest that
there was something not quite constitutional about such a procedure.
He carefully dissociated himself from all "isms." He accused Mr.
Bennett of failing to get at the heart of Canada's difficulties, and
talked somewhat vaguely about real democracy in industry. He also
made many references to disarmament and world peace, and criticized
the Conservative Government for restoring titles in Canada. Mr. King
advocated "recovery before reform," and denounced the "dictatorship" and "fascist" tendencies of his Conservative opponents. He
attacked the C.C.F. as Socialists, and criticized the party of H. H.
Stevens for its "ill-considered" principles and its political hypocrisy.

*Minor
parties*

Mr. Stevens, after his split with the Conservative party, to which
he had belonged for many years, had launched a Reconstruction
Party. "Stevens Clubs" were formed to carry its principles to the
voters. The party advocated what it described as a more honest and
thoroughgoing "New Deal," based on a great public works program
to employ all the young people of Canada. It favored a federal hous-

ing plan, lower interest rates, fair wages and fair business methods, and the development of the nation's resources by the Government. Mr. Stevens denounced the "handful of men" who had seized control of Canada's economic system, but he continued to defend democracy and free enterprise, much as President Roosevelt had done in his campaign of 1932.

The C.C.F., under the leadership of J. S. Woodsworth, carried on an honest campaign for state socialism. Quite frankly, the party *C.C.F.* favored replacing the capitalist system with a new economic order in which banks, packing plants, housing, public health and insurance would be socialized. The party recommended more public works, the reduction of the farmers' debts by statute, and a minimum wage on a nation-wide basis. As far as international policy was concerned, the C.C.F. pledged itself to maintain Canada's neutrality, and to keep the Dominion out of all capitalist wars in the future.

The new Social Credit party, whose activities in Alberta will be discussed in detail later, nominated candidates in the four western *Social Credit* provinces. Its leaders talked enthusiastically about a "basic dividend" of twenty-five dollars a month for all adults, to be promptly spent by them for food, shelter and clothing, the government to raise the money in some not clearly defined way from a levy on the unearned increment of the products derived from Canada's natural resources. The party refused to cooperate with the Reconstruction Party, and also rebuffed all overtures from the Liberals. Mr. Bennett's Government loaned Alberta $2,225,000 before the election to enable the province to meet some of its obligations. The Communists nominated only ten candidates, and of these, all were unsuccessful in the election.

With the Conservative party split, and suffering from poor organization, lack of funds, and Mr. Bennett's earlier illness and absence *The results* from the country, and forced to carry the dead weight of the worst depression the Dominion had ever experienced, the outcome seemed fairly certain long before the ballots were counted. About 75% of all the qualified voters in the Dominion went to the polls. The Liberals won a majority of ninety-seven over all other parties combined. They secured 171 seats, the Conservatives, 39, the Social Credit party, 17, the C.C.F., 7, the Reconstruction party, 1, and the rest were scattered among Independent Liberals, Liberal-Progressives, Independent Conservatives, and U.F.O. Liberals. Twelve of Mr. Bennett's ministers failed of reelection. The Liberal popular vote was 46.6% of the total. The party won all but one seat in the Maritimes, all but five in Quebec, and fifty-five of the eighty-two seats in Ontario. It carried Manitoba and Saskatchewan, but not Alberta and British Columbia.

Prime Minister King immediately reduced the size of his Cabinet from twenty-one to sixteen. Charles A. Dunning became Minister of *The King* Finance; Ernest Lapointe, Minister of Justice; W. D. Euler, Minister *government* of Trade and Commerce, and James G. Gardiner, Prime Minister of

Saskatchewan, was called into the federal Government as Minister of
Agriculture. A new Department of Transport was created by combining the Department of Railways and Canals with the Department
of Marine, and the civil aviation branch of the National Defense
Department. The new Department of Mines and Resources came into
being through a union of the Departments of Interior, Immigration,
Colonization, Soldier Settlement and Indian Affairs. Vincent Massey
succeeded G. Howard Ferguson as Canadian High Commissioner in
London.

*Trade
agreement
with the
United States*

On November 8, 1935, Mr. King was the guest of President Roosevelt, and presently it was announced that a new trade treaty had been
signed by the United States and Canada. A trade agreement was also
concluded with Japan. The treaty with the United States was really
the culmination of three years of discussion, for which considerable
credit must be given to the Conservative Government. Mr. Bennett
had expressed a desire for reciprocity with the United States as early
as 1933, and the hope that the London Economic Conference, which
President Roosevelt scuttled, would put an end to the mania of economic nationalism. He had sent up several trial balloons to test American sentiment and had carried on some discussions in Washington.
Mr. King had rather consistently maintained, ever since the Ottawa
Agreement of 1932, that raising tariffs was not the way to get world
markets. He had denounced "selfish nationalism" and "jingo
imperialism." His views and those of Cordell Hull, the American
Secretary of State, were fairly similar as far as tariffs and reciprocal
trade agreements were concerned. By the new treaty, Canada lowered
her tariff on 767 imports to about the pre-Bennett levels of 1930.
The list of articles included such products as automobiles, tractors,
radios, agricultural machinery, books, films, and a number of natural
products, such as cotton, fruits, meats, eggs, and vegetables. The
United States was also to receive most-favored nation treatment in
Canada, except for the special preferences granted the British Empire.
Canada in turn received trade concessions on over two hundred items
from the United States, or 44% of Canada's normal exports to the
United States, and two years later got the maximum tariff reduction
of 50% on items which constituted about half of Canada's total
exports to the United States. The benefits to Canada involved many
of her agricultural products, fisheries, lumber and minerals, such as
wood pulp, nickel and asbestos. It is difficult to state the precise provisions of the reciprocity agreement without going into a bewildering
mass of detail. Suffice it to say that, as always, the United States
wanted easier entry for her manufactured and semi-manufactured
goods into Canada, and Canada wanted free entry for her raw materials
in the United States. The proposed tariff changes were quite moderate
on both sides. As far as Canada was concerned, the new rates for the
most part simply transferred American goods from the highest to the

middle schedule of the Canadian tariff, and so far had economic
nationalism developed since the World War that the rates Canada got
were really higher under the reciprocity agreement than they had
been under the simple rates of the American Underwood Tariff of
1913. In the United States, the lumber and agricultural interests complained bitterly that they had been betrayed by their government; in
Canada, it was the textile, automobile and other manufacturers who
complained. Mr. Bennett, now leader of the Opposition, attacked the
reciprocity agreement on the ground that Canada's benefits were dis-
proportionately small, and many more neutral observers pointed out
that the United States had really driven a hard bargain. The agreement
was to continue for three years, and was renewed, with modifications,
effective January 1, 1939, for another three year period.

The newly elected Parliament assembled February 6, 1936 with the
Liberals in complete control. Pierre Casgrain was chosen speaker. He   *Session*
was attacked almost immediately by Mr. Bennett, who charged that   *of 1936*
he had dismissed 127 Parliamentary employees for purely political
reasons, thus transforming the Canadian speakership into a political,
partisan office, like that of the presiding officer of the American House
of Representatives. The charges were referred to the committee on
privileges and buried there. The speech from the throne urged ratification of the trade treaty with the United States, called for a national
commission on unemployment, and a royal commission to investigate
the coal and the textile industries, greater parliamentary control of
the commissions that controlled the railways and the radio, constitutional revision and government ownership of the Bank of Canada.
The Liberals rejected "pump priming" and the theory of spending the
country's way into prosperity, and proposed to concentrate on public
works which would produce revenue. The Minister of Labor, Mr.
Norman Rogers, announced that the labor camps would be closed,
and their occupants put to work for modest wages. Some unemployment relief work was stopped, but the monthly grants to the provinces
for direct relief were increased. A Dominion-provincial conference
had failed to produce significant results except to demand more
federal help for the provinces. As already pointed out, the Bank of
Canada was presently converted into a government owned corporation. The trade treaty with the United States was ratified. The
National Economic Council was abolished, and a National Employment Commission was assigned the task of studying the whole problem of unemployment. Mr. Bennett's social legislation was referred to
the courts, with the results already indicated. The budget showed an
overall deficit of $162,191,000. The deficit from the Canadian National
Railway was $48,000,000. Over $42,000,000 was loaned to the four
western provinces for relief. The corporate income tax was raised, the
sales tax increased two per cent, some changes were made in the excise
taxes, and the tariff was modified in line with the new trade

agreement. The next several years saw the business and employment curve both rise and fall, going up in 1937, and slipping back in 1938.

The problems of the Dominion will be better understood if we examine somewhat more in detail the conditions in several of the provinces. The Maritimes had passed through a severe crisis. In Nova Scotia, this was particularly true of the coal-mining industry, which continued to suffer in spite of federal subventions and efforts to get the Canadian National Railways to use more Nova Scotia coal. In the summer of 1933, a general election had overthrown the Conservative Government, and brought the Liberals, under Angus L. Macdonald, back into power. By 1937-1938, economic conditions in the Maritimes generally were improving, except for the fishing industry, the silver fox fur industry in Prince Edward Island, and recurring difficulties in the Nova Scotia coal fields. A provincial election held in New Brunswick in 1935 resulted in an overwhelming defeat of the Tilley Conservative Government and the accession to office of the Liberal leader, A. A. Dysart. In the same year, the elections in Prince Edward Island resulted in the choice of nothing but Liberals to the provincial parliament.

The Maritimes

Newfoundland, though not a part of the Dominion, had lost her status as an autonomous dominion because of the ravages of the depression. Canada could not assume its economic burdens, and so the British Secretary of State for the Dominions had announced in February, 1933 that a royal commission would be created to study Newfoundland's economic and financial plight. An Englishman was made chairman of the commission; the other two members were Canadians. The result of the investigation was a recommendation that Newfoundland be governed by a non-political commission which was charged, among other things, with reorganizing the finances. The government of Newfoundland thereafter consisted of a British governor, and three Britishers and three Newfoundlanders as commissioners. England agreed to give financial help to the stricken dominion. By the fall of 1935, there was a rising demand in Newfoundland for a return of responsible government and sharp protests against the regime of the commission.

Newfoundland

In the Western provinces, conditions were particularly acute during the whole period of the depression, and even a return to prosperity by the Dominion as a whole will no doubt have little effect upon some of the basic problems that beset the prairie provinces and concern its basic industry, agriculture. It is a distressing story of heavy wheat exports for a number of the post-war years, but steadily declining prices. Then followed a gradual shrinkage of the export trade, various attempts to provide relief for the farmer by enabling him to withhold his surplus from the market for a time and thus avoid further ruinous declines in income until, in the end, Canada had a storage

The West

of unsold wheat so large that practically all available storing space had been occupied.

Since December, 1930, the Canadian Government has virtually operated in margins and futures on the wheat exchange in vain attempts to bolster the market and farm income. By its operations, the Government kept Canadian wheat from ten to fifteen cents a bushel above the Liverpool price. By secret pegging devices, the Government expected to control the market to the advantage of the Canadian farmer until a world shortage would wipe out the Canadian surplus, a solution predicted by the optimists by the summer of 1935. The agricultural problem has challenged the ingenuity and courage of the Dominion Governments, whether Conservative or Liberal, ever since the crash of 1929. By international agreements, the operations of the Wheat Board, the payment of cash bonuses, and other devices intended to stabilize agriculture, the Government has struggled with what rapidly became an apparently insoluble problem. In the United States, during the same period, the Federal Farm Board bought up 330,000,000 bushels of wheat, at a cost of over $270,-000,000, and two years later when it liquidated its holdings, it took a loss of $160,000,000 with no visible effect on prices. *The wheat problem*

As early as 1931, the Canadian Government had offered a bonus to the wheat growers of five cents per bushel, at a time when the average price in Saskatchewan was thirty-five or thirty-eight cents a bushel. The Marketing Act of 1934 attempted to regulate exports and domestic consumption. In 1935, the Canadian Wheat Board Act was passed as another attempt to provide a buffer between the farmer and a chaotic world market. Wheat was accepted at a minimum price, and if sold later at a surplus, the profits were to go to the producers. If the wheat should eventually be sold at a loss, the Dominion Government would charge the amount to the national deficit. The loss on the 1935 crop proved to be nearly $12,000,000. By 1939, the Government was forced to limit its purchases from any one producer to five thousand bushels in any one year; seventy cents a bushel was fixed as the initial price for No. 1 Manitoba Northern, and the act was applied to all the wheat growing areas of the Dominion. Provision was made for the creation of cooperatives to sell wheat, under certain government guarantees. The empire preference for wheat, obtained by Prime Minister Bennett as an aftermath of the Ottawa agreements, proved to be a harmless and ineffective political gesture, and was removed in 1939. The wheat surplus continued to mount. By the end of July, 1940, the carry-over amounted to 300,000,000 bushels. The total storage capacity of all available elevators was only 424,000,000 bushels. So the Government began compensating farmers for constructing storage bins. By the end of the crop year of 1941, the carry-over was expected to exceed 575,-000,000 bushels of unsold wheat. Confronted with a financial obligation of $400,000,000 which represented the value of the wheat carry- *The Wheat Board* over, and faced with the necessity of finding still more storage space for the new crop which would be harvested in August, the federal Government, on March 12, 1941, presented a plan to the House of Commons, indicating that the Government would not take more than 230,000,000 bushels, and calling for a reduction in wheat acreage of 35%. According to this plan, the farmer would be paid for letting his land lie fallow, or planting it with other grains, grass or clover, at a rate varying from $2 to $4 per acre. As a basis for computation, the farm income sufficient to maintain the western economy was fixed at $325,000,000. The cost of the bonuses to the government was estimated at $30,000,000 to $36,000,000 per year. Mr. James A. MacKinnon, Minister of Trade and Commerce, announced quite frankly that the Cabinet had at last decided to "head into the wheat storm and tell the people the story in all its drab detail."

Prairie problems

That the prairie provinces were in almost constant financial difficulties needs little elaboration, and the federal treasury repeatedly had to help the four western provinces to meet their payments on maturing loans and interest charges, and for unemployment relief. Attempts to force the provinces to cut their expenses and accept some federal supervision of their provincial budgets, though partly successful, could not adequately deal with the financial problem, and promptly aroused political and sectional antagonisms, and bitter controversies over constitutional issues. Ontario and Quebec considered themselves the "milch-cows of the West," and Quebec blocked every attempt to bring about a more adequate redistribution of constitutional authority between the federal and the provincial governments. The drought and dust storms and grasshopper plagues which swept a large part of the United States and Canada in the summer of 1934 forced a large percentage of the western farmers on relief. Agricultural experts could accomplish little by way of a resettlement program or efforts to replenish the top soil, because most people, no matter how poor, refused to leave their homes. Some livestock was moved by the government to more fertile areas, and food and seed grain had to be distributed among the farmers.

Approaching bankruptcy

The burden was too much for the provinces to bear. Several declared mortgage and interest moratoria. Tax arrears in the drought areas of Saskatchewan had to be cancelled. In a sense, the three prairie provinces were overdeveloped, although they had fewer people than the American state of Kentucky. The farmers were "landlocked in a sea of wheat," and raising wheat no longer paid in a world gone mad with economic nationalism. Alberta's relief cost in 1933-34 amounted to $5,000,000. Strikes occurred in the hastily set up relief camps. In Calgary, in 1933, 6,061 telephones were taken out for non-payment of charges. Municipalities defaulted on their financial obligations. In Winnipeg, one out of every five persons was on relief in the fall of 1934. The only exception to this tale of misery was the mining business. Here there was a special boom in gold production because the United States had depreciated its dollar and was buying huge quantities of gold at higher prices.

The economic distress of the West was reflected in its politics. Alberta, in 1933, had a United Farmer Government, under J. E. *Depression* Brownlee, but soon moved farther to the left by embracing the Social *politics* Credit Government, to be described presently. In Manitoba, in the election of 1936, the Liberal Progressives emerged as the largest single group in the legislature, and counted on Social Credit support for a majority. In Saskatchewan, in 1934, every Government candidate lost his seat in the general election, and the Liberals won an overwhelming victory. The Conservatives were so completely routed that a Farm-Labor group of five members constituted the official opposition. The governments of all the western provinces were primarily occupied with economic affairs and relief for debtors throughout the 1930's, and with new appeals to the Dominion government for greater fiscal support. In British Columbia, where the Conservatives had been in power since 1928, the Liberals were returned to power in 1933 with overwhelming majorities. Although the province was near bankruptcy, the Liberal leader, T. D. Pattullo, promised "work with wages," instead of a dole, and appealed to Ottawa for "better terms," but he steadily refused to accept federal control of the province's budget and borrowing power.

Under these distressing circumstances, the C.C.F. continued to spread in the West, although its affiliations also extended eastward to *C.C.F.* include the United Farmers of Ontario. In a very real sense, the C.C.F. was the product of the depression. Its program was socialistic and looked toward a completely planned economy, except for a certain remainder of capitalistic individualism in agriculture. The C.C.F. claimed to be a genuine people's party, and denounced the two major parties as the tools of special privilege. It demanded the socialization of banks and key industries, government control of all foreign trade, and an extensive program of labor and social legislation. The party was ably led by J. S. Woodsworth, its president, a former minister and social worker, who had the respect of even his most conservative opponents. Woodsworth rejected all suggestions of violence; he was a pacifist, a humanitarian rebel, and believed completely in the efficacy of constitutional methods, persuasion and education. He recruited his followers among the organized farmers, among the more politically-minded labor groups, and among certain intellectual radicals and college professors who were described as "Woodsworth's Brain Trust." The vote of the C.C.F. grew sufficiently in the early 1930's to worry both major parties.

Developments in Alberta deserve somewhat more detailed discussion. In this unhappy province, the depression and the drought *William* produced Premier William Aberhart and the Social Credit League. *Aberhart*

On August 22, 1935, the candidates of the Social Credit party were successful in an election which ended a fourteen year regime of the United Farmers of Alberta. The prophet of the new dispensation was Aberhart, a former radio broadcaster, owner of the Prophetic Bible Institute, and principal of a Calgary high school. Aberhart has been described as a "cross betweeen William Jennings Bryan and Aimee Semple McPherson," the California woman evangelist. Some doubted his sincerity, but most people were willing to credit him with a full measure of devotion to the public service, and with an evangelical zeal that raised his political campaign to the fever pitch of a crusade. Aberhart had read the social credit theories of the Englishman, Major C. H. Douglas, *Credit, Power and Democracy*, by which he proposed to abolish poverty by an intricate plan which few students of economics have been able to follow, and which had some of the features of a number of American "ham and egg" proposals, like the Townsend plan to distribute two hundred dollars each month to the whole of the adult population, provided only that each person spend this amount each month and thereby keep prosperity in circulation. Aberhart took Major Douglas' ideas seriously. The latter accused the Calgary evangelist of oversimplifying them.

Social Credit

According to the version of Social Credit popularly believed in Alberta, the government would pay each adult twenty-five dollars a month; the state would manipulate credit and furnish interest-free loans to producers. Credit dividend books to this amount would be issued monthly; the government would fix the price of raw products and add a 10% tax on their turnover, such as, when wheat was sold to the miller, and flour to the baker, and bread to the consumer. Experts would fix a "just price," and keep it at that point. By some not fully explained economic magic, there would result a phenomenal increase in trade and every one would prosper because of the creation of new purchasing power. Aberhart inherited an empty treasury when he took office, a funded debt of $160,000,000, and a current deficit of $2,810,000. Alberta bonds began to fall, and their redemption had to be suspended. Expenses of government were reduced and heavier taxes were imposed. In 1936, Alberta defaulted on her bonded debt, and the interest rate on bonds was cut in half. Immediately, the bonds dropped 40% in market value. The Conservative federal government advanced a loan of $2,500,000 ($18,000,000 had been requested), but this proved inadequate to stop the downward spiral. Obviously, the times were not ripe for the inauguration of dividend payments to all adults. The prime minister had promised the distribution of social credit within eighteen months. A law was passed to stop mortgage foreclosures, and to keep creditors from going to court for relief. When the law was declared invalid by the courts, a general moratorium was declared.

It is impossible to follow all the differences of opinion which developed between Aberhart and the people of Alberta. Early in his

administration, he broke with Major Douglas. Playing on the bitter   *Demurrage*
sectionalism which existed between west and east, and the antago-   *money*
nism between big business and "St. James Street" and the suffering
farmer, the prime minister talked violently about freeing the people
"from economic bondage," and some of his followers even suggested
secession from the Dominion. Interest was described as ungodly usury,
and the sufferings of the people were attributed to the international
bankers who controlled the credit of the nation. Aberhart now turned
to the theories of Silvio Gesell concerning "demurrage money."
Stamp scrip, known as "prosperity certificates," were issued at one
dollar face value. Each holder had to put a one cent stamp on his certificates every Wednesday, so that in two years each certificate would
return $1.04 to the treasury in stamp sales. This scrip was issued to
pay for road relief work to the unemployed, and small amounts were
issued to the civil servants of the province. The plan was expected to
encourage spending by this "disappearing money scheme," though
the government refused to accept its own certificates in payment of
taxes. The scrip depreciated at once; banks refused to take it, and in
order to safeguard its value, the treasury had to redeem it once a
month, and eventually nearly the whole amount was retired. Codes
were designed for business and trade, but had to be abandoned when
the courts declared them unenforceable.

The social credit movement now degenerated into hopeless dis-
sension, and many of Aberhart's followers accused him of betraying   *Constitutional*
the cause of reform. Major Douglas and some of his aids were invited   *questions*
once more to Alberta, but with little success. In 1937, an act to license
all banks was disallowed. The constitutional controversies between
the provincial and the federal authorities continued under Mr. King
as they had begun with Mr. Bennett. Recall proceedings were initiated against Aberhart, but without success. Then, many of the acts
that had been invalidated were reënacted, a confiscatory tax was
imposed on bank reserves, and a Press Act, described as "a gag law,"
was passed by the Alberta legislature. All these measures were in turn
either disallowed by the Dominion Government, refused the assent
of the lieutenant-governor, or declared invalid by the Canadian Supreme Court. Aberhart tried to muzzle and control the unfriendly
press, and sought to prevent appeals to the courts. He was guilty of
studied discourtesies to the lieutenant-governor, and he justified all
he did on the ground that he was delivering the poor from under the
heels of the financial Pharaohs of St. James Street.

After eighteen months in office, the Prime Minister pleaded for
another trial period of six months. He continued to quarrel furiously   *Decline*
with his British advisors, and with the Liberal Government in
Ottawa. In 1938, he promised to raise the standard of living eight
fold, and to provide an average income of $1500, reduce taxes by half,
cut prices, and pay the promised dividend of twenty-five dollars a

month. He carried his propaganda into other parts of Canada, but it
proved to be ineffective in the Saskatchewan elections of 1938. Opposition continued to grow in Alberta itself, and in two of three by-
elections, Aberhart's disciples lost to so-called unity candidates.
Aberhart remained in office, but social credit was no nearer realization
than on the day when he left his Prophetic Bible Institute for the
arena of politics. Although none had received their monthly dividend, many still believed that the movement was an honest and necessary attack on the vested interests which held the farmer in their
clutches, and ground him down with the burdens of a mortgage structure which it was impossible to carry any longer. Alberta's experiences suggest a similarity with such schemes as the late Huey Long's
"Share the Wealth" movement, California's "$30 every Thursday,"
and the Townsend plan, in the United States.

Ontario

Ontario, like all the other provinces, struggled with increasing
debts and relief costs. Its government, under Prime Minister George
Stewart Henry, followed a conservative course in the early 1930's.
Mr. Henry, in 1933, denounced unemployment insurance as virtually
communistic and apparently believed its enactment would open the
gates of Ontario to Russian bolshevism. Two years earlier, the Communist headquarters in Toronto had been raided on orders of the
attorney-general, and the "red menace" continued to be uppermost
in the minds of many Ontario leaders. In 1934 there was another
political flurry over a bill to permit the sale of beer and wine by the
glass, but the Liberal leader, Mitchell F. Hepburn, refused to be
diverted from what he regarded as the real issues; namely, the debt,
maladministration and reform. In the general election of that year,
after a brief and bitterly fought campaign, the Conservatives were
defeated. After twenty-nine years in opposition, the Liberal party
returned to power in Ontario. The new prime minister was thirty-
eight years old, full of energy, motivated by great personal loyalties,
and described by some of his critics as "a small-time Huey Long in
speech and manners."

*Hepburn
government*

The new administration began with salary cuts, the selling off of
government automobiles, and the launching of a number of inquiries
into the activities of its predecessor. Hepburn fought for provincial
rights, accused the Dominion Government of invading the field of
income taxation to the detriment of the provinces, and demanded
more federal aid for the relief of the unemployed. The Prime Minister
precipitated a battle between the Ontario Hydroelectric Commission
and the Quebec power companies over contracts, and opposed the St.
Lawrence waterway development project in which the Roosevelt
administration continued to be interested. Mr. Hepburn sponsored
social legislation and tax reduction.

C. I. O.

When the C. I. O. automobile unions invaded Canada from the
United States and threatened a "sit-down" strike in the General

Motors plant at Oshawa, Hepburn undertook to save Ontario from "American lawlessness" and "foreign agitators." He denounced John L. Lewis, the American president of the C. I. O., as a gangster, and characterized American unionism as another Fenian invasion of Canada. As a matter of fact, the whole Oshawa affair passed off very peacefully, although Mr. Hepburn brought in the mounted police and special constables, and precipitated a cabinet crisis over the issues involved. The *New York Times* praised the Ontario leader for his courage, and the union eventually gained recognition. Prime Minister Hepburn, riding in on the C. I. O. issue, and stressing his battle with Quebec power interests, his balanced budget, lower taxes and improved business conditions, was reëlected in 1937 in an election in which his party carried 67 of the 90 seats, and the leftist parties lost out altogether. Premier King must have watched the activities of his stormy Liberal colleague in Ontario with increasing misgivings, but he remained silent, even when Mr. Hepburn closed out the "Government House" in which the lieutenant-governor resided, advertised the place for public sale, and finally turned it over for a children's hospital. Mr. Hepburn vigorously attacked the laissez-faire methods of Ottawa, quarreled with the federal leaders over constitutional questions, and was in turn accused by them of having entered into an unnatural political alliance with the fascist prime minister of Quebec to oust Mackenzie King as the national leader of the Liberal party.

In Alberta, the depression had produced Aberhart, in Ontario, Hepburn, and in Quebec, it brought Maurice L. Duplessis to power. *Quebec* M. Duplessis was a member of the Quebec Parliament for Three Rivers. Of patrician birth, cultured, witty and brilliant, he had been a Conservative, in a province in which the Liberal party had had virtually a monopoly of the government for more than a generation. In 1934, the tide began to turn against the Liberals. A young Liberal group was organized under Paul Gouin as the *Action Liberale Nationale*, and a somewhat similar group was formed by an offshoot from the Conservatives under the name of *Le Parti Franc*. The old party lines were beginning to break up, and the long regime of Premier Taschereau, who was always conservative and friendly to business, was in serious danger of collapse. In the election of 1935, Taschereau's majority was reduced to six. The Prime Minister resigned his leadership to a younger man. The election was marked by the revolt of the young against the older leaders, and by a great resurgence of French nationalism. The next year, the Liberal regime was overthrown, after about forty years of uninterrupted control, and a National Union Administration, *L'Union Nationale*, under Maurice Duplessis, took office. Duplessis controlled 76 of the 90 seats.

Some laudable social legislation was enacted by the Duplessis Government. The Prime Minister promised to protect the natural *The Duplessis* resources of the province, and he favored government ownership of *regime* hydroelectric power facilities. But there were increasing evidences of fascist trends in the new Government. Cardinal Villeneuve, primate of the Church in Canada, was a friend of Duplessis, and had repeatedly expressed his sympathy for the fascists in the Spanish Revolution and his misgivings about North American democracy, which seemed to contain certain elements that were incompatible with a Catholic social order. Under the Duplessis regime, labor was regimented in organizations under the influence of the Roman Catholic Church, and everything was done to foster French clericalism and nationalism. In some of the cities of the province, fascist groups began to drill and to express strong anti-Semitic views. Prime Minister Duplessis began to curtail civil liberties, and presently launched an hysterical campaign against communism. His *L'Union Nationale* attacked both England and the United States, and advocated the preservation of Quebec's natural resources for the French Canadians. Duplessis personally professed his loyalty to confederation and the British Crown, but a substantial part of the Church leadership seemed to encourage his nationalist campaign, and to favor a corporate state along the lines of Pope Pius XI's encyclical, *Quadragesimo Anno*. Legislation to establish joint committees of labor and employers in all industries had been initiated by Prime Minister Taschereau in 1934. Duplessis opposed labor unions of all kinds. In 1937, a Fair Wages Act was passed, looking toward the establishment of a corporate state and the enforcement of labor agreements. It left no room for collective bargaining or union representation on the boards created to determine hours and wages by industries and districts. Indeed, some of the Catholic Syndicates in the steel and textile industries struck against the new provisions. In 1938, an act was passed giving the Governor-in-Council the power to abrogate and change at will all collective labor agreements without consulting the interested parties, and to fix wages and hours. Duplessis denounced the C. I. O. and the closed shop, and his Fair Wages Board proceeded to fix minimum wages, raising the wages of the unskilled workers.

Quebec fascism

Meantime, the government became more and more anti-democratic, as well as anti-communist. Under the leadership of Arcand and others, fascist organizations grew in membership, like the *Jeunesse Patriote*, the *Parti Nationale Social Chrétien*, and the *Casques d'Acier* (steel helmets). Some of these organizations, and their weeklies, displayed the swastika, and anti-Semitism spread rapidly in Quebec. Probably the most notorious enactment of the Duplessis Government was the "padlock law" of 1937. This empowered the attorney-general, without recourse to the courts, to order premises padlocked for not more than a year if he thought they were being used for purposes of communist propaganda. The law prohibited the preparation and distribution of communist literature, and permitted its seizure and destruction by the police. Communism was not defined in the law, and one of the Government ministers remarked that "A lot of people are communists and don't know it." Under the law, newspaper offices in Montreal were padlocked, a school was raided, the textbooks confiscated and the children sent home; and some of Mr. J. S. Woodsworth's writings were seized. Those interested in the preservation of civil liberties protested vigorously, but M. Ernest Lapointe, French-Canadian Minister of Justice for the Dominion, who had not hesitated to invalidate the social credit legislation of Alberta, refused to recommend the disallowance of Quebec's padlock law.

The Liberal Government at Ottawa continued to devote its energies to economic legislation rather than politics. The business recession in the United States in 1937, after several years of recovery, immediately had its effect upon Canada. Crop failures in parts of the West made the farmer the Dominion's economic problem number one. The relief burden fell more and more on the federal government, and the Liberals found it necessary to initiate much of the Bennett program of social legislation which the courts had annulled. In 1938, Mr. Bennett relinquished the leadership of the opposition to Dr. R. J. Manion. In 1937, the Government had appointed a Royal Commission on Dominion-Provincial Relations. The tariff had been moderately reduced by tariff agreements. In 1937, Mackenzie King had visited Washington and also attended the Imperial Conference. On both occasions, he advocated economic appeasement and a revival of world trade, and he implemented his theories by concluding most-favored nation treaties with Latin-America and other countries. In 1938, a National Housing Act was enacted to stimulate low-cost housing projects by government loans to municipalities. A bill was passed for home improvement loans, with the government guaranteeing such loans to the bank, and new agricultural relief measures were enacted. Legislation was passed to strengthen the act dealing with monopolies and combinations in restraint of trade. A law was enacted to create the Trans-Canada Air Lines, with the government furnishing a subsidy and the Canadian National Railways holding a controlling interest in its shares. Mr. Bennett had favored outright government ownership. *Problems at Ottawa*

Labor remained restive, and 1937 saw an epidemic of strikes and lockouts in Ontario and Quebec, the largest since the end of the World War. The usual charges were made against "reds" and "foreign agitators." As far as communism as a national political force was concerned, it was of little significance, and its vote, although somewhat larger than formerly, was still quite negligible. In 1935, the Department of Labor reported a membership of 280,704 in trade unions; in 1929, the number had been 319,476. The figures indicate the usual decline in trade union membership in a time of depression and unemployment. *Labor*

Canadian Railways, like Canadian wheat, remained an apparently insoluble problem. Early in the Bennett regime, and at the suggestion *The railways* of Sir Henry Thornton, president of the Canadian National Railways, a Royal Commission on Transportation had been created. The existing public investment in the C. N. R. and the C. P. R., not counting the C. N. R. debts to the government on which no interest was paid, amounted to $2,200,000,000. Canada's entire war effort from 1914 to 1918, and the costs of demobilization, had amounted to only $1,695,-000,000. The report of the Royal Commission opposed the amalgamation of the C. N. R. and the C. P. R., as well as a lease of one to the other. It recommended that the C. N. R. be removed from political and community pressures, that coöperation be brought about between the two systems in order to eliminate waste and duplication in services, and it proposed a Board of Trustees of three members to operate the C. N. R. and control its budget. The Commission advised that Parliament meet the annual deficits out of its appropriations. An annual report to Parliament was suggested, as well as a continuous audit of accounts by parliamentary auditors; and no new securities were to be issued except for improvements to the system. The Board of Trustees was to appoint a President of the C. N. R., who should be directly responsible to them, and not to Parliament or the Government in power. Finally, a board of arbitration was recommended in order to provide and supervise coöperation between the two competing railway systems. The report discussed at length the competition of motor and trucking companies, pointed out that this was one of the major reasons, along with the depression, for the serious financial difficulties of both major railway systems. A plan was proposed to bring their bloated capital structures more in line with actual values, but this part of the report remained a dead letter.

Attempts at coöperation

The Canadian Senate promptly repudiated all suggestions of a merger, and the C. P. R. opposed the proposal for a joint board of arbitration. Some Montreal bankers urged that the Canadian Pacific should absorb the national lines, but the majority of the Canadian people still believed in public ownership and wanted no railroad monopoly. On March 21, 1933, the presidents of the two systems announced a pooling of passenger train services between Ottawa and Toronto, and Montreal and Toronto, and plans were worked out for certain joint operations in switching and cleaning cars, and in the use of freight sheds. Occasionally one road hauled traffic for the other. A study was also initiated to determine what railway mileage might be abandoned. Actually, none of these ventures in coöperation were of great importance, and proposals by government auditors to write off a billion dollars of capital indebtedness made no progress at all. Prime Minister Bennett's Minister of Railways and Canals, in 1935, argued that the Government should have permitted the Grand Trunk and the Canadian Northern to go into liquidation—a suggestion that was hardly helpful now. Mr. Bennett asserted that Canada's railway troubles resulted from a time when "in a moment of madness we thought we were a people of 50,000,000." Sir Edward Beatty, president of the C. P. R., declared that the experiment in public ownership was not honest and "nothing more than a sad accident." The bill to implement the report of the Royal Commission (the Duff report), initiated in the Senate by Arthur Meighen and sponsored in the House of Commons by Dr. R. J. Manion, was finally passed with many amendments. It was attacked by Mr. Mackenzie King as a possible forerunner of amalgamation and monopoly. Others feared the surrender of public ownership to a "self-perpetuating board," and predicted increased unemployment among railroad men. The Government gave specific assurances against amalgamation and against ill-considered abandonment of railroad mileage.

By 1937, most competent observers agreed that the coöperation *The future* suggested in the Duff report was a failure. The president of the C. P. R. admitted that savings were possible without change in ownership and proposed joint management and a division of the savings. Mr. S. J. Hungerford, president of the C. N. R., rejected the unification plan and advocated compulsory coöperation. He saw little possibility of reducing the total railway mileage of the Dominion, and he argued that the persistent heavy deficits were not due to operating costs, but to interest charges on three billion dollars of railway debts which the taxpayer had to pay. The Liberals made as little progress toward solving the problem as their predecessors in office had done. With a revival of business, and the extraordinary demands on the Dominion's transportation facilities by the new war, the situation is bound to improve, at least temporarily. But the fundamental difficulties remain.

Before turning to Canada's role in foreign policy and a second World War, something more should be said about certain consti- *Constitutional* tutional problems which, though not entirely due to the depression *reform* years, became more urgent in the decade when the Dominion was struggling to find a way out of the financial debacle of 1929. Reference has already been made to the constitutional crisis precipitated by Mr. Bennett's so-called "New Deal" program, but the same issues were present in a number of lesser controversies. Throughout the 1930's, Dominion-provincial conferences were held to discuss financial and economic problems, and on each occasion there were discussions of possible changes in the British North America Act, but without practical results. The Dominion Government, as has been pointed out before, has exclusive power to make laws for "the peace, order and good government of Canada in relation to all matters not coming within the classes of subjects assigned exclusively to the legislatures of the provinces." "Property and civil rights in the provinces" were left to the provinces. In general, and over a considerable period of years, the British Privy Council had been bolstering up the powers of the provinces to a point where the functional solution of national problems was becoming more difficult and almost impossible. The assumption by the federal government of the cost and responsibilities of relief, and the economic and social legislation necessitated by the depression decade, are examples in point. Nevertheless, in 1931, Canada had reaffirmed its intention to preserve the right of appeal to the British Privy Council. In 1934, Prime Minister Bennett urged the amending of the British North America Act so as to get the provinces to surrender to the Dominion government their jurisdiction over social legislation involving industry, old age, illness, and wages and hour laws. So Conservative a politician as Arthur Meighen described the constitution of 1867 as suitable only "for the horse and buggy period." But Quebec, ever restive about matters of provincial autonomy, together with several other provinces, opposed constitutional reform.

Report on Dominion-provincial relations

The year 1937 brought another attack on the Privy Council for annulling the Bennett legislation, although its author, now in opposition, staunchly defended the right of the Canadians to go directly to the throne in judicial appeals. Mr. Bennett agreed, however, with such Liberal leaders as M. Ernest Lapointe, that the British North America Act should be amended in order to get "uniform national laws." In 1940, the Report of a Royal Commission on Dominion-provincial relations was published at Ottawa. A Canadian reviewer quite properly called it the "first great inquest since 1867 into the working of Canadian federalism." The report was the result of two and a half years of study by a distinguished commission assisted by a large staff of experts. After reviewing the whole political, economic and constitutional development of the Dominion, and the stresses and strains on the Canadian system of the division of powers with the ebb and flow of prosperity since 1867, the Report concerned itself specifically with the trend since the World War and the depression toward increased governmental functions and the evolution of the Dominion into a "social service state." Rugged individualism had proved inadequate to cope with economic disaster, and the federal government had been compelled to come to the support of industry, agriculture and transportation. Provincial and municipal revenues had proved insufficient to carry the burdens of relief. The exigencies of public finance had forced a restudy of the whole constitutional structure of the Dominion. Finding the existing state of affairs intolerable, the Commission sought, within the framework of its instructions to preserve the federal system, to strike a new federal balance. It concluded that the Dominion should assume the relief burden, and that the "residual responsibility for social welfare functions should remain with the provinces." It proposed a redistribution of financial powers, urging that the provinces withdraw entirely from the area of income and inheritance taxes and surrender all existing federal subsidies, subject to possible adjusted emergency grants, the Dominion in turn to assume the provincial debts. The voluminous report of the Commission touched upon many other subjects, such as transportation, taxation, and a possible union of certain provinces. The Commission gave no final answer as to the ultimate fate of Canadian federalism. Summarizing the activities of the Commission in more practical terms, it may be said that the experts had been asked to submit a plan to relieve the provinces of what should be national charges, and in turn, had asked them to surrender certain sources of revenue to the federal government. The provincial debts to be assumed amounted to about $2,200,000,000 with a service cost of $62,000,000 annually. The costs of unemployment and relief which the Dominion would assume averaged perhaps $60,000,000 a year. The income and inheritance taxes to be surrendered as a field of taxation to the federal government had yielded about $64,000,000 annually, and the existing federal subsidies amounted to about $21,000,000. All the provinces except Ontario, Alberta and British Columbia were to receive, in place of these subsidies, federal adjustment grants totalling about $15,000,000 a year.

Early in 1941, a conference was called to discuss alteration of provincial-Dominion relations and status in the light of the Commission's recommendations (the Sirois Report). The conference lasted *Results* only a day or two. Prime Minister King encountered the flat refusal of the prime ministers of Ontario, Alberta, and British Columbia to discuss the issues. Six provincial leaders were ready to proceed with the Commission's recommendations; the others refused to sit on committees to consider them. The financial burdens of Canada had greatly increased in the meantime, due to the outbreak of war, and might easily total from 45% to 50% of the national income. Neither threats nor cajoling could move the opposition group, and Premier Hepburn of Ontario warned against smashing the confederation and stirring up racial feuds during a national crisis. In the end, Prime Minister King "postponed" the conference "until it may be that the Provinces themselves will ask for its resumption even before the war is over," and emphasized the "absolute unity of purpose with respect to Canada's war effort." The War undoubtedly will affect the whole future of Canadian federalism. It may well be that the greatest problem of the future in Canada is devising a new formula for Canadian federalism, which will provide for essential national regulations, and at the same time, satisfy all the forces of economic sectionalism and racial dualism which continue to complicate almost every significant Canadian national issue.

SELECTED BIBLIOGRAPHY FOR CHAPTER XXXIII

In addition to the volumes of *The Canadian Annual Review of Public Affairs*, consult the guides to periodical literature and the files of leading Canadian dailies. American and Canadian periodicals of special usefulness are *Business Week*, *The Canadian Forum*, *Foreign Affairs*, *Fortnightly*, *The Living Age*, *The Yale Review*, *Current History*, and *The New York Times Magazine*.

Leonard C. Marsh: *Canadians In and Out of Work* (Toronto, 1940) is excellent for an analysis of economic conditions. For constitutional discussions, see *Report of the Royal Commission on Dominion-Provincial Relations*, 3 vols. (Ottawa, 1940).

CHAPTER XXXIV

CANADA AND THE SECOND WORLD WAR

Isolation

CANADA emerged from the first World War a completely autonomous nation. Her status as such was officially confirmed by the Statute of Westminster, "the symbol of the free association of the members of the British Commonwealth of Nations." For a time, Canada participated actively in the experiment of collective security inaugurated by the Covenant of the League of Nations. Then, like her great neighbor to the South, the Dominion veered sharply toward a policy of isolationism and North Americanism, and her Governments saw little reason for diverting their attentions from the pressing problems of civil reëstablishment and reconstruction to the complicated and rather remote issues of post-war European diplomacy.

North Americanism

Canada continued to be represented in the councils of the League of Nations, but her Government, especially when the Liberal party was in power, emphasized Canadian isolation from world politics, and resolved to take a back seat in League affairs. Although resolute in her decision to remain British, the Dominion seemed to be steadily growing more North American. As Prime Minister King once put it, Canada has "too much geography," and the signal fact about her policy in the late 1920's and early 1930's was the necessity of preserving her national unity. Under Conservatives and Liberals alike, the emphasis was on domestic rather than foreign policy, although there was often a difference in degree between the attitudes of the major political groups. The keynote of Canadian policy before 1939 was to stress national independence and security, and to promote Canada's external trade. As Professor Underhill observed, the people of the Dominion seemed desirous of sailing "past the European siren, our ears stuffed with tax bills." As late as March, 1939, Mr. King denounced as sheer madness a policy which would automatically drag the Dominion every twenty years into a European war for democracy and the self-determination of small nations. Apparently the Prime Minister accepted with equanimity the Munich appeasement settlement which led to the dismembering of Czechoslovakia. The Monroe Doctrine and President Roosevelt's "good neighbor" policy were additional factors in encouraging the Dominion to retreat from the Empire and Europe. Canadian Governments insisted on being informed and consulted on all questions of Empire policy, but refused to accept any commitments to the British Empire, although it was quite apparent that Canada could not actually remain neutral if the mother country again became involved in a general European War. Canada, in the two decades following the first World War, withdrew more and more from her commitments to the system of collective

424

security. England's abandonment of Ethiopia to Italy, her hands-off policy toward Spain when Franco and his fascist allies attacked its republican government, and Britain's refusal to associate herself with the United States in an effort to block Japan's aggression in Manchuria, helped materially in bringing about the end of the authority of the League in world affairs. The Canadian "will to peace" during these years was as strong as the desire of the United States to remain completely clear of European entanglements. Canada continued to give lip service to the system of collective security, but she refused all commitments, including membership in the Pan-American Union. The Canadian people were divided into groups which advocated imperialism, collectivism and isolationism, and the Government therefore had to follow an opportunist course in external affairs.

In the Far East, Canada's policy was one of peace, trade development and the maintenance of a stable balance of power. Canada's *The Far East* representative at the League had spoken in 1932 in favor of a policy of conciliation and compromise with Japan, at the very time when that Oriental Empire was beginning its aggressions against China. The Canadian delegate merely echoed the sentiments of the British foreign minister in this respect. As Japan's conquests expanded and could not be held within reasonable bounds, the Canadian people became quite anti-Japanese in their feelings, but because of profitable trade relations with Japan, practically nothing was done to implement their emotions with a program of action. The private boycott of Japanese products had little effect, and the Government continued to give China its sympathy and Japan its nickel, scrap iron and other war materials. In 1938, Mr. Bennett attacked the Prime Minister's "passive policy" toward Japan, but the Conservative leader had done no better during his period in office.

Canada's relations with the United States became increasingly cordial in the years before war broke out again in 1939. President *Canada-* Roosevelt's gold revaluation law of 1933, raising the price of gold *United States* from $20 to $35 an ounce, started a mining boom in Canada, stimu- *relations* lated Canadian recovery, and made the American President the Santa Claus of the mining interests in the Dominion. Indeed, there was such a tremendous turn-over in mining stocks on the Toronto Exchange that the Ontario Government had to intervene with securities regulations in order to protect Canadian investors from the financial sharks and fly-by-night brokers who swarmed into the stock market. Canada's mining frontier expanded, new towns arose, old ones revived, and the gold exports of the Dominion helped to meet the interest payments on United States investments in Canada which formerly had been met by the export of goods and services. Canadian trade relations are in many ways closer with the United States than they are with the United Kingdom. In 1937, 41% of Canada's export trade and 58.7% of her import trade was with the United States, as contrasted with 38.4% of her exports which went to the mother country, and 19.3% of her imports which came from the United Kingdom. The negotiations between Ottawa and Washington for a St. Lawrence Waterway agreement had ended in failure for the time being, when the United States Senate in 1934 had defeated a proposed treaty, but the issue was to be revived under the stimulus of a new war. The agreement had provoked a sharp division of opinion in Canada as well as in the United States. Negotiations for a reciprocal trade agreement proved to be more successful, as has been pointed out in the preceding chapter.

The Monroe Doctrine   As the menace of Hitlerism and totalitarianism grew in Europe, the policy of Canadian-American *rapprochement* became more apparent, and received vigorous stimulation both from the American President and the Canadian Prime Minister. In 1936, President Roosevelt visited the Governor-General, Lord Tweedsmuir, at Quebec and undoubtedly discussed foreign policy with Mr. King on that occasion. In an address at Chautauqua, New York, in the same year, the President announced that the United States stood ready to defend itself and its neighborhood against all aggressors. On another occasion, when President Roosevelt received an honorary degree from Queen's University, he virtually promised that the United States would not stand idly by if Canada were ever attacked, thus virtually extending the Monroe Doctrine to the Dominion, with all that this implied as to the future of American isolationism. Some Canadians were not too happy to be forced to accept the paternal protection of their powerful neighbor, although, as a matter of fact, the United States was simply following a policy of intelligent self-interest in the face of the gathering storm clouds across the Atlantic. Canadian-American coöperation did not imply any weakening of the sentimental ties between the Dominion and the mother country. When Edward VIII abdicated in favor of his brother, George VI, Canada consented to the abdication by order-in-council because Parliament was not in session, thus demonstrating her complete autonomy by proclaiming the new monarch by her own independent will. For several months thereafter, the public officials of Canada were busy taking the new oath of allegiance. When the new king and his queen visited Canada, he was greeted by a passionate outburst of devotion and loyalty which was as marked in French Canada and the Canadian West as it was in Ontario.

The war begins   War broke out in Europe for the second time in twenty-five years in the summer of 1939. A detailed consideration of its causes can not be undertaken here. It was abundantly clear, long before 1939, that forces which might plunge the whole world into war were once more at work on the European continent. Some of these forces had their origins in the first World War, and in the provisions of the Peace of Versailles which contained the seeds of new international conflicts.

German nationalism, stirred to a fever pitch by Adolf Hitler and the Nazi movement, had as one of its aims the rearmament of Germany and the reincorporation into the Third German Reich of all German-speaking areas which had been surrendered to the victorious powers in 1919. German Austria, the Sudetenland of Czechoslovakia, Danzig, the Polish Corridor, and Memel had long been trouble spots in post-war Europe. Italian fascists, under the lash of Benito Mussolini, talked about an *Italia Irridenta*, which included Corsica, Nice and Savoy. Communist Russia looked with eager eyes toward areas inhabited by Russians and surrendered to Poland in 1920, and many of the smaller nations, like Hungary and Bulgaria, waited for a chance to regain their lost provinces. Germany demanded the return of her lost colonies, and manifested the old desire to dominate Central Europe by a *Drang nach Osten*, which was far more vigorous and ruthless under Hitler than it had ever been under Kaiser Wilhelm II. Germans and Italians demanded more *Lebensraum*, and Mussolini had his special plans to dominate the Mediterranean and carve out a new empire in Africa.

With irresistible cunning and daring, Hitler laid his plans to end German isolation in Europe. A *rapprochement* was worked out with Italy. In 1936, the Rome-Berlin Axis was extended to include Tokyo. By 1938, the great powers were again divided, as in 1914, into two great rival groups—the Axis powers with their policies of totalitarianism, militarism and aggression, and France, Britain and Russia, which were still more or less loyal to the League, and the first two of which represented a certain democratic way of life in contrast with fascist absolutism. Millions of men were called to the colors; Italy invaded Ethiopia with impunity; the democracies abandoned Spain to the fascists, and Japan began her march into China. In the growing conflict between the democracies and the Axis powers, events now moved with lightning rapidity. In 1938, Hitler absorbed Austria and entered his former home in triumph. Before long, Czechoslovakia was virtually isolated, and so that post-war democracy was carved up, the Poles and the Germans and the Magyars taking their respective slices of her territory. The French system of alliances in Central Europe collapsed, and the Franco-Russian agreement came to an end. The settlement at Munich, by which France and England abandoned Czechoslovakia to Hitler in the interest of "peace in our time," ended in bitter disillusionment when Hitler occupied all that was left of the Czechoslovak state. General Franco overthrew republicanism in Spain, with the aid of his fascist supporters in Rome and Berlin, and the United States, England and France stood idly by. Memel was recovered for the German Reich, and Italy absorbed Albania. *The record of aggression*

The Munich settlement postponed the war, but did not avoid it. France and England made belated and futile efforts to check Hitler's demands upon Poland, particularly his claims to Danzig and the *War breaks out*

Corridor, and announced new guarantees to Greece and Rumania. England concluded an agreement with Turkey, but last-minute French and English efforts to win the coöperation of Russia ended in failure, and Communist Russia presently startled the world by concluding an agreement with Nazi Germany. Meantime, Italy and Germany had concluded a formal military alliance. Events reached a breaking point in August, 1939, and early in September, German troops invaded Poland. After a remarkably efficient, ruthless and speedy campaign, Poland lay prostrate under the wheels of the German war machine, and was divided between Germany and Russia. England and France had declared war in support of Poland, but were able to give practically no aid to their stricken ally. Europe was headed toward a second World War.

German conquests

After the *Blitzkrieg* against Poland, there was such a lull in military operations, especially in the West, that many observers were misled into a sense of false security by what they chose to describe as a "phony war." Russia seized the opportunity to force concessions from Finland, although that little nation surrendered only after an heroic struggle, and then the Red Army of Stalin overran Estonia, Latvia and Lithuania in order to strengthen Russia's position on the Baltic. Hitler seized Denmark and Norway. Finally, on May 10, 1940, the "phony war" came to a sudden end and German troops crossed the frontiers of Holland, Belgium and Luxembourg. By June 25, the French and English armies had been so thoroughly defeated that a Franco-German armistice was concluded, giving Germany control of a large part of northern and western France and of all the channel ports. The British army, in one of the most heroic rear guard actions in the annals of war, managed to extricate itself from Dunkirk and make its way across the channel to England, leaving vast stores of equipment behind. Great Britain had seen five states, including her most important continental ally, crumble before the German war machine within a few weeks, but her Prime Minister, Winston Churchill, declared that Britain would go on fighting by herself, defending every village and city against the invader, should he decide to cross the Channel. The horrors of war, by sea and air and land, as the gigantic conflict between Germany and the British Empire developed and spread to other parts of Europe, Africa and the seven seas, has been a daily feature in the press and radio broadcasts in every land.

Canada declares war

Although the Dominions had steadfastly refused to bind themselves unconditionally to go to war, and Canada in particular had pursued what seemed to some an ultra-cautious international policy in order to avoid straining Canadian national unity, it was clear from the outset that the Dominion would not desert the mother country or the Empire in their hour of travail.)True to her constitutional convictions, however, Canada declared war in her own right for the first time in her history on September 10, 1939, by action of her own

ministers and the approval of the Canadian Parliament. England was
at war for a week before Canada joined the conflict. During that interval, the United States permitted the sale of war supplies to Canada,
and the German Consul-general continued to exercise his normal
functions in the Dominion. The Canadian Government has not yet
broken off relations with the French government at Vichy. A French
Minister remains at Ottawa, though diplomatic intercourse ceased
between London and Vichy on July 5, 1940.

The Canadian people, with few exceptions, viewed the war as
another great struggle in which fundamental moral issues were at *The*
stake. The war was regarded as a life and death struggle between *Canadian*
totalitarianism and democracy, between the forces of repression and *response*
ruthless aggression, and the forces of liberty, freedom, self-government, law and order, and the rights of small nations. Only Mr. Woodsworth spoke in Parliament against a declaration of war, and although
the vast majority of his colleagues did not share his views, they
seemed to respect the sincerity of his pacifist convictions. Canada was
poorly prepared to give aid to the Empire. Her per capita expenditures for defense purposes had been the lowest in the whole Commonwealth of Nations. Expenditures for national defense had risen, however, from $17,458,075 in 1933-34 to $27,378,541 in 1935-36, and in
succeeding budgets, significant additions were made. Canada's industry and manpower had to be geared to war. After the Munich crisis,
eleventh-hour plans were prepared to mobilize Canadian industries
and make the Dominion an "Empire arsenal." An air mission was dispatched to London to study the manufacture of aircraft and the training of pilots, and the Canadian militia was reorganized and plans
were made for coastal defense. The program of greater preparedness
was justified on grounds of home defense. British naval supremacy
was relied upon to keep open Canada's "life-line" with the rest of the
world. Slowly it dawned upon Canadians that the Dominion's
defensive frontiers might be in Europe. In the first few months of the
war, the Government acted with great caution and restraint in order
not to endanger Canada's national unity. During the first phase of the
war, Canada took over the task of defending Newfoundland and
Labrador (later this was extended to include Bermuda and Iceland),
of furnishing war supplies, providing for home defense, and training
air pilots for the entire Commonwealth. According to the Prime
Minister, all plans were worked out in accordance with the desires of
the British High Command. Canada's industrial mobilization proceeded slowly, but part of the responsibility must be charged to the
delays and mistakes of the British government. In the early stages of
the war, Great Britain asked Canada to train the men and expected
English factories to supply all the engines and planes which might be
needed. Little was done to tool up Canadian industry for war purposes, and as late as May, 1940, the Canadian Minister of Munitions

and Supply reported that British industry still refused to send designs and formulae to Canada. The Dominion was busy creating an army, when it should have been engaged in building a war industry, and for many months, the British plan continued to emphasize the production of war equipment in the British Isles.

Government by Council

Immediately upon Canada's declaration of war, the War Measures Act of the first World War was revived. This gave the Cabinet (the Governor-in-Council) vast powers to govern by executive order, including government in accordance with the Defense of Canada Regulations, which dealt with espionage, military matters, the channels of communication, and virtually authorized a rigid censorship and an abridgement of ordinary judicial safeguards, far more severe than the comparable British regulations.

Foreign exchange

In a nation whose national income was less than five billion dollars, and whose favorable trade balance was only $340,000,000, it was necessary to institute drastic exchange controls at once in order to freeze investments in Canada owned by Americans and Britishers, and thus prevent the flight of gold and capital from the Dominion. A Foreign Exchange Control Board was established and all holders of foreign exchange or securities had to declare their holdings and could not deal in them or use them except by permission of the Board. The purchase or sale of foreign exchange was rigidly controlled by the Board, and imports and exports were subjected to a system of licenses. The payment of exports in foreign currency could not be avoided, but imports from the United States were sharply curtailed. Some thirty categories of manufactured goods could not be imported at all and a secondary list of articles could come in only in limited quantities and by special permit, and subject to a special tax. By these restrictions, which included automobiles, spirits, tobacco, radios, phonographs, ornaments, and other luxury and semi-luxury articles, exchange could be saved to the amount of five or six million dollars a month. To discourage the consumption of the articles in question when produced in Canada, a special excise tax of 20% to 25% was imposed. The purpose of all these regulations was not to stimulate home industry, but to limit the production and consumption of non-essentials and thus preserve dollar balances. At the same time, the Canadian Government issued an urgent invitation to Americans to visit and vacation in the Dominion, for, in the words of the Prime Minister, "the American dollars you leave behind will be used . . . for purchases . . . in the United States," and "these purchases will be used for the defense of the ideals of justice and freedom, which we hold in common."

War budget

In the emergency session of Parliament, held in September, 1939, and lasting seven days, a war appropriation bill of $100,000,000 was passed, an excess profits tax was imposed, and a Department of Munitions and Supply was established. Huge war orders were placed within the next few months. As the war continued, price controls were imposed, a plan was provided for registering the Dominion's labor supply, and other regulations were imposed upon the economic life of the nation.

The Canadian army was described in 1938 as "a bow and arrow army running out of arrows." Expenditures on defense still totalled *The Army* only three dollars per capita, as compared with twenty-five dollars spent in Great Britain. The Conservative Government had drastically cut expenditures for defense purposes from 1930 to 1935, and in the latter year, Mr. Ian Mackenzie, Minister of National Defense in the King Government, insisted that Canada had not a single, modern anti-aircraft gun, no tanks, armored cars, tractors for heavy guns, or munition plants to produce rifles, machine guns or artillery, and that the ammunition available for field guns would last for about an hour and a half of firing. Nevertheless, Canada was better prepared for war than in 1914. Within a year of the outbreak of the second war, Canada had sent 55,000 men abroad for service in Iceland, Newfoundland and England. Canadian military headquarters were established in Great Britain under Major-General H. D. G. Crerar, and Major-General A. G. L. McNaughton commanded the First Canadian Division overseas.

On June 20, 1940, when it was clear that the war had entered upon a most critical phase for Great Britain, and the home country could *Conscription* no longer give Canada much aid by way of equipment and supplies, the Dominion Parliament passed a law, approved by the new Governor-general, the Earl of Athlone, conscripting the man power of Canada. In August, all men over sixteen had to register, and two months later, conscription for military service began with the training of 30,000 men per month between twenty-one and forty-five years of age for a training period of thirty days. The intention of the law was to provide a home defense force. In February, 1941, the training period was extended from thirty days to four months. No one was to be sent out of the country unless he volunteered for such service. Canada's permanent army of 4,000 men grew in nine months to 91,000, and in the following two months, to 154,000 men. Over two divisions had gone overseas by the end of the first year of war. Inside Canada, there was an active service force of 114,000, and the militia reserves comprised another 100,000 men. Finally, Home Guards, to a large extent veterans of the last war under fifty, were organized for guard duty within the Dominion. In February, 1941, Prime Minister King announced that the Canadian Army overseas, the air training plan, and the navy would be practically doubled in strength. A third division was to be sent overseas, as well as an armored division and an army tank brigade. 400,000 men were in active service or in the reserves at the time.

The Canadian Royal Navy increased its personnel in the same period from 1,774 to 9,000 men, and from 15 ships to 113, by August, 1940. *The Navy*

On May 28, 1940, seven destroyers of the Canadian Navy had sailed to help England in her desperate task of patrolling the English Channel against invasion. Canadian ship yards began turning out merchant ships, and small boats for the navy, such as mine sweepers, patrol boats, and corvettes, and many million tons of shipping were convoyed from Eastern Canadian ports on their way to the British Isles. The corvette is a stout little ship of about 800 tons, high in the bow, and broad in the beam, which is especially effective in anti-submarine work. It carries depth charges and anti-aircraft guns.

The Air Force

The Dominion's greatest war effort was the British Commonwealth Air Training Plan. This plan originally provided for the training in Canada annually of some 35,000 pilots, observers and gunners. Approximately one fifth of the men were to come from Australia and New Zealand, a few from elsewhere in the Empire, but the great majority were Canadians. Costs were to be divided among the participating nations. Training schools were established in Canada, new air fields were constructed, and the training staff was recruited primarily from the Royal Canadian Air Force and civilian flying instructors. The program was delayed greatly by England's inability to furnish enough planes, and by the tardy expansion of the Canadian aircraft industry. As a result, engines and planes were secured in quantities from the United States. Under the training program, pilots received instruction for twenty-five weeks, gunners and observers for twenty-six weeks. At the end of that period, the men were to be ready to proceed overseas. The program was timed to reach its zenith in 1942 when the number of trainees would have reached 40,000 men, but events in Europe speeded up the plan considerably. On February 19, 1941, the strength of the Royal Canadian Air Force was 50,385, composed of 3,136 officers, 39,805 airmen and 7,446 civilians. The air-training enterprise had grown into a billion dollar enterprise. Airports are being built through western Canada to Alaska, a development which is of great importance to the defense program of the United States. Many of the planes used in the air schools are of American manufacture, but by July, 1941, the new Canadian factories are expected to produce in quantity.

War orders

On the economic and industrial front, Canada began her war activities by placing orders abroad for equipment and munitions. It soon became apparent, however, that she must organize her own sources of production. The Canadian industrial tempo is now at the highest peak in history. Maximum production is expected by July, 1941. Vast quantities of machine tools have been bought from the United States in order to create new manufacturing capacity, and the Dominion remains largely dependent on its southern neighbor for steel. Sixteen shipyards are building corvettes and mine sweepers. By March 31, 1942, the Canadian Navy is expected to reach a strength of 413 ships and 27,000 men. Canada's output of planes is expected to reach 360 a month in 1941, but aeroplane engines, propellers and instruments are still largely imported. There has been a steady increase in the production of airplane bodies, automobiles, trucks and tanks, machine guns, rifles, and larger guns. One of the largest and most modern gun plants in the British Empire is in Canada. In the first year of the war, the Ministry of Munitions and Supply purchased enough woolen and cotton cloth to stretch from Ottawa to Berlin and back again, and all of this is being used for uniforms. The Government has created a number of new companies, which are really government owned, but staffed by business men. They act as agents of the Ministry of Munitions and Supply, and government controllers have been appointed for a number of the leading industries and raw materials. In some cases, the new plants are virtually branches of existing companies, with a provision that they may be bought from the government after the war. Labor was asked to work extra days and hours, and the response has been prompt and satisfying. Contracts have been intelligently and honestly drawn, for the most part, and there have been few charges of graft or mismanagement. Factory expansion has occasionally been encouraged by granting the owners exemption from the war profits tax. Among the leaders of this vast program of mobilizing the home front for war should be mentioned Defense Minister Rogers, who was killed in an airship crash in June, 1940, his successor, Colonel J. L. Ralston, and the American-born Minister of Munitions and Supply, C. D. Howe. The whole industrial and economic structure of Canada is being changed under the pressure of a war emergency, and many of the measures taken may well forecast still greater developments in the direction of state socialism during the remainder of the war and during the reconstruction that must follow a peace.

The strain on Canada's financial resources has been tremendous. The budget of 1940 was a billion dollar budget and made drastic additions to the income tax, imposed a heavy excise tax on automobiles, steeply graduated according to their value. The budget of 1941 was still larger and was passed without a record vote. Canadian taxes are still much lower than in Great Britain. Of the budget expenditures for 1940-41, estimated at $1,148,000,000, $760,000,000 was to come from taxation and other sources, leaving $390,000,000 to be borrowed. To this deficit must be added a credit of $200,000,000 advanced by the Canadian Government to finance British purchases in the Dominion. In February, 1941, when Finance Minister J. L. Ilsley presented a new war appropriations bill, he estimated that half of Canada's national income would go to the government. The first public war loan was raised in January, 1940,—a call for $200,000,000 at $3\frac{1}{4}\%$ interest. The loan was oversubscribed by 60%. In May, a campaign was launched for the sale of War Savings Certificates, which yielded $60,000,000 during the first year. In September, $300,000,000 was borrowed at

War budgets

$3\frac{1}{8}$%. The passage of the Unemployment Insurance Act was expected to result in the collection of large sums each year from employers and employees, and this fund also was invested in government securities to help finance the war. Great Britain paid for supplies bought in Canada by selling her Canadian securities to the Dominion, thus reducing the latter's indebtedness to the mother country. Various campaigns for war relief funds, like the Red Cross, were privately conducted and elicited generous responses. By the end of 1940, Canada expected to have no more unemployed employables. Her industries were booming, especially steel, textiles, pulp and paper, and the construction trades. Canada, to be sure, had lost one fifth of her normal foreign markets as a result of the war, but for the moment, with the exception of wheat and certain agricultural products, home consumption and war needs were adequate to keep the Canadian economic system running at top speed. Whether inflation is inevitable or not, a reduction in the standard of living seems unavoidable in the long run as a result of the war.

Canadian-American coöperation

Coöperation between the United States and Canada has become ever closer as the war progressed. An attempt was made to get each country to concentrate on the production of those supplies for which it seemed best fitted. Canada has concentrated on small arms and tanks, anti-tank guns and aircraft machine guns, Bren guns, and certain large naval guns and field pieces. 15,000 men were engaged in constructing the plant for a hundred million dollar chemical industry to produce explosives. In August, 1940, the Ogdensburg Agreement was announced by the United States and Canada. It was the culmination of discussions that had begun more than two years before the outbreak of the European War. The Agreement created a permanent Joint Canadian-American Board on Defense to provide for exchange of information, and coöperation between the general staffs of the two armies. Colonel O. M. Biggar became chairman of the Canadian section, and Mayor Fiorello LaGuardia of New York was made the American chairman of the Board. The Defense Board has been working hard on problems of continental strategy and defense, although obviously its reports can not be published in detail. Prime Minister King described the Ogdensburg Agreement as "no temporary axis. . . . It is part of the enduring foundation of a new world order, based on friendship and good will . . . ," and Mayor LaGuardia regarded the new defense policy as "the Monroe Doctrine translated into action." In January, 1941, the first United States troops sailed to man the new base which was being built at Newfoundland. Fifty American destroyers, overage, but fully equipped, were sent to England, in return for the lease to the United States of strategically located naval bases. There are some among the Canadian people who have been wondering whether the imperial tie would eventually be weakened by the increasing coöperation between Ottawa and Washington, but the vast majority seemed to be well satisfied with recent developments in Canadian-American relations. The passage of the "lend-lease bill" by the United States Congress in March, 1941, and the President's pledge of "all out" aid to Britain and the democracies for the duration of the war is but the final step toward the closest coöperation the two neighbor nations have ever experienced in all their history.

On March 19, 1941, the St. Lawrence Waterway project was revived by the signing of an agreement in Ottawa between the United States and Canada, calling for a construction project in the international rapids section of the St. Lawrence River at an estimated cost of $266,170,000. The agreement covers both power and navigation development in that area, and will not require ratification by the United States Senate since it is not in the form of a treaty. All that will be necessary to launch the enterprise is approval by a majority vote by the Canadian Parliament and the United States Congress. According to the estimates of engineers, the expenditures to be made primarily for navigation will amount to $38,578,000; the expenditures for power development will total $96,804,000, and the cost of work common to both purposes will be an additional $130,788,000. The exchange of notes between President Roosevelt and Prime Minister King emphasized the defense aspects of the plan as "a matter of vital necessity" and as part of the American program of aid to Britain and coöperation in defense with Canada. Under the proposed plan, the United States would pay about $206,000,000 of the total cost, and Canada's share would be $60,000,000, since the Dominion would be credited for money previously spent on the Welland Canal. President Roosevelt expects the work to be completed by 1945; expert engineers believe 1948 is the more likely date, and point out that Canada is still exporting surplus power, and that efficient steam plants can be built more rapidly to overcome a shortage of power for defense purposes than the St. Lawrence waterway could take care of the need. There are great engineering difficulties to be overcome, but the proposal will probably sufficiently capture the imagination of the Canadian and American peoples in war time to insure its adoption.

The St. Lawrence Waterway

Under the stress of war conditions, the United States government has permitted Canada to build naval vessels on the Great Lakes, and also to arm them before sending them to the Atlantic seaboard, thus again setting aside the old Rush-Bagot Agreement of 1817. The modification of the agreement was secured after two years of correspondence between the Ottawa and Washington governments. Both parties have been careful to preserve the spirit of the agreement which is now nearly a hundred and twenty-five years old. A temporary arrangement of a somewhat similar sort had been made during the first World War when American companies had wished to build mosquito boats on the Lakes.

The Rush-Bagot Agreement

The problem of civil liberties in a democracy in war time is always a difficult and delicate one, and Canada has not escaped the usual controversies over this issue. When the Canadian government declared war in 1939, that declaration immediately brought the War Measures Act, which had been dormant since the World War, into force. As already pointed out, this act gave vast powers to the executive branch of the government, powers which ordinarily are exercised by Parliament. In many respects, Canada was less sensitive to the necessity of preserving the democratic processes than England was in a much greater crisis. Conscription aroused comparatively little controversy because it concerned home defense primarily, and because only volunteers could be sent overseas. The Catholic Church gave the measure its blessing, and when Camillien Houde, Mayor of Montreal, tried to oppose conscription, he was clapped into a concentration camp. Adrien Arcand, the Quebec fascist leader, was likewise interned. In July, 1940, Parliament passed the Treachery Act, to apply to any one assisting the enemy. The Defense of Canada Regulations deal, among other things, with espionage, censorship and sabotage. Under these regulations, the Minister of Justice may detain or intern any person believed dangerous to the safety of the state, and the Royal Canadian Mounted Police are specially charged with running down "subversive elements." Several thousand Germans and Italians, and others suspected of fascist or communist sympathies, have been interned. There is a provision for the review of the Minister's orders, and for a report to Parliament. There have been several debates on the issue in the House of Commons, during which M. Lapointe has had to defend his conduct. Several regulations deal with freedom of speech and freedom of the press, although criticisms of the Government made in good faith are supposedly excepted. There have been several hundred prosecutions. The procedure is by indictment or summary trial. Sentences have varied from three months to three years. On the whole, these regulations have been enforced with moderation and intelligence and good sense, and a substantial amount of free discussion and criticism of Government policies remains. Several labor leaders have been interned for alleged Communist activities, and Jehovah's Witnesses have been in trouble because their religion does not permit them to salute the flag or sing the national anthem. Picketing has been curtailed, and Communist and fascist groups have been declared illegal, but no direct abrogation of the right of freedom of assembly seems to have occurred. Although the censorship regulations are quite drastic, results have been obtained largely by getting the voluntary cooperation of publishers. The importation of certain books and periodicals, including some "comics" from the United States, has been prohibited, in part to conserve dollar exchange. Thus far, there have been few individual injustices committed. The excellent example Great Britain has given by permitting complete freedom

of discussion in the midst of falling bombs can not help but have its
effect upon the Dominion.

The gigantic war effort described above touched off its full measure of political controversy. Ontario industrialists accused Prime   *Political*
Minister King of moving entirely too slowly, and the Conservative   *controversy*
Opposition charged that Canada was not only woefully unprepared,
but that attempts to deal with the situation were pitifully inadequate.
Conservative leaders expressed scepticism about the reports of progress that issued from the government departments and asked for more
detailed information, and C.C.F. leaders clamored against "big
business" and demanded a voice for labor in the defense program and
a hundred per cent excess profits tax. As a matter of fact, the King
Government had done everything the British Government had asked
it to do during the first six months of the war, and British industry
has been none too willing to send its designs across the ocean to
stimulate manufacturing in Canada.

On October 25, 1939, Prime Minister Duplessis held an election
in Quebec to get a mandate against certain war measures imposed   *A Quebec*
upon the French Canadian province. He charged the Liberal leader-   *election*
ship with imposing a centralized censorship and dictatorship upon
Quebec, and called for a defense of provincial rights. M. Lapointe
and three other federal ministers thereupon actively intervened in the
campaign and threatened to resign if their cause should be defeated.
At the same time, however, they promised the French Canadians that
there would be no military conscription for overseas service and that
they would resign if the Ottawa Government should attempt to initiate such a measure. The result of the Quebec election was a decisive
defeat for Duplessis and a landslide for the Liberals. Mr. King hailed
the outcome as a victory for Canada and the Empire. As a matter of
fact, it was as much a vote against conscription as it was a vote in
favor of participation in Canada's war program. French Canadians
seemed to accept the war, partly because Cardinal Villeneuve had
become an outspoken enemy of Hitlerism, and partly because of the
bold leadership of M. Lapointe and the other French-Canadian ministers. The fascist movement was suppressed in Quebec, apparently with
the full approval of the vast majority of the French-Canadians.
Duplessis was swept into political oblivion and was succeeded by
Adelard Godbout. French-Canadian enlistments and the decisive
defeat of the Duplessis non-participationist elements in the election
of 1939 are the best evidences of national unity in the present crisis.

A few months later, a second attack was launched on the Ottawa
Government. This time it came from Ontario where the legislature,   *The Ontario*
under Mr. Hepburn's leadership, in January, 1940 passed a vote of   *attack*
censure on Prime Minister King's war program. Both Liberals and
Conservatives voted for the measure, and Prime Minister Hepburn
indulged in considerable personal abuse of Mackenzie King. When

the Dominion Parliament assembled, the speech from the throne
announced an immediate appeal to the country, and Parliament was
sent home after a session of just four hours. Preparations were immediately made for a "snap election." This was Mr. King's answer to
Ontario. Dr. Manion, the Conservative leader, accused him of trick-
ery, dictatorship and unscrupulous politics. Mr. King's reply was
that he had to get rid of such obstruction in the interest of a total
war effort.

Election
of 1940

The election was ordered for March 26, 1940. The campaign turned
out to be extremely dull. Dr. Manion promised a government of the
best brains. Mr. King, with the advantage of a good political organization, ample funds, and the support of Quebec and business, had to
do very little except talk about national unity and the total war
program. Dr. Manion, a former Liberal, and an Irish-Roman Catholic
who had married a French Canadian wife, campaigned very ineffec-
tively under the label of a National Government. Mr. King steadfastly rejected all suggestions of a coalition. The Prime Minister
announced that he was too busy to do much campaigning and he made
only five addresses and some radio broadcasts. He asked for a popular
endorsement, and got it, in an election in which the Liberals got a
slightly larger majority than they had before, and in which such
prominent Conservatives as Manion, Stevens and Cahan lost their
seats. The C.C.F. strength increased from seven to eight, although its
popular vote was 400,000; and in Ontario, where the Liberals expected
to lose twenty seats, they actually gained one. The Social Credit
group at Ottawa fell from 16 to 9, and in an election in Alberta,
Premier Aberhart's party narrowly escaped defeat. The Liberals had
the support of the business interests, prospering from war orders, and
apparently the majority of the voters were satisfied with Mr. King's
war record and did not believe he would do either too little or too
much to injure Canada permanently. Mr. King once more had proved
that he was an expert conciliator and a clever manipulator, for he held
radicals and extreme conservatives together in a program of limited
participation in the war. The political Cassandras pronounced an
eulogy over the Conservative party and predicted it would never rise
again. Dr. Manion resigned his leadership and was succeeded by
Mr. R. B. Hanson. The C.C.F. suffered a heavy loss in the continued
serious illness of its leader, Mr. J. S. Woodsworth.

Greater
war efforts

Four months after the election just described, Hitler released his
Blitzkrieg against France and the Low Countries. As the crisis became
more alarming, the Canadian people demanded more action and the
Opposition clamored for a national coalition government. Mr. King
remained adamant. He promised the fullest coöperation with England
and reorganized and somewhat strengthened his Cabinet. When the
1939-40 budget showed a huge deficit, $600,000,000 was borrowed. A
special national defense tax of 2% was put on all incomes in excess of

$600 for single men and $1,200 for married men; the income taxes
were raised and the exemptions lowered, the excess profits tax scale
was raised to 75% and excises were imposed on many articles. Each
budget called for greater sacrifices. A man with an income of $200,000
a year in 1941 paid 64.8% to the government if he lived in Ontario,
74.8% if he lived in Montreal, and 85.2% if he lived in British Columbia. The proceedings of the House of Commons were curtailed
to permit only the consideration of what was important for the winning of the war, and Mr. King's ministers vigorously denied charges
of avoidable lags in the Canadian war effort. Shortcomings were
frankly admitted and steps were taken to eliminate the "bottle-necks"
in Canadian war production. In March, 1941, after an especially
frank address by C. D. Howe, Minister of Munitions and Supply,
which disarmed his critics by its unpretentious manner and truth-
telling, especially about the lag in airplane production, the Opposition leader virtually abandoned his demand for a National Government.

This narrative must be concluded at a time when no one can predict
the outcome of the second World War. Indeed, the struggle is just
entering upon its most violent phase. Canada is making a gallant
defense of her way of life. That her entire future will be materially
affected by the struggle is evident. Canada's autonomous powers, her
relation to the Empire, and her future as a Western Hemisphere nation
are all involved by events that will probably reach their final decision
on the battlefields of Europe. To that decision the two great Anglo-
Saxon neighbor nations in North America may make a contribution so
great as to prove decisive.

SELECTED BIBLIOGRAPHY FOR CHAPTER XXXIV

For a good summary of the events leading to war in 1939, F. Lee Benns' *Europe's
Return to War, 1938-1940* (New York, 1940) and Frederick L. Schuman's *Night Over
Europe: The Diplomacy of Nemesis, 1939-40* (New York, 1941) are useful and very readable.
Stimulating discussions of certain phases of Canadian policy will be found in Leslie
Roberts: *We Must Be Free* (Toronto, 1939); John MacCormac: *Canada: America's Problem*
(New York, 1940); and A. R. M. Lower: *Canada and the Far East, 1940* (New York,
1940).

Useful pamphlets are C. P. Stacey: *Canada and the Second World War* (Toronto, 1940)
and R. S. Lambert: *Canada's War Effort* (Toronto, 1940). Edgar P. Dean gives a brief
survey of "Canada's New Defense Program," in *Foreign Affairs*, October, 1940, pp. 1-17,
and there is a good discussion of "Civil Liberties in Canada during Wartime" by F. A.
Brewin in *The Bill of Rights Review*, I, No. 2, pp. 112-121. The only book length treatment thus far of Canada at war is edited by John W. Dafoe under the title *Canada Fights*
(New York, 1941).

APPENDIX

THE BRITISH NORTH AMERICA ACT, 1867

(30 & 31 Victoria, c. 3)

An Act for the Union of Canada, Nova Scotia, and New Brunswick, and the Government thereof: and for Purposes connected therewith.

[*March 29, 1867.*]

WHEREAS the Provinces of Canada, Nova Scotia, and New Brunswick, have expressed their desire to be federally united into one Dominion under the Crown of the United Kingdom of Great Britain and Ireland, with a Constitution similar in principle to that of the United Kingdom:

And whereas such a Union would conduce to the welfare of the Provinces and promote the interests of the British Empire:

And whereas on the establishment of the Union by authority of Parliament it is expedient, not only that the Constitution of the Legislative Authority in the Dominion be provided for, but also that the nature of the Executive Government therein be declared:

And whereas it is expedient that provision be made for the eventual admission into the Union of other parts of British North America:

Be it therefore enacted and declared by the Queen's most Excellent Majesty, by and with the advice and consent of the Lords Spiritual and Temporal, and Commons, in this present Parliament assembled, and by the authority of the same, as follows:

I.—PRELIMINARY

1. This Act may be cited as *The British North America Act, 1867.* *Short title*

2. The provisions of this Act referring to Her Majesty the Queen extend also to the heirs and successors of Her Majesty, Kings and Queens of the United Kingdom of Great Britain and Ireland. *Application of provisions referring to the Queen*

II.—UNION

3. It shall be lawful for the Queen, by and with the advice of Her Majesty's Most Honourable Privy Council, to declare by Proclamation that on and after a day herein appointed, not being more than six months after the passing of this Act, the Provinces of Canada, Nova Scotia, and New Brunswick shall form and be one Dominion under the name of Canada; and on and after that day those three *Declaration by proclamation of Union of Canada, Nova Scotia and New Brunswick, into one Dominion*

under name of Canada
Provinces shall form and be one Dominion under that name accordingly.

Commencement of subsequent provisions of Act. Meaning of Canada in such provisions
4. The subsequent provisions of this Act shall, unless it is otherwise expressed or implied, commence and have effect on and after the Union, that is to say, on and after the day appointed for the Union taking effect in the Queen's Proclamation; and in the same provisions, unless it is otherwise expressed or implied, the name Canada shall be taken to mean Canada as constituted under this Act.

Four Provinces
5. Canada shall be divided into four Provinces, named Ontario, Quebec, Nova Scotia, and New Brunswick.

Provinces of Ontario and Quebec
6. The parts of the Province of Canada (as it exists at the passing of this Act) which formerly constituted respectively the Provinces of Upper Canada and Lower Canada shall be deemed to be severed, and shall form two separate Provinces. The part which formerly constituted the Province of Upper Canada shall constitute the Province of Ontario, and the part which formerly constituted the Province of Lower Canada shall constitute the Province of Quebec.

Provinces of Nova Scotia and New Brunswick
7. The Provinces of Nova Scotia and New Brunswick shall have the same limits as at the passing of this Act.

Population of Provinces to be distinguished in decennial census
8. In the general census of the population of Canada which is hereby required to be taken in the year one thousand eight hundred and seventy-one, and in every tenth year thereafter, the respective populations of the four Provinces shall be distinguished.

III.—Executive Power

Executive Power to continue vested in the Queen
9. The Executive Government and authority of and over Canada is hereby declared to continue and be vested in the Queen.

Application of provisions referring to Governor-General
10. The provisions of this Act referring to the Governor-General extend and apply to the Governor-General for the time being of Canada, or other the Chief Executive Officer or Administrator for the time being carrying on the Government of Canada on behalf and in the name of the Queen, by whatever title he is designated.

Constitution of Privy Council for Canada
11. There shall be a Council to aid and advise in the Government of Canada, to be styled the Queen's Privy Council for Canada; and the persons who are to be members of that Council shall be from time to time chosen and summoned by the Governor-General and sworn in as Privy Councillors, and members thereof may be from time to time removed by the Governor-General.

All powers under Acts to be exercised by Governor-General with advice of Privy Council, or alone
12. All powers, authorities, and functions, which under any Act of the Parliament of Great Britain, or of the Parliament of the United Kingdom of Great Britain and Ireland, or of the Legislature of Upper Canada, Lower Canada, Canada, Nova Scotia, or New Brunswick, are at the Union vested in or exercisable by the respective Governors or Lieutenant-Governors of those Provinces, with the advice, or with the advice and consent, of the respective Executive

Councils thereof, or in conjunction with those Councils, or with any number of members thereof, or by those Governors, or Lieutenant-Governors individually, shall, as far as the same continue in existence and capable of being exercised after the Union in relation to the Government of Canada, be vested in and exercisable by the Governor-General, with the advice or with the advice and consent of or in connection with the Queen's Privy Council for Canada, or any members thereof, or by the Governor-General individually, as the case requires, subject nevertheless (except with respect to such as exist under Acts of the Parliament of Great Britain or of the Parliament of the United Kingdom of Great Britain and Ireland) to be abolished or altered by the Parliament of Canada.

13. The provisions of this Act referring to the Governor-General in Council shall be construed as referring to the Governor-General acting by and with the advice of the Queen's Privy Council for Canada. *Application of provisions referring to Governor-General in Council*

14. It shall be lawful for the Queen, if Her Majesty thinks fit, to authorize the Governor-General from time to time to appoint any person or any persons jointly or severally to be his Deputy or Deputies within any part or parts of Canada, and in that capacity to exercise during the pleasure of the Governor-General such of the powers, authorities, and functions of the Governor-General as the Governor-General deems it necessary or expedient to assign to him or them, subject to any limitations or directions expressed or given by the Queen; but the appointment of such a Deputy or Deputies shall not affect the exercise by the Governor-General himself of any power, authority or function. *Power to Her Majesty to authorize Governor-General to appoint Deputies*

15. The Command-in-Chief of the Land and Naval Militia, and of all Naval and Military Forces, of and in Canada, is hereby declared to continue and be vested in the Queen. *Command of armed forces to continue to be vested in the Queen*

16. Until the Queen otherwise directs the seat of Government of Canada shall be Ottawa. *Seat of Government of Canada*

IV.—Legislative Power

17. There shall be one Parliament for Canada, consisting of the Queen, an Upper House, styled the Senate, and the House of Commons. *Constitution of Parliament of Canada*

[*Section 18 was repealed by imperial Act 38 & 39 Vict., c. 38, and the following section substituted therefor.*

18. The privileges, immunities, and powers to be held, enjoyed and exercised by the Senate and by the House of Commons and by the members thereof respectively shall be such as are from time to time defined by Act of the Parliament of Canada, but so that any Act of the Parliament of Canada defining such privileges, immunities and powers shall not confer any privileges, immunities or powers exceeding those at the passing of such Act held, enjoyed, and exer- *Privileges, etc., of Houses*

cised by the Commons House of Parliament of the United Kingdom of Great Britain and Ireland and by the members thereof.]

First Session of the Parliament of Canada

19. The Parliament of Canada shall be called together not later than six months after the Union.

Yearly Session of the Parliament of Canada

20. There shall be a Session of the Parliament of Canada once at least in every year, so that twelve months shall not intervene between the last sitting of the Parliament in one Session and its first sitting in the next Session.

The Senate

Number of Senators

21. The Senate shall, subject to the provisions of this Act, consist of seventy-two members, who shall be styled Senators.

Representation of Provinces in Senate

22. In relation to the constitution of the Senate, Canada shall be deemed to consist of three divisions—

1. Ontario;
2. Quebec;
3. The Maritime Provinces, Nova Scotia and New Brunswick; which three divisions shall (subject to the provisions of this Act) be equally represented in the Senate as follows: Ontario by twenty-four Senators; Quebec by twenty-four Senators; and the Maritime Provinces by twenty-four Senators, twelve thereof representing Nova Scotia, and twelve thereof representing New Brunswick.

In the case of Quebec each of the twenty-four Senators representing that Province shall be appointed for one of the twenty-four Electoral Divisions of Lower Canada specified in Schedule A. to chapter one of the Consolidated Statutes of Canada.

Qualifications of Senator

23. The qualifications of a Senator shall be as follows:—

1. He shall be of the full age of thirty years;
2. He shall be either a natural-born subject of the Queen, or a subject of the Queen naturalized by an Act of the Parliament of Great Britain, or of the Parliament of the United Kingdom of Great Britain and Ireland, or of the Legislature of one of the Provinces of Upper Canada, Lower Canada, Canada, Nova Scotia, or New Brunswick, before the Union, or of the Parliament of Canada after the Union;
3. He shall be legally or equitably seised as of freehold for his own use and benefit of lands or tenements held in free and common socage, or seised or possessed for his own use and benefit of lands or tenements held in franc-aleu or in roture, within the Province for which he is appointed, of the value of $4,000, over and above all rents, dues, debts, charges, mortgages and incumbrances due or payable out of or charged on or affecting the same;
4. His real and personal property shall be together worth $4,000, over and above his debts and liabilities;

5. He shall be resident in the Province for which he is appointed;

6. In the case of Quebec he shall have his real property qualification in the Electoral Division for which he is appointed, or shall be resident in that Division.

24. The Governor-General shall from time to time, in the Queen's name, by instrument under the Great Seal of Canada, summon qualified persons to the Senate; and, subject to the provisions of this Act, every person so summoned shall become and be a member of the Senate and a Senator. *Summoning of Senators*

25. Such persons shall be first summoned to the Senate as the Queen by warrant under Her Majesty's Royal Sign Manual thinks fit to approve, and their names shall be inserted in the Queen's Proclamation of Union. *Summons of first body of Senators*

26. If at any time on the recommendation of the Governor-General the Queen thinks fit to direct that three or six members be added to the Senate, the Governor-General may by summons to three or six qualified persons (as the case may be), representing equally the three divisions of Canada, add to the Senate accordingly. *Additions of Senators in certain cases*

27. In case of such addition being at any time made the Governor-General shall not summon any person to the Senate, except on a further like direction by the Queen on the like recommendation, until each of the three divisions of Canada is represented by twenty-four Senators and no more. *Reduction of Senate to normal number*

28. The number of Senators shall not at any time exceed seventy-eight. *Maximum number of Senators*

29. A Senator shall, subject to the provisions of this Act, hold his place in the Senate for life. *Tenure of place in Senate*

30. A Senator may by writing under his hand addressed to the Governor-General resign his place in the Senate, and thereupon the same shall be vacant. *Resignation of place in Senate*

31. The place of a Senator shall become vacant in any of the following cases: *Disqualification of Senators*

1. If for two consecutive Sessions of the Parliament he fails to give his attendance in the Senate;

2. If he takes an oath or makes a declaration or acknowledgment of allegiance, obedience, or adherence to a foreign power, or does an act whereby he becomes a subject or citizen, or entitled to the rights or privileges of a subject or citizen, of a foreign power;

3. If he is adjudged bankrupt or insolvent, or applies for the benefit of any law relating to insolvent debtors, or becomes a public defaulter;

4. If he is attainted of treason or convicted of felony or of any infamous crime;

5. If he ceases to be qualified in respect of property or of residence; provided, that a Senator shall not be deemed to have ceased to be qualified in respect of residence by reason only of his

residing at the seat of the Government of Canada while holding an office under that Government requiring his presence
there.

32. When a vacancy happens in the Senate by resignation, death,
or otherwise, the Governor-General shall by summons to a fit and
qualified person fill the vacancy.

33. If any question arises respecting the qualification of a Senator
or a vacancy in the Senate, the same shall be heard and determined
by the Senate.

34. The Governor-General may from time to time, by instrument
under the Great Seal of Canada, appoint a Senator to be Speaker of
the Senate, and may remove him and appoint another in his stead.

35. Until the Parliament of Canada otherwise provides, the
presence of at least fifteen Senators, including the Speaker, shall be
necessary to constitute a meeting of the Senate for the exercise of its
powers.

36. Questions arising in the Senate shall be decided by a majority
of voices, and the Speaker shall in all cases have a vote, and when
the voices are equal the decision shall be deemed to be in the negative.

The House of Commons

37. The House of Commons shall, subject to the provisions of
this Act, consist of one hundred and eighty-one members, of whom
eighty-two shall be elected for Ontario, sixty-five for Quebec, nineteen for Nova Scotia and fifteen for New Brunswick.

38. The Governor-General shall from time to time, in the Queen's
name, by instrument under the Great Seal of Canada, summon and
call together the House of Commons.

39. A Senator shall not be capable of being elected or of sitting or
voting as a member of the House of Commons.

40. Until the Parliament of Canada otherwise provides, Ontario,
Quebec, Nova Scotia, and New Brunswick shall, for the purposes of
the election of members to serve in the House of Commons, be divided
into Electoral Districts as follows:—

1.—ONTARIO

Ontario shall be divided into the Counties, Ridings of Counties,
Cities, parts of Cities, and Towns enumerated in the first Schedule
to this Act, each whereof shall be an Electoral District, each such
District as numbered in that Schedule being entitled to return one
member.

2.—QUEBEC

Quebec shall be divided into sixty-five Electoral Districts, composed of the sixty-five Electoral Divisions into which Lower Canada
is at the passing of this Act divided under chapter two of the Con-

solidated Statutes of Canada, chapter seventy-five of the Consolidated Statutes of Lower Canada, and the Act of the Province of Canada of the twenty-third year of the Queen, chapter one, or any other Act amending the same in force at the Union, so that each such Electoral Division shall be for the purposes of this Act an Electoral District entitled to return one member.

3.—Nova Scotia

Each of the eighteen Counties of Nova Scotia shall be an Electoral District. The County of Halifax shall be entitled to return two members, and each of the other Counties one member.

4.—New Brunswick

Each of the fourteen Counties into which New Brunswick is divided, including the City and County of St. John, shall be an Electoral District; the City of St. John shall also be a separate Electoral District. Each of those fifteen Electoral Districts shall be entitled to return one member.

41. Until the Parliament of Canada otherwise provides, all laws in force in the several Provinces at the Union relative to the following matters or any of them, namely,—the qualifications and disqualifications of persons to be elected or to sit or vote as members of the House of Assembly or Legislative Assembly in the several Provinces, the voters at elections of such members, the oaths to be taken by voters, the Returning Officers, their powers and duties, the proceedings at elections, the periods during which elections may be continued, the trial of controverted elections, and proceedings incident thereto, the vacating of seats of members, and the execution of new writs in case of seats vacated otherwise than by dissolution,— shall respectively apply to elections of members to serve in the House of Commons for the same several Provinces. *Continuance of existing election laws until Parliament of Canada otherwise provides*

Provided that, until the Parliament of Canada otherwise provides, at any election for a Member of the House of Commons for the District of Algoma, in addition to persons qualified by the law of the Province of Canada to vote, every male British subject aged twenty-one years or upwards, being a householder, shall have a vote.

42. For the first election of members to serve in the House of Commons the Governor-General shall cause writs to be issued by such persons, in such form, and addressed to such Returning Officers as he thinks fit. *Writs for first election*

The person issuing writs under this section shall have the like powers as are possessed at the Union by the officers charged with the issuing of writs for the election of members to serve in the respective House of Assembly or Legislative Assembly of the Province of Canada, Nova Scotia, or New Brunswick; and the Returning Officers to whom writs are directed under this section shall have the like powers as are possessed at the Union by the officers charged with the returning of writs for the election of members to serve in the same respective House of Assembly or Legislative Assembly.

43. In case a vacancy in the representation in the House of Commons of any Electoral District happens before the meeting of the Parliament, or after the meeting of the Parliament before provision is made by the Parliament in this behalf, the provisions of the last foregoing section of this Act shall extend and apply to the issuing and returning of a writ in respect of such vacant District.

44. The House of Commons on its first assembling after a general election shall proceed with all practicable speed to elect one of its members to be Speaker.

45. In case of a vacancy happening in the office of Speaker by death, resignation or otherwise, the House of Commons shall with all practicable speed proceed to elect another of its members to be Speaker.

46. The Speaker shall preside at all meetings of the House of Commons.

47. Until the Parliament of Canada otherwise provides, in case of the absence for any reason of the Speaker from the chair of the House of Commons for a period of forty-eight consecutive hours, the House may elect another of its members to act as Speaker, and the member so elected shall during the continuance of such absence of the Speaker have and execute all the powers, privileges, and duties of Speaker.

48. The presence of at least twenty members of the House of Commons shall be necessary to constitute a meeting of the House for the exercise of its powers, and for that purpose the Speaker shall be reckoned as a member.

49. Questions arising in the House of Commons shall be decided by a majority of voices other than that of the Speaker, and when the voices are equal, but not otherwise, the Speaker shall have a vote.

50. Every House of Commons shall continue for five years from the day of the return of the writs for choosing the House (subject to be sooner dissolved by the Governor-General), and no longer.

51. On the completion of the census in the year one thousand eight hundred and seventy-one, and of each subsequent decennial census, the representation of the four Provinces shall be re-adjusted by such authority, in such manner and from such time as the Parliament of Canada from time to time provides, subject and according to the following rules:—

1. Quebec shall have the fixed number of sixty-five members.
2. There shall be assigned to each of the other Provinces such a number of members as will bear the same proportion to the number of its population (ascertained at such census) as the number of sixty-five bears to the number of the population of Quebec (so ascertained).
3. In the computation of the number of members for a Province

a fractional part not exceeding one-half of the whole number requisite for entitling the Province to a member shall be disregarded; but a fractional part exceeding one-half of that number shall be equivalent to the whole number.

4. On any such re-adjustment the number of members for a Province shall not be reduced unless the proportion which the number of the population of the Province bore to the number of the aggregate population of Canada at the then last preceding re-adjustment of the number of members for the Province is ascertained at the then latest census to be diminished by one-twentieth part or upwards.

5. Such re-adjustment shall not take effect until the termination of the then existing Parliament.

52. The number of members of the House of Commons may be from time to time increased by the Parliament of Canada, provided the proportionate representation of the Provinces prescribed by this Act is not thereby disturbed. *Increase of number of House of Commons*

Money Votes; Royal Assent

53. Bills for appropriating any part of the public revenue, or for imposing any tax or impost, shall originate in the House of Commons. *Appropriation and tax bills*

54. It shall not be lawful for the House of Commons to adopt or pass any vote, resolution, address, or bill for the appropriation of any part of the public revenue, or of any tax or impost, to any purpose that has not been first recommended to that House by message of the Governor-General in the Session in which such vote, resolution, address, or bill is proposed. *Recommendation of money votes*

55. Where a bill passed by the Houses of the Parliament is presented to the Governor-General for the Queen's assent, he shall declare according to his discretion, but subject to the provisions of this Act and to Her Majesty's instructions, either that he assents thereto in the Queen's name, or that he withholds the Queen's assent, or that he reserves the bill for the signification of the Queen's pleasure. *Royal assent to bills, etc.*

56. Where the Governor-General assents to a bill in the Queen's name, he shall by the first convenient opportunity send an authentic copy of the Act to one of Her Majesty's Principal Secretaries of State; and if the Queen in Council within two years after the receipt thereof by the Secretary of State thinks fit to disallow the Act, such disallowance (with a certificate of the Secretary of State of the day on which the Act was received by him) being signified by the Governor-General by speech or message to each of the Houses of the Parliament, or by proclamation, shall annul the Act from and after the day of such signification. *Disallowance by Order in Council of Act, assented to by Governor-General*

57. A bill reserved for the signification of the Queen's pleasure shall not have any force unless and until within two years from the day on which it was presented to the Governor-General for the Queen's assent, the Governor-General signifies, by speech or message *Signification of Queen's pleasure on bill reserved*

to each of the Houses of the Parliament or by proclamation, that it has received the assent of the Queen in Council.

An entry of every such speech, message, or proclamation shall be made in the Journal of each House, and a duplicate thereof duly attested shall be delivered to the proper officer to be kept among the Records of Canada.

V.—PROVINCIAL CONSTITUTIONS

Executive Power

Appointment of Lieutenant-Governors of Provinces

58. For each Province there shall be an officer, styled the Lieutenant-Governor, appointed by the Governor-General in Council by instrument under the Great Seal of Canada.

Tenure of office of Lieutenant-Governor

59. A Lieutenant-Governor shall hold office during the pleasure of the Governor-General; but any Lieutenant-Governor appointed after the commencement of the first Session of the Parliament of Canada shall not be removable within five years from his appointment, except for cause assigned, which shall be communicated to him in writing within one month after the order for his removal is made, and shall be communicated by message to the Senate and to the House of Commons within one week thereafter if the Parliament is then sitting, and if not then within one week after the commencement of the next Session of the Parliament.

Salaries of Lieutenant-Governors

60. The salaries of the Lieutenant-Governors shall be fixed and provided by the Parliament of Canada.

Oaths, etc., of Lieutenant-Governor

61. Every Lieutenant-Governor shall, before assuming the duties of his office, make and subscribe before the Governor-General or some person authorized by him, oaths of allegiance and office similar to those taken by the Governor-General.

Application of provisions referring to Lieutenant-Governor

62. The provisions of this Act referring to the Lieutenant-Governor extend and apply to the Lieutenant-Governor for the time being of each Province or other the chief executive officer or administrator for the time being carrying on the government of the Province, by whatever title he is designated.

Appointment of executive officers for Ontario and Quebec

63. The Executive Council of Ontario and of Quebec shall be composed of such persons as the Lieutenant-Governor from time to time thinks fit, and in the first instance of the following officers, namely:—the Attorney-General, the Secretary and Registrar of the Province, the Treasurer of the Province, the Commissioner of Crown Lands, and the Commissioner of Agriculture and Public Works, with, in Quebec, the Speaker of the Legislative Council and the Solicitor-General.

Government of Nova Scotia and New Brunswick

64. The Constitution of the Executive Authority in each of the Provinces of Nova Scotia and New Brunswick shall, subject to the provisions of this Act, continue as it exists at the Union, until altered under the authority of this Act.

65. All powers, authorities, and functions which under any Act of the Parliament of Great Britain, or of the Parliament of the United Kingdom of Great Britain and Ireland, or of the Legislature of Upper Canada, Lower Canada, or Canada, were or are before or at the Union vested in or exercisable by the respective Governors or Lieutenant-Governors of those Provinces, with the advice, or with the advice and consent, of the respective Executive Councils thereof, or in conjunction with those Councils or with any number of members thereof, or by those Governors or Lieutenant-Governors individually, shall, as far as the same are capable of being exercised after the Union in relation to the Government of Ontario and Quebec respectively, be vested in and shall or may be exercised by the Lieutenant-Governor of Ontario and Quebec respectively, with the advice or with the advice and consent of, or in conjunction with the respective Executive Councils, or any members thereof, or by the Lieutenant-Governor individually, as the case requires, subject nevertheless (except with respect to such as exist under Acts of the Parliament of Great Britain, or of the Parliament of the United Kingdom of Great Britain and Ireland) to be abolished or altered by the respective Legislatures of Ontario and Quebec.

All powers under Acts to be exercised by Lieutenant-Governor of Ontario or Quebec with advice of Executive Council or alone

66. The provisions of this Act referring to the Lieutenant-Governor in Council shall be construed as referring to the Lieutenant-Governor of the Province acting by and with the advice of the Executive Council thereof.

Application of provisions referring to Lieutenant-Governor in Council

67. The Governor-General in Council may from time to time appoint an administrator to execute the office and functions of Lieutenant-Governor during his absence, illness, or other inability.

Administration in absence, etc., of Lieutenant-Governor

68. Unless and until the Executive Government of any Province otherwise directs with respect to that Province, the seats of Government of the Provinces shall be as follows, namely,—of Ontario, the City of Toronto; of Quebec, the City of Quebec; of Nova Scotia, the City of Halifax; and of New Brunswick, the City of Fredericton.

Seats of Provincial Governments

Legislative Power

1.—ONTARIO

69. There shall be a Legislature for Ontario consisting of the Lieutenant-Governor and of one House, styled the Legislative Assembly cf Ontario.

Legislature for Ontario

70. The Legislative Assembly of Ontario shall be composed of eighty-two members to be elected to represent the eighty-two Electoral Districts set forth in the first Schedule to this Act.

Electoral districts

2.—QUEBEC

71. There shall be a Legislature for Quebec consisting of the Lieutenant-Governor and of two Houses, styled the Legislative Council of Quebec and the Legislative Assembly of Quebec.

Legislature for Quebec

*Constitution
of Legislative
Council*
72. The Legislative Council of Quebec shall be composed of twenty-four members, to be appointed by the Lieutenant-Governor in the Queen's name by Instrument under the Great Seal of Quebec, one being appointed to represent each of the twenty-four electoral divisions of Lower Canada in this Act referred to, and each holding office for the term of his life, unless the Legislature of Quebec otherwise provides under the provisions of this Act.

*Qualification
of Legislative
Councillors*

*Resignation,
Disqualifica-
tion, etc.*
73. The qualifications of the Legislative Councillors of Quebec shall be the same as those of the Senators for Quebec.

74. The place of a Legislative Councillor of Quebec shall become vacant in the cases *mutatis mutandis*, in which the place of Senator becomes vacant.

Vacancies
75. When a vacancy happens in the Legislative Council of Quebec, by resignation, death, or otherwise, the Lieutenant-Governor, in the Queen's name by Instrument under the Great Seal of Quebec, shall appoint a fit and qualified person to fill the vacancy.

*Questions as to
Vacancies, etc.*
76. If any question arises respecting the qualification of a Legislative Councillor of Quebec, or a vacancy in the Legislative Council of Quebec, the same shall be heard and determined by the Legislative Council.

*Speaker of
Legislative
Council*
77. The Lieutenant-Governor may from time to time, by Instrument under the Great Seal of Quebec, appoint a member of the Legislative Council of Quebec to be Speaker thereof, and may remove him and appoint another in his stead.

*Quorum of
Legislative
Council*
78. Until the Legislature of Quebec otherwise provides, the presence of at least ten members of the Legislative Council, including the Speaker, shall be necessary to constitute a meeting for the exercise of its powers.

*Voting in
Legislative
Council*
79. Questions arising in the Legislative Council of Quebec shall be decided by a majority of voices, and the Speaker shall in all cases have a vote, and when the voices are equal the decision shall be deemed to be in the negative.

*Constitution
of Legislative
Assembly of
Quebec*
80. The Legislative Assembly of Quebec shall be composed of sixty-five members, to be elected to represent the sixty-five electoral divisions or districts of Lower Canada in this Act referred to, subject to alteration thereof by the Legislature of Quebec: Provided that it shall not be lawful to present to the Lieutenant-Governor of Quebec for assent any bill for altering the limits of any of the Electoral Divisions or Districts mentioned in the second Schedule to this Act, unless the second and third readings of such bill have been passed in the Legislative Assembly with the concurrence of the majority of the members representing all those Electoral Divisions or Districts, and the assent shall not be given to such bill unless an address has been presented by the Legislative Assembly to the Lieutenant-Governor stating that it has been so passed.

3.—ONTARIO AND QUEBEC

81. The Legislatures of Ontario and Quebec respectively shall be called together not later than six months after the Union. *First Session of Legislatures*

82. The Lieutenant-Governor of Ontario and of Quebec shall, from time to time, in the Queen's name, by Instrument under the Great Seal of the Province, summon and call together the Legislative Assembly of the Province. *Summoning of Legislative Assemblies*

83. Until the Legislature of Ontario or of Quebec otherwise provides, a person accepting or holding in Ontario or in Quebec any office, commission, or employment, permanent or temporary, at the nomination of the Lieutenant-Governor, to which an annual salary, or any fee, allowance, emolument, or profit of any kind or amount whatever from the Province is attached, shall not be eligible as a member of the Legislative Assembly of the respective Province, nor shall he sit or vote as such; but nothing in this Section shall make ineligible any person being a member of the Executive Council of the respective Province, or holding any of the following offices, that is to say, the offices of Attorney-General, Secretary and Registrar of the Province, Treasurer of the Province, Commissioner of Crown Lands, and Commissioner of Agriculture and Public Works, and, in Quebec, Solicitor-General, or shall disqualify him to sit or vote in the House for which he is elected, provided he is elected while holding such office. *Restriction on election of holders of office*

84. Until the Legislatures of Ontario and Quebec respectively otherwise provide, all laws which at the Union are in force in those Provinces respectively, relative to the following matters, or any of them, namely,—the qualifications and disqualifications of persons to be elected or to sit or vote as members of the Assembly of Canada, the qualifications or disqualifications of voters, the oaths to be taken by voters, the Returning Officers, their powers and duties, the proceedings at elections, the periods during which such elections may be continued, and the trial of controverted elections and the proceedings incident thereto, the vacating of the seats of members and the issuing and execution of new writs in case of seats vacated otherwise than by dissolution, shall respectively apply to elections of members to serve in the respective Legislative Assemblies of Ontario and Quebec. *Continuance of existing election laws*

Provided that until the Legislature of Ontario otherwise provides, at any election for a member of the Legislative Assembly of Ontario for the District of Algoma, in addition to persons qualified by the law of the Province of Canada to vote, every male British Subject, aged twenty-one years or upwards, being a householder, shall have a vote.

85. Every Legislative Assembly of Ontario and every Legislative Assembly of Quebec shall continue for four years from the day of the

*Duration of
Legislative
Assemblies*

return of the writs for choosing the same (subject nevertheless to either the Legislative Assembly of Ontario or the Legislative Assembly of Quebec being sooner dissolved by the Lieutenant-Governor of the Province), and no longer.

86. There shall be a Session of the Legislature of Ontario and of that of Quebec once at least in every year, so that twelve months *Yearly Sessions* shall not intervene between the last sitting of the Legislature in *of Legislature* each Province in one Session and its first sitting in the next Session.

87. The following provisions of this Act respecting the House of Commons of Canada shall extend and apply to the Legislative *Speaker,* Assemblies of Ontario and Quebec, that is to say,—the provisions *Quorum, etc.* relating to the election of a Speaker originally and on vacancies, the duties of the Speaker, the absence of the Speaker, the quorum, and the mode of voting, as if those provisions were here re-enacted and made applicable in terms to each such Legislative Assembly.

4.—Nova Scotia and New Brunswick

*Constitutions
of Legislatures
of Nova Scotia
and New
Brunswick*

88. The constitution of the Legislature of each of the Provinces of Nova Scotia and New Brunswick shall, subject to the provisions of this Act, continue as it exists at the Union until altered under the authority of this Act; and the House of Assembly of New Brunswick existing at the passing of this Act shall, unless sooner dissolved, continue for the period for which it was elected.

5.—Ontario, Quebec, and Nova Scotia

First elections

89. Each of the Lieutenant-Governors of Ontario, Quebec, and Nova Scotia shall cause writs to be issued for the first election of members of the Legislative Assembly thereof in such form and by such person as he thinks fit, and at such time and addressed to such Returning Officer as the Governor-General directs, and so that the first election of members of Assembly for any Electoral District or any subdivision thereof shall be held at the same time and at the same places as the election for a member to serve in the House of Commons of Canada for that Electoral District.

6.—The Four Provinces

*Application
to Legislatures
of provisions
respecting
money votes,
etc.*

90. The following provisions of this Act respecting the Parliament of Canada, namely,—the provisions relating to appropriation and tax bills, the recommendation of money votes, the assent to bills, the disallowance of Acts, and the signification of pleasure on bills reserved,—shall extend and apply to the Legislatures of the several Provinces as if those provisions were here re-enacted and made applicable in terms to the respective Provinces and the Legislatures thereof, with the substitution of the Lieutenant-Governor of the Province for the Governor-General, of the Governor-General for

the Queen and for a Secretary of State, of one year for two years, and of the Province for Canada.

VI.—DISTRIBUTION OF LEGISLATIVE POWERS

Powers of the Parliament

91. It shall be lawful for the Queen, by and with the advice and consent of the Senate and House of Commons, to make laws for the peace, order, and good government of Canada, in relation to all matters not coming within the classes of subjects by this Act assigned exclusively to the Legislatures of the Provinces; and for greater certainty, but not so as to restrict the generality of the foregoing terms of this section, it is hereby declared that (notwithstanding anything in this Act) the exclusive Legislative Authority of the Parliament of Canada extends to all matters coming within the classes of subjects next hereinafter enumerated, that is to say:— *Legislative authority of Parliament of Canada*

1. The Public Debt and Property.
2. The regulation of Trade and Commerce.
3. The raising of money by any mode or system of Taxation.
4. The borrowing of money on the public credit.
5. Postal service.
6. The Census and Statistics.
7. Militia, Military and Naval Service, and Defence.
8. The fixing of and providing for the salaries and allowances of civil and other officers of the Government of Canada.
9. Beacons, Buoys, Lighthouses, and Sable Island.
10. Navigation and Shipping.
11. Quarantine and the establishment and maintenance of Marine Hospitals.
12. Sea Coast and Inland Fisheries.
13. Ferries between a Province and any British or Foreign country or between two Provinces.
14. Currency and Coinage.
15. Banking, incorporation of banks, and the issue of paper money.
16. Savings Banks.
17. Weights and Measures.
18. Bills of Exchange and Promissory Notes.
19. Interest.
20. Legal tender.
21. Bankruptcy and Insolvency.
22. Patents of Invention and Discovery.
23. Copyrights.
24. Indians, and lands reserved for the Indians.
25. Naturalization and Aliens.
26. Marriage and Divorce.
27. The Criminal Law, except the Constitution of Courts of Criminal Jurisdiction, but including the Procedure in Criminal Matters.

28. The establishment, maintenance, and management of Penitentiaries.

29. Such classes of subjects as are expressly excepted in the enumeration of the classes of subjects by this Act assigned exclusively to the Legislatures of the Provinces:

And any matter coming within any of the classes of subjects enumerated in this section shall not be deemed to come within the class of matters of a local or private nature comprised in the enumeration of the classes of subjects by this Act assigned exclusively to the Legislatures of the Provinces.

Exclusive Powers of Provincial Legislatures

Exclusive Provincial Legislation

92. In each Province the Legislature may exclusively make laws in relation to matters coming within the classes of subjects next hereinafter enumerated, that is to say,—

1. The amendment from time to time, notwithstanding anything in this Act, of the Constitution of the Province, except as regards the office of Lieutenant-Governor.
2. Direct Taxation within the Province in order to the raising of a Revenue for Provincial purposes.
3. The borrowing of money on the sole credit of the Province.
4. The establishment and tenure of Provincial offices and the appointment and payment of Provincial officers.
5. The management and sale of the Public Lands belonging to the Province, and of the timber and wood thereon.
6. The establishment, maintenance, and management of public and reformatory prisons in and for the Province.
7. The establishment, maintenance, and management of hospitals, asylums, charities, and eleemosynary institutions in and for the Province, other than marine hospitals.
8. Municipal institutions in the Province.
9. Shop, saloon, tavern, auctioneer, and other licenses, in order to the raising of a revenue for Provincial, local, or municipal purposes.
10. Local works and undertakings other than such as are of the following classes,—
a. Lines of steam or other ships, railways, canals, telegraphs, and other works and undertakings connecting the Province with any other or others of the Provinces, or extending beyond the limits of the Province;
b. Lines of steam ships between the Province and any British or Foreign country;
c. Such works as, although wholly situate within the Province, are before or after their execution declared by the Parliament of Canada to be for the general advantage of Canada or for the advantage of two or more of the Provinces.
11. The incorporation of companies with Provincial objects.

12. The solemnization of marriage in the Province.
13. Property and civil rights in the Province.
14. The administration of justice in the Province, including the constitution, maintenance, and organization of Provincial Courts, both of civil and of criminal jurisdiction, and including procedure in civil matters in those Courts.
15. The imposition of punishment by fine, penalty, or imprisonment for enforcing any law of the Province made in relation to any matter coming within any of the classes of subjects enumerated in this section.
16. Generally all matters of a merely local or private nature in the Province.

Education

93. In and for each Province the Legislature may exclusively make laws in relation to education, subject and according to the following provisions:— *Legislation respecting education*

1. Nothing in any such law shall prejudicially affect any right or privilege with respect to denominational schools which any class of persons have by law in the Province at the union.
2. All the powers, privileges, and duties at the union by law conferred and imposed in Upper Canada on the separate schools and school trustees of the Queen's Roman Catholic subjects shall be and the same are hereby extended to the dissentient schools of the Queen's Protestant and Roman Catholic subjects in Quebec.
3. Where in any Province a system of separate or dissentient schools exists by law at the Union or is thereafter established by the Legislature of the Province, an appeal shall lie to the Governor-General in Council from any Act or decision of any Provincial authority affecting any right or privilege of the Protestant or Roman Catholic minority of the Queen's subjects in relation to education.
4. In case any such Provincial law as from time to time seems to the Governor-General in Council requisite for the due execution of the provisions of this section is not made, or in case any decision of the Governor-General in Council on any appeal under this section is not duly executed by the proper Provincial authority in that behalf, then and in every such case, and as far only as the circumstances of each case require, the Parliament of Canada may make remedial laws for the due execution of the provisions of this section and of any decision of the Governor-General in Council under this section.

Uniformity of Laws in Ontario, Nova Scotia and New Brunswick

94. Notwithstanding anything in this Act, the Parliament of Canada may make provisions for the uniformity of all or any of the

laws relative to property and civil rights in Ontario, Nova Scotia, and New Brunswick, and of the procedure of all or any of the Courts in those three Provinces; and from and after the passing of any Act in that behalf the power of the Parliament of Canada to make laws in relation to any matter comprised in any such Act shall, notwithstanding anything in this Act, be unrestricted; but any Act of the Parliament of Canada making provision for such uniformity shall not have effect in any Province unless and until it is adopted and enacted as law by the Legislature thereof.

Agriculture and Immigration

95. In each Province the Legislature may make laws in relation to Agriculture in the Province, and to Immigration into the Province; and it is hereby declared that the Parliament of Canada may from time to time make laws in relation to Agriculture in all or any of the Provinces, and to Immigration into all or any of the Provinces; and any law of the Legislature of a Province relative to Agriculture or to Immigration shall have effect in and for the Province as long and as far only as it is not repugnant to any Act of the Parliament of Canada.

VII.—JUDICATURE

96. The Governor-General shall appoint the Judges of the Superior, District, and County Courts in each Province, except those of the Courts of Probate in Nova Scotia and New Brunswick.

97. Until the laws relative to property and civil rights in Ontario, Nova Scotia, and New Brunswick, and the procedure of the Courts of those Provinces, are made uniform, the Judges of the Courts of those Provinces appointed by the Governor-General shall be selected from the respective Bars of those Provinces.

98. The Judges of the Courts of Quebec shall be selected from the Bar of that Province.

99. The Judges of the Superior Courts shall hold office during good behaviour, but shall be removable by the Governor-General on address of the Senate and House of Commons.

100. The salaries, allowances and pensions of the Judges of the Superior, District, and County Courts (except the Courts of Probate in Nova Scotia and New Brunswick), and of the Admiralty Courts in cases where the Judges thereof are for the time being paid by salary, shall be fixed and provided by the Parliament of Canada.

101. The Parliament of Canada may, notwithstanding anything in this Act, from time to time, provide for the constitution, maintenance, and organization of a general Court of Appeal for Canada, and for the establishment of any additional Courts for the better administration of the Laws of Canada.

VIII.—REVENUES; DEBTS; ASSETS; TAXATION

102. All duties and revenues over which the respective Legislatures of Canada, Nova Scotia, and New Brunswick before and at the

Union had and have power of appropriation, except such portions thereof as are by this Act reserved to the respective Legislatures of the Provinces, or are raised by them in accordance with the special powers conferred on them by this Act, shall form one Consolidated Revenue Fund, to be appropriated for the public service of Canada in the manner and subject to the charges in this Act provided. *Creation of Consolidated Revenue Fund*

103. The Consolidated Revenue Fund of Canada shall be permanently charged with the costs, charges, and expenses incident to the collection, management, and receipt thereof, and the same shall form the first charge thereon, subject to be reviewed and audited in such manner as shall be ordered by the Governor-General in Council until the Parliament otherwise provides. *Expenses of collection, etc.*

104. The annual interest of the public debts of the several Provinces of Canada, Nova Scotia, and New Brunswick at the Union shall form the second charge on the Consolidated Revenue Fund of Canada. *Interest of Provincial public debts*

105. Unless altered by the Parliament of Canada, the salary of the Governor-General shall be ten thousand pounds sterling money of the United Kingdom of Great Britain and Ireland, payable out of the Consolidated Revenue Fund of Canada, and the same shall form the third charge thereon. *Salary of Governor-General*

106. Subject to the several payments by this Act charged on the Consolidated Revenue Fund of Canada, the same shall be appropriated by the Parliament of Canada for the public service. *Appropriation of fund subject to charges*

107. All stocks, cash, banker's balances, and securities for money belonging to each Province at the time of the Union, except as in this Act mentioned, shall be the property of Canada, and shall be taken in reduction of the amount of the respective debts of the Provinces at the Union. *Transfer to Canada of stocks, etc., belonging to two Provinces*

108. The public works and property of each Province, enumerated in the third Schedule to this Act, shall be the property of Canada. *Transfer of property in schedule*

109. All lands, mines, minerals, and royalties belonging to the several Provinces of Canada, Nova Scotia and New Brunswick at the Union, and all sums then due or payable for such lands, mines, minerals, or royalties, shall belong to the several Provinces of Ontario, Quebec, Nova Scotia and New Brunswick in which the same are situate or arise, subject to any trusts existing in respect thereof, and to any interest other than of the Province in the same. *Lands, mines, etc., belonging to Provinces to belong to them*

110. All assets connected with such portions of the public debt of each Province as are assumed by that Province shall belong to that Province. *Assets connected with Provincial debts*

111. Canada shall be liable for the debts and liabilities of each Province existing at the Union. *Canada to be liable for Provincial debts*

112. Ontario and Quebec conjointly shall be liable to Canada for the amount (if any) by which the debt of the Province of Canada exceeds at the Union $62,500,000, and shall be charged with interest at the rate of five per centum per annum thereon. *Liability of Ontario and Quebec to Canada*

Assets of Ontario and Quebec

113. The assets enumerated in the fourth Schedule to this Act belonging at the Union to the Province of Canada shall be the property of Ontario and Quebec conjointly.

Liability of Nova Scotia to Canada

114. Nova Scotia shall be liable to Canada for the amount (if any) by which its public debt exceeds at the Union $8,000,000, and shall be charged with interest at the rate of five per centum per annum thereon.

Liability of New Brunswick to Canada

115. New Brunswick shall be liable to Canada for the amount (if any) by which its public debt exceeds at the Union $7,000,000, and shall be charged with interest at the rate of five per centum per annum thereon.

Payment of interest to Nova Scotia and New Brunswick if their public debts are less than the stipulated amounts

116. In case the public debts of Nova Scotia and New Brunswick do not at the Union amount to $8,000,000 and $7,000,000 respectively, they shall respectively receive by half-yearly payments in advance from the Government of Canada interest at five per centum per annum on the difference between the actual amounts of their respective debts and such stipulated amounts.

Provincial public property

117. The several Provinces shall retain all their respective public property not otherwise disposed of in this Act, subject to the right of Canada to assume any lands or public property required for fortifications or for the defence of the country.

Grants to Provinces

118. The following sums shall be paid yearly by Canada to the several Provinces for the support of their Governments and Legislatures:—

	Dollars
Ontario	Eighty thousand
Quebec	Seventy thousand
Nova Scotia	Sixty thousand
New Brunswick	Fifty thousand
	Two hundred and sixty thousand

And an annual grant in aid of each Province shall be made, equal to eighty cents per head of the population as ascertained by the Census of 1861, and in case of Nova Scotia and New Brunswick, by each subsequent decennial census, until the population of each of those two Provinces amounts to four hundred thousand souls, at which rate such grant shall thereafter remain. Such grants shall be in full settlement of all future demands on Canada, and shall be paid half-yearly in advance to each Province; but the Government of Canada shall deduct from such grants, as against any Province, all sums chargeable as interest on the Public Debt of that Province in excess of the several amounts stipulated in this Act.

Further grant to New Brunswick for ten years

119. New Brunswick shall receive, by half-yearly payments in advance from Canada, for the period of ten years from the Union, an additional allowance of $63,000 per annum; but as long as the Public Debt of that Province remains under $7,000,000, a deduction

equal to the interest at five per centum per annum on such deficiency shall be made from that allowance of $63,000.

120. All payments to be made under this Act, or in discharge in liabilities created under any Act of the Provinces of Canada, Nova Scotia and New Brunswick respectively, and assumed by Canada, shall, until the Parliament of Canada otherwise directs, be made of such form and manner as may from time to time be ordered by the Governor-General in Council. *Form of payments*

121. All articles of the growth, produce, or manufacture of any of the Provinces shall, from and after the Union, be admitted free into each of the other Provinces. *Manufactures, etc., of one Province to be admitted free into the others*

122. The Customs and Excise Laws of each Province shall, subject to the provisions of this Act, continue in force until altered by the Parliament of Canada. *Continuance of Customs and Excise Laws*

123. Where Customs duties are, at the Union, leviable on any goods, wares, or merchandises in any two Provinces, those goods, wares, and merchandises may, from and after the Union, be imported from one of those Provinces into the other of them on proof of payment of the Customs duty leviable thereon in the Province of exportation, and on payment of such further amount (if any) of Customs duty as is leviable thereon in the Province of importation. *Exportation and importation as between two Provinces*

124. Nothing in this Act shall affect the right of New Brunswick to levy the lumber dues provided in chapter fifteen of title three of the Revised Statutes of New Brunswick, or in any Act amending that Act before or after the Union, and not increasing the amount of such dues; but the lumber of any of the Provinces other than New Brunswick shall not be subjected to such dues. *Lumber dues in New Brunswick*

125. No lands or property belonging to Canada or any Province shall be liable to taxation. *Exemption of public lands, etc., from taxation*

126. Such portions of the duties and revenues over which the respective Legislatures of Canada, Nova Scotia and New Brunswick had before the Union power of appropriation as are by this Act reserved to the respective Governments or Legislatures of the Provinces, and all duties and revenues raised by them in accordance with the special powers conferred upon them by this Act, shall in each Province form one Consolidated Revenue Fund to be appropriated for the public service of the Province. *Provincial Consolidated Revenue Funds*

IX.—Miscellaneous Provisions

General

127. If any person being at the passing of this Act a Member of the Legislative Council of Canada, Nova Scotia, or New Brunswick, to whom a place in the Senate is offered, does not within thirty days thereafter, by writing under his hand, addressed to the Governor-General of the Province of Canada, or to the Lieutenant-Governor of Nova Scotia or New Brunswick (as the case may be), accept the *As to Legislative Councillors of Provinces becoming Senators*

same, he shall be deemed to have declined the same; and any person who, being at the passing of this Act a member of the Legislative Council of Nova Scotia or New Brunswick, accepts a place in the Senate, shall thereby vacate his seat in such Legislative Council.

Oath of allegiance, etc.

128. Every member of the Senate or House of Commons of Canada shall, before taking his seat therein, take and subscribe before the Governor-General or some person authorized by him, and every member of a Legislative Council or Legislative Assembly of any Province shall, before taking his seat therein, take and subscribe before the Lieutenant-Governor of the Province or some person authorized by him, the oath of allegiance contained in the fifth Schedule to this Act; and every member of the Senate of Canada and every member of the Legislative Council of Quebec shall also, before taking his seat therein, take and subscribe before the Governor-General or some person authorized by him, the declaration of qualification contained in the same Schedule.

Continuance of existing laws, courts, officers, etc.

129. Except as otherwise provided by this Act, all laws in force in Canada, Nova Scotia or New Brunswick at the Union, and all Courts of civil and military jurisdiction, and all legal commissions, powers and authorities, and all officers, judicial, administrative and ministerial, existing therein at the Union, shall continue in Ontario, Quebec, Nova Scotia and New Brunswick respectively, as if the Union had not been made; subject nevertheless (except with respect to such as are enacted by or exist under Acts of the Parliament of Great Britain or of the Parliament of the United Kingdom of Great Britain and Ireland) to be repealed, abolished or altered by the Parliament of Canada, or by the Legislature of the respective Province, according to the authority of the Parliament or of that Legislature under this Act.

Transfer of officers to Canada

130. Until the Parliament of Canada otherwise provides, all officers of the several Provinces having duties to discharge in relation to matters other than those coming within the classes of subjects by this Act assigned exclusively to the Legislatures of the Provinces shall be officers of Canada, and shall continue to discharge the duties of their respective offices under the same liabilities, responsibilities and penalties as if the Union had not been made.

Appointment of new officers

131. Until the Parliament of Canada otherwise provides, the Governor-General in Council may from time to time appoint such officers as the Governor-General in Council deems necessary or proper for the effectual execution of this Act.

Power for performance of treaty obligations by Canada as part of British Empire

132. The Parliament and Government of Canada shall have all powers necessary or proper for performing the obligations of Canada or of any Province thereof, as part of the British Empire, towards foreign countries, arising under treaties between the Empire and such foreign countries.

133. Either the English or the French language may be used by any person in the debates of the Houses of the Parliament of Canada

and of the Houses of the Legislature of Quebec; and both those *Use of English* languages shall be used in the respective records and journals of *and French* those Houses; and either of those languages may be used by any *languages* person or in any pleading or process in or issuing from any Court of Canada established under this Act, and in or from all or any of the Courts of Quebec.

The Acts of the Parliament of Canada and of the Legislature of Quebec shall be printed and published in both those languages.

Ontario and Quebec

134. Until the Legislature of Ontario or of Quebec otherwise provides, the Lieutenant-Governors of Ontario and Quebec may each *Appointment* appoint under the Great Seal of the Province the following officers, *of executive* to hold office during pleasure, that is to say:—the Attorney-General, *officers for* the Secretary and Registrar of the Province, the Treasurer of the *Ontario and* Province, the Commissioner of Crown Lands, and the Commissioner *Quebec* of Agriculture and Public Works, and in the case of Quebec the Solicitor-General; and may, by order of the Lieutenant-Governor in Council, from time to time prescribe the duties of those officers and of the several departments over which they shall preside or to which they shall belong, and of the officers and clerks thereof; and may also appoint other and additional officers to hold office during pleasure, and may from time to time prescribe the duties of those officers, and of the several departments over which they shall preside or to which they shall belong, and of the officers and clerks thereof.

135. Until the Legislature of Ontario or Quebec otherwise provides, all rights, powers, duties, functions, responsibilities or authorities at *Powers, duties,* the passing of this Act vested in or imposed on the Attorney-General, *etc., of* Solicitor-General, Secretary and Registrar of the Province of Canada, *executive* Minister of Finance, Commissioner of Crown Lands, Commissioner *officers* of Public Works, and Minister of Agriculture and Receiver-General, by any law, statute or ordinance of Upper Canada, Lower Canada, or Canada, and not repugnant to this Act, shall be vested in or imposed on any officer to be appointed by the Lieutenant-Governor for the discharge of the same or any of them; and the Commissioner of Agriculture and Public Works shall perform the duties and functions of the office of Minister of Agriculture at the passing of this Act imposed by the law of the Province of Canada, as well as those of the Commissioner of Public Works.

136. Until altered by the Lieutenant-Governor in Council, the Great Seals of Ontario and of Quebec respectively shall be the same, *Great Seals* or of the same design, as those used in the Provinces of Upper Canada and Lower Canada respectively before their Union as the Province of Canada.

137. The words 'and from thence to the end of the then next *Construction* ensuing Session of the Legislature,' or words to the same effect, *of temporary* used in any temporary Act of the Province of Canada not expired *Acts*

before the Union, shall be construed to extend and apply to the next Session of the Parliament of Canada, if the subject-matter of the Act is within the powers of the same, as defined by this Act, or to the next Sessions of the Legislatures of Ontario and Quebec respectively, if the subject-matter of the Act is within the powers of the same as defined by this Act.

As to errors in names

138. From and after the Union, the use of the words 'Upper Canada' instead of 'Ontario,' or 'Lower Canada' instead of 'Quebec,' in any deed, writ, process, pleading, document, matter or thing, shall not invalidate the same.

As to issue of Proclamations before Union, to commence after Union

139. Any Proclamation under the Great Seal of the Province of Canada issued before the Union to take effect at a time which is subsequent to the Union, whether relating to that Province, or to Upper Canada, or to Lower Canada, and the several matters and things therein proclaimed, shall be and continue of like force and effect as if the Union had not been made.

As to issue of Proclamations after Union under authority of Acts before Union

140. Any Proclamation which is authorized by any Act of the Legislature of the Province of Canada to be issued under the Great Seal of the Province of Canada, whether relating to that Province, or to Upper Canada, or to Lower Canada, and which is not issued before the Union, may be issued by the Lieutenant-Governor of Ontario or of Quebec, as its subject-matter requires, under the Great Seal thereof; and from and after the issue of such Proclamation the same and the several matters and things therein proclaimed shall be and continue of the like force and effect in Ontario or Quebec as if the Union had not been made.

Penitentiary

141. The Penitentiary of the Province of Canada shall, until the Parliament of Canada otherwise provides, be and continue the Penitentiary of Ontario and of Quebec.

Arbitration respecting debts, etc.

142. The division and adjustment of the debts, credits, liabilities, properties and assets of Upper Canada and Lower Canada shall be referred to the arbitrament of three arbitrators, one chosen by the Government of Ontario, one by the Government of Quebec and one by the Government of Canada; and the selection of the arbitrators shall not be made until the Parliament of Canada and the Legislatures of Ontario and Quebec have met; and the arbitrator chosen by the Government of Canada shall not be a resident either in Ontario or in Quebec.

Division of records

143. The Governor-General in Council may from time to time order that such and so many of the records, books, and documents of the Province of Canada as he thinks fit shall be appropriated and delivered either to Ontario or to Quebec, and the same shall henceforth be the property of that Province; and any copy thereof or extract therefrom, duly certified by the officer having charge of the original thereof, shall be admitted as evidence.

144. The Lieutenant-Governor of Quebec may from time to time, by Proclamation under the Great Seal of the Province, to take effect

from a day to be appointed therein, constitute townships in those *Constitution* parts of the Province of Quebec in which townships are not then *of townships* already constituted, and fix the metes and bounds thereof. *in Quebec*

X.—INTERCOLONIAL RAILWAY

145. Inasmuch as the Provinces of Canada, Nova Scotia, and New Brunswick have joined in a declaration that the construction of the *Duty of* Intercolonial Railway is essential to the consolidation of the Union *Government and* of British North America, and to the assent thereto of Nova Scotia *Parliament of* and New Brunswick, and have consequently agreed that provision *make railway* should be made for its immediate construction by the Government of *herein described* Canada: Therefore, in order to give effect to that agreement, it shall be the duty of the Government and Parliament of Canada to provide for the commencement within six months after the Union, of a railway connecting the River St. Lawrence with the City of Halifax in Nova Scotia, and for the construction thereof without intermission, and the completion thereof with all practicable speed.

XI.—ADMISSION OF OTHER COLONIES

146. It shall be lawful for the Queen, by and with the advice of Her Majesty's Most Honourable Privy Council, on Addresses from *Power to admit* the Houses of the Parliament of Canada, and from the Houses of the *Newfoundland,* respective Legislatures of the Colonies or Provinces of Newfoundland, *Prince Edward Island, British* Prince Edward Island, and British Columbia, to admit those Colonies *Columbia,* or Provinces, or any of them, into the Union, and on Address from *Rupert's Land* the Houses of the Parliament of Canada to admit Rupert's Land and *and* the North-western Territory, or either of them, into the Union, on *Northwestern* such terms and conditions in each case as are in the Addresses ex- *Territory into* pressed and as the Queen thinks fit to approve, subject to the pro- *the Union by* visions of this Act; and the provisions of any Order in Council in *Order of* that behalf shall have effect as if they had been enacted by the Parlia- *Council* ment of the United Kingdom of Great Britain and Ireland.

147. In case of the admission of Newfoundland and Prince Edward Island, or either of them, each shall be entitled to a representation *As to* in the Senate of Canada of four members, and (notwithstanding *representation of* anything in this Act) in case of the admission of Newfoundland the *Newfoundland* normal number of Senators shall be seventy-six and their maximum *Prince Edward* number shall be eighty-two; but Prince Edward Island when admitted *Island in* shall be deemed to be comprised in the third of the three divisions *Senate* into which Canada is, in relation to the constitution of the Senate, divided by this Act, and accordingly, after the admission of Prince Edward Island, whether Newfoundland is admitted or not, the representation of Nova Scotia and New Brunswick in the Senate shall, as vacancies occur, be reduced from twelve to ten members respectively, and the representation of each of those Provinces shall

not be increased at any time beyond ten, except under the provisions of this Act for the appointment of three or six additional Senators under the direction of the Queen.

THE BRITISH NORTH AMERICA ACT, 1871
(34 and 35 Victoria, c. 28)

An Act respecting the Establishment of Provinces in the Dominion of Canada.

29th June, 1871

Whereas doubts have been entertained respecting the powers of the Parliament of Canada to establish Provinces in territories admitted, or which may hereafter be admitted, into the Dominion of Canada, and to provide for the representation of such Provinces in the said Parliament, and it is expedient to remove such doubts, and to vest such powers in the said Parliament:

Be it enacted by the Queen's Most Excellent Majesty, by and with the advice and consent of the Lords, Spiritual and Temporal, and Commons in this present Parliament assembled, and by the authority of the same, as follows:—

Short title
1. This Act may be cited for all purposes as *The British North America Act, 1871*.

Parliament's authority to establish new Provinces
2. The Parliament of Canada may from time to time establish new Provinces in any territories forming for the time being part of the Dominion of Canada, but not included in any Province thereof, and may, at the time of such establishment, make provision for the constitution and administration of any such Province, and for the passing of laws for the peace, order and good government of such Province, and for its representation in the said Parliament.

Alteration of limits of Provinces
3. The Parliament of Canada may from time to time, with the consent of the Legislature of any Province of the said Dominion, increase, diminish, or otherwise alter the limits of such Province, upon such terms and conditions as may be agreed to by the said Legislature, and may, with the like consent, make provision respecting the effect and operation of any such increase or diminution or alteration of territory in relation to any Province affected thereby.

Parliament of Canada may legislate for any territory not included in a Province
4. The Parliament of Canada may from time to time make provision for the administration, peace, order and good government of any territory not for the time being included in any Province.

5. The following Acts passed by the said Parliament of Canada, and intituled respectively:

"An Act for the temporary government of Rupert's Land and the North-Western Territory when united with Canada;" and

"An Act to amend and continue the Act thirty-two and thirty-three Victoria, chapter three, and to establish and provide for the government of the Province of Manitoba.''

shall be and be deemed to have been valid and effectual for all purposes whatsoever from the date at which they respectively received the assent, in the Queen's name, of the Governor-General of the said Dominion of Canada.

6. Except as provided for by the third section of this Act, it shall not be competent for the Parliament of Canada to alter the provisions *Limitations* of the last mentioned Act of the said Parliament in so far as it relates *of powers of* to the Province of Manitoba or of any other Act hereafter establish- *Parliament* ing new Provinces in the said Dominion, subject always to the right *over established* of the Legislature of the Province of Manitoba to alter from time *Province* to time the provisions of any law respecting the qualification of electors and members of the Legislative Assembly, and to make laws respecting elections in the said Province.

THE BRITISH NORTH AMERICA ACT, 1886
(49 and 50 Victoria, c. 35)

An Act respecting the Representation in the Parliament of Canada of Terri-
tories which for the time being form part of the Dominion of Canada, but
are not included in any Province.

25th June, 1886

Whereas it is expedient to empower the Parliament of Canada to provide for the representation in the Senate and House of Commons of Canada, or either of them, of any territory which for the time being forms part of the Dominion of Canada, but is not included in any Province:

Be it therefore enacted by the Queen's Most Excellent Majesty, by and with the advice and consent of the Lords Spiritual and Temporal, and Commons, in the present Parliament assembled, and by the authority of the same, as follows:—

1. The Parliament of Canada may from time to time make provision for the representation in the Senate and House of Commons of *Provision for* Canada, or in either of them, of any territories which for the time *representation* being form part of the Dominion of Canada, but are not included in *of territories* any Province thereof.

2. Any Act passed by the Parliament of Canada before the passing of this Act for the purpose mentioned in this Act, shall, if not dis- *Effect of Acts* allowed by the Queen, be, and shall be deemed to have been, valid *of Parliament* and effectual from the date at which it received the assent, in Her *of Canada* Majesty's name, of the Governor-General of Canada.

It is hereby declared that any Act passed by the Parliament of Canada, whether before or after the passing of this Act, for the purpose mentioned in this Act, or in *The British North America Act, 1871,* has effect, notwithstanding anything in *The British North America Act, 1867,* and the number of Senators or the number of Members of the House of Commons specified in the last-mentioned Act is increased by the number of Senators or of Members, as the case may be, provided by any such Act of the Parliament of Canada for the representation of any provinces or territories of Canada.

Short title 3. This Act may be cited as *The British North America Act, 1886*.

This Act, and *The British North America Act, 1867*, and *The British North America Act, 1871*, shall be construed together, and may be cited together as *The British North America Acts, 1867 to 1886*.

THE BRITISH NORTH AMERICA ACT, 1907
(7 Edward VII, c. 11)

An Act to make further provision with respect to the sums to be paid by Canada to the several Provinces of the Dominion.

9th August, 1907

Whereas an address has been presented to His Majesty by the Senate and Commons of Canada in the terms set forth in the schedule of this Act:

Be it therefore enacted by the King's Most Excellent Majesty, by and with the advice and consent of the Lords Spiritual and Temporal, and Commons, in this present Parliament assembled, and by the authority of the same, as follows:

Payments to be made by Canada to Provinces 1. (1) The following grants shall be made yearly by Canada to every province, which at the commencement of this Act is a province of the Dominion, for its local purposes and the support of its Government and Legislature:

(a) A fixed grant—

Where the population of the province is under one hundred and fifty thousand, of one hundred thousand dollars;

Where the population of the province is one hundred and fifty thousand, but does not exceed two hundred thousand, of one hundred and fifty thousand dollars;

Where the population of the province is two hundred thousand, but does not exceed four hundred thousand, of one hundred and eighty thousand dollars;

Where the population of the province is four hundred thousand, but does not exceed eight hundred thousand, of one hundred and ninety thousand dollars;

Where the population of the province is eight hundred thousand, but does not exceed one million five hundred thousand, of two hundred and twenty thousand dollars;

Where the population of the province exceeds one million five hundred thousand, of two hundred and forty thousand dollars; and

(b) Subject to the special provisions of this Act as to the provinces of British Columbia and Prince Edward Island, a grant at the rate of eighty cents per head of the population of the province up to the number of two million five hundred thousand, and at the rate of sixty cents per head of so much of the population as exceeds that number.

(2) An additional grant of one hundred thousand dollars shall be made yearly to the province of British Columbia for a period of ten years from the commencement of this Act.

(3) The population of a province shall be ascertained from time to time in the case of the provinces of Manitoba, Saskatchewan, and Alberta respectively by the last quinquennial census of statutory estimate of population made under the Acts establishing those provinces or any other Act of the Parliament of Canada making provision for the purpose, and in the case of any other province by the last decennial census for the time being.

(4) The grants payable under this Act shall be paid half-yearly in advance to each province.

(5) The grants payable under this Act shall be substituted for the grants or subsidies (in this Act referred to as existing grants) payable for the like purposes at the commencement of this Act to the several provinces of the Dominion under the provisions of section one hundred and eighteen of the British North America Act, 1867, or of any Order in Council establishing a province, or of any Act of the Parliament of Canada containing directions for the payment of any such grant or subsidy, and those provisions shall cease to have effect.

(6) The Government of Canada shall have the same power of deducting sums charged against a province on account of the interest of public debt in the case of the grant payable under this Act to the province as they have in the case of the existing grant.

(7) Nothing in this Act shall affect the obligation of the Government of Canada to pay to any province any grant which is payable to that province other than the existing grant for which the grant under this Act is substituted.

(8) In the case of the provinces of British Columbia and Prince Edward Island, the amount paid on account of the grant payable per head of the population to the provinces under this Act shall not at any time be less than the amount of the corresponding grant payable at the commencement of this Act; and if it is found on any decennial census that the population of the province has decreased since the last decennial census, the amount paid on account of the grant shall not be decreased below the amount then payable, notwithstanding the decrease of the population.

2. This Act may be cited as the British North America Act, 1907, and shall take effect as from the first day of July nineteen hundred and seven. *Short title*

THE BRITISH NORTH AMERICA ACT, 1915

(5 and 6 George V, c. 45)

19th May, 1915

Alteration of constitution of Senate

Be it enacted by the King's Most Excellent Majesty, by and with the advice and consent of the Lords Spiritual and Temporal, and Commons, in this present Parliament assembled, and by the authority of the same, as follows:

1.—(1) Notwithstanding anything in the British North America Act, 1867, or in any Act amending the same, or in any Order in Council or terms or conditions of union made or approved under the said Acts or in any Act of the Canadian Parliament—

(i) The number of senators provided for under section twenty-one of the British North America Act, 1867, is increased from seventy-two to ninety-six:

(ii) The Divisions of Canada in relation to the constitution of the Senate provided for by section twenty-two of the said Act are increased from three to four, the fourth Division to comprise the Western Provinces of Manitoba, British Columbia, Saskatchewan, and Alberta, which four Divisions shall (subject to the provisions of the said Act and of this Act) be equally represented in the Senate as follows: Ontario by twenty-four senators; Quebec by twenty-four senators; the Maritime Provinces and Prince Edward Island by twenty-four senators, ten thereof representing Nova Scotia, ten thereof representing New Brunswick, and four thereof representing Prince Edward Island; the Western Provinces by twenty-four senators, six thereof representing Manitoba, six thereof representing British Columbia, six thereof representing Saskatchewan, and six thereof representing Alberta:

(iii) The number of persons whom by section twenty-six of the said Act the Governor-General of Canada, may, upon the direction of His Majesty the King, add to the Senate is increased from three or six to four or eight, representing equally the four Divisions of Canada:

(iv) In case of such addition being at any time made the Governor-General of Canada shall not summon any person to the Senate except upon a further like direction by His Majesty the King on the like recommendation to represent one of the four Divisions until such Division is represented by twenty-four senators and no more:

(v) The number of senators shall not at any time exceed one hundred and four:

(vi) The representation in the Senate to which by section one hundred and forty-seven of the British North America Act, 1867, Newfoundland would be entitled, in case of its admission to the Union, is increased from four to six members, and in case of the admission of Newfoundland into the Union, notwithstanding anything in the said Act or in this Act, the normal number of senators shall be one hundred and two, and their maximum number one hundred and ten:

(vii) Nothing herein contained shall affect the powers of the Canadian Parliament under the British North America Act, 1886.

(2) Paragraphs (i) to (vi) inclusive of subsection (1) of this section shall not take effect before the termination of the now existing Canadian Parliament.

2. The British North America Act, 1867, is amended by adding *Constitution* thereto the following section immediately after section fifty-one of *of House of* the said Act: *Commons*

51A. Notwithstanding anything in this Act, a province shall always be entitled to a number of members in the House of Commons not less than the number of senators representing such province.

3. This Act may be cited as the British North America Act, 1915; *Short title* and the British North America Acts, 1867 to 1886, and this Act may be cited together as the British North America Acts, 1867 to 1915.

INDEX

INDEX TO CHAPTERS XXXIII AND XXXIV